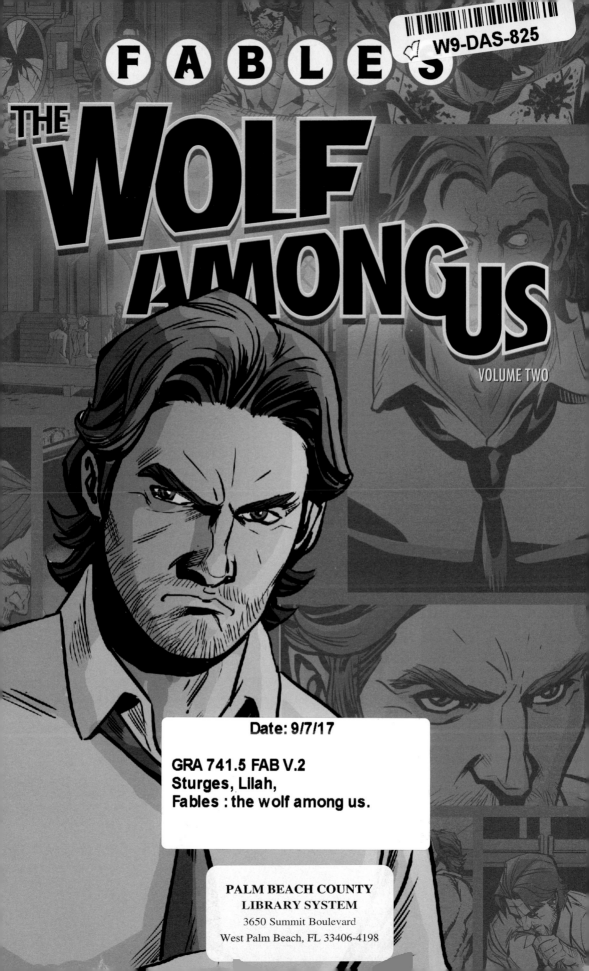

FABLES

THE WOLF AMONG US

VOLUME TWO

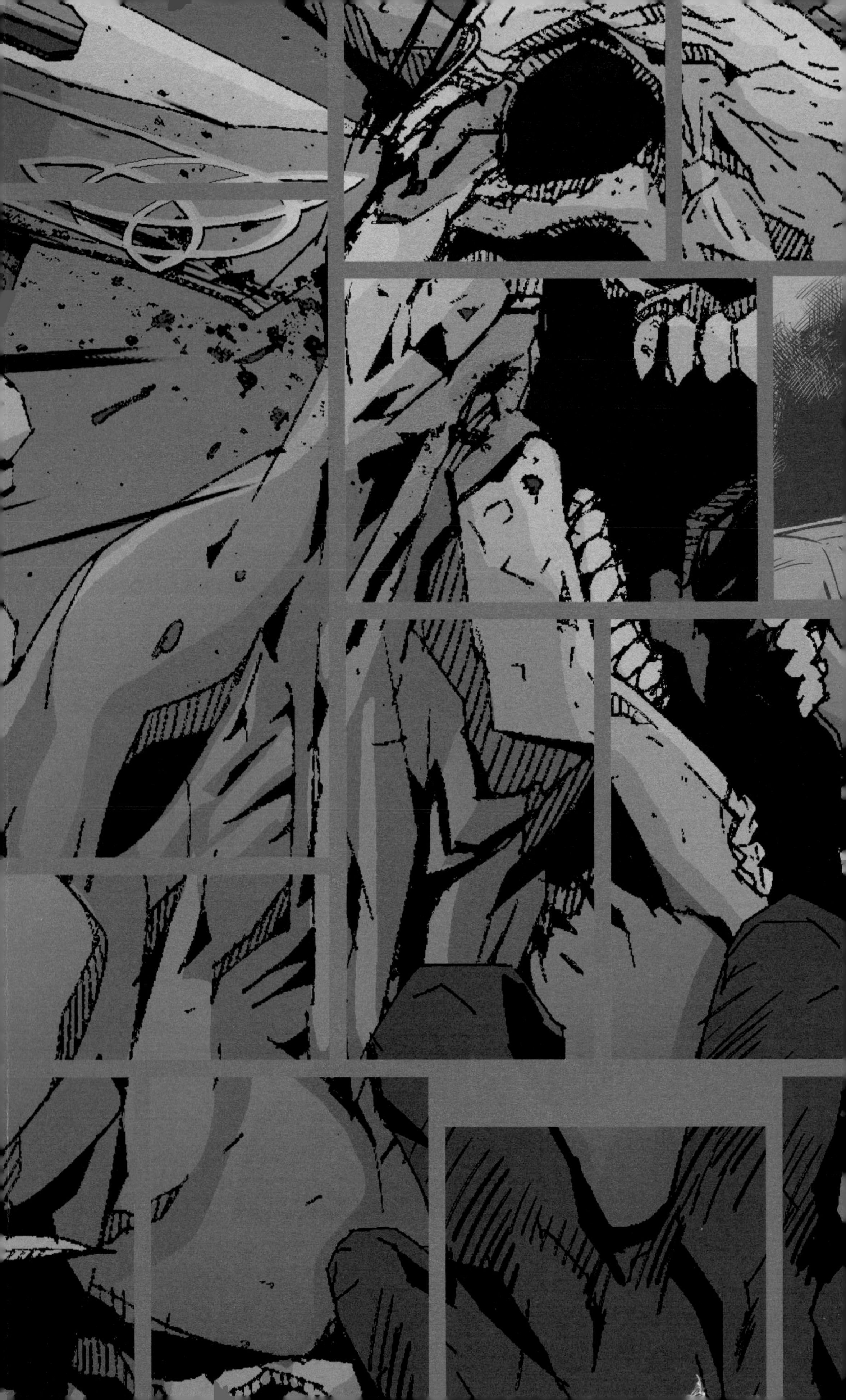

FABLES
THE WOLF AMONG US

VOLUME TWO

WRITERS
MATTHEW STURGES & DAVE JUSTUS

ARTISTS

TRAVIS MOORE
Issues #8-16: Pages 21-30

JOËLLE JONES
Issue #9: Pages 11-20

SHAWN McMANUS
Issues #8, #10-12, #14-16: Pages 11-20

MEGAN LEVENS
Issue #13: Pages 11-20

ERIC NGUYEN
Issues #8-9, #11, #13, #15: Pages 1-10

CHRISTOPHER MITTEN
Issue #14: Pages 8-10

STEVE SADOWSKI
Issue #10: Pages 1-10
Issue #12: Pages 1-10
Issue #14: Pages 1-7
Issue #16: Pages 1-7

ANDREW PEPOY
Issue #16: Pages 8-10

COLORIST
LEE LOUGHRIDGE

LETTERERS
SAL CIPRIANO *(Issue #9)*
TOM NAPOLITANO *(Issues #10-11)*
MARILYN PATRIZIO *(Issues #11-12)*

COVER ART AND ORIGINAL SERIES COVERS
CHRISSIE ZULLO

FABLES created by BILL WILLINGHAM

ROWENA YOW EDITOR – ORIGINAL SERIES
JEB WOODARD GROUP EDITOR – COLLECTED EDITIONS
SCOTT NYBAKKEN EDITOR – COLLECTED EDITION
STEVE COOK DESIGN DIRECTOR – BOOKS
CURTIS KING JR. PUBLICATION DESIGN

SHELLY BOND VP & EXECUTIVE EDITOR – VERTIGO

DIANE NELSON PRESIDENT
DAN DIDIO AND JIM LEE CO-PUBLISHERS
GEOFF JOHNS CHIEF CREATIVE OFFICER
AMIT DESAI SENIOR VP – MARKETING & GLOBAL FRANCHISE MANAGEMENT
NAIRI GARDINER SENIOR VP – FINANCE
SAM ADES VP – DIGITAL MARKETING
BOBBIE CHASE VP – TALENT DEVELOPMENT
MARK CHIARELLO SENIOR VP – ART, DESIGN & COLLECTED EDITIONS
JOHN CUNNINGHAM VP – CONTENT STRATEGY
ANNE DEPIES VP – STRATEGY PLANNING & REPORTING
DON FALLETTI VP – MANUFACTURING OPERATIONS
LAWRENCE GANEM VP – EDITORIAL ADMINISTRATION & TALENT RELATIONS
ALISON GILL SENIOR VP – MANUFACTURING & OPERATIONS
HANK KANALZ SENIOR VP – EDITORIAL STRATEGY & ADMINISTRATION
JAY KOGAN VP – LEGAL AFFAIRS
DEREK MADDALENA SENIOR VP – SALES & BUSINESS DEVELOPMENT
JACK MAHAN VP – BUSINESS AFFAIRS
DAN MIRON VP – SALES PLANNING & TRADE DEVELOPMENT
NICK NAPOLITANO VP – MANUFACTURING ADMINISTRATION
CAROL ROEDER VP – MARKETING
EDDIE SCANNELL VP – MASS ACCOUNT & DIGITAL SALES
COURTNEY SIMMONS SENIOR VP – PUBLICITY & COMMUNICATIONS
JIM (SKI) SOKOLOWSKI VP – COMIC BOOK SPECIALTY & NEWSSTAND SALES
SANDY YI SENIOR VP – GLOBAL FRANCHISE MANAGEMENT

LOGO DESIGN BY BRAINCHILD STUDIOS/NYC

FABLES: THE WOLF AMONG US VOL. 2

PUBLISHED DC COMICS. COMPILATION AND ALL NEW MATERIAL COPYRIGHT © 2016 BILL WILLINGHAM AND
DC COMICS. ALL RIGHTS RESERVED.

ORIGINALLY PUBLISHED IN SINGLE MAGAZINE FORM AS FABLES: THE WOLF AMONG US 8-16 AND ONLINE AS FABLES: THE
WOLF AMONG US DIGITAL CHAPTERS 22-48. COPYRIGHT © 2015, 2016 BILL WILLINGHAM AND DC COMICS. ALL RIGHTS
RESERVED. ALL CHARACTERS, THEIR DISTINCTIVE LIKENESSES AND RELATED ELEMENTS FEATURED IN THIS PUBLICATION
ARE TRADEMARKS OF BILL WILLINGHAM. VERTIGO IS A TRADEMARK OF DC COMICS. THE STORIES, CHARACTERS
AND INCIDENTS FEATURED IN THIS PUBLICATION ARE ENTIRELY FICTIONAL. DC COMICS DOES NOT READ OR ACCEPT
UNSOLICITED SUBMISSIONS OF IDEAS, STORIES OR ARTWORK.

DC COMICS
2900 WEST ALAMEDA AVENUE
BURBANK, CA 91505
PRINTED IN THE USA. FIRST PRINTING.
ISBN: 978-1-4012-6137-5

LIBRARY OF CONGRESS CATALOGING-IN-PUBLICATION DATA IS AVAILABLE.

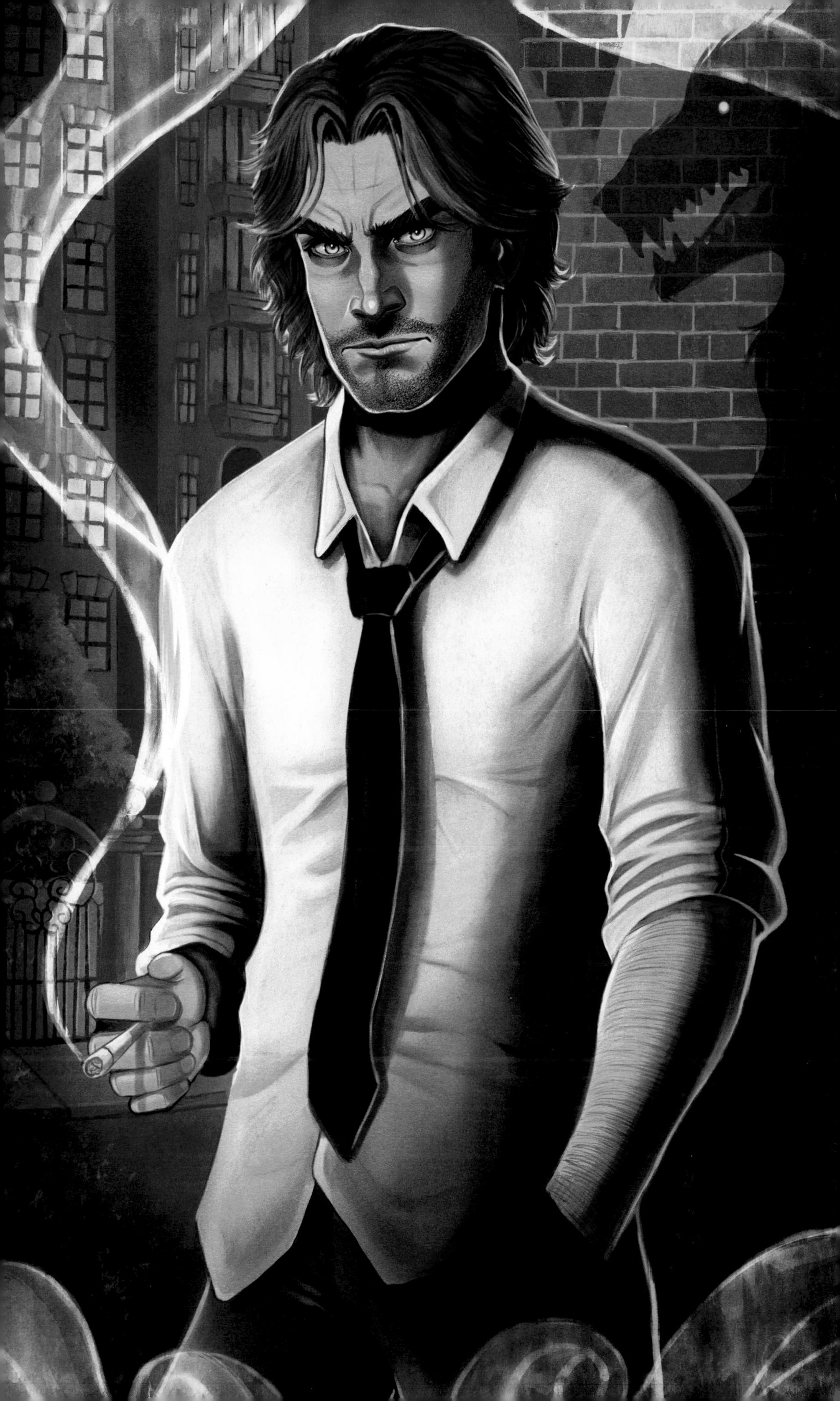

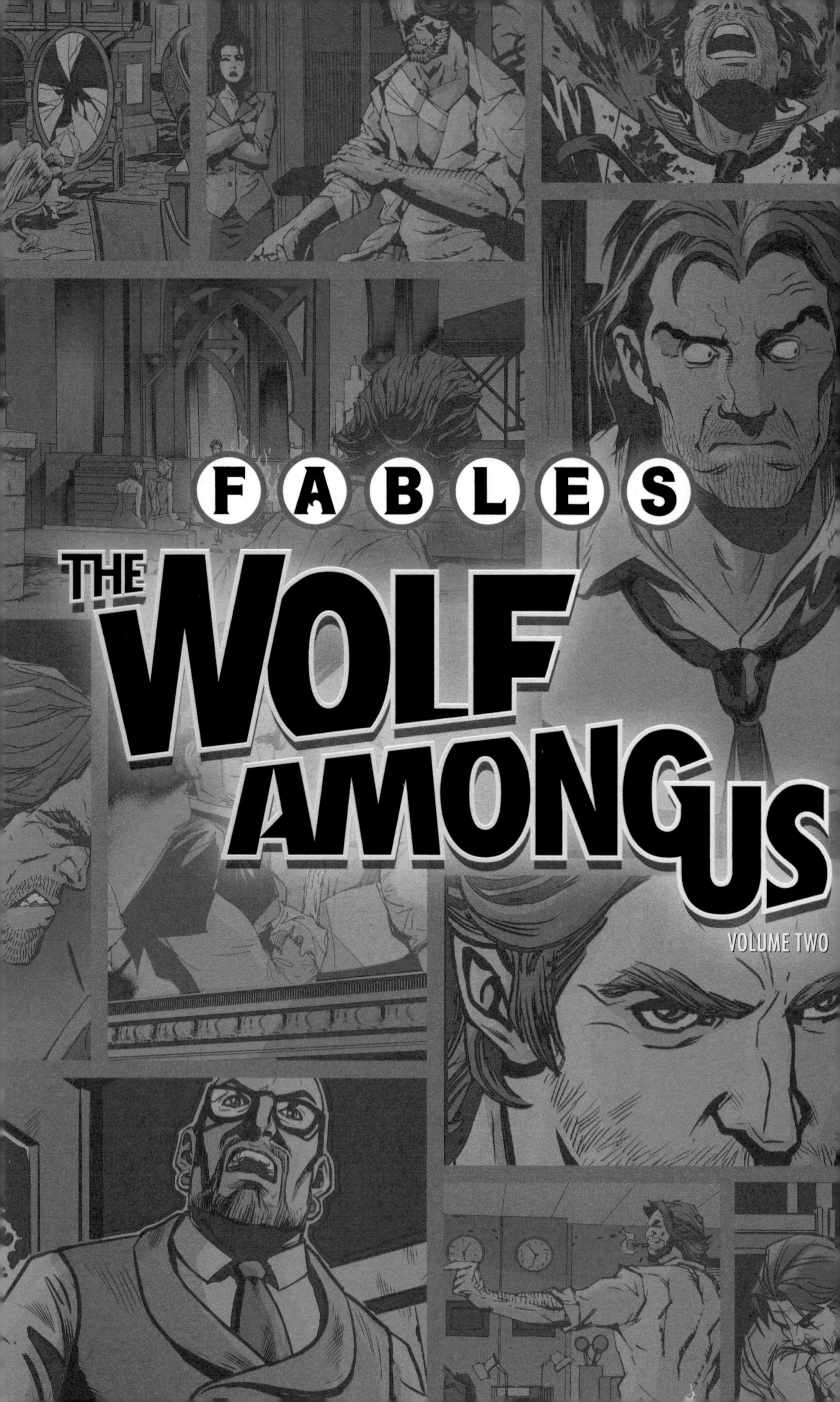
FABLES
THE WOLF AMONG US
VOLUME TWO

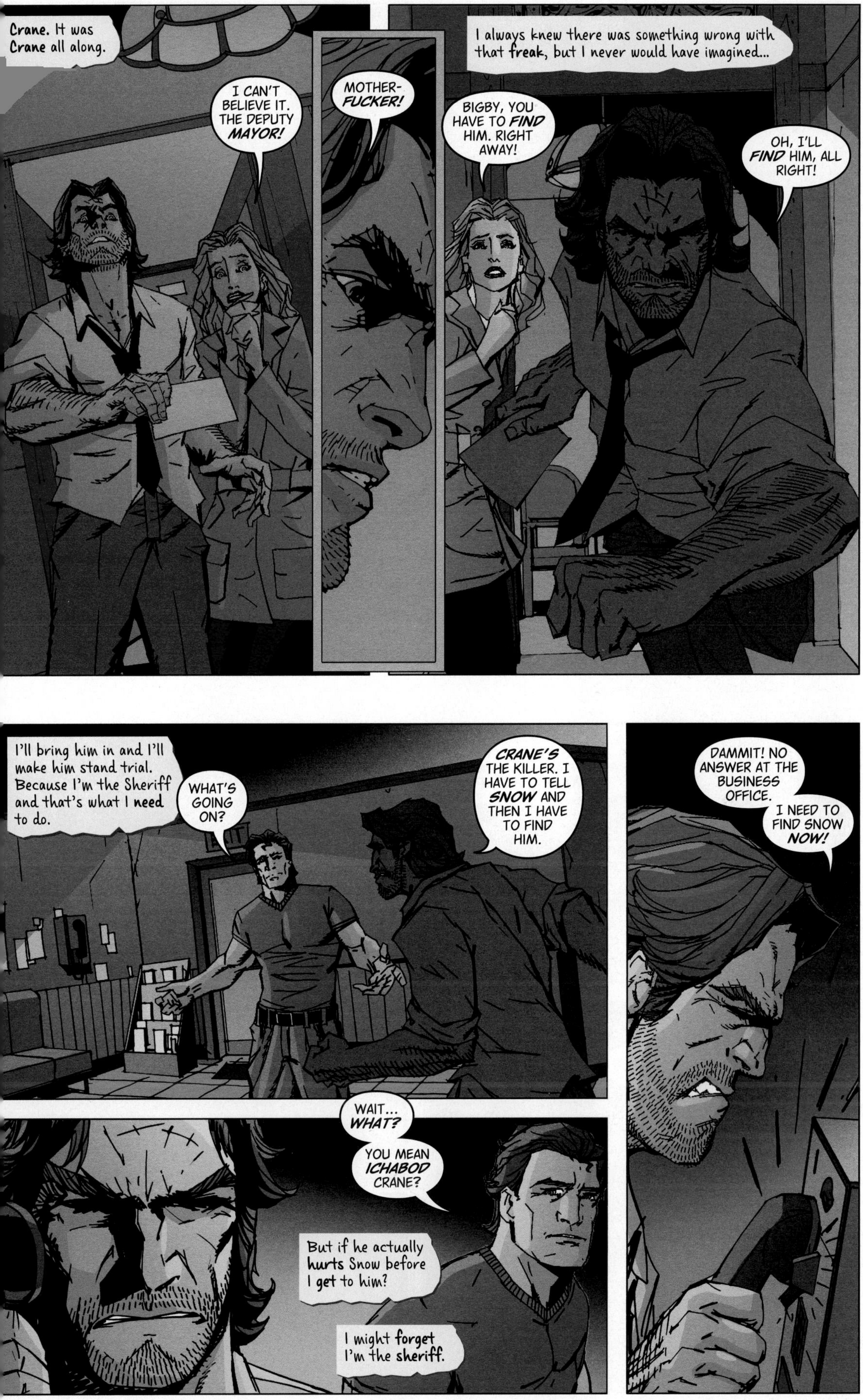

Crane. It was Crane all along.
I CAN'T BELIEVE IT. THE DEPUTY MAYOR!
MOTHER-FUCKER!
I always knew there was something wrong with that freak, but I never would have imagined...
BIGBY, YOU HAVE TO FIND HIM. RIGHT AWAY!
OH, I'LL FIND HIM, ALL RIGHT!
I'll bring him in and I'll make him stand trial. Because I'm the Sheriff and that's what I need to do.
WHAT'S GOING ON?
CRANE'S THE KILLER. I HAVE TO TELL SNOW AND THEN I HAVE TO FIND HIM.
DAMMIT! NO ANSWER AT THE BUSINESS OFFICE.
I NEED TO FIND SNOW NOW!
WAIT... WHAT?
YOU MEAN ICHABOD CRANE?
But if he actually hurts Snow before I get to him?
I might forget I'm the sheriff.

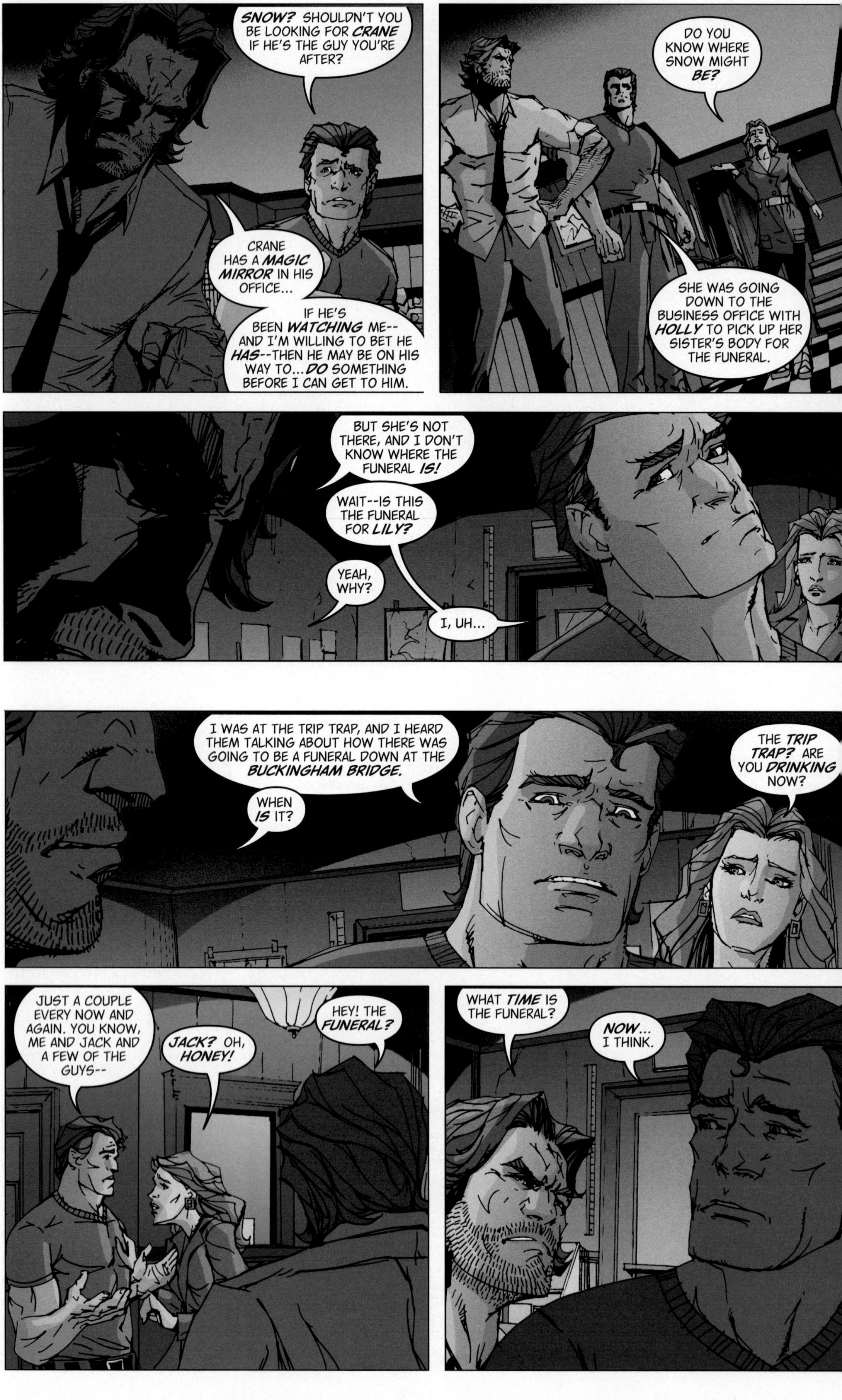
SNOW? SHOULDN'T YOU BE LOOKING FOR CRANE IF HE'S THE GUY YOU'RE AFTER?
CRANE HAS A MAGIC MIRROR IN HIS OFFICE...
IF HE'S BEEN WATCHING ME--AND I'M WILLING TO BET HE HAS--THEN HE MAY BE ON HIS WAY TO...DO SOMETHING BEFORE I CAN GET TO HIM.
DO YOU KNOW WHERE SNOW MIGHT BE?
SHE WAS GOING DOWN TO THE BUSINESS OFFICE WITH HOLLY TO PICK UP HER SISTER'S BODY FOR THE FUNERAL.
BUT SHE'S NOT THERE, AND I DON'T KNOW WHERE THE FUNERAL IS!
WAIT--IS THIS THE FUNERAL FOR LILY?
YEAH, WHY?
I, UH...
I WAS AT THE TRIP TRAP, AND I HEARD THEM TALKING ABOUT HOW THERE WAS GOING TO BE A FUNERAL DOWN AT THE BUCKINGHAM BRIDGE.
WHEN IS IT?
THE TRIP TRAP? ARE YOU DRINKING NOW?
JUST A COUPLE EVERY NOW AND AGAIN. YOU KNOW, ME AND JACK AND A FEW OF THE GUYS--
JACK? OH, HONEY!
HEY! THE FUNERAL?
WHAT TIME IS THE FUNERAL?
NOW... I THINK.

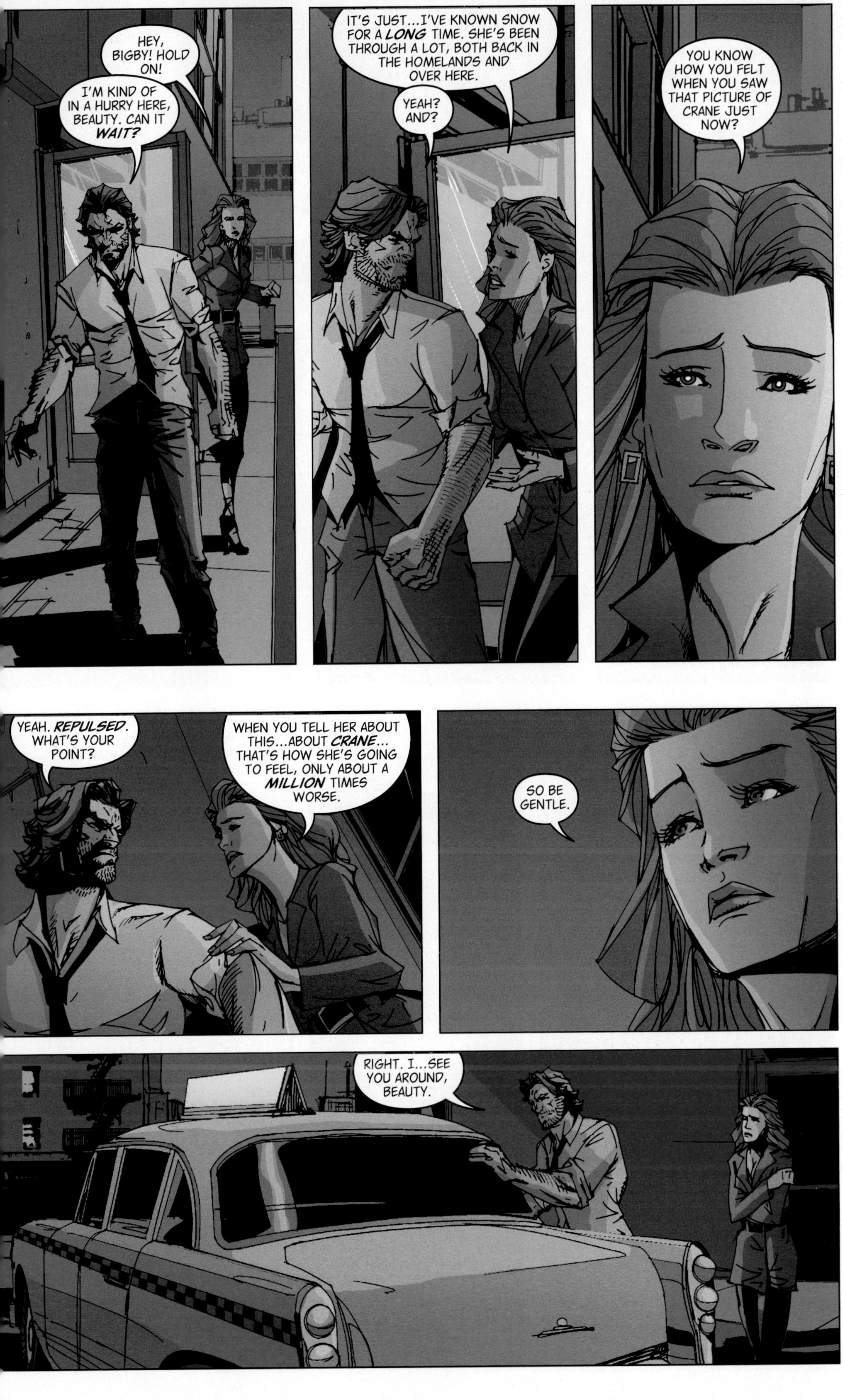
HEY, BIGBY! HOLD ON!
I'M KIND OF IN A HURRY HERE, BEAUTY. CAN IT *WAIT?*
IT'S JUST...I'VE KNOWN SNOW FOR A *LONG* TIME. SHE'S BEEN THROUGH A LOT, BOTH BACK IN THE HOMELANDS AND OVER HERE.
YEAH? AND?
YOU KNOW HOW YOU FELT WHEN YOU SAW THAT PICTURE OF CRANE JUST NOW?
YEAH. *REPULSED*. WHAT'S YOUR POINT?
WHEN YOU TELL HER ABOUT THIS...ABOUT *CRANE*... THAT'S HOW SHE'S GOING TO FEEL, ONLY ABOUT A *MILLION* TIMES WORSE.
SO BE GENTLE.
RIGHT. I...SEE YOU AROUND, BEAUTY.

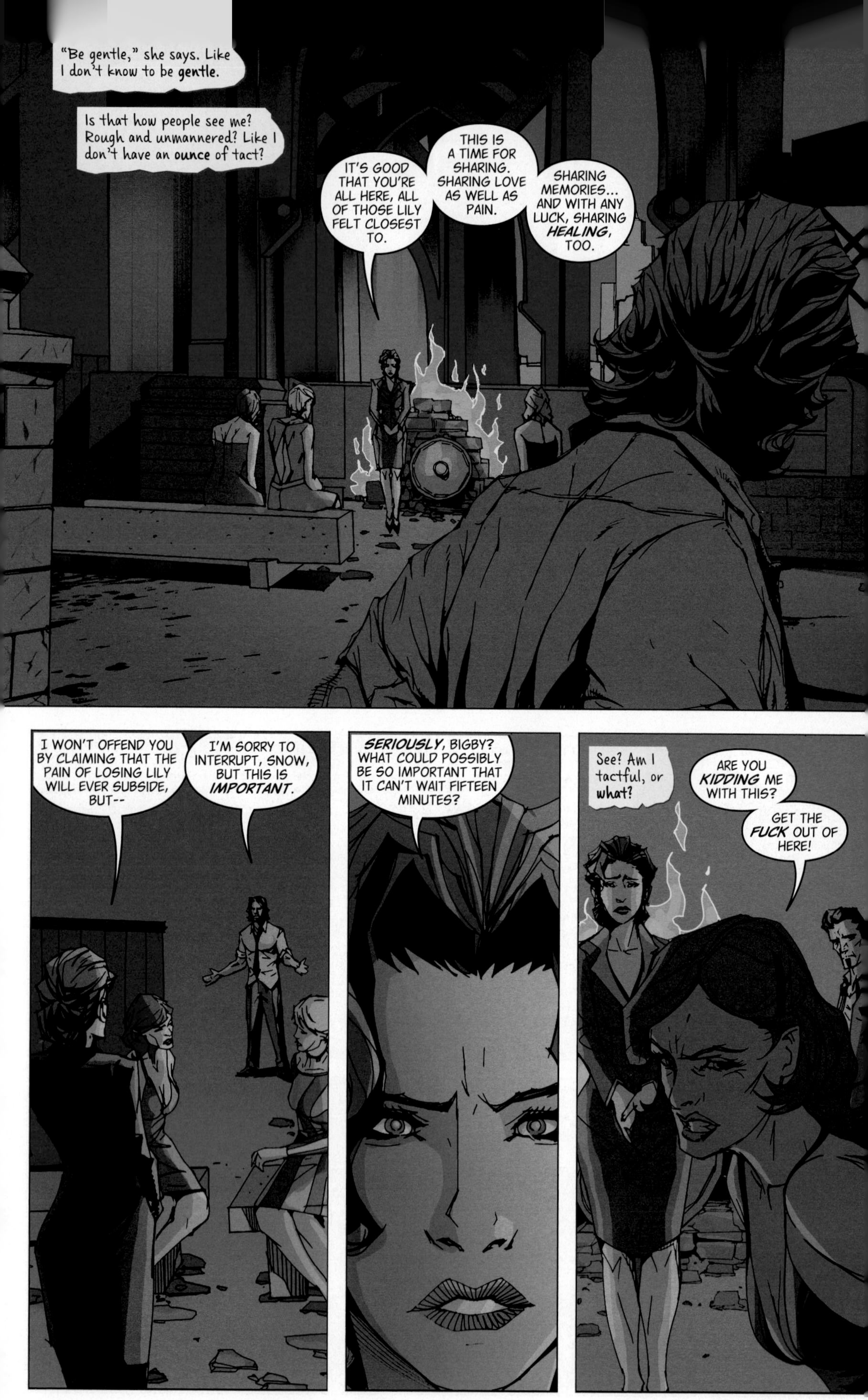
"Be gentle," she says. Like I don't know to be **gentle**.
Is that how people see me? Rough and unmannered? Like I don't have an **ounce** of tact?
IT'S GOOD THAT YOU'RE ALL HERE, ALL OF THOSE LILY FELT CLOSEST TO.
THIS IS A TIME FOR SHARING. SHARING LOVE AS WELL AS PAIN.
SHARING MEMORIES... AND WITH ANY LUCK, SHARING *HEALING*, TOO.
I WON'T OFFEND YOU BY CLAIMING THAT THE PAIN OF LOSING LILY WILL EVER SUBSIDE, BUT--
I'M SORRY TO INTERRUPT, SNOW, BUT THIS IS *IMPORTANT*.
SERIOUSLY, BIGBY? WHAT COULD POSSIBLY BE SO IMPORTANT THAT IT CAN'T WAIT FIFTEEN MINUTES?
See? Am I tactful, or **what**?
ARE YOU *KIDDING* ME WITH THIS?
GET THE *FUCK* OUT OF HERE!

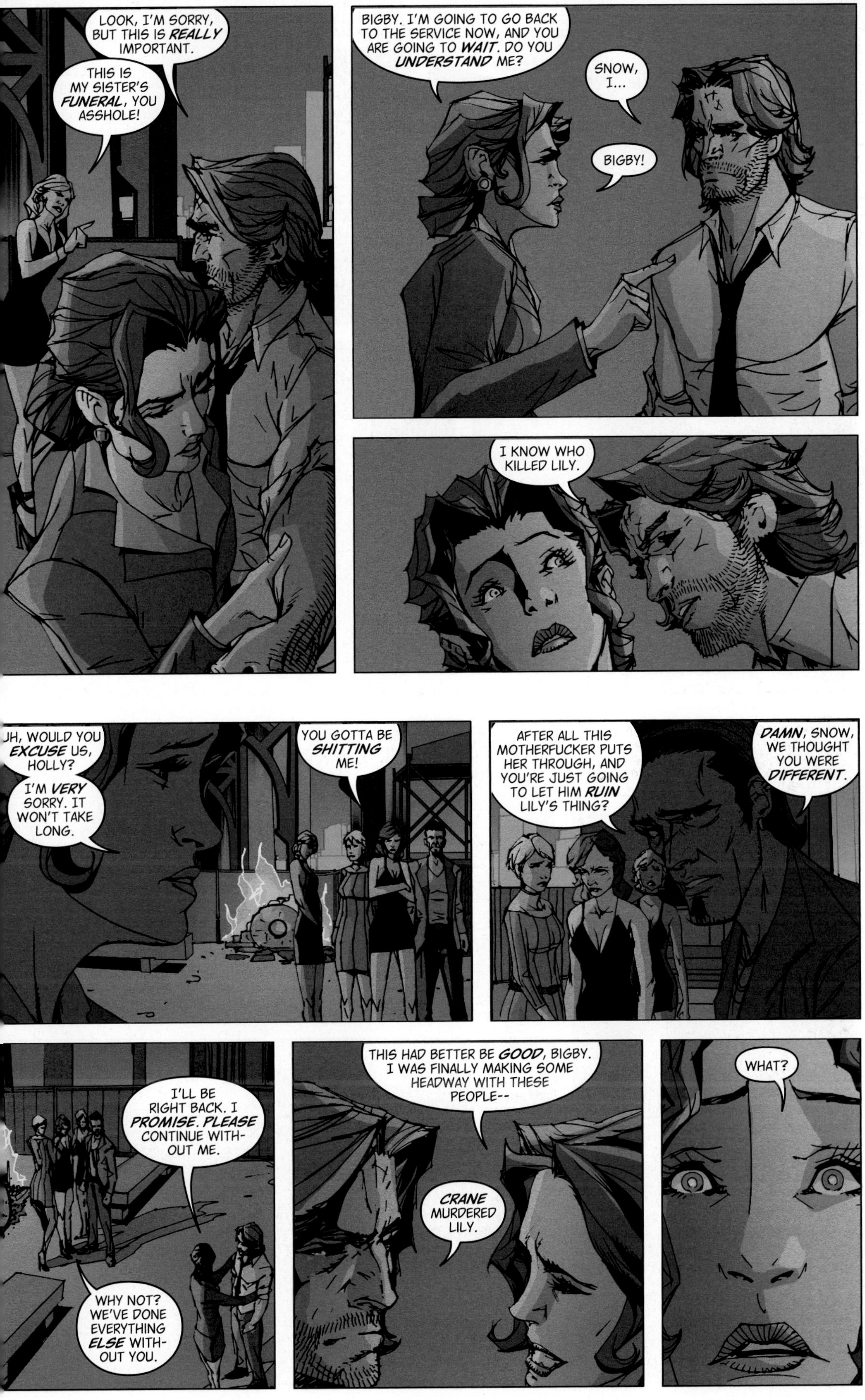
LOOK, I'M SORRY, BUT THIS IS REALLY IMPORTANT.
THIS IS MY SISTER'S FUNERAL, YOU ASSHOLE!
BIGBY. I'M GOING TO GO BACK TO THE SERVICE NOW, AND YOU ARE GOING TO WAIT. DO YOU UNDERSTAND ME?
SNOW, I...
BIGBY!
I KNOW WHO KILLED LILY.
UH, WOULD YOU EXCUSE US, HOLLY?
I'M VERY SORRY. IT WON'T TAKE LONG.
YOU GOTTA BE SHITTING ME!
AFTER ALL THIS MOTHERFUCKER PUTS HER THROUGH, AND YOU'RE JUST GOING TO LET HIM RUIN LILY'S THING?
DAMN, SNOW, WE THOUGHT YOU WERE DIFFERENT.
I'LL BE RIGHT BACK. I PROMISE. PLEASE CONTINUE WITHOUT ME.
WHY NOT? WE'VE DONE EVERYTHING ELSE WITHOUT YOU.
THIS HAD BETTER BE GOOD, BIGBY. I WAS FINALLY MAKING SOME HEADWAY WITH THESE PEOPLE--
CRANE MURDERED LILY.
WHAT?

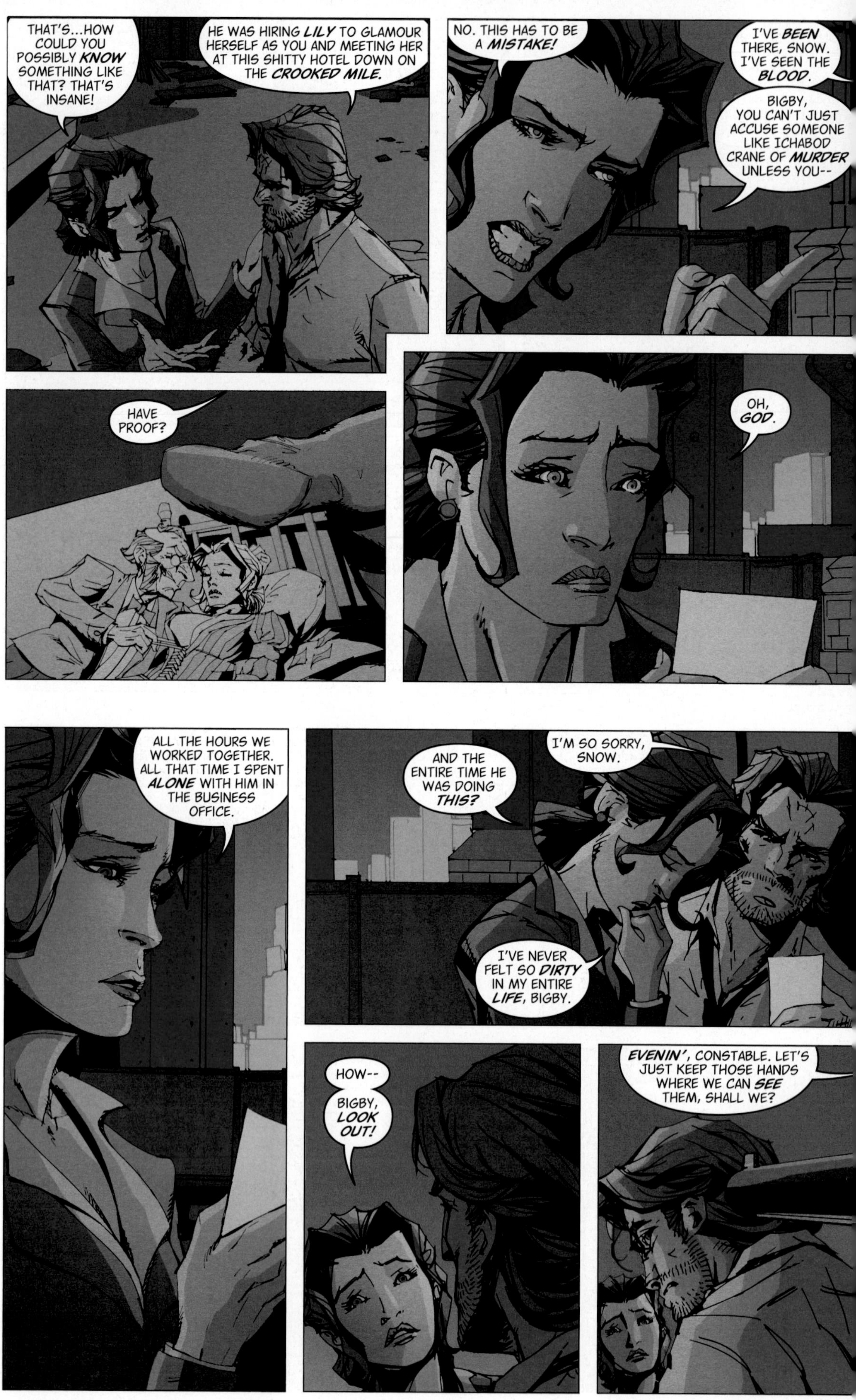
THAT'S...HOW COULD YOU POSSIBLY KNOW SOMETHING LIKE THAT? THAT'S INSANE!
HE WAS HIRING LILY TO GLAMOUR HERSELF AS YOU AND MEETING HER AT THIS SHITTY HOTEL DOWN ON THE CROOKED MILE.
NO. THIS HAS TO BE A MISTAKE!
I'VE BEEN THERE, SNOW. I'VE SEEN THE BLOOD.
BIGBY, YOU CAN'T JUST ACCUSE SOMEONE LIKE ICHABOD CRANE OF MURDER UNLESS YOU--
HAVE PROOF?
OH, GOD.
ALL THE HOURS WE WORKED TOGETHER. ALL THAT TIME I SPENT ALONE WITH HIM IN THE BUSINESS OFFICE.
AND THE ENTIRE TIME HE WAS DOING THIS?
I'M SO SORRY, SNOW.
I'VE NEVER FELT SO DIRTY IN MY ENTIRE LIFE, BIGBY.
HOW--
BIGBY, LOOK OUT!
EVENIN', CONSTABLE. LET'S JUST KEEP THOSE HANDS WHERE WE CAN SEE THEM, SHALL WE?

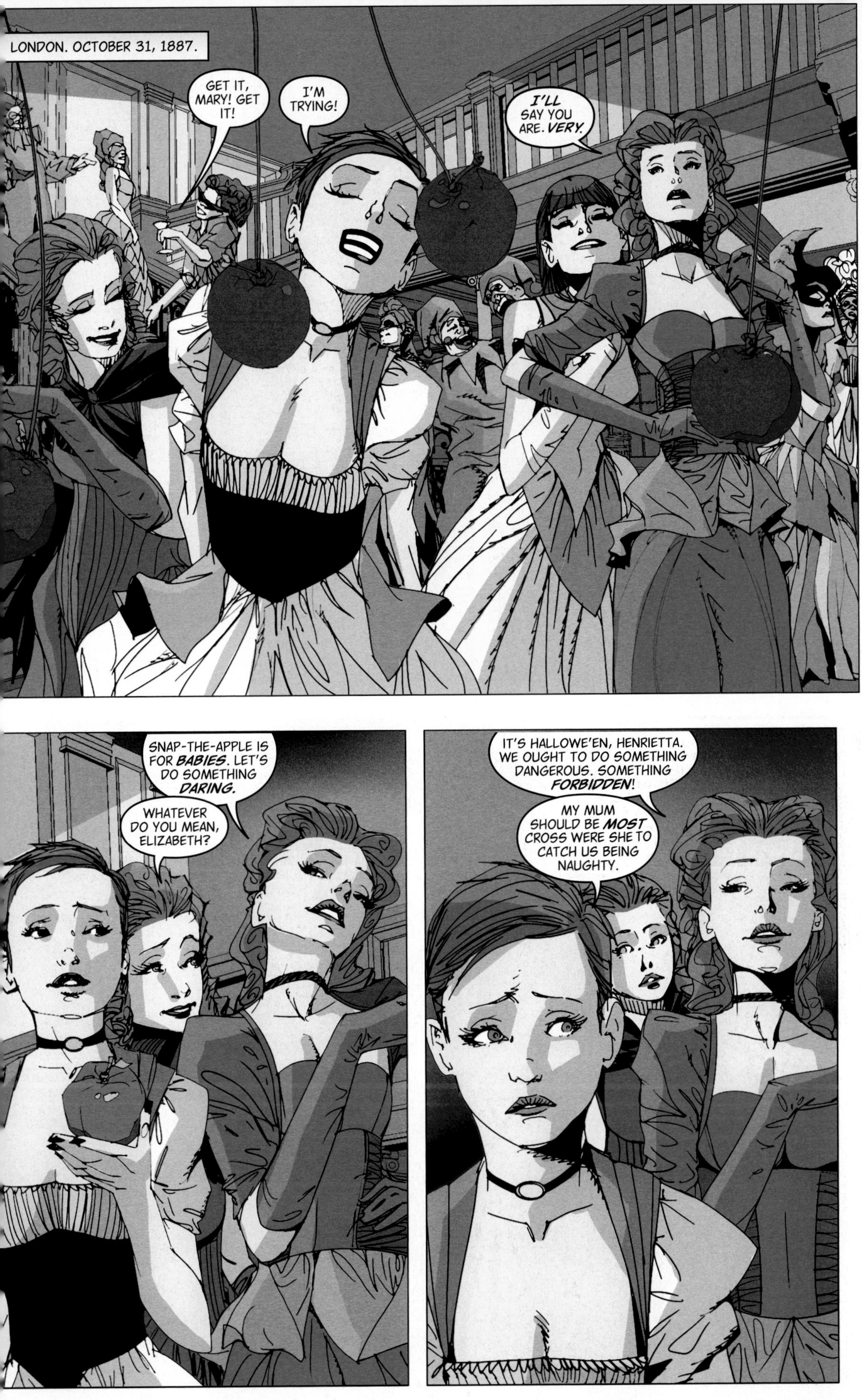
LONDON. OCTOBER 31, 1887.
GET IT, MARY! GET IT!
I'M TRYING!
I'LL SAY YOU ARE. VERY.
SNAP-THE-APPLE IS FOR BABIES. LET'S DO SOMETHING DARING.
WHATEVER DO YOU MEAN, ELIZABETH?
IT'S HALLOWE'EN, HENRIETTA. WE OUGHT TO DO SOMETHING DANGEROUS. SOMETHING FORBIDDEN!
MY MUM SHOULD BE MOST CROSS WERE SHE TO CATCH US BEING NAUGHTY.

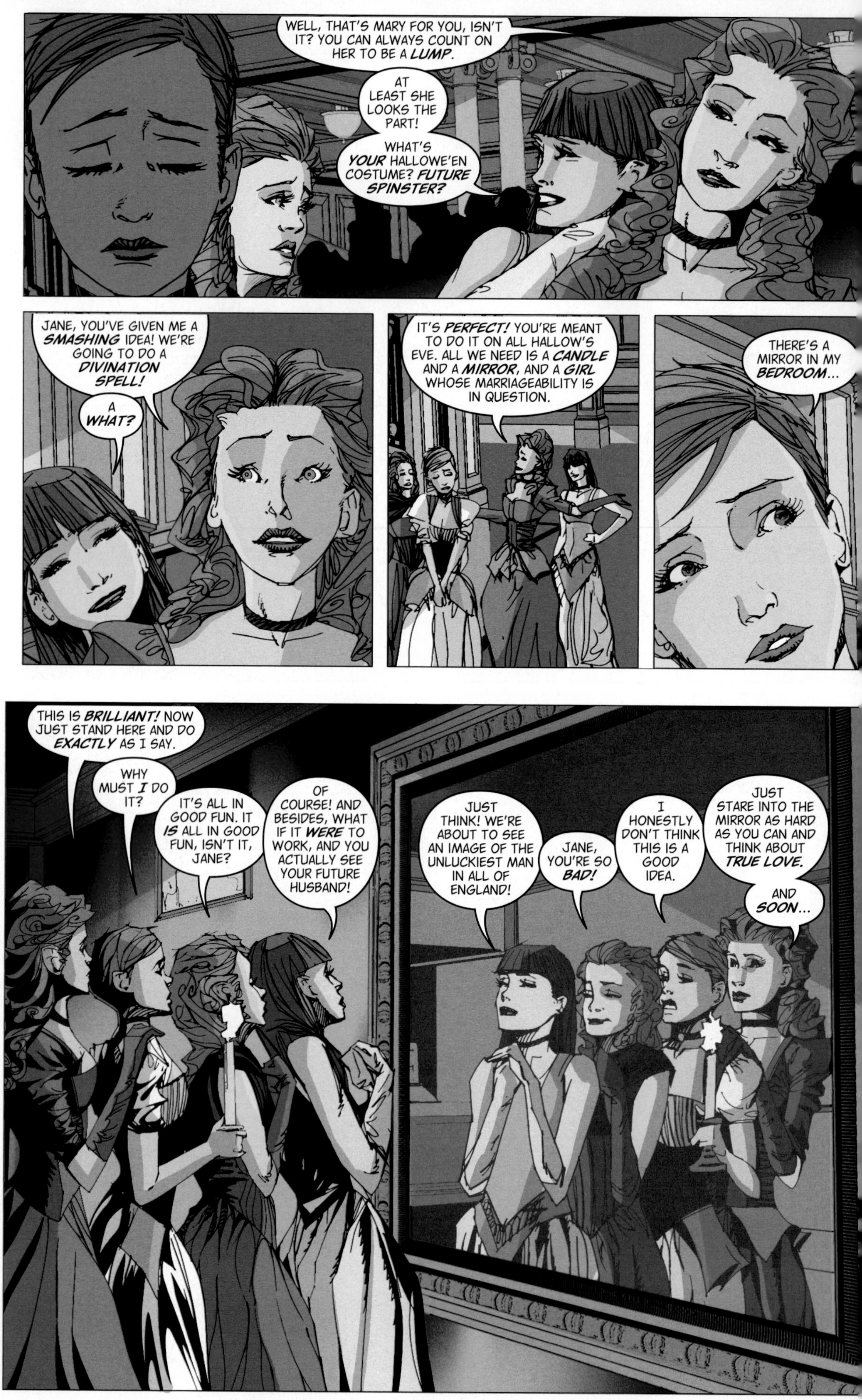
WELL, THAT'S MARY FOR YOU, ISN'T IT? YOU CAN ALWAYS COUNT ON HER TO BE A LUMP.
AT LEAST SHE LOOKS THE PART!
WHAT'S YOUR HALLOWE'EN COSTUME? FUTURE SPINSTER?
JANE, YOU'VE GIVEN ME A SMASHING IDEA! WE'RE GOING TO DO A DIVINATION SPELL!
A WHAT?
IT'S PERFECT! YOU'RE MEANT TO DO IT ON ALL HALLOW'S EVE. ALL WE NEED IS A CANDLE AND A MIRROR, AND A GIRL WHOSE MARRIAGEABILITY IS IN QUESTION.
THERE'S A MIRROR IN MY BEDROOM...
THIS IS BRILLIANT! NOW JUST STAND HERE AND DO EXACTLY AS I SAY.
WHY MUST I DO IT?
IT'S ALL IN GOOD FUN. IT IS ALL IN GOOD FUN, ISN'T IT, JANE?
OF COURSE! AND BESIDES, WHAT IF IT WERE TO WORK, AND YOU ACTUALLY SEE YOUR FUTURE HUSBAND!
JUST THINK! WE'RE ABOUT TO SEE AN IMAGE OF THE UNLUCKIEST MAN IN ALL OF ENGLAND!
JANE, YOU'RE SO BAD!
I HONESTLY DON'T THINK THIS IS A GOOD IDEA.
JUST STARE INTO THE MIRROR AS HARD AS YOU CAN AND THINK ABOUT TRUE LOVE.
AND SOON...

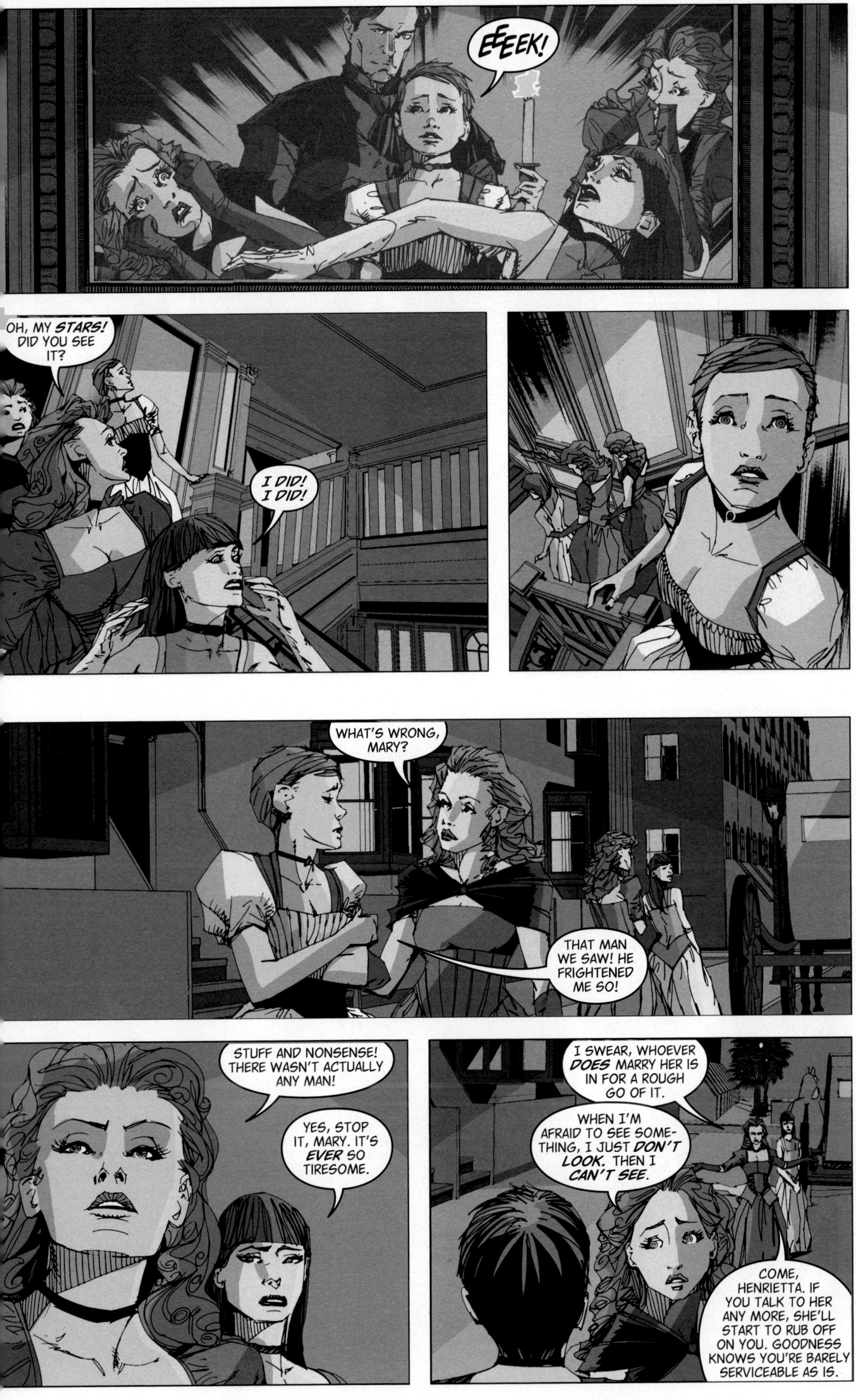

EEEEK!
OH, MY STARS! DID YOU SEE IT?
I DID! I DID!
WHAT'S WRONG, MARY?
THAT MAN WE SAW! HE FRIGHTENED ME SO!
STUFF AND NONSENSE! THERE WASN'T ACTUALLY ANY MAN!
YES, STOP IT, MARY. IT'S EVER SO TIRESOME.
I SWEAR, WHOEVER DOES MARRY HER IS IN FOR A ROUGH GO OF IT.
WHEN I'M AFRAID TO SEE SOME-THING, I JUST DON'T LOOK. THEN I CAN'T SEE.
COME, HENRIETTA. IF YOU TALK TO HER ANY MORE, SHE'LL START TO RUB OFF ON YOU. GOODNESS KNOWS YOU'RE BARELY SERVICEABLE AS IS.

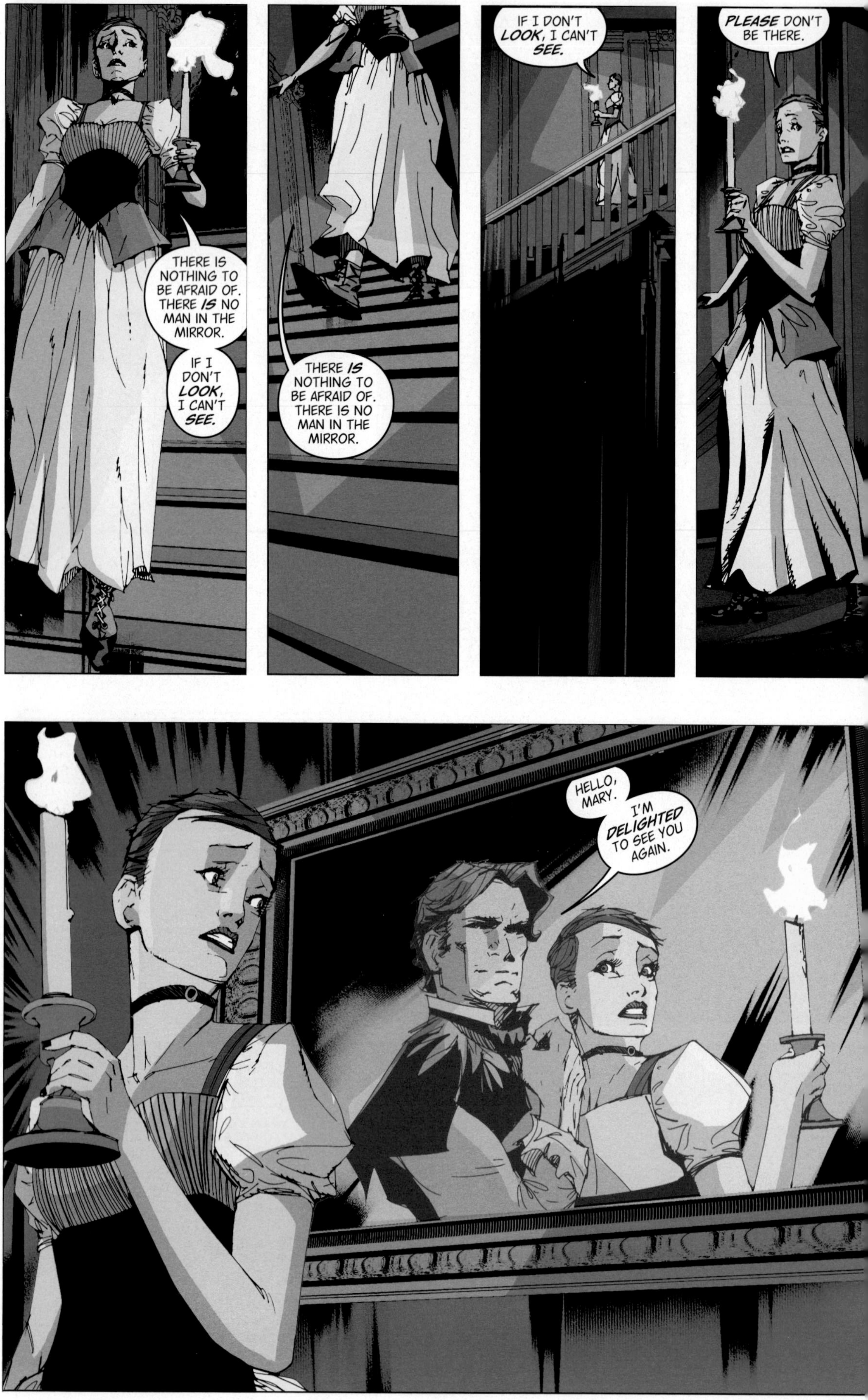
THERE IS NOTHING TO BE AFRAID OF. THERE *IS* NO MAN IN THE MIRROR.
IF I DON'T *LOOK,* I CAN'T *SEE.*
THERE *IS* NOTHING TO BE AFRAID OF. THERE IS NO MAN IN THE MIRROR.
IF I DON'T *LOOK*, I CAN'T *SEE.*
PLEASE DON'T BE THERE.
HELLO, MARY.
I'M *DELIGHTED* TO SEE YOU AGAIN.

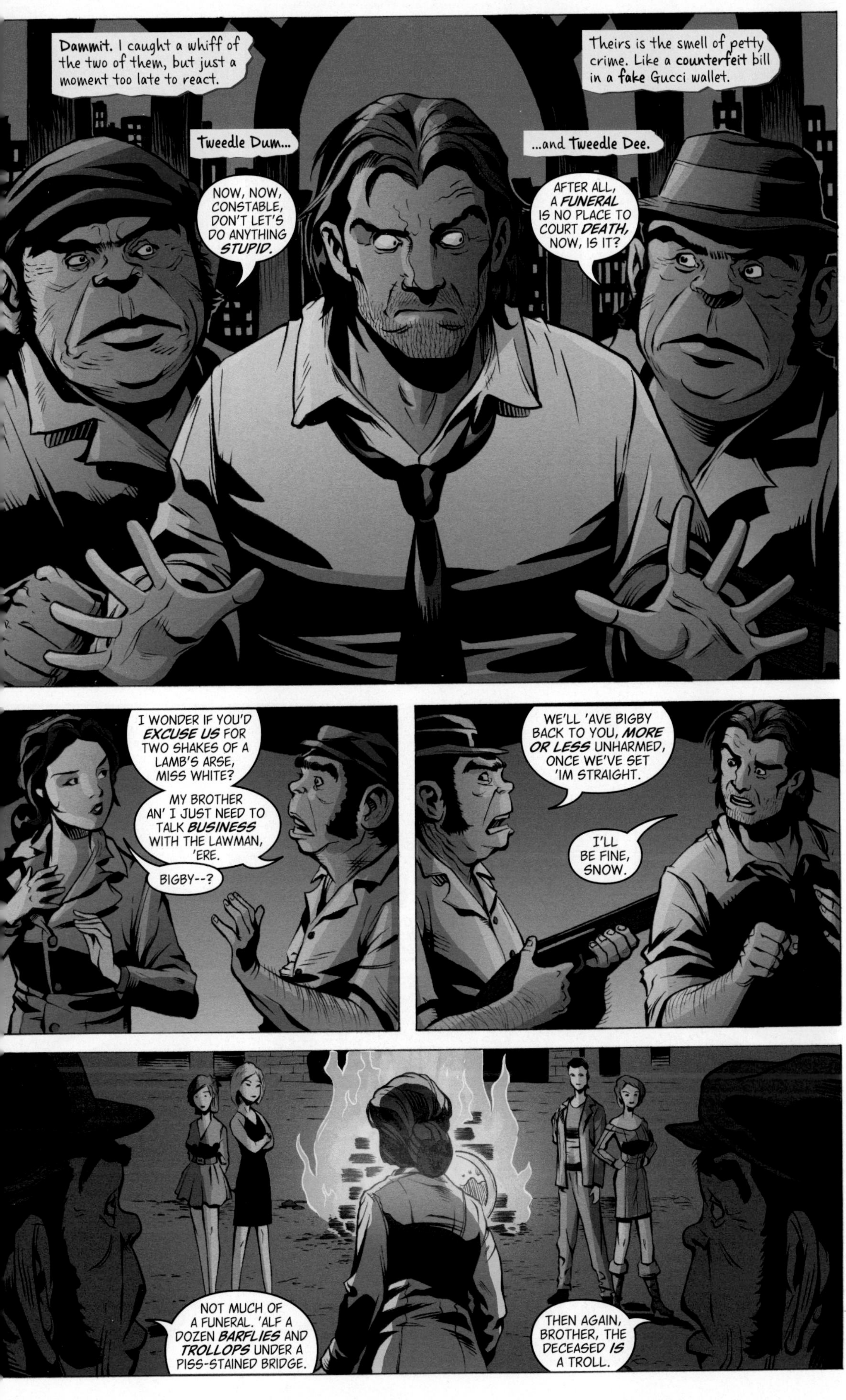

Dammit. I caught a whiff of the two of them, but just a moment too late to react.
Theirs is the smell of petty crime. Like a counterfeit bill in a fake Gucci wallet.
Tweedle Dum...
...and Tweedle Dee.
NOW, NOW, CONSTABLE, DON'T LET'S DO ANYTHING STUPID.
AFTER ALL, A FUNERAL IS NO PLACE TO COURT DEATH, NOW, IS IT?
I WONDER IF YOU'D EXCUSE US FOR TWO SHAKES OF A LAMB'S ARSE, MISS WHITE?
MY BROTHER AN' I JUST NEED TO TALK BUSINESS WITH THE LAWMAN, 'ERE.
BIGBY--?
WE'LL 'AVE BIGBY BACK TO YOU, MORE OR LESS UNHARMED, ONCE WE'VE SET 'IM STRAIGHT.
I'LL BE FINE, SNOW.
NOT MUCH OF A FUNERAL. 'ALF A DOZEN BARFLIES AND TROLLOPS UNDER A PISS-STAINED BRIDGE.
THEN AGAIN, BROTHER, THE DECEASED IS A TROLL.

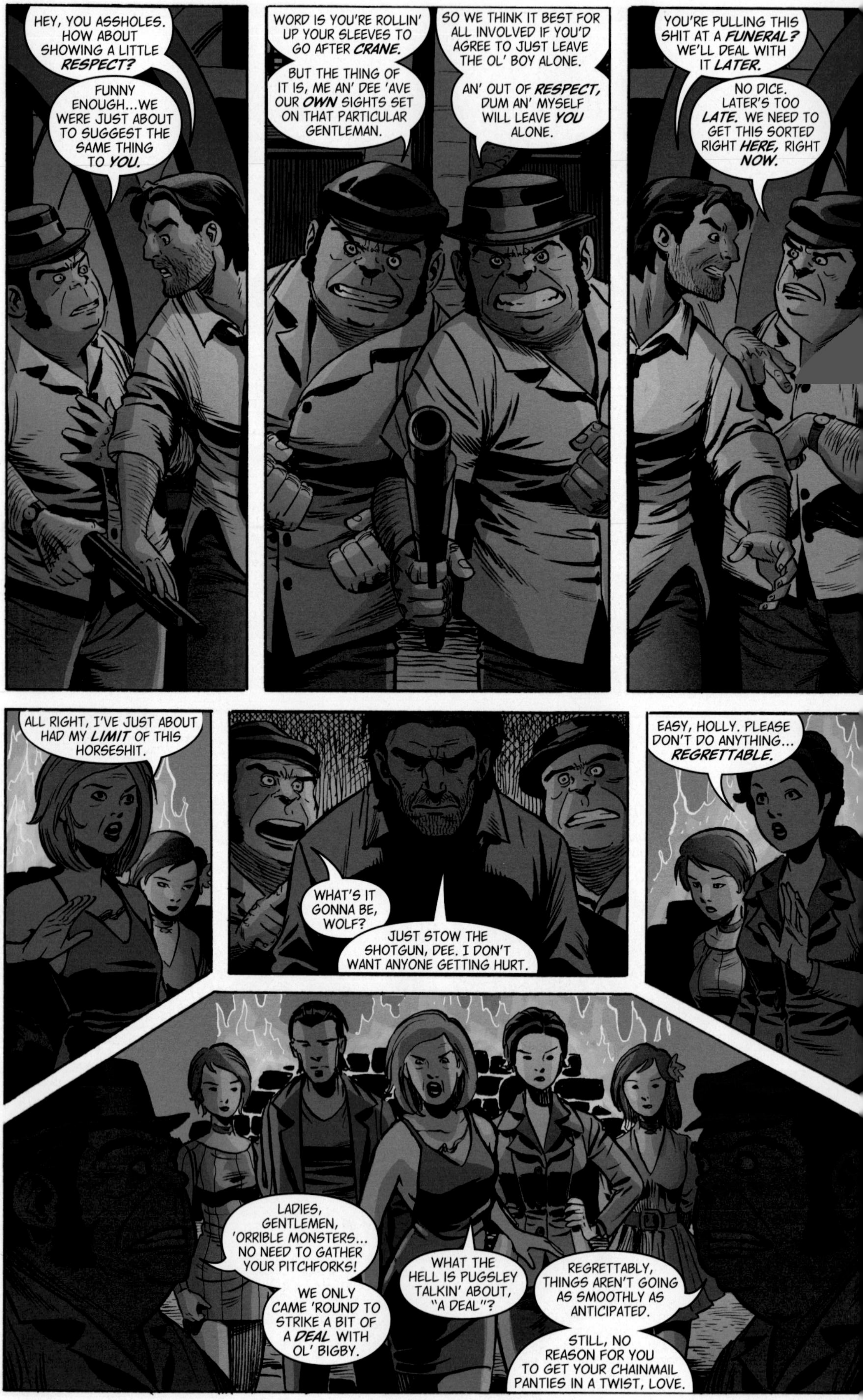
HEY, YOU ASSHOLES. HOW ABOUT SHOWING A LITTLE RESPECT?
FUNNY ENOUGH...WE WERE JUST ABOUT TO SUGGEST THE SAME THING TO YOU.
WORD IS YOU'RE ROLLIN' UP YOUR SLEEVES TO GO AFTER CRANE.
BUT THE THING OF IT IS, ME AN' DEE 'AVE OUR OWN SIGHTS SET ON THAT PARTICULAR GENTLEMAN.
SO WE THINK IT BEST FOR ALL INVOLVED IF YOU'D AGREE TO JUST LEAVE THE OL' BOY ALONE.
AN' OUT OF RESPECT, DUM AN' MYSELF WILL LEAVE YOU ALONE.
YOU'RE PULLING THIS SHIT AT A FUNERAL? WE'LL DEAL WITH IT LATER.
NO DICE. LATER'S TOO LATE. WE NEED TO GET THIS SORTED RIGHT HERE, RIGHT NOW.
ALL RIGHT, I'VE JUST ABOUT HAD MY LIMIT OF THIS HORSESHIT.
WHAT'S IT GONNA BE, WOLF?
JUST STOW THE SHOTGUN, DEE. I DON'T WANT ANYONE GETTING HURT.
EASY, HOLLY. PLEASE DON'T DO ANYTHING... REGRETTABLE.
LADIES, GENTLEMEN, 'ORRIBLE MONSTERS... NO NEED TO GATHER YOUR PITCHFORKS!
WE ONLY CAME 'ROUND TO STRIKE A BIT OF A DEAL WITH OL' BIGBY.
WHAT THE HELL IS PUGSLEY TALKIN' ABOUT, "A DEAL"?
REGRETTABLY, THINGS AREN'T GOING AS SMOOTHLY AS ANTICIPATED.
STILL, NO REASON FOR YOU TO GET YOUR CHAINMAIL PANTIES IN A TWIST, LOVE.

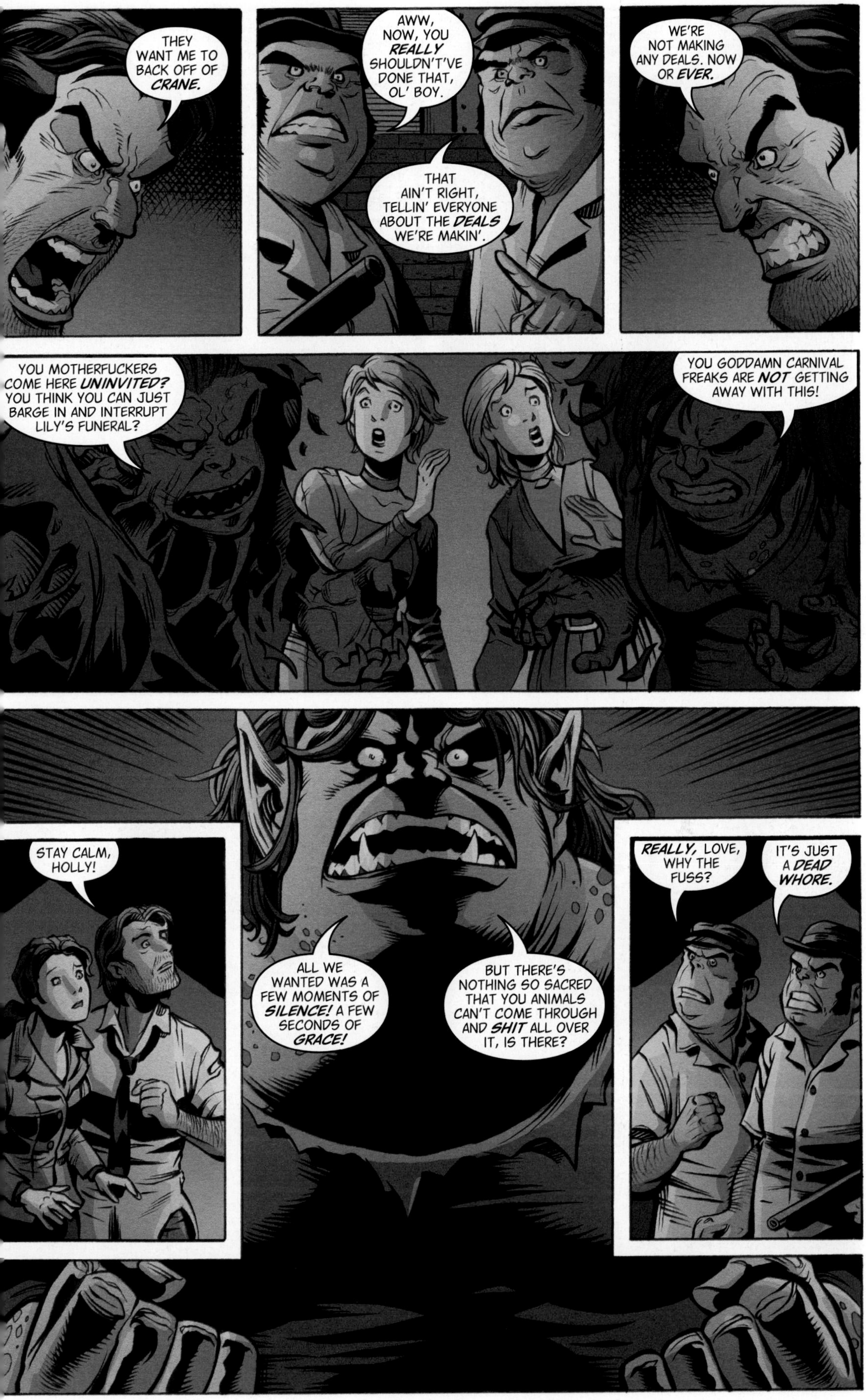
THEY WANT ME TO BACK OFF OF CRANE.
AWW, NOW, YOU REALLY SHOULDN'T'VE DONE THAT, OL' BOY.
THAT AIN'T RIGHT, TELLIN' EVERYONE ABOUT THE DEALS WE'RE MAKIN'.
WE'RE NOT MAKING ANY DEALS. NOW OR EVER.
YOU MOTHERFUCKERS COME HERE UNINVITED? YOU THINK YOU CAN JUST BARGE IN AND INTERRUPT LILY'S FUNERAL?
YOU GODDAMN CARNIVAL FREAKS ARE NOT GETTING AWAY WITH THIS!
STAY CALM, HOLLY!
ALL WE WANTED WAS A FEW MOMENTS OF SILENCE! A FEW SECONDS OF GRACE!
BUT THERE'S NOTHING SO SACRED THAT YOU ANIMALS CAN'T COME THROUGH AND SHIT ALL OVER IT, IS THERE?
REALLY, LOVE, WHY THE FUSS?
IT'S JUST A DEAD WHORE.

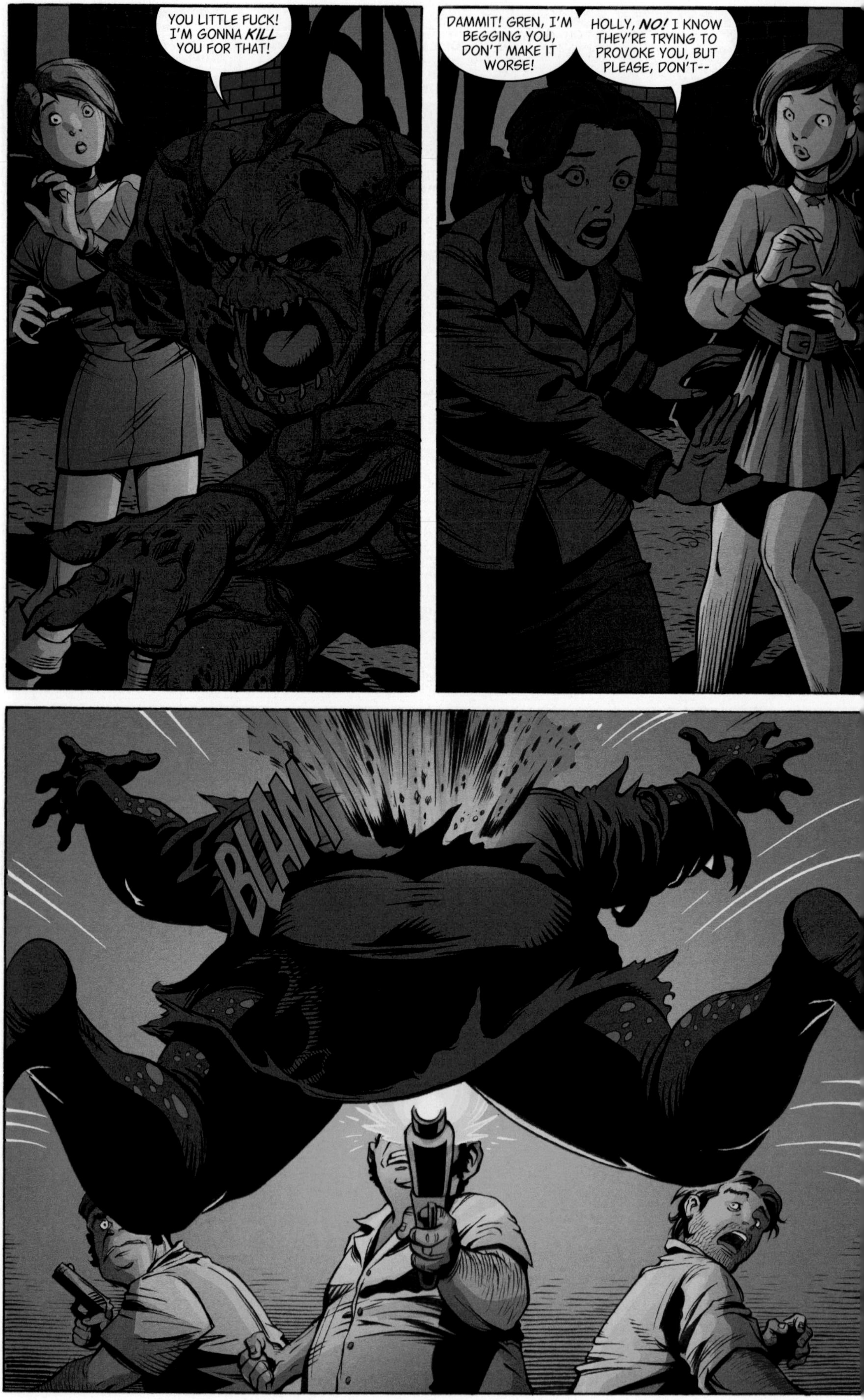
YOU LITTLE FUCK! I'M GONNA *KILL* YOU FOR THAT!
DAMMIT! GREN, I'M BEGGING YOU, DON'T MAKE IT WORSE!
HOLLY, ***NO!*** I KNOW THEY'RE TRYING TO PROVOKE YOU, BUT PLEASE, DON'T--
BLAM!

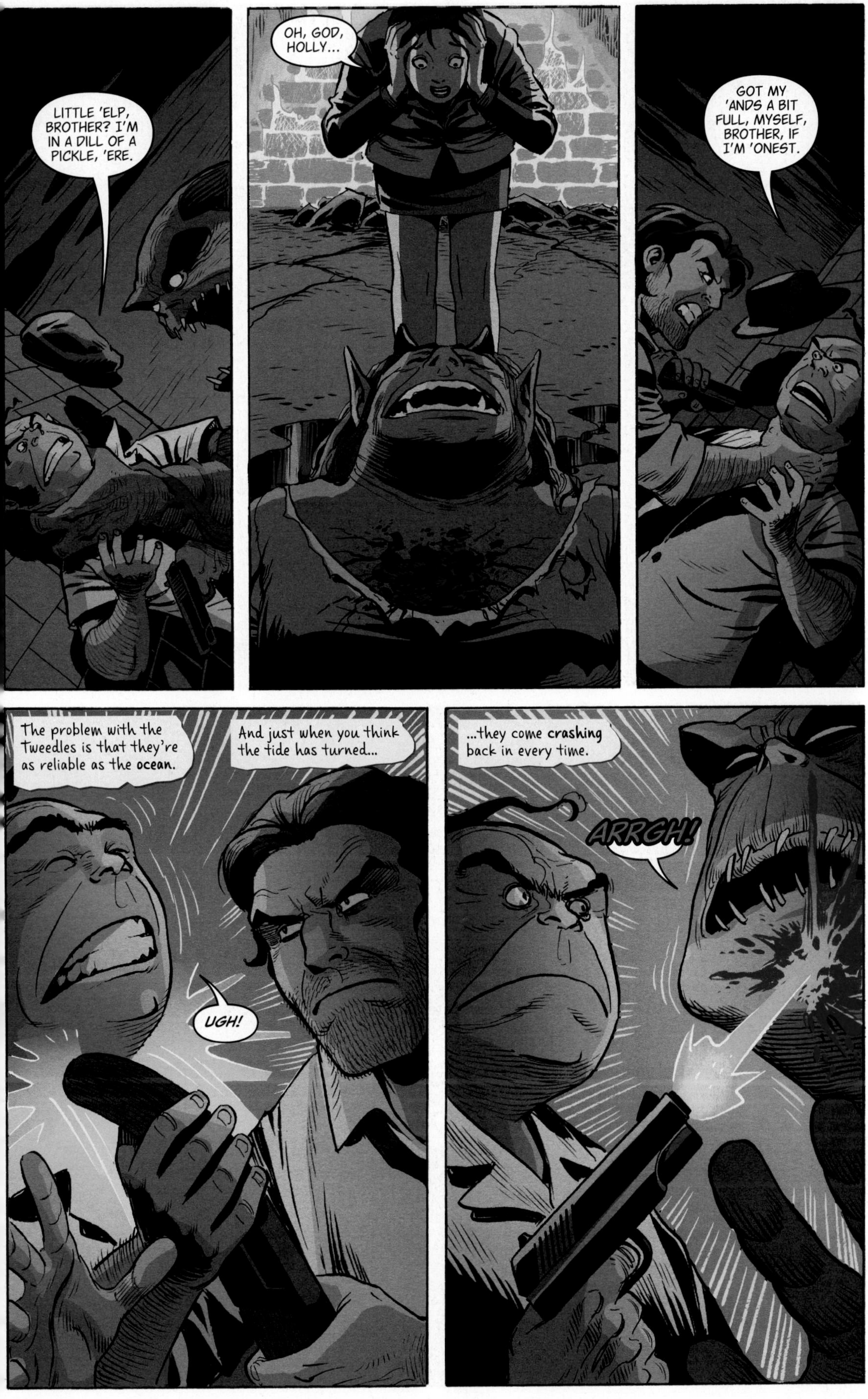
LITTLE 'ELP, BROTHER? I'M IN A DILL OF A PICKLE, 'ERE.
OH, GOD, HOLLY...
GOT MY 'ANDS A BIT FULL, MYSELF, BROTHER, IF I'M 'ONEST.
The problem with the Tweedles is that they're as reliable as the **ocean**.
And just when you think the tide has turned...
UGH!
...they come **crashing** back in every time.
ARRGH!

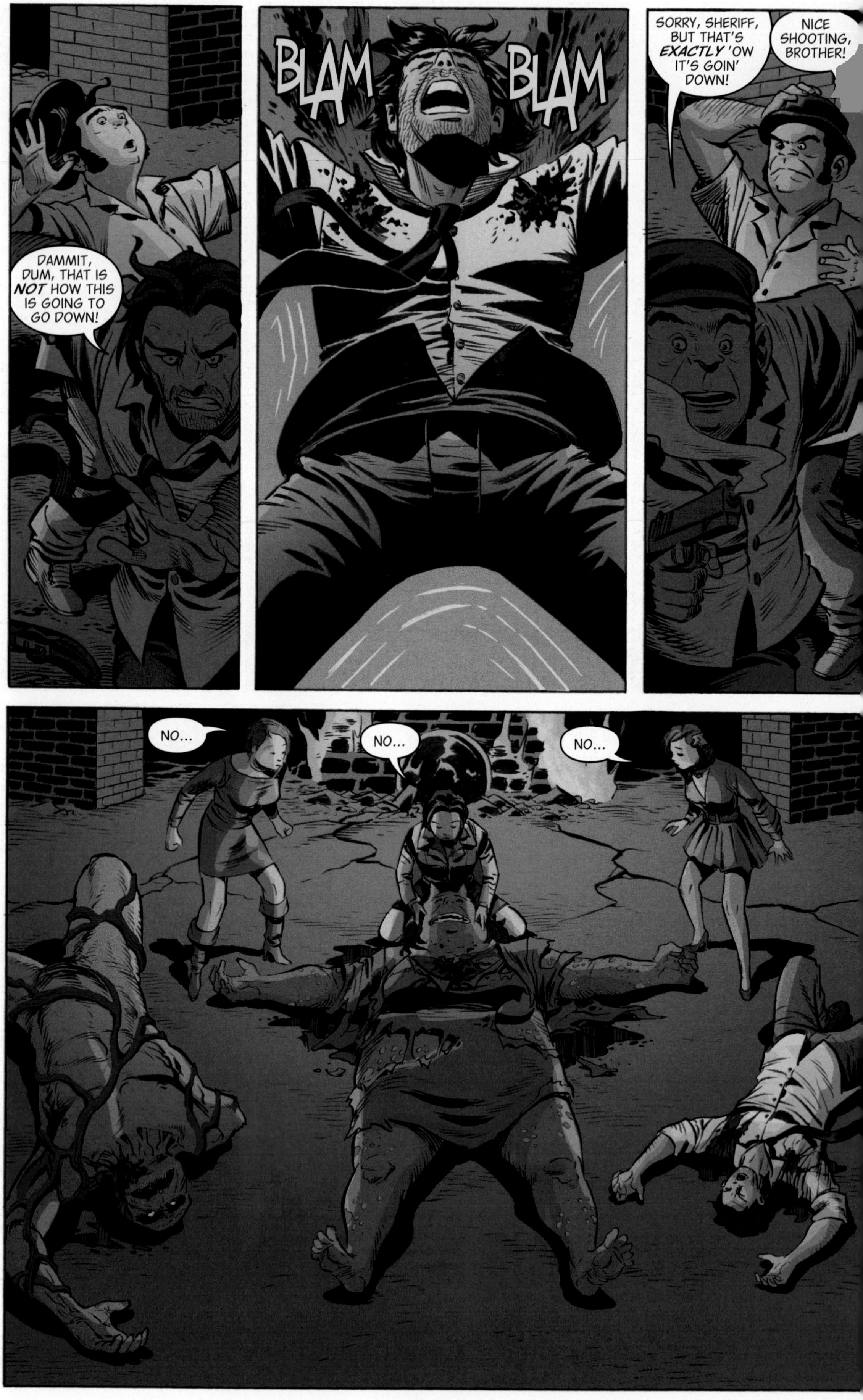
DAMMIT, DUM, THAT IS NOT HOW THIS IS GOING TO GO DOWN!
BLAM
BLAM
SORRY, SHERIFF, BUT THAT'S EXACTLY 'OW IT'S GOIN' DOWN!
NICE SHOOTING, BROTHER!
NO...
NO...
NO...

LONDON. NOVEMBER 1, 1887.

OF COURSE I HAVE *DELIGHTED* IN YOUR COMPANY ALL THIS DAY, MY CAPTIVATING *MARY*.

BUT SURELY ONE AS *RADIANT* AS YOURSELF IS NEEDED OUTDOORS, WHERE THE LONDON SUN FAILS TO PRY THROUGH THE AUTUMN CLOUDS.

YOU ARE *KIND* TO SAY IT, SIR... BUT I HAVE NOT BEEN MISSED AT ALL TODAY.

MY *SCHOOL CHUMS* HAVE NOT RUNG FOR ME, NOR EVEN MY *PARENTS* CALLED ME TO TEA.

I FEEL *GREEDY*, KEEPING YOUR ATTENTION ALL TO MYSELF.

YOU ARE SUCH A RESPLENDENT BUTTERFLY, YET I FEAR THAT I HAVE RENDERED YOU TRAPPED BEHIND THIS *GLASS*.

BUTTERFLY? HARDLY! I AM AT BEST A *MOTH*, DIRECTIONLESS AND DRAB OF COLOR AND CERTAINLY A HAZARD TO ANY DECENT CLOTHING I ENCOUNTER!

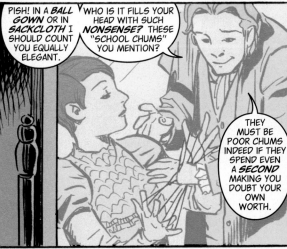

PISH! IN A *BALL GOWN* OR IN *SACKCLOTH* I SHOULD COUNT YOU EQUALLY ELEGANT.

WHO IS IT FILLS YOUR HEAD WITH SUCH *NONSENSE?* THESE "SCHOOL CHUMS" YOU MENTION?

THEY MUST BE POOR CHUMS INDEED IF THEY SPEND EVEN A *SECOND* MAKING YOU DOUBT YOUR OWN WORTH.

YOU ARE... KIND TO SAY IT, SIR.

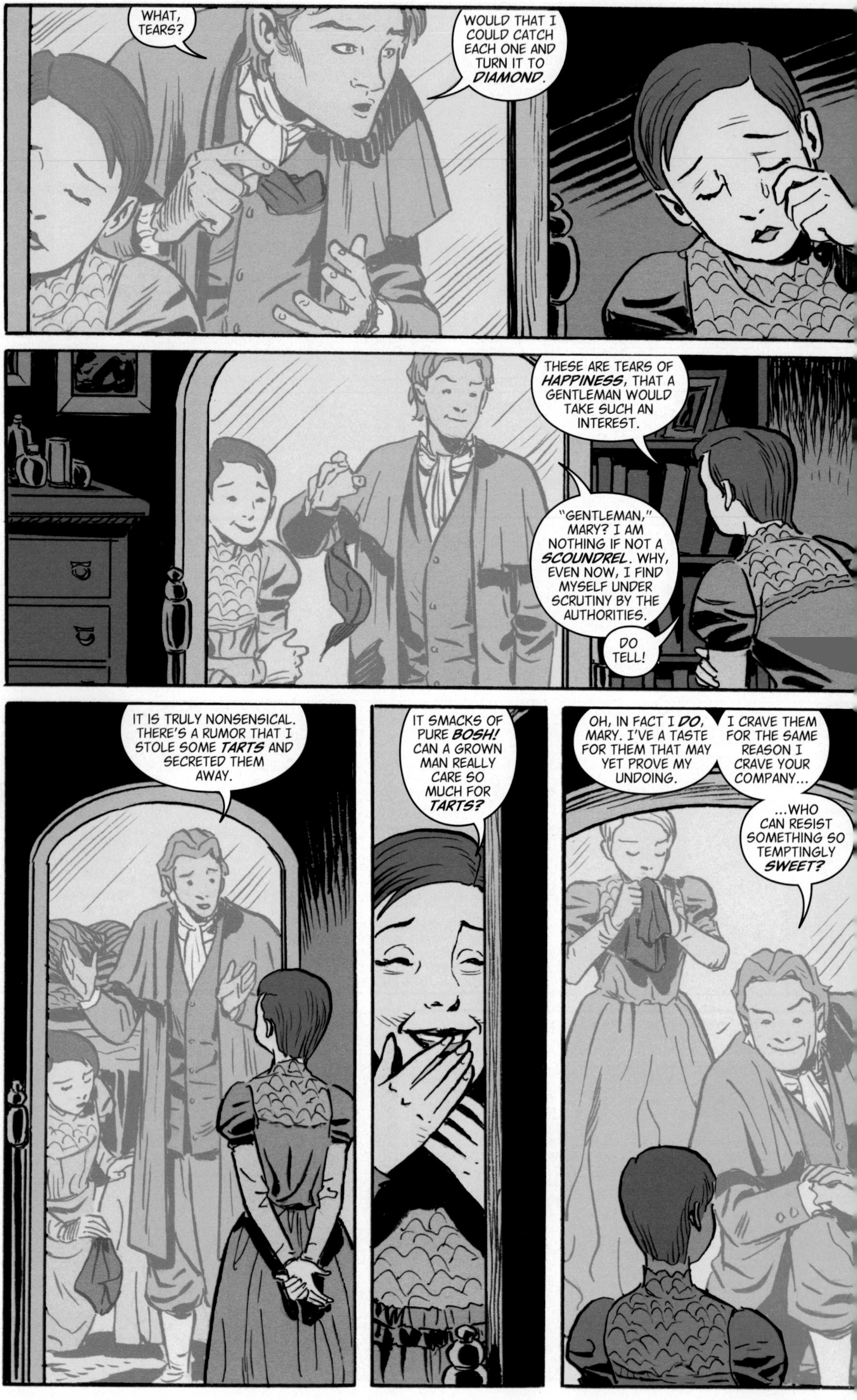
WHAT, TEARS?
WOULD THAT I COULD CATCH EACH ONE AND TURN IT TO **DIAMOND**.
THESE ARE TEARS OF **HAPPINESS**, THAT A GENTLEMAN WOULD TAKE SUCH AN INTEREST.
"GENTLEMAN," MARY? I AM NOTHING IF NOT A **SCOUNDREL**. WHY, EVEN NOW, I FIND MYSELF UNDER SCRUTINY BY THE AUTHORITIES.
DO TELL!
IT IS TRULY NONSENSICAL. THERE'S A RUMOR THAT I STOLE SOME **TARTS** AND SECRETED THEM AWAY.
IT SMACKS OF PURE **BOSH!** CAN A GROWN MAN REALLY CARE SO MUCH FOR **TARTS?**
OH, IN FACT I **DO**, MARY. I'VE A TASTE FOR THEM THAT MAY YET PROVE MY UNDOING.
I CRAVE THEM FOR THE SAME REASON I CRAVE YOUR COMPANY...
...WHO CAN RESIST SOMETHING SO TEMPTINGLY **SWEET?**

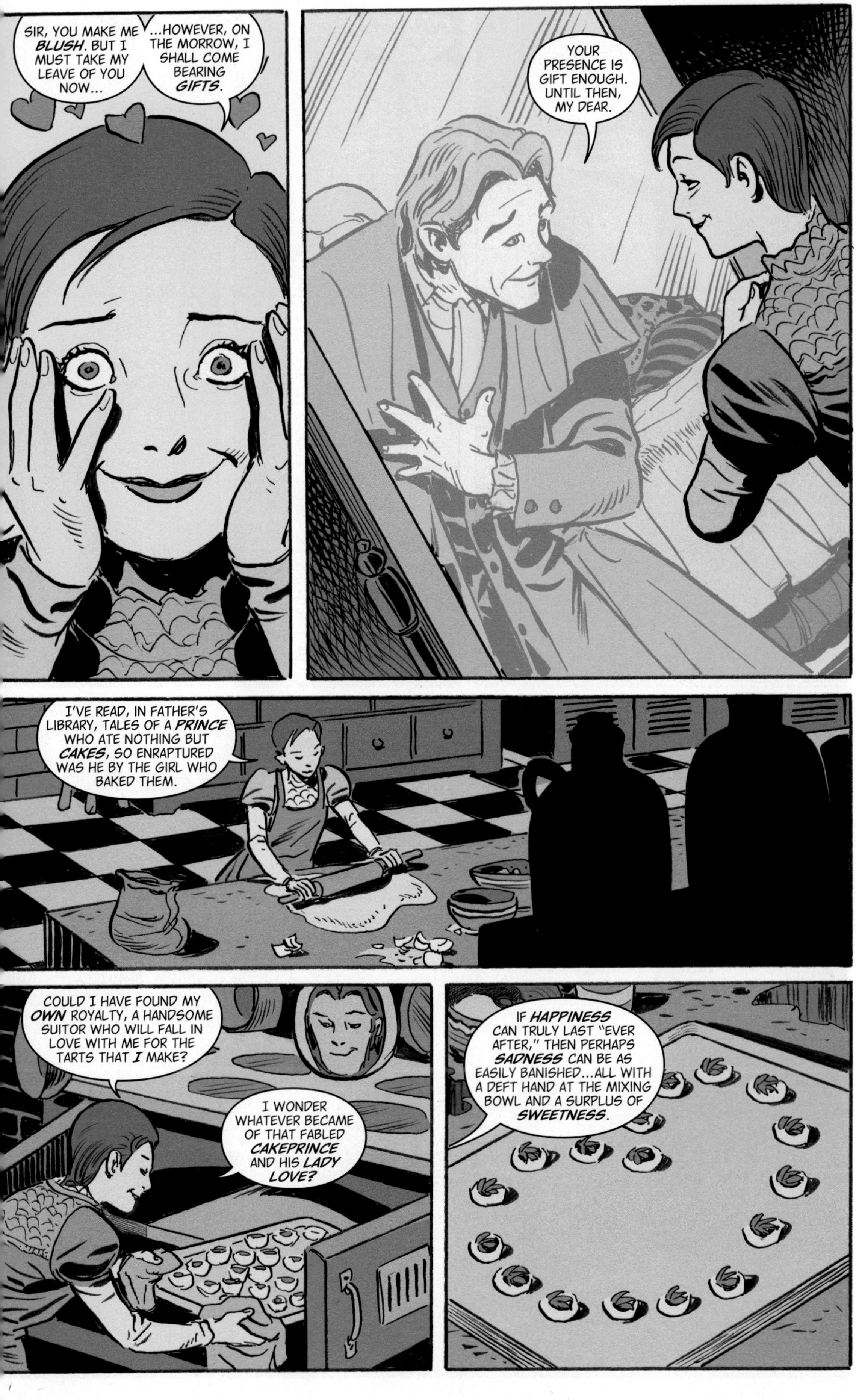
SIR, YOU MAKE ME *BLUSH*. BUT I MUST TAKE MY LEAVE OF YOU NOW...
...HOWEVER, ON THE MORROW, I SHALL COME BEARING *GIFTS*.
YOUR PRESENCE IS GIFT ENOUGH. UNTIL THEN, MY DEAR.
I'VE READ, IN FATHER'S LIBRARY, TALES OF A *PRINCE* WHO ATE NOTHING BUT *CAKES*, SO ENRAPTURED WAS HE BY THE GIRL WHO BAKED THEM.
COULD I HAVE FOUND MY *OWN* ROYALTY, A HANDSOME SUITOR WHO WILL FALL IN LOVE WITH ME FOR THE TARTS THAT *I* MAKE?
I WONDER WHATEVER BECAME OF THAT FABLED *CAKEPRINCE* AND HIS *LADY LOVE?*
IF *HAPPINESS* CAN TRULY LAST "EVER AFTER," THEN PERHAPS *SADNESS* CAN BE AS EASILY BANISHED...ALL WITH A DEFT HAND AT THE MIXING BOWL AND A SURPLUS OF *SWEETNESS*.

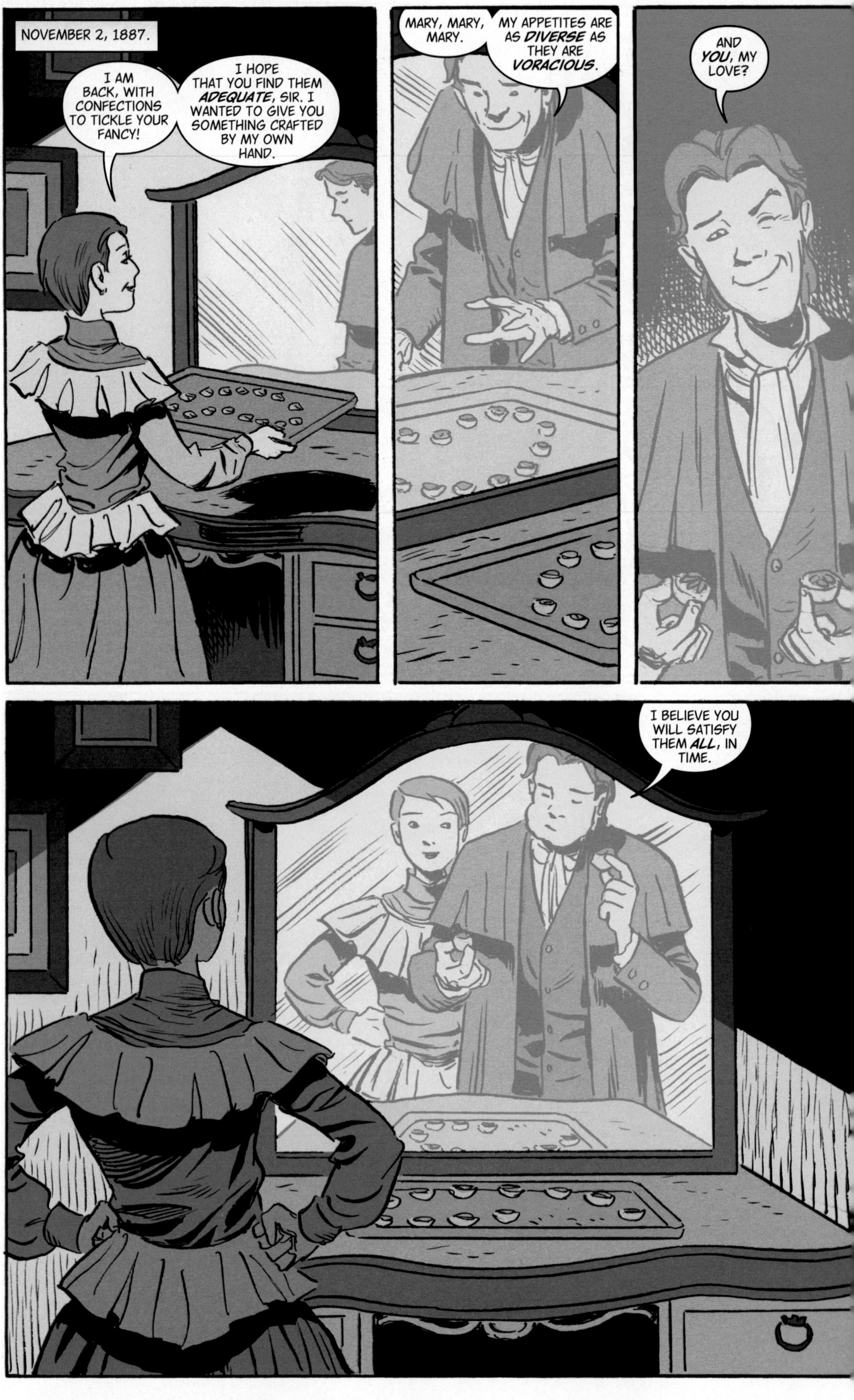

NOVEMBER 2, 1887.
I AM BACK, WITH CONFECTIONS TO TICKLE YOUR FANCY!
I HOPE THAT YOU FIND THEM ADEQUATE, SIR. I WANTED TO GIVE YOU SOMETHING CRAFTED BY MY OWN HAND.
MARY, MARY, MARY.
MY APPETITES ARE AS DIVERSE AS THEY ARE VORACIOUS.
AND YOU, MY LOVE?
I BELIEVE YOU WILL SATISFY THEM ALL, IN TIME.

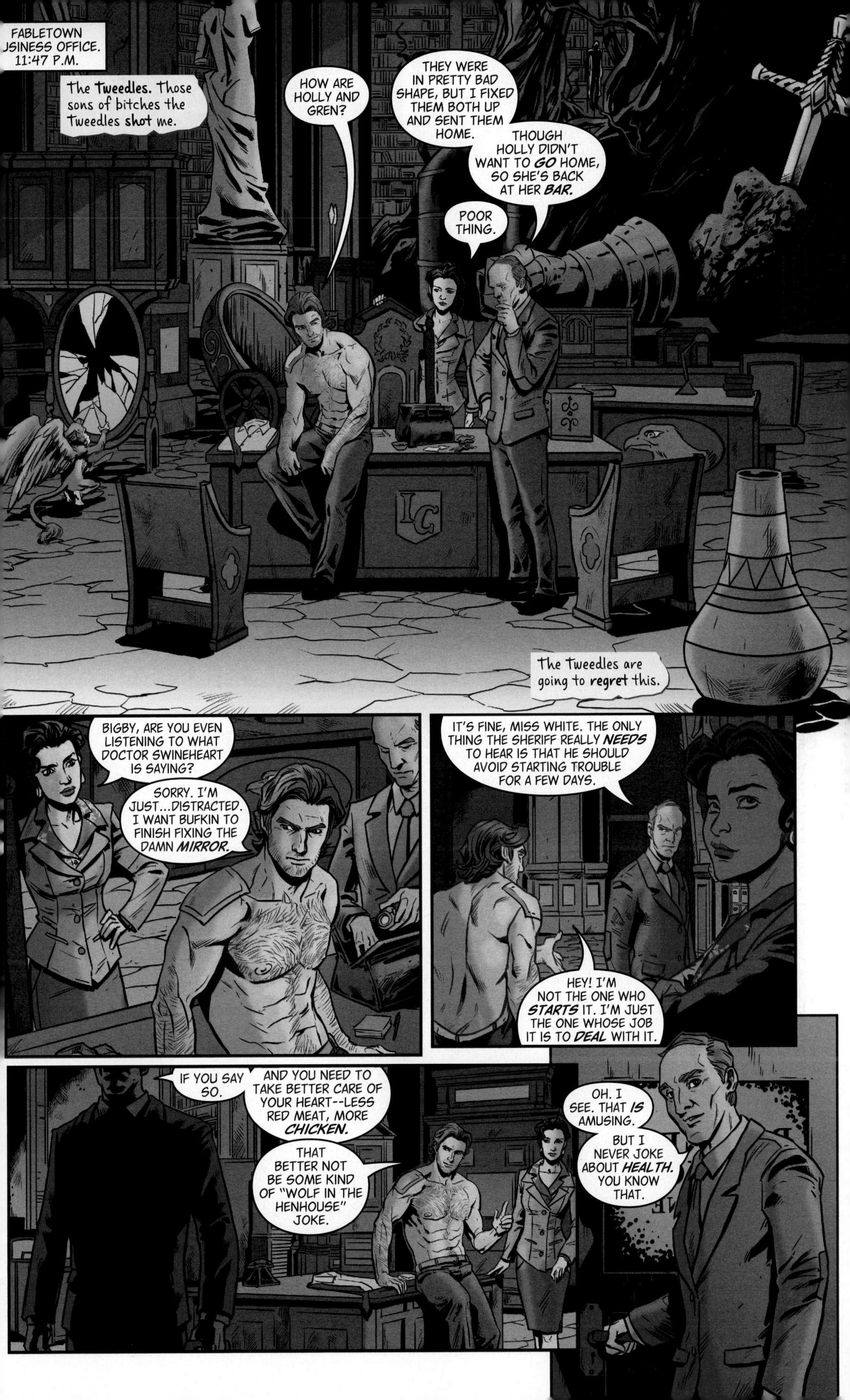
FABLETOWN
JSINESS OFFICE.
11:47 P.M.
The Tweedles. Those sons of bitches the Tweedles shot me.
HOW ARE HOLLY AND GREN?
THEY WERE IN PRETTY BAD SHAPE, BUT I FIXED THEM BOTH UP AND SENT THEM HOME.
THOUGH HOLLY DIDN'T WANT TO GO HOME, SO SHE'S BACK AT HER BAR.
POOR THING.
The Tweedles are going to regret this.
BIGBY, ARE YOU EVEN LISTENING TO WHAT DOCTOR SWINEHEART IS SAYING?
SORRY. I'M JUST...DISTRACTED. I WANT BUFKIN TO FINISH FIXING THE DAMN MIRROR.
IT'S FINE, MISS WHITE. THE ONLY THING THE SHERIFF REALLY NEEDS TO HEAR IS THAT HE SHOULD AVOID STARTING TROUBLE FOR A FEW DAYS.
HEY! I'M NOT THE ONE WHO STARTS IT. I'M JUST THE ONE WHOSE JOB IT IS TO DEAL WITH IT.
IF YOU SAY SO.
AND YOU NEED TO TAKE BETTER CARE OF YOUR HEART--LESS RED MEAT, MORE CHICKEN.
THAT BETTER NOT BE SOME KIND OF "WOLF IN THE HENHOUSE" JOKE.
OH. I SEE. THAT IS AMUSING.
BUT I NEVER JOKE ABOUT HEALTH. YOU KNOW THAT.

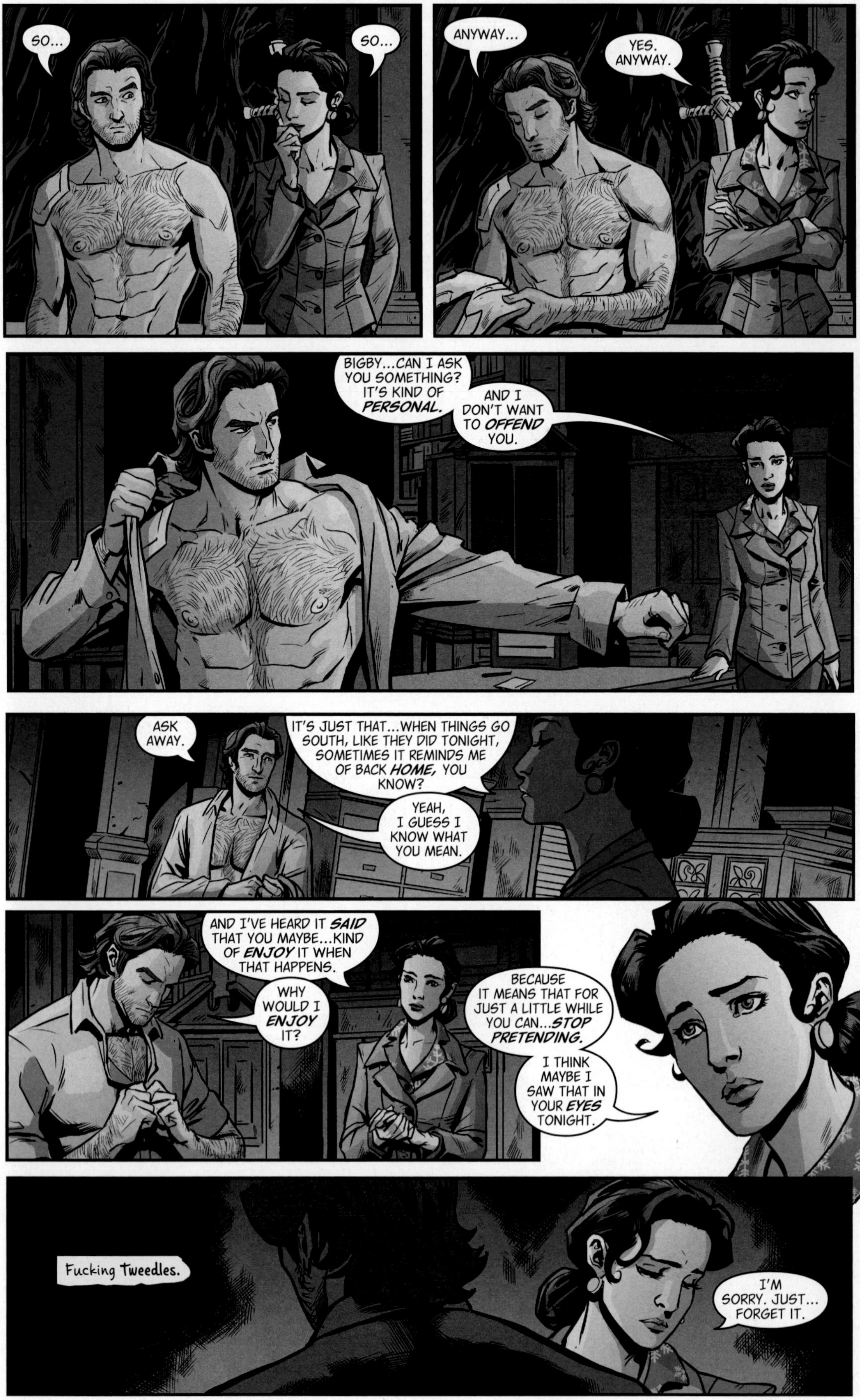
SO...
SO...
ANYWAY...
YES. ANYWAY.
BIGBY...CAN I ASK YOU SOMETHING? IT'S KIND OF PERSONAL.
AND I DON'T WANT TO OFFEND YOU.
ASK AWAY.
IT'S JUST THAT...WHEN THINGS GO SOUTH, LIKE THEY DID TONIGHT, SOMETIMES IT REMINDS ME OF BACK HOME, YOU KNOW?
YEAH, I GUESS I KNOW WHAT YOU MEAN.
AND I'VE HEARD IT SAID THAT YOU MAYBE...KIND OF ENJOY IT WHEN THAT HAPPENS.
WHY WOULD I ENJOY IT?
BECAUSE IT MEANS THAT FOR JUST A LITTLE WHILE YOU CAN...STOP PRETENDING.
I THINK MAYBE I SAW THAT IN YOUR EYES TONIGHT.
Fucking Tweedles.
I'M SORRY. JUST... FORGET IT.

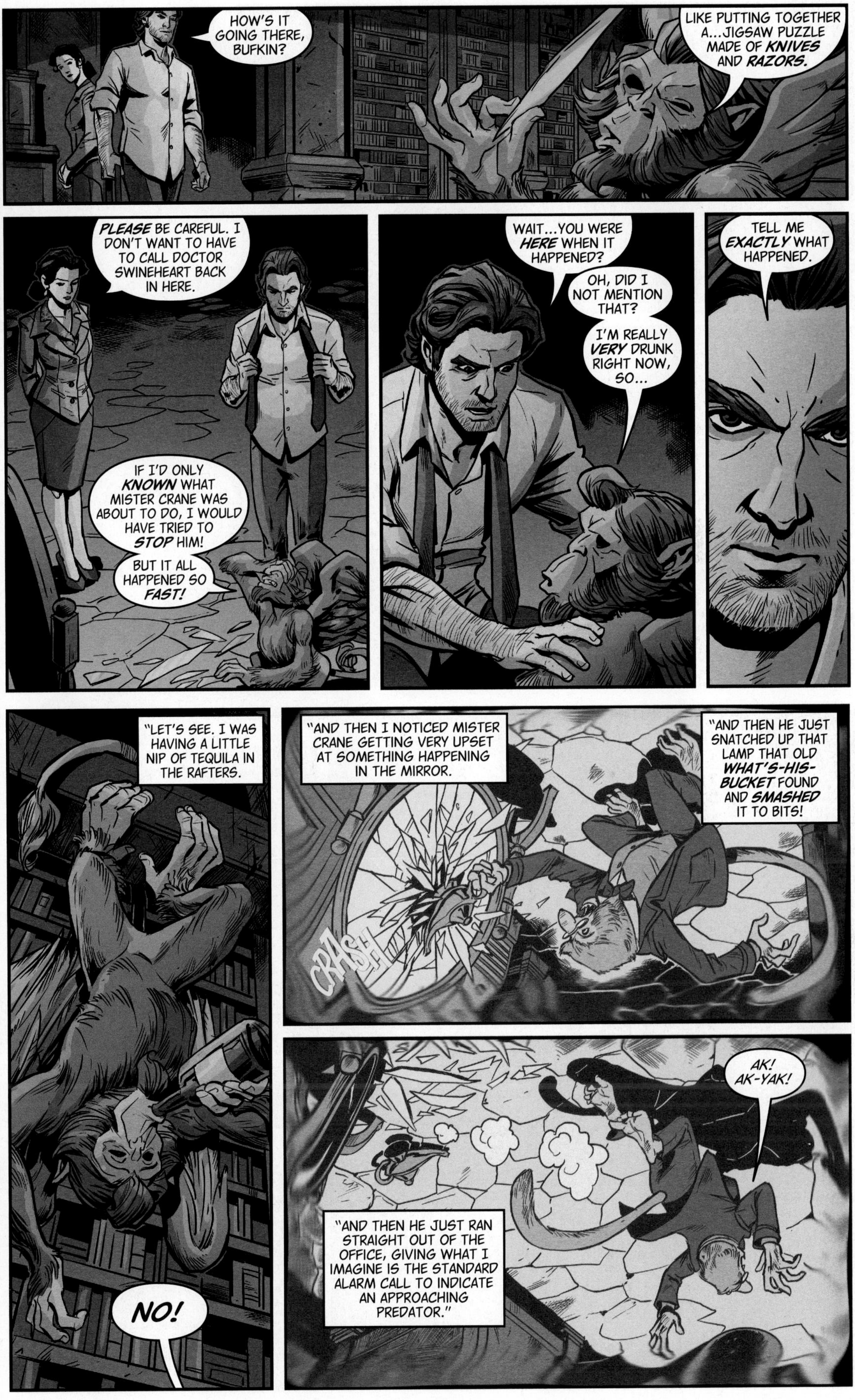
HOW'S IT GOING THERE, BUFKIN?
LIKE PUTTING TOGETHER A...JIGSAW PUZZLE MADE OF KNIVES AND RAZORS.
PLEASE BE CAREFUL. I DON'T WANT TO HAVE TO CALL DOCTOR SWINEHEART BACK IN HERE.
IF I'D ONLY KNOWN WHAT MISTER CRANE WAS ABOUT TO DO, I WOULD HAVE TRIED TO STOP HIM!
BUT IT ALL HAPPENED SO FAST!
WAIT...YOU WERE HERE WHEN IT HAPPENED?
OH, DID I NOT MENTION THAT?
I'M REALLY VERY DRUNK RIGHT NOW, SO...
TELL ME EXACTLY WHAT HAPPENED.
"LET'S SEE. I WAS HAVING A LITTLE NIP OF TEQUILA IN THE RAFTERS.
NO!
"AND THEN I NOTICED MISTER CRANE GETTING VERY UPSET AT SOMETHING HAPPENING IN THE MIRROR.
"AND THEN HE JUST SNATCHED UP THAT LAMP THAT OLD WHAT'S-HIS-BUCKET FOUND AND SMASHED IT TO BITS!
CRASH
AK! AK-YAK!
"AND THEN HE JUST RAN STRAIGHT OUT OF THE OFFICE, GIVING WHAT I IMAGINE IS THE STANDARD ALARM CALL TO INDICATE AN APPROACHING PREDATOR."

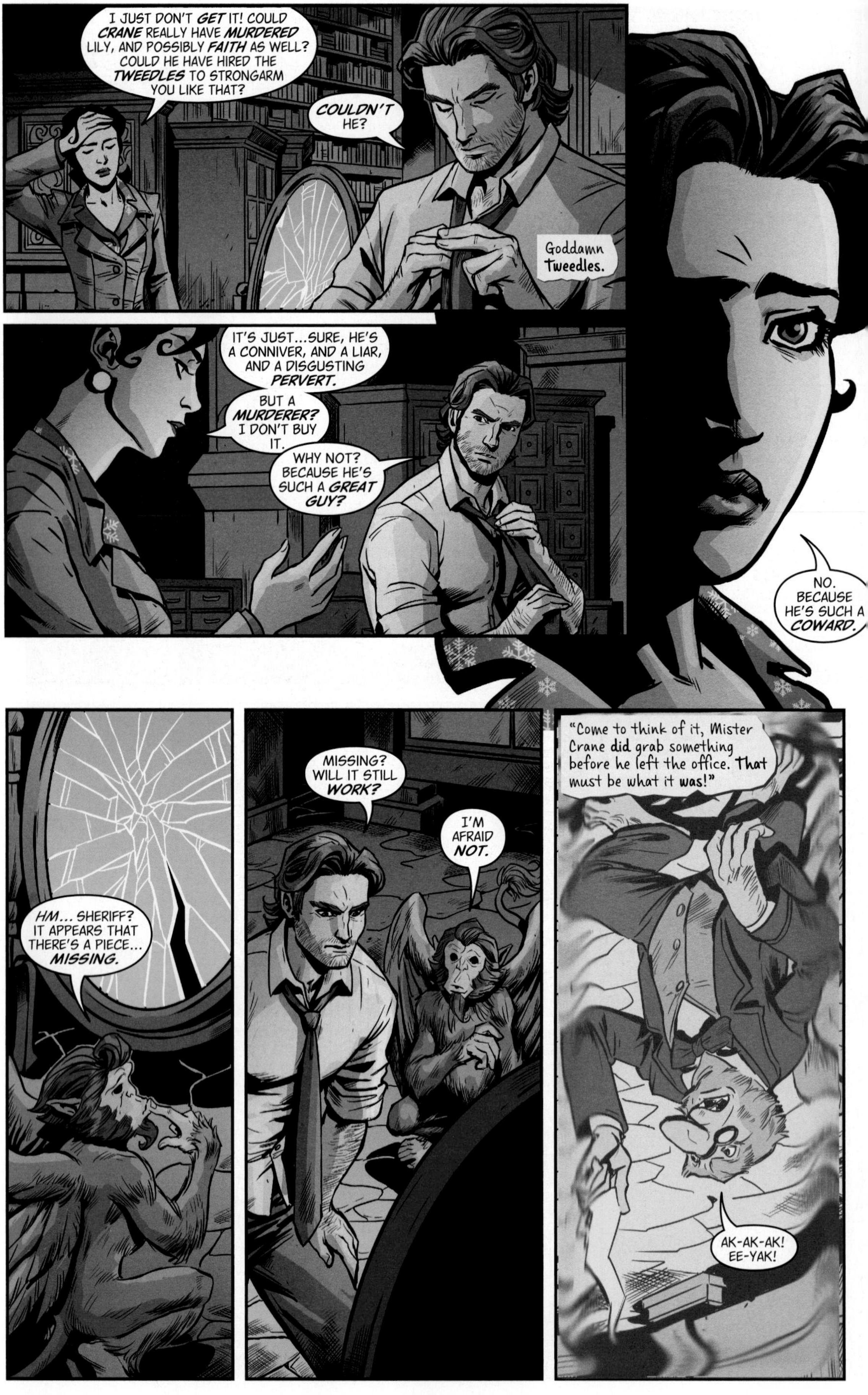
I JUST DON'T GET IT! COULD CRANE REALLY HAVE MURDERED LILY, AND POSSIBLY FAITH AS WELL? COULD HE HAVE HIRED THE TWEEDLES TO STRONGARM YOU LIKE THAT?
COULDN'T HE?
Goddamn Tweedles.
IT'S JUST...SURE, HE'S A CONNIVER, AND A LIAR, AND A DISGUSTING PERVERT.
BUT A MURDERER? I DON'T BUY IT.
WHY NOT? BECAUSE HE'S SUCH A GREAT GUY?
NO. BECAUSE HE'S SUCH A COWARD.
HM... SHERIFF? IT APPEARS THAT THERE'S A PIECE... MISSING.
MISSING? WILL IT STILL WORK?
I'M AFRAID NOT.
"Come to think of it, Mister Crane did grab something before he left the office. That must be what it was!"
AK-AK-AK! EE-YAK!

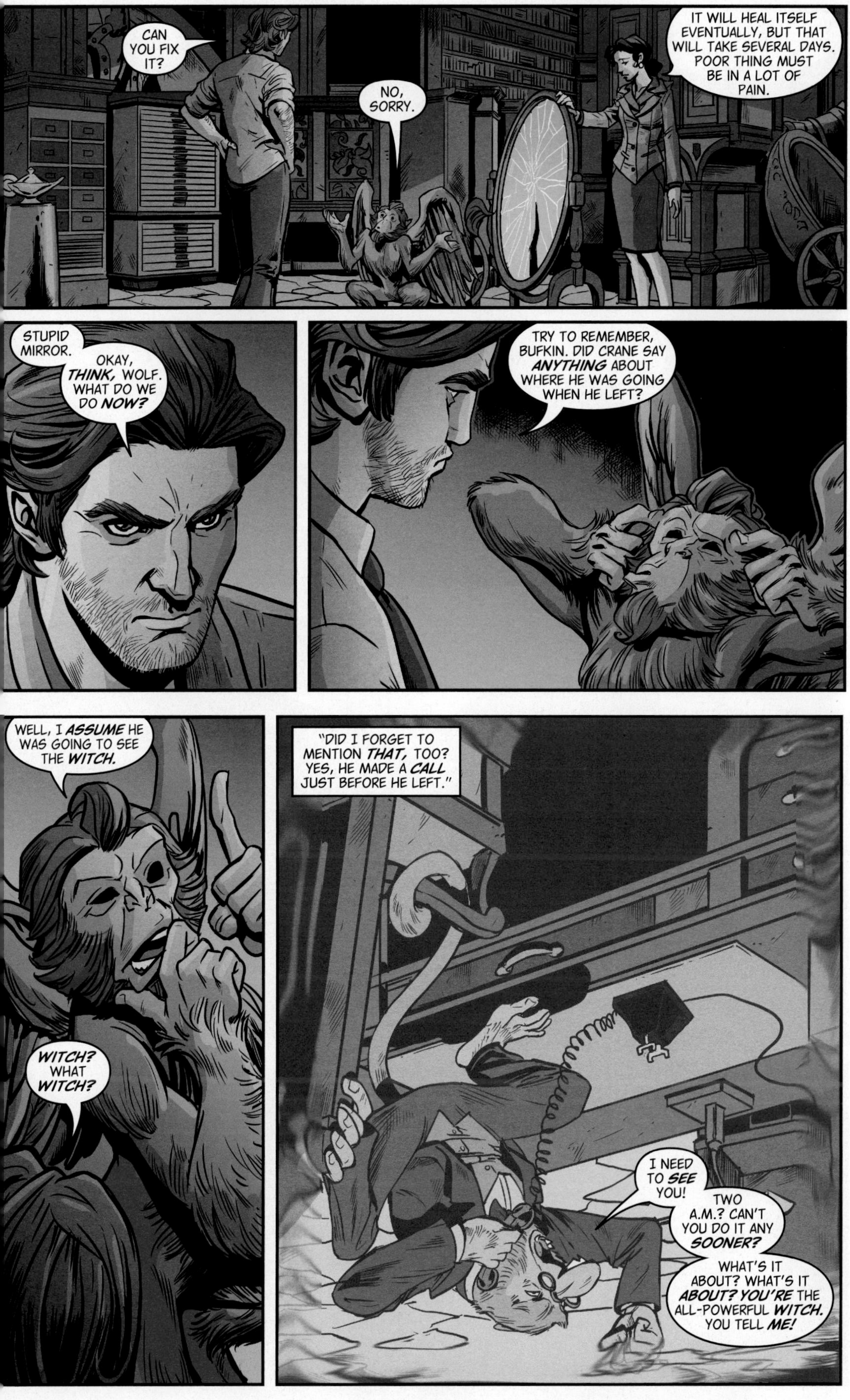
CAN YOU FIX IT?
NO, SORRY.
IT WILL HEAL ITSELF EVENTUALLY, BUT THAT WILL TAKE SEVERAL DAYS. POOR THING MUST BE IN A LOT OF PAIN.
STUPID MIRROR.
OKAY, THINK, WOLF. WHAT DO WE DO NOW?
TRY TO REMEMBER, BUFKIN. DID CRANE SAY ANYTHING ABOUT WHERE HE WAS GOING WHEN HE LEFT?
WELL, I ASSUME HE WAS GOING TO SEE THE WITCH.
WITCH? WHAT WITCH?
"DID I FORGET TO MENTION THAT, TOO? YES, HE MADE A CALL JUST BEFORE HE LEFT."
I NEED TO SEE YOU!
TWO A.M.? CAN'T YOU DO IT ANY SOONER?
WHAT'S IT ABOUT? WHAT'S IT ABOUT? YOU'RE THE ALL-POWERFUL WITCH. YOU TELL ME!

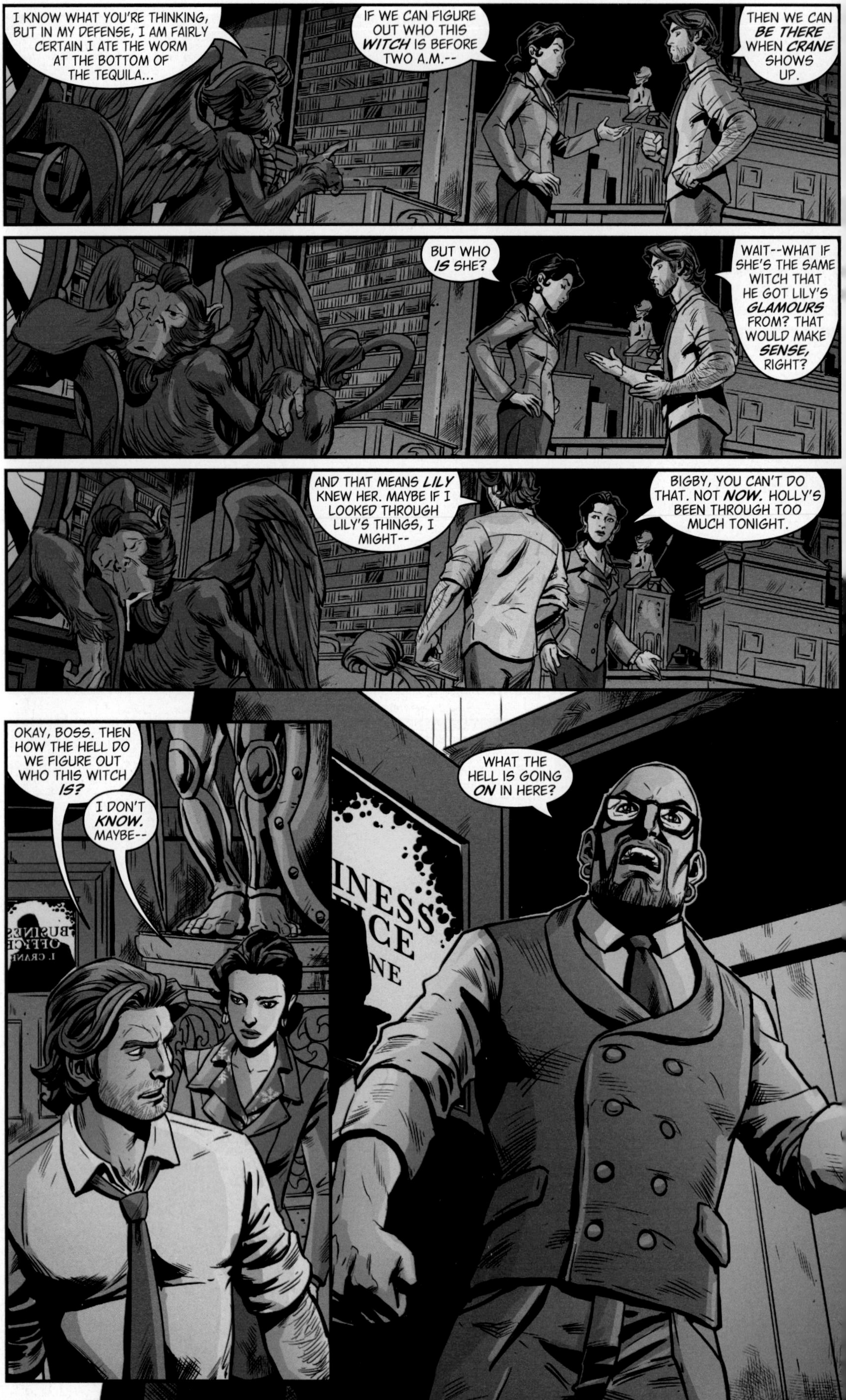
I KNOW WHAT YOU'RE THINKING, BUT IN MY DEFENSE, I AM FAIRLY CERTAIN I ATE THE WORM AT THE BOTTOM OF THE TEQUILA...
IF WE CAN FIGURE OUT WHO THIS *WITCH* IS BEFORE TWO A.M.--
THEN WE CAN *BE THERE* WHEN *CRANE* SHOWS UP.
BUT WHO *IS* SHE?
WAIT--WHAT IF SHE'S THE SAME WITCH THAT HE GOT LILY'S *GLAMOURS* FROM? THAT WOULD MAKE *SENSE,* RIGHT?
AND THAT MEANS *LILY* KNEW HER. MAYBE IF I LOOKED THROUGH LILY'S THINGS, I MIGHT--
BIGBY, YOU CAN'T DO THAT. NOT *NOW.* HOLLY'S BEEN THROUGH TOO MUCH TONIGHT.
OKAY, BOSS. THEN HOW THE HELL DO WE FIGURE OUT WHO THIS WITCH *IS?*
I DON'T *KNOW.* MAYBE--
WHAT THE HELL IS GOING *ON* IN HERE?

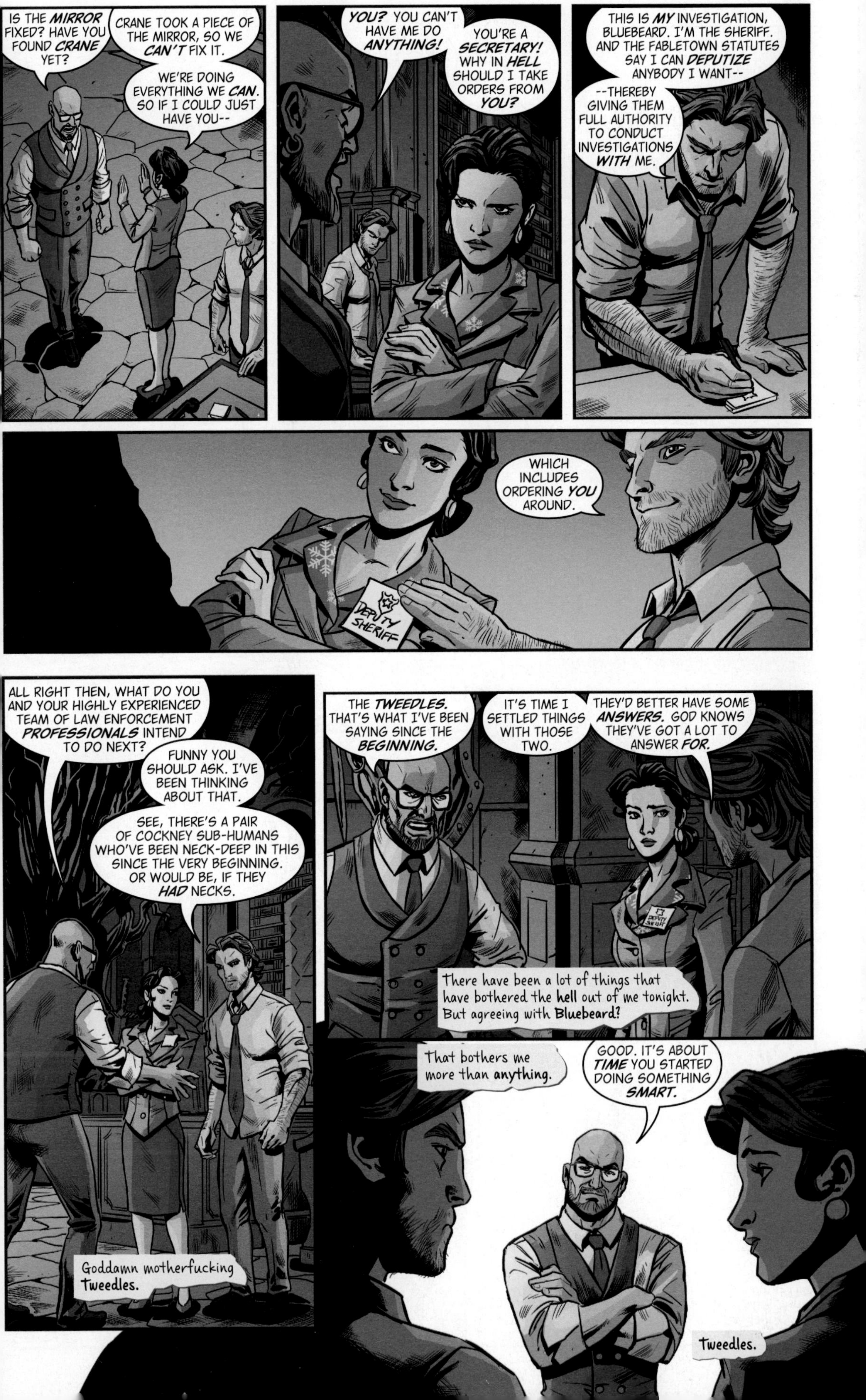
IS THE MIRROR FIXED? HAVE YOU FOUND CRANE YET?
CRANE TOOK A PIECE OF THE MIRROR, SO WE CAN'T FIX IT.
WE'RE DOING EVERYTHING WE CAN. SO IF I COULD JUST HAVE YOU--
YOU? YOU CAN'T HAVE ME DO ANYTHING!
YOU'RE A SECRETARY! WHY IN HELL SHOULD I TAKE ORDERS FROM YOU?
THIS IS MY INVESTIGATION, BLUEBEARD. I'M THE SHERIFF. AND THE FABLETOWN STATUTES SAY I CAN DEPUTIZE ANYBODY I WANT--
--THEREBY GIVING THEM FULL AUTHORITY TO CONDUCT INVESTIGATIONS WITH ME.
WHICH INCLUDES ORDERING YOU AROUND.
DEPUTY SHERIFF
ALL RIGHT THEN, WHAT DO YOU AND YOUR HIGHLY EXPERIENCED TEAM OF LAW ENFORCEMENT PROFESSIONALS INTEND TO DO NEXT?
FUNNY YOU SHOULD ASK. I'VE BEEN THINKING ABOUT THAT.
SEE, THERE'S A PAIR OF COCKNEY SUB-HUMANS WHO'VE BEEN NECK-DEEP IN THIS SINCE THE VERY BEGINNING. OR WOULD BE, IF THEY HAD NECKS.
Goddamn motherfucking Tweedles.
THE TWEEDLES. THAT'S WHAT I'VE BEEN SAYING SINCE THE BEGINNING.
IT'S TIME I SETTLED THINGS WITH THOSE TWO.
THEY'D BETTER HAVE SOME ANSWERS. GOD KNOWS THEY'VE GOT A LOT TO ANSWER FOR.
There have been a lot of things that have bothered the hell out of me tonight. But agreeing with Bluebeard?
That bothers me more than anything.
GOOD. IT'S ABOUT TIME YOU STARTED DOING SOMETHING SMART.
Tweedles.

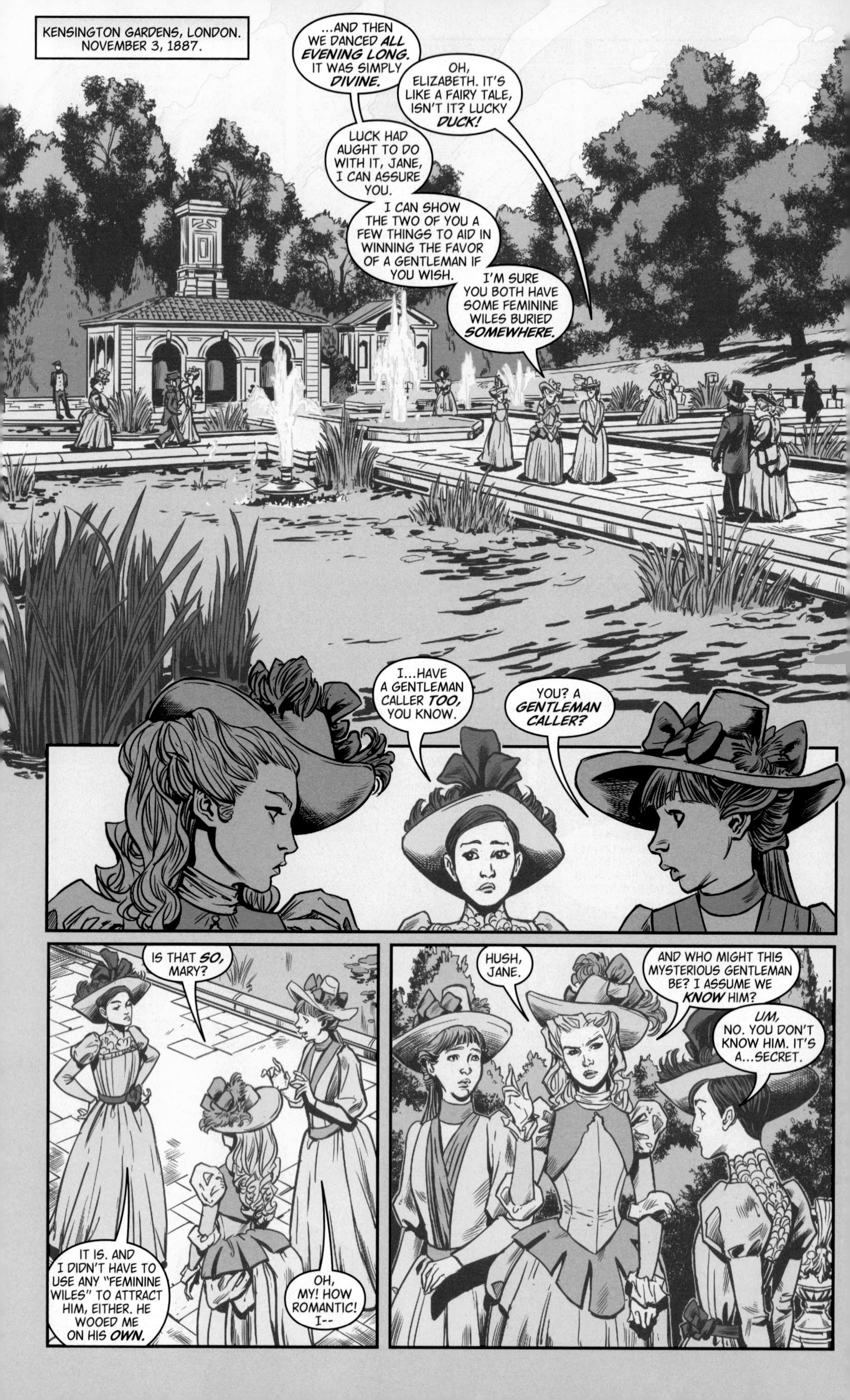
KENSINGTON GARDENS, LONDON. NOVEMBER 3, 1887.
...AND THEN WE DANCED ALL EVENING LONG. IT WAS SIMPLY DIVINE.
OH, ELIZABETH. IT'S LIKE A FAIRY TALE, ISN'T IT? LUCKY DUCK!
LUCK HAD AUGHT TO DO WITH IT, JANE, I CAN ASSURE YOU.
I CAN SHOW THE TWO OF YOU A FEW THINGS TO AID IN WINNING THE FAVOR OF A GENTLEMAN IF YOU WISH.
I'M SURE YOU BOTH HAVE SOME FEMININE WILES BURIED SOMEWHERE.
I...HAVE A GENTLEMAN CALLER TOO, YOU KNOW.
YOU? A GENTLEMAN CALLER?
IS THAT SO, MARY?
IT IS. AND I DIDN'T HAVE TO USE ANY "FEMININE WILES" TO ATTRACT HIM, EITHER. HE WOOED ME ON HIS OWN.
OH, MY! HOW ROMANTIC! I--
HUSH, JANE.
AND WHO MIGHT THIS MYSTERIOUS GENTLEMAN BE? I ASSUME WE KNOW HIM?
UM, NO. YOU DON'T KNOW HIM. IT'S A...SECRET.

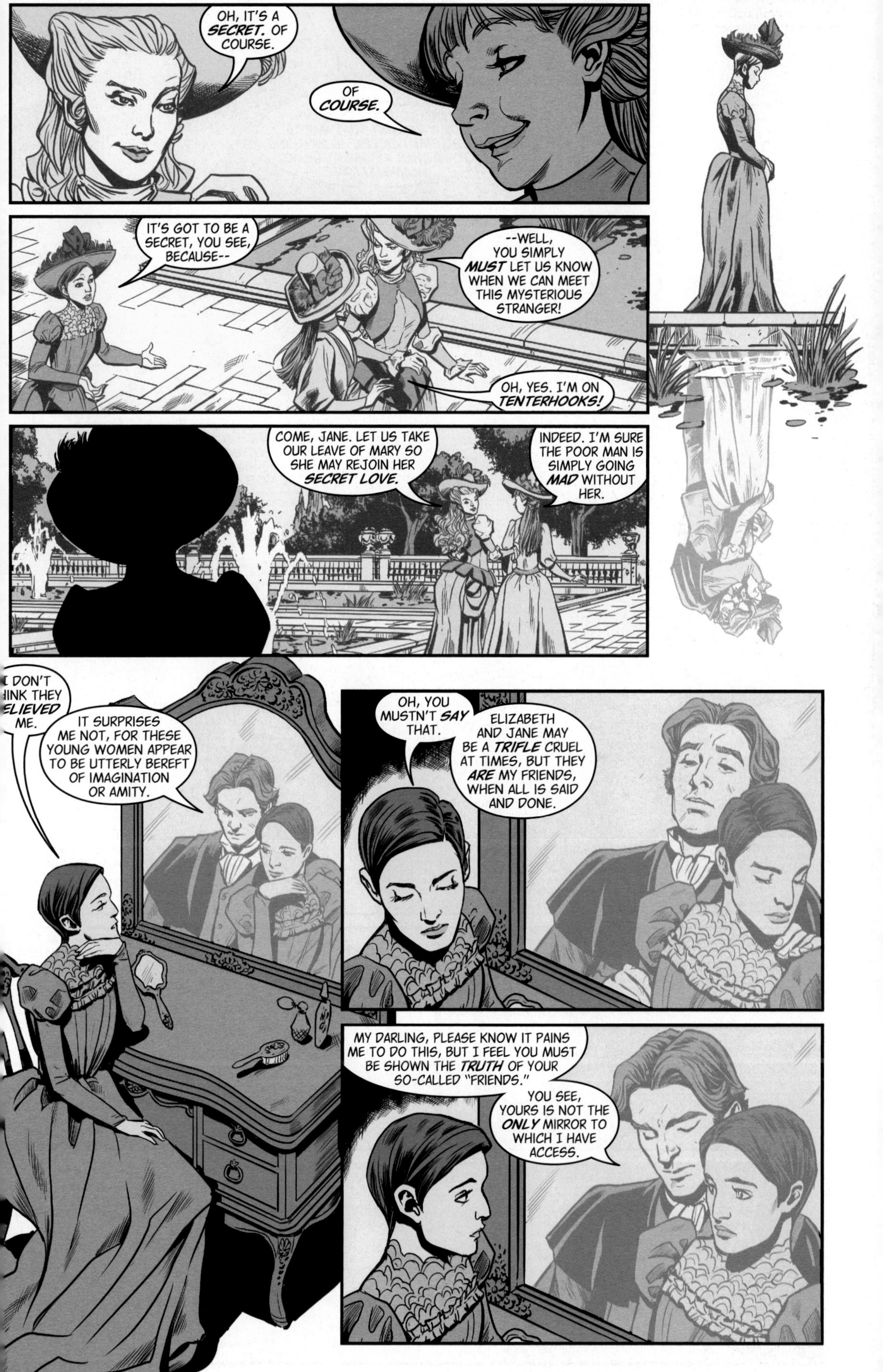

OH, IT'S A SECRET. OF COURSE.
OF COURSE.
IT'S GOT TO BE A SECRET, YOU SEE, BECAUSE--
--WELL, YOU SIMPLY MUST LET US KNOW WHEN WE CAN MEET THIS MYSTERIOUS STRANGER!
OH, YES. I'M ON TENTERHOOKS!
COME, JANE. LET US TAKE OUR LEAVE OF MARY SO SHE MAY REJOIN HER SECRET LOVE.
INDEED. I'M SURE THE POOR MAN IS SIMPLY GOING MAD WITHOUT HER.
I DON'T THINK THEY BELIEVED ME.
IT SURPRISES ME NOT, FOR THESE YOUNG WOMEN APPEAR TO BE UTTERLY BEREFT OF IMAGINATION OR AMITY.
OH, YOU MUSTN'T SAY THAT.
ELIZABETH AND JANE MAY BE A TRIFLE CRUEL AT TIMES, BUT THEY ARE MY FRIENDS, WHEN ALL IS SAID AND DONE.
MY DARLING, PLEASE KNOW IT PAINS ME TO DO THIS, BUT I FEEL YOU MUST BE SHOWN THE TRUTH OF YOUR SO-CALLED "FRIENDS."
YOU SEE, YOURS IS NOT THE ONLY MIRROR TO WHICH I HAVE ACCESS.

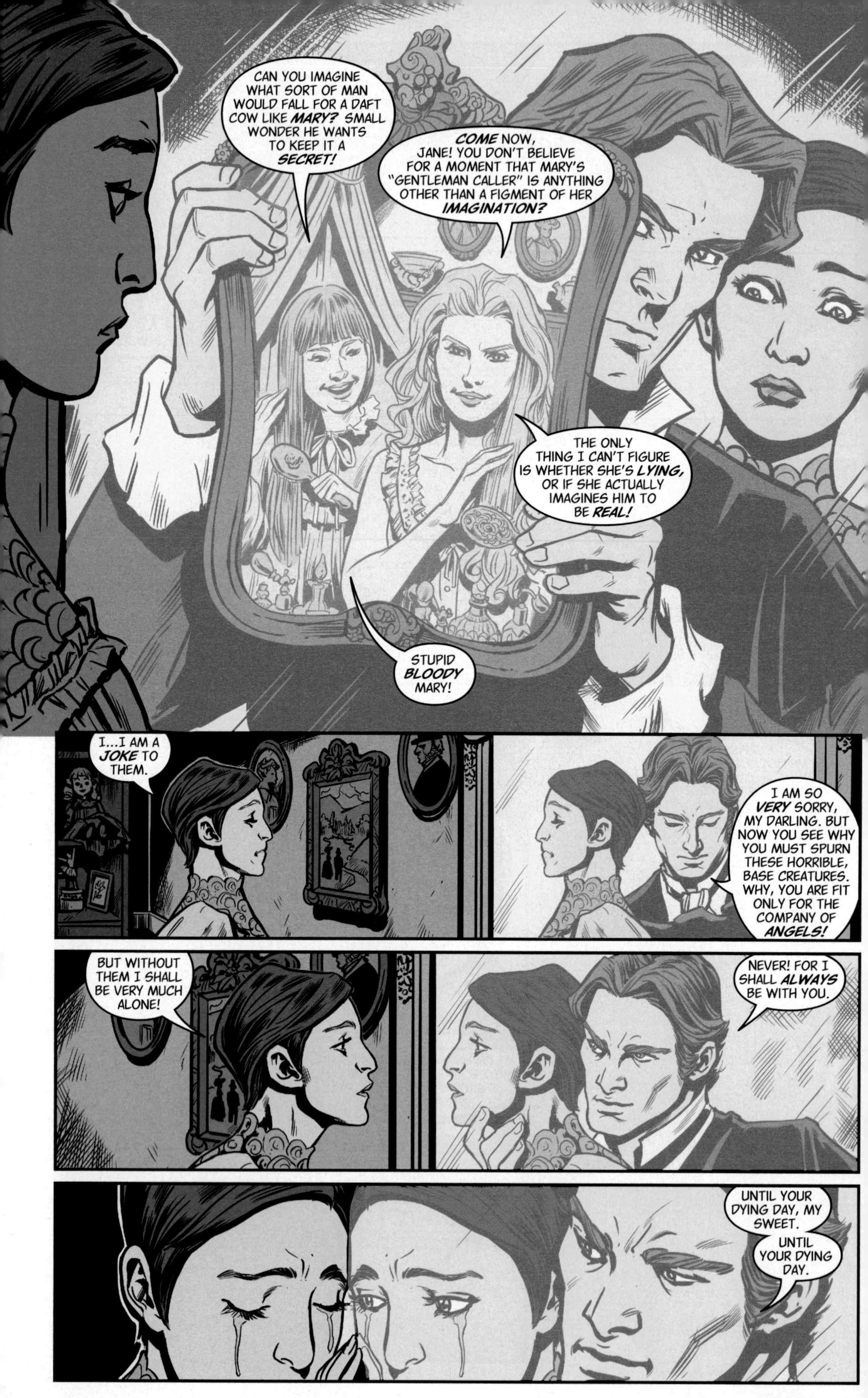
CAN YOU IMAGINE WHAT SORT OF MAN WOULD FALL FOR A DAFT COW LIKE MARY? SMALL WONDER HE WANTS TO KEEP IT A SECRET!
COME NOW, JANE! YOU DON'T BELIEVE FOR A MOMENT THAT MARY'S "GENTLEMAN CALLER" IS ANYTHING OTHER THAN A FIGMENT OF HER IMAGINATION?
THE ONLY THING I CAN'T FIGURE IS WHETHER SHE'S LYING, OR IF SHE ACTUALLY IMAGINES HIM TO BE REAL!
STUPID BLOODY MARY!
I...I AM A JOKE TO THEM.
I AM SO VERY SORRY, MY DARLING. BUT NOW YOU SEE WHY YOU MUST SPURN THESE HORRIBLE, BASE CREATURES. WHY, YOU ARE FIT ONLY FOR THE COMPANY OF ANGELS!
BUT WITHOUT THEM I SHALL BE VERY MUCH ALONE!
NEVER! FOR I SHALL ALWAYS BE WITH YOU.
UNTIL YOUR DYING DAY, MY SWEET.
UNTIL YOUR DYING DAY.

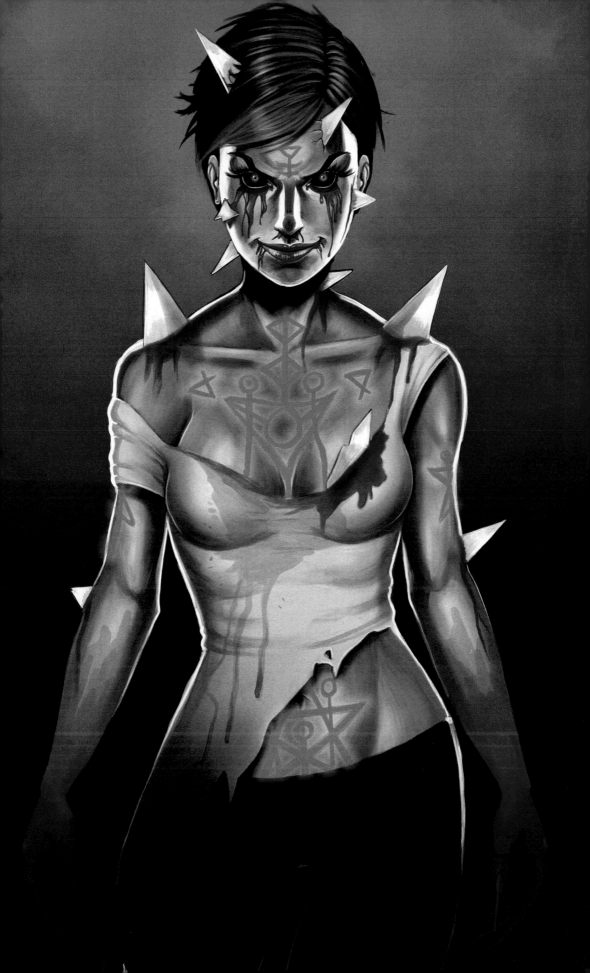

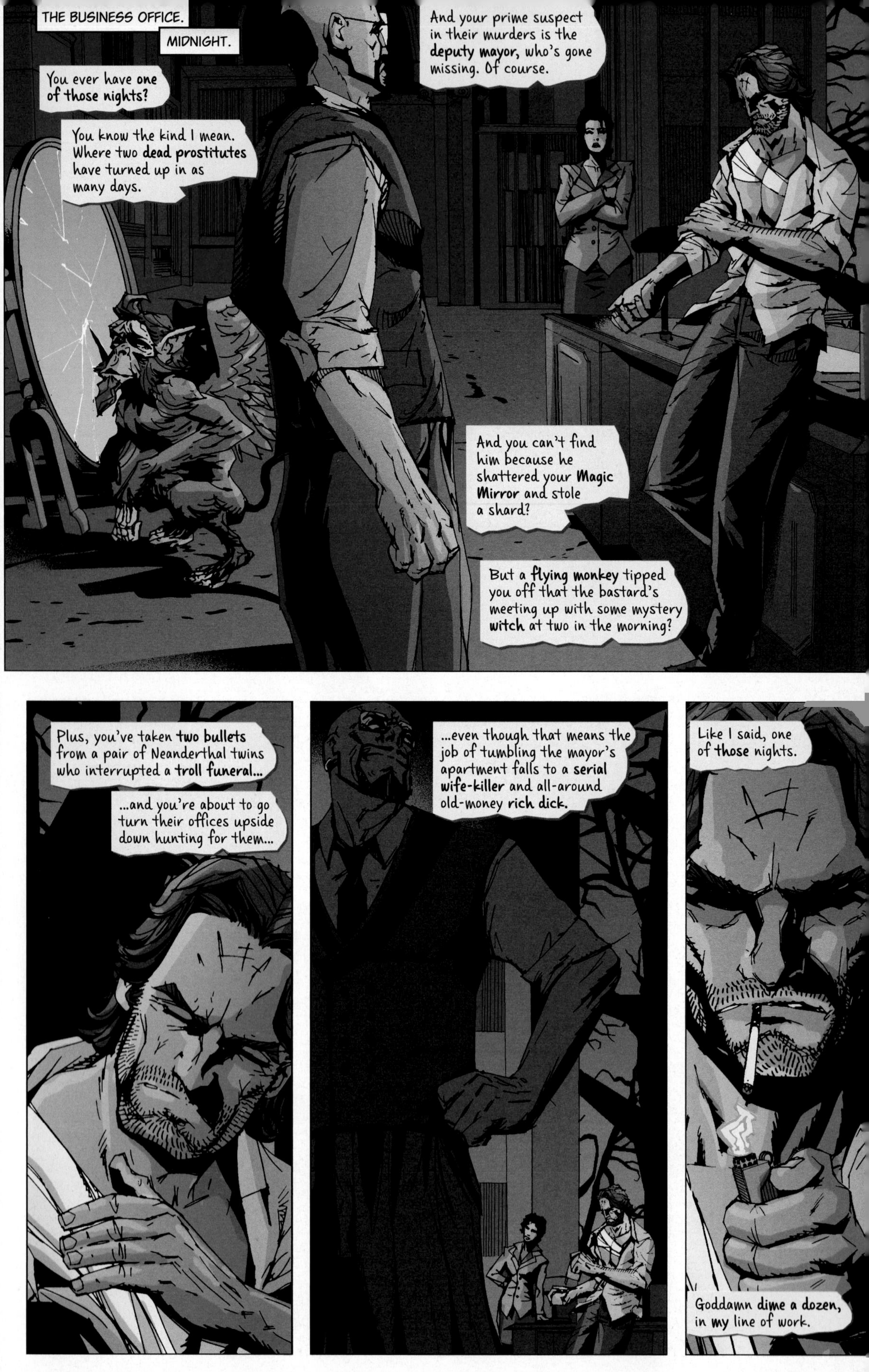
THE BUSINESS OFFICE.
MIDNIGHT.
You ever have one of those nights?
You know the kind I mean. Where two dead prostitutes have turned up in as many days.
And your prime suspect in their murders is the deputy mayor, who's gone missing. Of course.
And you can't find him because he shattered your Magic Mirror and stole a shard?
But a flying monkey tipped you off that the bastard's meeting up with some mystery witch at two in the morning?
Plus, you've taken two bullets from a pair of Neanderthal twins who interrupted a troll funeral...
...and you're about to go turn their offices upside down hunting for them...
...even though that means the job of tumbling the mayor's apartment falls to a serial wife-killer and all-around old-money rich dick.
Like I said, one of those nights.
Goddamn dime a dozen, in my line of work.

YOU KNOW I *HATE* THAT WE'RE INVOLVING THAT PRICK *BLUEBEARD* IN THIS INVESTIGATION.

BIGBY! COULD YOU AT LEAST *TRY* TO KEEP YOUR VOICE DOWN?

IF YOU FUCK THIS UP FOR ME, ALL THE MONEY IN THE *WORLD* ISN'T GOING TO PROTECT YOU.

IF YOU *THREATEN* ME AGAIN, YOU'LL WORK THIS CASE *PRO BONO*.

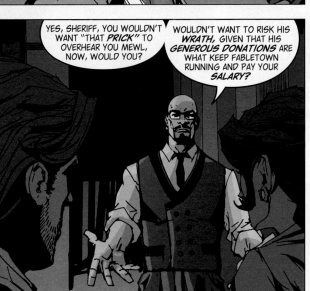

YES, SHERIFF, YOU WOULDN'T WANT "THAT *PRICK*" TO OVERHEAR YOU MEWL, NOW, WOULD YOU?

WOULDN'T WANT TO RISK HIS *WRATH*, GIVEN THAT HIS *GENEROUS DONATIONS* ARE WHAT KEEP FABLETOWN RUNNING AND PAY YOUR *SALARY*?

PRICK.

IF WE'RE GOING BY THE PHONE CALL THAT *BUFKIN* OVERHEARD, WE'VE GOT TWO HOURS TO FIGURE OUT WHO THIS WITCH IS...

...AND INTERCEPT *CRANE* THERE, HOPEFULLY BEFORE HE DOES ANY *MORE* DAMAGE TO THE COMMUNITY HE'S SWORN TO PROTECT.

WHICH MEANS THAT EVERY MOMENT WE SPEND HERE IS A MOMENT *WASTED!*

I'M OFF TO THE BLACKGUARD'S QUARTERS.

IF I FIND ANYTHING OF *INTEREST*, YOU TWO WILL BE THE FIRST TO KNOW.

WITHOUT A *KEY?*

I'VE YET TO MEET THE LOCK THAT COULD *STOP* ME, MS. WHITE.

A LENGTHY SERIES OF *CHASTITY BELTS* WILL ATTEST TO THAT.

I DON'T TRUST HIM ANY FARTHER THAN I CAN *THROW* HIM.

SEE, THAT'S WHERE WE PART WAYS, SNOW.

I COULD THROW THAT SONUVABITCH *MUCH* FARTHER THAN I TRUST HIM.

WITH ANY LUCK, I'LL GET TO DO EXACTLY THAT, BEFORE THE NIGHT IS OVER.

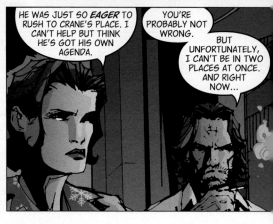

HE WAS JUST SO *EAGER* TO RUSH TO CRANE'S PLACE. I CAN'T HELP BUT THINK HE'S GOT HIS OWN AGENDA.

YOU'RE PROBABLY NOT WRONG.

BUT UNFORTUNATELY, I CAN'T BE IN TWO PLACES AT ONCE. AND RIGHT NOW...

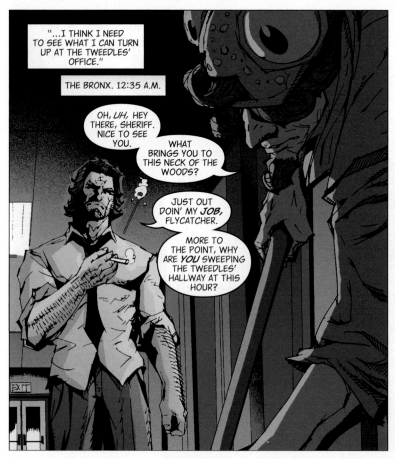

"...I THINK I NEED TO SEE WHAT I CAN TURN UP AT THE TWEEDLES' OFFICE."

THE BRONX. 12:35 A.M.

OH, *UH*, HEY THERE, SHERIFF. NICE TO SEE YOU.

WHAT BRINGS YOU TO THIS NECK OF THE WOODS?

JUST OUT DOIN' MY *JOB*, FLYCATCHER.

MORE TO THE POINT, WHY ARE *YOU* SWEEPING THE TWEEDLES' HALLWAY AT THIS HOUR?

EXIT

I'M JUST DOING *MY* JOB, TOO, SHERIFF.

CRANE, UH, *LET ME GO* FROM THE WOODLAND RECENTLY, AND THE TWEEDLES WERE NICE ENOUGH TO HIRE ME RIGHT AWAY.

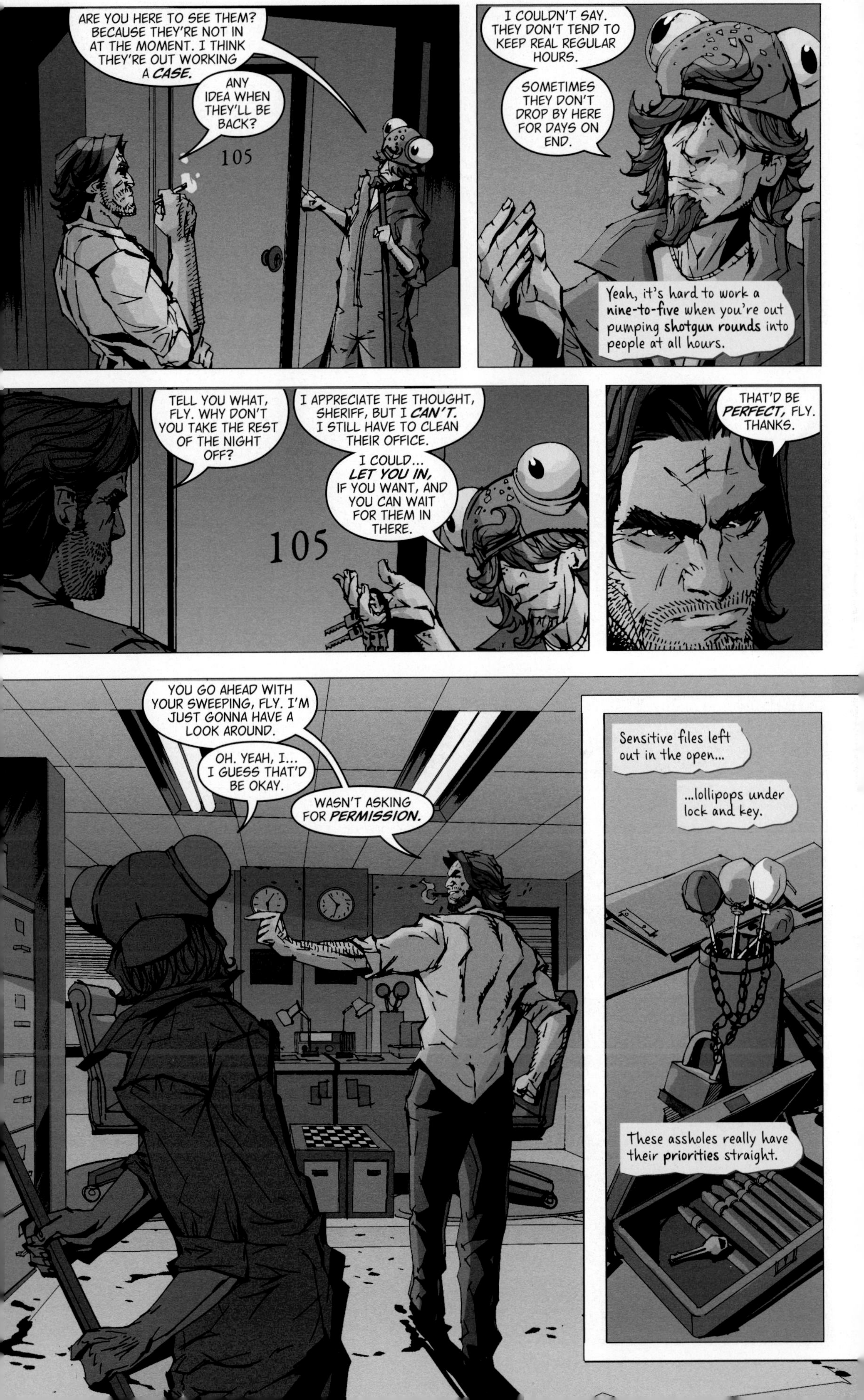

ARE YOU HERE TO SEE THEM? BECAUSE THEY'RE NOT IN AT THE MOMENT. I THINK THEY'RE OUT WORKING A CASE.
ANY IDEA WHEN THEY'LL BE BACK?
105
I COULDN'T SAY. THEY DON'T TEND TO KEEP REAL REGULAR HOURS.
SOMETIMES THEY DON'T DROP BY HERE FOR DAYS ON END.
Yeah, it's hard to work a nine-to-five when you're out pumping shotgun rounds into people at all hours.
TELL YOU WHAT, FLY. WHY DON'T YOU TAKE THE REST OF THE NIGHT OFF?
I APPRECIATE THE THOUGHT, SHERIFF, BUT I CAN'T. I STILL HAVE TO CLEAN THEIR OFFICE.
I COULD... LET YOU IN, IF YOU WANT, AND YOU CAN WAIT FOR THEM IN THERE.
105
THAT'D BE PERFECT, FLY. THANKS.
YOU GO AHEAD WITH YOUR SWEEPING, FLY. I'M JUST GONNA HAVE A LOOK AROUND.
OH. YEAH, I... I GUESS THAT'D BE OKAY.
WASN'T ASKING FOR PERMISSION.
Sensitive files left out in the open...
...lollipops under lock and key.
These assholes really have their priorities straight.

These cigars are far too nice for a couple of mouth-breathers like the Tweedles.

I figure I'll enter a couple into "evidence" and get to the bottom of them later.

Hello, what's this?

No telling when this might come in handy.

WOW. I'D'VE LAID EVEN MONEY THAT THESE JACKASSES DIDN'T KNOW WHAT ORDER THE **ALPHABET** CAME IN.

LET'S SEE WHETHER THEY'VE GOT A FILE ON **CRANE**.

SHIT. JUST LIKE **BEAUTY**, CRANE'S IN DEBT UP TO HIS BEADY LITTLE EYEBALLS WITH THE CROOKED MAN.

HOW WAS HE **EVER** PLANNING TO PAY ALL THIS BACK?

quest for Property
Acquisition

Daily Task:
Find Compromising Photo.
$500 Bill.

Debt to Crooked Man
$1000 x 12 x 75
Current Payment Plan:
month to month
Items Procured from the
Business Office:

Warlock Fossil $3,000
Williams Enigmalith $400
Stone Footprint $3,500

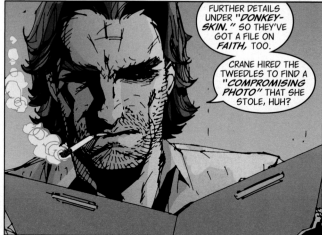

FURTHER DETAILS UNDER *"DONKEY-SKIN."* SO THEY'VE GOT A FILE ON **FAITH**, TOO.

CRANE HIRED THE TWEEDLES TO FIND A *"COMPROMISING PHOTO"* THAT SHE STOLE, HUH?

THAT EXPLAINS WHY THEY WERE AT HER APARTMENT... AND AT THE **WOODSMAN'S** PLACE.

OF COURSE, THEIR METHOD OF FINDING A **NEEDLE** IN A **HAYSTACK**...

...IS TO BURN THE HAYSTACK TO THE GROUND AND THEN SIFT THROUGH THE **ASHES**.

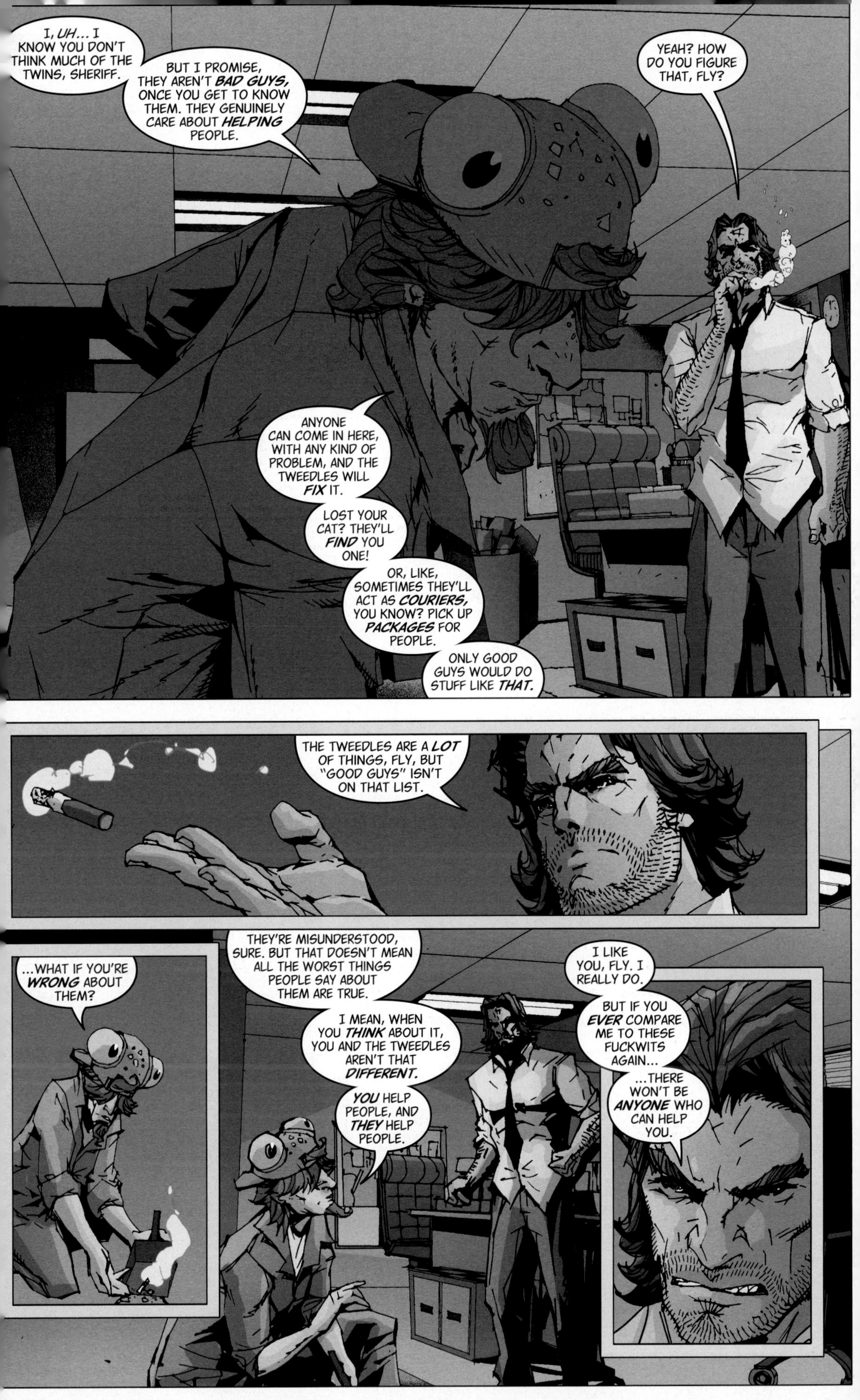
I, UH... I KNOW YOU DON'T THINK MUCH OF THE TWINS, SHERIFF.
BUT I PROMISE, THEY AREN'T BAD GUYS, ONCE YOU GET TO KNOW THEM. THEY GENUINELY CARE ABOUT HELPING PEOPLE.
YEAH? HOW DO YOU FIGURE THAT, FLY?
ANYONE CAN COME IN HERE, WITH ANY KIND OF PROBLEM, AND THE TWEEDLES WILL FIX IT.
LOST YOUR CAT? THEY'LL FIND YOU ONE!
OR, LIKE, SOMETIMES THEY'LL ACT AS COURIERS, YOU KNOW? PICK UP PACKAGES FOR PEOPLE.
ONLY GOOD GUYS WOULD DO STUFF LIKE THAT.
THE TWEEDLES ARE A LOT OF THINGS, FLY, BUT "GOOD GUYS" ISN'T ON THAT LIST.
...WHAT IF YOU'RE WRONG ABOUT THEM?
THEY'RE MISUNDERSTOOD, SURE. BUT THAT DOESN'T MEAN ALL THE WORST THINGS PEOPLE SAY ABOUT THEM ARE TRUE.
I MEAN, WHEN YOU THINK ABOUT IT, YOU AND THE TWEEDLES AREN'T THAT DIFFERENT.
YOU HELP PEOPLE, AND THEY HELP PEOPLE.
I LIKE YOU, FLY. I REALLY DO.
BUT IF YOU EVER COMPARE ME TO THESE FUCKWITS AGAIN...
...THERE WON'T BE ANYONE WHO CAN HELP YOU.

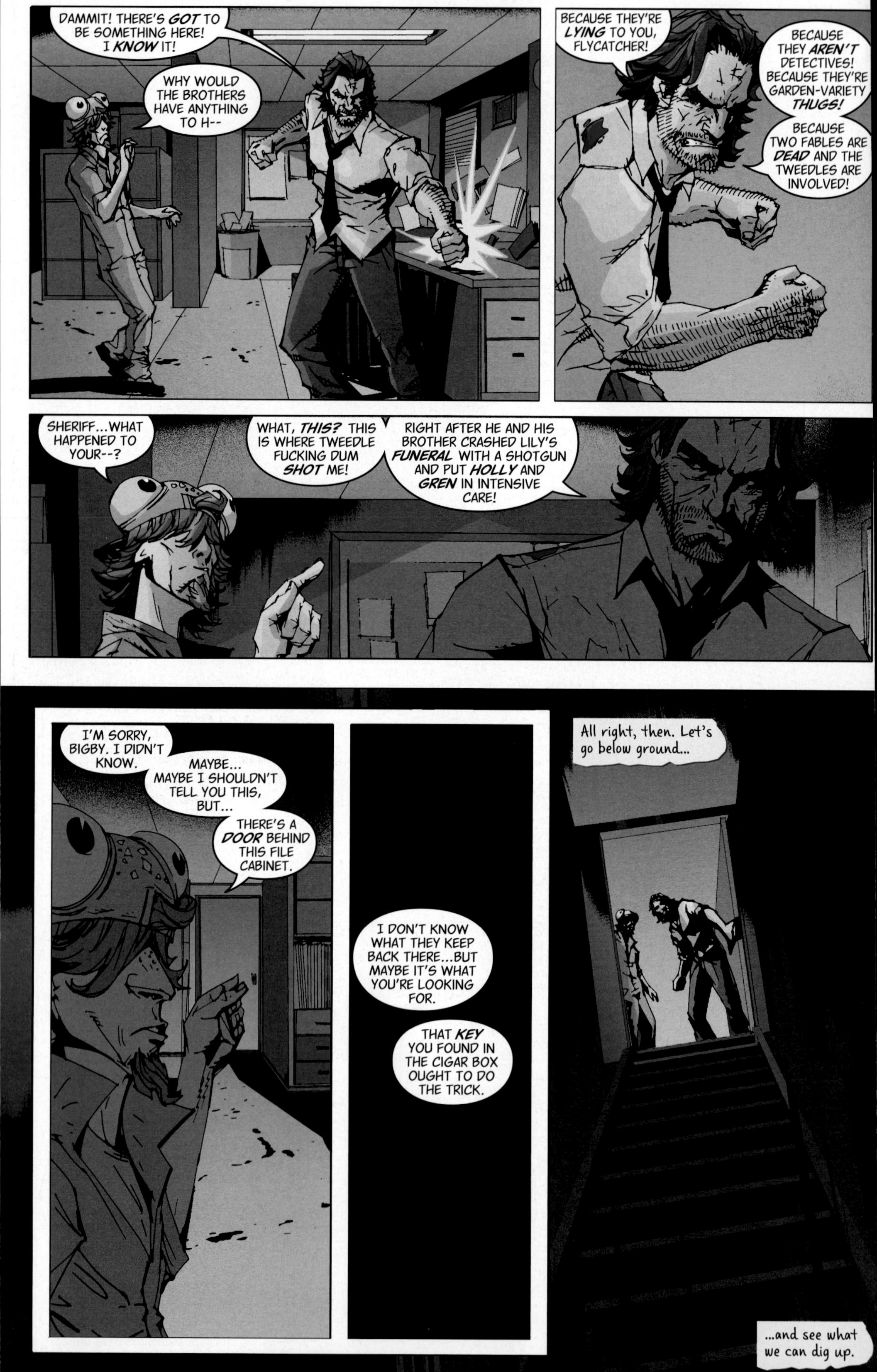
DAMMIT! THERE'S GOT TO BE SOMETHING HERE! I KNOW IT!
WHY WOULD THE BROTHERS HAVE ANYTHING TO H--
BECAUSE THEY'RE LYING TO YOU, FLYCATCHER!
BECAUSE THEY AREN'T DETECTIVES! BECAUSE THEY'RE GARDEN-VARIETY THUGS!
BECAUSE TWO FABLES ARE DEAD AND THE TWEEDLES ARE INVOLVED!
SHERIFF...WHAT HAPPENED TO YOUR--?
WHAT, THIS? THIS IS WHERE TWEEDLE FUCKING DUM SHOT ME!
RIGHT AFTER HE AND HIS BROTHER CRASHED LILY'S FUNERAL WITH A SHOTGUN AND PUT HOLLY AND GREN IN INTENSIVE CARE!
I'M SORRY, BIGBY. I DIDN'T KNOW.
MAYBE... MAYBE I SHOULDN'T TELL YOU THIS, BUT...
THERE'S A DOOR BEHIND THIS FILE CABINET.
I DON'T KNOW WHAT THEY KEEP BACK THERE...BUT MAYBE IT'S WHAT YOU'RE LOOKING FOR.
THAT KEY YOU FOUND IN THE CIGAR BOX OUGHT TO DO THE TRICK.
All right, then. Let's go below ground...
...and see what we can dig up.

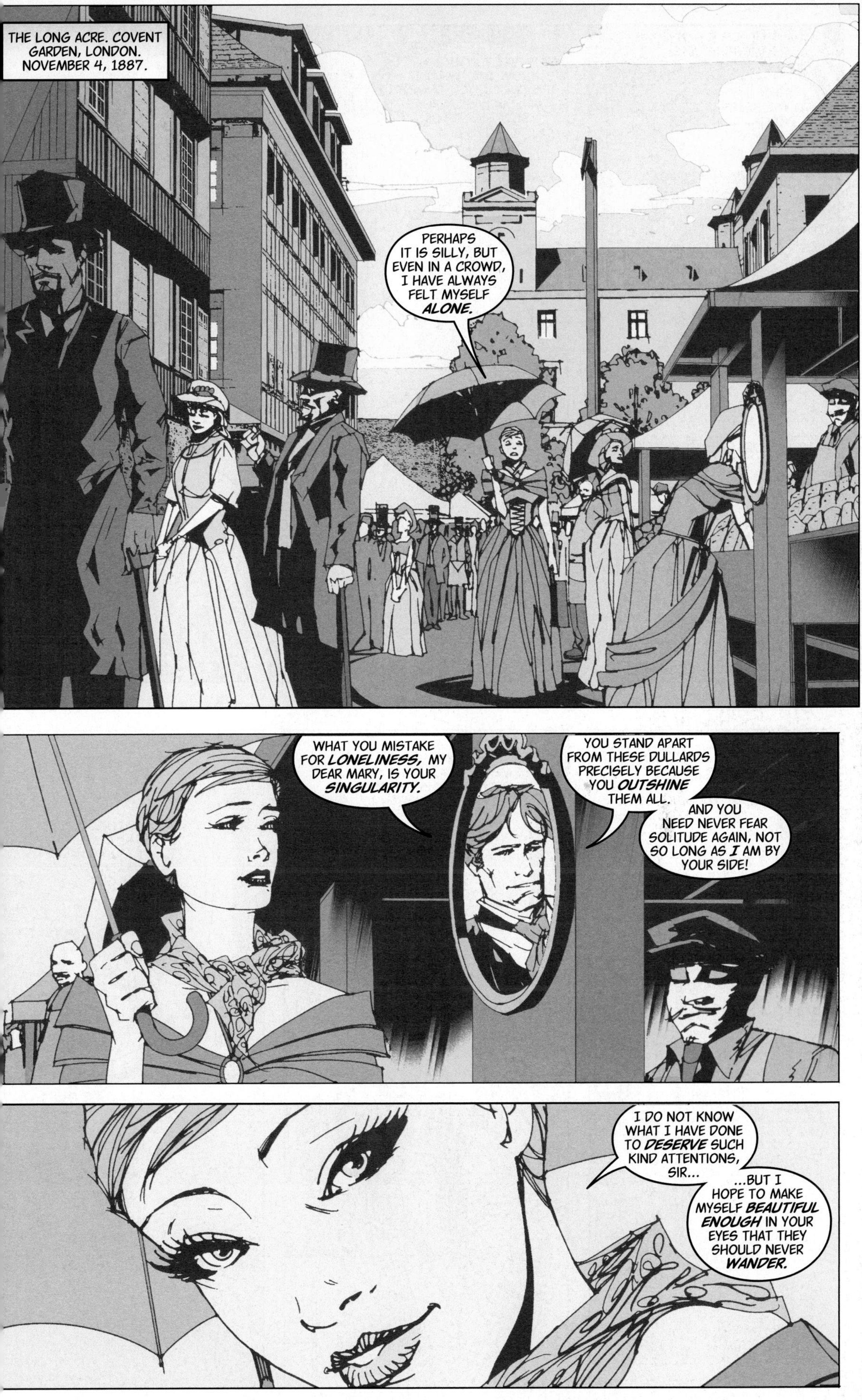
THE LONG ACRE. COVENT GARDEN, LONDON. NOVEMBER 4, 1887.
PERHAPS IT IS SILLY, BUT EVEN IN A CROWD, I HAVE ALWAYS FELT MYSELF ALONE.
WHAT YOU MISTAKE FOR LONELINESS, MY DEAR MARY, IS YOUR SINGULARITY.
YOU STAND APART FROM THESE DULLARDS PRECISELY BECAUSE YOU OUTSHINE THEM ALL.
AND YOU NEED NEVER FEAR SOLITUDE AGAIN, NOT SO LONG AS I AM BY YOUR SIDE!
I DO NOT KNOW WHAT I HAVE DONE TO DESERVE SUCH KIND ATTENTIONS, SIR...
...BUT I HOPE TO MAKE MYSELF BEAUTIFUL ENOUGH IN YOUR EYES THAT THEY SHOULD NEVER WANDER.

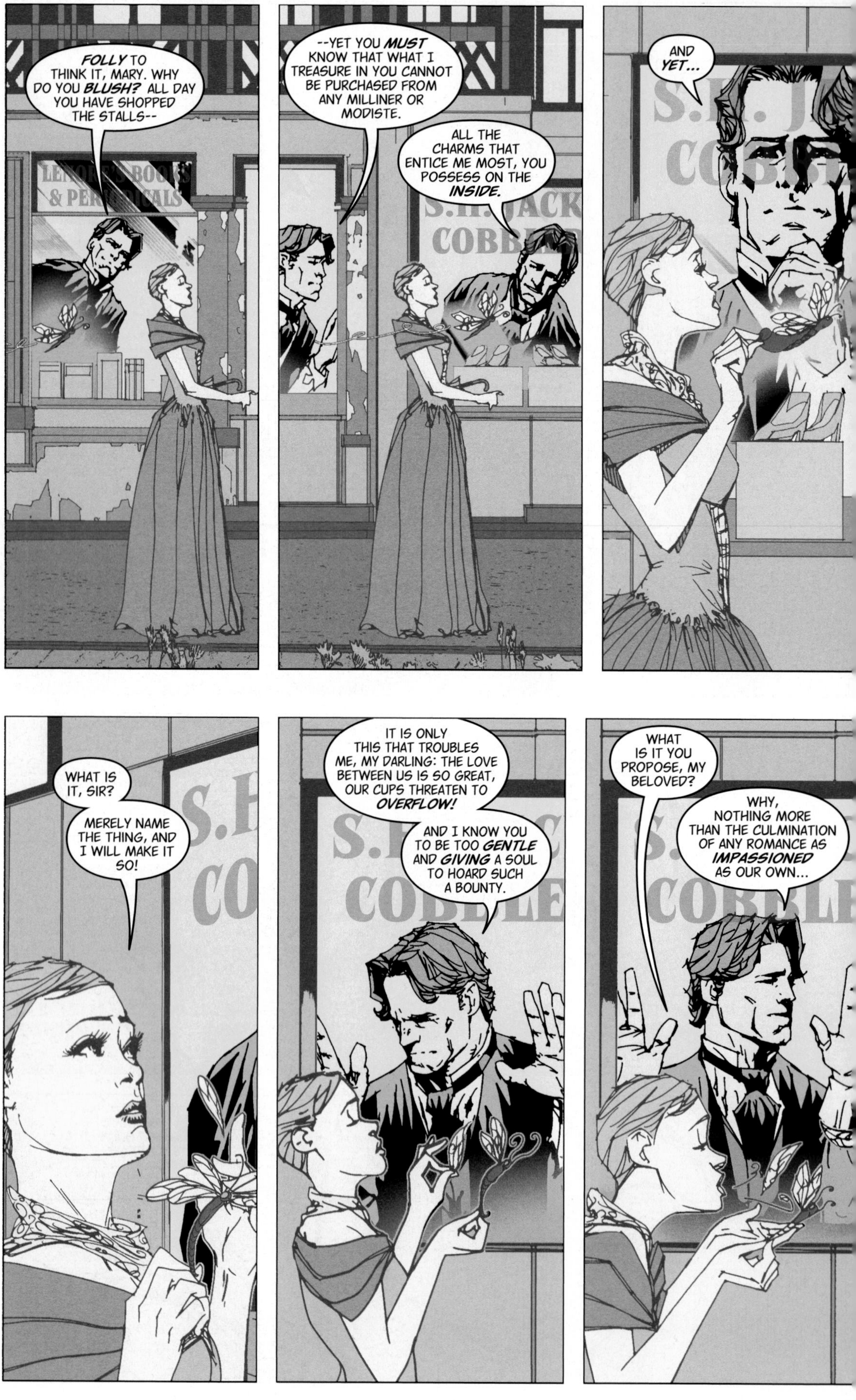
FOLLY TO THINK IT, MARY. WHY DO YOU BLUSH? ALL DAY YOU HAVE SHOPPED THE STALLS--
LENORE'S BOOKS & PERIODICALS
--YET YOU MUST KNOW THAT WHAT I TREASURE IN YOU CANNOT BE PURCHASED FROM ANY MILLINER OR MODISTE.
ALL THE CHARMS THAT ENTICE ME MOST, YOU POSSESS ON THE INSIDE.
AND YET...
WHAT IS IT, SIR?
MERELY NAME THE THING, AND I WILL MAKE IT SO!
IT IS ONLY THIS THAT TROUBLES ME, MY DARLING: THE LOVE BETWEEN US IS SO GREAT, OUR CUPS THREATEN TO OVERFLOW!
AND I KNOW YOU TO BE TOO GENTLE AND GIVING A SOUL TO HOARD SUCH A BOUNTY.
WHAT IS IT YOU PROPOSE, MY BELOVED?
WHY, NOTHING MORE THAN THE CULMINATION OF ANY ROMANCE AS IMPASSIONED AS OUR OWN...

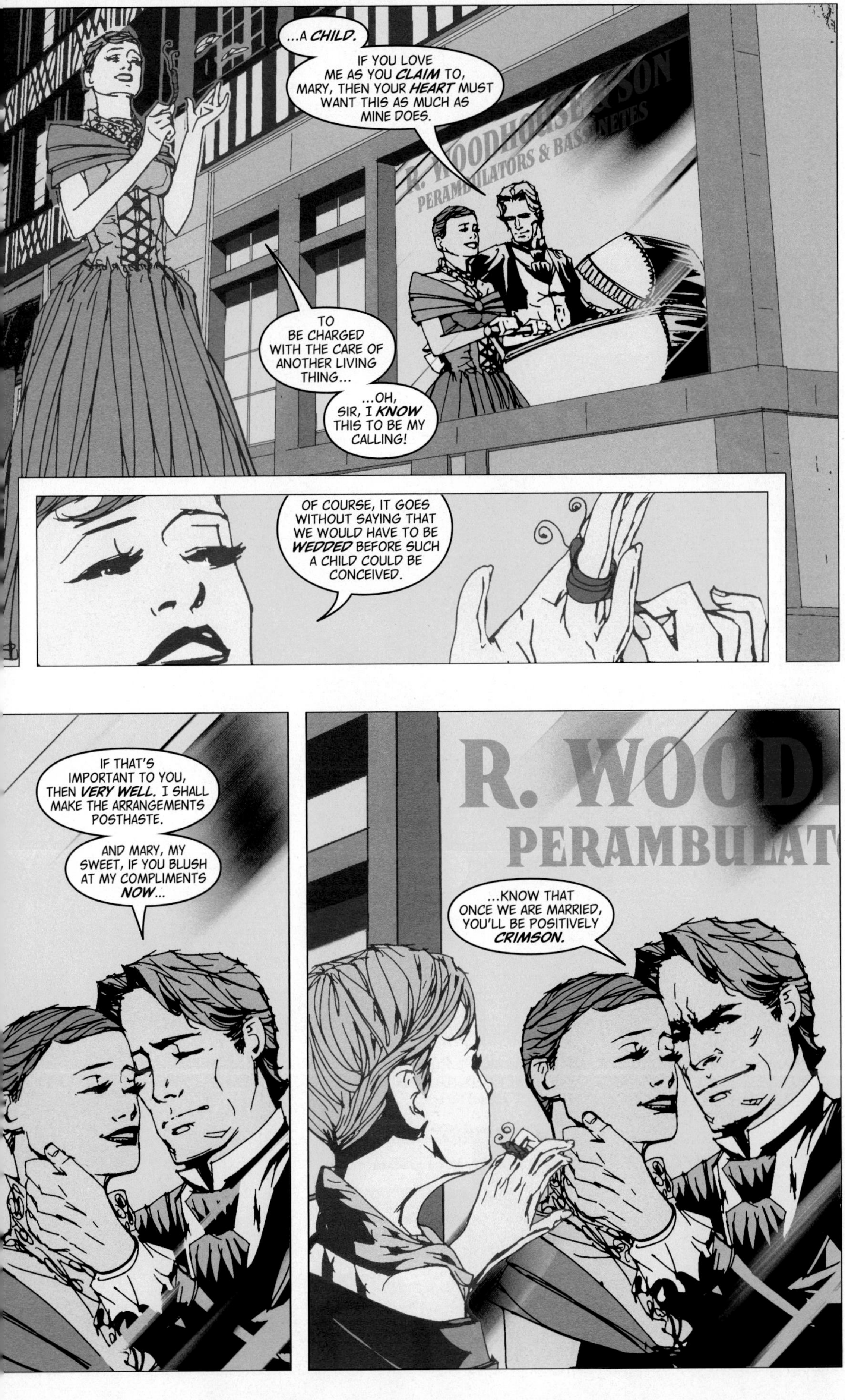

...A CHILD.
IF YOU LOVE ME AS YOU CLAIM TO, MARY, THEN YOUR HEART MUST WANT THIS AS MUCH AS MINE DOES.
TO BE CHARGED WITH THE CARE OF ANOTHER LIVING THING...
...OH, SIR, I KNOW THIS TO BE MY CALLING!
OF COURSE, IT GOES WITHOUT SAYING THAT WE WOULD HAVE TO BE WEDDED BEFORE SUCH A CHILD COULD BE CONCEIVED.
IF THAT'S IMPORTANT TO YOU, THEN VERY WELL. I SHALL MAKE THE ARRANGEMENTS POSTHASTE.
AND MARY, MY SWEET, IF YOU BLUSH AT MY COMPLIMENTS NOW...
...KNOW THAT ONCE WE ARE MARRIED, YOU'LL BE POSITIVELY CRIMSON.

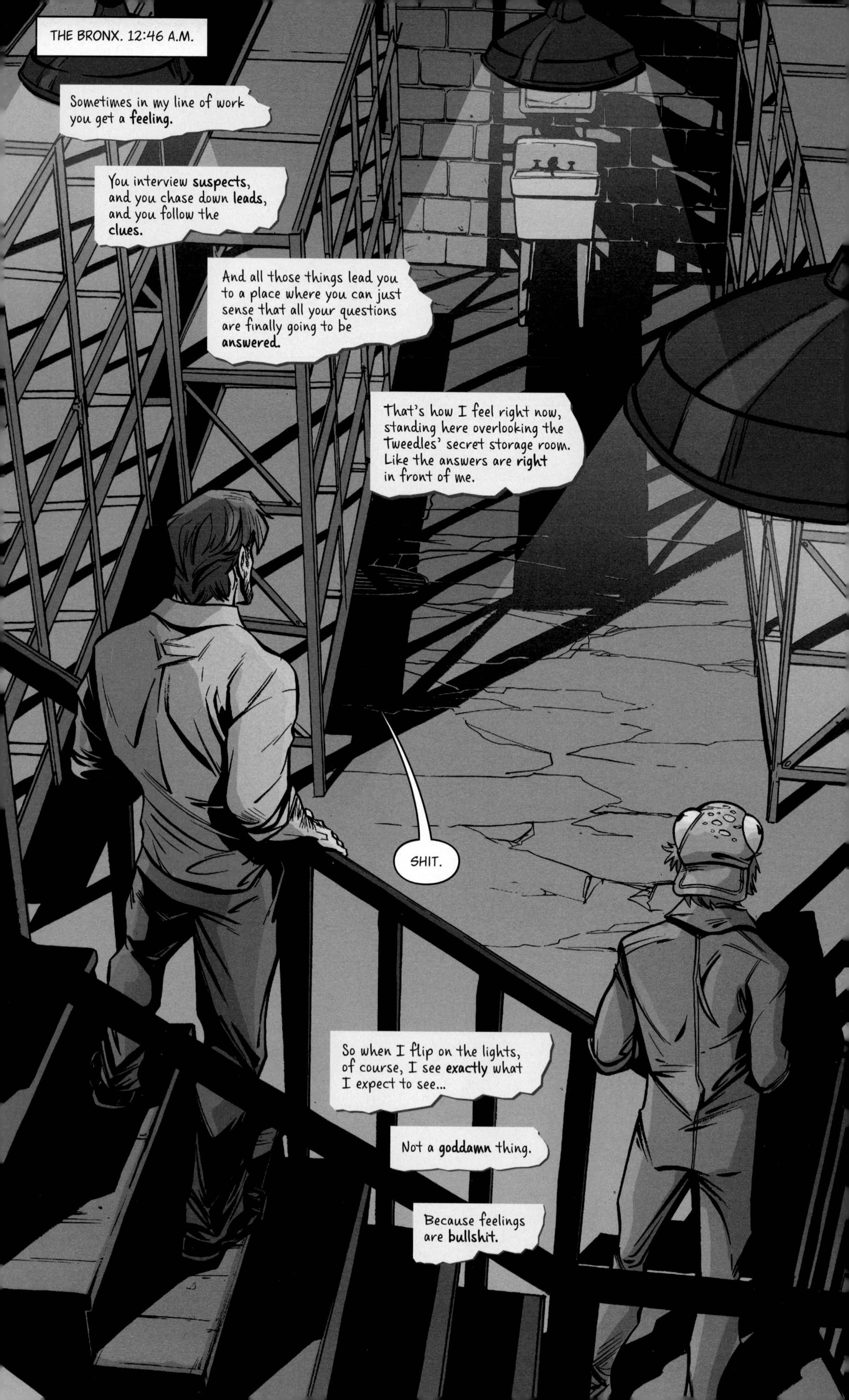
THE BRONX. 12:46 A.M.
Sometimes in my line of work you get a feeling.
You interview suspects, and you chase down leads, and you follow the clues.
And all those things lead you to a place where you can just sense that all your questions are finally going to be answered.
That's how I feel right now, standing here overlooking the Tweedles' secret storage room. Like the answers are right in front of me.
SHIT.
So when I flip on the lights, of course, I see exactly what I expect to see...
Not a goddamn thing.
Because feelings are bullshit.

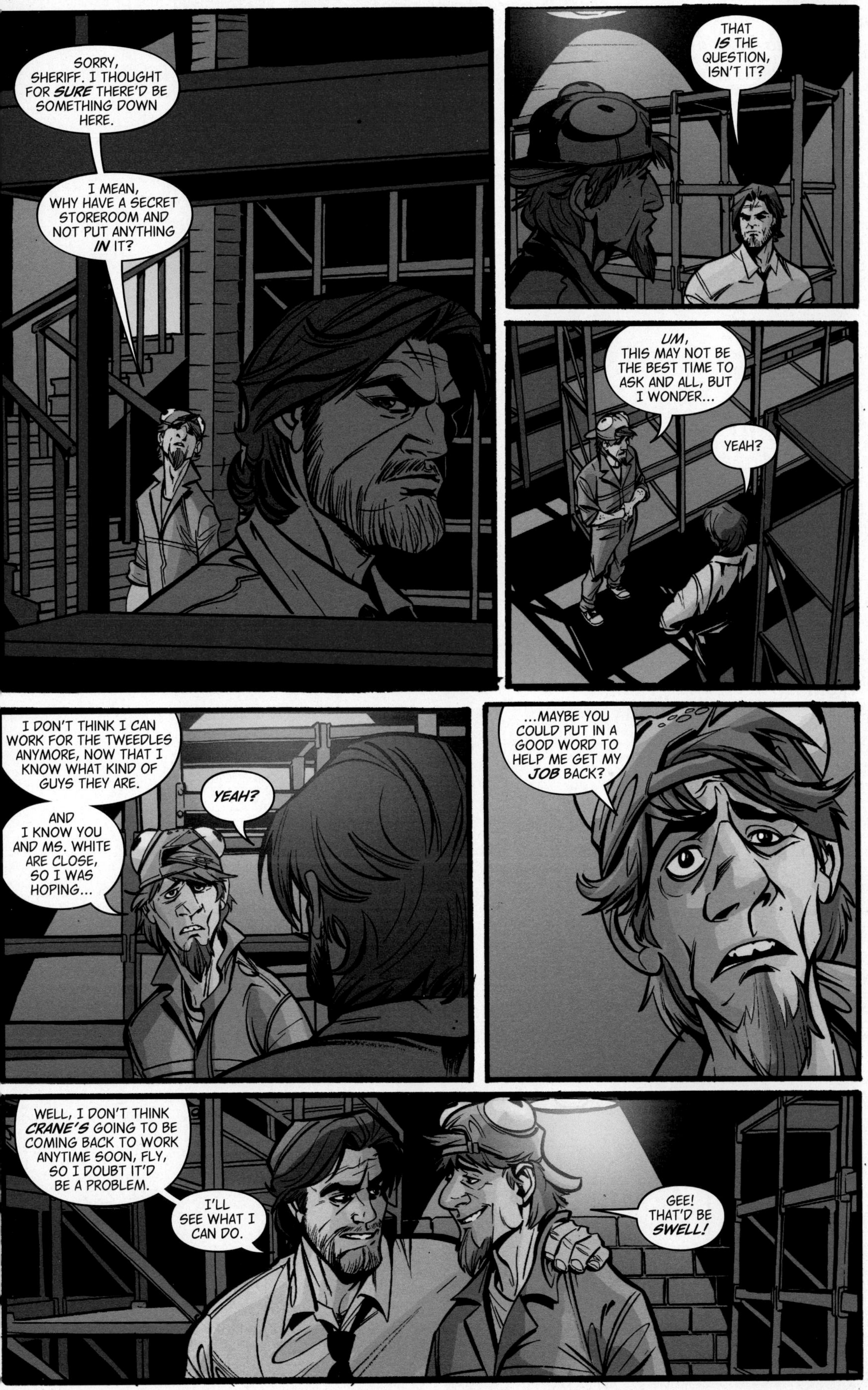
SORRY, SHERIFF. I THOUGHT FOR SURE THERE'D BE SOMETHING DOWN HERE.
I MEAN, WHY HAVE A SECRET STOREROOM AND NOT PUT ANYTHING IN IT?
THAT IS THE QUESTION, ISN'T IT?
UM, THIS MAY NOT BE THE BEST TIME TO ASK AND ALL, BUT I WONDER...
YEAH?
I DON'T THINK I CAN WORK FOR THE TWEEDLES ANYMORE, NOW THAT I KNOW WHAT KIND OF GUYS THEY ARE.
YEAH?
AND I KNOW YOU AND MS. WHITE ARE CLOSE, SO I WAS HOPING...
...MAYBE YOU COULD PUT IN A GOOD WORD TO HELP ME GET MY JOB BACK?
WELL, I DON'T THINK CRANE'S GOING TO BE COMING BACK TO WORK ANYTIME SOON, FLY, SO I DOUBT IT'D BE A PROBLEM.
I'LL SEE WHAT I CAN DO.
GEE! THAT'D BE SWELL!

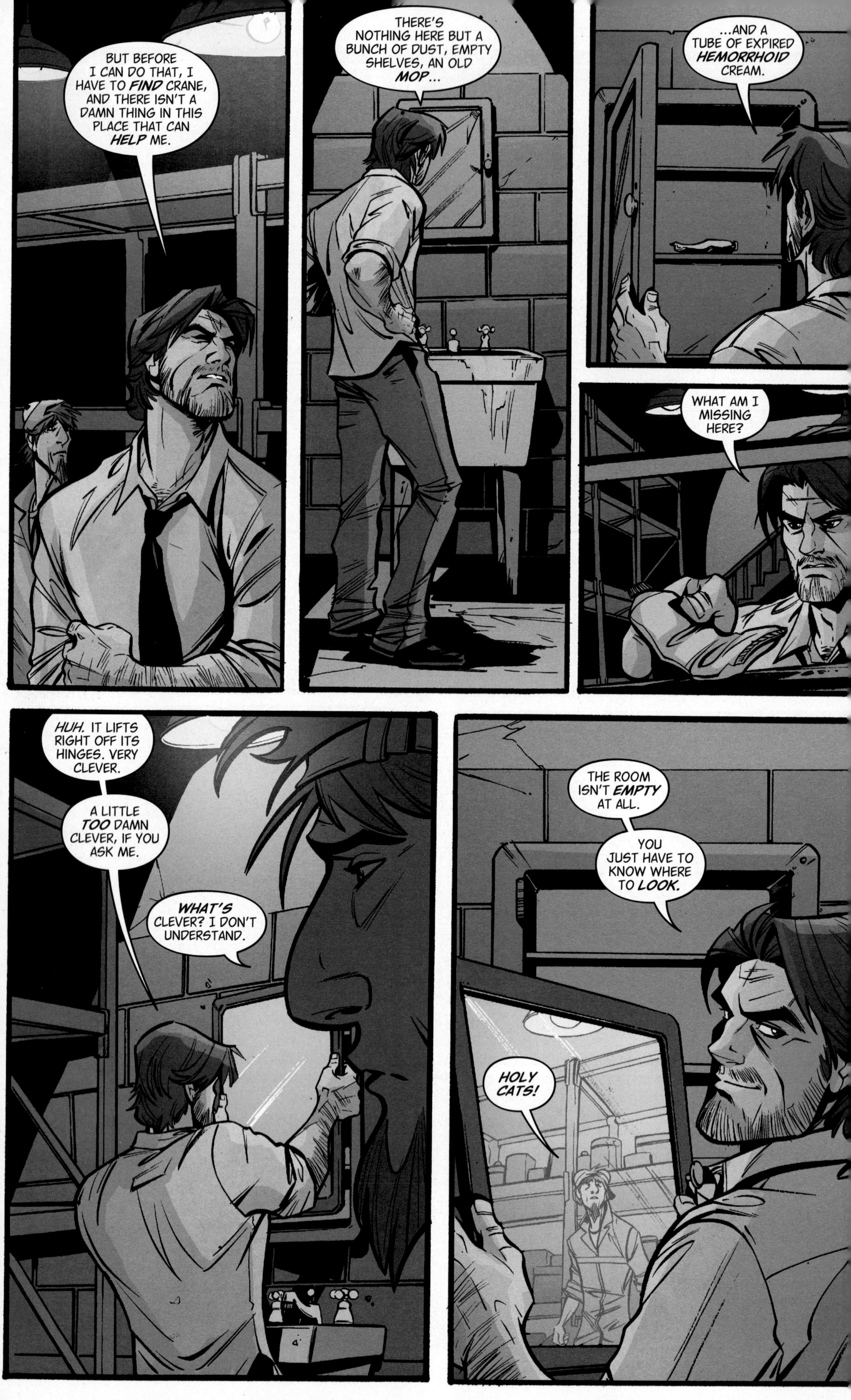
BUT BEFORE I CAN DO THAT, I HAVE TO FIND CRANE, AND THERE ISN'T A DAMN THING IN THIS PLACE THAT CAN HELP ME.
THERE'S NOTHING HERE BUT A BUNCH OF DUST, EMPTY SHELVES, AN OLD MOP...
...AND A TUBE OF EXPIRED HEMORRHOID CREAM.
WHAT AM I MISSING HERE?
HUH. IT LIFTS RIGHT OFF ITS HINGES. VERY CLEVER.
A LITTLE TOO DAMN CLEVER, IF YOU ASK ME.
WHAT'S CLEVER? I DON'T UNDERSTAND.
THE ROOM ISN'T EMPTY AT ALL.
YOU JUST HAVE TO KNOW WHERE TO LOOK.
HOLY CATS!

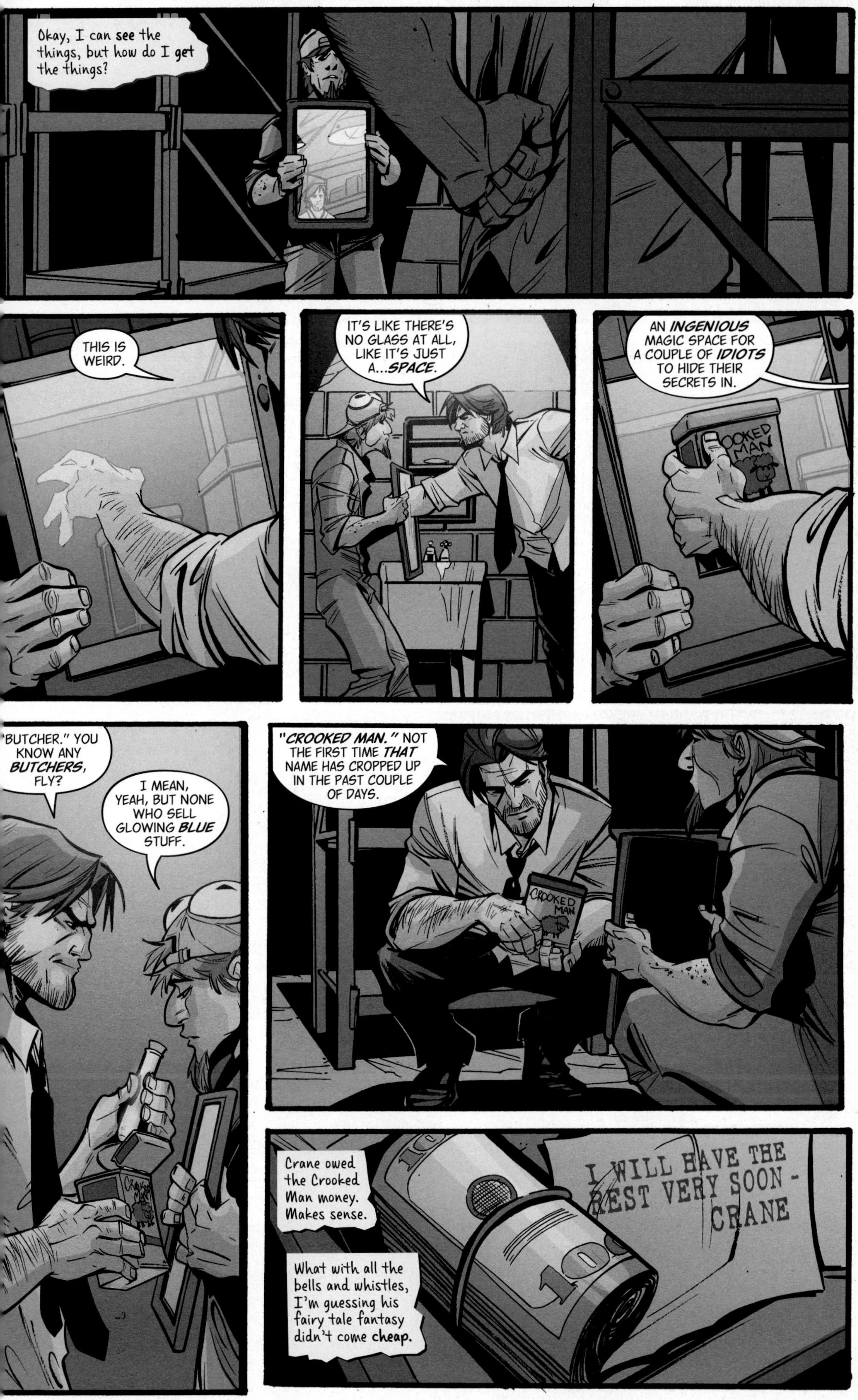

Okay, I can see the things, but how do I get the things?
THIS IS WEIRD.
IT'S LIKE THERE'S NO GLASS AT ALL, LIKE IT'S JUST A...SPACE.
AN INGENIOUS MAGIC SPACE FOR A COUPLE OF IDIOTS TO HIDE THEIR SECRETS IN.
CROOKED MAN
"BUTCHER." YOU KNOW ANY BUTCHERS, FLY?
I MEAN, YEAH, BUT NONE WHO SELL GLOWING BLUE STUFF.
"CROOKED MAN." NOT THE FIRST TIME THAT NAME HAS CROPPED UP IN THE PAST COUPLE OF DAYS.
CROOKED MAN
Crane owed the Crooked Man money. Makes sense.
I WILL HAVE THE REST VERY SOON - CRANE
What with all the bells and whistles, I'm guessing his fairy tale fantasy didn't come cheap.

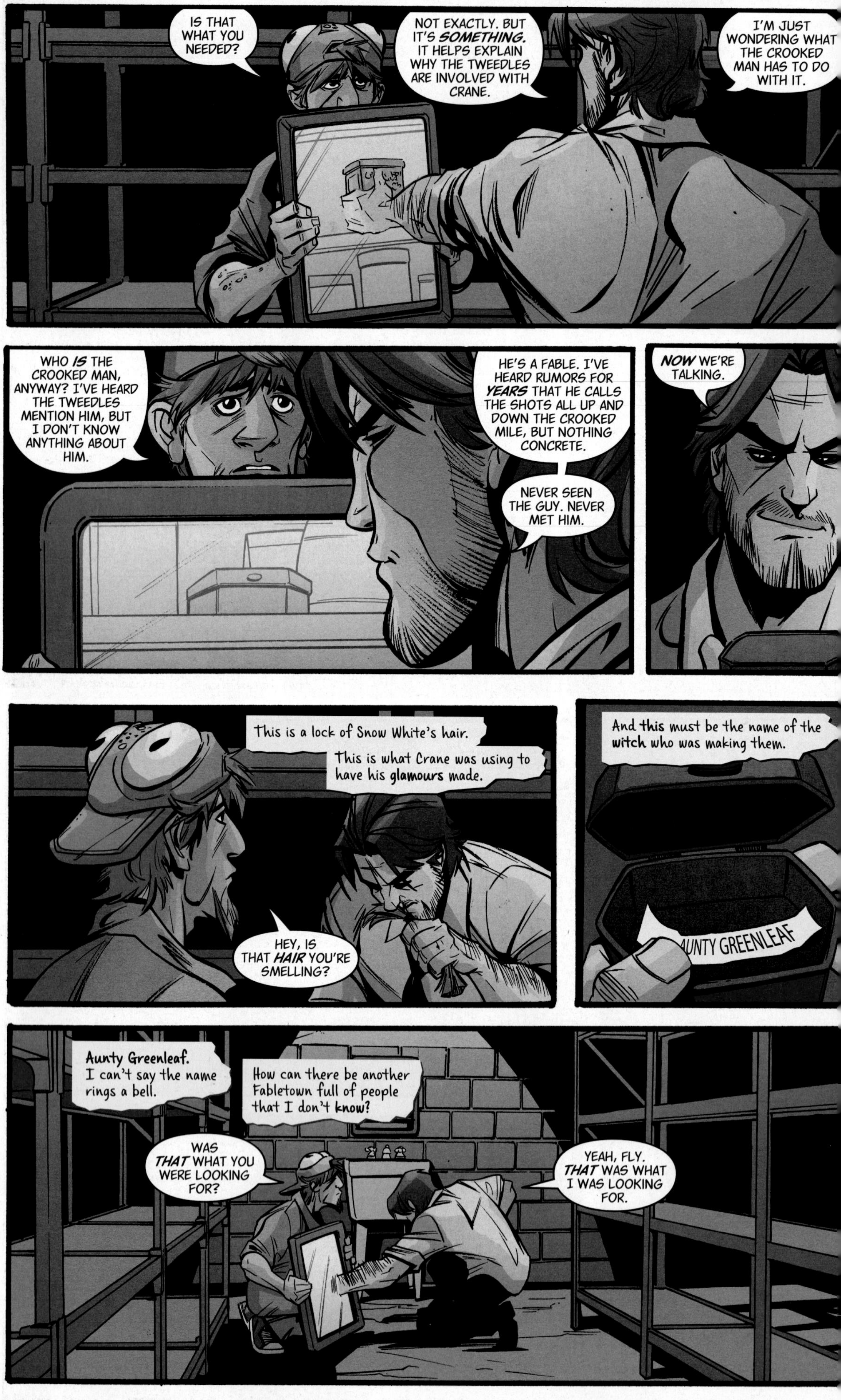

IS THAT WHAT YOU NEEDED?
NOT EXACTLY. BUT IT'S SOMETHING. IT HELPS EXPLAIN WHY THE TWEEDLES ARE INVOLVED WITH CRANE.
I'M JUST WONDERING WHAT THE CROOKED MAN HAS TO DO WITH IT.
WHO IS THE CROOKED MAN, ANYWAY? I'VE HEARD THE TWEEDLES MENTION HIM, BUT I DON'T KNOW ANYTHING ABOUT HIM.
HE'S A FABLE. I'VE HEARD RUMORS FOR YEARS THAT HE CALLS THE SHOTS ALL UP AND DOWN THE CROOKED MILE, BUT NOTHING CONCRETE.
NEVER SEEN THE GUY. NEVER MET HIM.
NOW WE'RE TALKING.
This is a lock of Snow White's hair.
This is what Crane was using to have his glamours made.
HEY, IS THAT HAIR YOU'RE SMELLING?
And this must be the name of the witch who was making them.
AUNTY GREENLEAF
Aunty Greenleaf. I can't say the name rings a bell.
How can there be another Fabletown full of people that I don't know?
WAS THAT WHAT YOU WERE LOOKING FOR?
YEAH, FLY. THAT WAS WHAT I WAS LOOKING FOR.

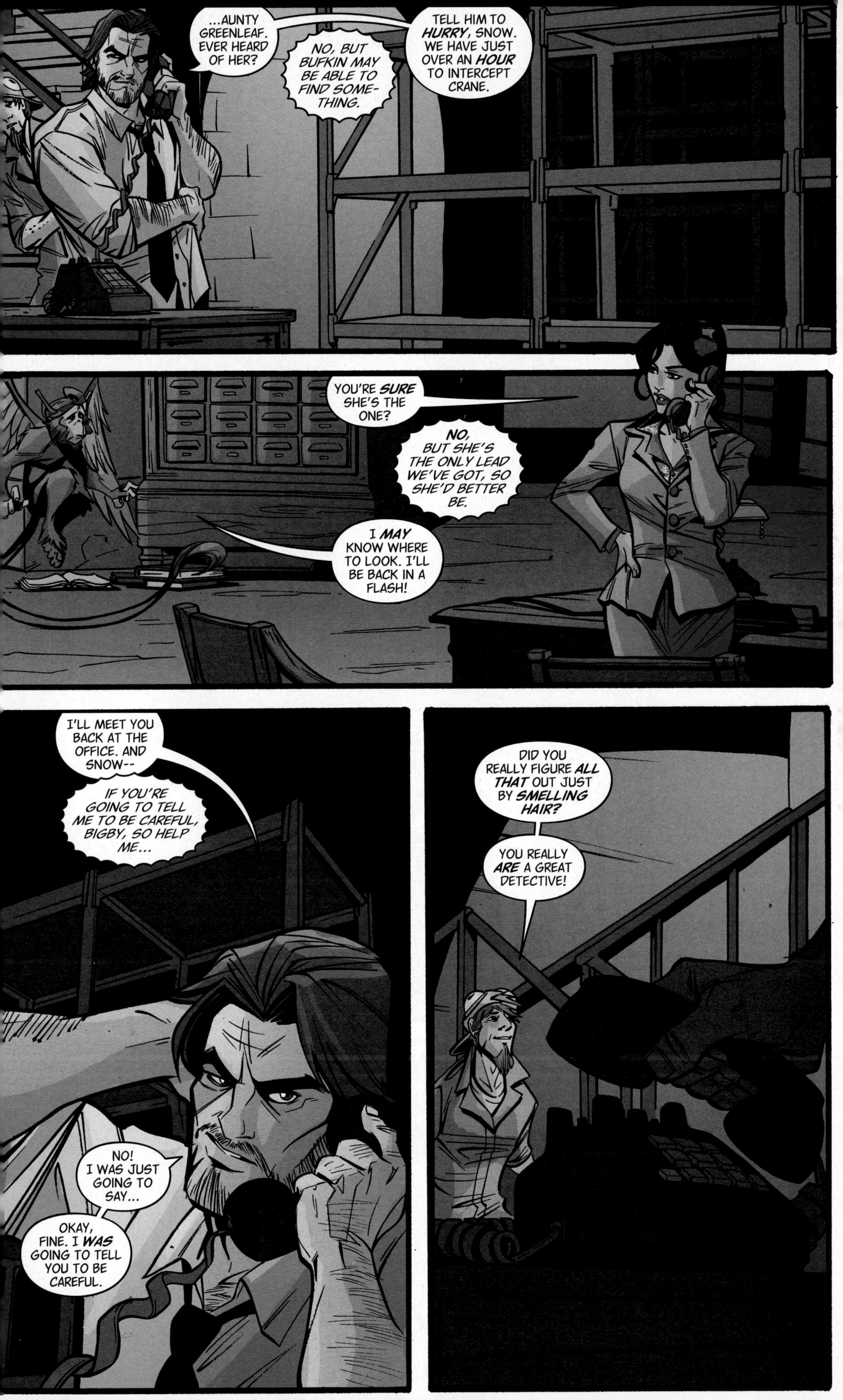
...AUNTY GREENLEAF. EVER HEARD OF HER?
NO, BUT BUFKIN MAY BE ABLE TO FIND SOMETHING.
TELL HIM TO HURRY, SNOW. WE HAVE JUST OVER AN HOUR TO INTERCEPT CRANE.
YOU'RE SURE SHE'S THE ONE?
NO, BUT SHE'S THE ONLY LEAD WE'VE GOT, SO SHE'D BETTER BE.
I MAY KNOW WHERE TO LOOK. I'LL BE BACK IN A FLASH!
I'LL MEET YOU BACK AT THE OFFICE. AND SNOW--
IF YOU'RE GOING TO TELL ME TO BE CAREFUL, BIGBY, SO HELP ME...
NO! I WAS JUST GOING TO SAY...
OKAY, FINE. I WAS GOING TO TELL YOU TO BE CAREFUL.
DID YOU REALLY FIGURE ALL THAT OUT JUST BY SMELLING HAIR?
YOU REALLY ARE A GREAT DETECTIVE!

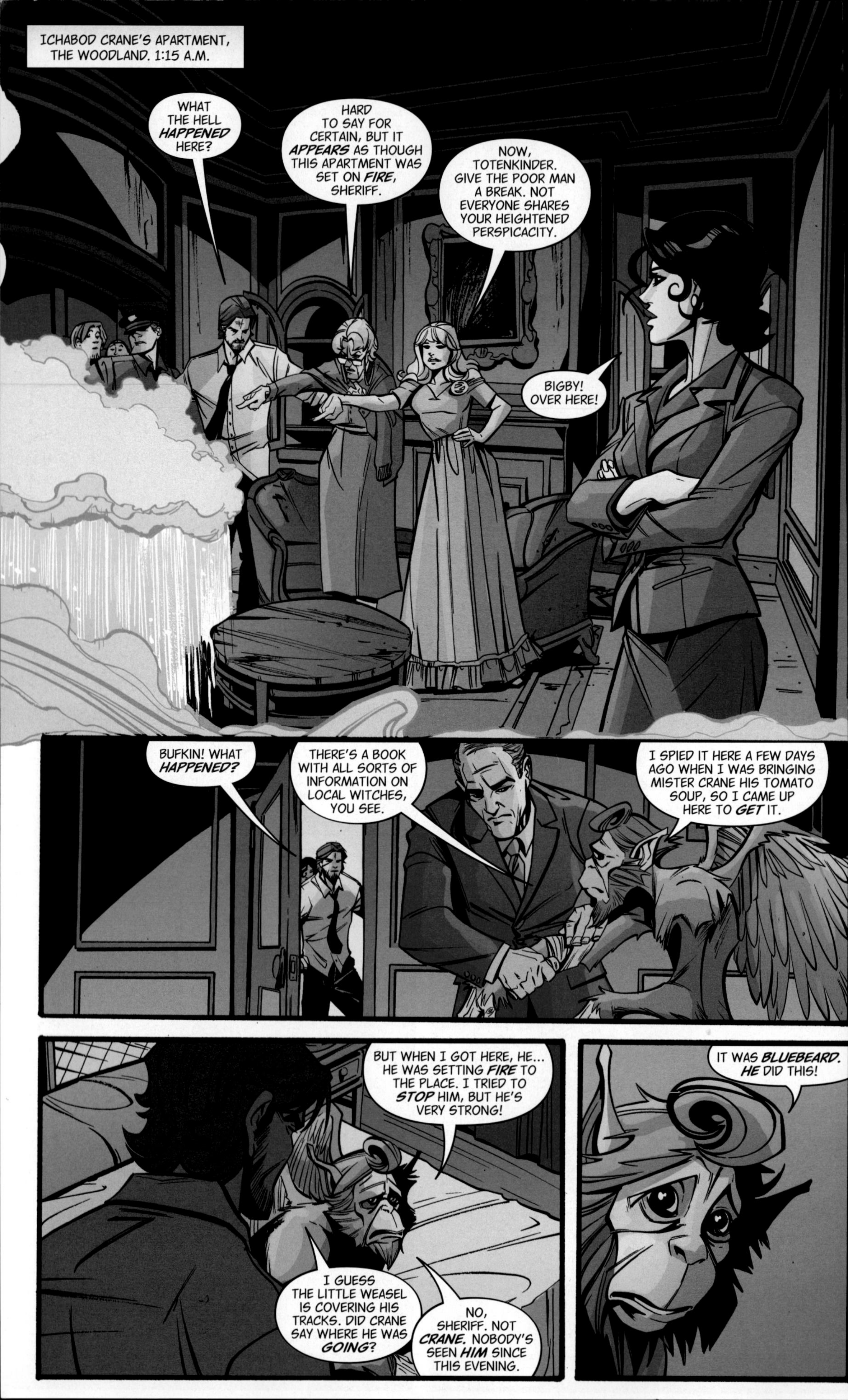
ICHABOD CRANE'S APARTMENT, THE WOODLAND. 1:15 A.M.
WHAT THE HELL *HAPPENED* HERE?
HARD TO SAY FOR CERTAIN, BUT IT *APPEARS* AS THOUGH THIS APARTMENT WAS SET ON *FIRE*, SHERIFF.
NOW, TOTENKINDER. GIVE THE POOR MAN A BREAK. NOT EVERYONE SHARES YOUR HEIGHTENED PERSPICACITY.
BIGBY! OVER HERE!
BUFKIN! WHAT *HAPPENED?*
THERE'S A BOOK WITH ALL SORTS OF INFORMATION ON LOCAL WITCHES, YOU SEE.
I SPIED IT HERE A FEW DAYS AGO WHEN I WAS BRINGING MISTER CRANE HIS TOMATO SOUP, SO I CAME UP HERE TO *GET* IT.
BUT WHEN I GOT HERE, HE... HE WAS SETTING *FIRE* TO THE PLACE. I TRIED TO *STOP* HIM, BUT HE'S VERY STRONG!
I GUESS THE LITTLE WEASEL IS COVERING HIS TRACKS. DID CRANE SAY WHERE HE WAS *GOING*?
NO, SHERIFF. NOT *CRANE.* NOBODY'S SEEN *HIM* SINCE THIS EVENING.
IT WAS *BLUEBEARD. HE* DID THIS!

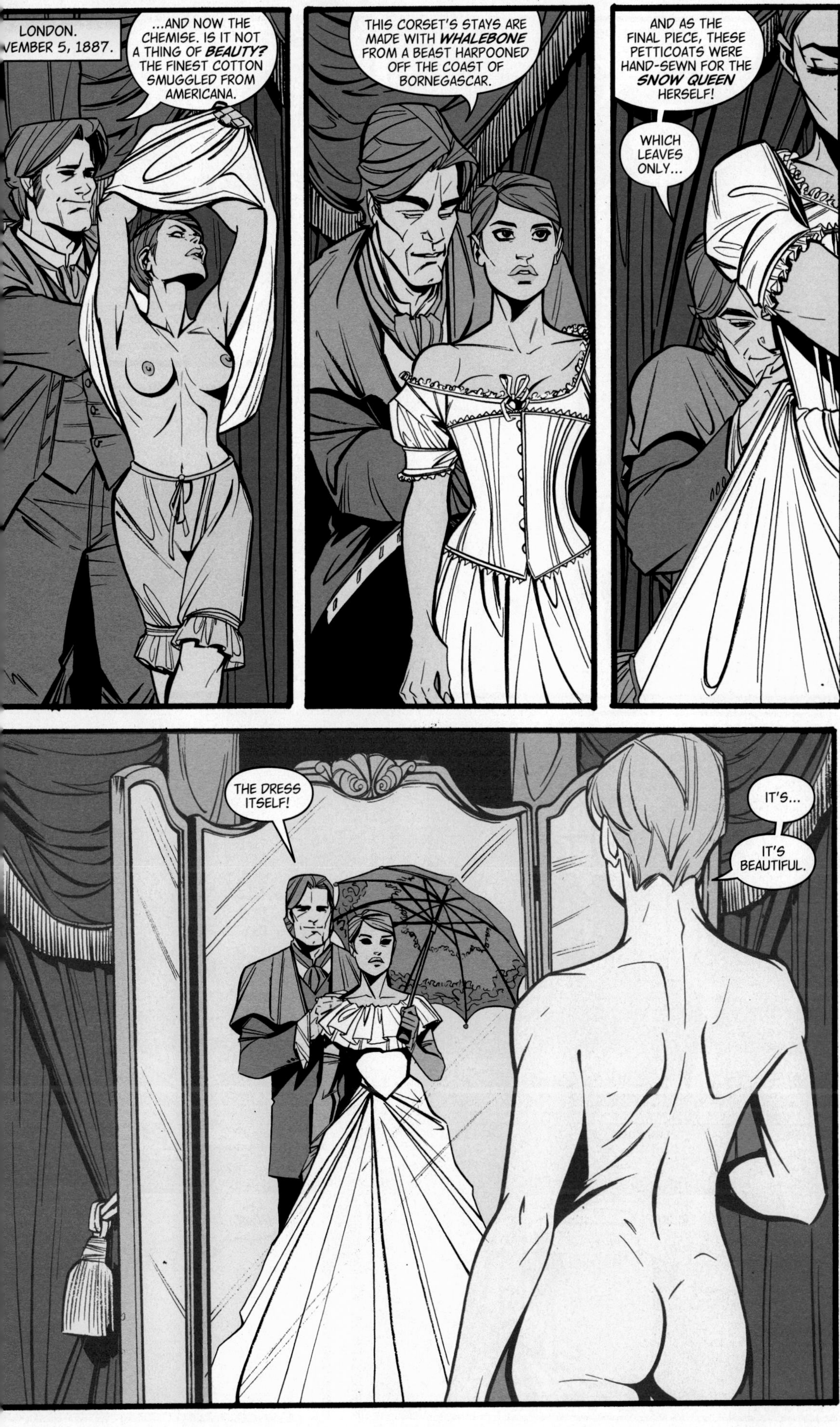
LONDON.
VEMBER 5, 1887.
...AND NOW THE CHEMISE. IS IT NOT A THING OF BEAUTY? THE FINEST COTTON SMUGGLED FROM AMERICANA.
THIS CORSET'S STAYS ARE MADE WITH WHALEBONE FROM A BEAST HARPOONED OFF THE COAST OF BORNEGASCAR.
AND AS THE FINAL PIECE, THESE PETTICOATS WERE HAND-SEWN FOR THE SNOW QUEEN HERSELF!
WHICH LEAVES ONLY...
THE DRESS ITSELF!
IT'S...
IT'S BEAUTIFUL.

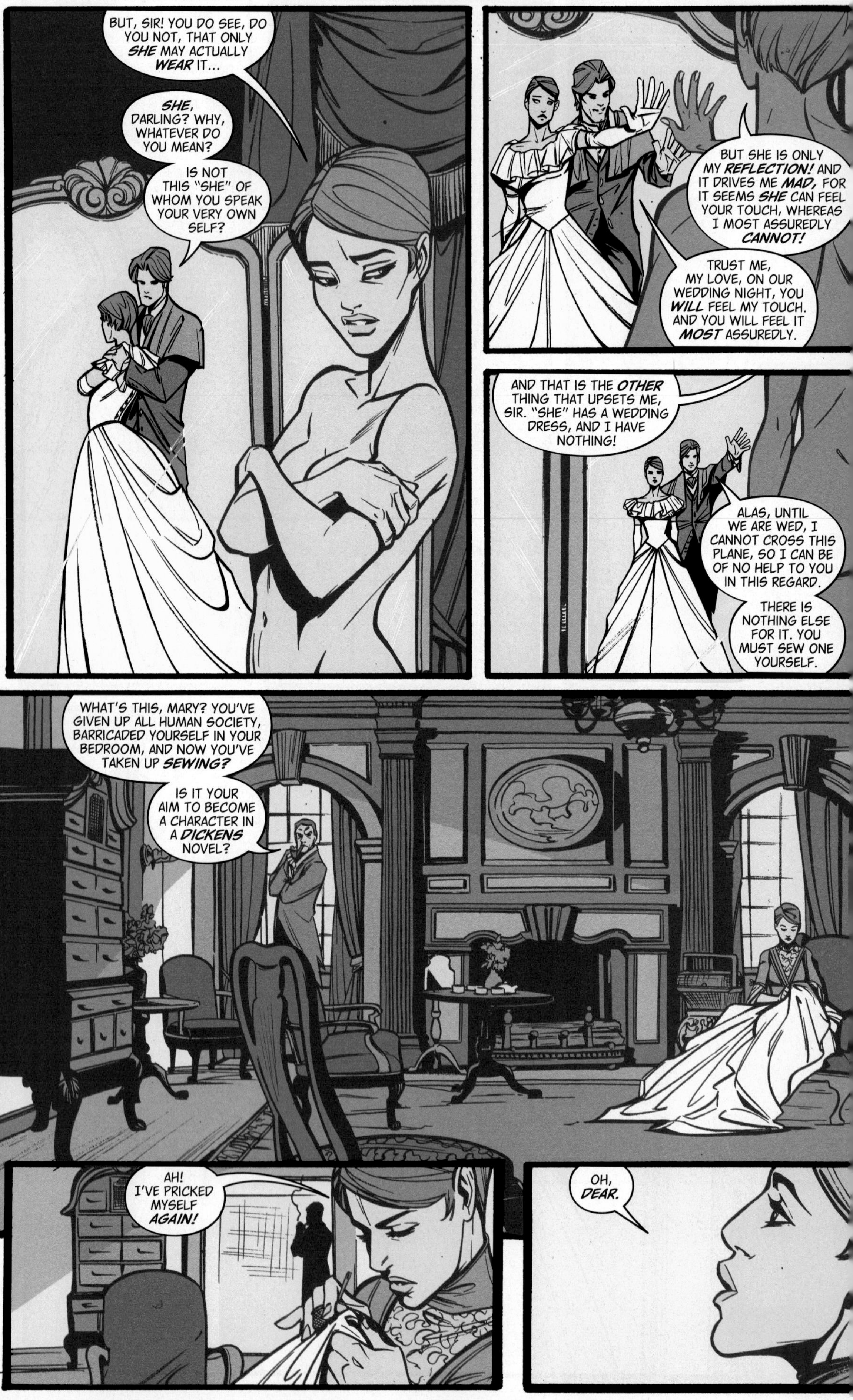
BUT, SIR! YOU DO SEE, DO YOU NOT, THAT ONLY SHE MAY ACTUALLY WEAR IT...
SHE, DARLING? WHY, WHATEVER DO YOU MEAN?
IS NOT THIS "SHE" OF WHOM YOU SPEAK YOUR VERY OWN SELF?
BUT SHE IS ONLY MY REFLECTION! AND IT DRIVES ME MAD, FOR IT SEEMS SHE CAN FEEL YOUR TOUCH, WHEREAS I MOST ASSUREDLY CANNOT!
TRUST ME, MY LOVE, ON OUR WEDDING NIGHT, YOU WILL FEEL MY TOUCH. AND YOU WILL FEEL IT MOST ASSUREDLY.
AND THAT IS THE OTHER THING THAT UPSETS ME, SIR. "SHE" HAS A WEDDING DRESS, AND I HAVE NOTHING!
ALAS, UNTIL WE ARE WED, I CANNOT CROSS THIS PLANE, SO I CAN BE OF NO HELP TO YOU IN THIS REGARD.
THERE IS NOTHING ELSE FOR IT. YOU MUST SEW ONE YOURSELF.
WHAT'S THIS, MARY? YOU'VE GIVEN UP ALL HUMAN SOCIETY, BARRICADED YOURSELF IN YOUR BEDROOM, AND NOW YOU'VE TAKEN UP SEWING?
IS IT YOUR AIM TO BECOME A CHARACTER IN A DICKENS NOVEL?
AH! I'VE PRICKED MYSELF AGAIN!
OH, DEAR.

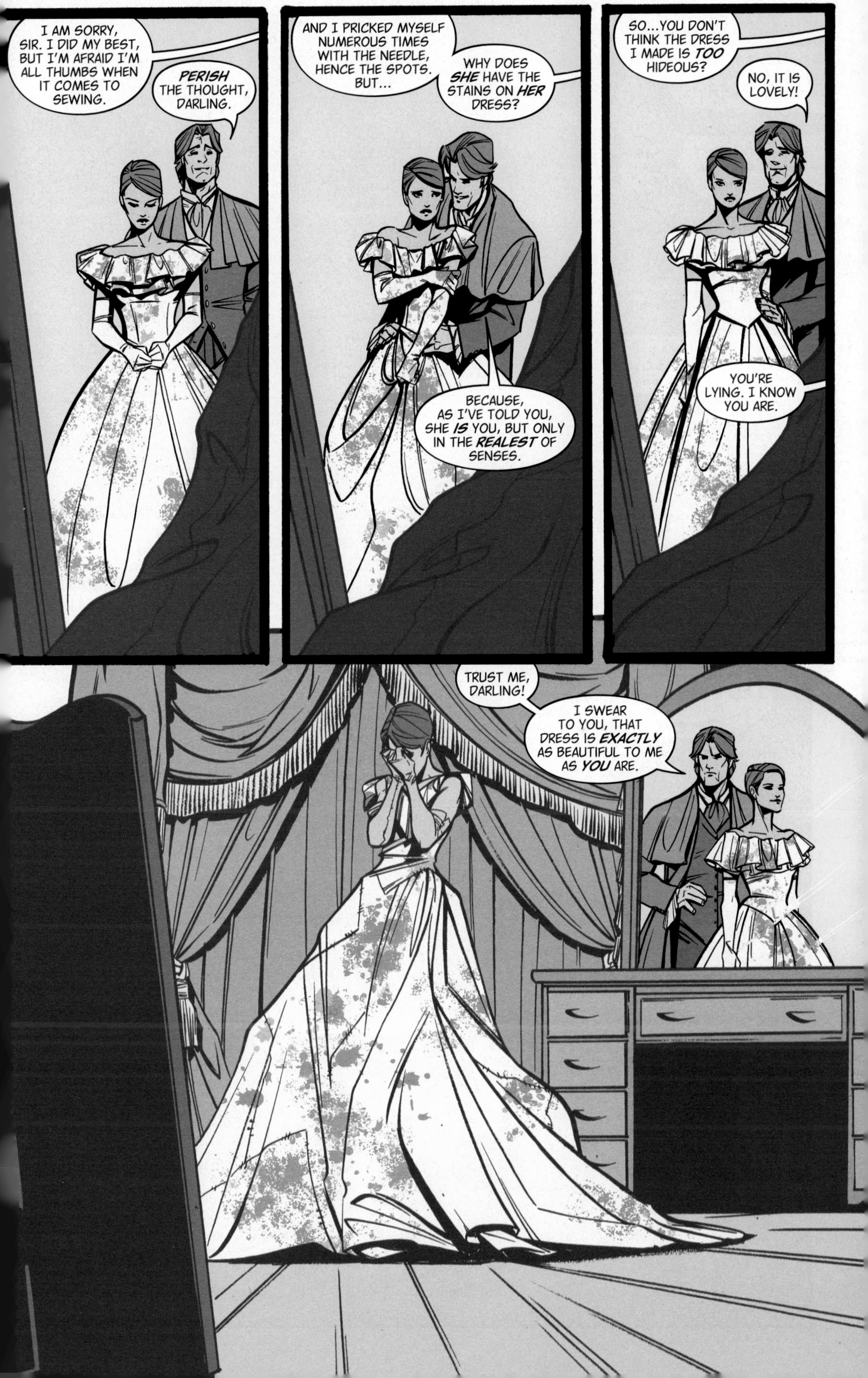
I AM SORRY, SIR. I DID MY BEST, BUT I'M AFRAID I'M ALL THUMBS WHEN IT COMES TO SEWING.
PERISH THE THOUGHT, DARLING.
AND I PRICKED MYSELF NUMEROUS TIMES WITH THE NEEDLE, HENCE THE SPOTS. BUT...
WHY DOES SHE HAVE THE STAINS ON HER DRESS?
BECAUSE, AS I'VE TOLD YOU, SHE IS YOU, BUT ONLY IN THE REALEST OF SENSES.
SO...YOU DON'T THINK THE DRESS I MADE IS TOO HIDEOUS?
NO, IT IS LOVELY!
YOU'RE LYING. I KNOW YOU ARE.
TRUST ME, DARLING!
I SWEAR TO YOU, THAT DRESS IS EXACTLY AS BEAUTIFUL TO ME AS YOU ARE.

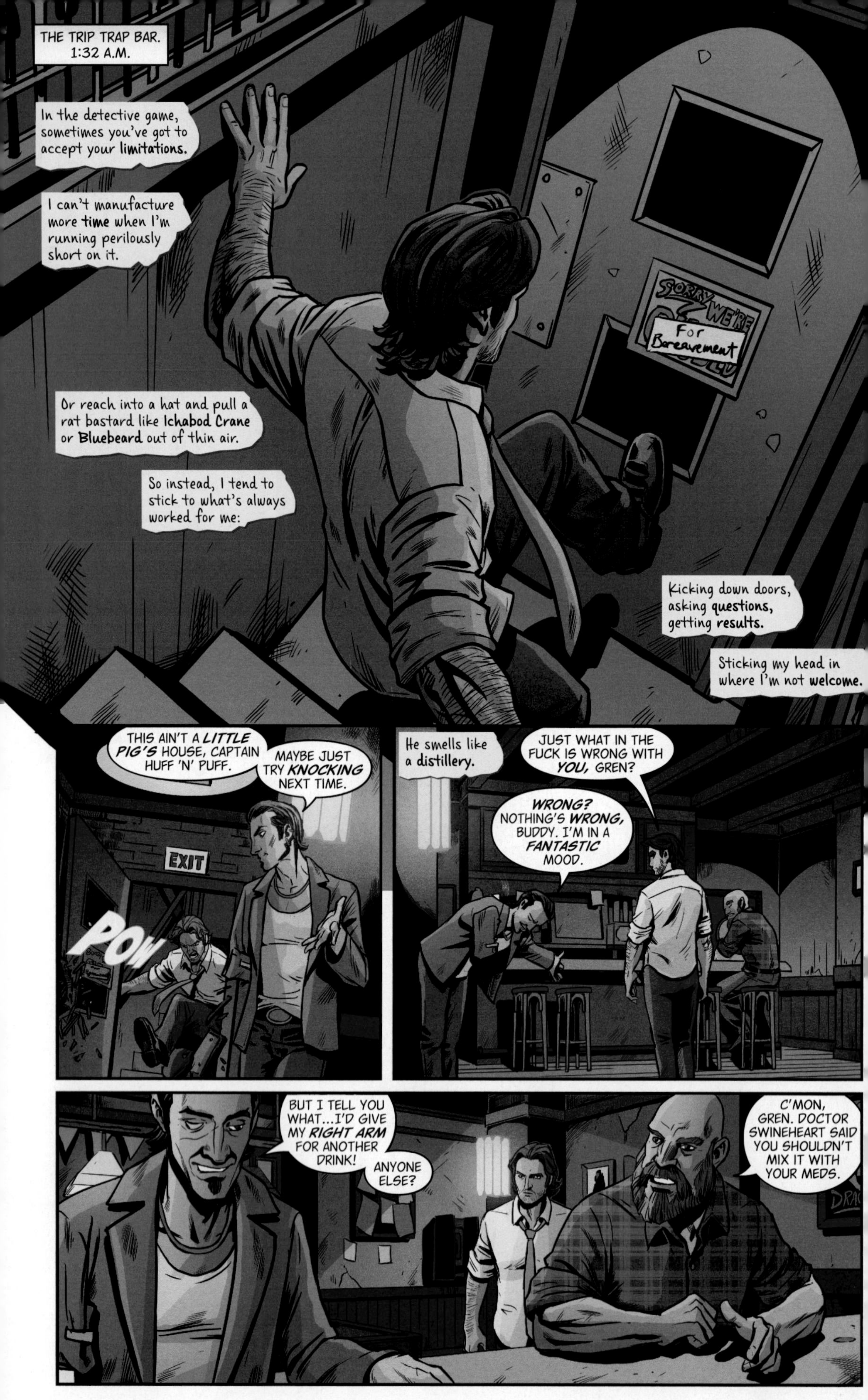

THE TRIP TRAP BAR. 1:32 A.M.
In the detective game, sometimes you've got to accept your **limitations.**
I can't manufacture more **time** when I'm running perilously short on it.
SORRY WE'RE
For Bereavement
Or reach into a hat and pull a rat bastard like **Ichabod Crane** or **Bluebeard** out of thin air.
So instead, I tend to stick to what's always worked for me:
Kicking down doors, asking **questions,** getting **results.**
Sticking my head in where I'm not **welcome.**
THIS AIN'T A ***LITTLE PIG'S*** HOUSE, CAPTAIN HUFF 'N' PUFF.
MAYBE JUST TRY ***KNOCKING*** NEXT TIME.
EXIT
POW
He smells like a **distillery.**
JUST WHAT IN THE FUCK IS WRONG WITH ***YOU,*** GREN?
WRONG? NOTHING'S ***WRONG,*** BUDDY. I'M IN A ***FANTASTIC*** MOOD.
BUT I TELL YOU WHAT...I'D GIVE MY ***RIGHT ARM*** FOR ANOTHER DRINK!
ANYONE ELSE?
C'MON, GREN. DOCTOR SWINEHEART SAID YOU SHOULDN'T MIX IT WITH YOUR MEDS.

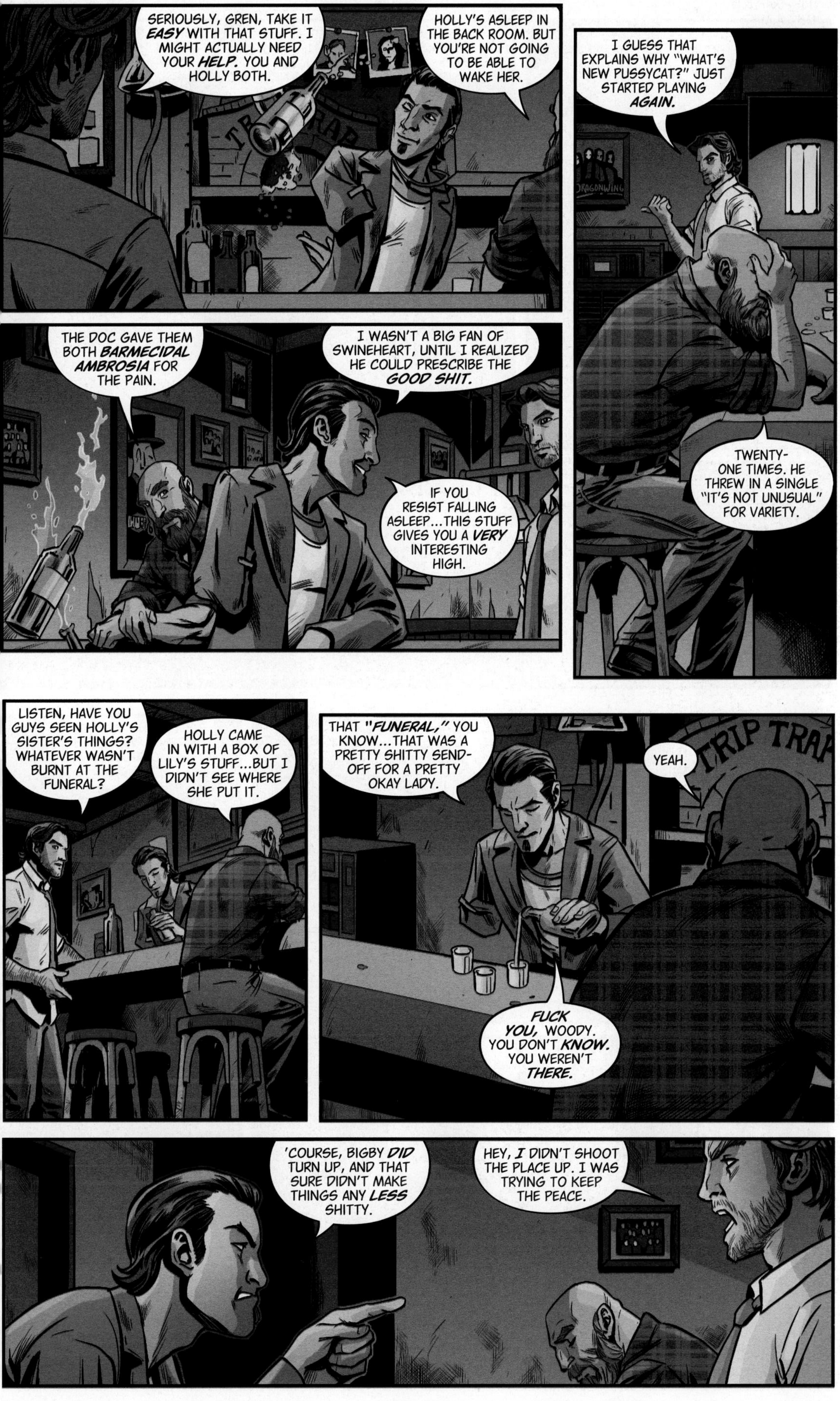
SERIOUSLY, GREN, TAKE IT EASY WITH THAT STUFF. I MIGHT ACTUALLY NEED YOUR HELP. YOU AND HOLLY BOTH.
HOLLY'S ASLEEP IN THE BACK ROOM. BUT YOU'RE NOT GOING TO BE ABLE TO WAKE HER.
I GUESS THAT EXPLAINS WHY "WHAT'S NEW PUSSYCAT?" JUST STARTED PLAYING AGAIN.
DRAGONWING
TRIP TRAP
THE DOC GAVE THEM BOTH BARMECIDAL AMBROSIA FOR THE PAIN.
I WASN'T A BIG FAN OF SWINEHEART, UNTIL I REALIZED HE COULD PRESCRIBE THE GOOD SHIT.
IF YOU RESIST FALLING ASLEEP...THIS STUFF GIVES YOU A VERY INTERESTING HIGH.
TWENTY-ONE TIMES. HE THREW IN A SINGLE "IT'S NOT UNUSUAL" FOR VARIETY.
LISTEN, HAVE YOU GUYS SEEN HOLLY'S SISTER'S THINGS? WHATEVER WASN'T BURNT AT THE FUNERAL?
HOLLY CAME IN WITH A BOX OF LILY'S STUFF...BUT I DIDN'T SEE WHERE SHE PUT IT.
THAT "FUNERAL," YOU KNOW...THAT WAS A PRETTY SHITTY SEND-OFF FOR A PRETTY OKAY LADY.
YEAH.
FUCK YOU, WOODY. YOU DON'T KNOW. YOU WEREN'T THERE.
'COURSE, BIGBY DID TURN UP, AND THAT SURE DIDN'T MAKE THINGS ANY LESS SHITTY.
HEY, I DIDN'T SHOOT THE PLACE UP. I WAS TRYING TO KEEP THE PEACE.

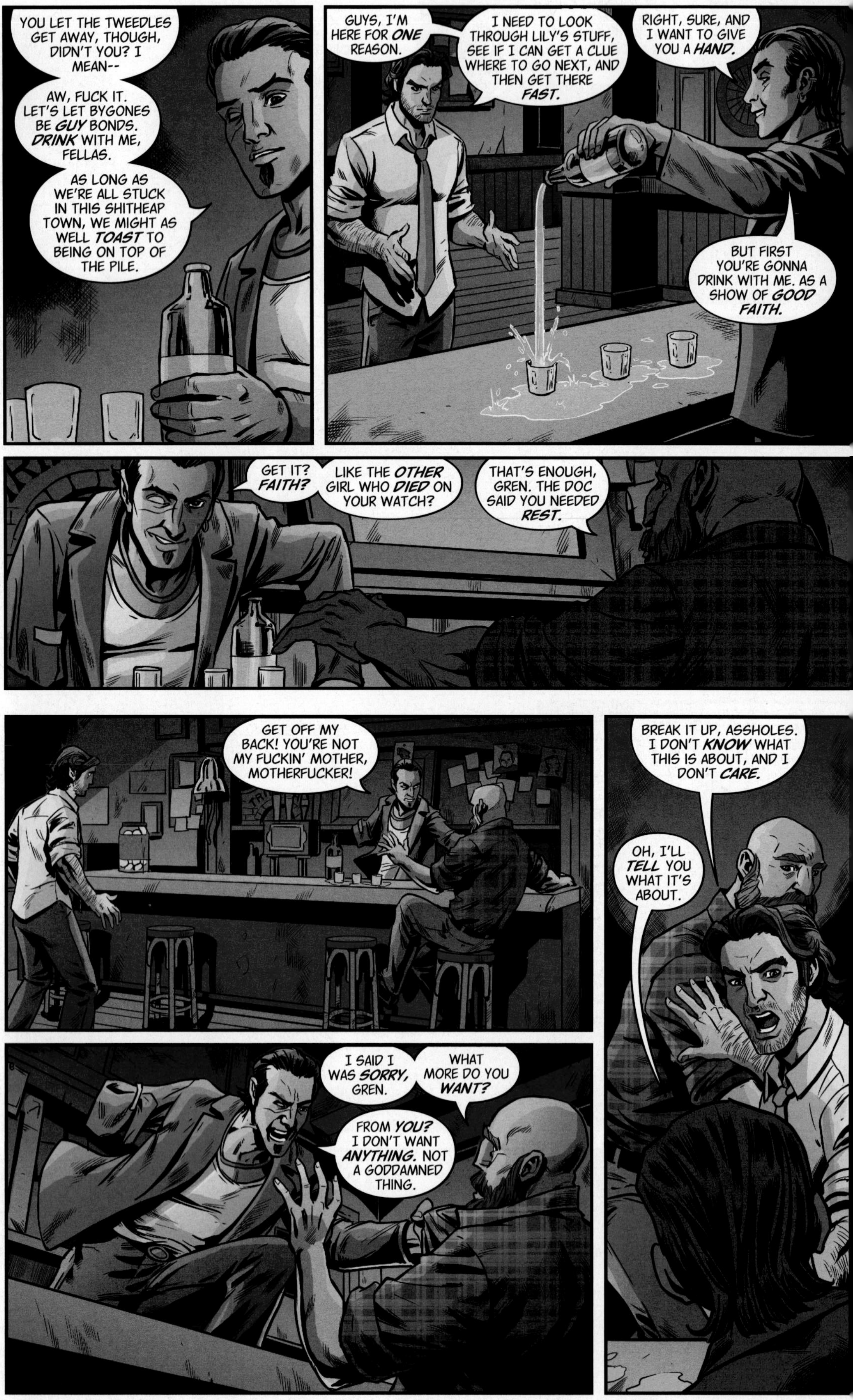
YOU LET THE TWEEDLES GET AWAY, THOUGH, DIDN'T YOU? I MEAN--
AW, FUCK IT. LET'S LET BYGONES BE GUY BONDS. DRINK WITH ME, FELLAS.
AS LONG AS WE'RE ALL STUCK IN THIS SHITHEAP TOWN, WE MIGHT AS WELL TOAST TO BEING ON TOP OF THE PILE.
GUYS, I'M HERE FOR ONE REASON.
I NEED TO LOOK THROUGH LILY'S STUFF, SEE IF I CAN GET A CLUE WHERE TO GO NEXT, AND THEN GET THERE FAST.
RIGHT, SURE, AND I WANT TO GIVE YOU A HAND.
BUT FIRST YOU'RE GONNA DRINK WITH ME. AS A SHOW OF GOOD FAITH.
GET IT? FAITH?
LIKE THE OTHER GIRL WHO DIED ON YOUR WATCH?
THAT'S ENOUGH, GREN. THE DOC SAID YOU NEEDED REST.
GET OFF MY BACK! YOU'RE NOT MY FUCKIN' MOTHER, MOTHERFUCKER!
I SAID I WAS SORRY, GREN.
WHAT MORE DO YOU WANT?
FROM YOU? I DON'T WANT ANYTHING. NOT A GODDAMNED THING.
BREAK IT UP, ASSHOLES. I DON'T KNOW WHAT THIS IS ABOUT, AND I DON'T CARE.
OH, I'LL TELL YOU WHAT IT'S ABOUT.

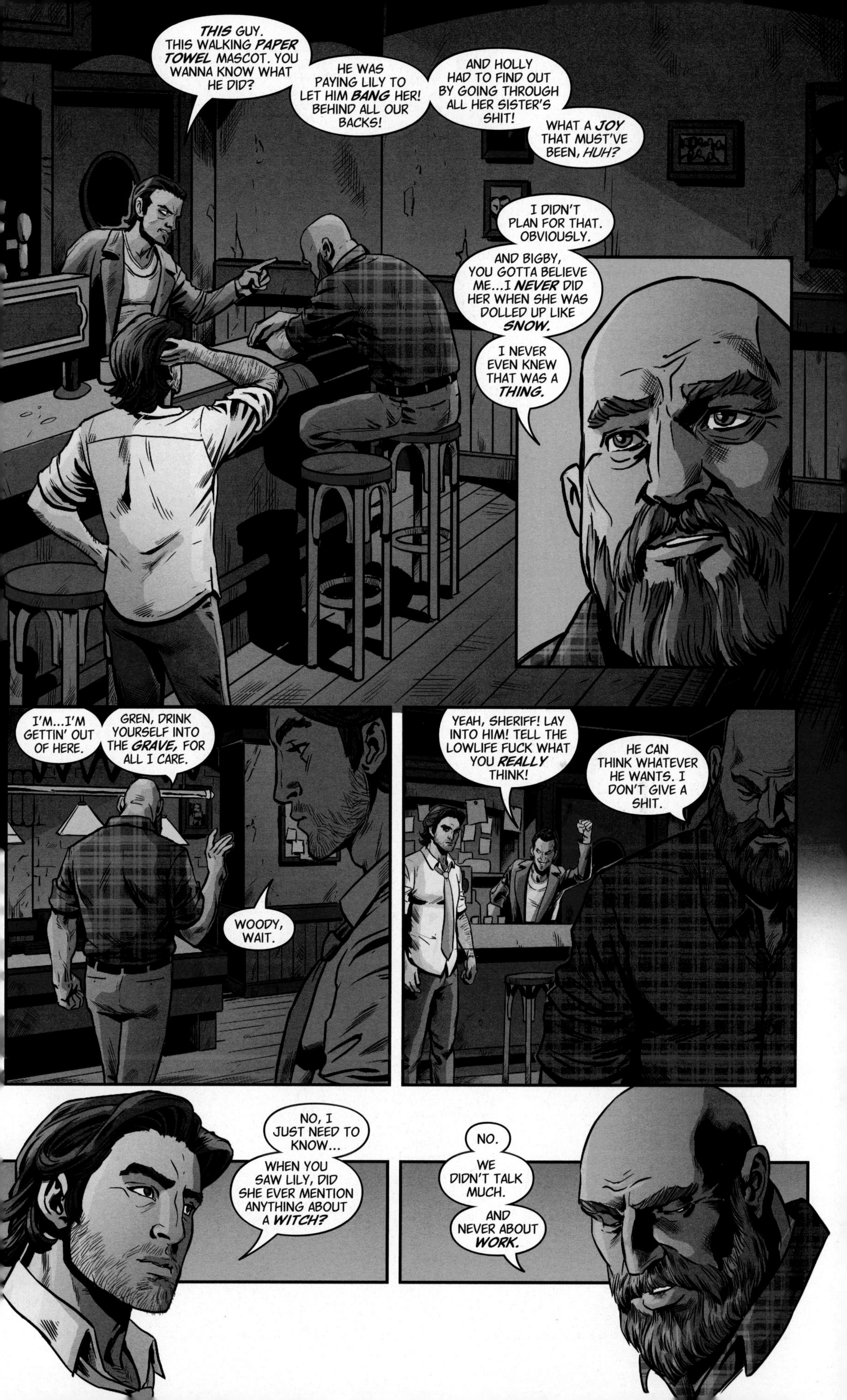
THIS GUY. THIS WALKING PAPER TOWEL MASCOT. YOU WANNA KNOW WHAT HE DID?
HE WAS PAYING LILY TO LET HIM BANG HER! BEHIND ALL OUR BACKS!
AND HOLLY HAD TO FIND OUT BY GOING THROUGH ALL HER SISTER'S SHIT!
WHAT A JOY THAT MUST'VE BEEN, HUH?
I DIDN'T PLAN FOR THAT. OBVIOUSLY.
AND BIGBY, YOU GOTTA BELIEVE ME...I NEVER DID HER WHEN SHE WAS DOLLED UP LIKE SNOW.
I NEVER EVEN KNEW THAT WAS A THING.
I'M...I'M GETTIN' OUT OF HERE.
GREN, DRINK YOURSELF INTO THE GRAVE, FOR ALL I CARE.
WOODY, WAIT.
YEAH, SHERIFF! LAY INTO HIM! TELL THE LOWLIFE FUCK WHAT YOU REALLY THINK!
HE CAN THINK WHATEVER HE WANTS. I DON'T GIVE A SHIT.
NO, I JUST NEED TO KNOW...
WHEN YOU SAW LILY, DID SHE EVER MENTION ANYTHING ABOUT A WITCH?
NO.
WE DIDN'T TALK MUCH.
AND NEVER ABOUT WORK.

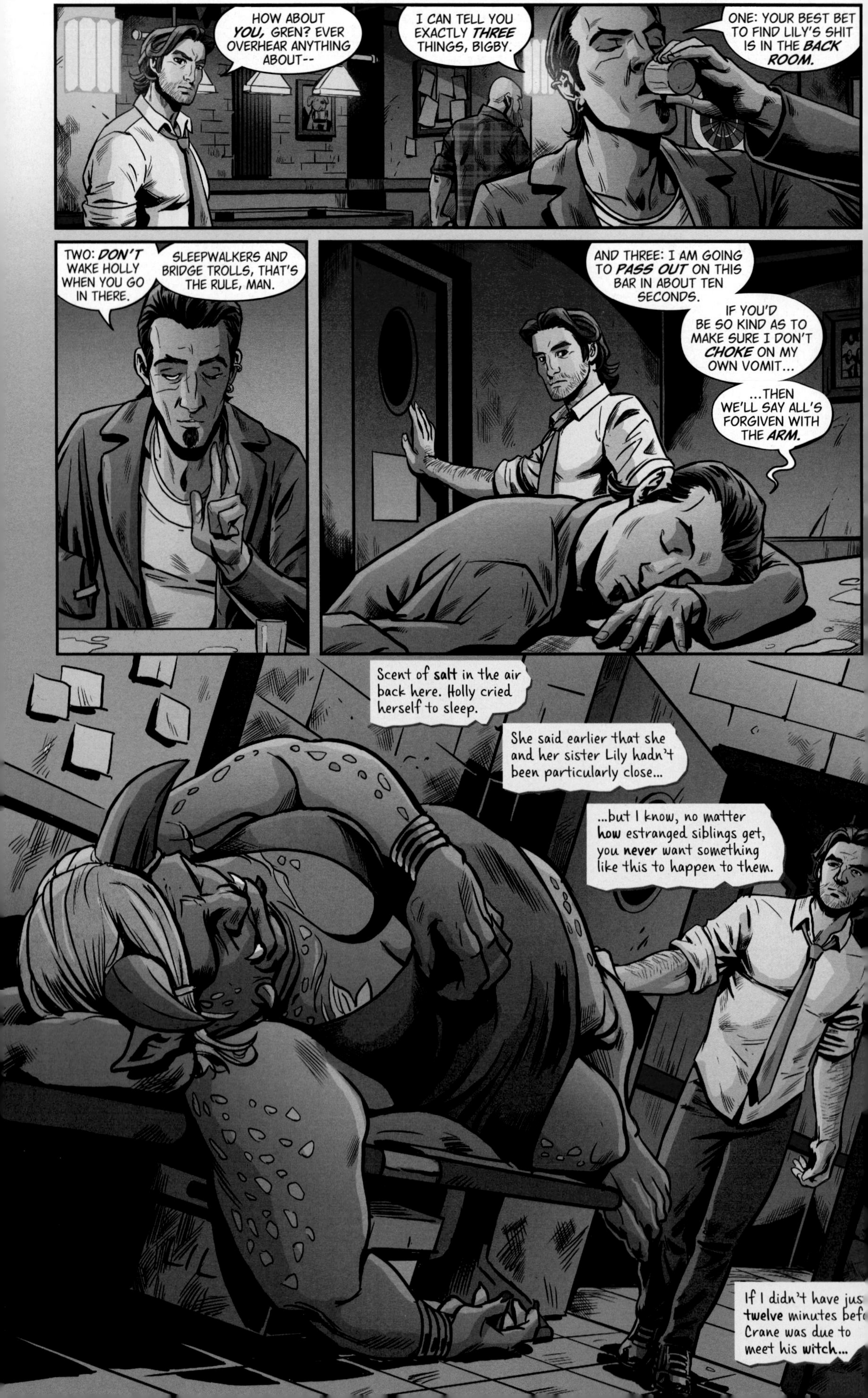

HOW ABOUT YOU, GREN? EVER OVERHEAR ANYTHING ABOUT--
I CAN TELL YOU EXACTLY THREE THINGS, BIGBY.
ONE: YOUR BEST BET TO FIND LILY'S SHIT IS IN THE BACK ROOM.
TWO: DON'T WAKE HOLLY WHEN YOU GO IN THERE.
SLEEPWALKERS AND BRIDGE TROLLS, THAT'S THE RULE, MAN.
AND THREE: I AM GOING TO PASS OUT ON THIS BAR IN ABOUT TEN SECONDS.
IF YOU'D BE SO KIND AS TO MAKE SURE I DON'T CHOKE ON MY OWN VOMIT...
...THEN WE'LL SAY ALL'S FORGIVEN WITH THE ARM.
Scent of salt in the air back here. Holly cried herself to sleep.
She said earlier that she and her sister Lily hadn't been particularly close...
...but I know, no matter how estranged siblings get, you never want something like this to happen to them.
If I didn't have jus twelve minutes bef Crane was due to meet his witch...

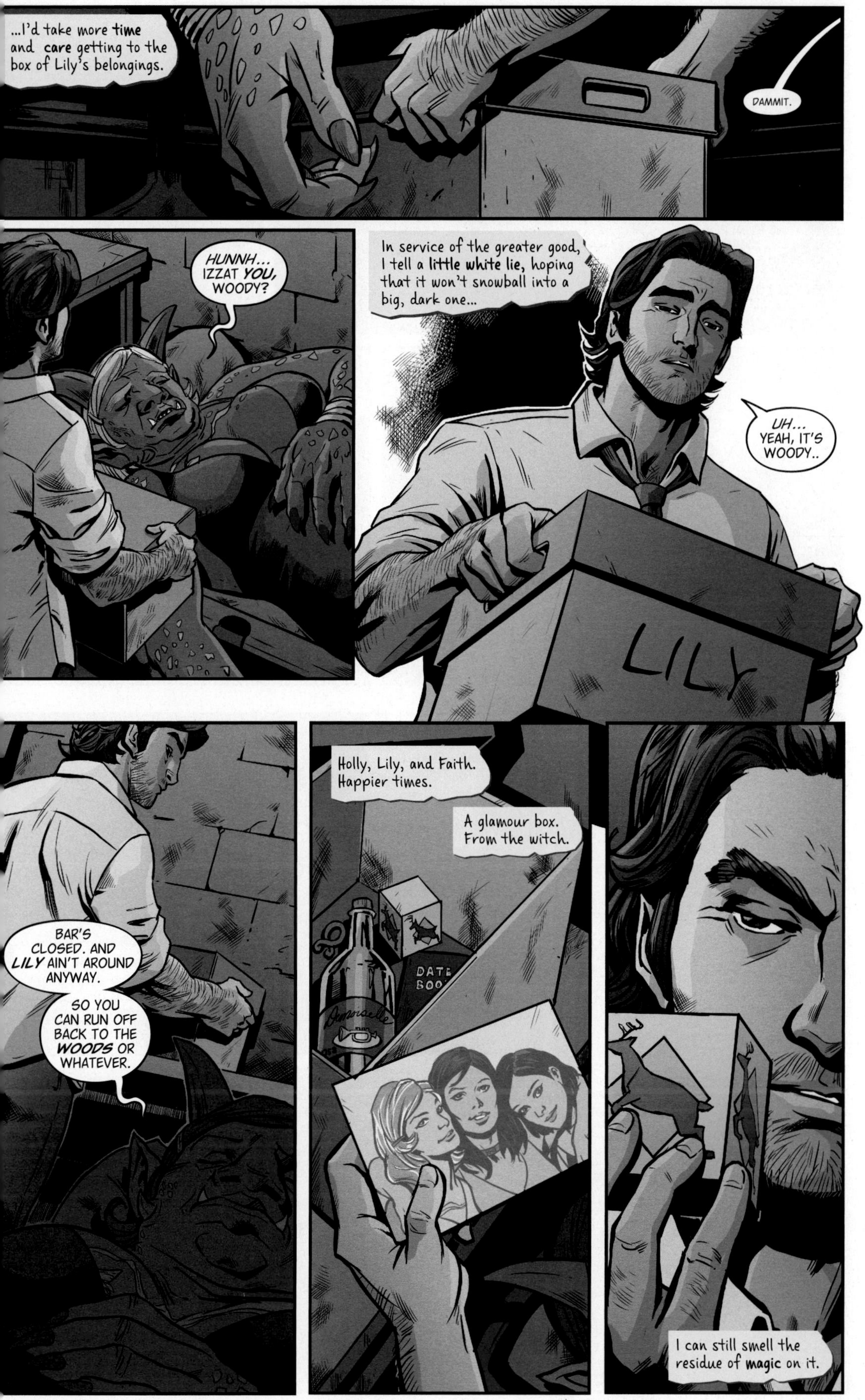
...I'd take more time and care getting to the box of Lily's belongings.
DAMMIT.
HUNNH... IZZAT YOU, WOODY?
In service of the greater good, I tell a little white lie, hoping that it won't snowball into a big, dark one...
UH... YEAH, IT'S WOODY..
LILY
BAR'S CLOSED. AND LILY AIN'T AROUND ANYWAY.
SO YOU CAN RUN OFF BACK TO THE WOODS OR WHATEVER.
Holly, Lily, and Faith. Happier times.
A glamour box. From the witch.
DATE BOO
I can still smell the residue of magic on it.

I DON'T KNOW WHY YOU CAME HERE TONIGHT, WOODY.

LILY'S FUNERAL...IT WAS JUST SO *FUCKED*. BUT...I WISH YOU COULD'VE BEEN THERE.

I WISH I UNDERSTOOD WHAT *BIGBY'S* DOING. IF HE EVEN REALLY *CARES*.

HE CARES ABOUT THIS, HOLLY. ABOUT LILY. ABOUT FAITH.

I *KNOW* HE DOES.

YEAH? WELL...YOU KNOW HIM BETTER THAN ANYONE, SO...

...I'LL TAKE YOUR...WORD FOR IT.

She's passed out again. And I've got what I need.

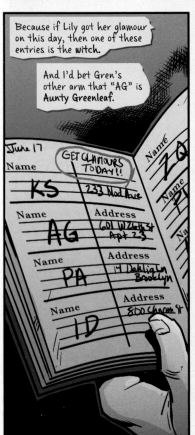

Because if Lily got her glamour on this day, then one of these entries is the witch.

And I'd bet Gren's other arm that "AG" is Aunty Greenleaf.

June 17

GET GLAMOURS TODAY!!

Name
KS   233 Mad Ave

Name
AG   601 W 26th St Apt 23

Name
PA   4 Dahlia Brooklyn

Name
ID   800 Charm St

Name
Z.Q.

Name
P.

Name
N

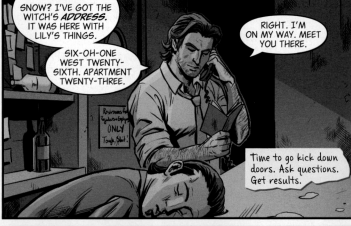

SNOW? I'VE GOT THE WITCH'S *ADDRESS*. IT WAS HERE WITH LILY'S THINGS.

SIX-OH-ONE WEST TWENTY-SIXTH. APARTMENT TWENTY-THREE.

RIGHT. I'M ON MY WAY. MEET YOU THERE.

Time to go kick down doors. Ask questions. Get results.

Time to stick my head in where I am most definitely not welcome.

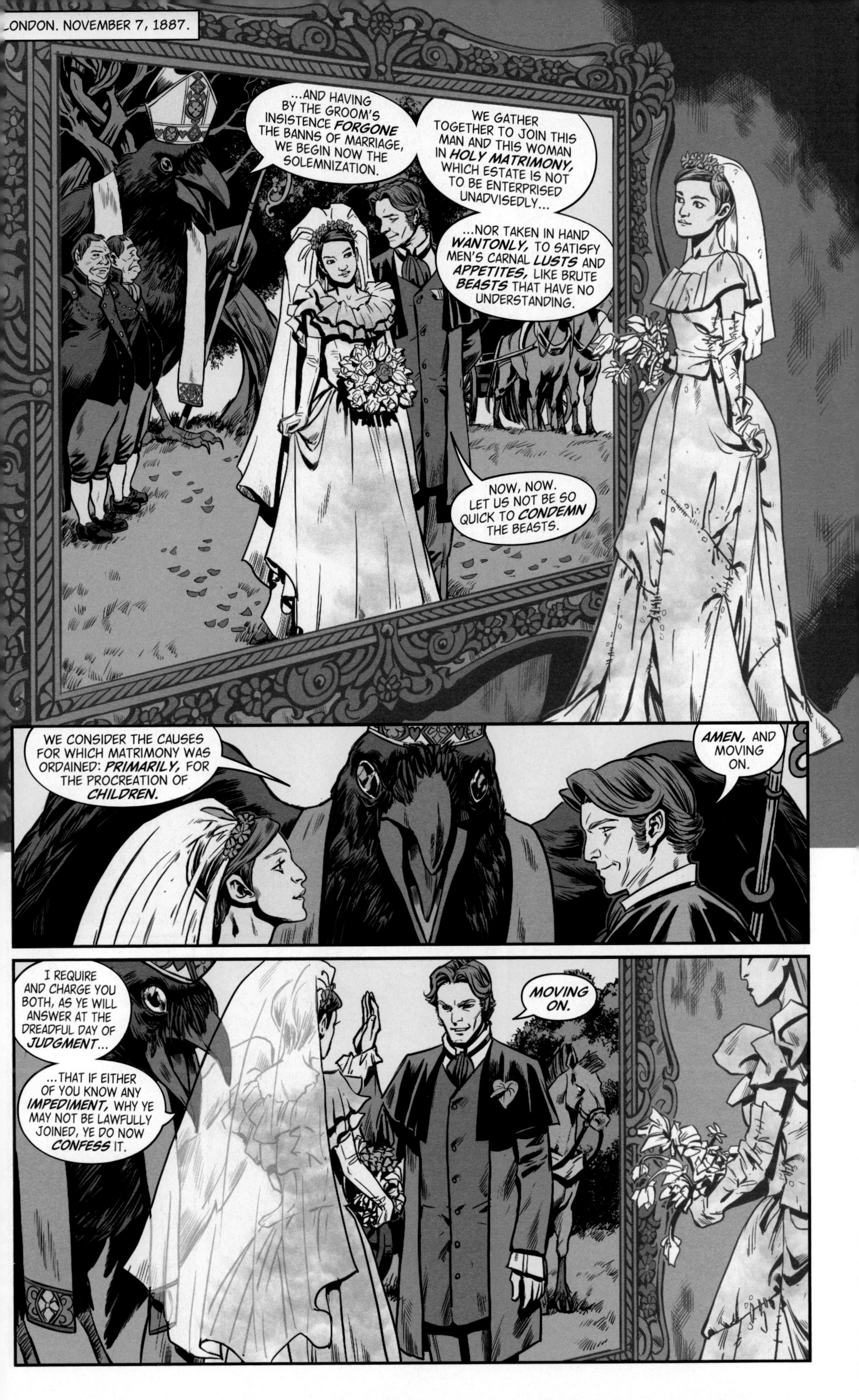
LONDON. NOVEMBER 7, 1887.
...AND HAVING BY THE GROOM'S INSISTENCE FORGONE THE BANNS OF MARRIAGE, WE BEGIN NOW THE SOLEMNIZATION.
WE GATHER TOGETHER TO JOIN THIS MAN AND THIS WOMAN IN HOLY MATRIMONY, WHICH ESTATE IS NOT TO BE ENTERPRISED UNADVISEDLY...
...NOR TAKEN IN HAND WANTONLY, TO SATISFY MEN'S CARNAL LUSTS AND APPETITES, LIKE BRUTE BEASTS THAT HAVE NO UNDERSTANDING.
NOW, NOW. LET US NOT BE SO QUICK TO CONDEMN THE BEASTS.
WE CONSIDER THE CAUSES FOR WHICH MATRIMONY WAS ORDAINED: PRIMARILY, FOR THE PROCREATION OF CHILDREN.
AMEN, AND MOVING ON.
I REQUIRE AND CHARGE YOU BOTH, AS YE WILL ANSWER AT THE DREADFUL DAY OF JUDGMENT...
...THAT IF EITHER OF YOU KNOW ANY IMPEDIMENT, WHY YE MAY NOT BE LAWFULLY JOINED, YE DO NOW CONFESS IT.
MOVING ON.

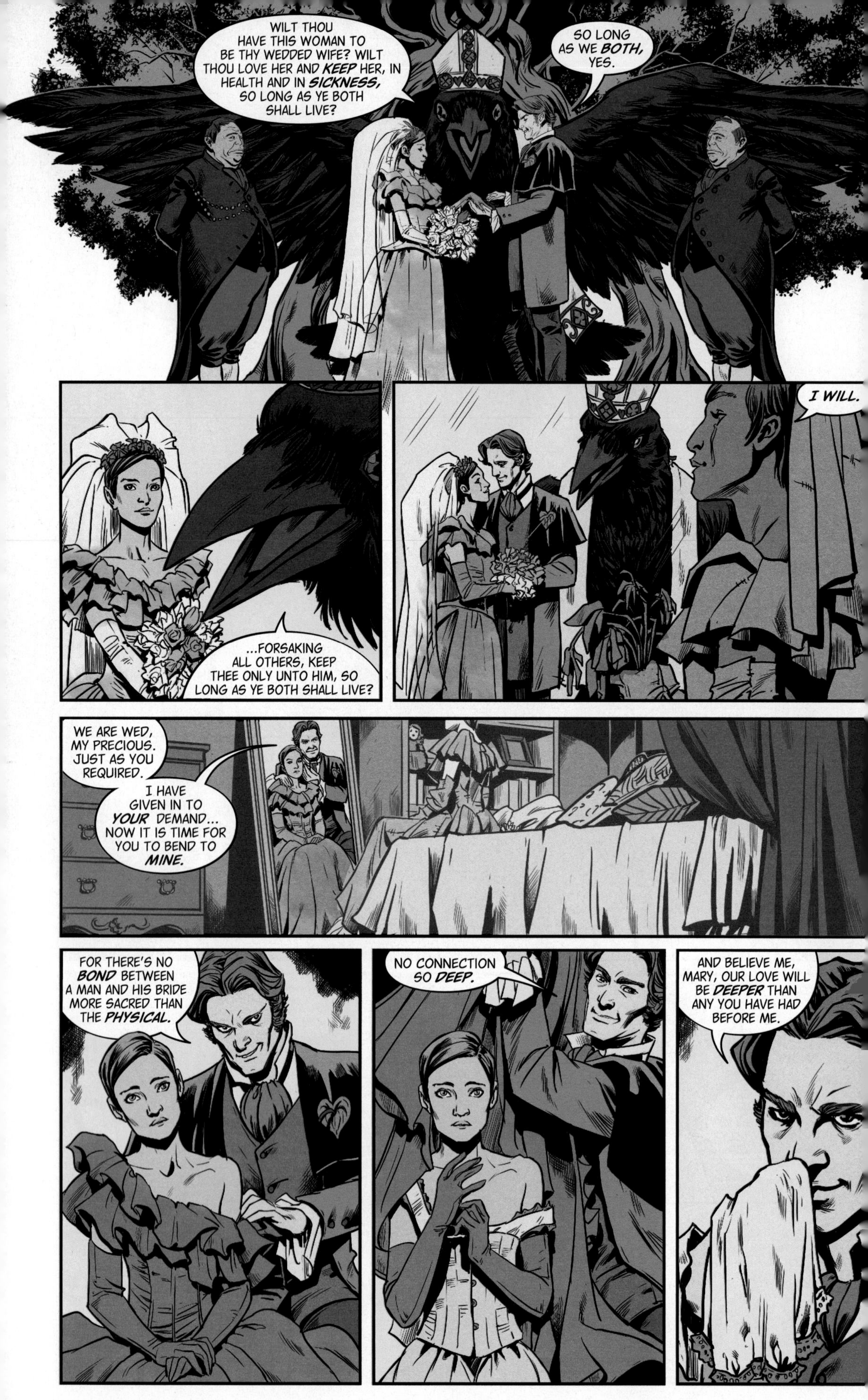
WILT THOU HAVE THIS WOMAN TO BE THY WEDDED WIFE? WILT THOU LOVE HER AND KEEP HER, IN HEALTH AND IN SICKNESS, SO LONG AS YE BOTH SHALL LIVE?
SO LONG AS WE BOTH, YES.
...FORSAKING ALL OTHERS, KEEP THEE ONLY UNTO HIM, SO LONG AS YE BOTH SHALL LIVE?
I WILL.
WE ARE WED, MY PRECIOUS. JUST AS YOU REQUIRED.
I HAVE GIVEN IN TO YOUR DEMAND... NOW IT IS TIME FOR YOU TO BEND TO MINE.
FOR THERE'S NO BOND BETWEEN A MAN AND HIS BRIDE MORE SACRED THAN THE PHYSICAL.
NO CONNECTION SO DEEP.
AND BELIEVE ME, MARY, OUR LOVE WILL BE DEEPER THAN ANY YOU HAVE HAD BEFORE ME.

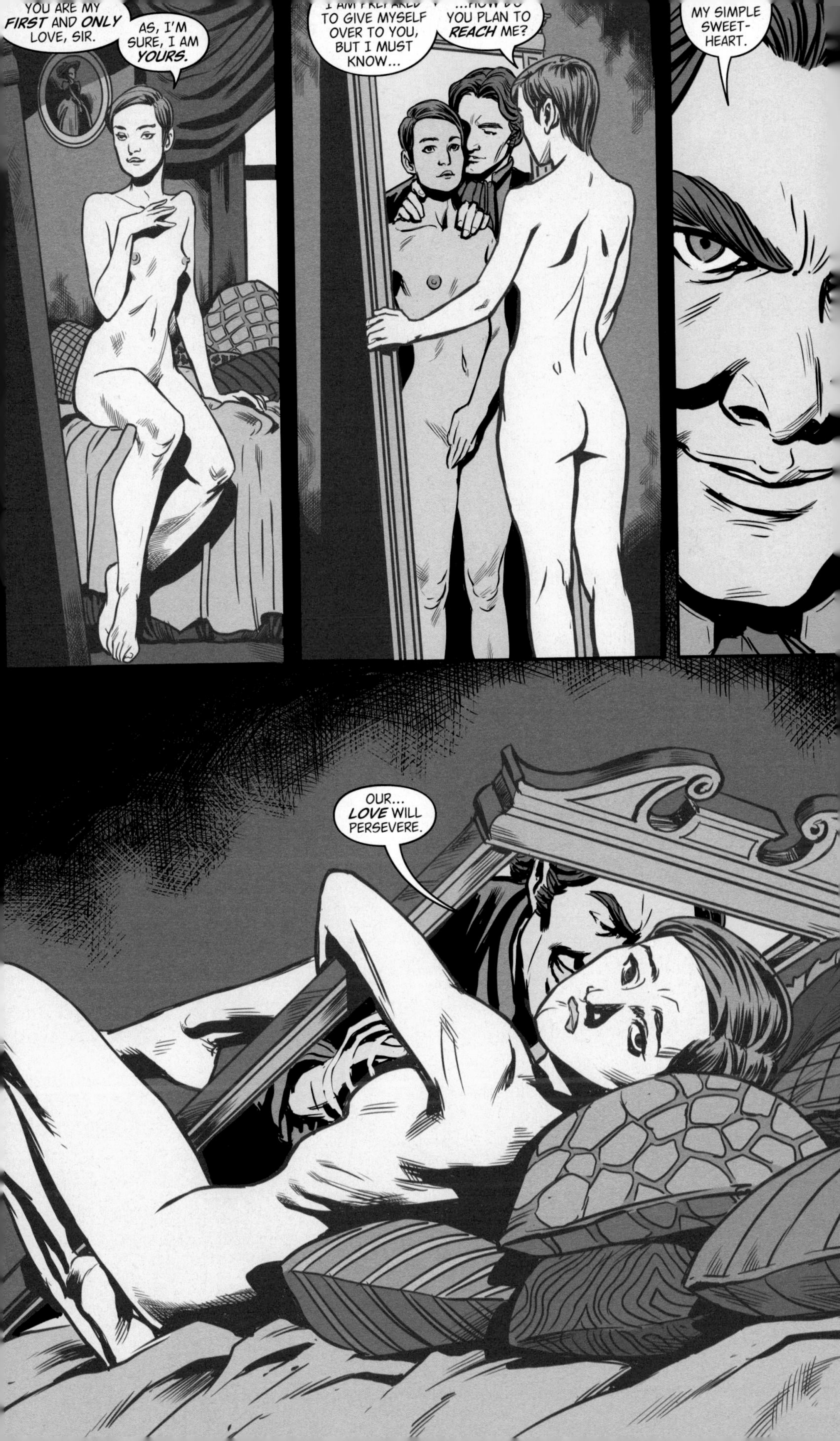

YOU ARE MY FIRST AND ONLY LOVE, SIR.
AS, I'M SURE, I AM YOURS.
TO GIVE MYSELF OVER TO YOU, BUT I MUST KNOW...
YOU PLAN TO REACH ME?
MY SIMPLE SWEET-HEART.
OUR... LOVE WILL PERSEVERE.

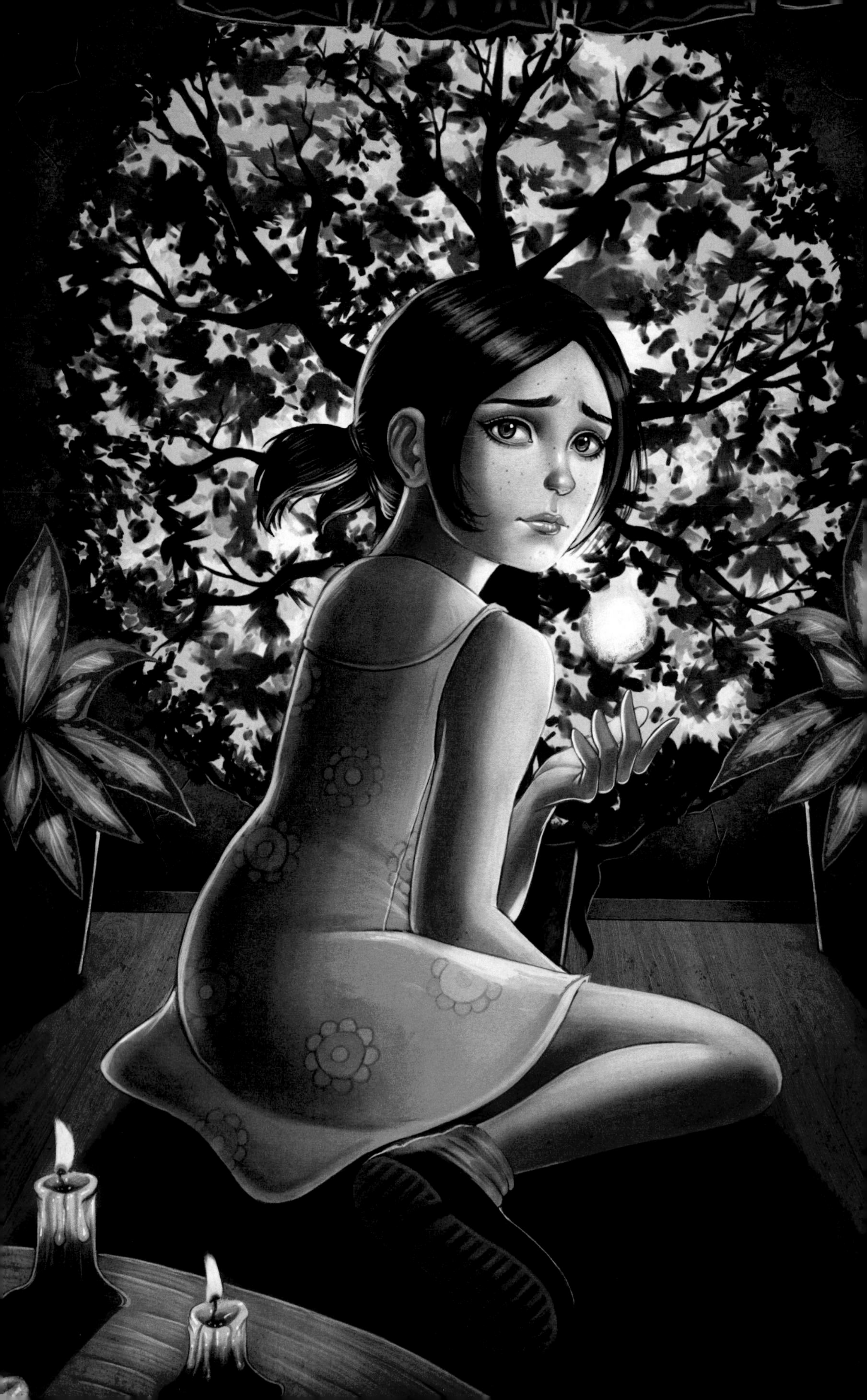

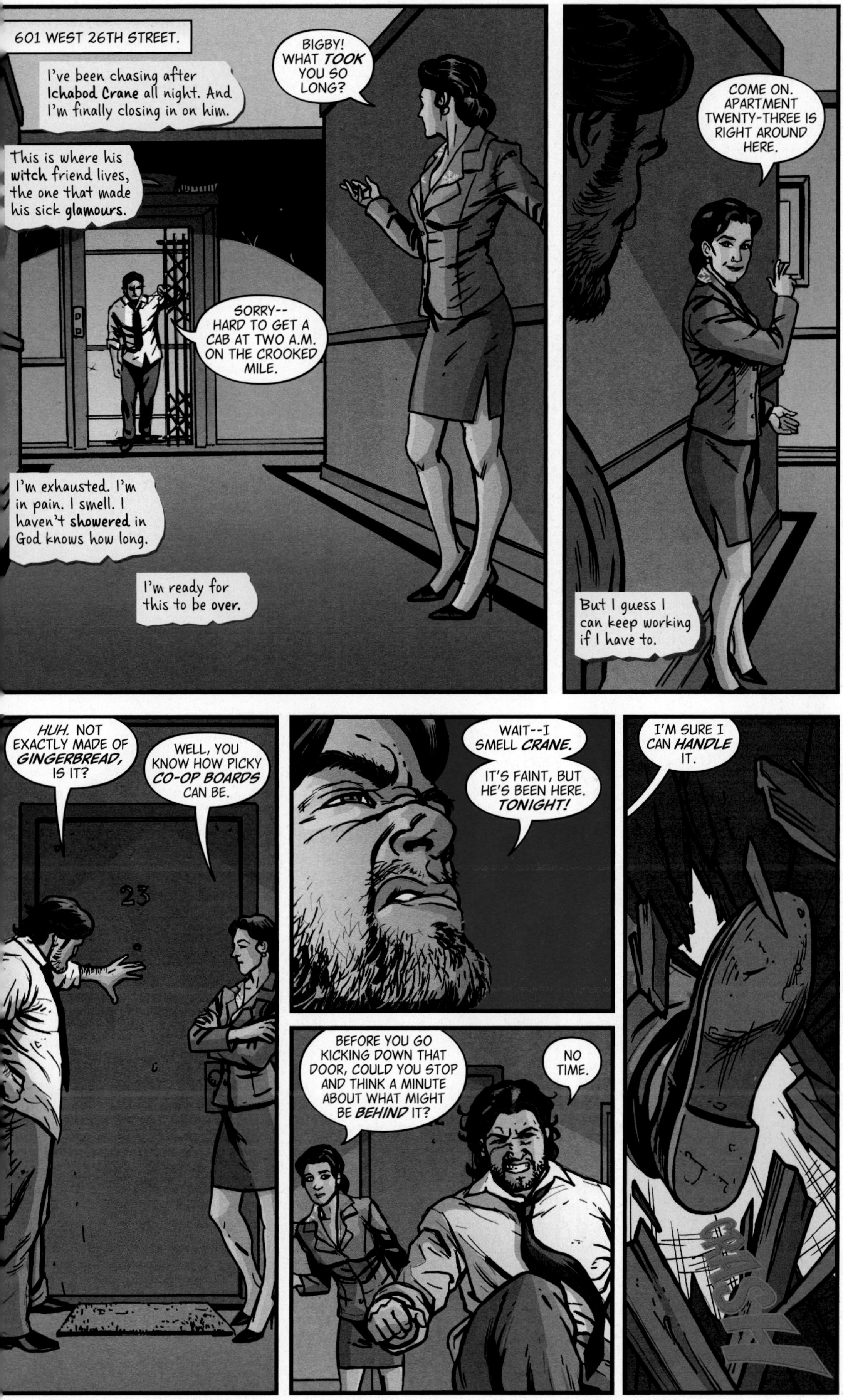
601 WEST 26TH STREET.
I've been chasing after Ichabod Crane all night. And I'm finally closing in on him.
This is where his witch friend lives, the one that made his sick glamours.
BIGBY! WHAT TOOK YOU SO LONG?
SORRY-- HARD TO GET A CAB AT TWO A.M. ON THE CROOKED MILE.
I'm exhausted. I'm in pain. I smell. I haven't showered in God knows how long.
I'm ready for this to be over.
COME ON. APARTMENT TWENTY-THREE IS RIGHT AROUND HERE.
But I guess I can keep working if I have to.
HUH. NOT EXACTLY MADE OF GINGERBREAD, IS IT?
WELL, YOU KNOW HOW PICKY CO-OP BOARDS CAN BE.
23
WAIT--I SMELL CRANE.
IT'S FAINT, BUT HE'S BEEN HERE. TONIGHT!
BEFORE YOU GO KICKING DOWN THAT DOOR, COULD YOU STOP AND THINK A MINUTE ABOUT WHAT MIGHT BE BEHIND IT?
NO TIME.
I'M SURE I CAN HANDLE IT.
CRASH

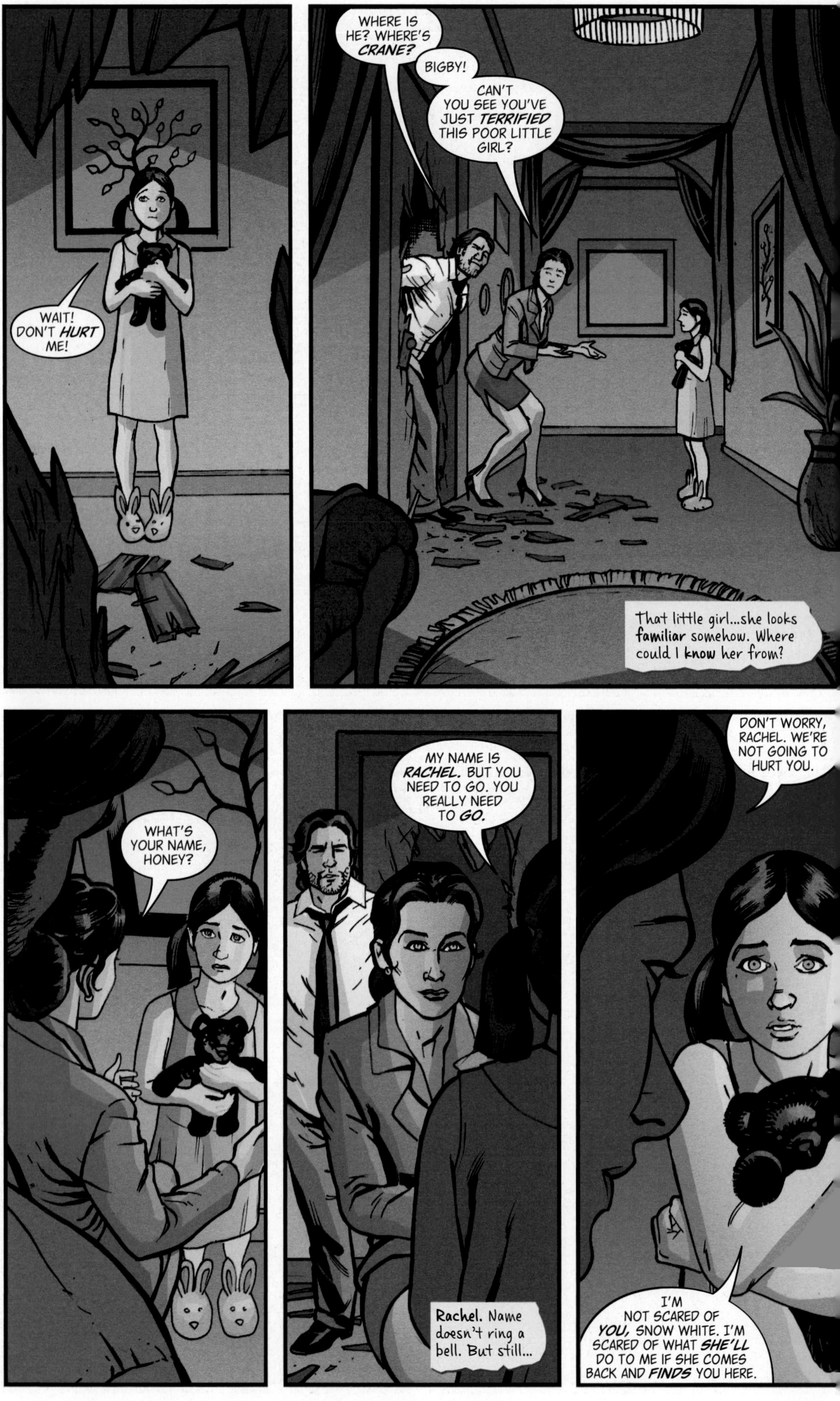

WAIT! DON'T HURT ME!
WHERE IS HE? WHERE'S CRANE?
BIGBY!
CAN'T YOU SEE YOU'VE JUST TERRIFIED THIS POOR LITTLE GIRL?
That little girl...she looks familiar somehow. Where could I know her from?
WHAT'S YOUR NAME, HONEY?
MY NAME IS RACHEL. BUT YOU NEED TO GO. YOU REALLY NEED TO GO.
Rachel. Name doesn't ring a bell. But still...
DON'T WORRY, RACHEL. WE'RE NOT GOING TO HURT YOU.
I'M NOT SCARED OF YOU, SNOW WHITE. I'M SCARED OF WHAT SHE'LL DO TO ME IF SHE COMES BACK AND FINDS YOU HERE.

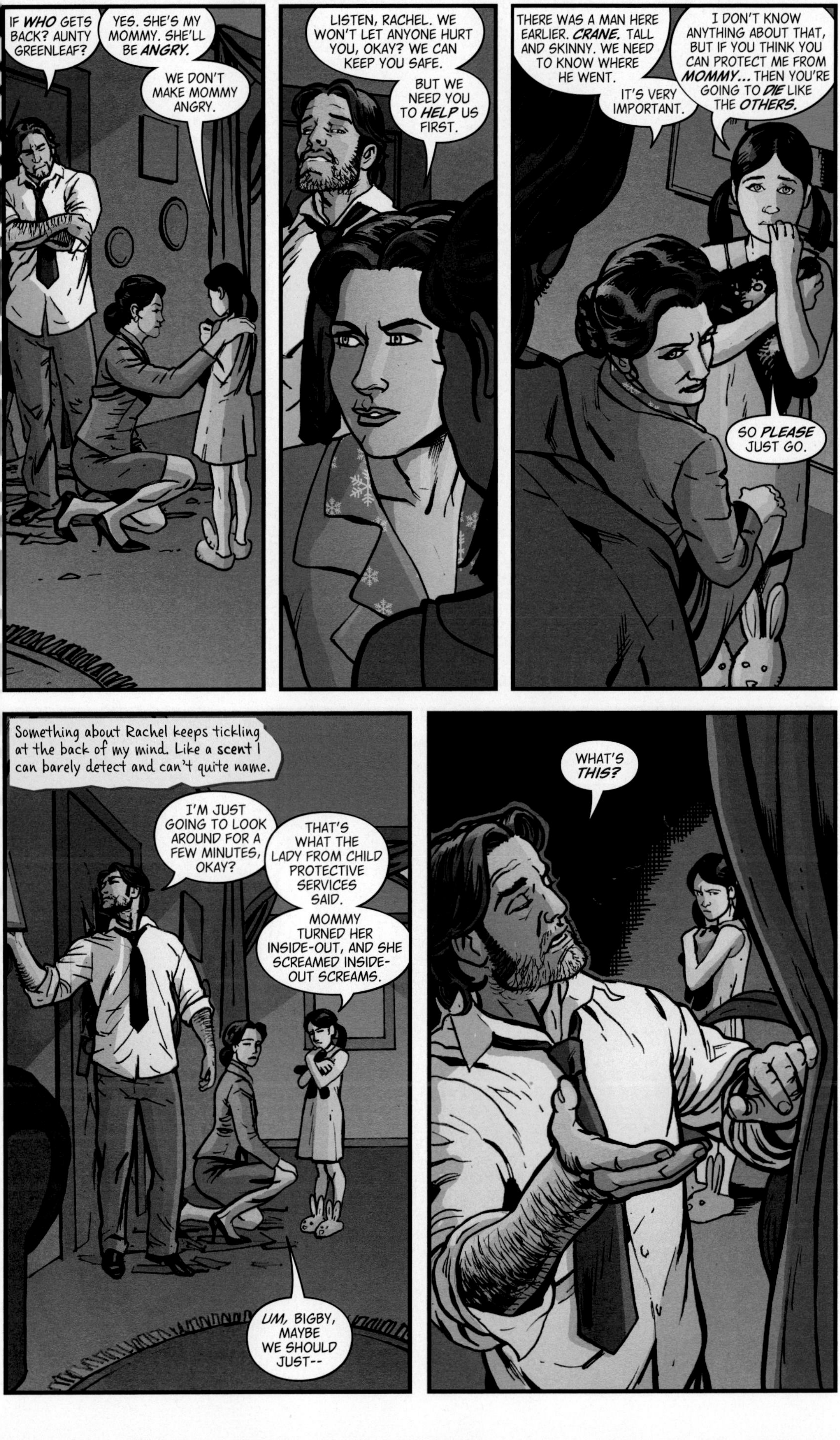
IF WHO GETS BACK? AUNTY GREENLEAF?
YES. SHE'S MY MOMMY. SHE'LL BE ANGRY.
WE DON'T MAKE MOMMY ANGRY.
LISTEN, RACHEL. WE WON'T LET ANYONE HURT YOU, OKAY? WE CAN KEEP YOU SAFE.
BUT WE NEED YOU TO HELP US FIRST.
THERE WAS A MAN HERE EARLIER. CRANE. TALL AND SKINNY. WE NEED TO KNOW WHERE HE WENT.
IT'S VERY IMPORTANT.
I DON'T KNOW ANYTHING ABOUT THAT, BUT IF YOU THINK YOU CAN PROTECT ME FROM MOMMY... THEN YOU'RE GOING TO DIE LIKE THE OTHERS.
SO PLEASE JUST GO.
Something about Rachel keeps tickling at the back of my mind. Like a scent I can barely detect and can't quite name.
I'M JUST GOING TO LOOK AROUND FOR A FEW MINUTES, OKAY?
THAT'S WHAT THE LADY FROM CHILD PROTECTIVE SERVICES SAID.
MOMMY TURNED HER INSIDE-OUT, AND SHE SCREAMED INSIDE-OUT SCREAMS.
UM, BIGBY, MAYBE WE SHOULD JUST--
WHAT'S THIS?

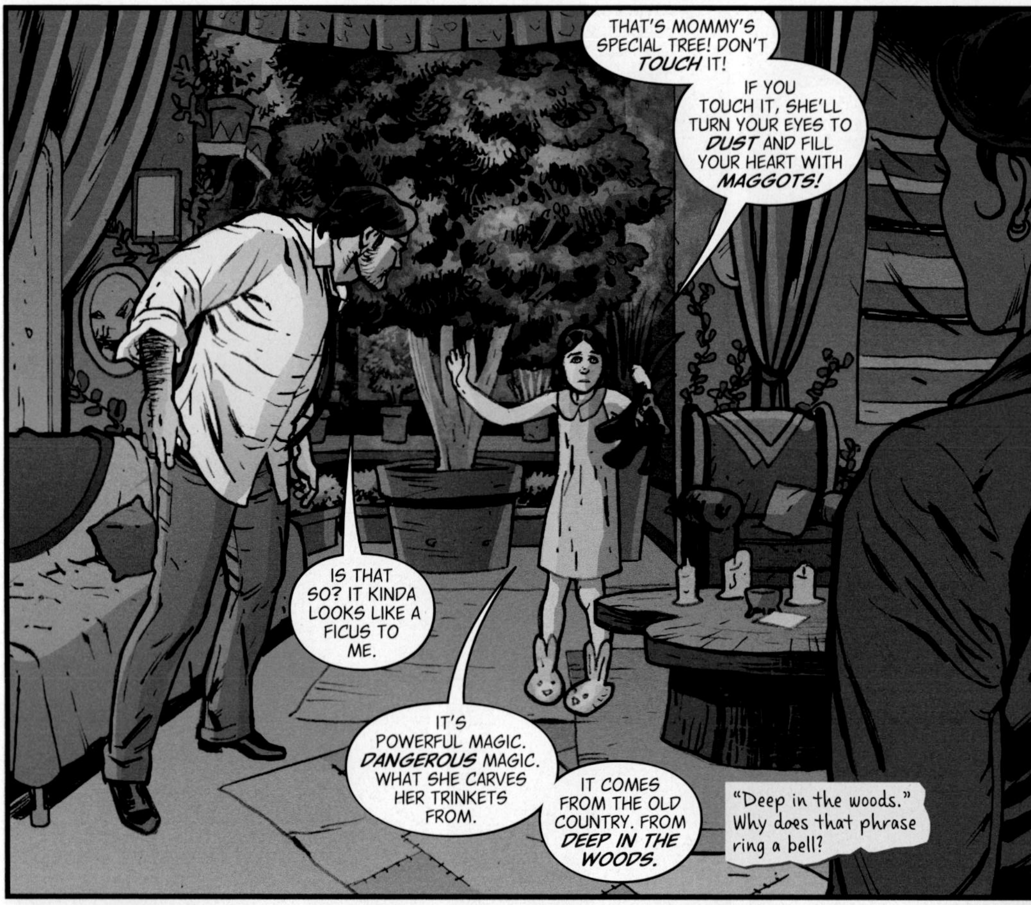
THAT'S MOMMY'S SPECIAL TREE! DON'T *TOUCH* IT!
IF YOU TOUCH IT, SHE'LL TURN YOUR EYES TO *DUST* AND FILL YOUR HEART WITH *MAGGOTS!*
IS THAT SO? IT KINDA LOOKS LIKE A FICUS TO ME.
IT'S POWERFUL MAGIC. *DANGEROUS* MAGIC. WHAT SHE CARVES HER TRINKETS FROM.
IT COMES FROM THE OLD COUNTRY. FROM *DEEP IN THE WOODS.*
"Deep in the woods." Why does that phrase ring a bell?

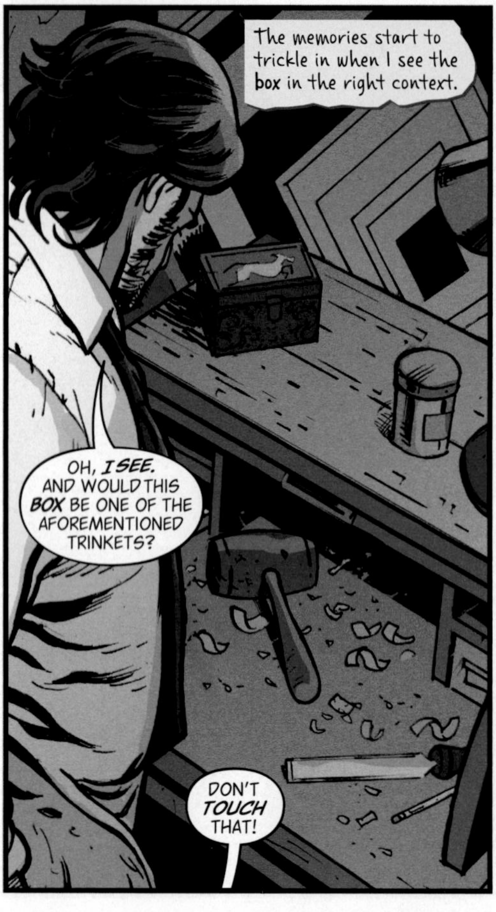
The memories start to trickle in when I see the **box** in the right context.
OH, *I SEE.* AND WOULD THIS *BOX* BE ONE OF THE AFOREMENTIONED TRINKETS?
DON'T *TOUCH* THAT!

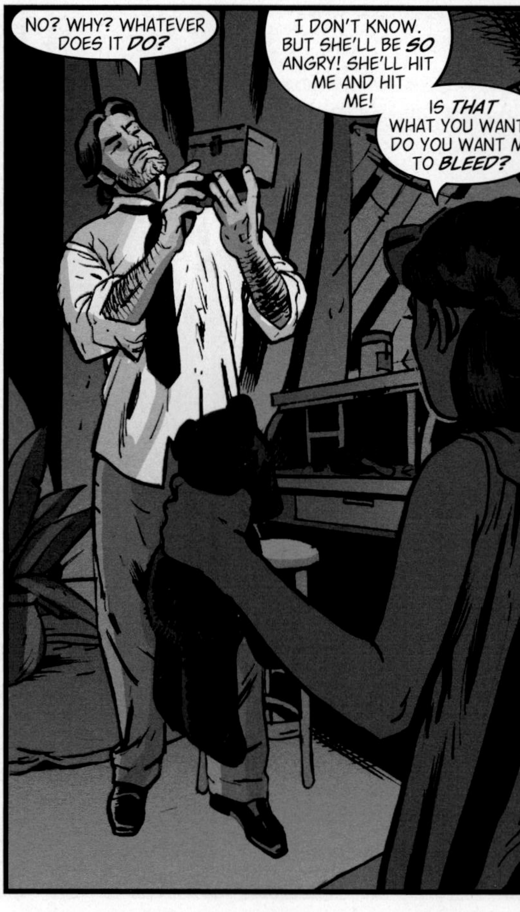
NO? WHY? WHATEVER DOES IT *DO?*
I DON'T KNOW. BUT SHE'LL BE *SO* ANGRY! SHE'LL HIT ME AND HIT ME!
IS *THAT* WHAT YOU WANT? DO YOU WANT ME TO *BLEED?*

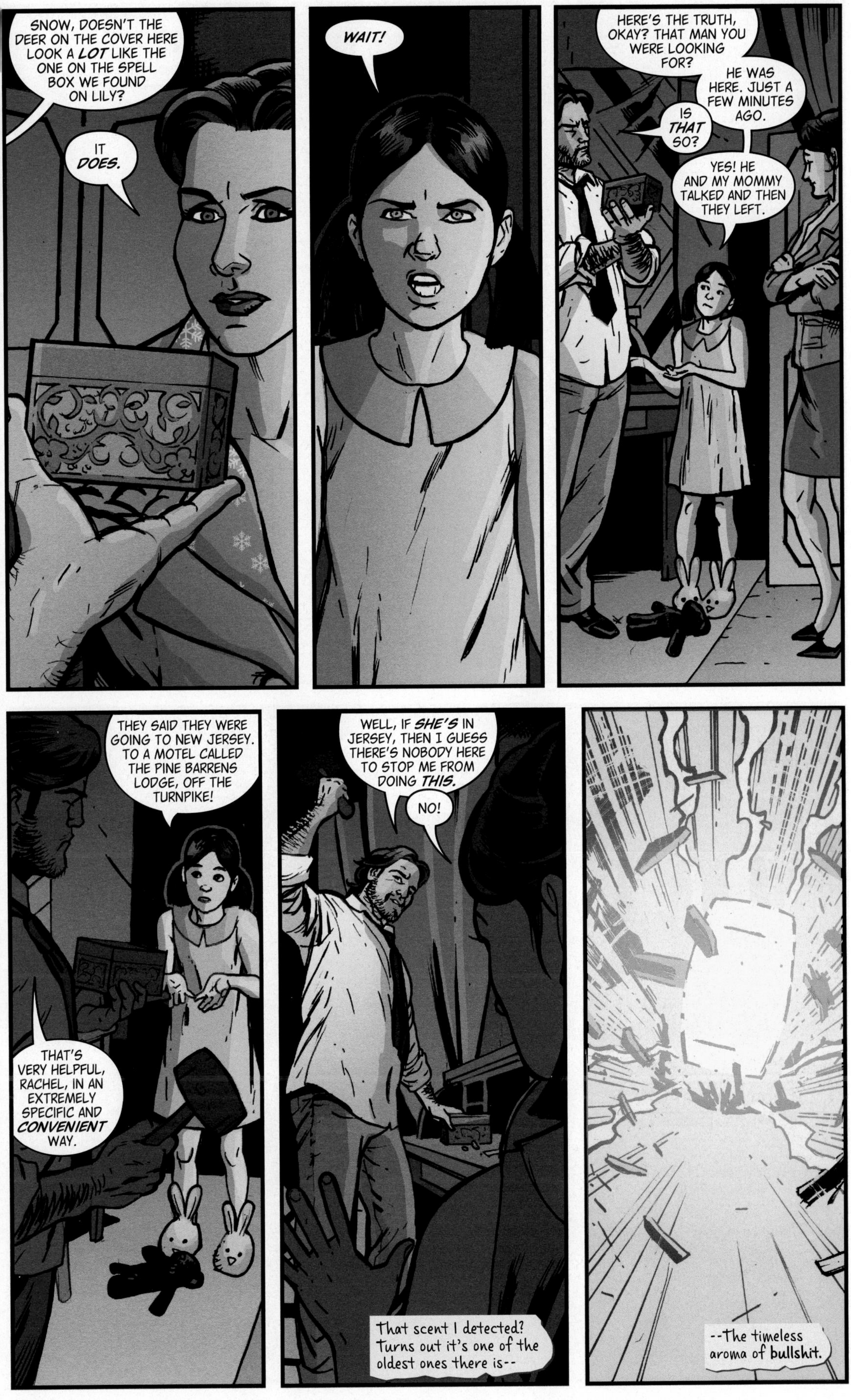
SNOW, DOESN'T THE DEER ON THE COVER HERE LOOK A LOT LIKE THE ONE ON THE SPELL BOX WE FOUND ON LILY?
IT DOES.
WAIT!
HERE'S THE TRUTH, OKAY? THAT MAN YOU WERE LOOKING FOR?
HE WAS HERE. JUST A FEW MINUTES AGO.
IS THAT SO?
YES! HE AND MY MOMMY TALKED AND THEN THEY LEFT.
THEY SAID THEY WERE GOING TO NEW JERSEY. TO A MOTEL CALLED THE PINE BARRENS LODGE, OFF THE TURNPIKE!
THAT'S VERY HELPFUL, RACHEL, IN AN EXTREMELY SPECIFIC AND CONVENIENT WAY.
WELL, IF SHE'S IN JERSEY, THEN I GUESS THERE'S NOBODY HERE TO STOP ME FROM DOING THIS.
NO!
That scent I detected? Turns out it's one of the oldest ones there is--
--The timeless aroma of bullshit.

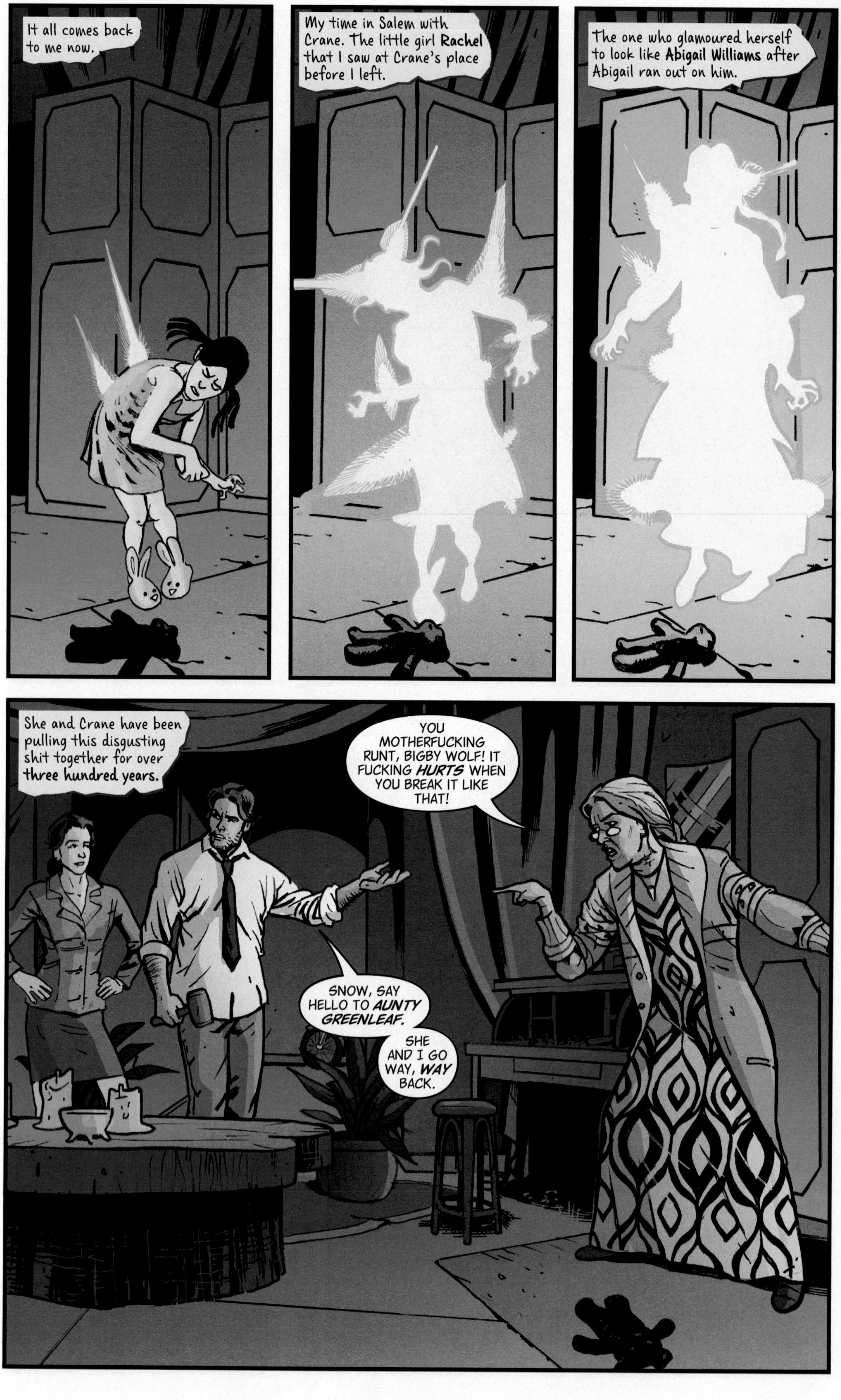
It all comes back to me now.
My time in Salem with Crane. The little girl **Rachel** that I saw at Crane's place before I left.
The one who glamoured herself to look like **Abigail Williams** after Abigail ran out on him.
She and Crane have been pulling this disgusting shit together for over **three hundred years.**
YOU MOTHERFUCKING RUNT, BIGBY WOLF! IT FUCKING ***HURTS*** WHEN YOU BREAK IT LIKE THAT!
SNOW, SAY HELLO TO ***AUNTY GREENLEAF.***
SHE AND I GO WAY, ***WAY*** BACK.

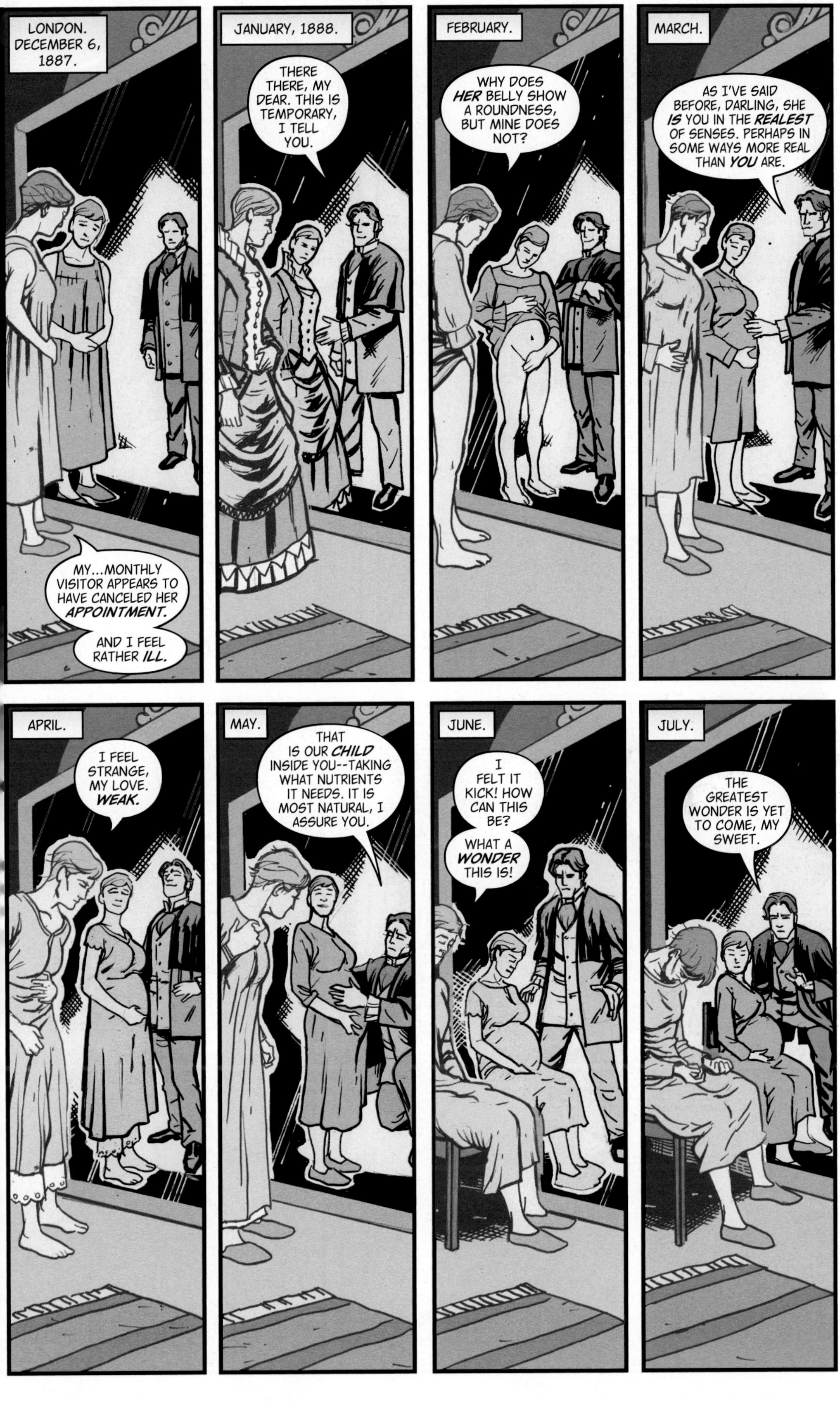

LONDON. DECEMBER 6, 1887.
MY...MONTHLY VISITOR APPEARS TO HAVE CANCELED HER APPOINTMENT.
AND I FEEL RATHER ILL.
JANUARY, 1888.
THERE THERE, MY DEAR. THIS IS TEMPORARY, I TELL YOU.
FEBRUARY.
WHY DOES HER BELLY SHOW A ROUNDNESS, BUT MINE DOES NOT?
MARCH.
AS I'VE SAID BEFORE, DARLING, SHE IS YOU IN THE REALEST OF SENSES. PERHAPS IN SOME WAYS MORE REAL THAN YOU ARE.
APRIL.
I FEEL STRANGE, MY LOVE. WEAK.
MAY.
THAT IS OUR CHILD INSIDE YOU--TAKING WHAT NUTRIENTS IT NEEDS. IT IS MOST NATURAL, I ASSURE YOU.
JUNE.
I FELT IT KICK! HOW CAN THIS BE?
WHAT A WONDER THIS IS!
JULY.
THE GREATEST WONDER IS YET TO COME, MY SWEET.

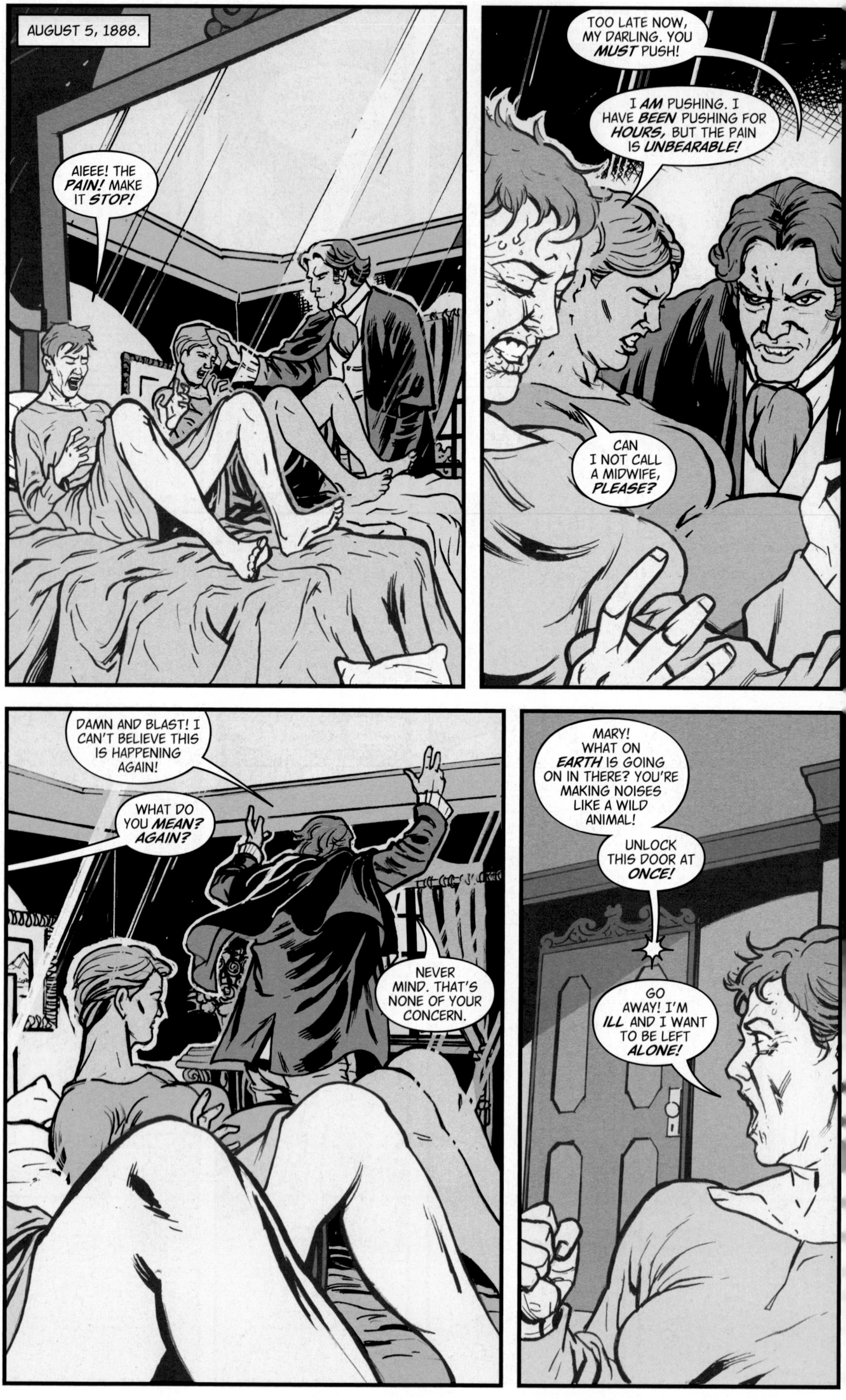
AUGUST 5, 1888.
AIEEE! THE PAIN! MAKE IT STOP!
TOO LATE NOW, MY DARLING. YOU MUST PUSH!
I AM PUSHING. I HAVE BEEN PUSHING FOR HOURS, BUT THE PAIN IS UNBEARABLE!
CAN I NOT CALL A MIDWIFE, PLEASE?
DAMN AND BLAST! I CAN'T BELIEVE THIS IS HAPPENING AGAIN!
WHAT DO YOU MEAN? AGAIN?
NEVER MIND. THAT'S NONE OF YOUR CONCERN.
MARY! WHAT ON EARTH IS GOING ON IN THERE? YOU'RE MAKING NOISES LIKE A WILD ANIMAL!
UNLOCK THIS DOOR AT ONCE!
GO AWAY! I'M ILL AND I WANT TO BE LEFT ALONE!

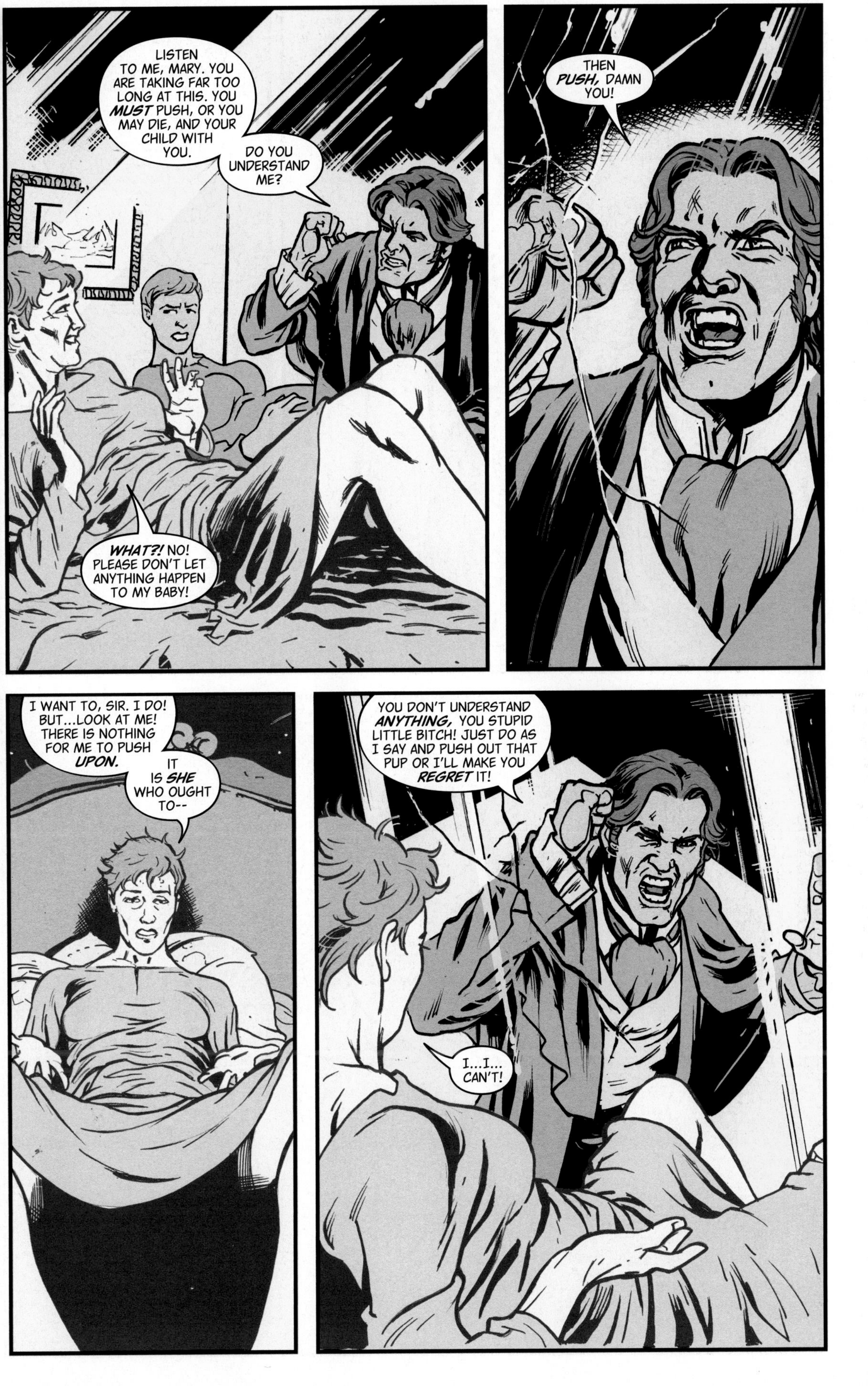
LISTEN TO ME, MARY. YOU ARE TAKING FAR TOO LONG AT THIS. YOU MUST PUSH, OR YOU MAY DIE, AND YOUR CHILD WITH YOU.
DO YOU UNDERSTAND ME?
WHAT?! NO! PLEASE DON'T LET ANYTHING HAPPEN TO MY BABY!
THEN PUSH, DAMN YOU!
I WANT TO, SIR. I DO! BUT...LOOK AT ME! THERE IS NOTHING FOR ME TO PUSH UPON.
IT IS SHE WHO OUGHT TO--
YOU DON'T UNDERSTAND ANYTHING, YOU STUPID LITTLE BITCH! JUST DO AS I SAY AND PUSH OUT THAT PUP OR I'LL MAKE YOU REGRET IT!
I...I... CAN'T!

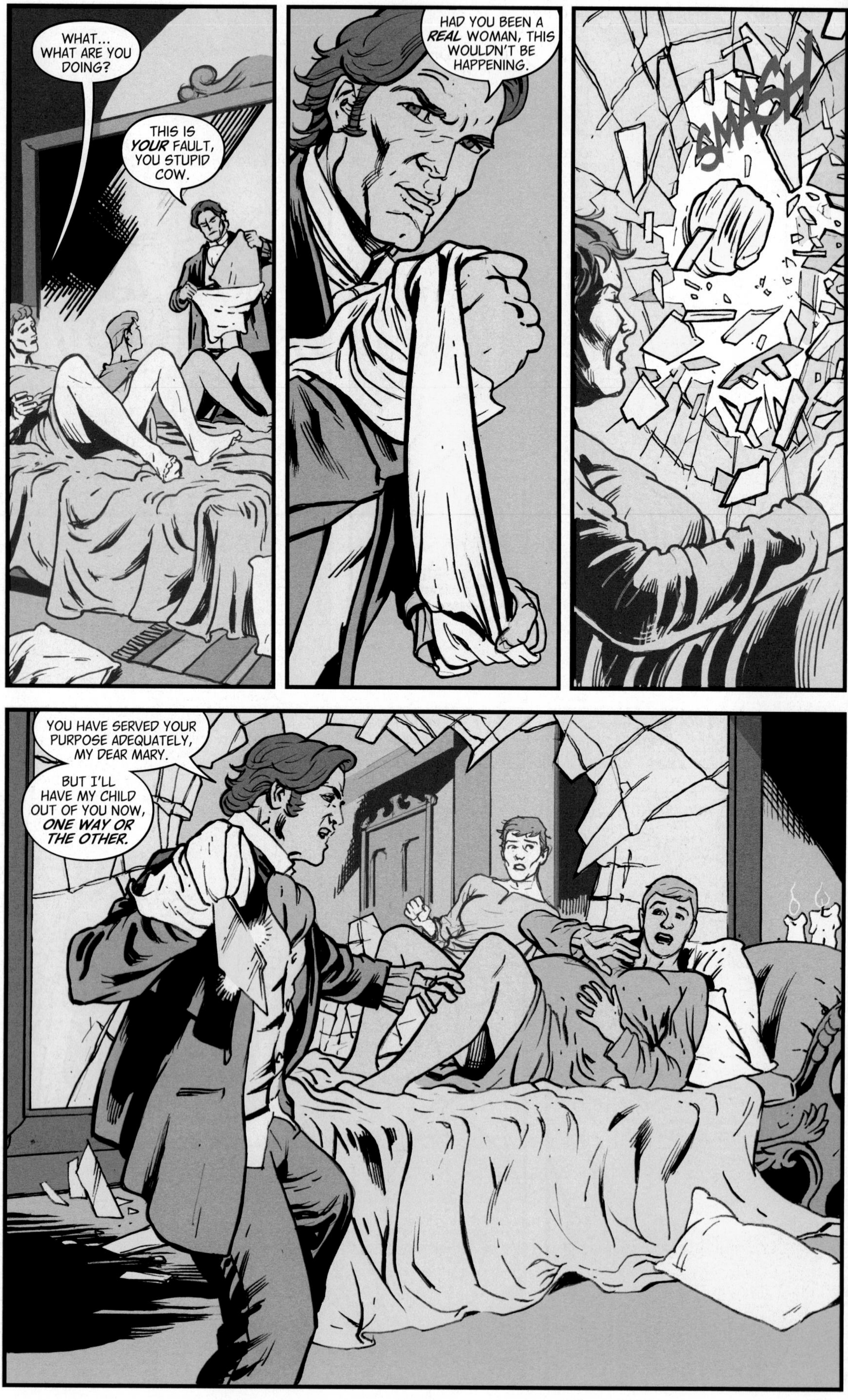
WHAT... WHAT ARE YOU DOING?
THIS IS *YOUR* FAULT, YOU STUPID COW.
HAD YOU BEEN A *REAL* WOMAN, THIS WOULDN'T BE HAPPENING.
SMASH
YOU HAVE SERVED YOUR PURPOSE ADEQUATELY, MY DEAR MARY.
BUT I'LL HAVE MY CHILD OUT OF YOU NOW, ***ONE WAY OR THE OTHER.***

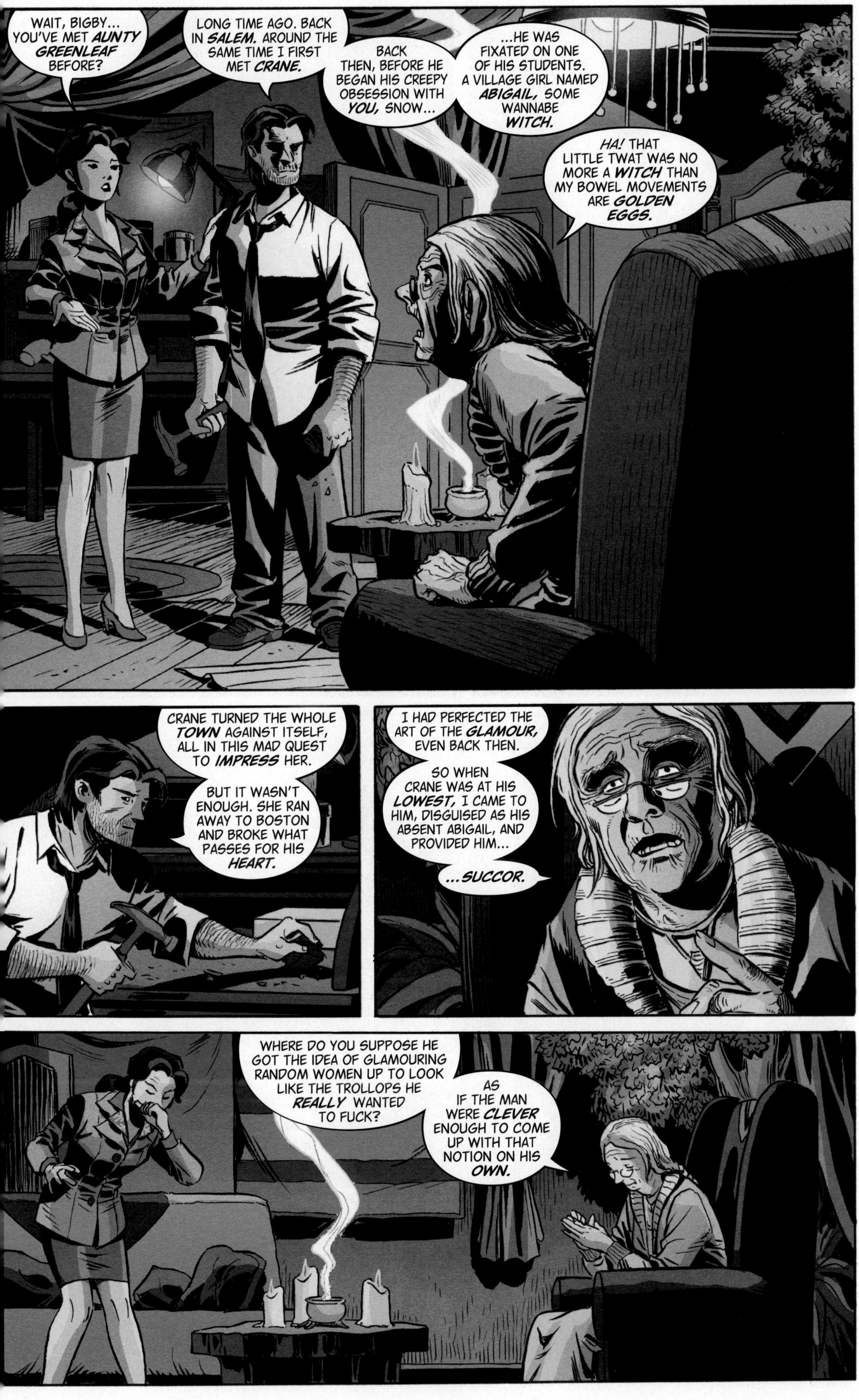
WAIT, BIGBY... YOU'VE MET AUNTY GREENLEAF BEFORE?
LONG TIME AGO. BACK IN SALEM. AROUND THE SAME TIME I FIRST MET CRANE.
BACK THEN, BEFORE HE BEGAN HIS CREEPY OBSESSION WITH YOU, SNOW...
...HE WAS FIXATED ON ONE OF HIS STUDENTS. A VILLAGE GIRL NAMED ABIGAIL, SOME WANNABE WITCH.
HA! THAT LITTLE TWAT WAS NO MORE A WITCH THAN MY BOWEL MOVEMENTS ARE GOLDEN EGGS.
CRANE TURNED THE WHOLE TOWN AGAINST ITSELF, ALL IN THIS MAD QUEST TO IMPRESS HER.
BUT IT WASN'T ENOUGH. SHE RAN AWAY TO BOSTON AND BROKE WHAT PASSES FOR HIS HEART.
I HAD PERFECTED THE ART OF THE GLAMOUR, EVEN BACK THEN.
SO WHEN CRANE WAS AT HIS LOWEST, I CAME TO HIM, DISGUISED AS HIS ABSENT ABIGAIL, AND PROVIDED HIM...
...SUCCOR.
WHERE DO YOU SUPPOSE HE GOT THE IDEA OF GLAMOURING RANDOM WOMEN UP TO LOOK LIKE THE TROLLOPS HE REALLY WANTED TO FUCK?
AS IF THE MAN WERE CLEVER ENOUGH TO COME UP WITH THAT NOTION ON HIS OWN.

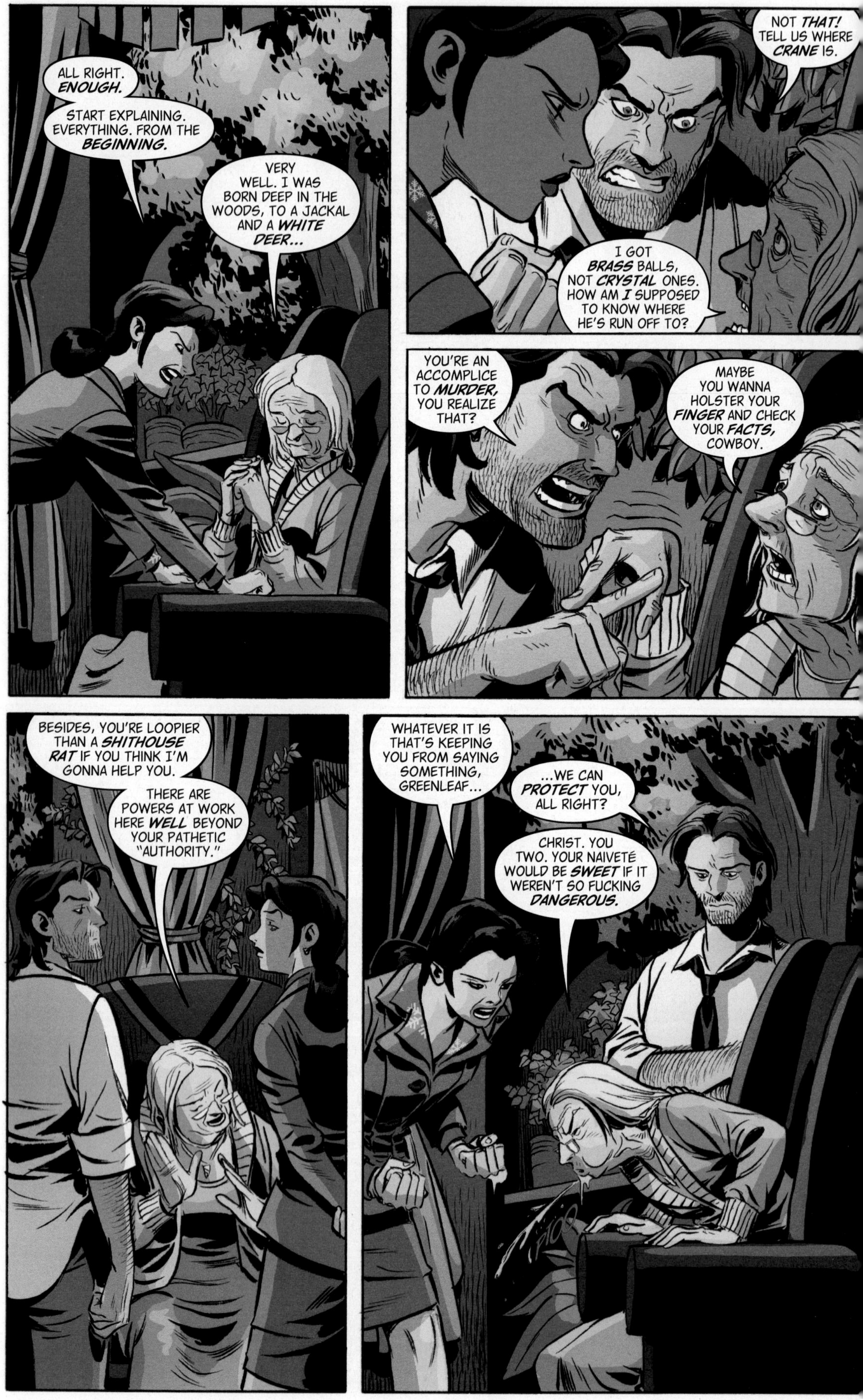
ALL RIGHT. ENOUGH.
START EXPLAINING. EVERYTHING. FROM THE BEGINNING.
VERY WELL. I WAS BORN DEEP IN THE WOODS, TO A JACKAL AND A WHITE DEER...
NOT THAT! TELL US WHERE CRANE IS.
I GOT BRASS BALLS, NOT CRYSTAL ONES. HOW AM I SUPPOSED TO KNOW WHERE HE'S RUN OFF TO?
YOU'RE AN ACCOMPLICE TO MURDER, YOU REALIZE THAT?
MAYBE YOU WANNA HOLSTER YOUR FINGER AND CHECK YOUR FACTS, COWBOY.
BESIDES, YOU'RE LOOPIER THAN A SHITHOUSE RAT IF YOU THINK I'M GONNA HELP YOU.
THERE ARE POWERS AT WORK HERE WELL BEYOND YOUR PATHETIC "AUTHORITY."
WHATEVER IT IS THAT'S KEEPING YOU FROM SAYING SOMETHING, GREENLEAF...
...WE CAN PROTECT YOU, ALL RIGHT?
CHRIST. YOU TWO. YOUR NAIVETÉ WOULD BE SWEET IF IT WEREN'T SO FUCKING DANGEROUS.

YOU KNOW WHAT *I* THINK? I THINK WE'VE BEEN *MORE* THAN PATIENT.

YOU'VE BEEN SELLING *ILLEGAL GLAMOURS* THAT UNDERMINE *EVERYTHING* WE'VE BUILT.

YOU'RE HARBORING A *FUGITIVE* WHO TOOK ADVANTAGE OF THOSE GLAMOURS.

AND NOW YOU'RE RESISTING EVERY OPPORTUNITY TO MAKE THINGS *RIGHT.*

OOH, THIS ONE'S GOT SOME *FEIST* TO HER!

FRANKLY, I DON'T GIVE *TWO SHITS* IF YOU'RE AFRAID FOR YOUR LIFE, LADY.

Wow. Snow's wires must be *really* frayed by this whole thing, to break out *that* kinda talk.

BECAUSE AT LEAST WE CAN MAKE SURE YOU *NEVER* HURT US AGAIN.

OH? AND JUST *HOW* DO YOU PLAN TO DO *THAT,* PRINCESS PUMP 'N' DUMP?

WE'RE *DESTROYING THE TREE.*

WHAT?! *NO!*

HOW *DARE* YOU COME IN HERE AND THREATEN TO TAKE FROM ME THE *ONE* THING...

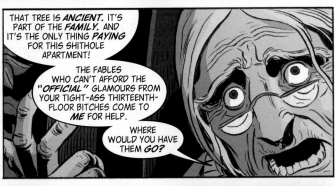

THAT TREE IS *ANCIENT.* IT'S PART OF THE *FAMILY.* AND IT'S THE ONLY THING *PAYING* FOR THIS SHITHOLE APARTMENT!

THE FABLES WHO CAN'T AFFORD THE *"OFFICIAL"* GLAMOURS FROM YOUR TIGHT-ASS THIRTEENTH-FLOOR *BITCHES* COME TO *ME* FOR HELP.

WHERE WOULD YOU HAVE THEM *GO?*

SPARE ME THE *SOB STORY.* YOU'RE SPINNING OTHER PEOPLE'S MISERY INTO *GOLD.*

TWO FABLES ARE *DEAD* BECAUSE OF THIS.

YOU'RE *INSANE* IF YOU THINK WE'RE LEAVING SOMETHING THIS POWERFUL IN YOUR HANDS.

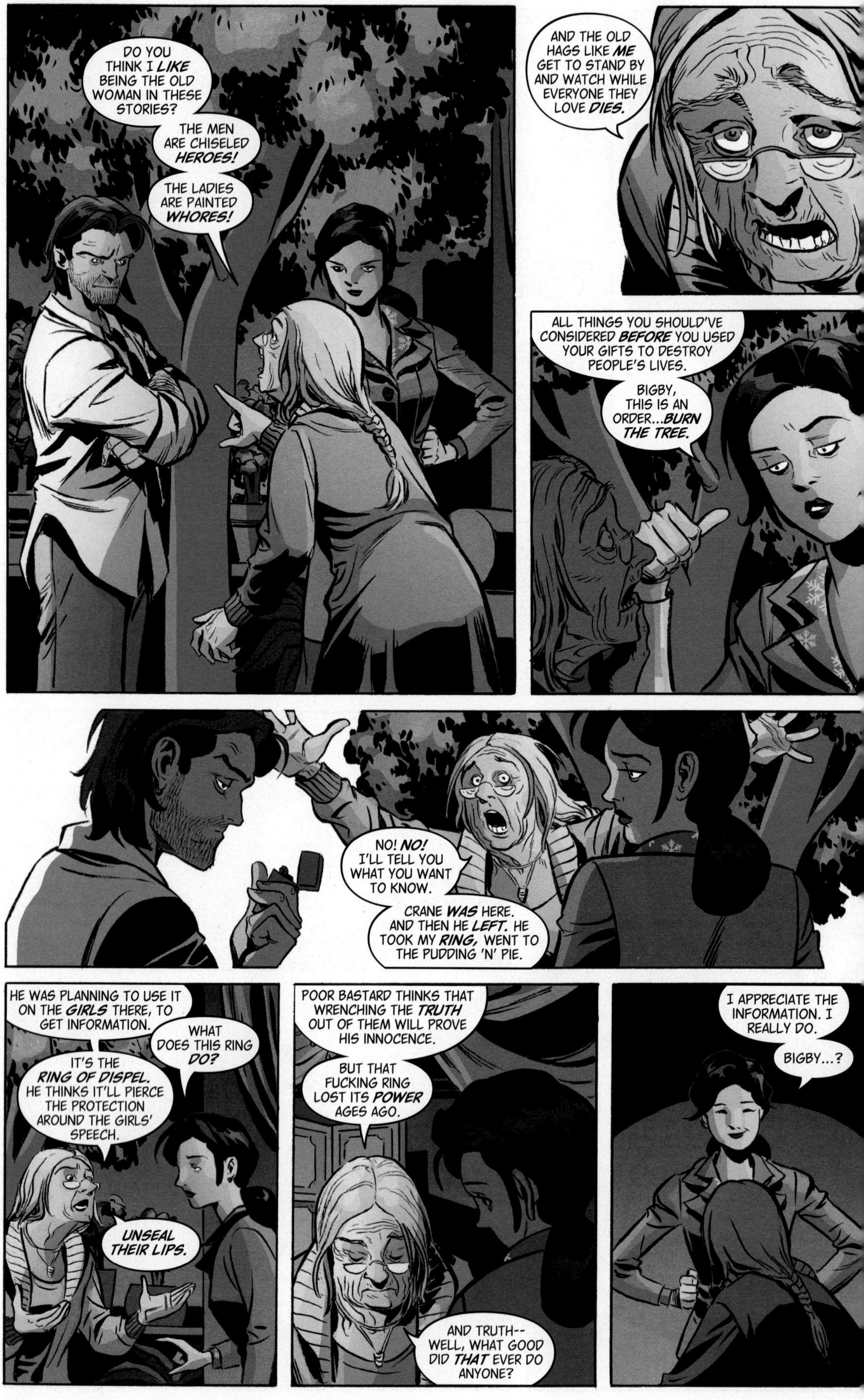

DO YOU THINK I LIKE BEING THE OLD WOMAN IN THESE STORIES?
THE MEN ARE CHISELED HEROES!
THE LADIES ARE PAINTED WHORES!
AND THE OLD HAGS LIKE ME GET TO STAND BY AND WATCH WHILE EVERYONE THEY LOVE DIES.
ALL THINGS YOU SHOULD'VE CONSIDERED BEFORE YOU USED YOUR GIFTS TO DESTROY PEOPLE'S LIVES.
BIGBY, THIS IS AN ORDER...BURN THE TREE.
NO! NO! I'LL TELL YOU WHAT YOU WANT TO KNOW.
CRANE WAS HERE. AND THEN HE LEFT. HE TOOK MY RING, WENT TO THE PUDDING 'N' PIE.
HE WAS PLANNING TO USE IT ON THE GIRLS THERE, TO GET INFORMATION.
WHAT DOES THIS RING DO?
IT'S THE RING OF DISPEL. HE THINKS IT'LL PIERCE THE PROTECTION AROUND THE GIRLS' SPEECH.
UNSEAL THEIR LIPS.
POOR BASTARD THINKS THAT WRENCHING THE TRUTH OUT OF THEM WILL PROVE HIS INNOCENCE.
BUT THAT FUCKING RING LOST ITS POWER AGES AGO.
AND TRUTH--WELL, WHAT GOOD DID THAT EVER DO ANYONE?
I APPRECIATE THE INFORMATION. I REALLY DO.
BIGBY...?

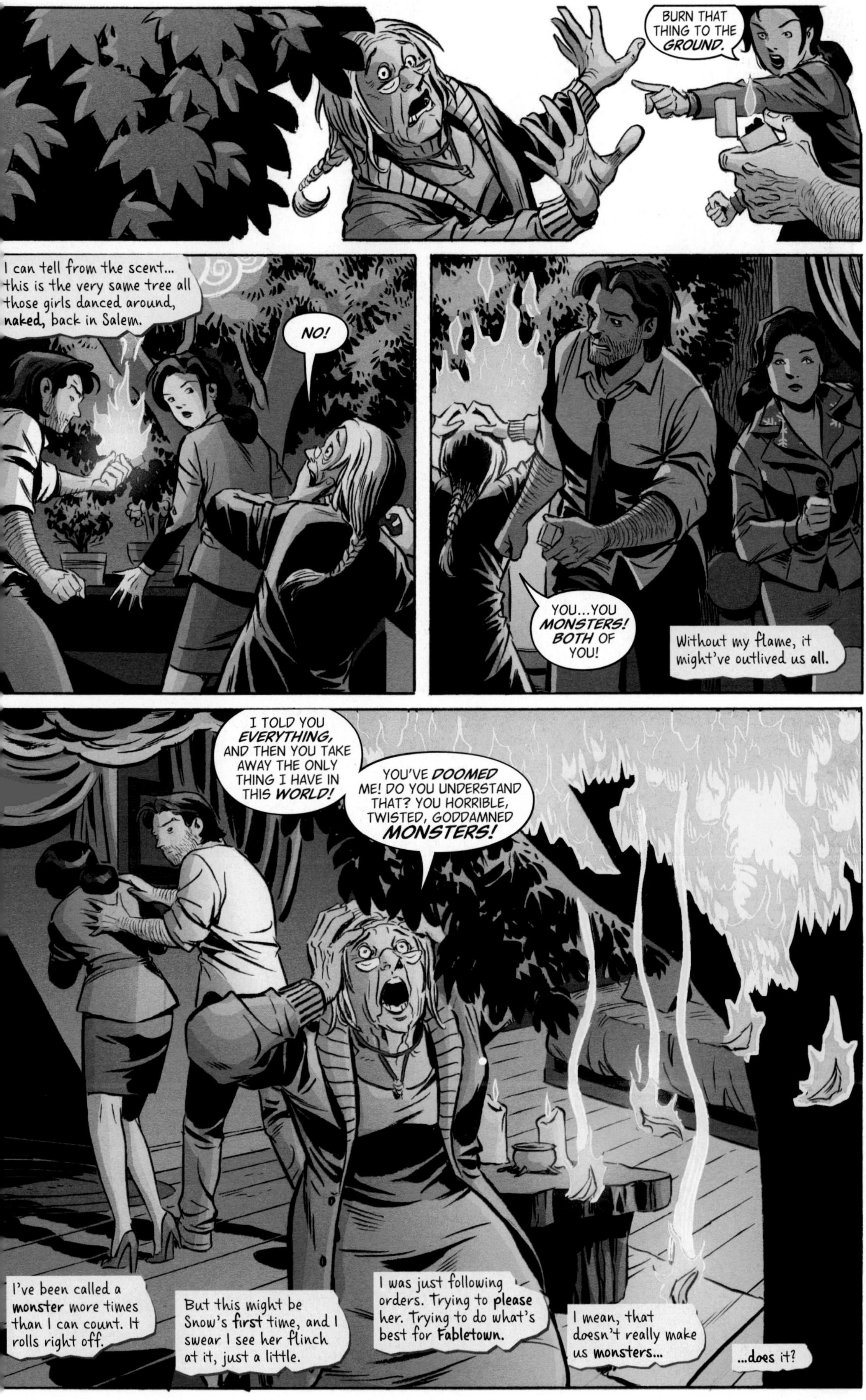
BURN THAT THING TO THE **GROUND.**
I can tell from the scent... this is the very same tree all those girls danced around, **naked,** back in Salem.
NO!
YOU...YOU **MONSTERS! BOTH** OF YOU!
Without my flame, it might've outlived us **all.**
I TOLD YOU **EVERYTHING,** AND THEN YOU TAKE AWAY THE ONLY THING I HAVE IN THIS **WORLD!**
YOU'VE **DOOMED** ME! DO YOU UNDERSTAND THAT? YOU HORRIBLE, TWISTED, GODDAMNED **MONSTERS!**
I've been called a **monster** more times than I can count. It rolls right off.
But this might be Snow's **first** time, and I swear I see her flinch at it, just a little.
I was just following orders. Trying to **please** her. Trying to do what's best for **Fabletown.**
I mean, that doesn't really make us **monsters...**
...does it?

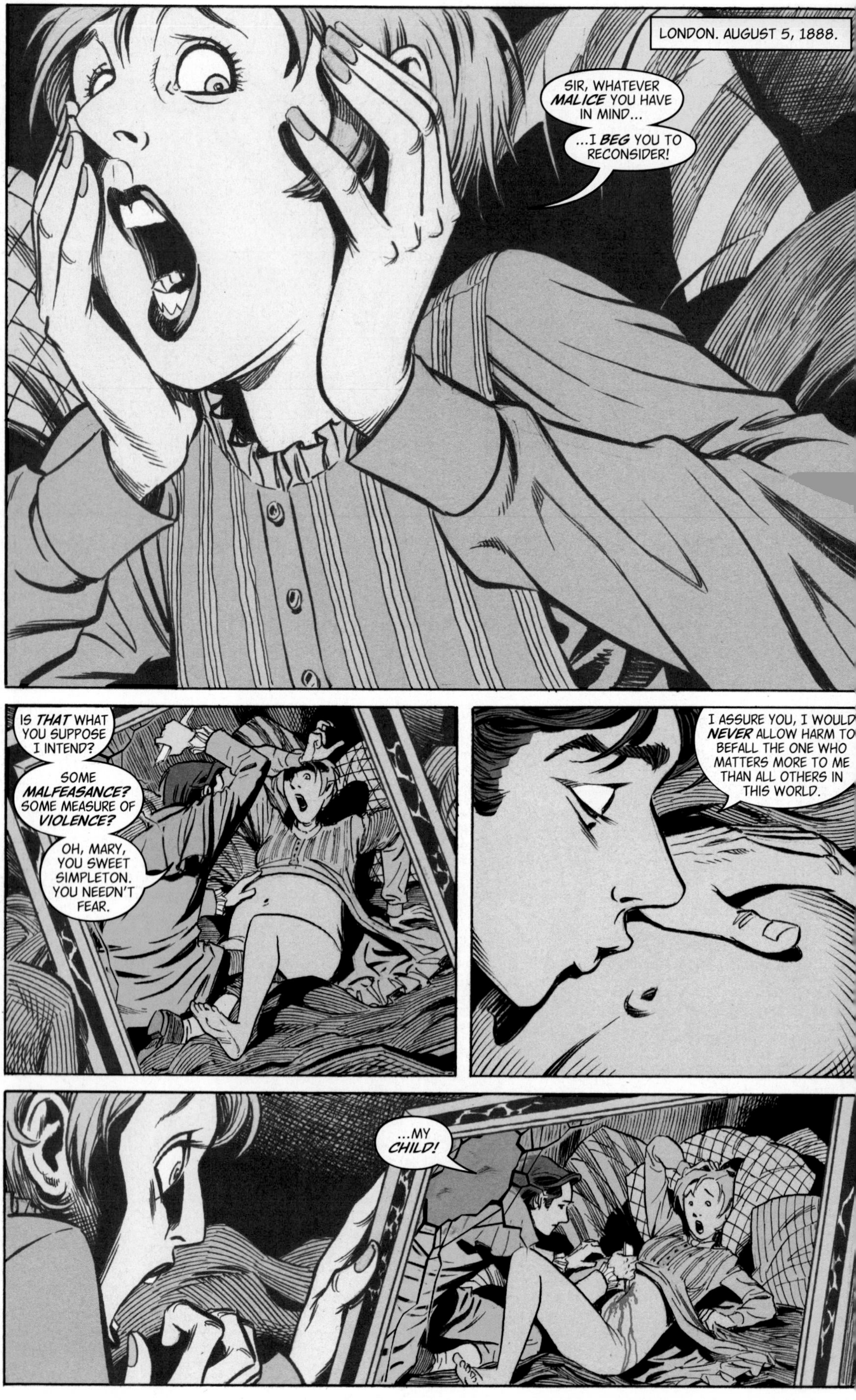
LONDON. AUGUST 5, 1888.
SIR, WHATEVER MALICE YOU HAVE IN MIND...
...I BEG YOU TO RECONSIDER!
IS THAT WHAT YOU SUPPOSE I INTEND?
SOME MALFEASANCE? SOME MEASURE OF VIOLENCE?
OH, MARY, YOU SWEET SIMPLETON. YOU NEEDN'T FEAR.
I ASSURE YOU, I WOULD NEVER ALLOW HARM TO BEFALL THE ONE WHO MATTERS MORE TO ME THAN ALL OTHERS IN THIS WORLD.
...MY CHILD!

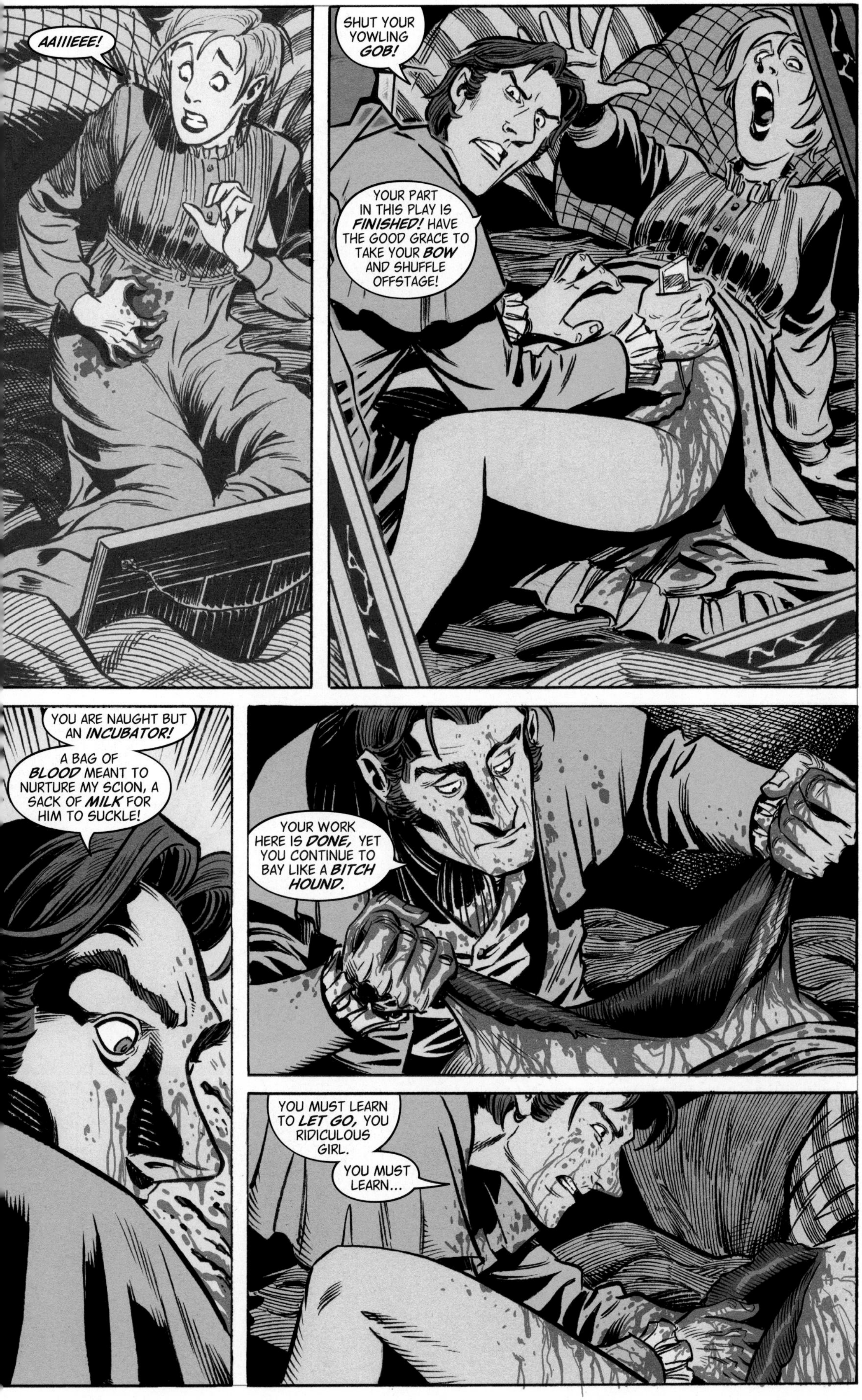
AAIIIEEE!
SHUT YOUR YOWLING GOB!
YOUR PART IN THIS PLAY IS FINISHED! HAVE THE GOOD GRACE TO TAKE YOUR BOW AND SHUFFLE OFFSTAGE!
YOU ARE NAUGHT BUT AN INCUBATOR!
A BAG OF BLOOD MEANT TO NURTURE MY SCION, A SACK OF MILK FOR HIM TO SUCKLE!
YOUR WORK HERE IS DONE, YET YOU CONTINUE TO BAY LIKE A BITCH HOUND.
YOU MUST LEARN TO LET GO, YOU RIDICULOUS GIRL.
YOU MUST LEARN...

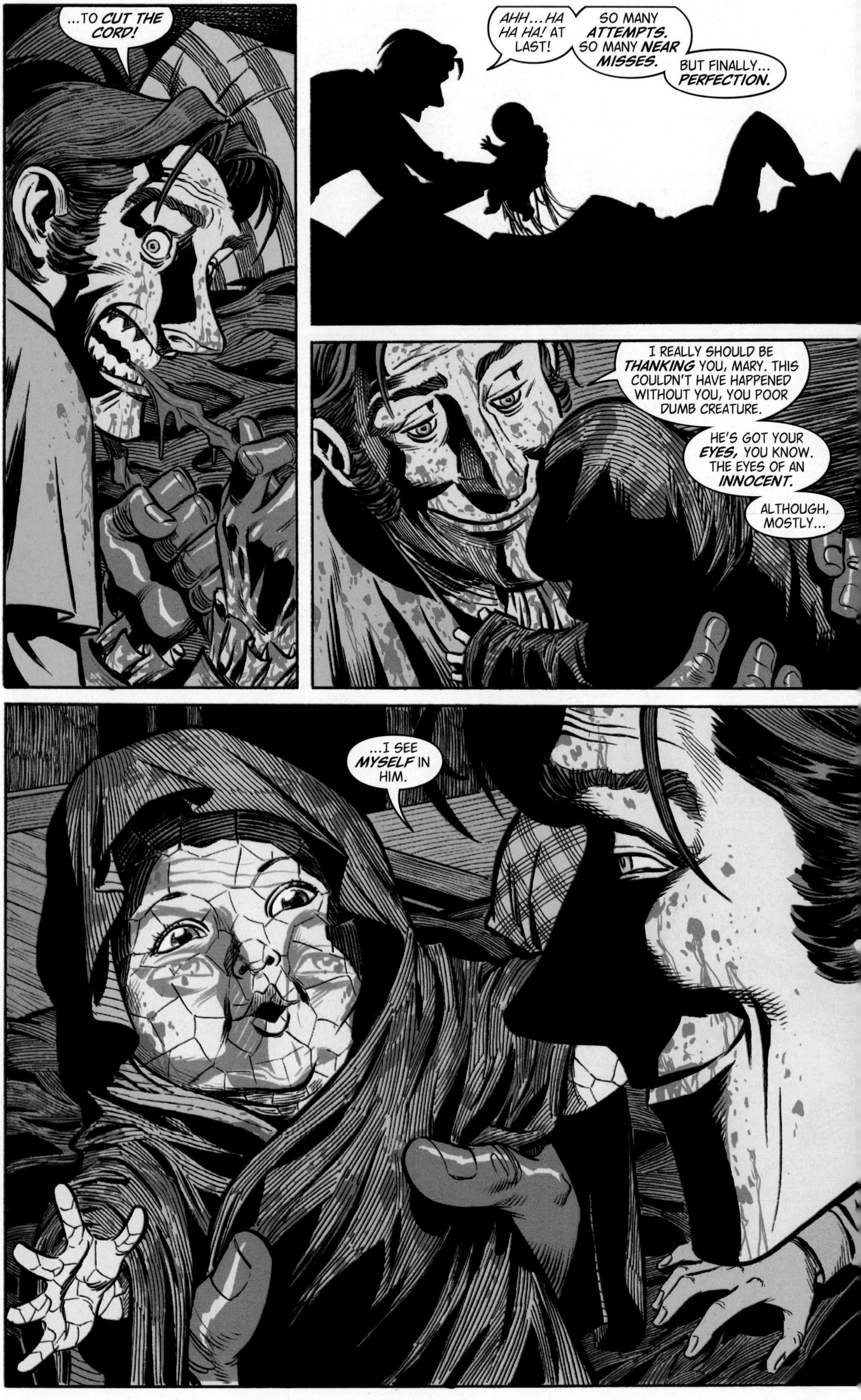

...TO CUT THE CORD!
AHH...HA HA HA! AT LAST!
SO MANY ATTEMPTS. SO MANY NEAR MISSES.
BUT FINALLY... PERFECTION.
I REALLY SHOULD BE THANKING YOU, MARY. THIS COULDN'T HAVE HAPPENED WITHOUT YOU, YOU POOR DUMB CREATURE.
HE'S GOT YOUR EYES, YOU KNOW. THE EYES OF AN INNOCENT.
ALTHOUGH, MOSTLY...
...I SEE MYSELF IN HIM.

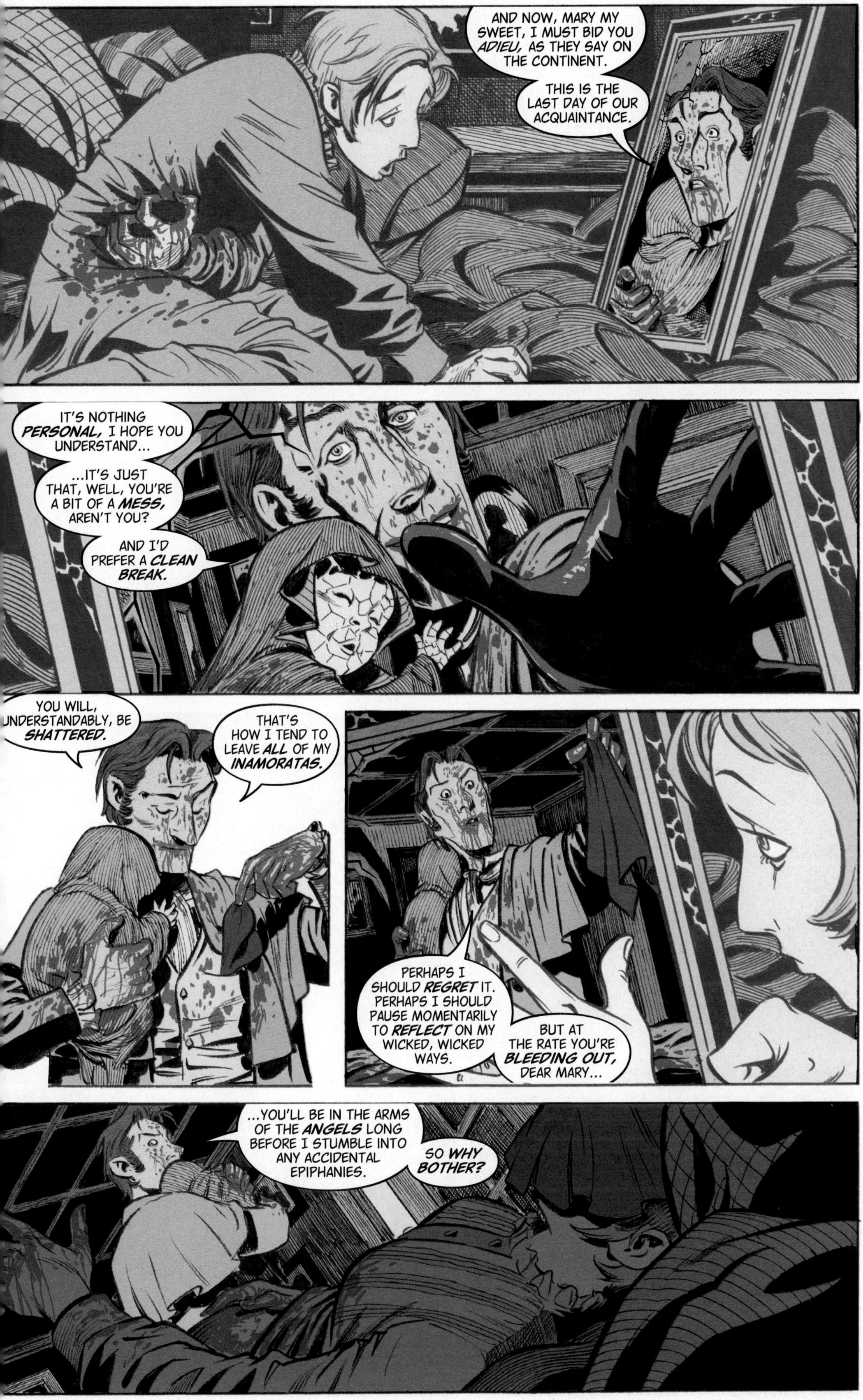
AND NOW, MARY MY SWEET, I MUST BID YOU ADIEU, AS THEY SAY ON THE CONTINENT.
THIS IS THE LAST DAY OF OUR ACQUAINTANCE.
IT'S NOTHING PERSONAL, I HOPE YOU UNDERSTAND...
...IT'S JUST THAT, WELL, YOU'RE A BIT OF A MESS, AREN'T YOU?
AND I'D PREFER A CLEAN BREAK.
YOU WILL, UNDERSTANDABLY, BE SHATTERED.
THAT'S HOW I TEND TO LEAVE ALL OF MY INAMORATAS.
PERHAPS I SHOULD REGRET IT. PERHAPS I SHOULD PAUSE MOMENTARILY TO REFLECT ON MY WICKED, WICKED WAYS.
BUT AT THE RATE YOU'RE BLEEDING OUT, DEAR MARY...
...YOU'LL BE IN THE ARMS OF THE ANGELS LONG BEFORE I STUMBLE INTO ANY ACCIDENTAL EPIPHANIES.
SO WHY BOTHER?

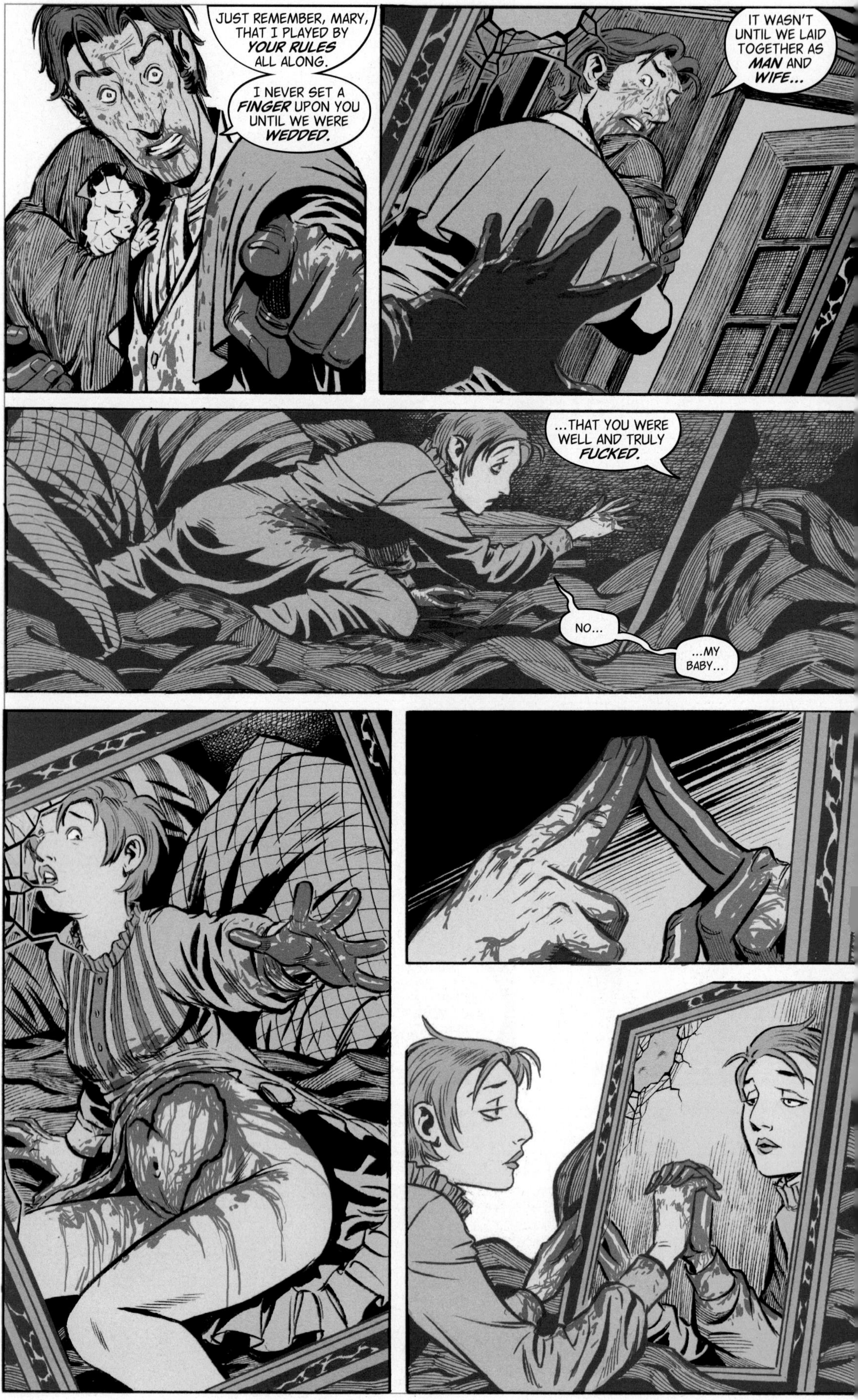
JUST REMEMBER, MARY, THAT I PLAYED BY YOUR RULES ALL ALONG.
I NEVER SET A FINGER UPON YOU UNTIL WE WERE WEDDED.
IT WASN'T UNTIL WE LAID TOGETHER AS MAN AND WIFE...
...THAT YOU WERE WELL AND TRULY FUCKED.
NO...
...MY BABY...

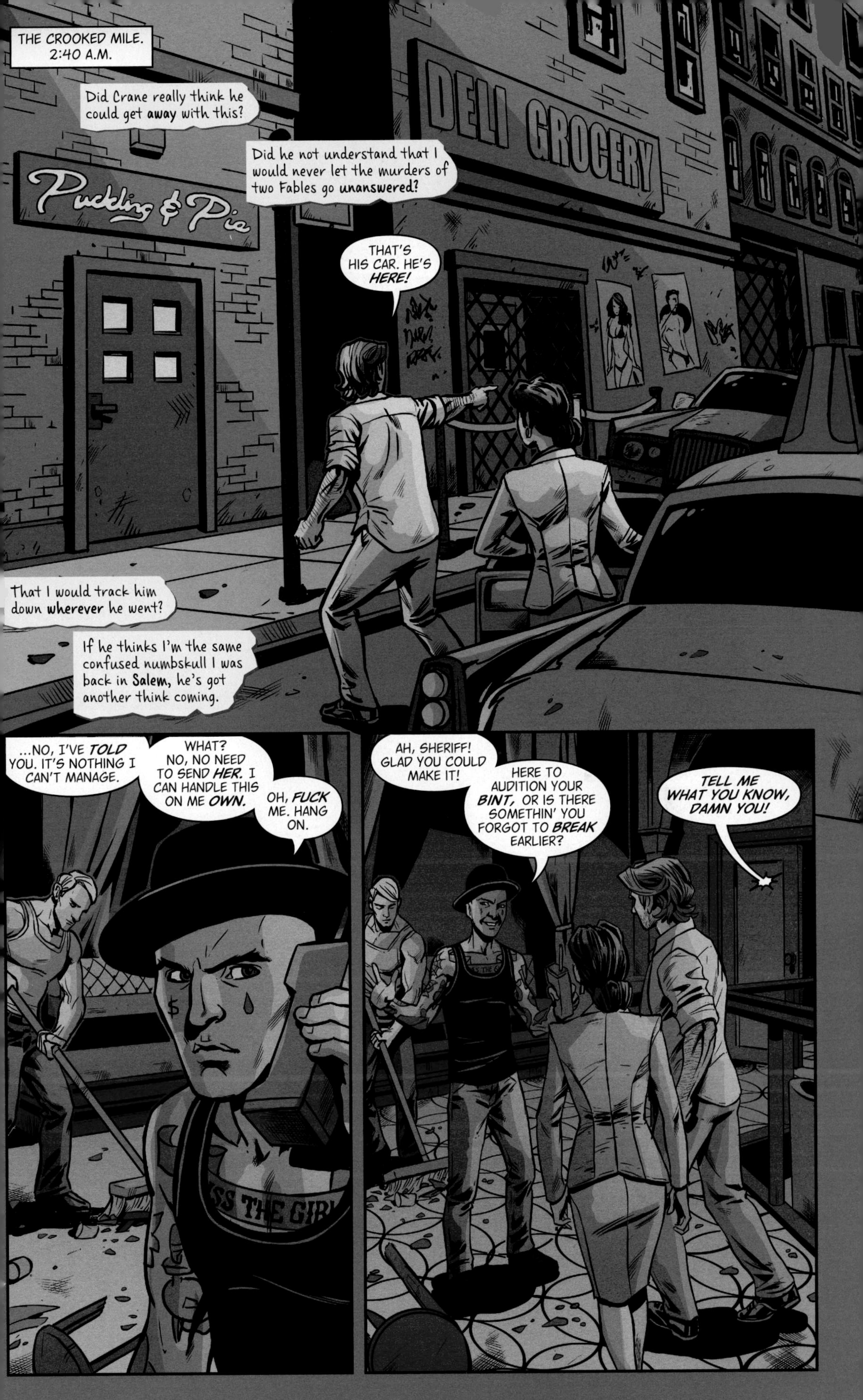
THE CROOKED MILE. 2:40 A.M.
Did Crane really think he could get away with this?
Did he not understand that I would never let the murders of two Fables go unanswered?
DELI GROCERY
Pudding & Pie
THAT'S HIS CAR. HE'S HERE!
That I would track him down wherever he went?
If he thinks I'm the same confused numbskull I was back in Salem, he's got another think coming.
...NO, I'VE TOLD YOU. IT'S NOTHING I CAN'T MANAGE.
WHAT? NO, NO NEED TO SEND HER. I CAN HANDLE THIS ON ME OWN.
OH, FUCK ME. HANG ON.
AH, SHERIFF! GLAD YOU COULD MAKE IT!
HERE TO AUDITION YOUR BINT, OR IS THERE SOMETHIN' YOU FORGOT TO BREAK EARLIER?
TELL ME WHAT YOU KNOW, DAMN YOU!

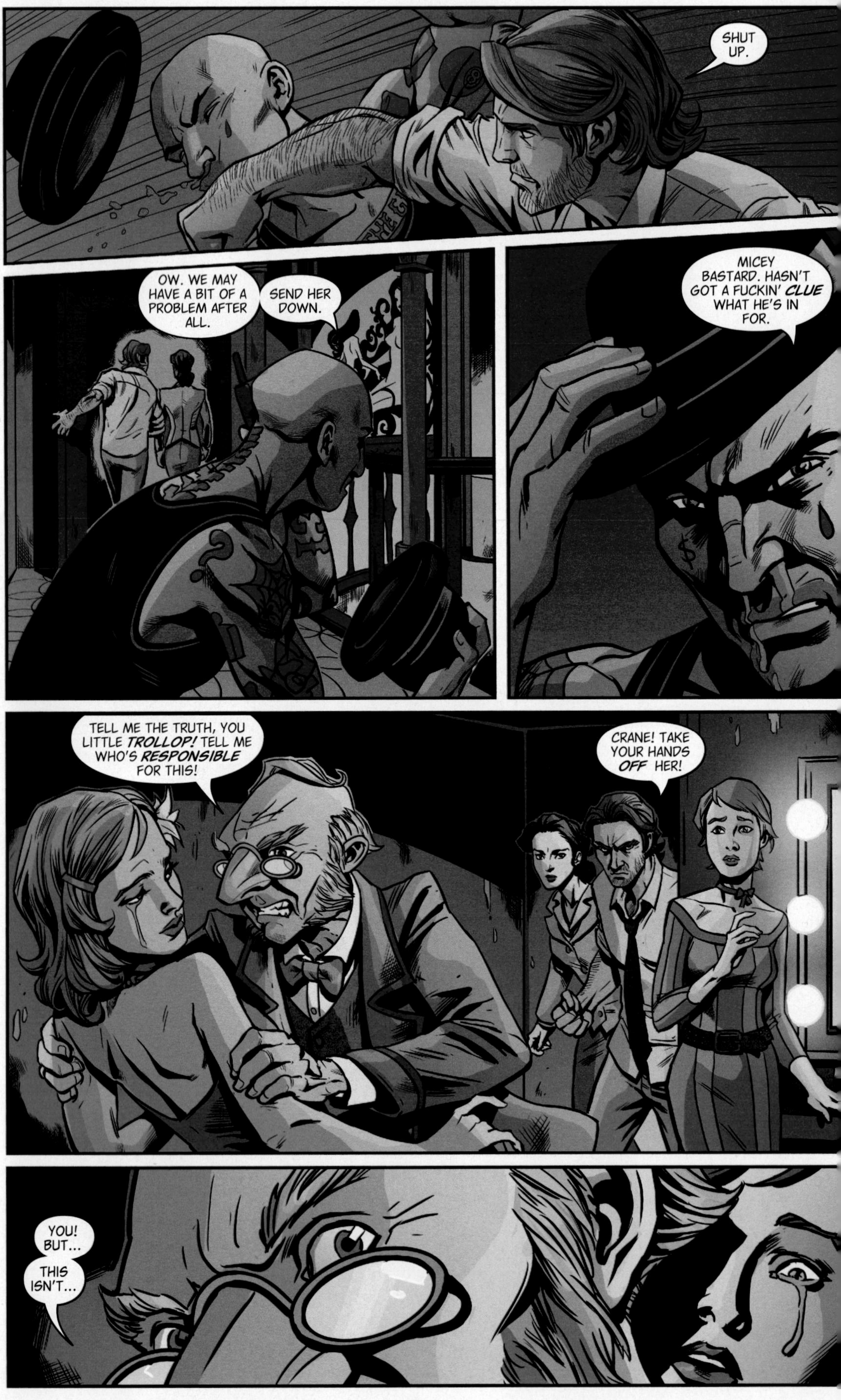

SHUT UP.
OW. WE MAY HAVE A BIT OF A PROBLEM AFTER ALL.
SEND HER DOWN.
MICEY BASTARD. HASN'T GOT A FUCKIN' *CLUE* WHAT HE'S IN FOR.
TELL ME THE TRUTH, YOU LITTLE *TROLLOP!* TELL ME WHO'S *RESPONSIBLE* FOR THIS!
CRANE! TAKE YOUR HANDS *OFF* HER!
YOU! BUT...
THIS ISN'T...

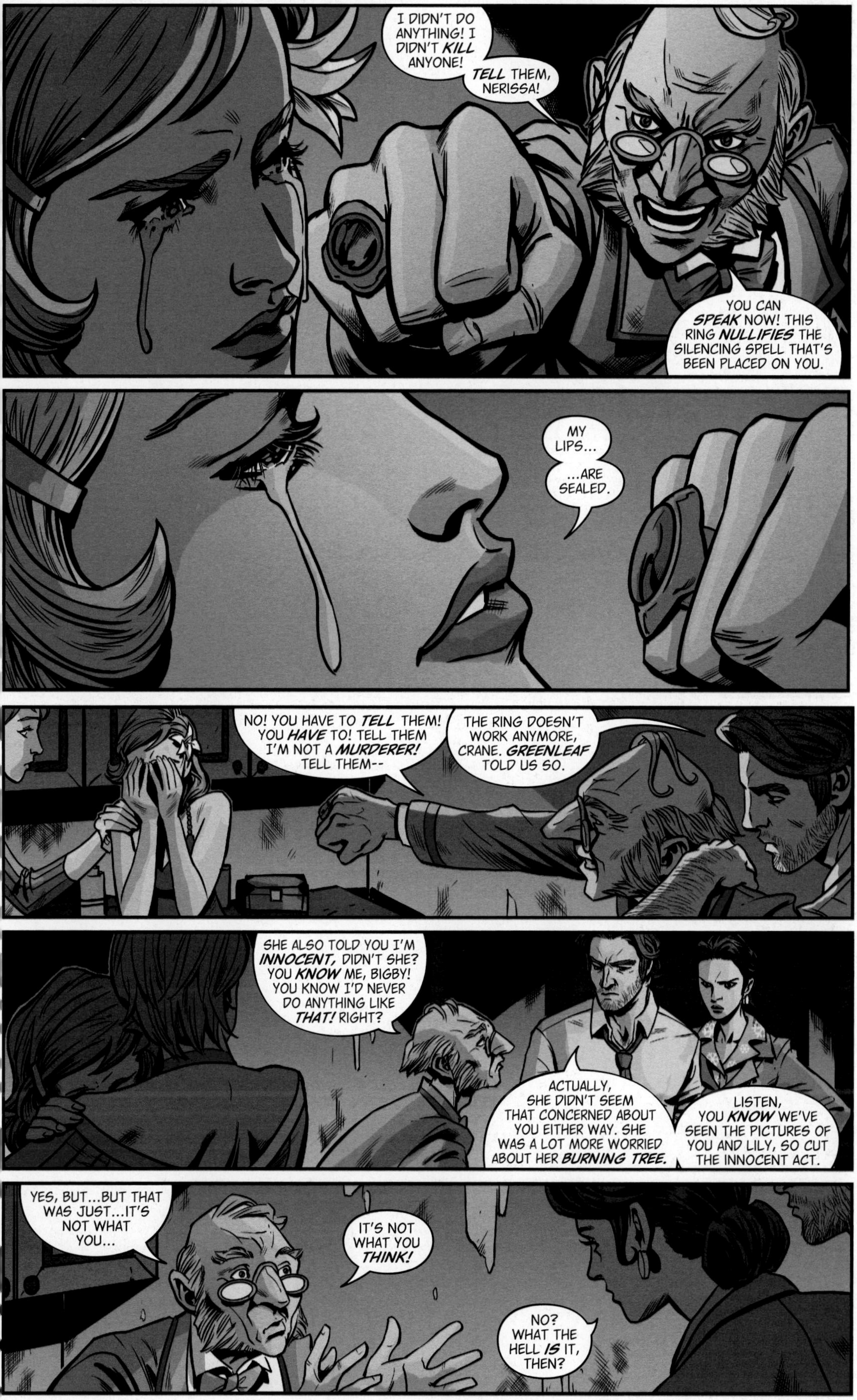

I DIDN'T DO ANYTHING! I DIDN'T KILL ANYONE!
TELL THEM, NERISSA!
YOU CAN SPEAK NOW! THIS RING NULLIFIES THE SILENCING SPELL THAT'S BEEN PLACED ON YOU.
MY LIPS...
...ARE SEALED.
NO! YOU HAVE TO TELL THEM! YOU HAVE TO! TELL THEM I'M NOT A MURDERER! TELL THEM--
THE RING DOESN'T WORK ANYMORE, CRANE. GREENLEAF TOLD US SO.
SHE ALSO TOLD YOU I'M INNOCENT, DIDN'T SHE? YOU KNOW ME, BIGBY! YOU KNOW I'D NEVER DO ANYTHING LIKE THAT! RIGHT?
ACTUALLY, SHE DIDN'T SEEM THAT CONCERNED ABOUT YOU EITHER WAY. SHE WAS A LOT MORE WORRIED ABOUT HER BURNING TREE.
LISTEN, YOU KNOW WE'VE SEEN THE PICTURES OF YOU AND LILY, SO CUT THE INNOCENT ACT.
YES, BUT...BUT THAT WAS JUST...IT'S NOT WHAT YOU...
IT'S NOT WHAT YOU THINK!
NO? WHAT THE HELL IS IT, THEN?

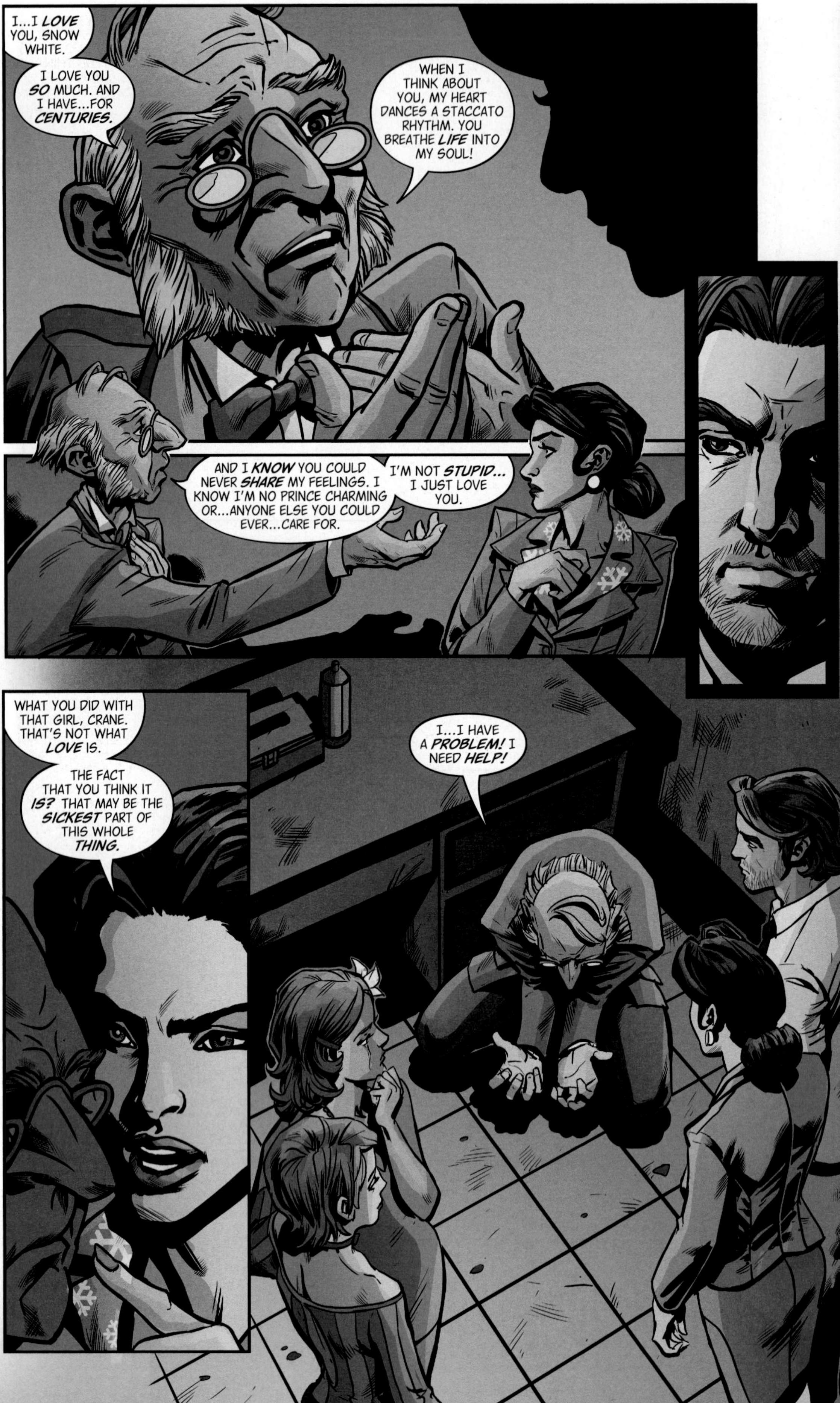
I...I LOVE YOU, SNOW WHITE.
I LOVE YOU SO MUCH. AND I HAVE...FOR CENTURIES.
WHEN I THINK ABOUT YOU, MY HEART DANCES A STACCATO RHYTHM. YOU BREATHE LIFE INTO MY SOUL!
AND I KNOW YOU COULD NEVER SHARE MY FEELINGS. I KNOW I'M NO PRINCE CHARMING OR...ANYONE ELSE YOU COULD EVER...CARE FOR.
I'M NOT STUPID... I JUST LOVE YOU.
WHAT YOU DID WITH THAT GIRL, CRANE. THAT'S NOT WHAT LOVE IS.
THE FACT THAT YOU THINK IT IS? THAT MAY BE THE SICKEST PART OF THIS WHOLE THING.
I...I HAVE A PROBLEM! I NEED HELP!

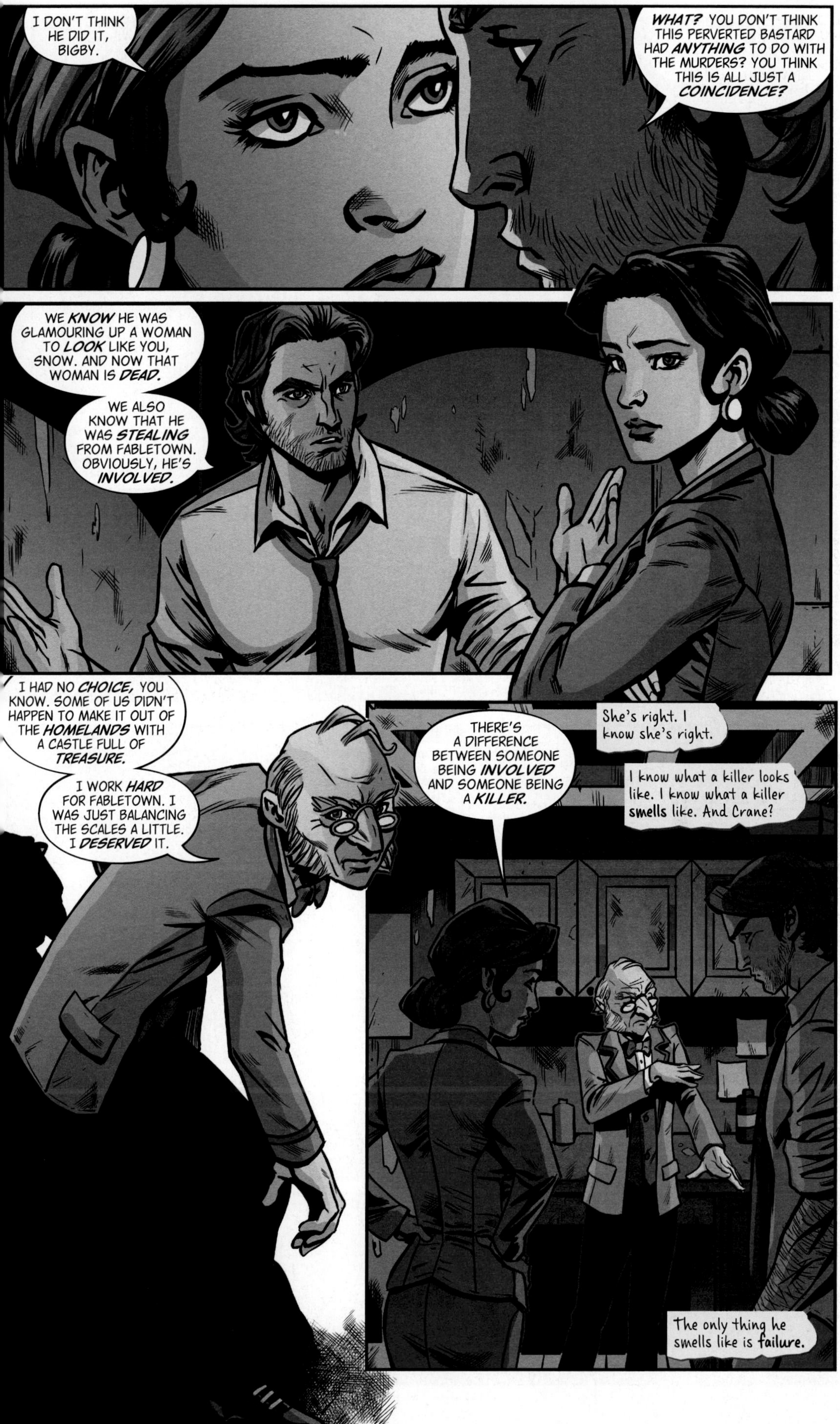

I DON'T THINK HE DID IT, BIGBY.
WHAT? YOU DON'T THINK THIS PERVERTED BASTARD HAD ANYTHING TO DO WITH THE MURDERS? YOU THINK THIS IS ALL JUST A COINCIDENCE?
WE KNOW HE WAS GLAMOURING UP A WOMAN TO LOOK LIKE YOU, SNOW. AND NOW THAT WOMAN IS DEAD.
WE ALSO KNOW THAT HE WAS STEALING FROM FABLETOWN. OBVIOUSLY, HE'S INVOLVED.
I HAD NO CHOICE, YOU KNOW. SOME OF US DIDN'T HAPPEN TO MAKE IT OUT OF THE HOMELANDS WITH A CASTLE FULL OF TREASURE.
I WORK HARD FOR FABLETOWN. I WAS JUST BALANCING THE SCALES A LITTLE. I DESERVED IT.
THERE'S A DIFFERENCE BETWEEN SOMEONE BEING INVOLVED AND SOMEONE BEING A KILLER.
She's right. I know she's right.
I know what a killer looks like. I know what a killer smells like. And Crane?
The only thing he smells like is failure.

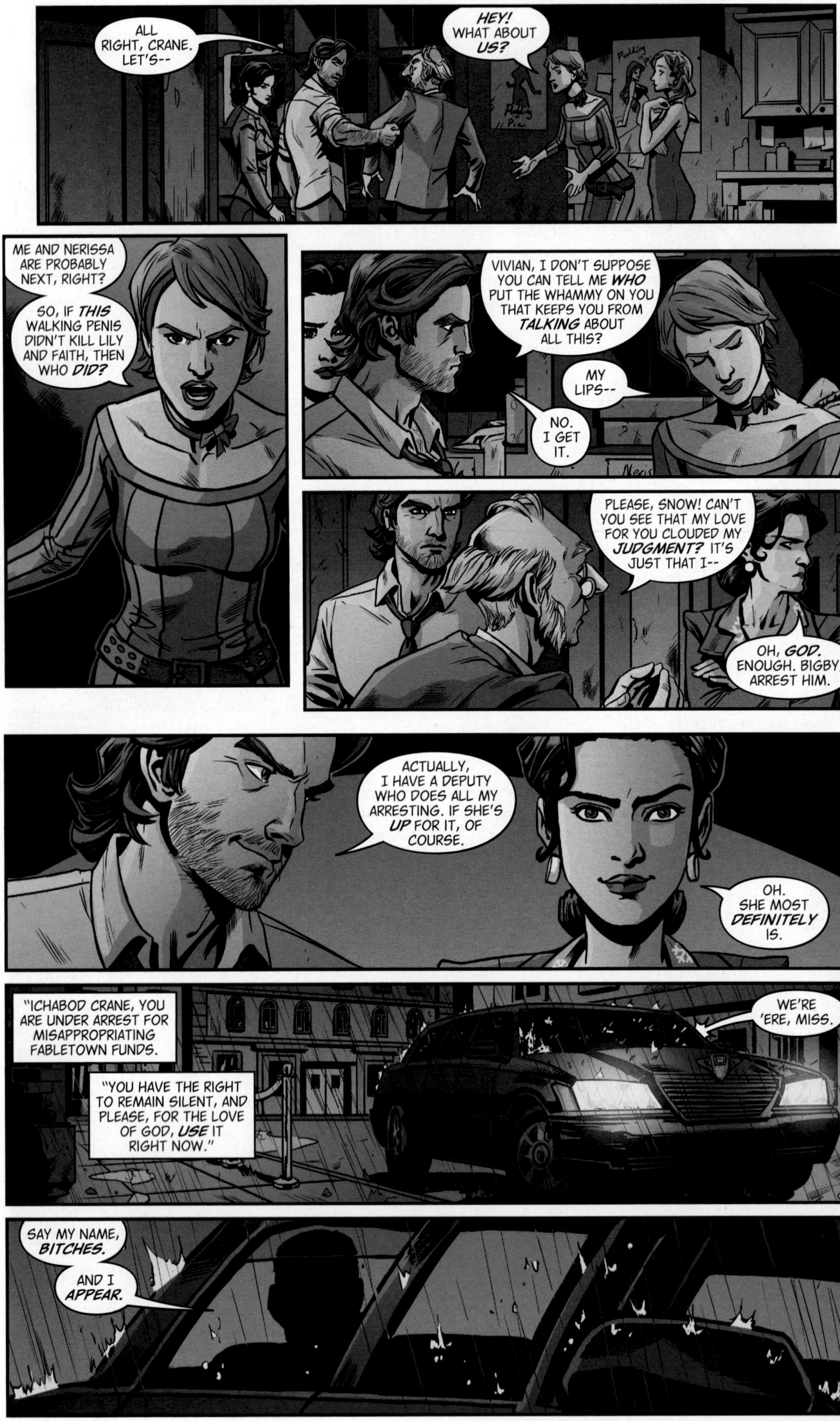

ALL RIGHT, CRANE. LET'S--
HEY! WHAT ABOUT US?
Pudding 'n' Pie
ME AND NERISSA ARE PROBABLY NEXT, RIGHT?
SO, IF THIS WALKING PENIS DIDN'T KILL LILY AND FAITH, THEN WHO DID?
VIVIAN, I DON'T SUPPOSE YOU CAN TELL ME WHO PUT THE WHAMMY ON YOU THAT KEEPS YOU FROM TALKING ABOUT ALL THIS?
MY LIPS--
NO. I GET IT.
PLEASE, SNOW! CAN'T YOU SEE THAT MY LOVE FOR YOU CLOUDED MY JUDGMENT? IT'S JUST THAT I--
OH, GOD. ENOUGH. BIGBY, ARREST HIM.
ACTUALLY, I HAVE A DEPUTY WHO DOES ALL MY ARRESTING. IF SHE'S UP FOR IT, OF COURSE.
OH. SHE MOST DEFINITELY IS.
"ICHABOD CRANE, YOU ARE UNDER ARREST FOR MISAPPROPRIATING FABLETOWN FUNDS.
"YOU HAVE THE RIGHT TO REMAIN SILENT, AND PLEASE, FOR THE LOVE OF GOD, USE IT RIGHT NOW."
WE'RE 'ERE, MISS.
SAY MY NAME, BITCHES.
AND I APPEAR.

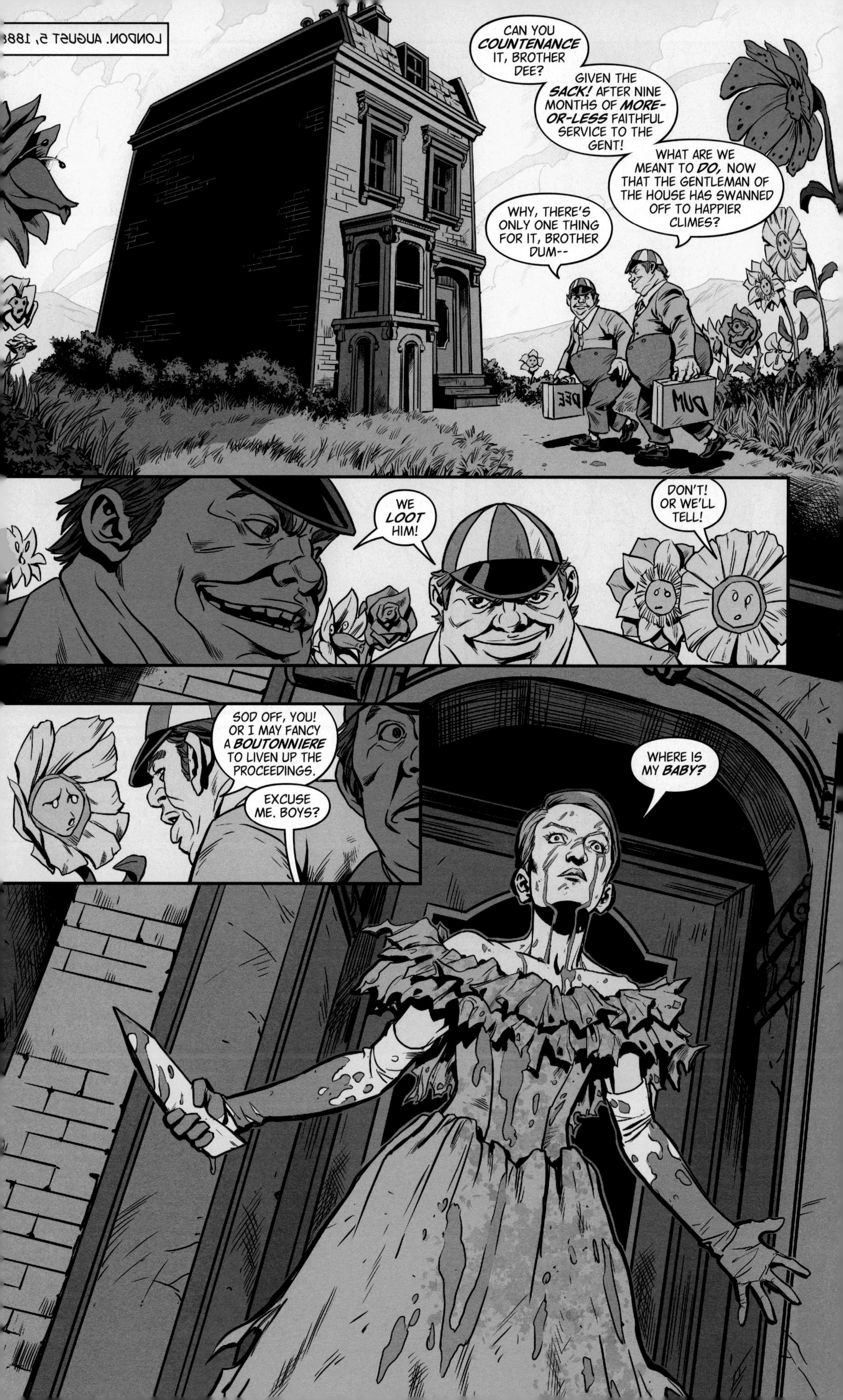
LONDON. AUGUST 5, 188
CAN YOU COUNTENANCE IT, BROTHER DEE?
GIVEN THE SACK! AFTER NINE MONTHS OF MORE-OR-LESS FAITHFUL SERVICE TO THE GENT!
WHAT ARE WE MEANT TO DO, NOW THAT THE GENTLEMAN OF THE HOUSE HAS SWANNED OFF TO HAPPIER CLIMES?
WHY, THERE'S ONLY ONE THING FOR IT, BROTHER DUM--
DEE
DUM
WE LOOT HIM!
DON'T! OR WE'LL TELL!
SOD OFF, YOU! OR I MAY FANCY A BOUTONNIERE TO LIVEN UP THE PROCEEDINGS.
EXCUSE ME. BOYS?
WHERE IS MY BABY?

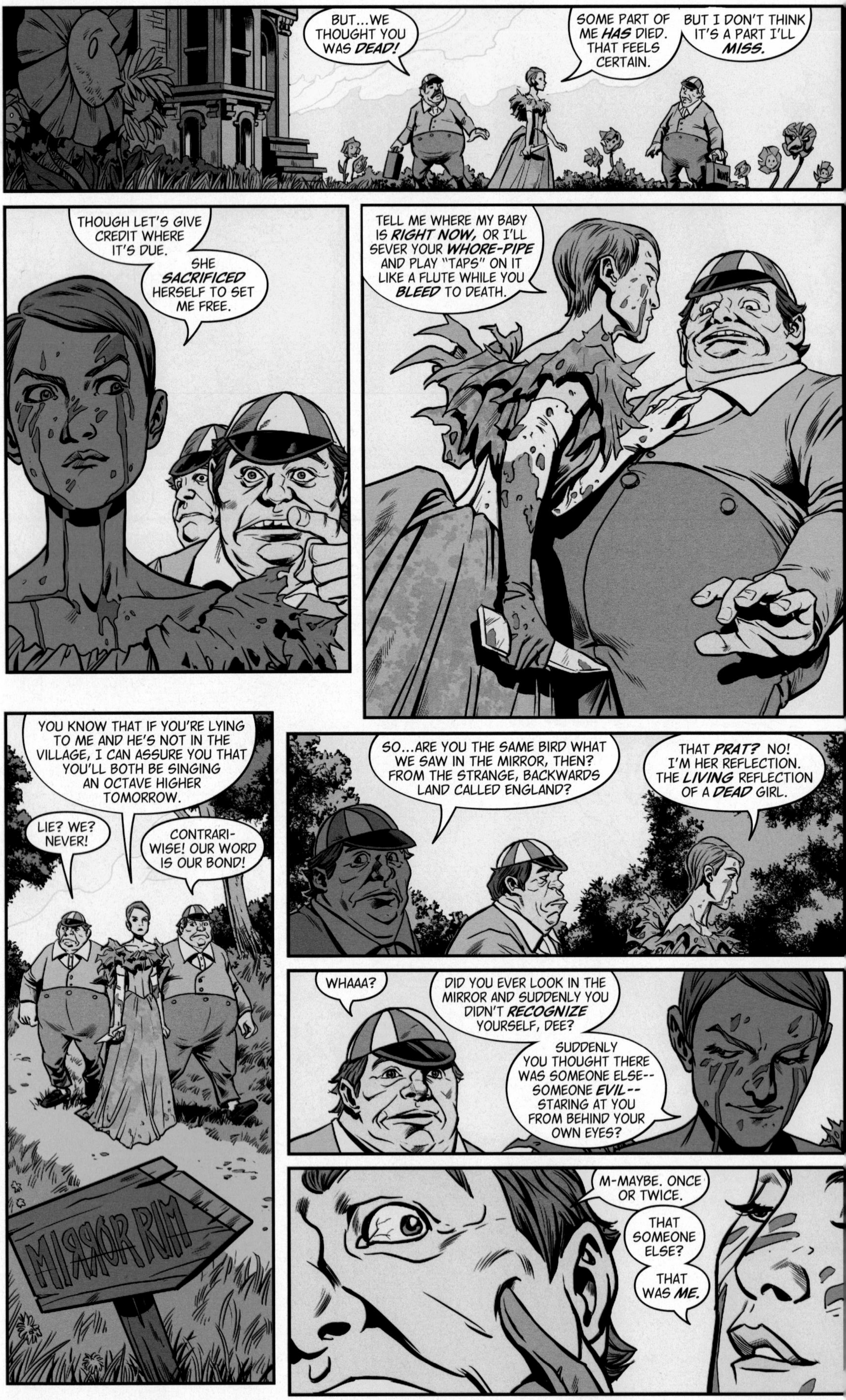

BUT...WE THOUGHT YOU WAS DEAD!
SOME PART OF ME HAS DIED. THAT FEELS CERTAIN.
BUT I DON'T THINK IT'S A PART I'LL MISS.
THOUGH LET'S GIVE CREDIT WHERE IT'S DUE.
SHE SACRIFICED HERSELF TO SET ME FREE.
TELL ME WHERE MY BABY IS RIGHT NOW, OR I'LL SEVER YOUR WHORE-PIPE AND PLAY "TAPS" ON IT LIKE A FLUTE WHILE YOU BLEED TO DEATH.
YOU KNOW THAT IF YOU'RE LYING TO ME AND HE'S NOT IN THE VILLAGE, I CAN ASSURE YOU THAT YOU'LL BOTH BE SINGING AN OCTAVE HIGHER TOMORROW.
LIE? WE? NEVER!
CONTRARI-WISE! OUR WORD IS OUR BOND!
SO...ARE YOU THE SAME BIRD WHAT WE SAW IN THE MIRROR, THEN? FROM THE STRANGE, BACKWARDS LAND CALLED ENGLAND?
THAT PRAT? NO! I'M HER REFLECTION. THE LIVING REFLECTION OF A DEAD GIRL.
WHAAA?
DID YOU EVER LOOK IN THE MIRROR AND SUDDENLY YOU DIDN'T RECOGNIZE YOURSELF, DEE?
SUDDENLY YOU THOUGHT THERE WAS SOMEONE ELSE-- SOMEONE EVIL-- STARING AT YOU FROM BEHIND YOUR OWN EYES?
M-MAYBE. ONCE OR TWICE.
THAT SOMEONE ELSE?
THAT WAS ME.

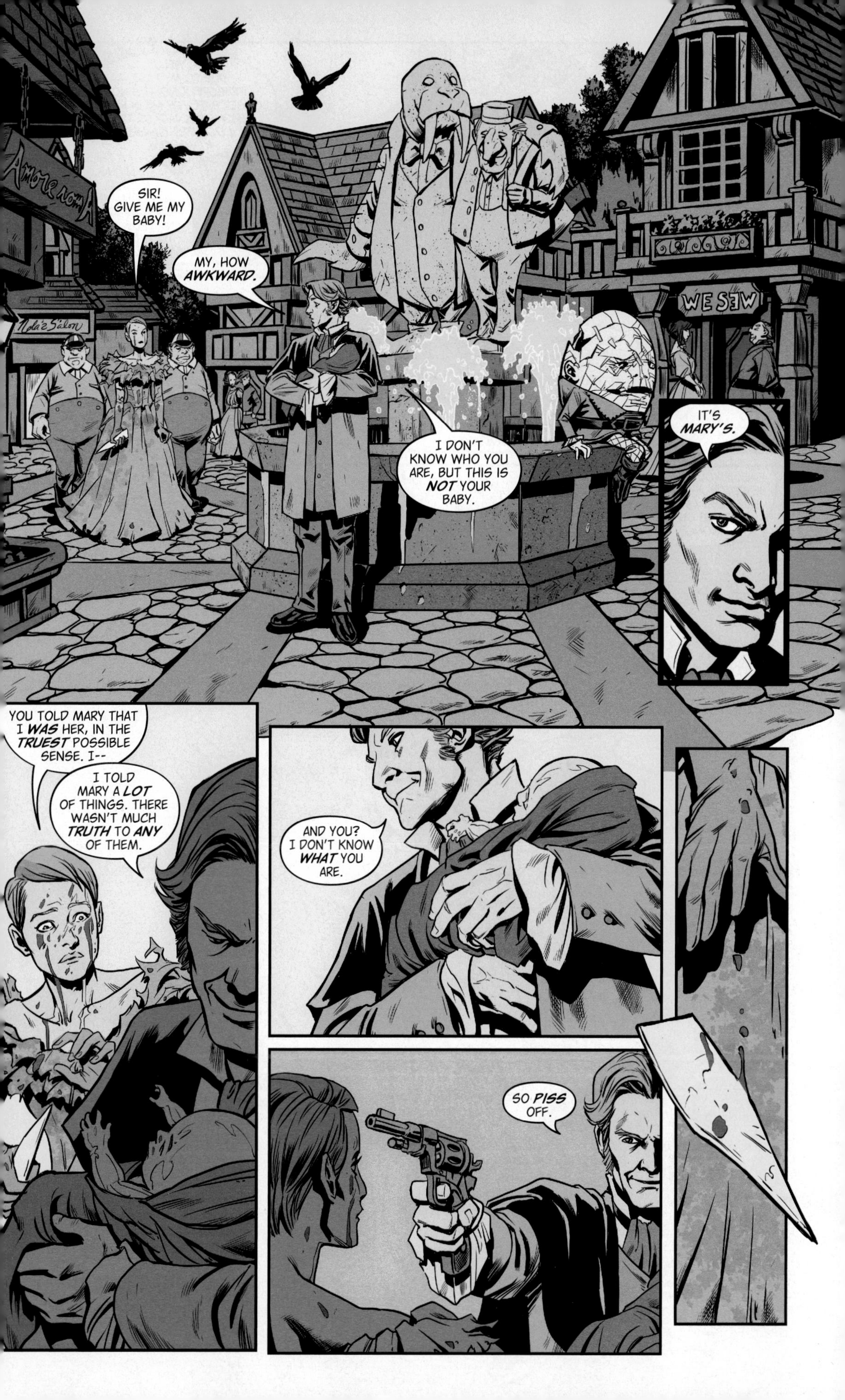
SIR! GIVE ME MY BABY!
MY, HOW AWKWARD.
I DON'T KNOW WHO YOU ARE, BUT THIS IS NOT YOUR BABY.
IT'S MARY'S.
YOU TOLD MARY THAT I WAS HER, IN THE TRUEST POSSIBLE SENSE. I--
I TOLD MARY A LOT OF THINGS. THERE WASN'T MUCH TRUTH TO ANY OF THEM.
AND YOU? I DON'T KNOW WHAT YOU ARE.
SO PISS OFF.

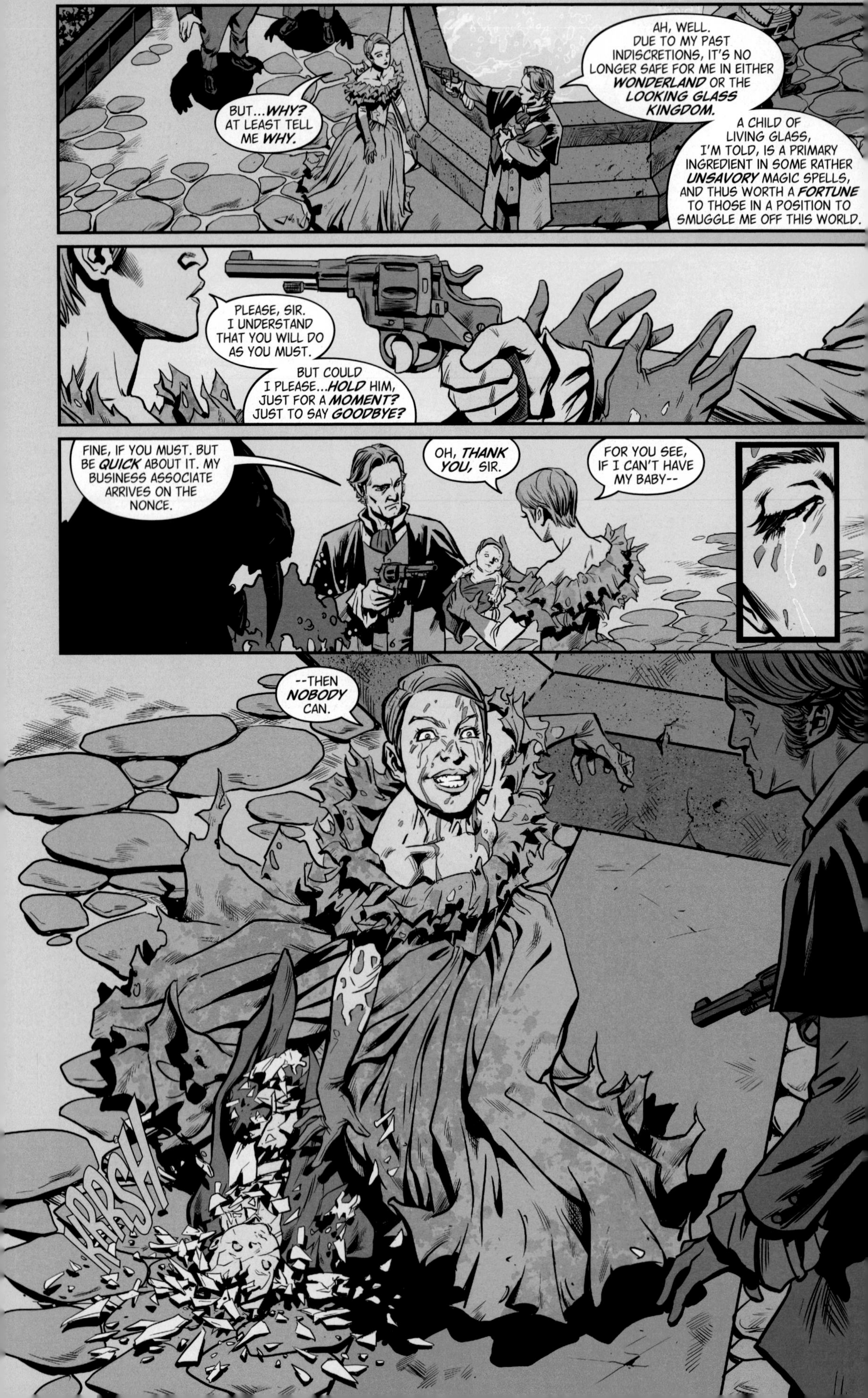
BUT...WHY? AT LEAST TELL ME WHY.
AH, WELL. DUE TO MY PAST INDISCRETIONS, IT'S NO LONGER SAFE FOR ME IN EITHER WONDERLAND OR THE LOOKING GLASS KINGDOM.
A CHILD OF LIVING GLASS, I'M TOLD, IS A PRIMARY INGREDIENT IN SOME RATHER UNSAVORY MAGIC SPELLS, AND THUS WORTH A FORTUNE TO THOSE IN A POSITION TO SMUGGLE ME OFF THIS WORLD.
PLEASE, SIR. I UNDERSTAND THAT YOU WILL DO AS YOU MUST.
BUT COULD I PLEASE...HOLD HIM, JUST FOR A MOMENT? JUST TO SAY GOODBYE?
FINE, IF YOU MUST. BUT BE QUICK ABOUT IT. MY BUSINESS ASSOCIATE ARRIVES ON THE NONCE.
OH, THANK YOU, SIR.
FOR YOU SEE, IF I CAN'T HAVE MY BABY--
--THEN NOBODY CAN.
KRRSH

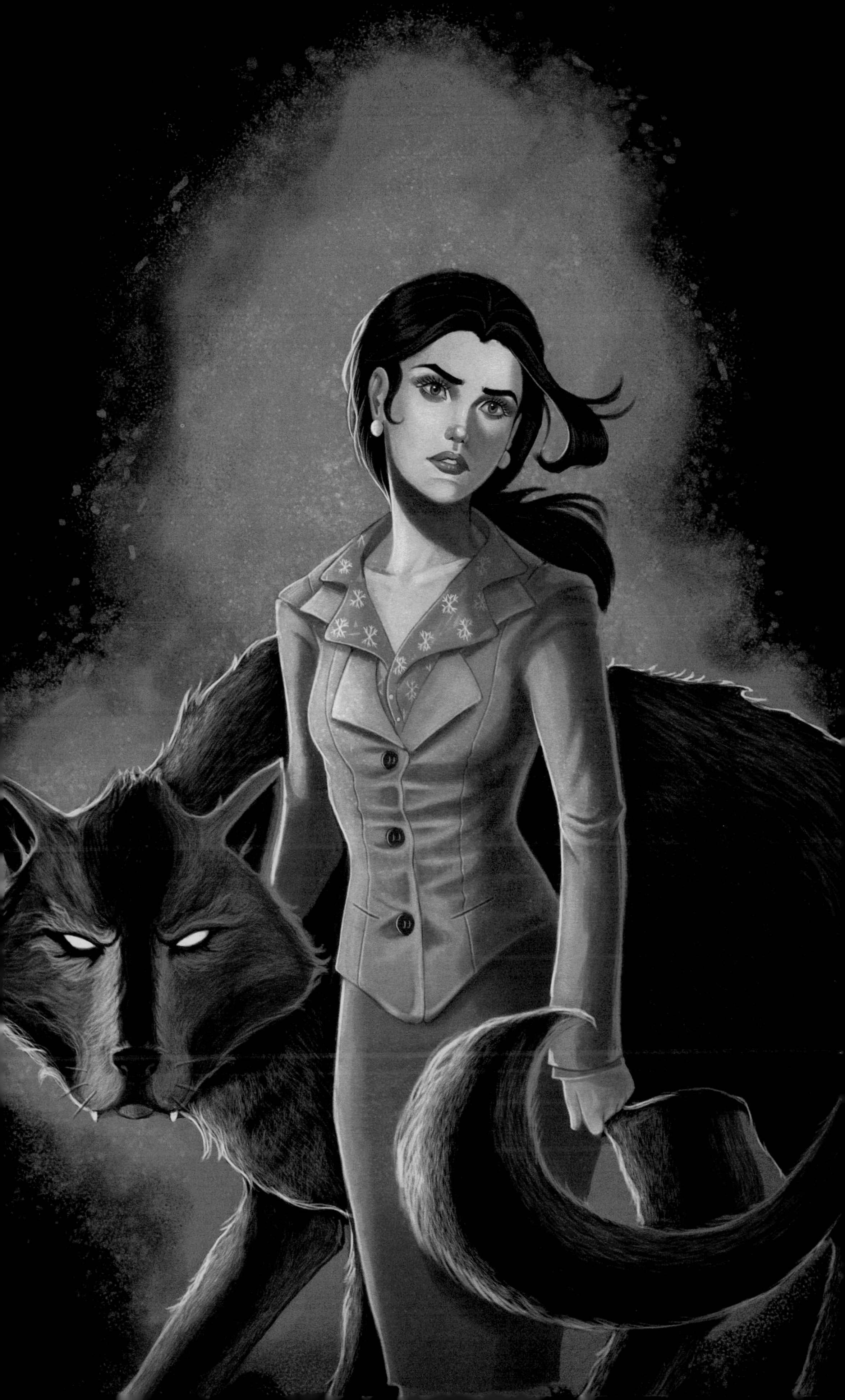

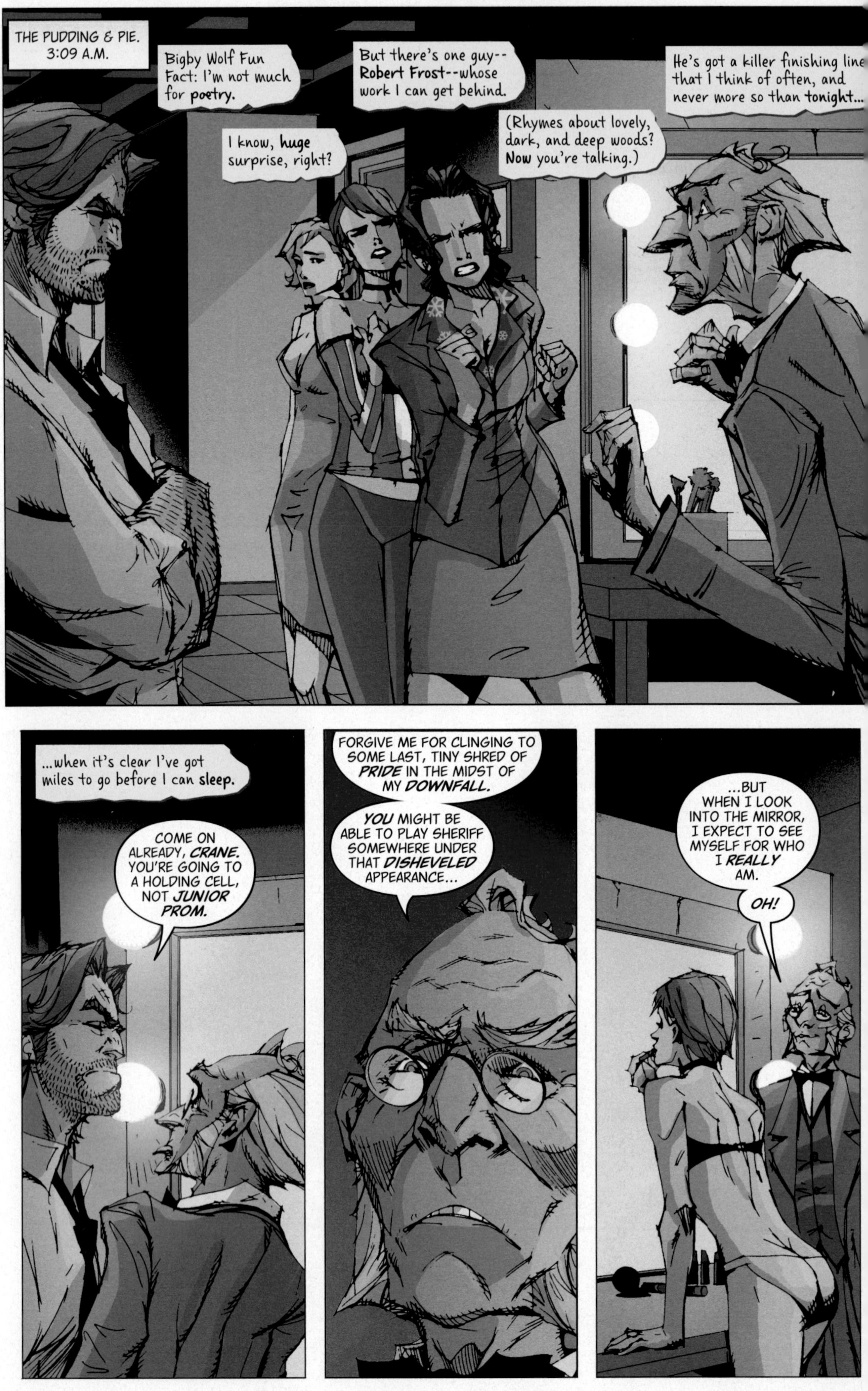

THE PUDDING & PIE. 3:09 A.M.
Bigby Wolf Fun Fact: I'm not much for poetry.
I know, huge surprise, right?
But there's one guy--Robert Frost--whose work I can get behind.
(Rhymes about lovely, dark, and deep woods? Now you're talking.)
He's got a killer finishing line that I think of often, and never more so than tonight...
...when it's clear I've got miles to go before I can sleep.
COME ON ALREADY, CRANE. YOU'RE GOING TO A HOLDING CELL, NOT JUNIOR PROM.
FORGIVE ME FOR CLINGING TO SOME LAST, TINY SHRED OF PRIDE IN THE MIDST OF MY DOWNFALL.
YOU MIGHT BE ABLE TO PLAY SHERIFF SOMEWHERE UNDER THAT DISHEVELED APPEARANCE...
...BUT WHEN I LOOK INTO THE MIRROR, I EXPECT TO SEE MYSELF FOR WHO I REALLY AM.
OH!

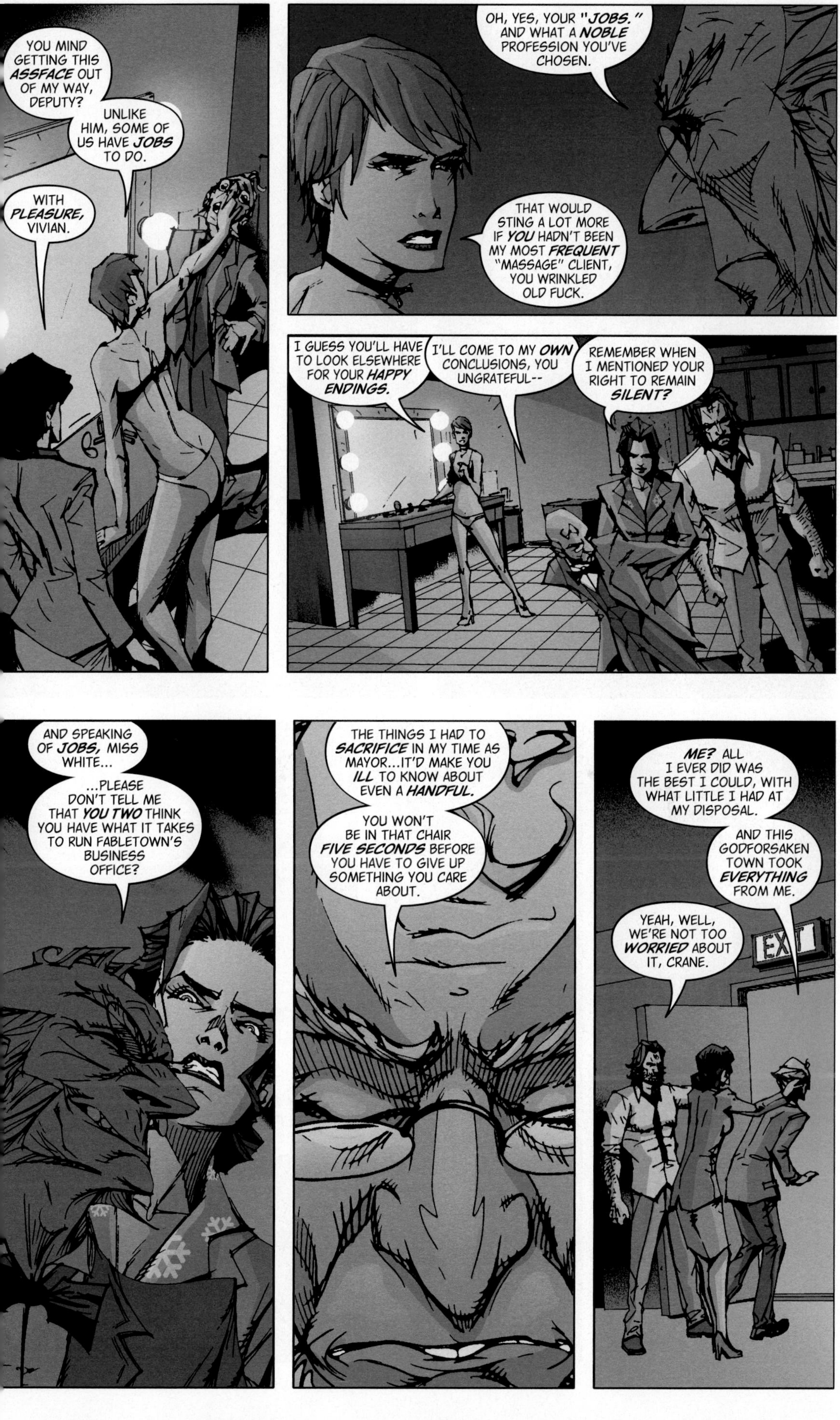
YOU MIND GETTING THIS ASSFACE OUT OF MY WAY, DEPUTY?
UNLIKE HIM, SOME OF US HAVE JOBS TO DO.
WITH PLEASURE, VIVIAN.
OH, YES, YOUR "JOBS." AND WHAT A NOBLE PROFESSION YOU'VE CHOSEN.
THAT WOULD STING A LOT MORE IF YOU HADN'T BEEN MY MOST FREQUENT "MASSAGE" CLIENT, YOU WRINKLED OLD FUCK.
I GUESS YOU'LL HAVE TO LOOK ELSEWHERE FOR YOUR HAPPY ENDINGS.
I'LL COME TO MY OWN CONCLUSIONS, YOU UNGRATEFUL--
REMEMBER WHEN I MENTIONED YOUR RIGHT TO REMAIN SILENT?
AND SPEAKING OF JOBS, MISS WHITE...
...PLEASE DON'T TELL ME THAT YOU TWO THINK YOU HAVE WHAT IT TAKES TO RUN FABLETOWN'S BUSINESS OFFICE?
THE THINGS I HAD TO SACRIFICE IN MY TIME AS MAYOR...IT'D MAKE YOU ILL TO KNOW ABOUT EVEN A HANDFUL.
YOU WON'T BE IN THAT CHAIR FIVE SECONDS BEFORE YOU HAVE TO GIVE UP SOMETHING YOU CARE ABOUT.
ME? ALL I EVER DID WAS THE BEST I COULD, WITH WHAT LITTLE I HAD AT MY DISPOSAL.
AND THIS GODFORSAKEN TOWN TOOK EVERYTHING FROM ME.
YEAH, WELL, WE'RE NOT TOO WORRIED ABOUT IT, CRANE.
EXIT

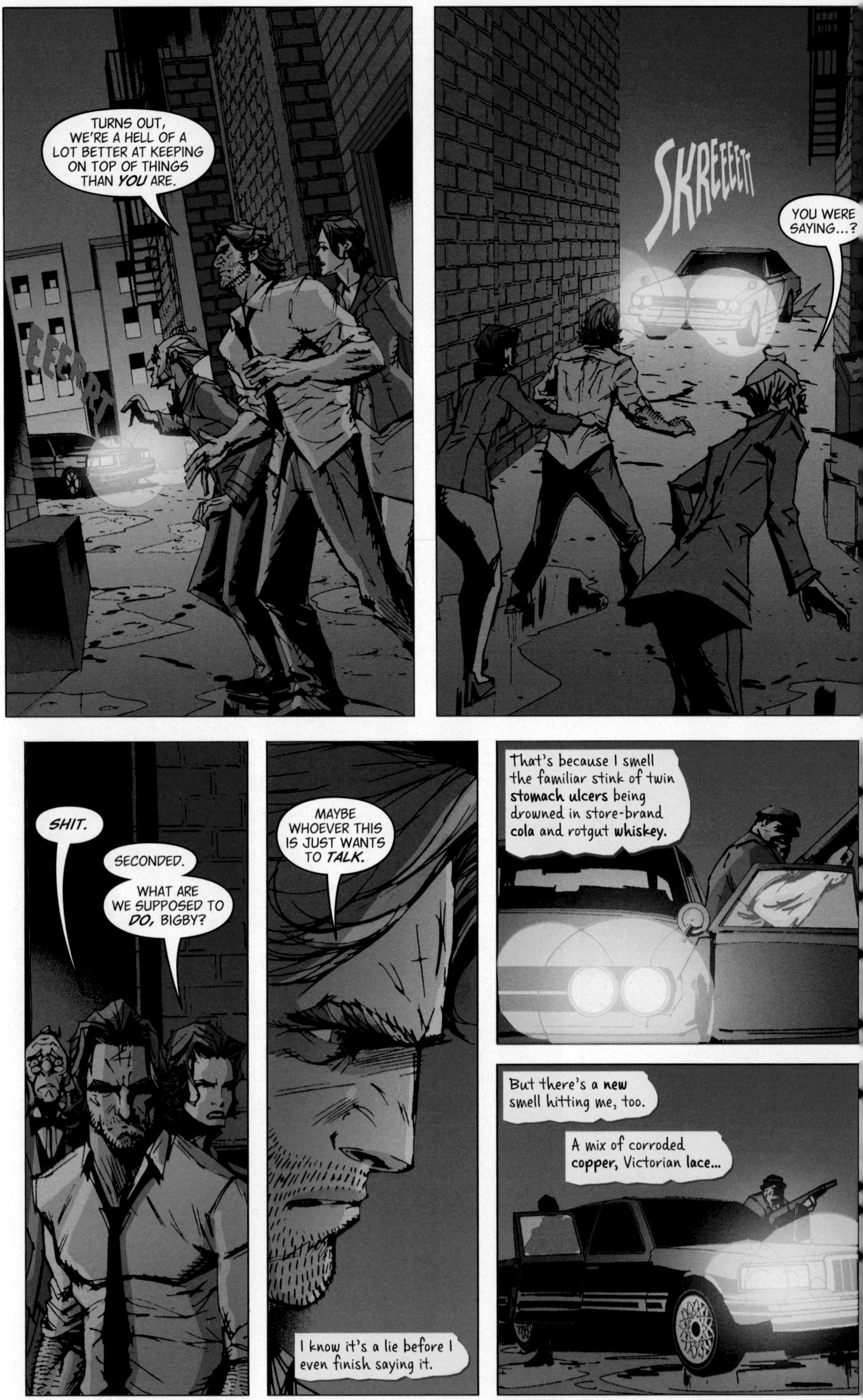

TURNS OUT, WE'RE A HELL OF A LOT BETTER AT KEEPING ON TOP OF THINGS THAN *YOU* ARE.
EEERRRT
SKREEEEETT
YOU WERE SAYING...?
SHIT.
SECONDED.
WHAT ARE WE SUPPOSED TO *DO,* BIGBY?
MAYBE WHOEVER THIS IS JUST WANTS TO *TALK.*
I know it's a lie before I even finish saying it.
That's because I smell the familiar stink of twin **stomach ulcers** being drowned in store-brand **cola** and rotgut **whiskey.**
But there's a **new** smell hitting me, too.
A mix of corroded **copper,** Victorian **lace...**

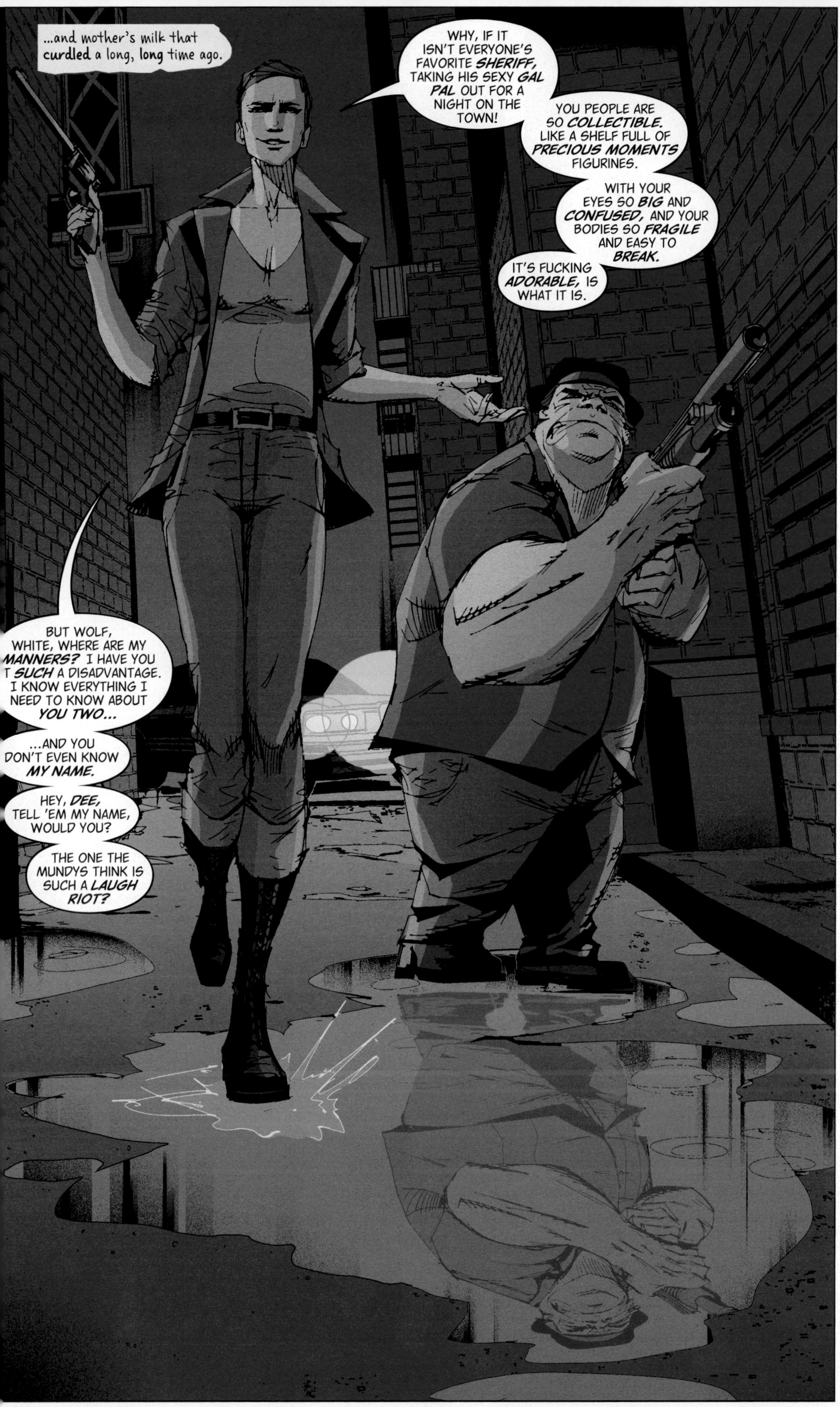
...and mother's milk that curdled a long, long time ago.
WHY, IF IT ISN'T EVERYONE'S FAVORITE SHERIFF, TAKING HIS SEXY GAL PAL OUT FOR A NIGHT ON THE TOWN!
YOU PEOPLE ARE SO COLLECTIBLE. LIKE A SHELF FULL OF PRECIOUS MOMENTS FIGURINES.
WITH YOUR EYES SO BIG AND CONFUSED, AND YOUR BODIES SO FRAGILE AND EASY TO BREAK.
IT'S FUCKING ADORABLE, IS WHAT IT IS.
BUT WOLF, WHITE, WHERE ARE MY MANNERS? I HAVE YOU T SUCH A DISADVANTAGE. I KNOW EVERYTHING I NEED TO KNOW ABOUT YOU TWO...
...AND YOU DON'T EVEN KNOW MY NAME.
HEY, DEE, TELL 'EM MY NAME, WOULD YOU?
THE ONE THE MUNDYS THINK IS SUCH A LAUGH RIOT?

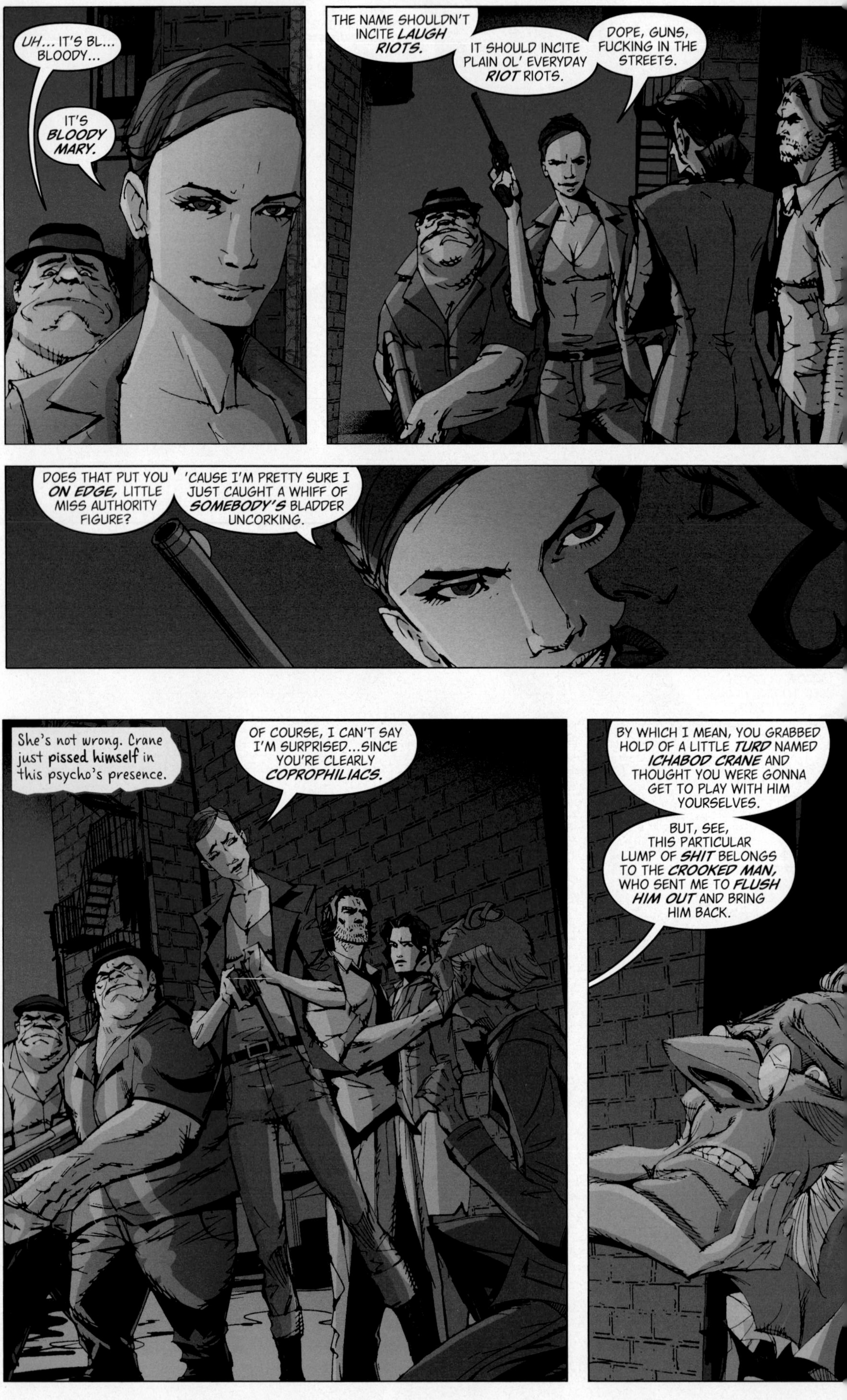
UH... IT'S BL... BLOODY...
IT'S BLOODY MARY.
THE NAME SHOULDN'T INCITE LAUGH RIOTS.
IT SHOULD INCITE PLAIN OL' EVERYDAY RIOT RIOTS.
DOPE, GUNS, FUCKING IN THE STREETS.
DOES THAT PUT YOU ON EDGE, LITTLE MISS AUTHORITY FIGURE?
'CAUSE I'M PRETTY SURE I JUST CAUGHT A WHIFF OF SOMEBODY'S BLADDER UNCORKING.
She's not wrong. Crane just pissed himself in this psycho's presence.
OF COURSE, I CAN'T SAY I'M SURPRISED...SINCE YOU'RE CLEARLY COPROPHILIACS.
BY WHICH I MEAN, YOU GRABBED HOLD OF A LITTLE TURD NAMED ICHABOD CRANE AND THOUGHT YOU WERE GONNA GET TO PLAY WITH HIM YOURSELVES.
BUT, SEE, THIS PARTICULAR LUMP OF SHIT BELONGS TO THE CROOKED MAN, WHO SENT ME TO FLUSH HIM OUT AND BRING HIM BACK.

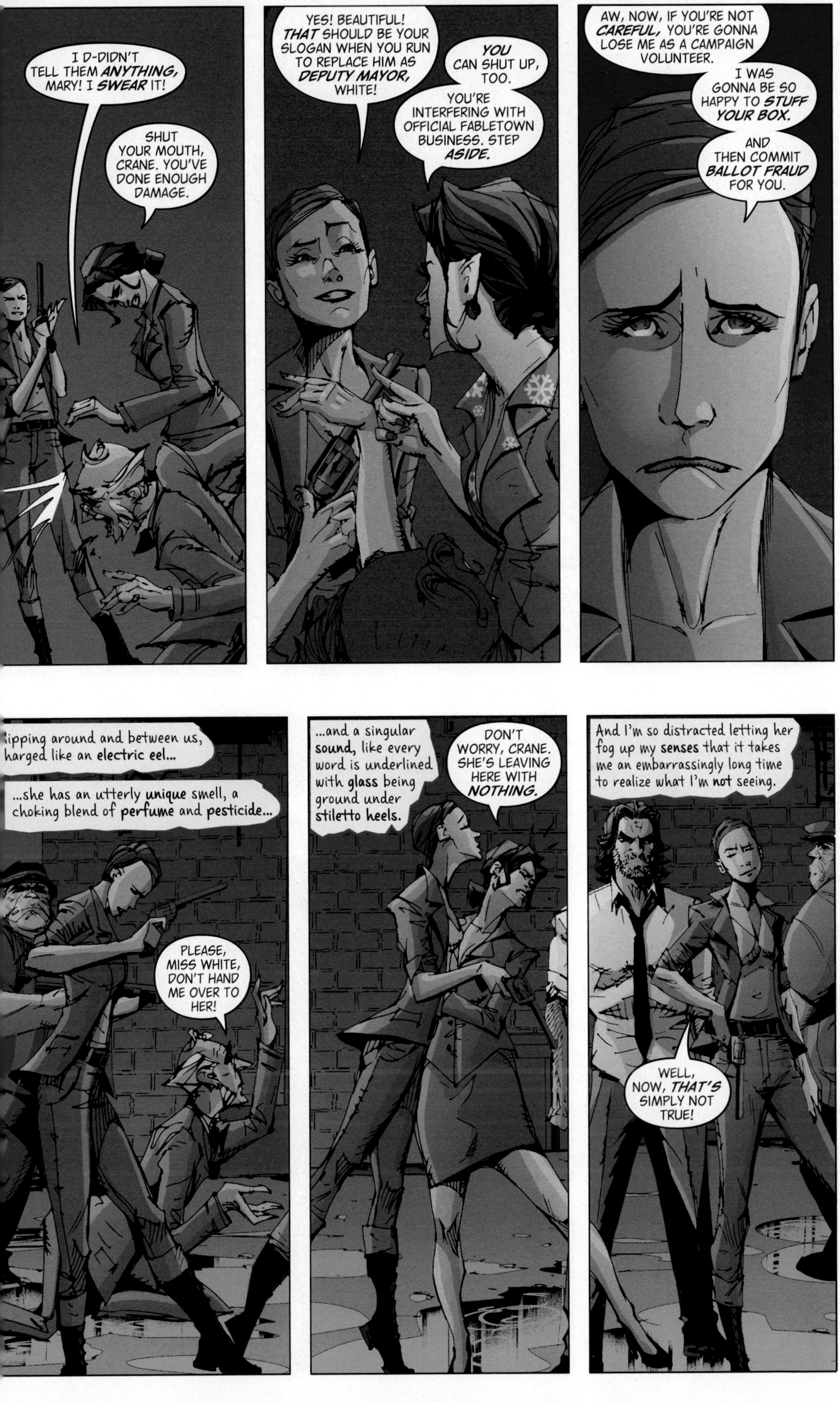
I D-DIDN'T TELL THEM ANYTHING, MARY! I SWEAR IT!
SHUT YOUR MOUTH, CRANE. YOU'VE DONE ENOUGH DAMAGE.
YES! BEAUTIFUL! THAT SHOULD BE YOUR SLOGAN WHEN YOU RUN TO REPLACE HIM AS DEPUTY MAYOR, WHITE!
YOU CAN SHUT UP, TOO.
YOU'RE INTERFERING WITH OFFICIAL FABLETOWN BUSINESS. STEP ASIDE.
AW, NOW, IF YOU'RE NOT CAREFUL, YOU'RE GONNA LOSE ME AS A CAMPAIGN VOLUNTEER.
I WAS GONNA BE SO HAPPY TO STUFF YOUR BOX.
AND THEN COMMIT BALLOT FRAUD FOR YOU.
ipping around and between us, harged like an electric eel...
...she has an utterly unique smell, a choking blend of perfume and pesticide...
PLEASE, MISS WHITE, DON'T HAND ME OVER TO HER!
...and a singular sound, like every word is underlined with glass being ground under stiletto heels.
DON'T WORRY, CRANE. SHE'S LEAVING HERE WITH NOTHING.
And I'm so distracted letting her fog up my senses that it takes me an embarrassingly long time to realize what I'm not seeing.
WELL, NOW, THAT'S SIMPLY NOT TRUE!

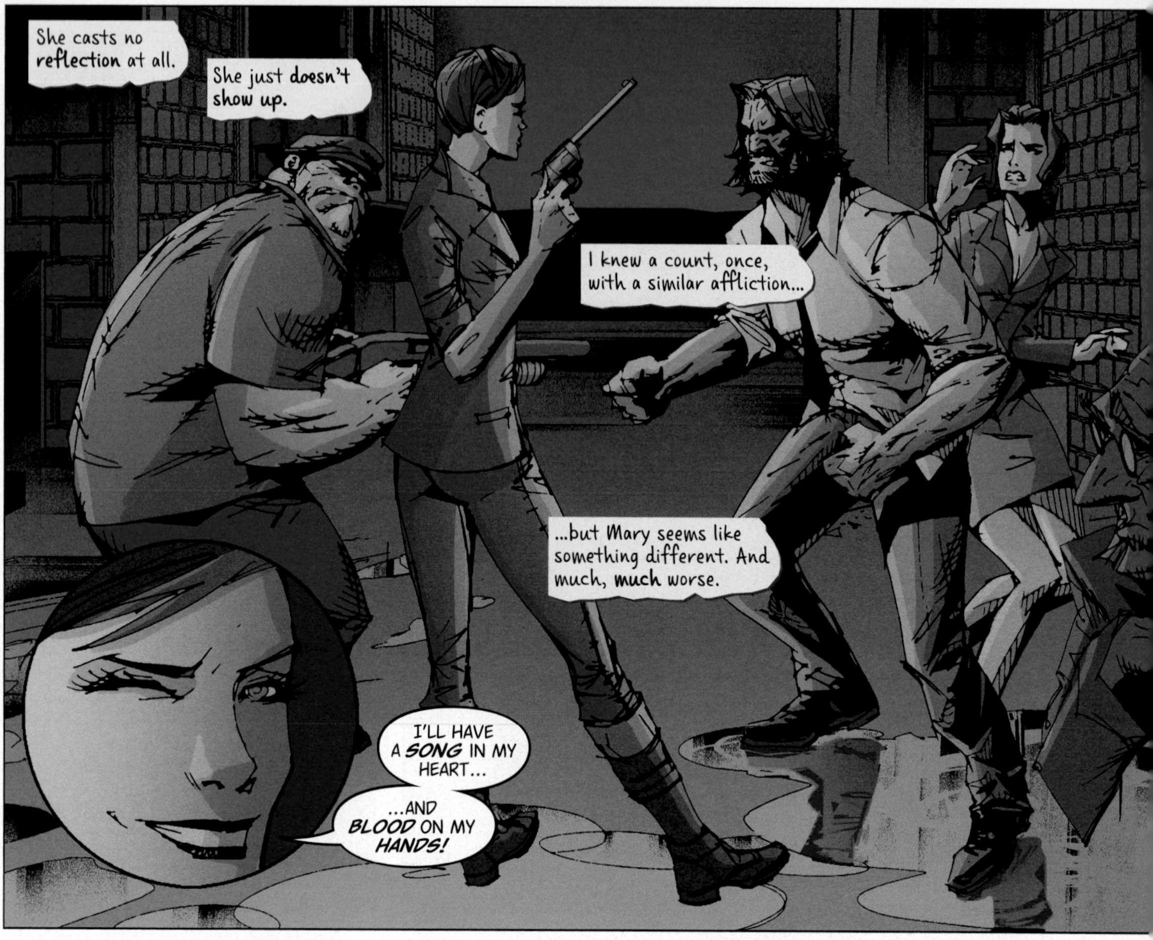
She casts no reflection at all.
She just doesn't show up.
I knew a count, once, with a similar affliction...
...but Mary seems like something different. And much, much worse.
I'LL HAVE A SONG IN MY HEART...
...AND BLOOD ON MY HANDS!

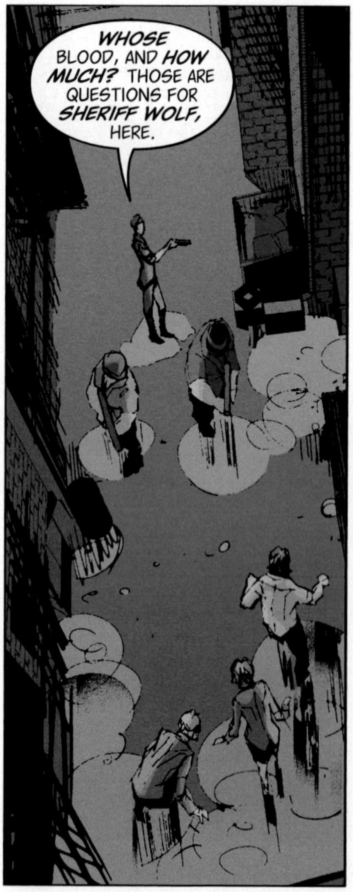
WHOSE BLOOD, AND HOW MUCH? THOSE ARE QUESTIONS FOR SHERIFF WOLF, HERE.

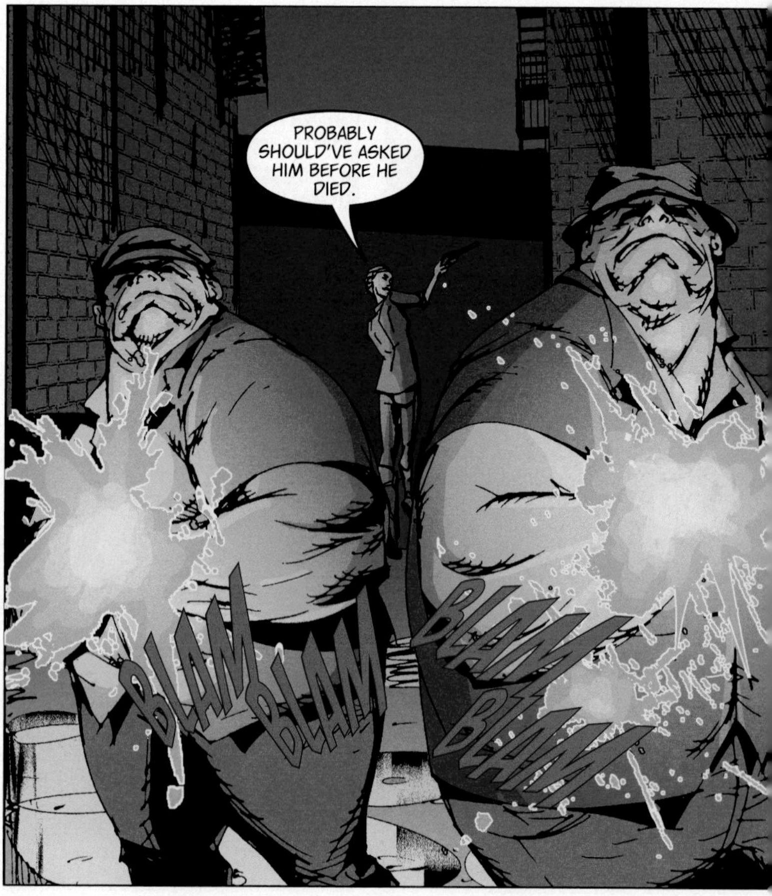
PROBABLY SHOULD'VE ASKED HIM BEFORE HE DIED.
BLAM
BLAM
BLAM
BLAM

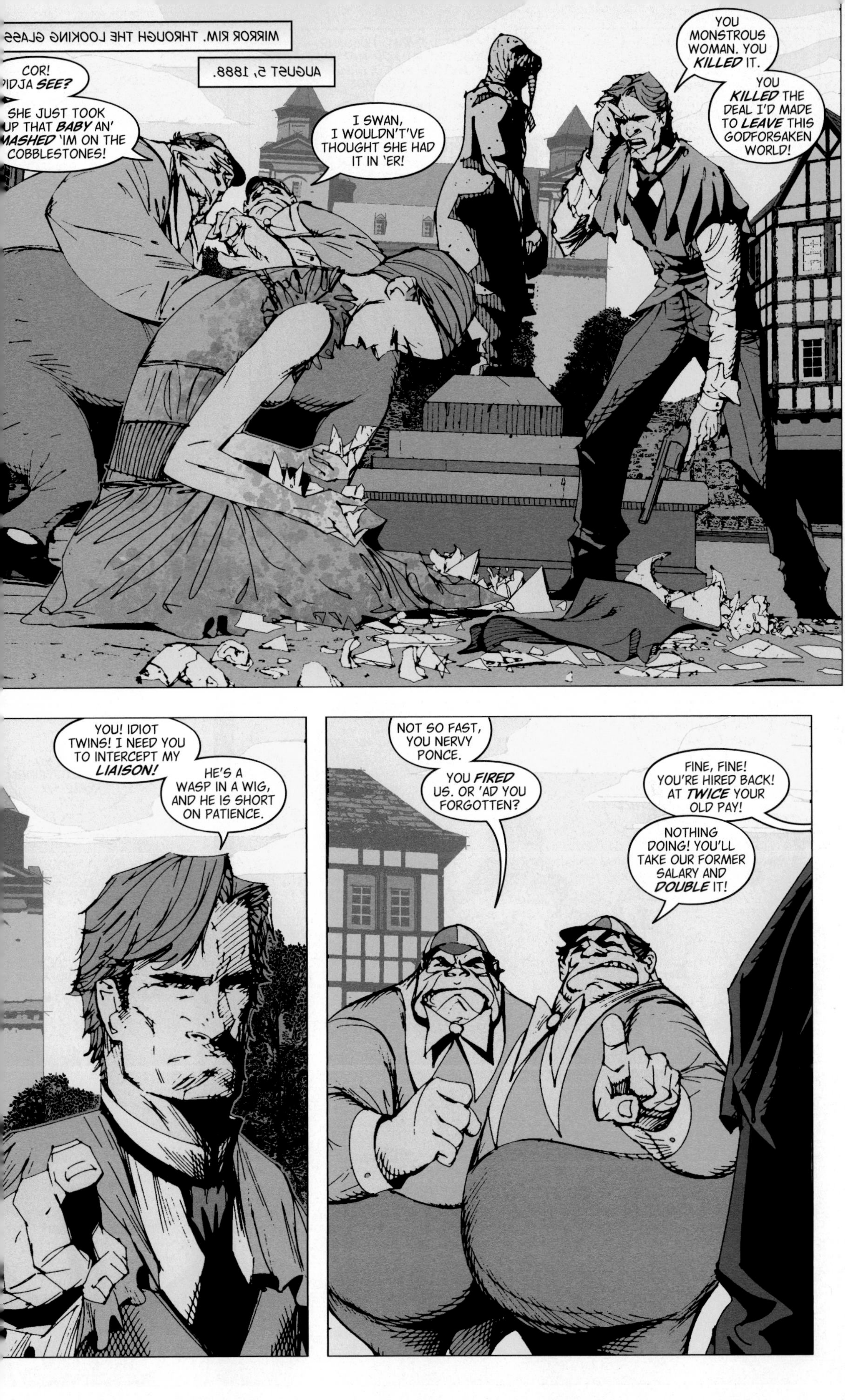
MIRROR RIM. THROUGH THE LOOKING GLASS
AUGUST 5, 1888.
COR! DIDJA SEE?
SHE JUST TOOK UP THAT BABY AN' MASHED 'IM ON THE COBBLESTONES!
I SWAN, I WOULDN'T'VE THOUGHT SHE HAD IT IN 'ER!
YOU MONSTROUS WOMAN. YOU KILLED IT.
YOU KILLED THE DEAL I'D MADE TO LEAVE THIS GODFORSAKEN WORLD!
YOU! IDIOT TWINS! I NEED YOU TO INTERCEPT MY LIAISON!
HE'S A WASP IN A WIG, AND HE IS SHORT ON PATIENCE.
NOT SO FAST, YOU NERVY PONCE.
YOU FIRED US. OR 'AD YOU FORGOTTEN?
FINE, FINE! YOU'RE HIRED BACK! AT TWICE YOUR OLD PAY!
NOTHING DOING! YOU'LL TAKE OUR FORMER SALARY AND DOUBLE IT!

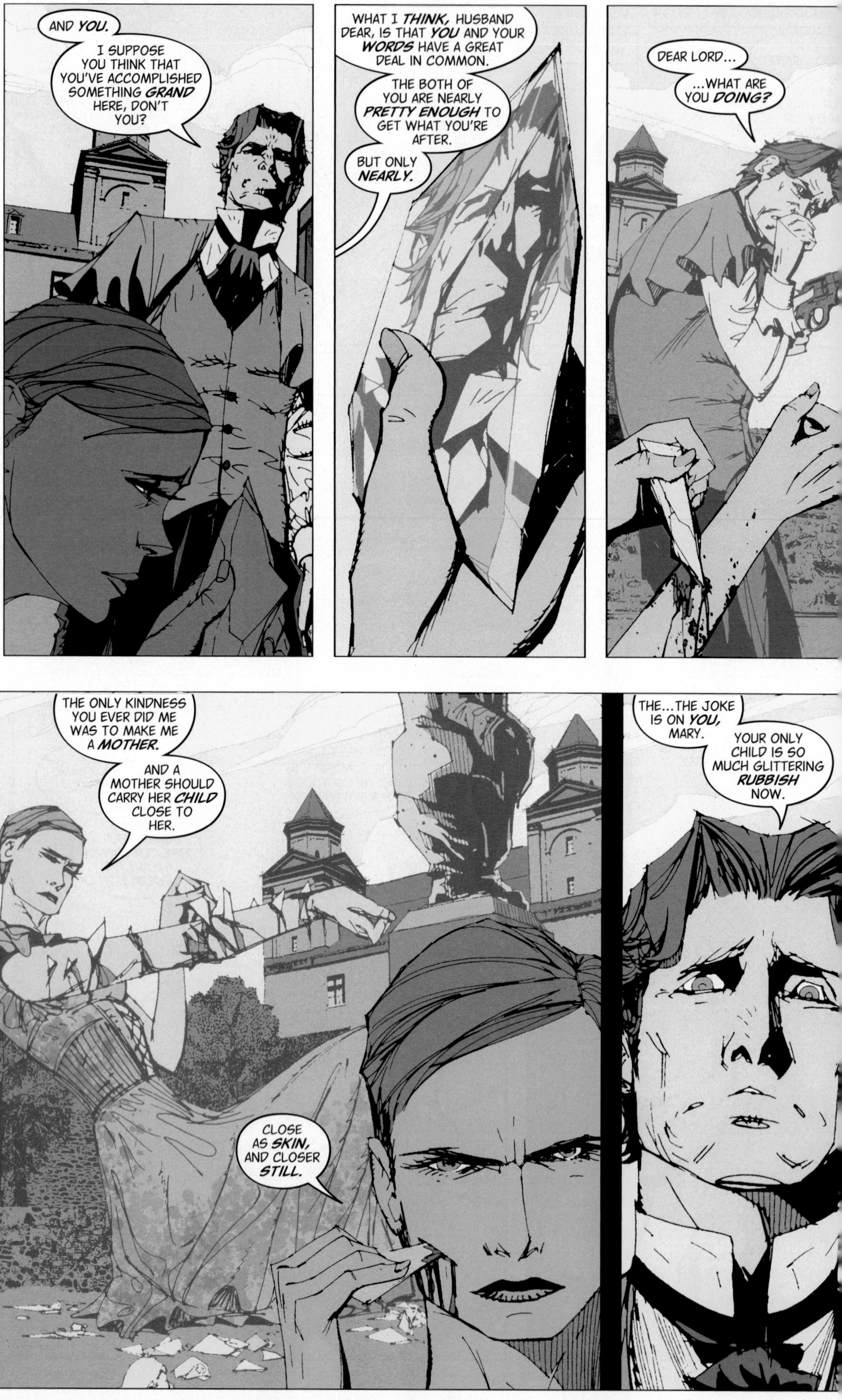
AND YOU.
I SUPPOSE YOU THINK THAT YOU'VE ACCOMPLISHED SOMETHING GRAND HERE, DON'T YOU?
WHAT I THINK, HUSBAND DEAR, IS THAT YOU AND YOUR WORDS HAVE A GREAT DEAL IN COMMON.
THE BOTH OF YOU ARE NEARLY PRETTY ENOUGH TO GET WHAT YOU'RE AFTER.
BUT ONLY NEARLY.
DEAR LORD...
...WHAT ARE YOU DOING?
THE ONLY KINDNESS YOU EVER DID ME WAS TO MAKE ME A MOTHER.
AND A MOTHER SHOULD CARRY HER CHILD CLOSE TO HER.
CLOSE AS SKIN, AND CLOSER STILL.
THE...THE JOKE IS ON YOU, MARY.
YOUR ONLY CHILD IS SO MUCH GLITTERING RUBBISH NOW.

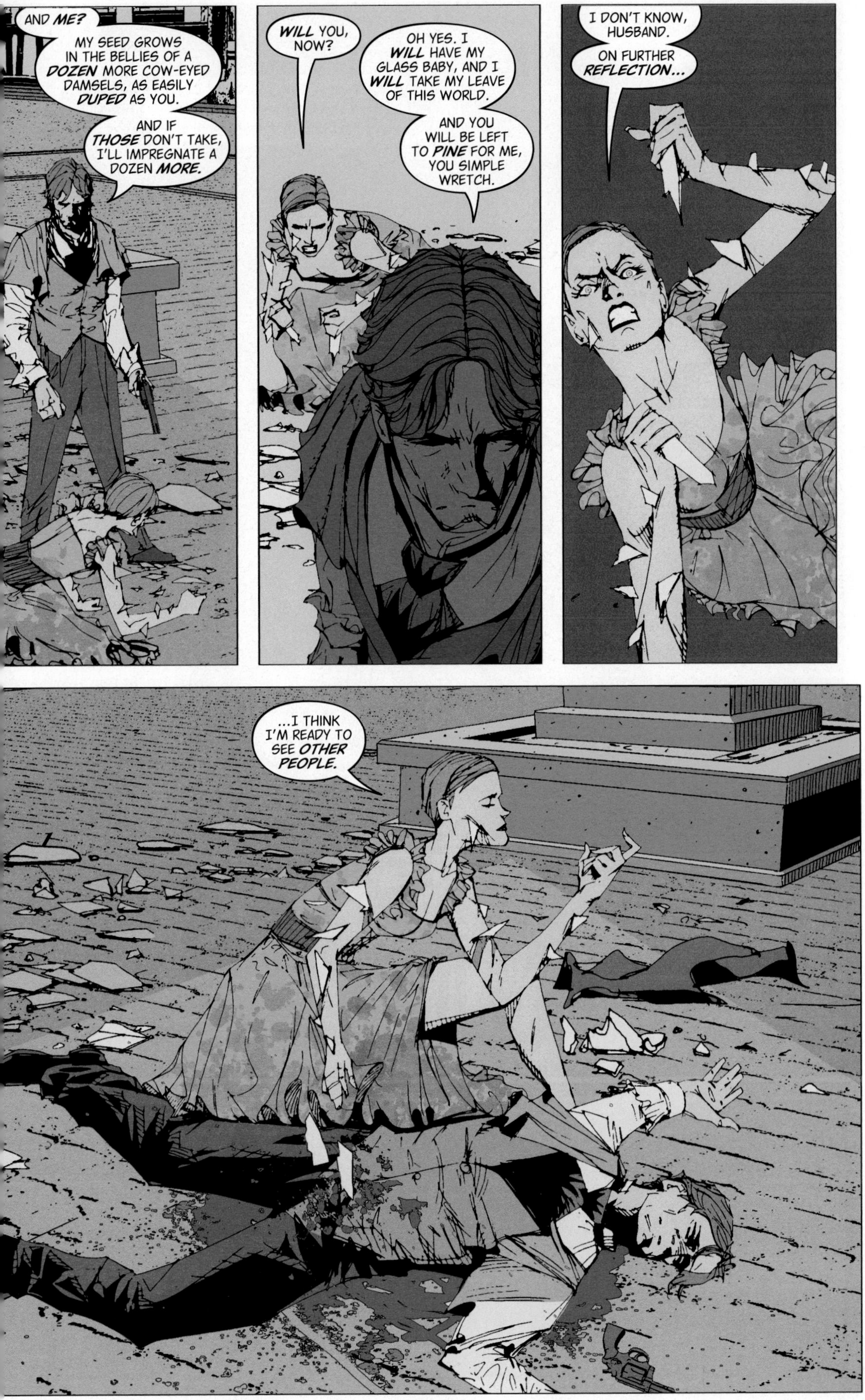
AND ***ME?***
MY SEED GROWS IN THE BELLIES OF A ***DOZEN*** MORE COW-EYED DAMSELS, AS EASILY ***DUPED*** AS YOU.
AND IF ***THOSE*** DON'T TAKE, I'LL IMPREGNATE A DOZEN ***MORE.***
WILL YOU, NOW?
OH YES. I ***WILL*** HAVE MY GLASS BABY, AND I ***WILL*** TAKE MY LEAVE OF THIS WORLD.
AND YOU WILL BE LEFT TO ***PINE*** FOR ME, YOU SIMPLE WRETCH.
I DON'T KNOW, HUSBAND.
ON FURTHER ***REFLECTION...***
...I THINK I'M READY TO SEE ***OTHER PEOPLE.***

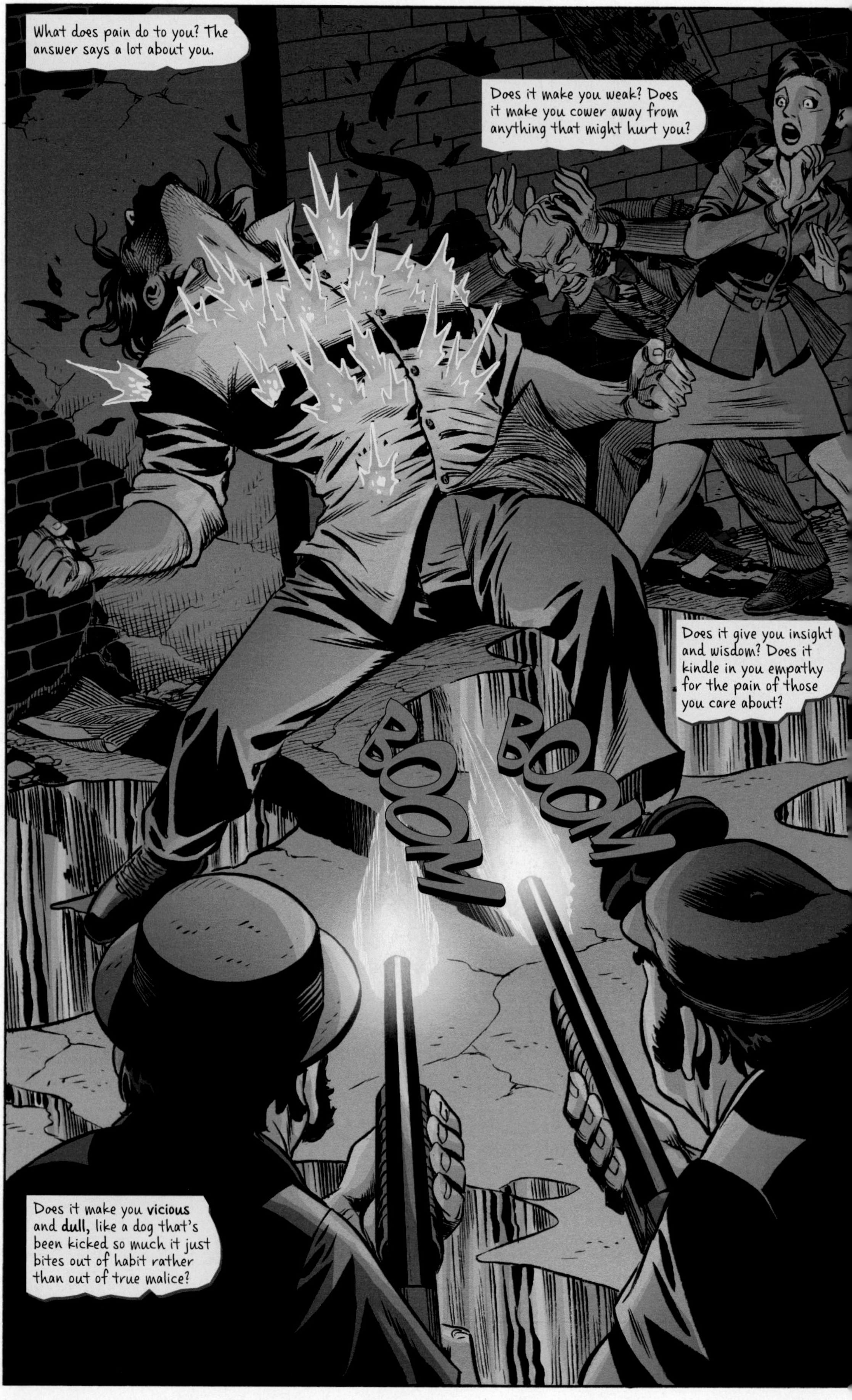
What does pain do to you? The answer says a lot about you.
Does it make you weak? Does it make you cower away from anything that might hurt you?
Does it give you insight and wisdom? Does it kindle in you empathy for the pain of those you care about?
BOOM
BOOM
Does it make you **vicious** and **dull,** like a dog that's been kicked so much it just bites out of habit rather than out of true malice?

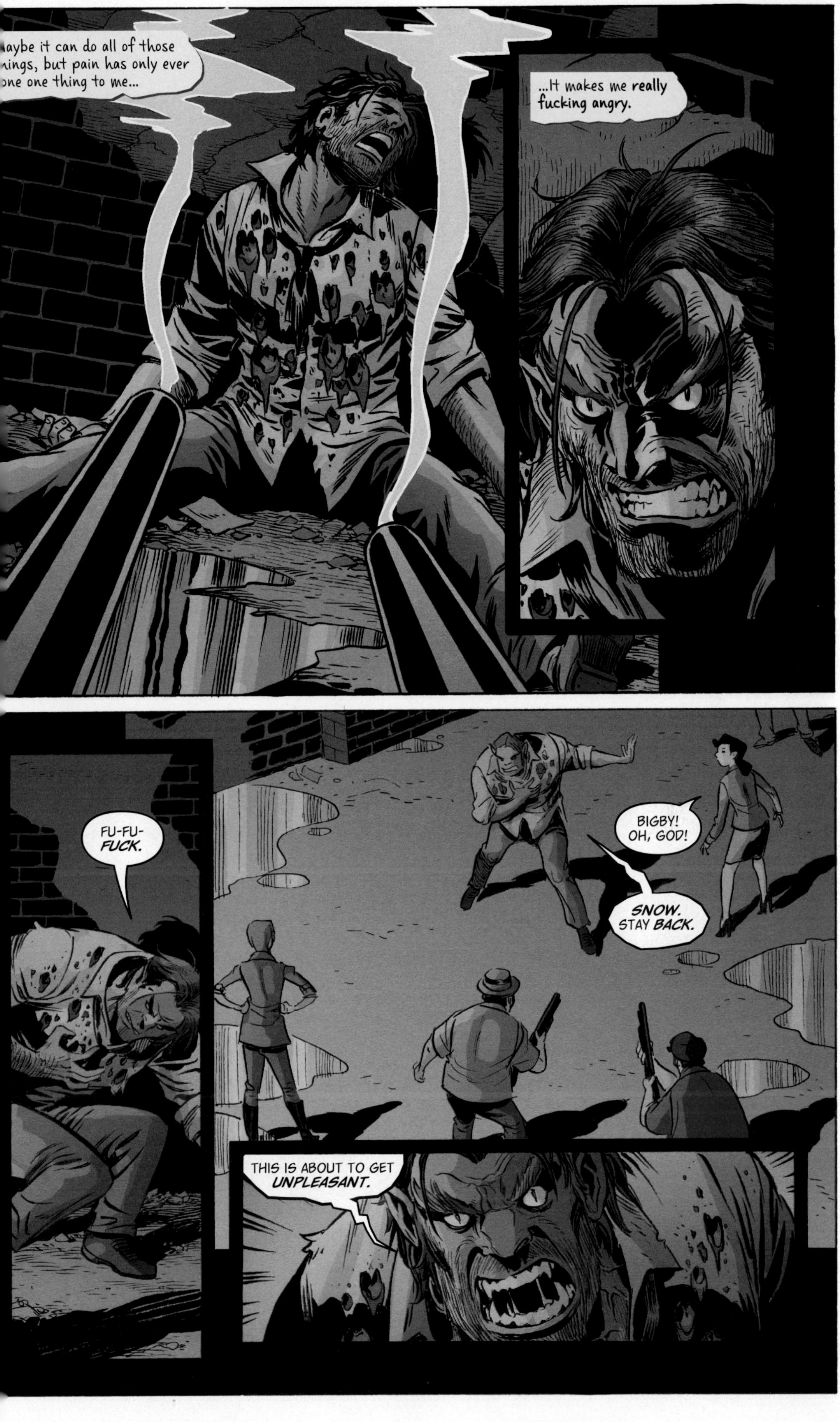
aybe it can do all of those ings, but pain has only ever one one thing to me...
...It makes me really fucking angry.
FU-FU-FUCK.
BIGBY! OH, GOD!
SNOW. STAY BACK.
THIS IS ABOUT TO GET UNPLEASANT.

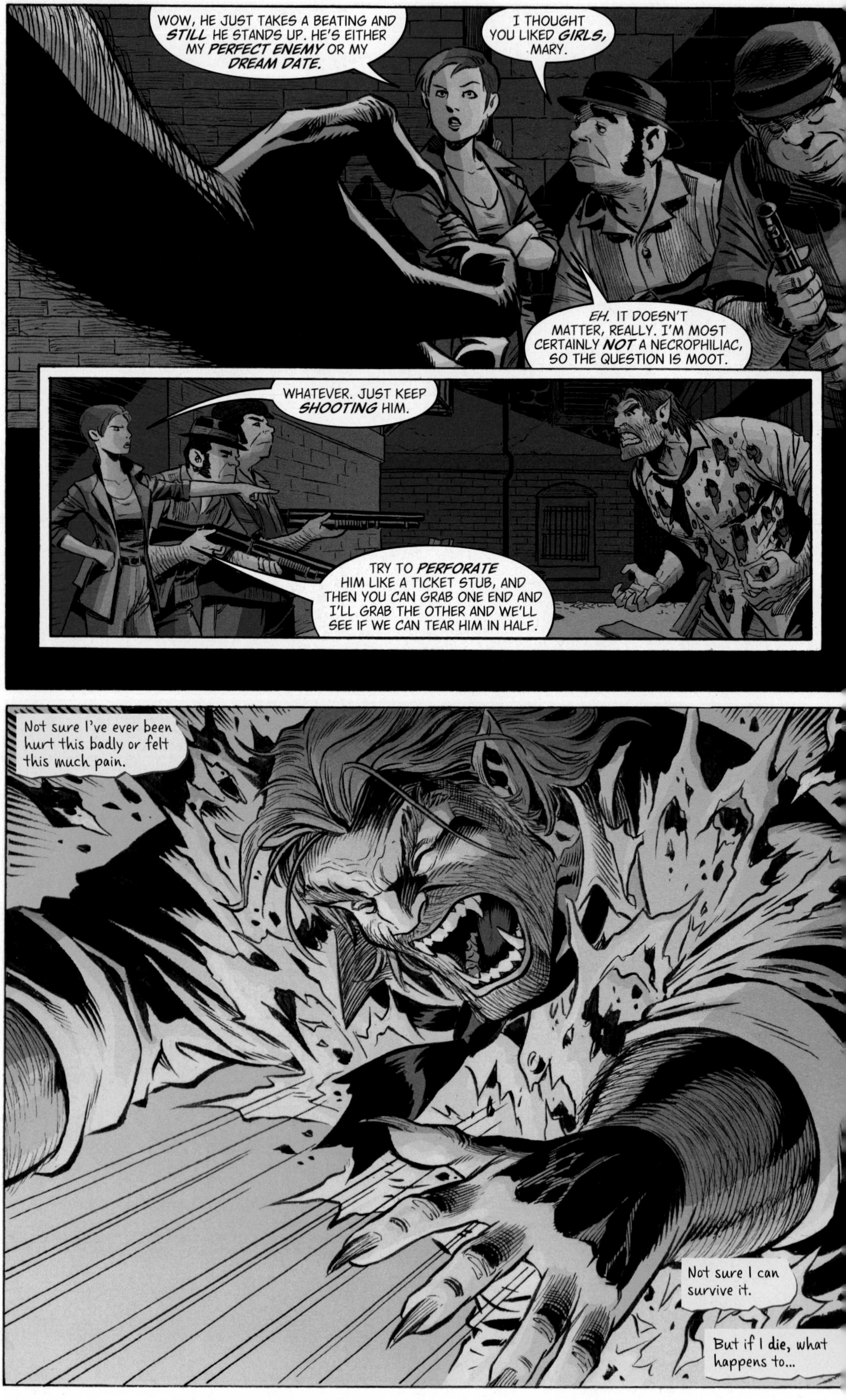
WOW, HE JUST TAKES A BEATING AND STILL HE STANDS UP. HE'S EITHER MY PERFECT ENEMY OR MY DREAM DATE.
I THOUGHT YOU LIKED GIRLS, MARY.
EH. IT DOESN'T MATTER, REALLY. I'M MOST CERTAINLY NOT A NECROPHILIAC, SO THE QUESTION IS MOOT.
WHATEVER. JUST KEEP SHOOTING HIM.
TRY TO PERFORATE HIM LIKE A TICKET STUB, AND THEN YOU CAN GRAB ONE END AND I'LL GRAB THE OTHER AND WE'LL SEE IF WE CAN TEAR HIM IN HALF.
Not sure I've ever been hurt this badly or felt this much pain.
Not sure I can survive it.
But if I die, what happens to...

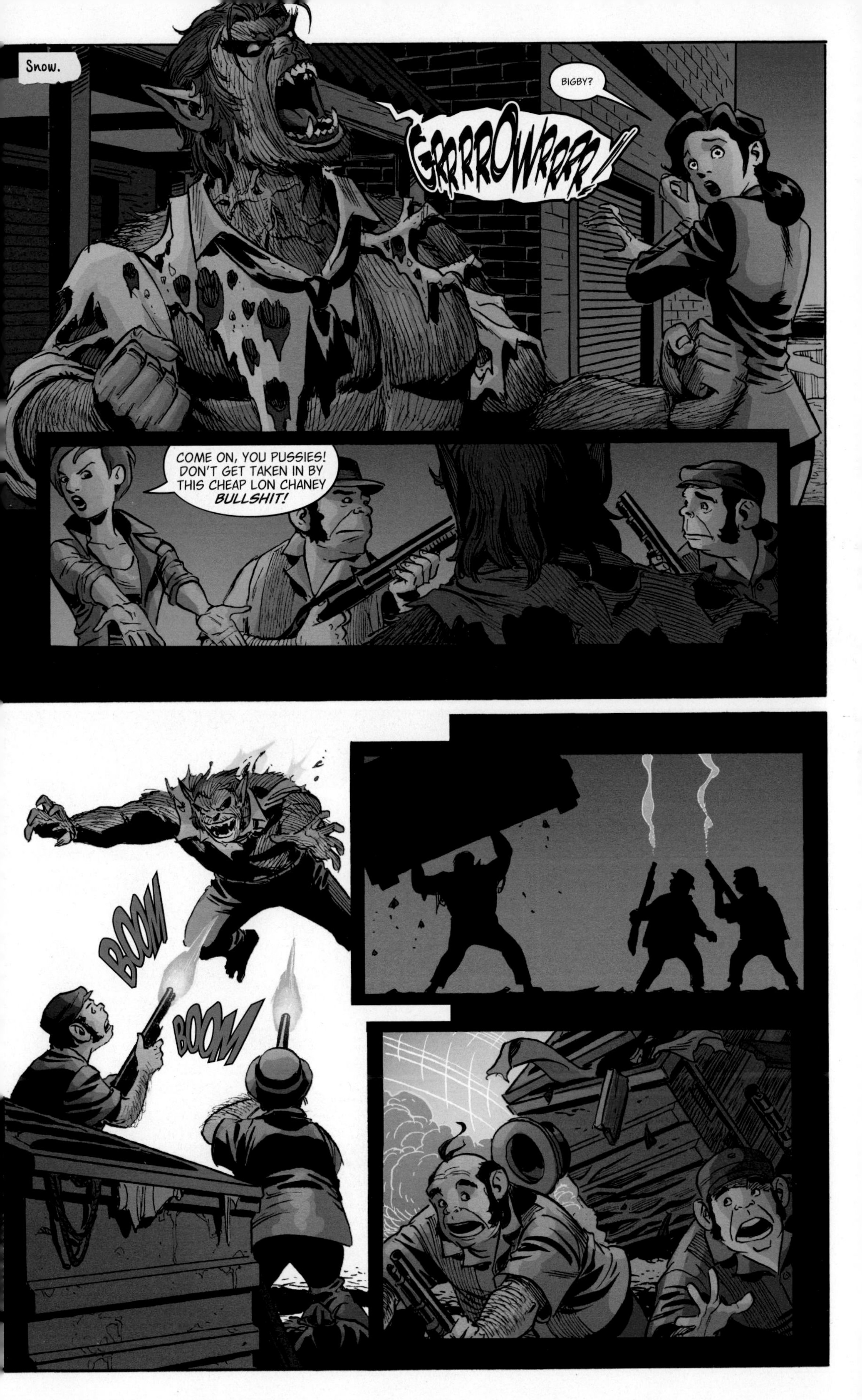
Snow.
BIGBY?
GRRRROWRRRR!
COME ON, YOU PUSSIES! DON'T GET TAKEN IN BY THIS CHEAP LON CHANEY BULLSHIT!
BOOM
BOOM

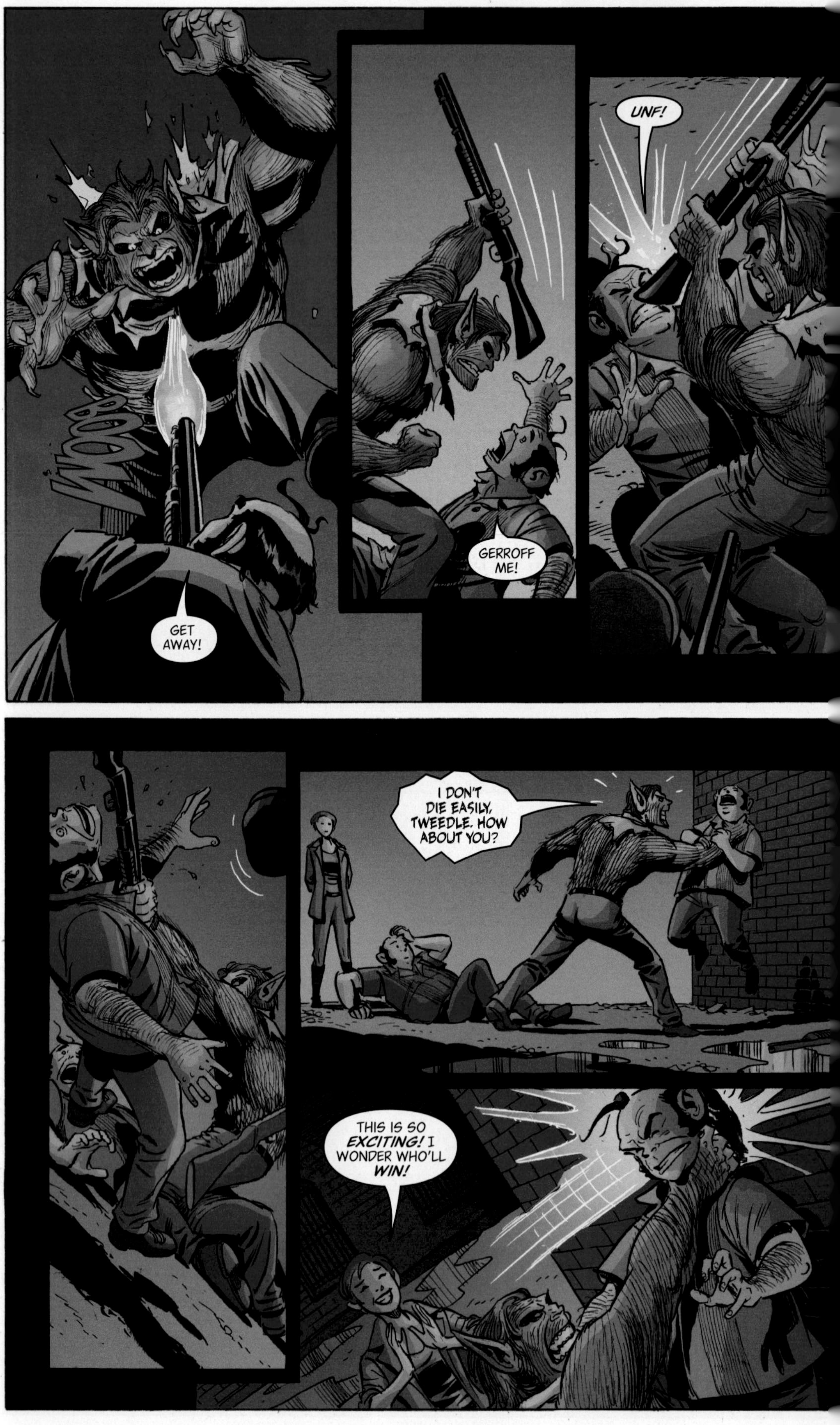
BOOM
GET AWAY!
GERROFF ME!
UNF!
I DON'T DIE EASILY, TWEEDLE. HOW ABOUT YOU?
THIS IS SO EXCITING! I WONDER WHO'LL WIN!

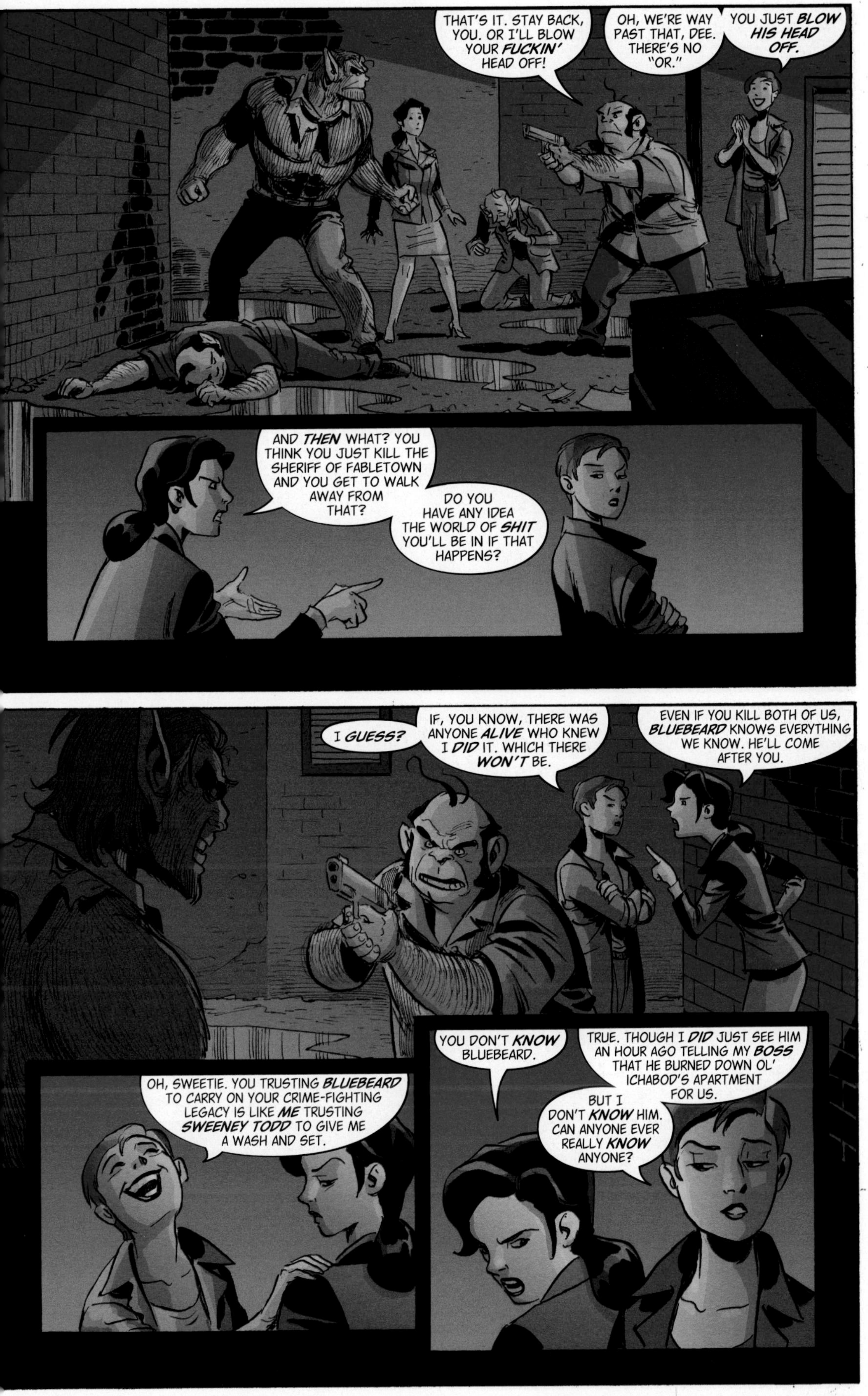
THAT'S IT. STAY BACK, YOU. OR I'LL BLOW YOUR FUCKIN' HEAD OFF!
OH, WE'RE WAY PAST THAT, DEE. THERE'S NO "OR."
YOU JUST BLOW HIS HEAD OFF.
AND THEN WHAT? YOU THINK YOU JUST KILL THE SHERIFF OF FABLETOWN AND YOU GET TO WALK AWAY FROM THAT?
DO YOU HAVE ANY IDEA THE WORLD OF SHIT YOU'LL BE IN IF THAT HAPPENS?
I GUESS?
IF, YOU KNOW, THERE WAS ANYONE ALIVE WHO KNEW I DID IT. WHICH THERE WON'T BE.
EVEN IF YOU KILL BOTH OF US, BLUEBEARD KNOWS EVERYTHING WE KNOW. HE'LL COME AFTER YOU.
OH, SWEETIE. YOU TRUSTING BLUEBEARD TO CARRY ON YOUR CRIME-FIGHTING LEGACY IS LIKE ME TRUSTING SWEENEY TODD TO GIVE ME A WASH AND SET.
YOU DON'T KNOW BLUEBEARD.
TRUE. THOUGH I DID JUST SEE HIM AN HOUR AGO TELLING MY BOSS THAT HE BURNED DOWN OL' ICHABOD'S APARTMENT FOR US.
BUT I DON'T KNOW HIM. CAN ANYONE EVER REALLY KNOW ANYONE?

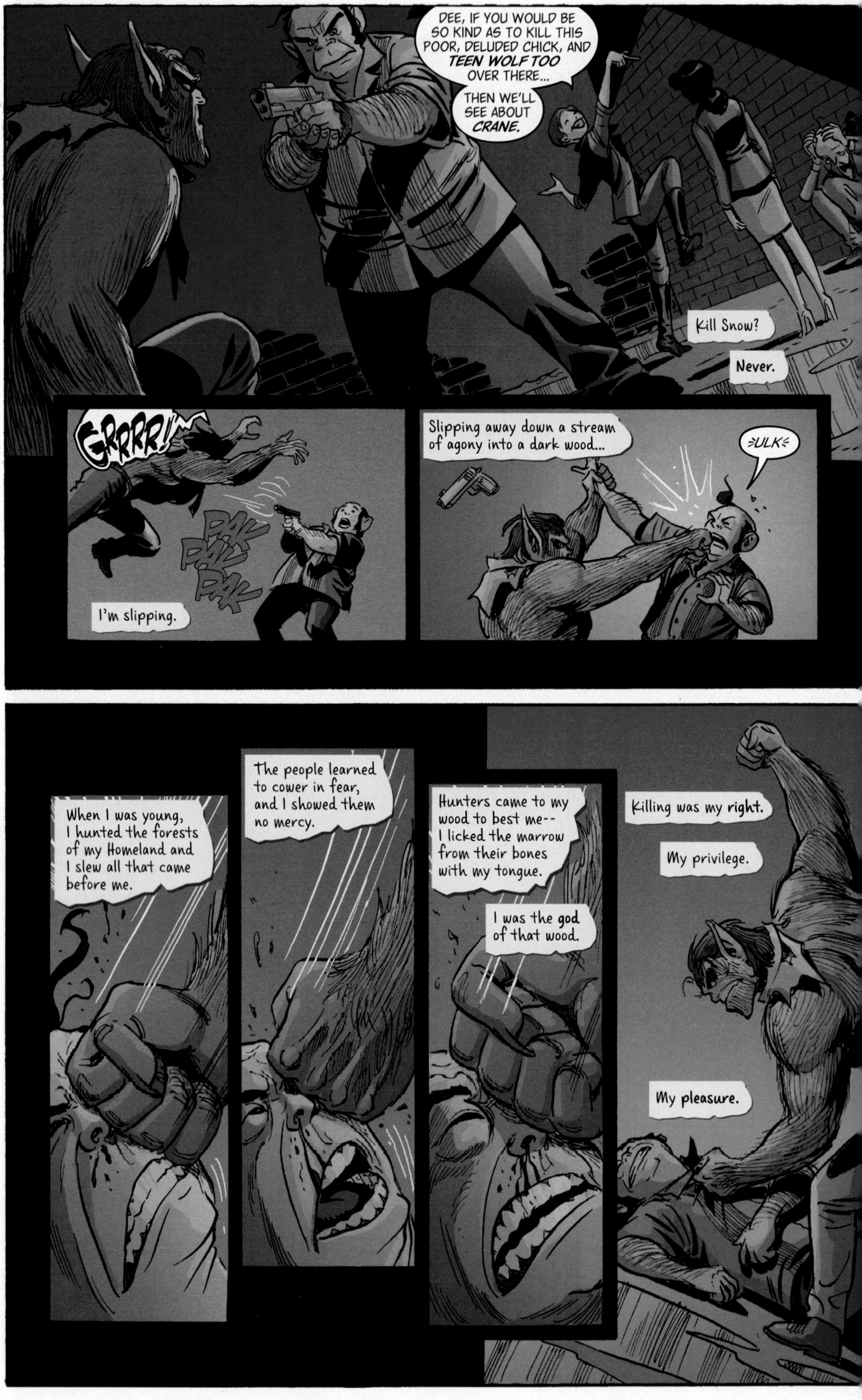

DEE, IF YOU WOULD BE SO KIND AS TO KILL THIS POOR, DELUDED CHICK, AND TEEN WOLF TOO OVER THERE...
THEN WE'LL SEE ABOUT CRANE.
Kill Snow?
Never.
GRRRR!
PAK PAK PAK
I'm slipping.
Slipping away down a stream of agony into a dark wood...
ULK
When I was young, I hunted the forests of my Homeland and I slew all that came before me.
The people learned to cower in fear, and I showed them no mercy.
Hunters came to my wood to best me-- I licked the marrow from their bones with my tongue.
I was the god of that wood.
Killing was my right.
My privilege.
My pleasure.

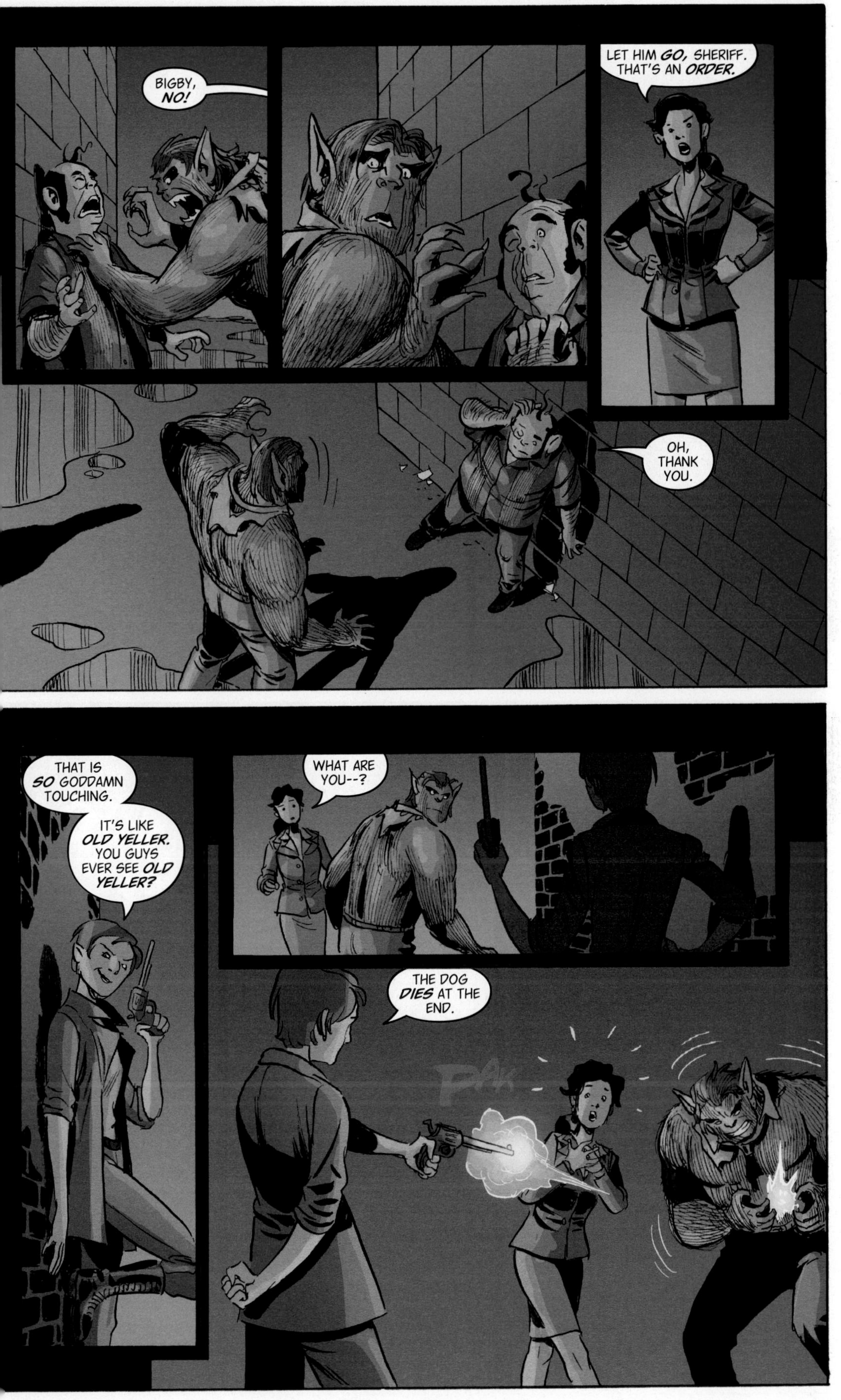
BIGBY, NO!
LET HIM GO, SHERIFF. THAT'S AN ORDER.
OH, THANK YOU.
THAT IS SO GODDAMN TOUCHING.
IT'S LIKE OLD YELLER. YOU GUYS EVER SEE OLD YELLER?
WHAT ARE YOU--?
THE DOG DIES AT THE END.

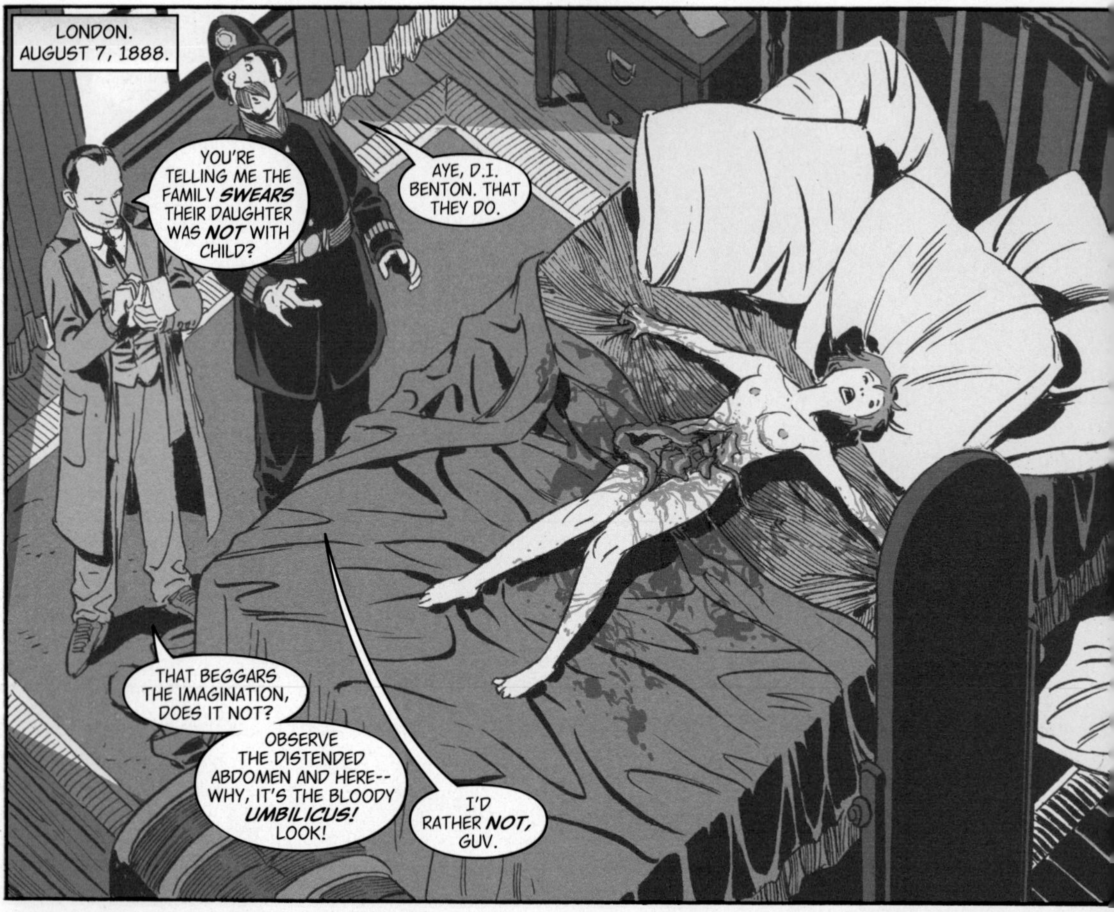
LONDON. AUGUST 7, 1888.
YOU'RE TELLING ME THE FAMILY **SWEARS** THEIR DAUGHTER WAS **NOT** WITH CHILD?
AYE, D.I. BENTON. THAT THEY DO.
THAT BEGGARS THE IMAGINATION, DOES IT NOT?
OBSERVE THE DISTENDED ABDOMEN AND HERE-- WHY, IT'S THE BLOODY **UMBILICUS!** LOOK!
I'D RATHER **NOT,** GUV.

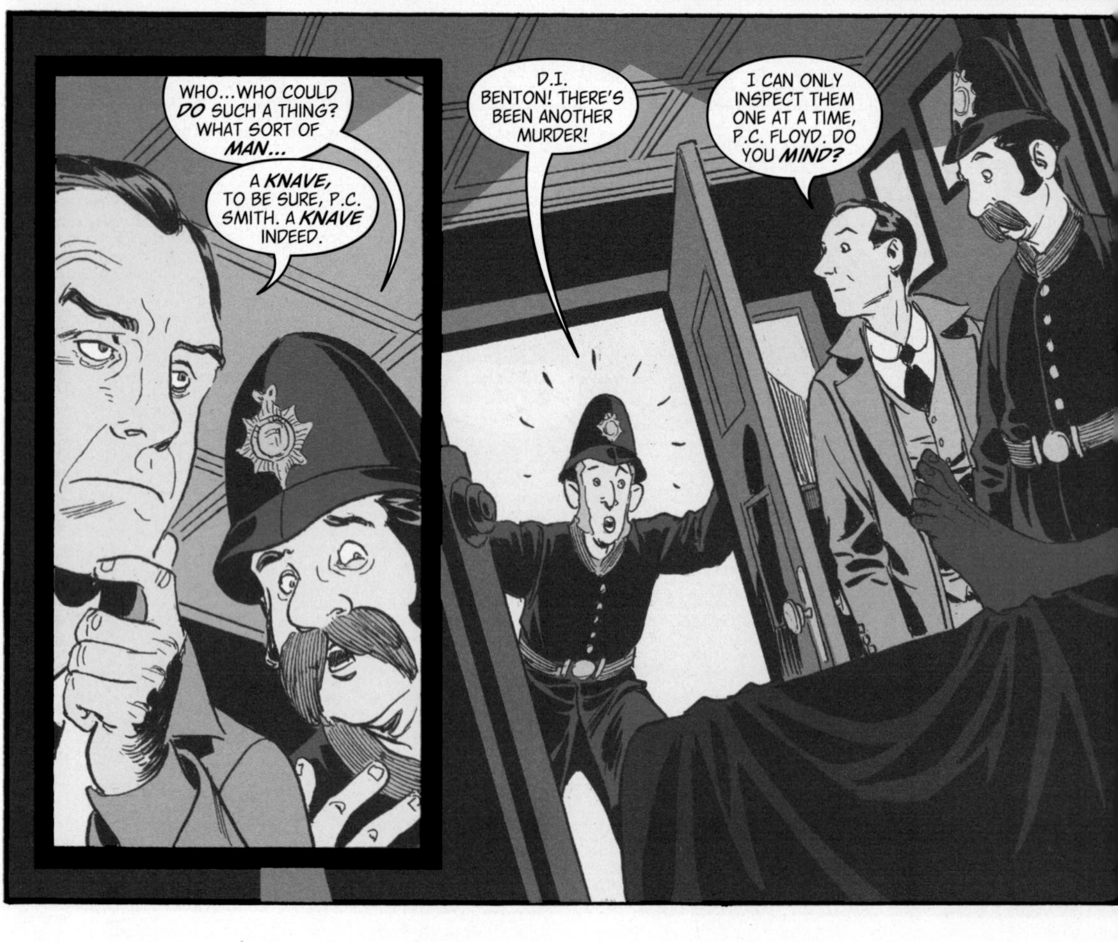
WHO...WHO COULD **DO** SUCH A THING? WHAT SORT OF **MAN...**
A **KNAVE,** TO BE SURE, P.C. SMITH. A **KNAVE** INDEED.
D.I. BENTON! THERE'S BEEN ANOTHER MURDER!
I CAN ONLY INSPECT THEM ONE AT A TIME, P.C. FLOYD. DO YOU **MIND?**

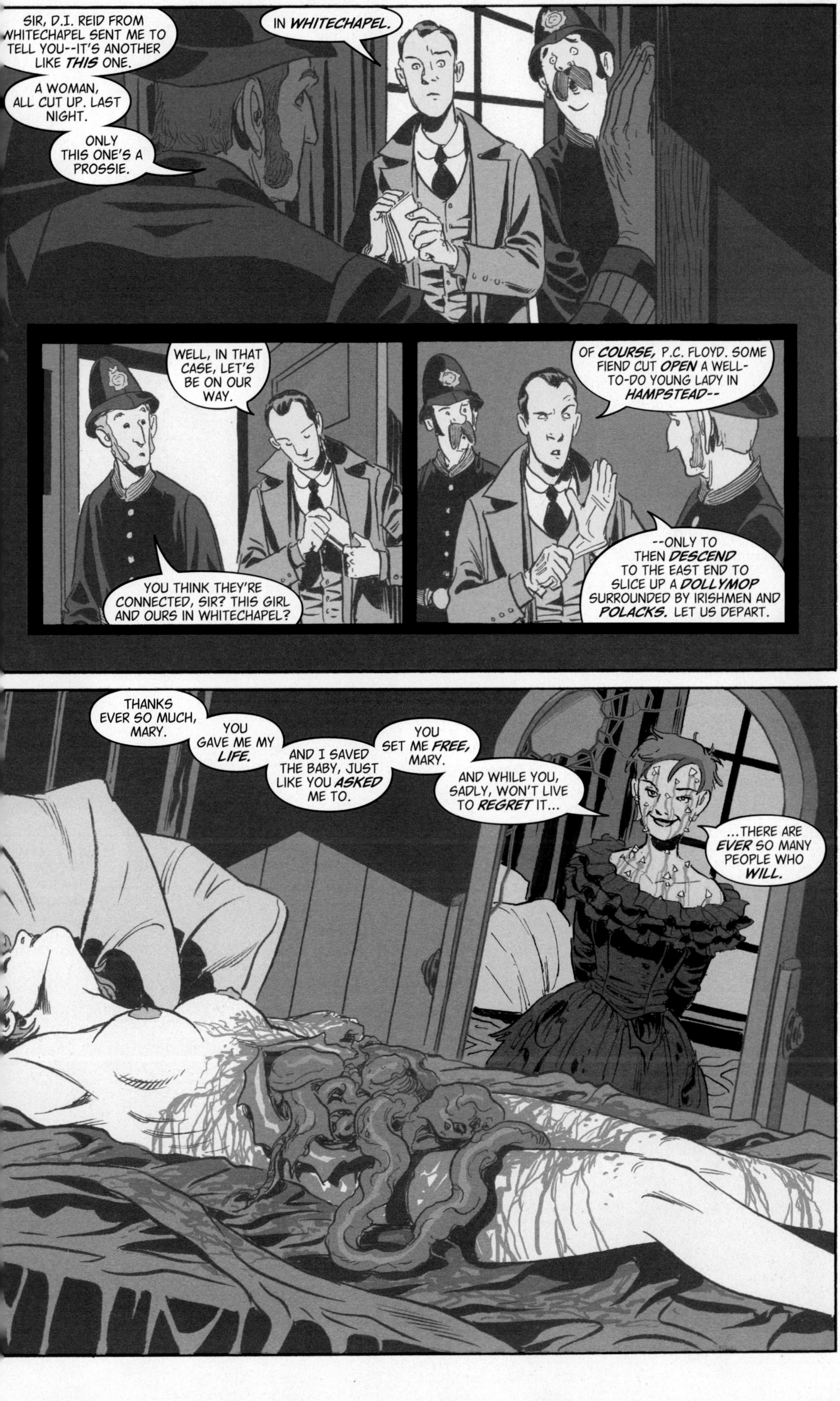
SIR, D.I. REID FROM WHITECHAPEL SENT ME TO TELL YOU--IT'S ANOTHER LIKE THIS ONE.
IN WHITECHAPEL.
A WOMAN, ALL CUT UP. LAST NIGHT.
ONLY THIS ONE'S A PROSSIE.
WELL, IN THAT CASE, LET'S BE ON OUR WAY.
YOU THINK THEY'RE CONNECTED, SIR? THIS GIRL AND OURS IN WHITECHAPEL?
OF COURSE, P.C. FLOYD. SOME FIEND CUT OPEN A WELL-TO-DO YOUNG LADY IN HAMPSTEAD--
--ONLY TO THEN DESCEND TO THE EAST END TO SLICE UP A DOLLYMOP SURROUNDED BY IRISHMEN AND POLACKS. LET US DEPART.
THANKS EVER SO MUCH, MARY.
YOU GAVE ME MY LIFE.
AND I SAVED THE BABY, JUST LIKE YOU ASKED ME TO.
YOU SET ME FREE, MARY.
AND WHILE YOU, SADLY, WON'T LIVE TO REGRET IT...
...THERE ARE EVER SO MANY PEOPLE WHO WILL.

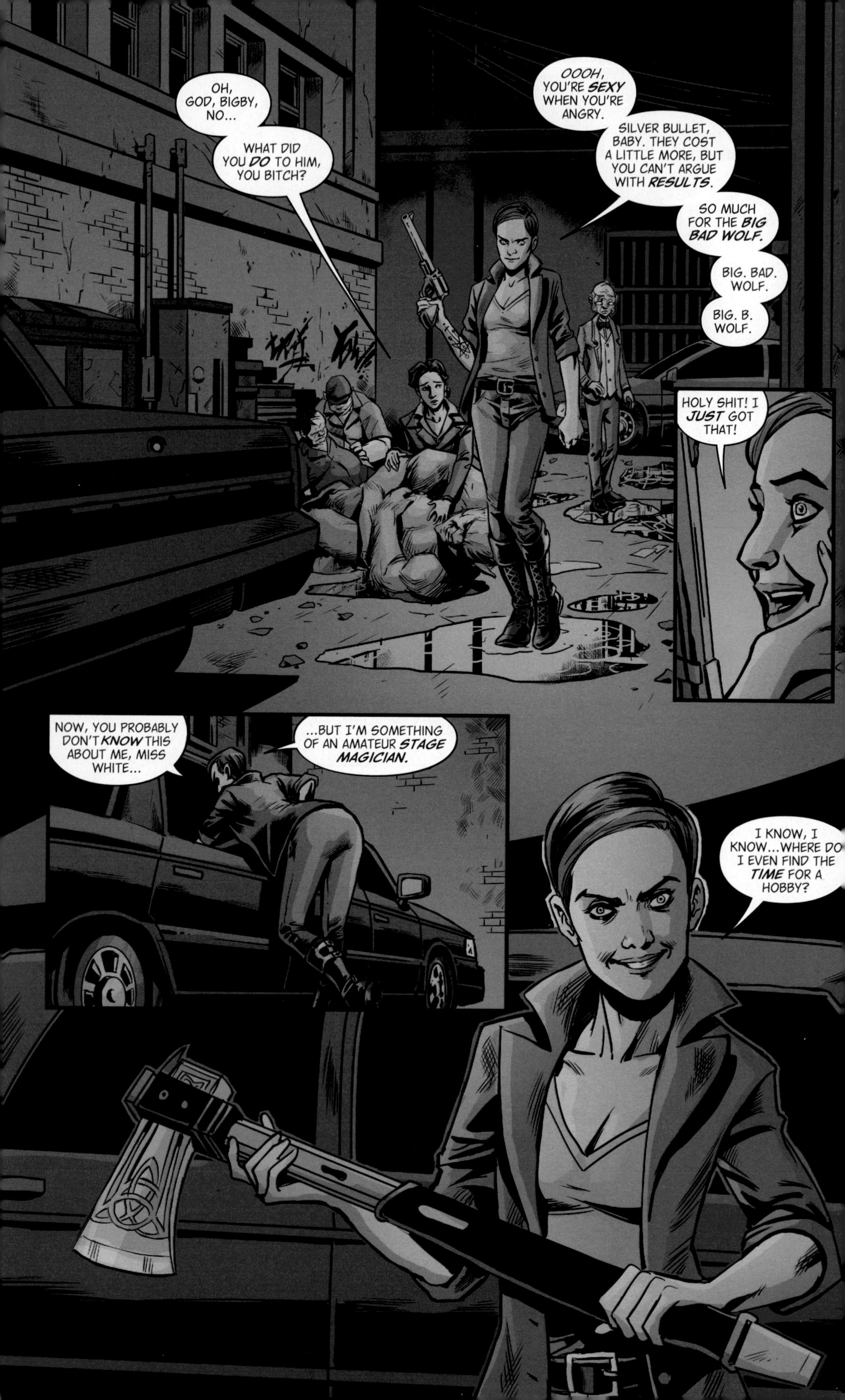
OH, GOD, BIGBY, NO...
WHAT DID YOU DO TO HIM, YOU BITCH?
OOOH, YOU'RE SEXY WHEN YOU'RE ANGRY.
SILVER BULLET, BABY. THEY COST A LITTLE MORE, BUT YOU CAN'T ARGUE WITH RESULTS.
SO MUCH FOR THE BIG BAD WOLF.
BIG. BAD. WOLF.
BIG. B. WOLF.
HOLY SHIT! I JUST GOT THAT!
NOW, YOU PROBABLY DON'T KNOW THIS ABOUT ME, MISS WHITE...
...BUT I'M SOMETHING OF AN AMATEUR STAGE MAGICIAN.
I KNOW, I KNOW...WHERE DO I EVEN FIND THE TIME FOR A HOBBY?

THE THING ABOUT MAGIC IS, THERE ARE **SO MANY ELEMENTS** THAT YOU'VE GOT TO PERFECT.

YOU GOTTA HAVE SOME **PYROTECHNICS**, TO REALLY START THINGS OFF WITH A **BANG!**

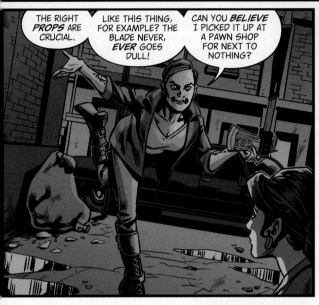

THE RIGHT **PROPS** ARE CRUCIAL.

LIKE THIS THING, FOR EXAMPLE? THE BLADE NEVER, **EVER** GOES DULL!

CAN YOU **BELIEVE** I PICKED IT UP AT A PAWN SHOP FOR NEXT TO NOTHING?

IT HELPS TO HAVE A SMOKIN' HOT **ASSISTANT.**

YOU EVER CONSIDERED **FISHNETS,** WHITE?

POP THE TOP COUPLE **BUTTONS** ON THAT BLOUSE, GIVE THE CROWD WHAT THEY **REALLY** WANT?

ANYWAY, GOTTA WORK UP SOME **STAGE PATTER,** OF COURSE.

LAAAADIES AND GENTLEMEN! SCUMBAG DEPUTY MAYORS OF ALL AGES!

THE GREAT **BLOODY MARY** WILL PERFORM A FEAT OF PRESTIDIT...

...PRESTIDIGITIZ...

...FUCKIN' **MAGIC!**

WATCH IN WONDER AS I SAW THIS SHERIFF IN **HALF** BEFORE YOUR VERY EYES!

NO SMOKE! NO MIRRORS!

AND THEN, OF COURSE, THE SUBTLE ART OF MISDIRECTION...

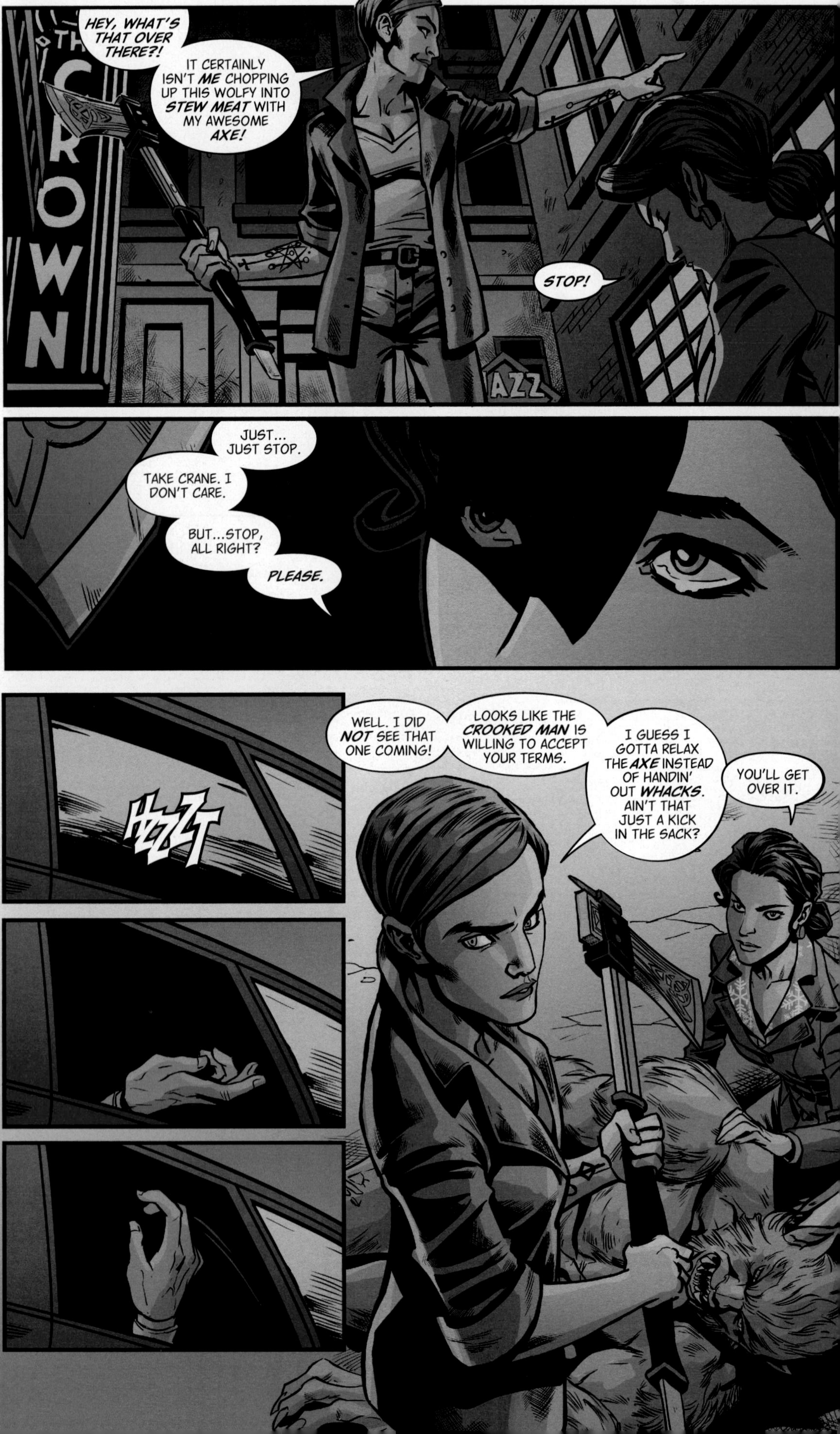
HEY, WHAT'S THAT OVER THERE?!
IT CERTAINLY ISN'T ME CHOPPING UP THIS WOLFY INTO STEW MEAT WITH MY AWESOME AXE!
STOP!
JUST... JUST STOP.
TAKE CRANE. I DON'T CARE.
BUT...STOP, ALL RIGHT?
PLEASE.
HZZZT
WELL. I DID NOT SEE THAT ONE COMING!
LOOKS LIKE THE CROOKED MAN IS WILLING TO ACCEPT YOUR TERMS.
I GUESS I GOTTA RELAX THE AXE INSTEAD OF HANDIN' OUT WHACKS. AIN'T THAT JUST A KICK IN THE SACK?
YOU'LL GET OVER IT.

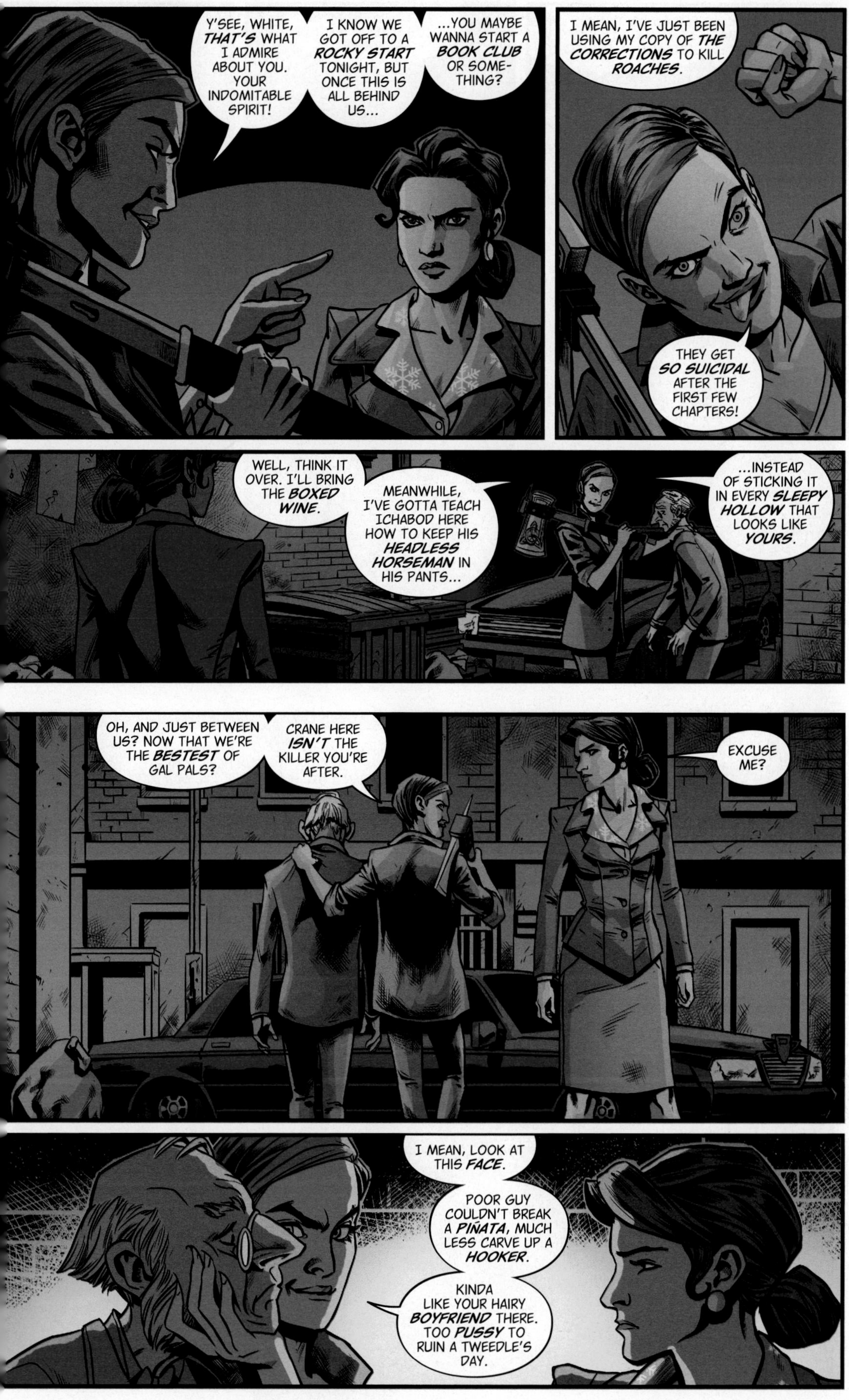
Y'SEE, WHITE, THAT'S WHAT I ADMIRE ABOUT YOU. YOUR INDOMITABLE SPIRIT!
I KNOW WE GOT OFF TO A ROCKY START TONIGHT, BUT ONCE THIS IS ALL BEHIND US...
...YOU MAYBE WANNA START A BOOK CLUB OR SOME-THING?
I MEAN, I'VE JUST BEEN USING MY COPY OF THE CORRECTIONS TO KILL ROACHES.
THEY GET SO SUICIDAL AFTER THE FIRST FEW CHAPTERS!
WELL, THINK IT OVER. I'LL BRING THE BOXED WINE.
MEANWHILE, I'VE GOTTA TEACH ICHABOD HERE HOW TO KEEP HIS HEADLESS HORSEMAN IN HIS PANTS...
...INSTEAD OF STICKING IT IN EVERY SLEEPY HOLLOW THAT LOOKS LIKE YOURS.
OH, AND JUST BETWEEN US? NOW THAT WE'RE THE BESTEST OF GAL PALS?
CRANE HERE ISN'T THE KILLER YOU'RE AFTER.
EXCUSE ME?
I MEAN, LOOK AT THIS FACE.
POOR GUY COULDN'T BREAK A PIÑATA, MUCH LESS CARVE UP A HOOKER.
KINDA LIKE YOUR HAIRY BOYFRIEND THERE. TOO PUSSY TO RUIN A TWEEDLE'S DAY.

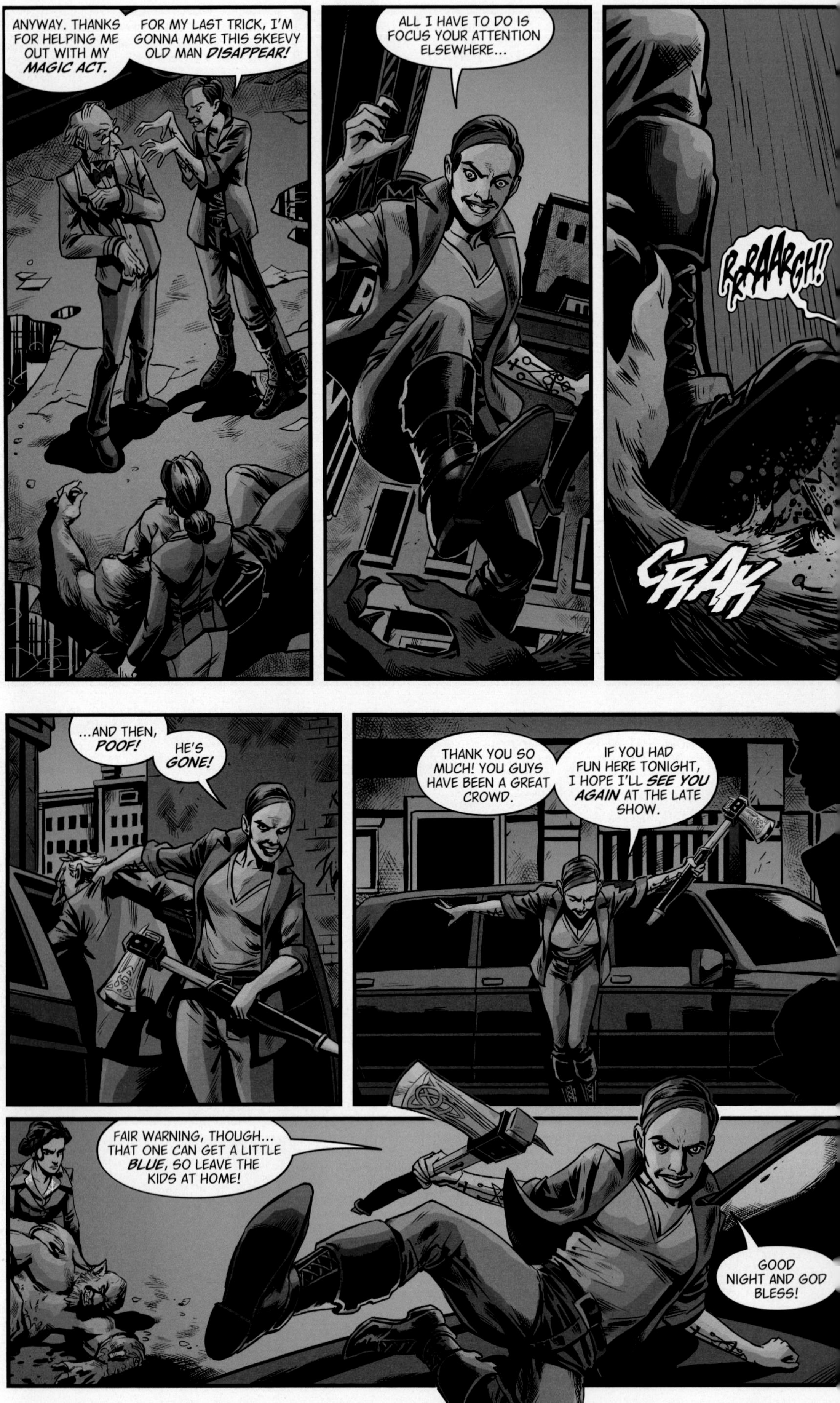
ANYWAY. THANKS FOR HELPING ME OUT WITH MY MAGIC ACT.
FOR MY LAST TRICK, I'M GONNA MAKE THIS SKEEVY OLD MAN DISAPPEAR!
ALL I HAVE TO DO IS FOCUS YOUR ATTENTION ELSEWHERE...
RRRAAARGH!
CRAK
...AND THEN, POOF!
HE'S GONE!
THANK YOU SO MUCH! YOU GUYS HAVE BEEN A GREAT CROWD.
IF YOU HAD FUN HERE TONIGHT, I HOPE I'LL SEE YOU AGAIN AT THE LATE SHOW.
FAIR WARNING, THOUGH... THAT ONE CAN GET A LITTLE BLUE, SO LEAVE THE KIDS AT HOME!
GOOD NIGHT AND GOD BLESS!

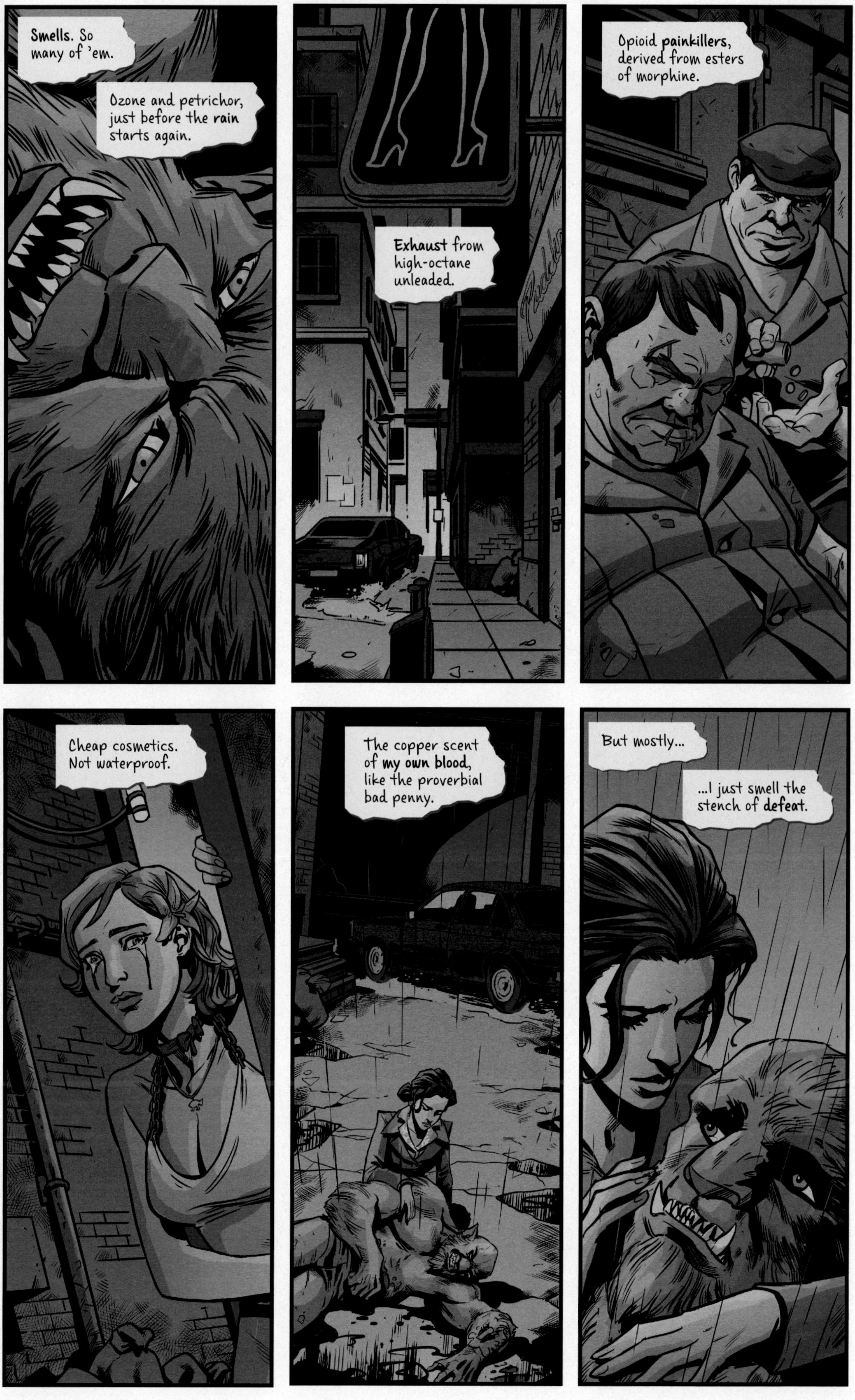
Smells. So many of 'em.
Ozone and petrichor, just before the rain starts again.
Exhaust from high-octane unleaded.
Opioid painkillers, derived from esters of morphine.
Cheap cosmetics. Not waterproof.
The copper scent of my own blood, like the proverbial bad penny.
But mostly...
...I just smell the stench of defeat.

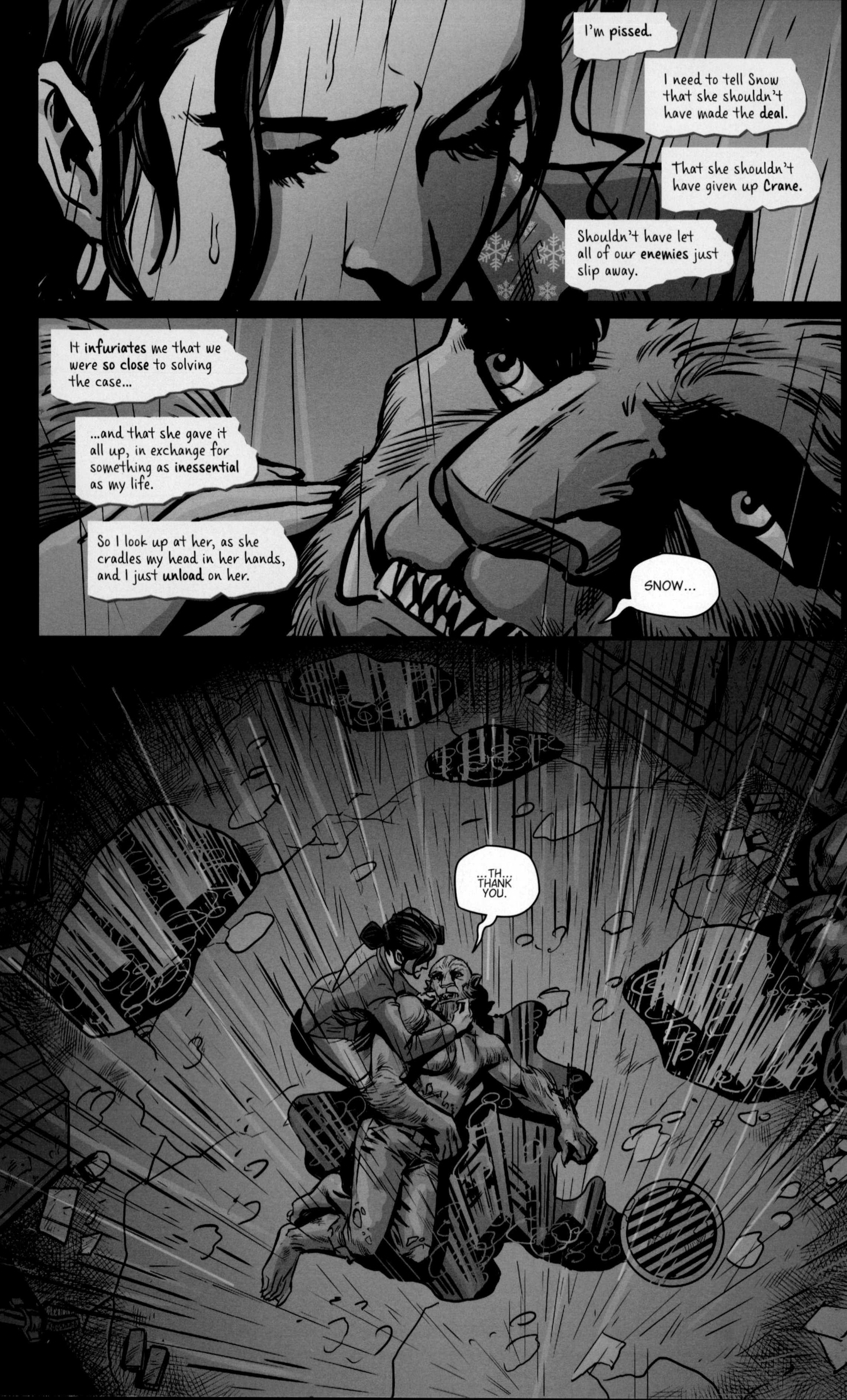
I'm pissed.
I need to tell Snow that she shouldn't have made the deal.
That she shouldn't have given up Crane.
Shouldn't have let all of our enemies just slip away.
It infuriates me that we were so close to solving the case...
...and that she gave it all up, in exchange for something as inessential as my life.
So I look up at her, as she cradles my head in her hands, and I just unload on her.
SNOW...
...TH... THANK YOU.

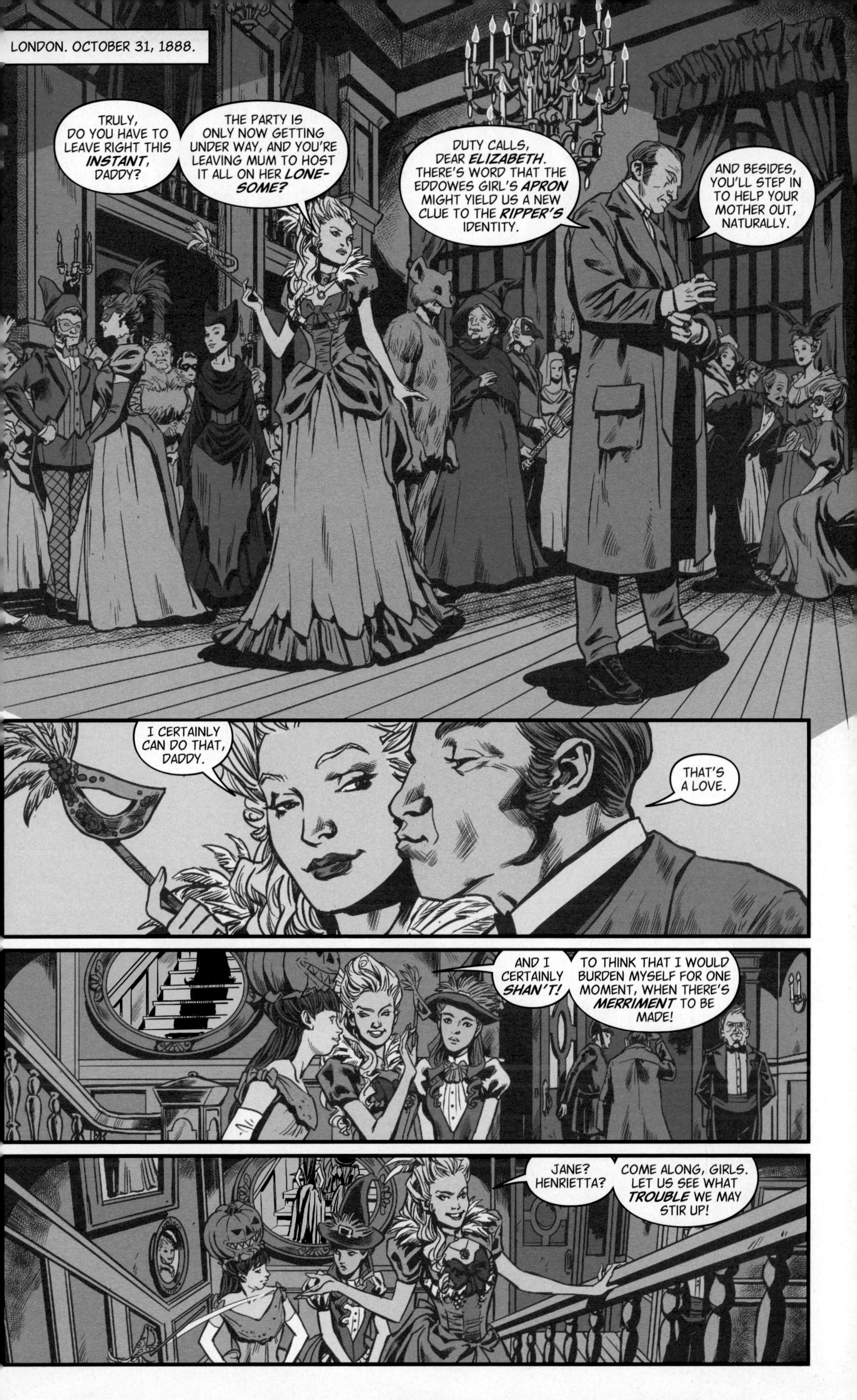
LONDON. OCTOBER 31, 1888.
TRULY, DO YOU HAVE TO LEAVE RIGHT THIS INSTANT, DADDY?
THE PARTY IS ONLY NOW GETTING UNDER WAY, AND YOU'RE LEAVING MUM TO HOST IT ALL ON HER LONESOME?
DUTY CALLS, DEAR ELIZABETH. THERE'S WORD THAT THE EDDOWES GIRL'S APRON MIGHT YIELD US A NEW CLUE TO THE RIPPER'S IDENTITY.
AND BESIDES, YOU'LL STEP IN TO HELP YOUR MOTHER OUT, NATURALLY.
I CERTAINLY CAN DO THAT, DADDY.
THAT'S A LOVE.
AND I CERTAINLY SHAN'T!
TO THINK THAT I WOULD BURDEN MYSELF FOR ONE MOMENT, WHEN THERE'S MERRIMENT TO BE MADE!
JANE? HENRIETTA?
COME ALONG, GIRLS. LET US SEE WHAT TROUBLE WE MAY STIR UP!

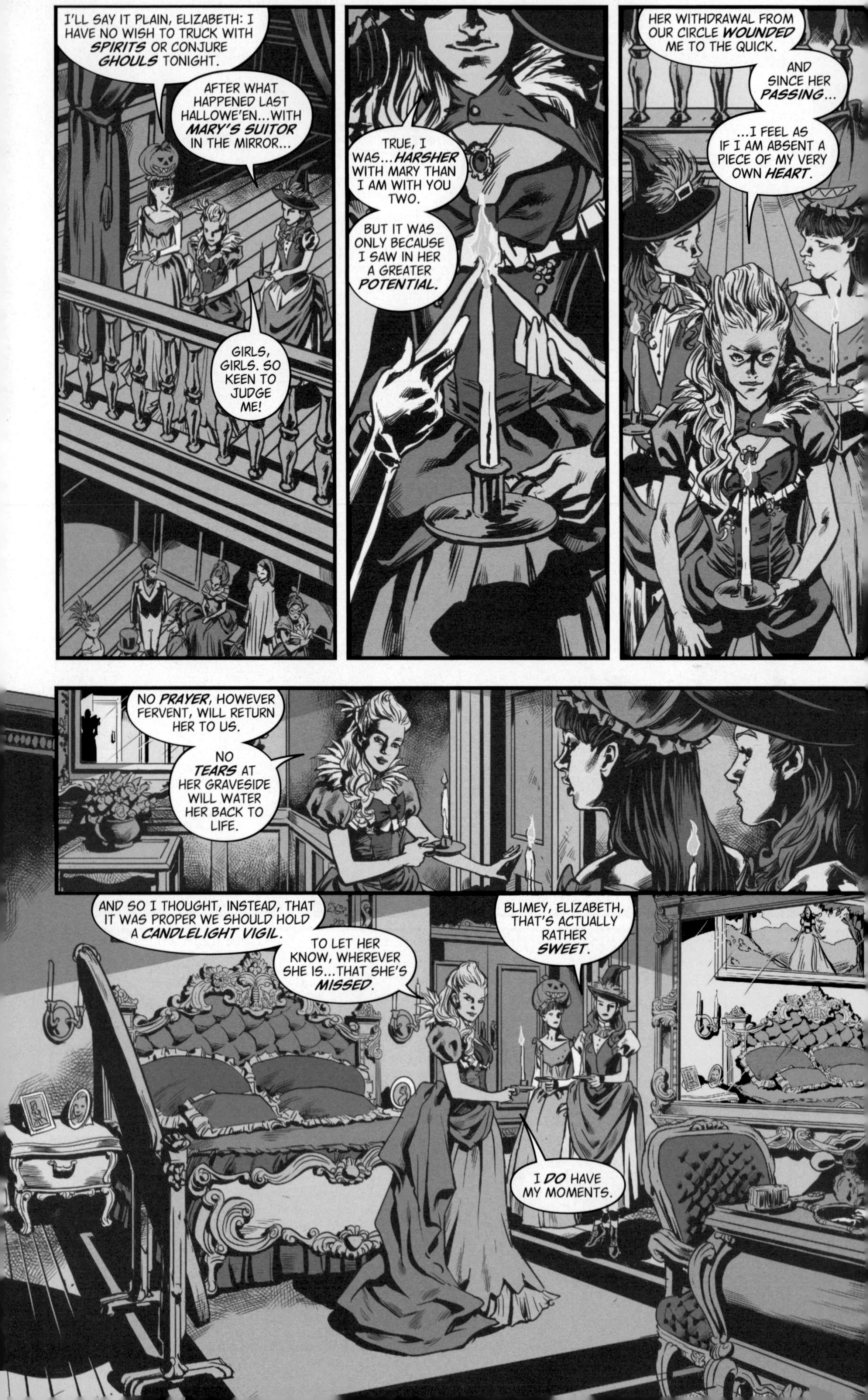
I'LL SAY IT PLAIN, ELIZABETH: I HAVE NO WISH TO TRUCK WITH SPIRITS OR CONJURE GHOULS TONIGHT.
AFTER WHAT HAPPENED LAST HALLOWE'EN...WITH MARY'S SUITOR IN THE MIRROR...
GIRLS, GIRLS. SO KEEN TO JUDGE ME!
TRUE, I WAS...HARSHER WITH MARY THAN I AM WITH YOU TWO.
BUT IT WAS ONLY BECAUSE I SAW IN HER A GREATER POTENTIAL.
HER WITHDRAWAL FROM OUR CIRCLE WOUNDED ME TO THE QUICK.
AND SINCE HER PASSING...
...I FEEL AS IF I AM ABSENT A PIECE OF MY VERY OWN HEART.
NO PRAYER, HOWEVER FERVENT, WILL RETURN HER TO US.
NO TEARS AT HER GRAVESIDE WILL WATER HER BACK TO LIFE.
AND SO I THOUGHT, INSTEAD, THAT IT WAS PROPER WE SHOULD HOLD A CANDLELIGHT VIGIL.
TO LET HER KNOW, WHEREVER SHE IS...THAT SHE'S MISSED.
BLIMEY, ELIZABETH, THAT'S ACTUALLY RATHER SWEET.
I DO HAVE MY MOMENTS.

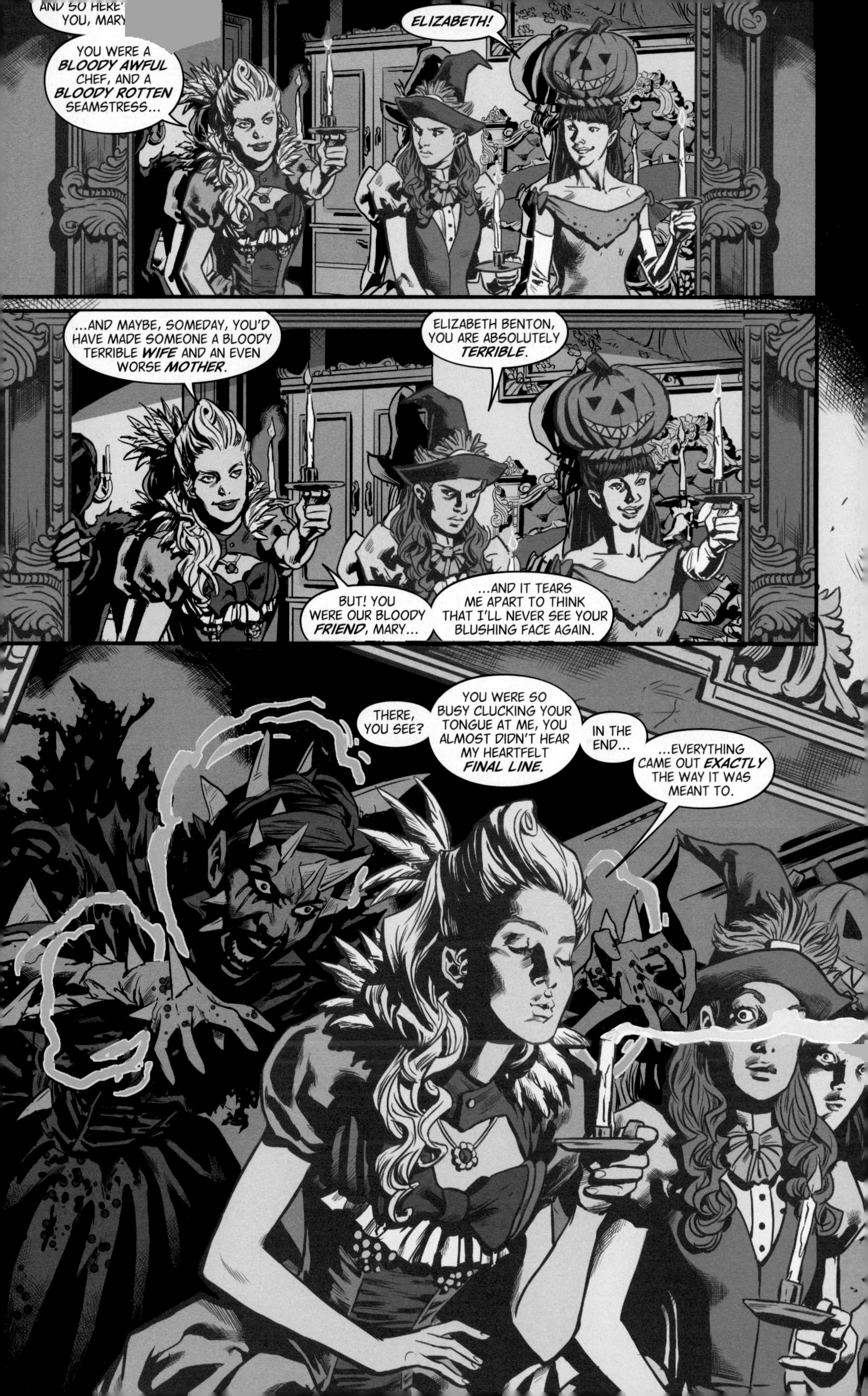
AND SO HERE
YOU, MARY
YOU WERE A BLOODY AWFUL CHEF, AND A BLOODY ROTTEN SEAMSTRESS...
ELIZABETH!
...AND MAYBE, SOMEDAY, YOU'D HAVE MADE SOMEONE A BLOODY TERRIBLE WIFE AND AN EVEN WORSE MOTHER.
ELIZABETH BENTON, YOU ARE ABSOLUTELY TERRIBLE.
BUT! YOU WERE OUR BLOODY FRIEND, MARY...
...AND IT TEARS ME APART TO THINK THAT I'LL NEVER SEE YOUR BLUSHING FACE AGAIN.
THERE, YOU SEE?
YOU WERE SO BUSY CLUCKING YOUR TONGUE AT ME, YOU ALMOST DIDN'T HEAR MY HEARTFELT FINAL LINE.
IN THE END...
...EVERYTHING CAME OUT EXACTLY THE WAY IT WAS MEANT TO.

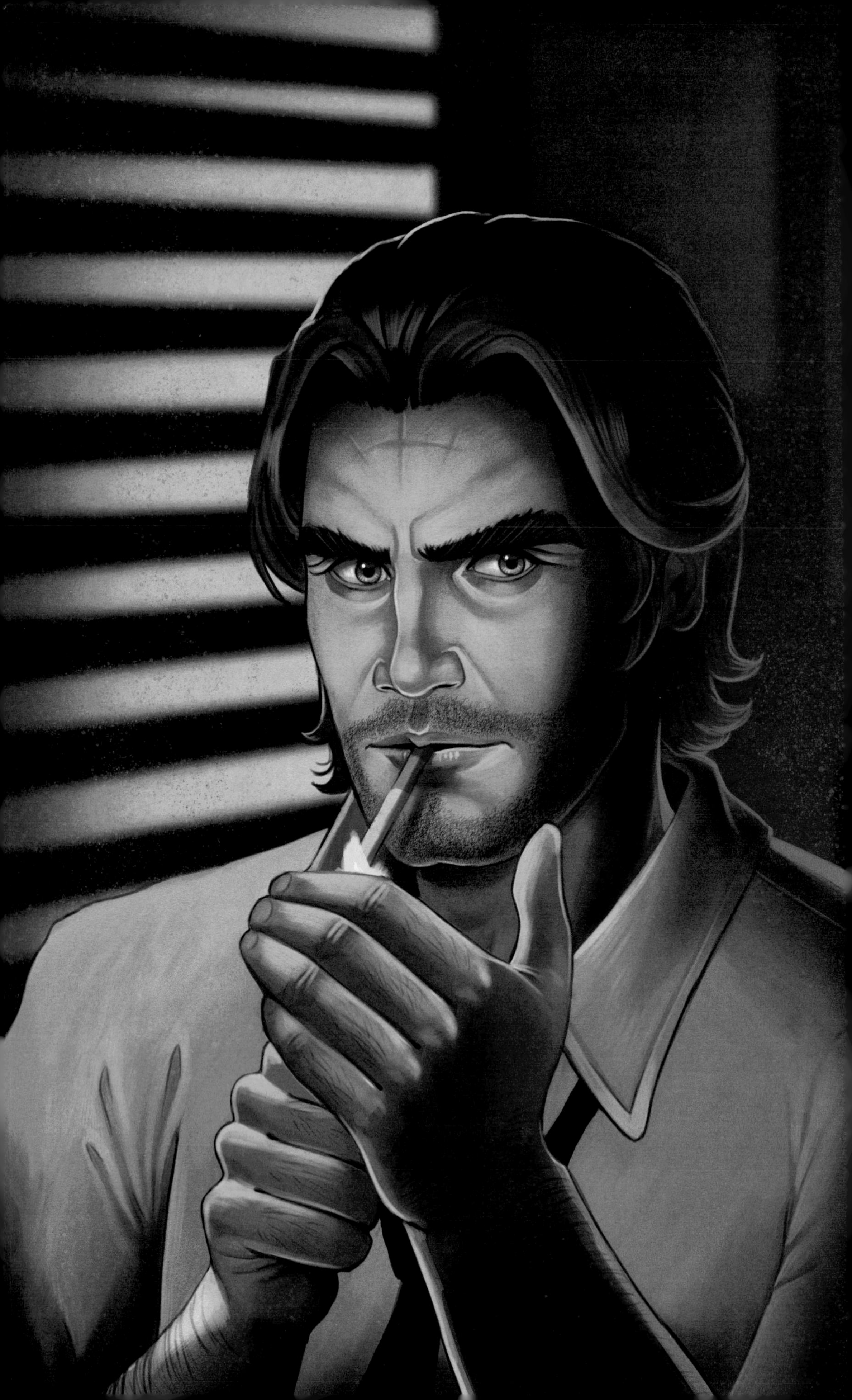

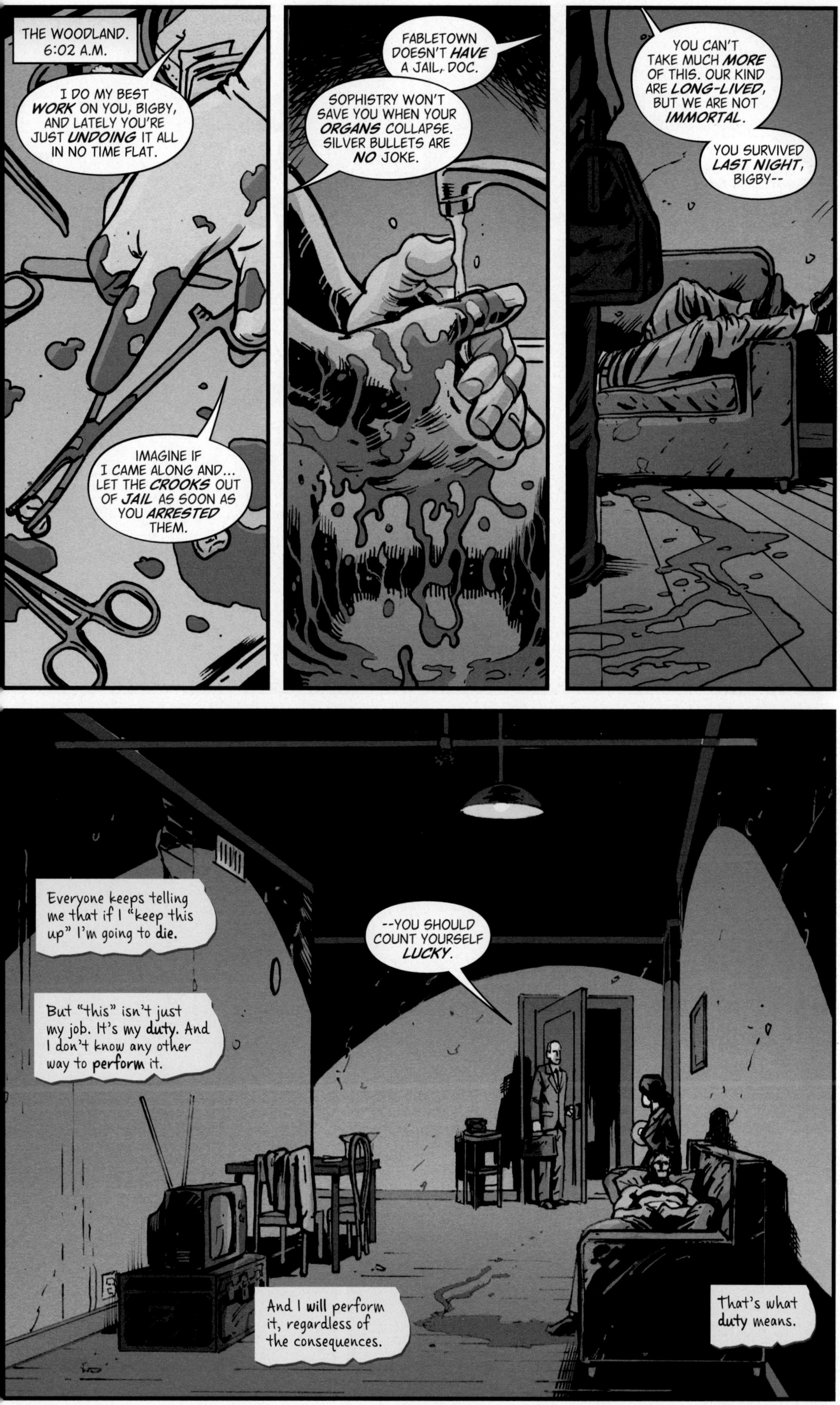
THE WOODLAND. 6:02 A.M.
I DO MY BEST WORK ON YOU, BIGBY, AND LATELY YOU'RE JUST UNDOING IT ALL IN NO TIME FLAT.
IMAGINE IF I CAME ALONG AND... LET THE CROOKS OUT OF JAIL AS SOON AS YOU ARRESTED THEM.
FABLETOWN DOESN'T HAVE A JAIL, DOC.
SOPHISTRY WON'T SAVE YOU WHEN YOUR ORGANS COLLAPSE. SILVER BULLETS ARE NO JOKE.
YOU CAN'T TAKE MUCH MORE OF THIS. OUR KIND ARE LONG-LIVED, BUT WE ARE NOT IMMORTAL.
YOU SURVIVED LAST NIGHT, BIGBY--
Everyone keeps telling me that if I "keep this up" I'm going to die.
--YOU SHOULD COUNT YOURSELF LUCKY.
But "this" isn't just my job. It's my duty. And I don't know any other way to perform it.
And I will perform it, regardless of the consequences.
That's what duty means.

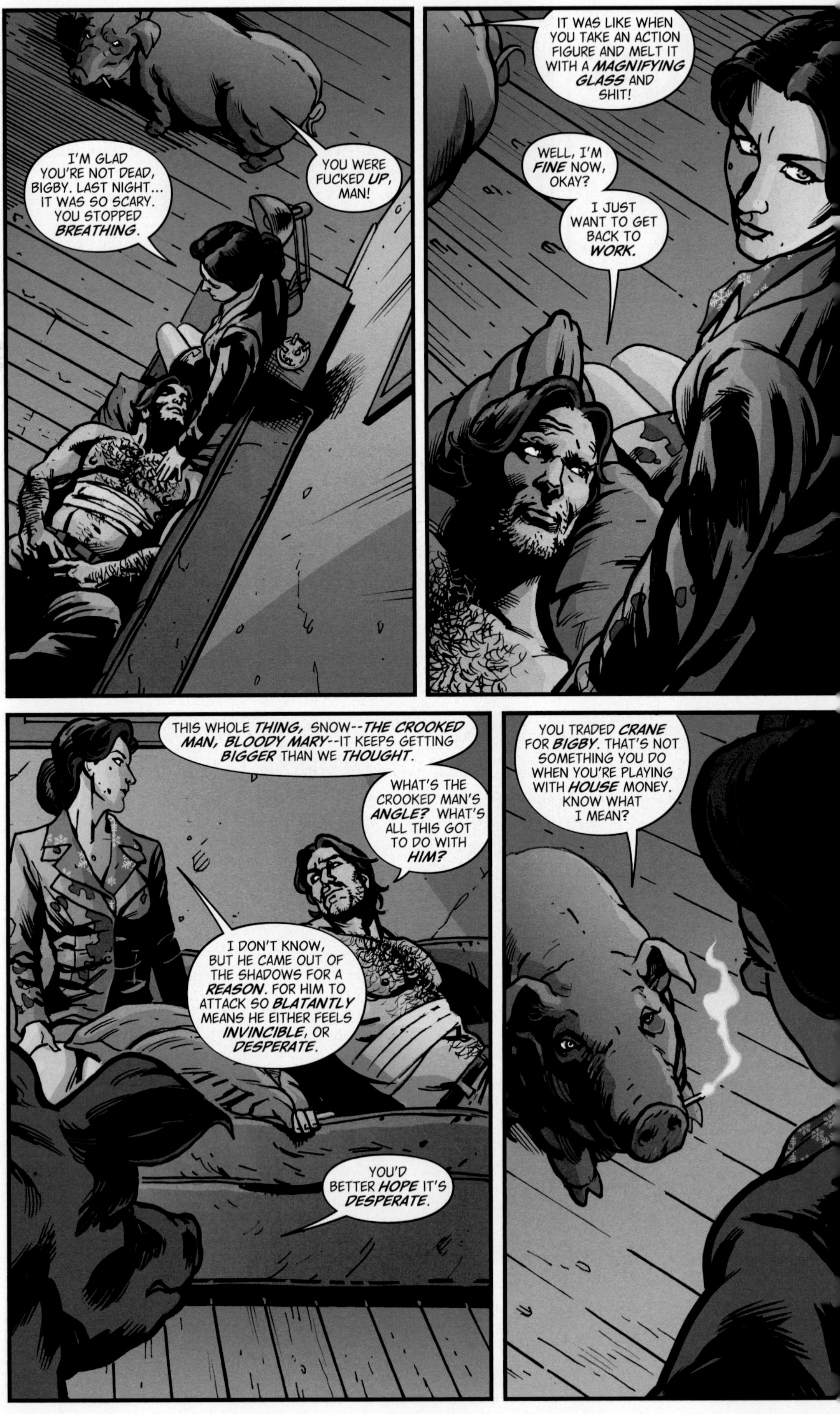
I'M GLAD YOU'RE NOT DEAD, BIGBY. LAST NIGHT... IT WAS SO SCARY. YOU STOPPED *BREATHING*.
YOU WERE FUCKED *UP*, MAN!
IT WAS LIKE WHEN YOU TAKE AN ACTION FIGURE AND MELT IT WITH A *MAGNIFYING GLASS* AND SHIT!
WELL, I'M *FINE* NOW, OKAY?
I JUST WANT TO GET BACK TO *WORK.*
THIS WHOLE *THING,* SNOW--*THE CROOKED MAN, BLOODY MARY*--IT KEEPS GETTING *BIGGER* THAN WE *THOUGHT*.
WHAT'S THE CROOKED MAN'S *ANGLE?* WHAT'S ALL THIS GOT TO DO WITH *HIM?*
I DON'T KNOW, BUT HE CAME OUT OF THE SHADOWS FOR A *REASON*. FOR HIM TO ATTACK SO *BLATANTLY* MEANS HE EITHER FEELS *INVINCIBLE*, OR *DESPERATE*.
YOU'D BETTER *HOPE* IT'S *DESPERATE*.
YOU TRADED *CRANE* FOR *BIGBY*. THAT'S NOT SOMETHING YOU DO WHEN YOU'RE PLAYING WITH *HOUSE* MONEY. KNOW WHAT I MEAN?

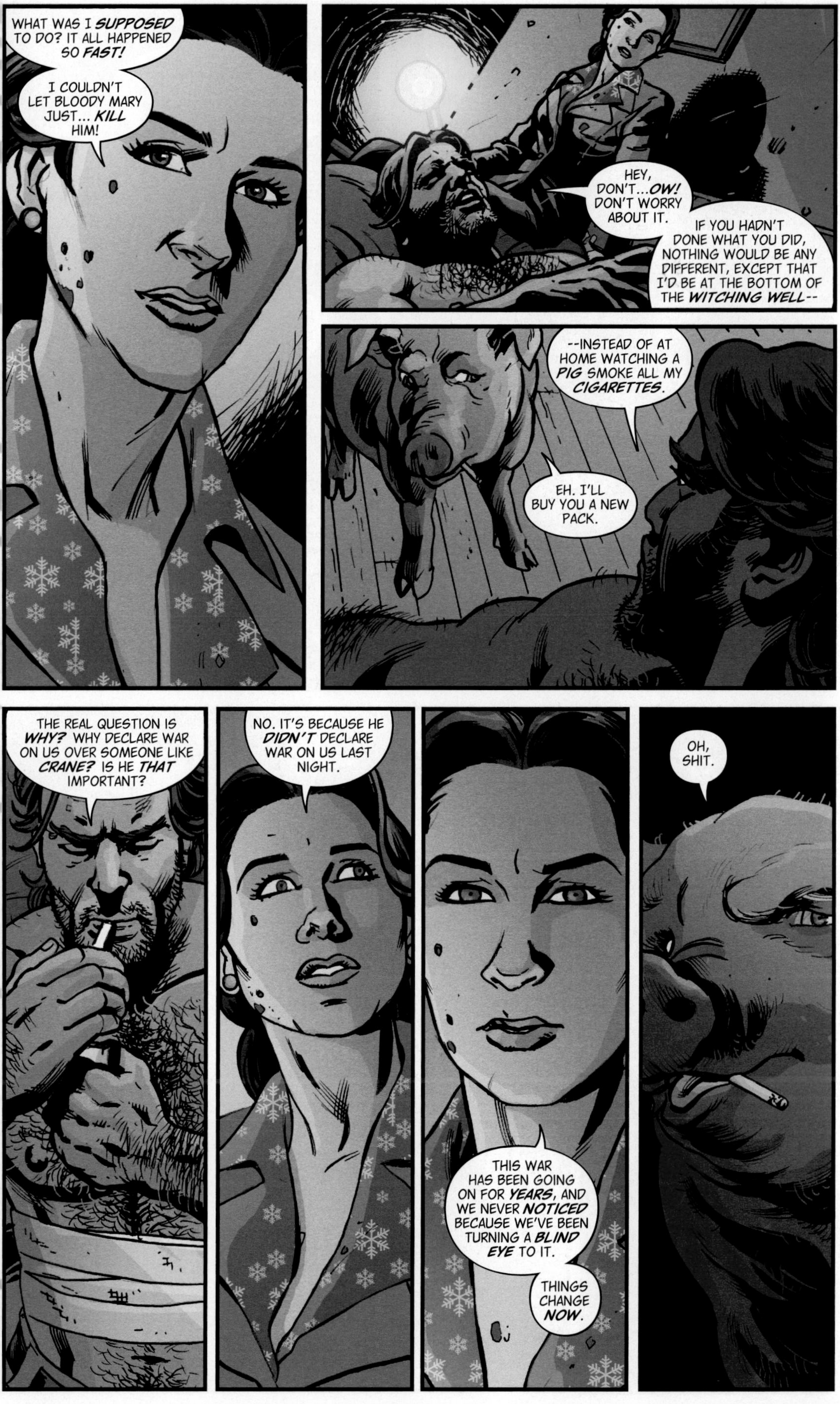

WHAT WAS I SUPPOSED TO DO? IT ALL HAPPENED SO FAST!
I COULDN'T LET BLOODY MARY JUST... KILL HIM!
HEY, DON'T...OW! DON'T WORRY ABOUT IT.
IF YOU HADN'T DONE WHAT YOU DID, NOTHING WOULD BE ANY DIFFERENT, EXCEPT THAT I'D BE AT THE BOTTOM OF THE WITCHING WELL--
--INSTEAD OF AT HOME WATCHING A PIG SMOKE ALL MY CIGARETTES.
EH. I'LL BUY YOU A NEW PACK.
THE REAL QUESTION IS WHY? WHY DECLARE WAR ON US OVER SOMEONE LIKE CRANE? IS HE THAT IMPORTANT?
NO. IT'S BECAUSE HE DIDN'T DECLARE WAR ON US LAST NIGHT.
THIS WAR HAS BEEN GOING ON FOR YEARS, AND WE NEVER NOTICED BECAUSE WE'VE BEEN TURNING A BLIND EYE TO IT.
THINGS CHANGE NOW.
OH, SHIT.

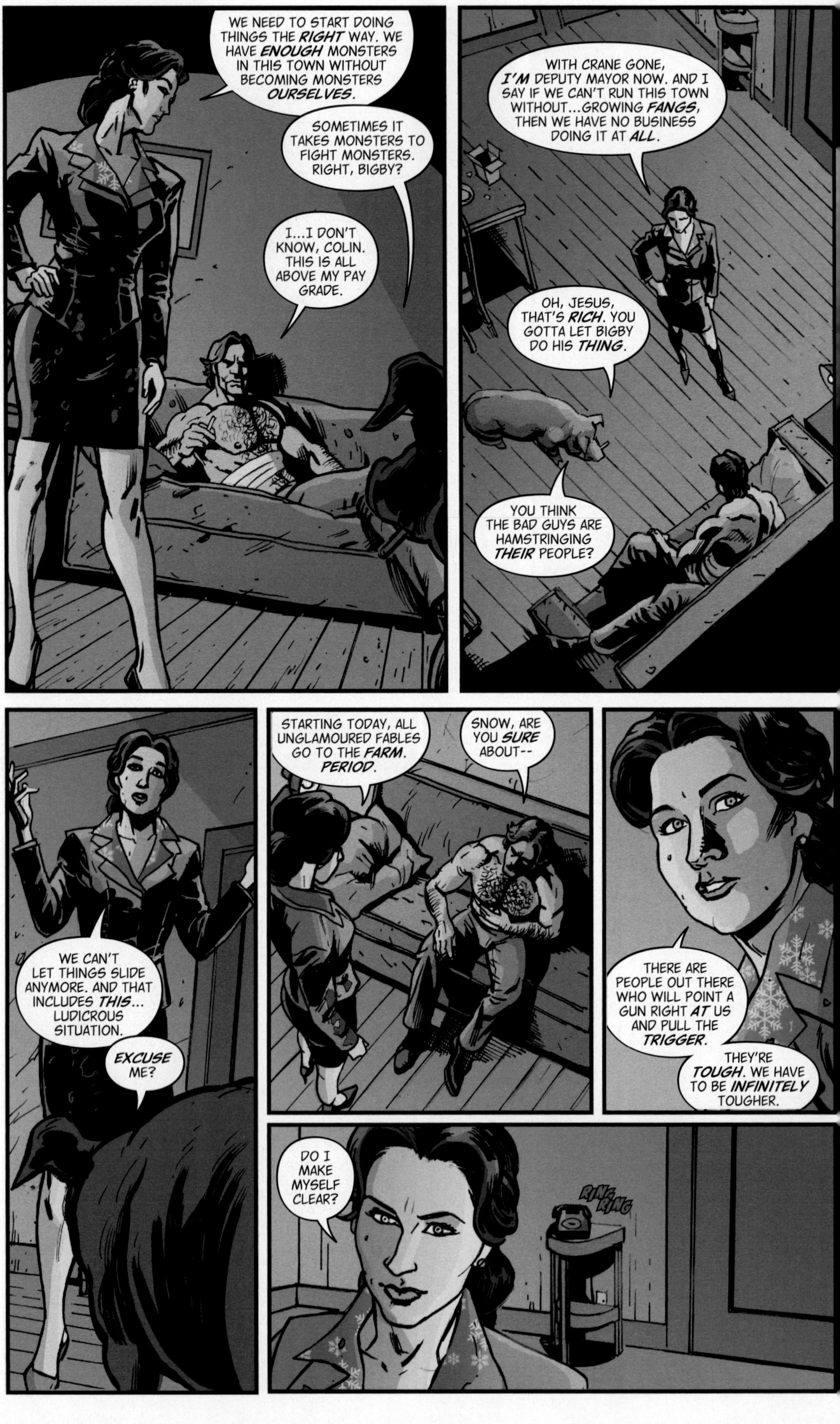

WE NEED TO START DOING THINGS THE ***RIGHT*** WAY. WE HAVE ***ENOUGH*** MONSTERS IN THIS TOWN WITHOUT BECOMING MONSTERS ***OURSELVES***.
SOMETIMES IT TAKES MONSTERS TO FIGHT MONSTERS. RIGHT, BIGBY?
I...I DON'T KNOW, COLIN. THIS IS ALL ABOVE MY PAY GRADE.
WITH CRANE GONE, ***I'M*** DEPUTY MAYOR NOW. AND I SAY IF WE CAN'T RUN THIS TOWN WITHOUT...GROWING ***FANGS***, THEN WE HAVE NO BUSINESS DOING IT AT ***ALL***.
OH, JESUS, THAT'S ***RICH***. YOU GOTTA LET BIGBY DO HIS ***THING***.
YOU THINK THE BAD GUYS ARE HAMSTRINGING ***THEIR*** PEOPLE?
WE CAN'T LET THINGS SLIDE ANYMORE. AND THAT INCLUDES ***THIS***... LUDICROUS SITUATION.
EXCUSE ME?
STARTING TODAY, ALL UNGLAMOURED FABLES GO TO THE ***FARM***. ***PERIOD***.
SNOW, ARE YOU ***SURE*** ABOUT--
THERE ARE PEOPLE OUT THERE WHO WILL POINT A GUN RIGHT ***AT*** US AND PULL THE ***TRIGGER***.
THEY'RE ***TOUGH***. WE HAVE TO BE ***INFINITELY*** TOUGHER.
DO I MAKE MYSELF CLEAR?
RING RING

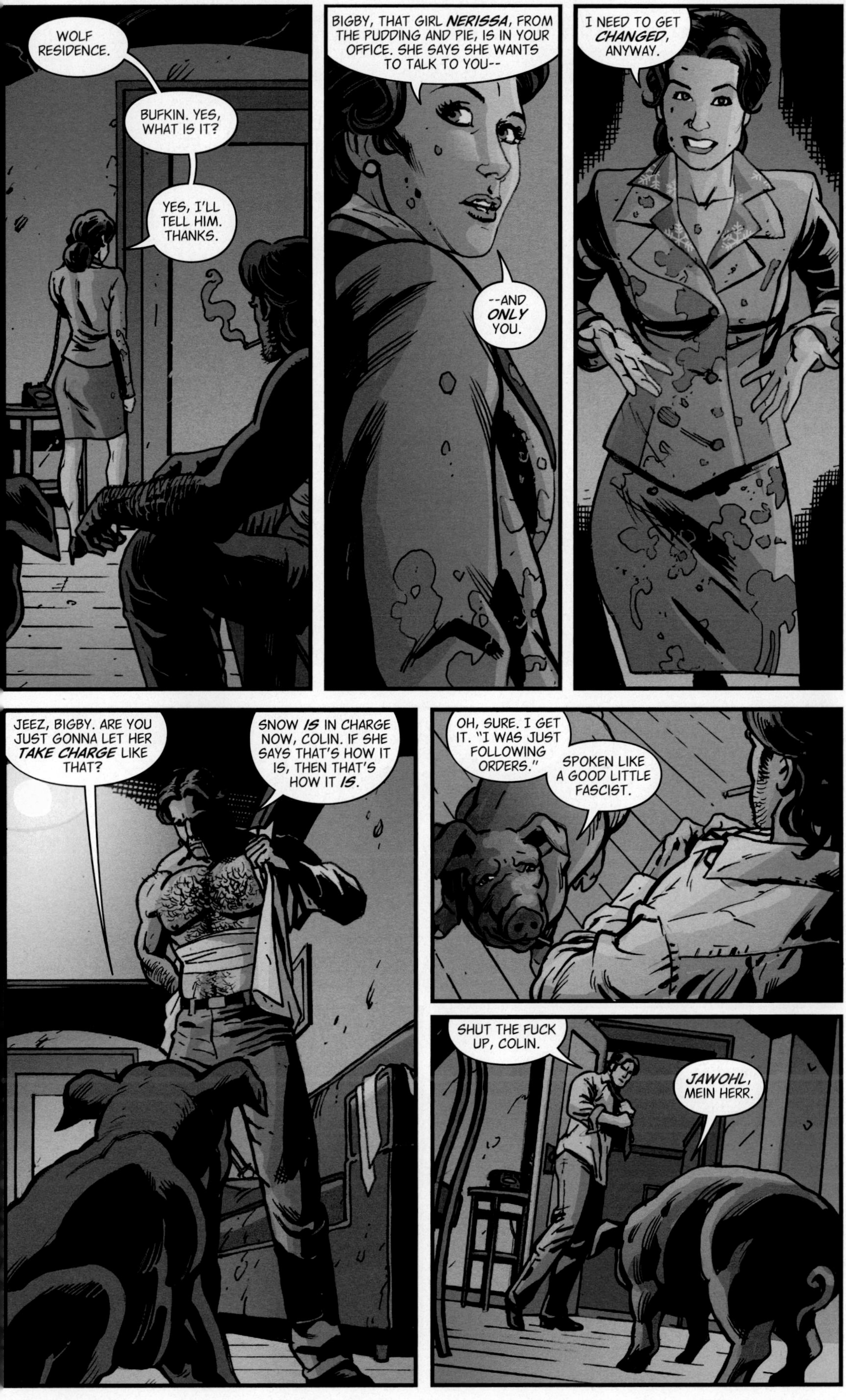
WOLF RESIDENCE.
BUFKIN. YES, WHAT IS IT?
YES, I'LL TELL HIM. THANKS.
BIGBY, THAT GIRL NERISSA, FROM THE PUDDING AND PIE, IS IN YOUR OFFICE. SHE SAYS SHE WANTS TO TALK TO YOU--
--AND ONLY YOU.
I NEED TO GET CHANGED, ANYWAY.
JEEZ, BIGBY. ARE YOU JUST GONNA LET HER TAKE CHARGE LIKE THAT?
SNOW IS IN CHARGE NOW, COLIN. IF SHE SAYS THAT'S HOW IT IS, THEN THAT'S HOW IT IS.
OH, SURE. I GET IT. "I WAS JUST FOLLOWING ORDERS."
SPOKEN LIKE A GOOD LITTLE FASCIST.
SHUT THE FUCK UP, COLIN.
JAWOHL, MEIN HERR.

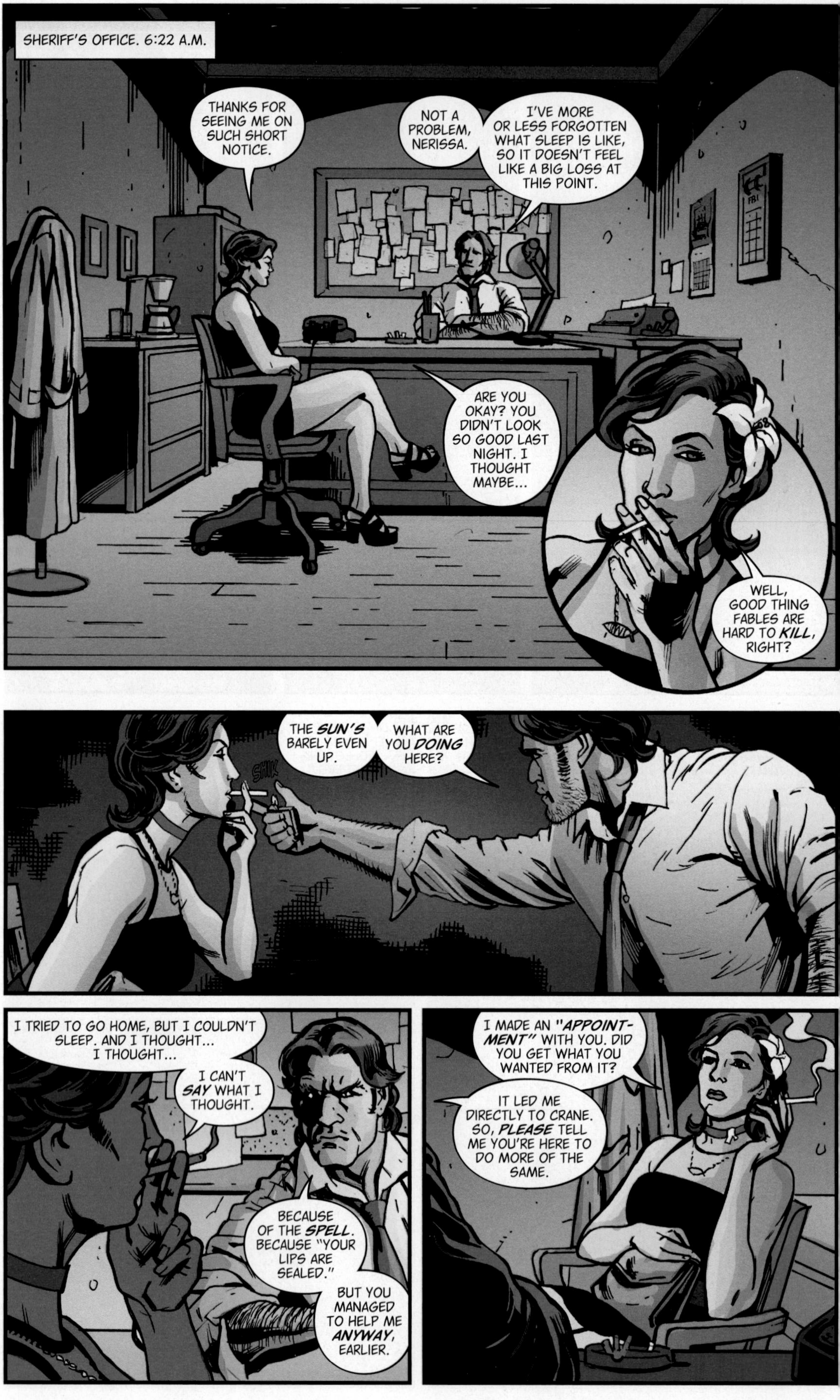

SHERIFF'S OFFICE. 6:22 A.M.
THANKS FOR SEEING ME ON SUCH SHORT NOTICE.
NOT A PROBLEM, NERISSA.
I'VE MORE OR LESS FORGOTTEN WHAT SLEEP IS LIKE, SO IT DOESN'T FEEL LIKE A BIG LOSS AT THIS POINT.
ARE YOU OKAY? YOU DIDN'T LOOK SO GOOD LAST NIGHT. I THOUGHT MAYBE...
WELL, GOOD THING FABLES ARE HARD TO KILL, RIGHT?
THE SUN'S BARELY EVEN UP.
WHAT ARE YOU DOING HERE?
SHIK
I TRIED TO GO HOME, BUT I COULDN'T SLEEP. AND I THOUGHT... I THOUGHT...
I CAN'T SAY WHAT I THOUGHT.
BECAUSE OF THE SPELL. BECAUSE "YOUR LIPS ARE SEALED."
BUT YOU MANAGED TO HELP ME ANYWAY, EARLIER.
I MADE AN "APPOINTMENT" WITH YOU. DID YOU GET WHAT YOU WANTED FROM IT?
IT LED ME DIRECTLY TO CRANE. SO, PLEASE TELL ME YOU'RE HERE TO DO MORE OF THE SAME.

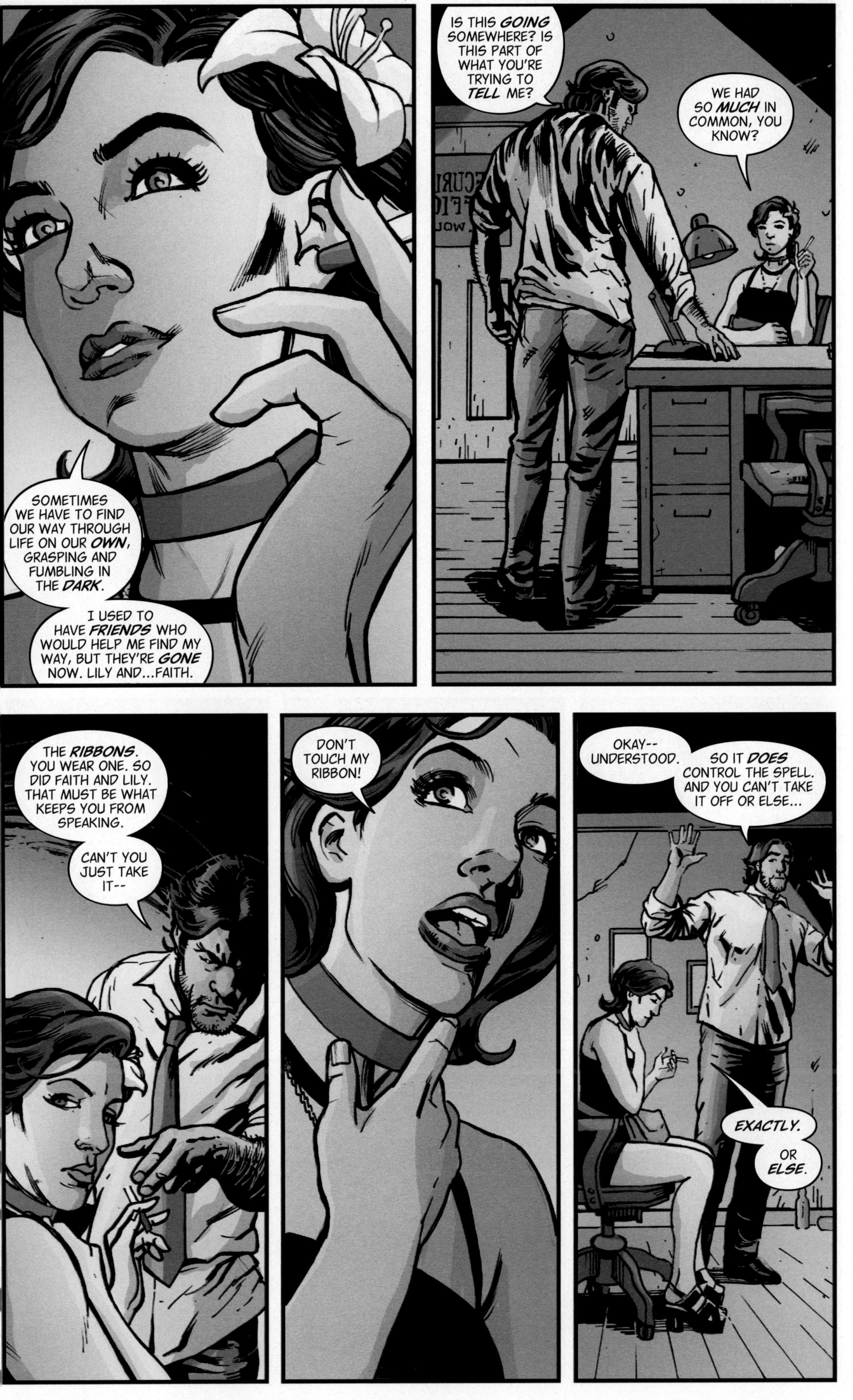
SOMETIMES WE HAVE TO FIND OUR WAY THROUGH LIFE ON OUR *OWN*, GRASPING AND FUMBLING IN THE *DARK*.
I USED TO HAVE *FRIENDS* WHO WOULD HELP ME FIND MY WAY, BUT THEY'RE *GONE* NOW. LILY AND...FAITH.
IS THIS *GOING* SOMEWHERE? IS THIS PART OF WHAT YOU'RE TRYING TO *TELL* ME?
WE HAD SO *MUCH* IN COMMON, YOU KNOW?
THE *RIBBONS*. YOU WEAR ONE. SO DID FAITH AND LILY. THAT MUST BE WHAT KEEPS YOU FROM SPEAKING.
CAN'T YOU JUST TAKE IT--
DON'T TOUCH MY RIBBON!
OKAY-- UNDERSTOOD.
SO IT *DOES* CONTROL THE SPELL. AND YOU CAN'T TAKE IT OFF OR ELSE...
EXACTLY.
OR *ELSE*.

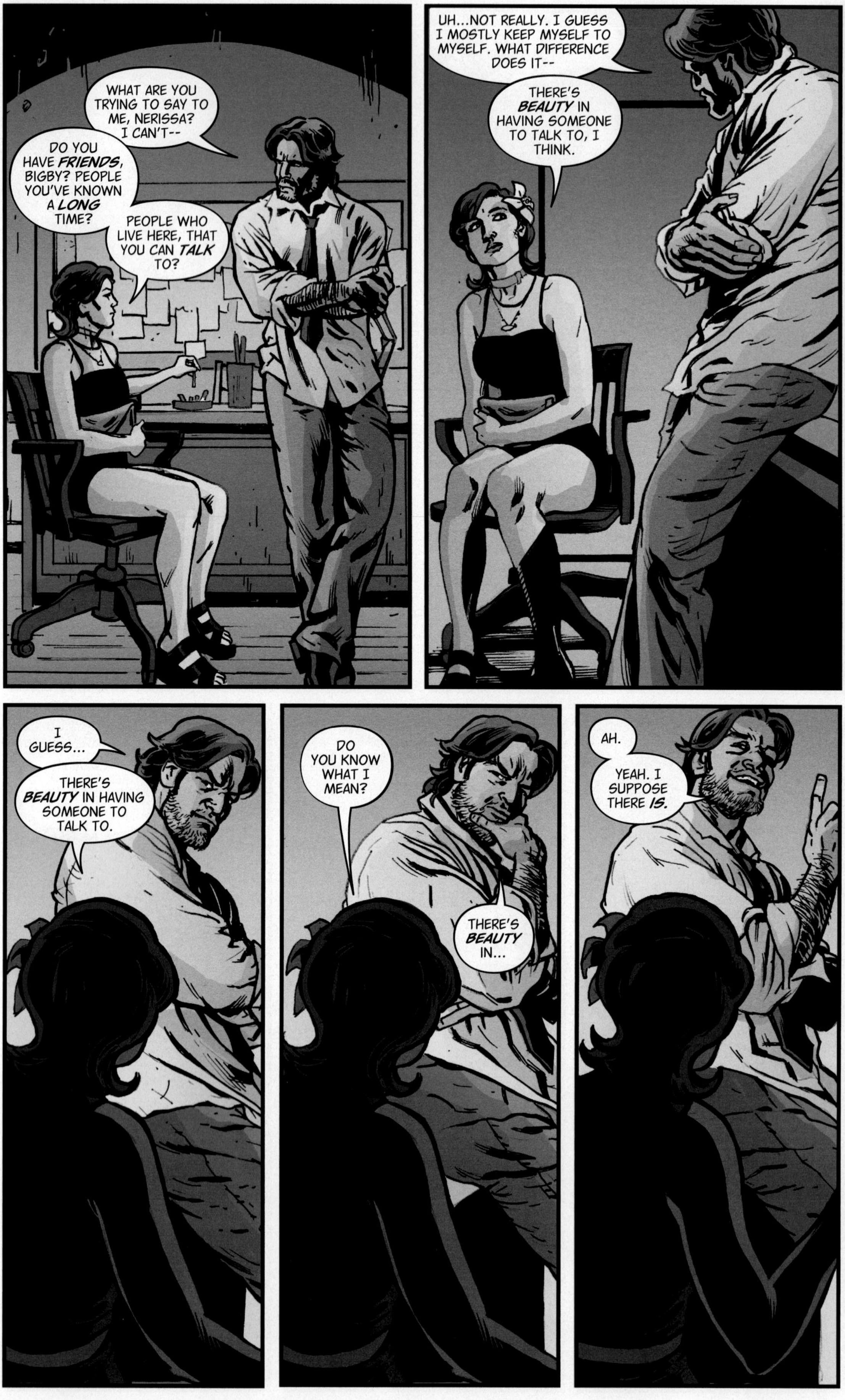
WHAT ARE YOU TRYING TO SAY TO ME, NERISSA? I CAN'T--
DO YOU HAVE *FRIENDS*, BIGBY? PEOPLE YOU'VE KNOWN A *LONG* TIME?
PEOPLE WHO LIVE HERE, THAT YOU CAN *TALK* TO?
UH...NOT REALLY. I GUESS I MOSTLY KEEP MYSELF TO MYSELF. WHAT DIFFERENCE DOES IT--
THERE'S *BEAUTY* IN HAVING SOMEONE TO TALK TO, I THINK.
I GUESS...
THERE'S *BEAUTY* IN HAVING SOMEONE TO TALK TO.
DO YOU KNOW WHAT I MEAN?
THERE'S *BEAUTY* IN...
AH.
YEAH. I SUPPOSE THERE *IS*.

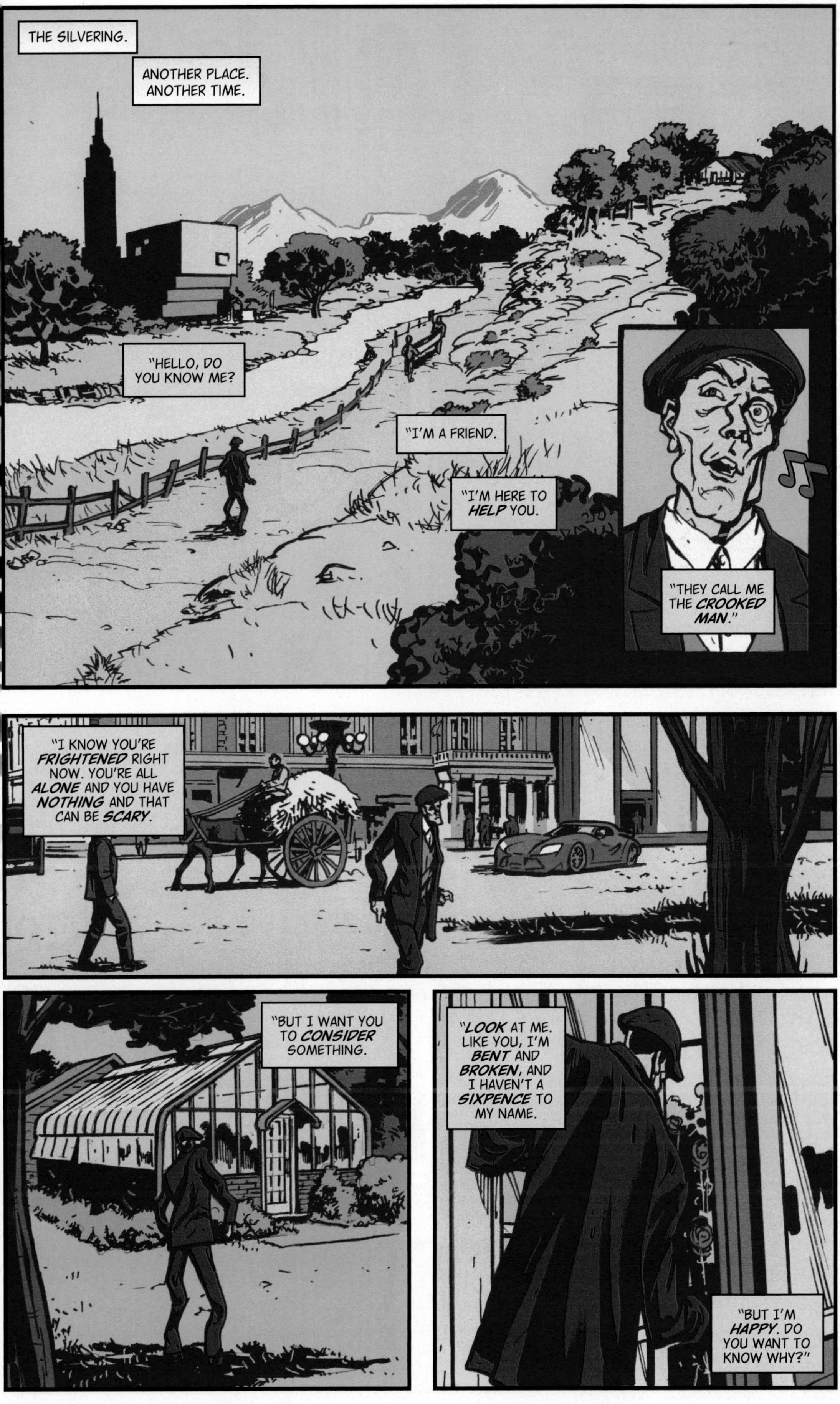
THE SILVERING.
ANOTHER PLACE. ANOTHER TIME.
"HELLO, DO YOU KNOW ME?
"I'M A FRIEND.
"I'M HERE TO HELP YOU.
"THEY CALL ME THE CROOKED MAN."
"I KNOW YOU'RE FRIGHTENED RIGHT NOW. YOU'RE ALL ALONE AND YOU HAVE NOTHING AND THAT CAN BE SCARY.
"BUT I WANT YOU TO CONSIDER SOMETHING.
"LOOK AT ME. LIKE YOU, I'M BENT AND BROKEN, AND I HAVEN'T A SIXPENCE TO MY NAME.
"BUT I'M HAPPY. DO YOU WANT TO KNOW WHY?"

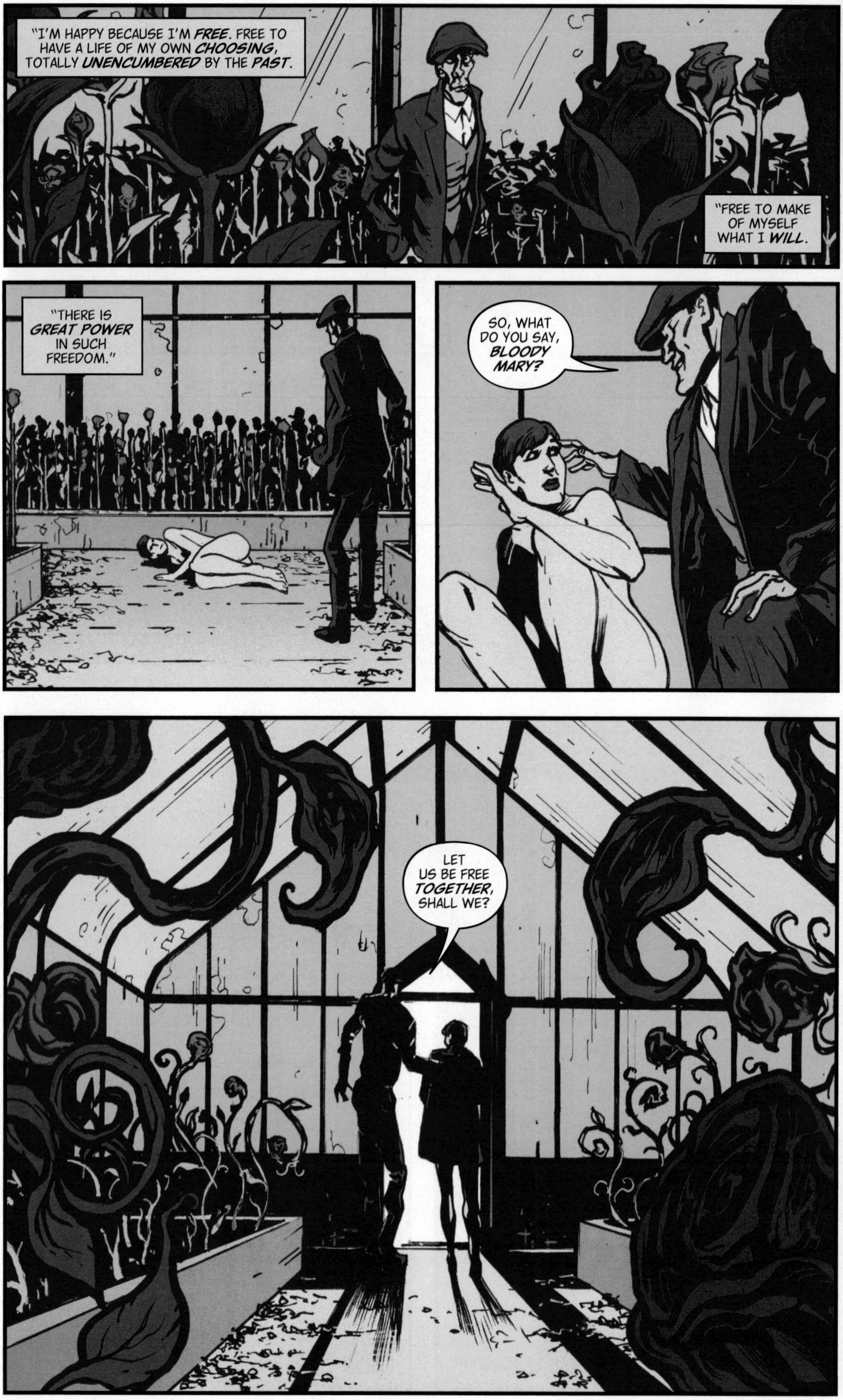
"I'M HAPPY BECAUSE I'M FREE. FREE TO HAVE A LIFE OF MY OWN CHOOSING, TOTALLY UNENCUMBERED BY THE PAST.
"FREE TO MAKE OF MYSELF WHAT I WILL.
"THERE IS GREAT POWER IN SUCH FREEDOM."
SO, WHAT DO YOU SAY, BLOODY MARY?
LET US BE FREE TOGETHER, SHALL WE?

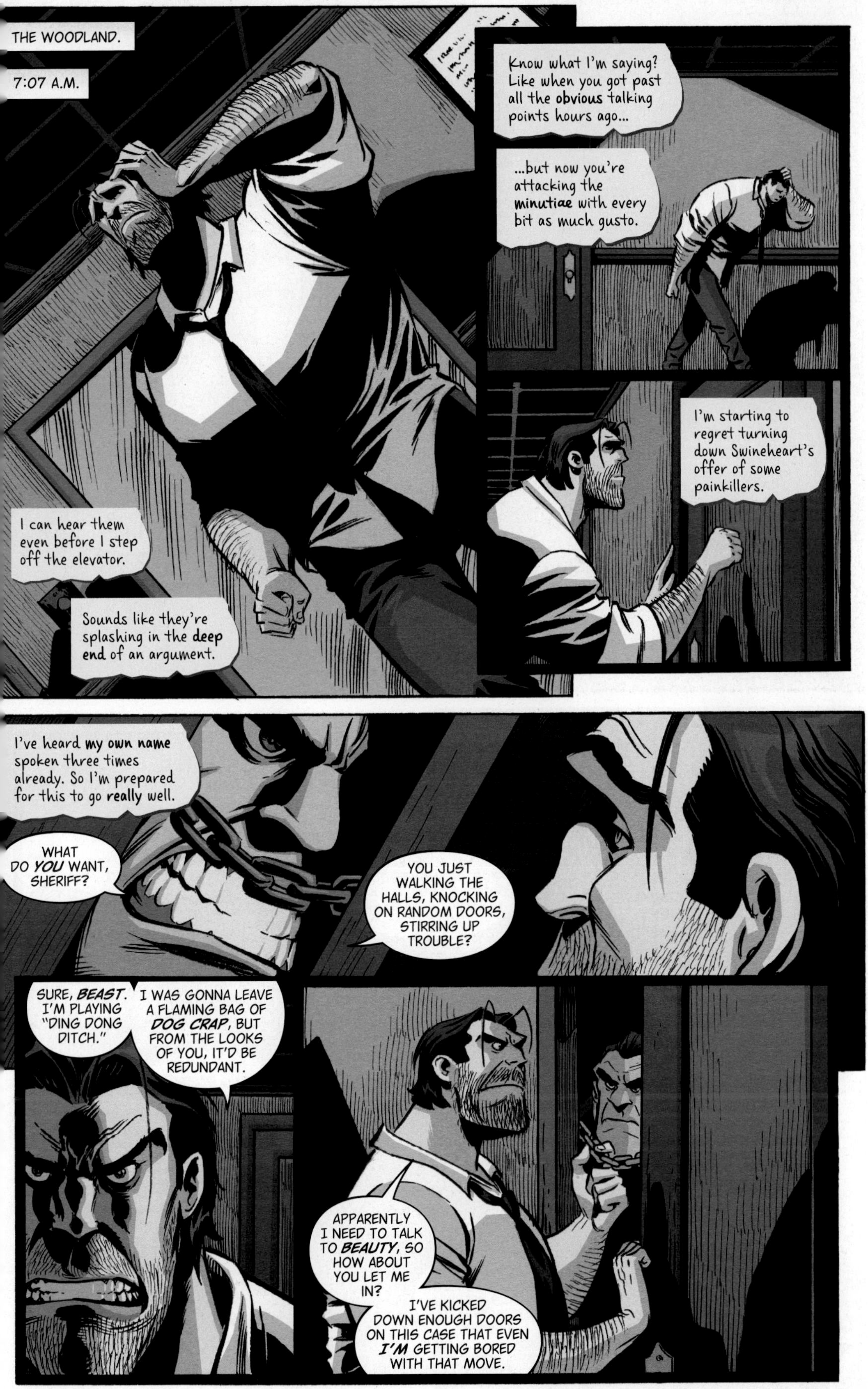
THE WOODLAND.
7:07 A.M.
I can hear them even before I step off the elevator.
Sounds like they're splashing in the deep end of an argument.
Know what I'm saying? Like when you got past all the obvious talking points hours ago...
...but now you're attacking the minutiae with every bit as much gusto.
I'm starting to regret turning down Swineheart's offer of some painkillers.
I've heard my own name spoken three times already. So I'm prepared for this to go really well.
WHAT DO YOU WANT, SHERIFF?
YOU JUST WALKING THE HALLS, KNOCKING ON RANDOM DOORS, STIRRING UP TROUBLE?
SURE, BEAST. I'M PLAYING "DING DONG DITCH."
I WAS GONNA LEAVE A FLAMING BAG OF DOG CRAP, BUT FROM THE LOOKS OF YOU, IT'D BE REDUNDANT.
APPARENTLY I NEED TO TALK TO BEAUTY, SO HOW ABOUT YOU LET ME IN?
I'VE KICKED DOWN ENOUGH DOORS ON THIS CASE THAT EVEN I'M GETTING BORED WITH THAT MOVE.

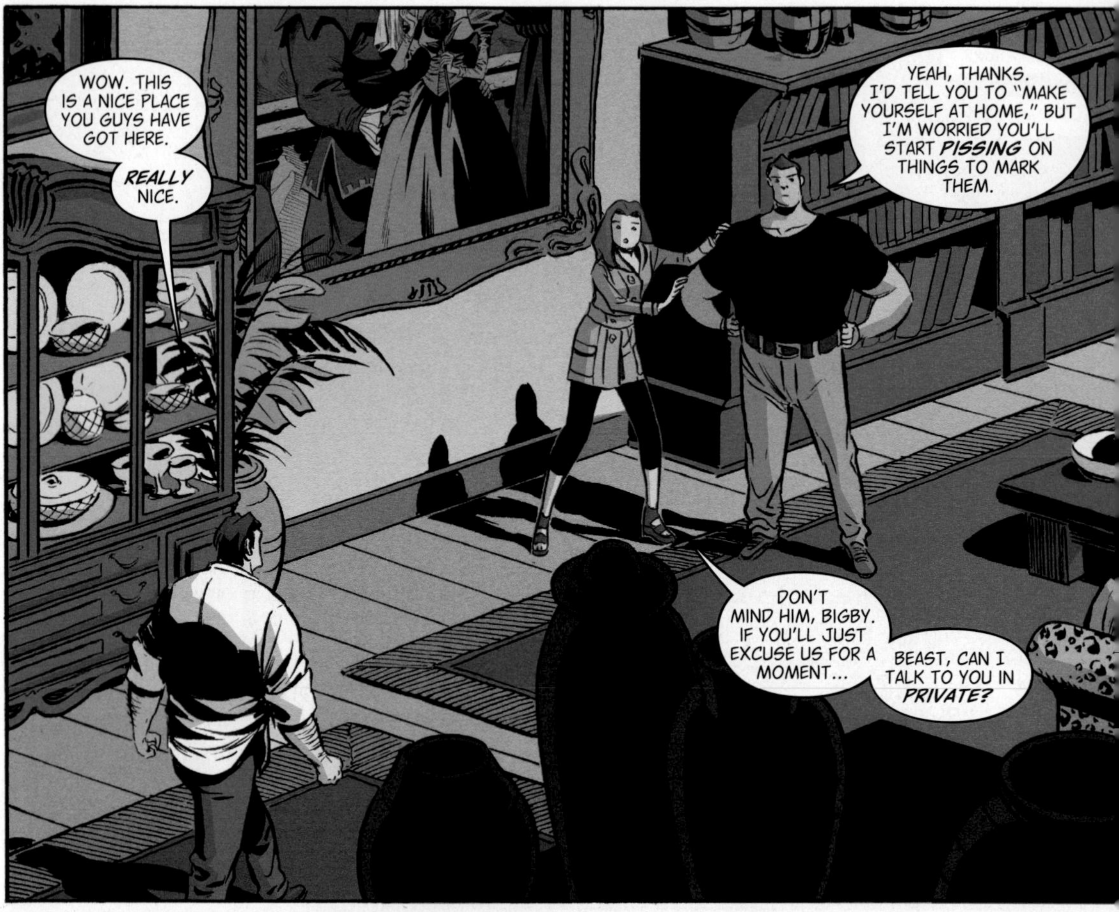
WOW. THIS IS A NICE PLACE YOU GUYS HAVE GOT HERE.
REALLY NICE.
YEAH, THANKS. I'D TELL YOU TO "MAKE YOURSELF AT HOME," BUT I'M WORRIED YOU'LL START PISSING ON THINGS TO MARK THEM.
DON'T MIND HIM, BIGBY. IF YOU'LL JUST EXCUSE US FOR A MOMENT...
BEAST, CAN I TALK TO YOU IN PRIVATE?

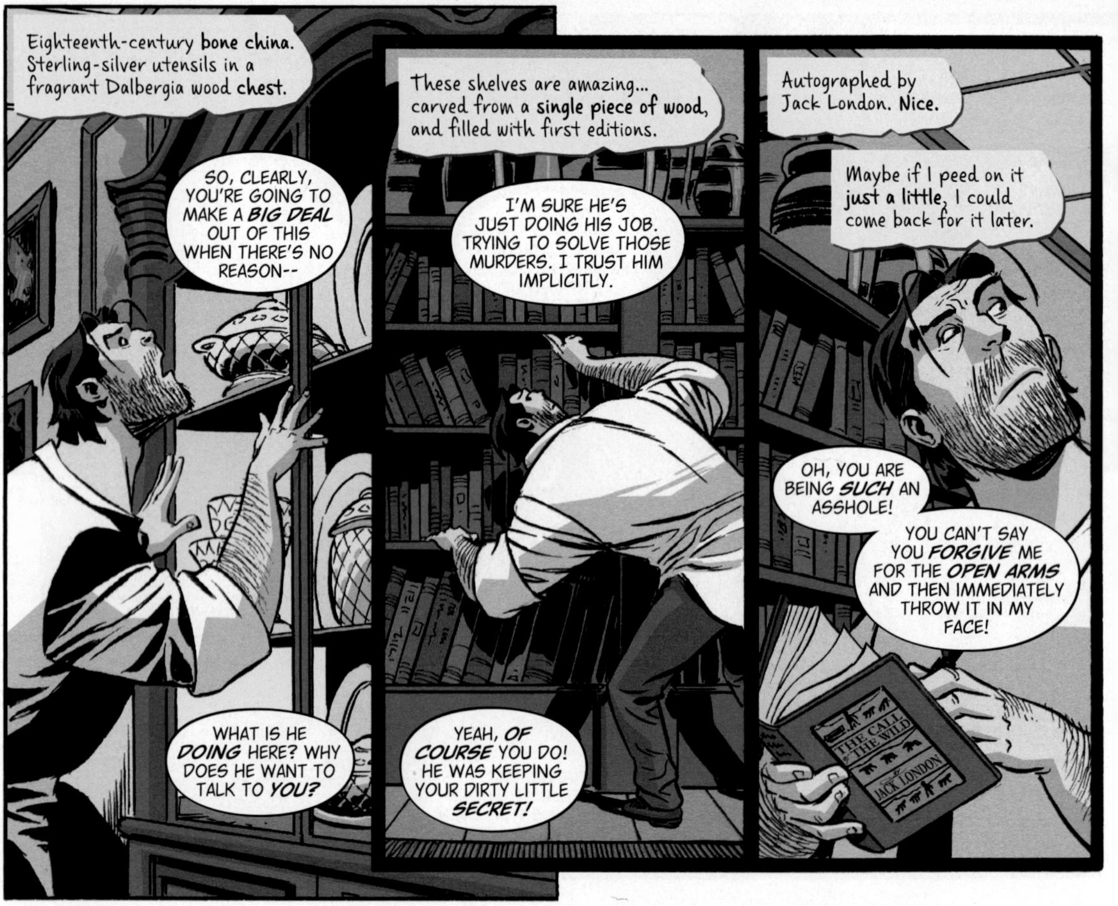
Eighteenth-century bone china. Sterling-silver utensils in a fragrant Dalbergia wood chest.
SO, CLEARLY, YOU'RE GOING TO MAKE A BIG DEAL OUT OF THIS WHEN THERE'S NO REASON--
WHAT IS HE DOING HERE? WHY DOES HE WANT TO TALK TO YOU?
These shelves are amazing... carved from a single piece of wood, and filled with first editions.
I'M SURE HE'S JUST DOING HIS JOB. TRYING TO SOLVE THOSE MURDERS. I TRUST HIM IMPLICITLY.
YEAH, OF COURSE YOU DO! HE WAS KEEPING YOUR DIRTY LITTLE SECRET!
Autographed by Jack London. Nice.
Maybe if I peed on it just a little, I could come back for it later.
OH, YOU ARE BEING SUCH AN ASSHOLE!
YOU CAN'T SAY YOU FORGIVE ME FOR THE OPEN ARMS AND THEN IMMEDIATELY THROW IT IN MY FACE!
THE CALL OF THE WILD
JACK LONDON

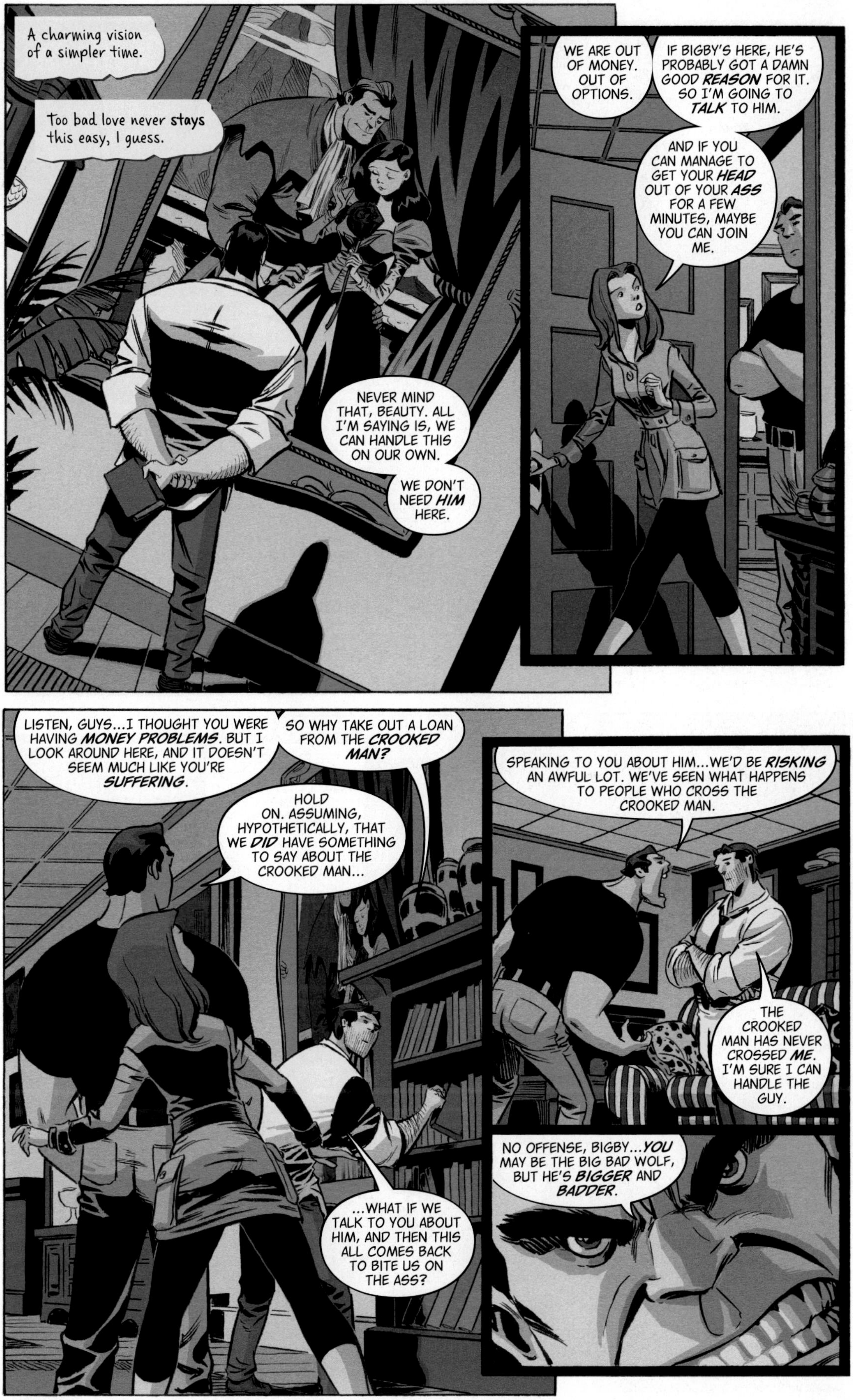
A charming vision of a simpler time.
Too bad love never stays this easy, I guess.
NEVER MIND THAT, BEAUTY. ALL I'M SAYING IS, WE CAN HANDLE THIS ON OUR OWN.
WE DON'T NEED *HIM* HERE.
WE ARE OUT OF MONEY. OUT OF OPTIONS.
IF BIGBY'S HERE, HE'S PROBABLY GOT A DAMN GOOD *REASON* FOR IT. SO I'M GOING TO *TALK* TO HIM.
AND IF YOU CAN MANAGE TO GET YOUR *HEAD* OUT OF YOUR *ASS* FOR A FEW MINUTES, MAYBE YOU CAN JOIN ME.
LISTEN, GUYS...I THOUGHT YOU WERE HAVING *MONEY PROBLEMS*. BUT I LOOK AROUND HERE, AND IT DOESN'T SEEM MUCH LIKE YOU'RE *SUFFERING*.
SO WHY TAKE OUT A LOAN FROM THE *CROOKED MAN?*
HOLD ON. ASSUMING, HYPOTHETICALLY, THAT WE *DID* HAVE SOMETHING TO SAY ABOUT THE CROOKED MAN...
...WHAT IF WE TALK TO YOU ABOUT HIM, AND THEN THIS ALL COMES BACK TO BITE US ON THE ASS?
SPEAKING TO YOU ABOUT HIM...WE'D BE *RISKING* AN AWFUL LOT. WE'VE SEEN WHAT HAPPENS TO PEOPLE WHO CROSS THE CROOKED MAN.
THE CROOKED MAN HAS NEVER CROSSED *ME*. I'M SURE I CAN HANDLE THE GUY.
NO OFFENSE, BIGBY...*YOU* MAY BE THE BIG BAD WOLF, BUT HE'S *BIGGER* AND *BADDER*.

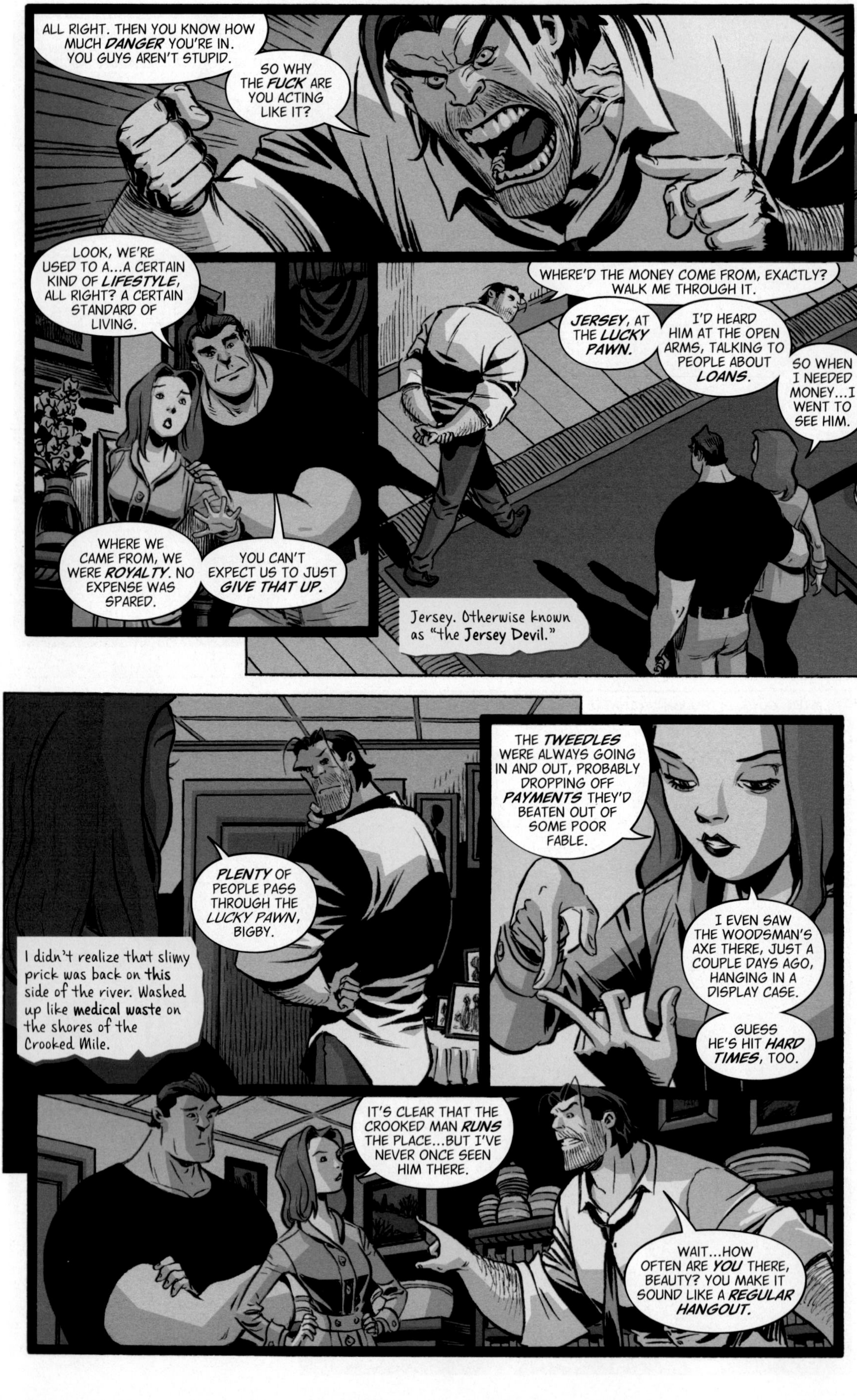
ALL RIGHT. THEN YOU KNOW HOW MUCH DANGER YOU'RE IN. YOU GUYS AREN'T STUPID.
SO WHY THE FUCK ARE YOU ACTING LIKE IT?
LOOK, WE'RE USED TO A...A CERTAIN KIND OF LIFESTYLE, ALL RIGHT? A CERTAIN STANDARD OF LIVING.
WHERE WE CAME FROM, WE WERE ROYALTY. NO EXPENSE WAS SPARED.
YOU CAN'T EXPECT US TO JUST GIVE THAT UP.
WHERE'D THE MONEY COME FROM, EXACTLY? WALK ME THROUGH IT.
JERSEY, AT THE LUCKY PAWN.
I'D HEARD HIM AT THE OPEN ARMS, TALKING TO PEOPLE ABOUT LOANS.
SO WHEN I NEEDED MONEY...I WENT TO SEE HIM.
Jersey. Otherwise known as "the Jersey Devil."
PLENTY OF PEOPLE PASS THROUGH THE LUCKY PAWN, BIGBY.
I didn't realize that slimy prick was back on this side of the river. Washed up like medical waste on the shores of the Crooked Mile.
THE TWEEDLES WERE ALWAYS GOING IN AND OUT, PROBABLY DROPPING OFF PAYMENTS THEY'D BEATEN OUT OF SOME POOR FABLE.
I EVEN SAW THE WOODSMAN'S AXE THERE, JUST A COUPLE DAYS AGO, HANGING IN A DISPLAY CASE.
GUESS HE'S HIT HARD TIMES, TOO.
IT'S CLEAR THAT THE CROOKED MAN RUNS THE PLACE...BUT I'VE NEVER ONCE SEEN HIM THERE.
WAIT...HOW OFTEN ARE YOU THERE, BEAUTY? YOU MAKE IT SOUND LIKE A REGULAR HANGOUT.

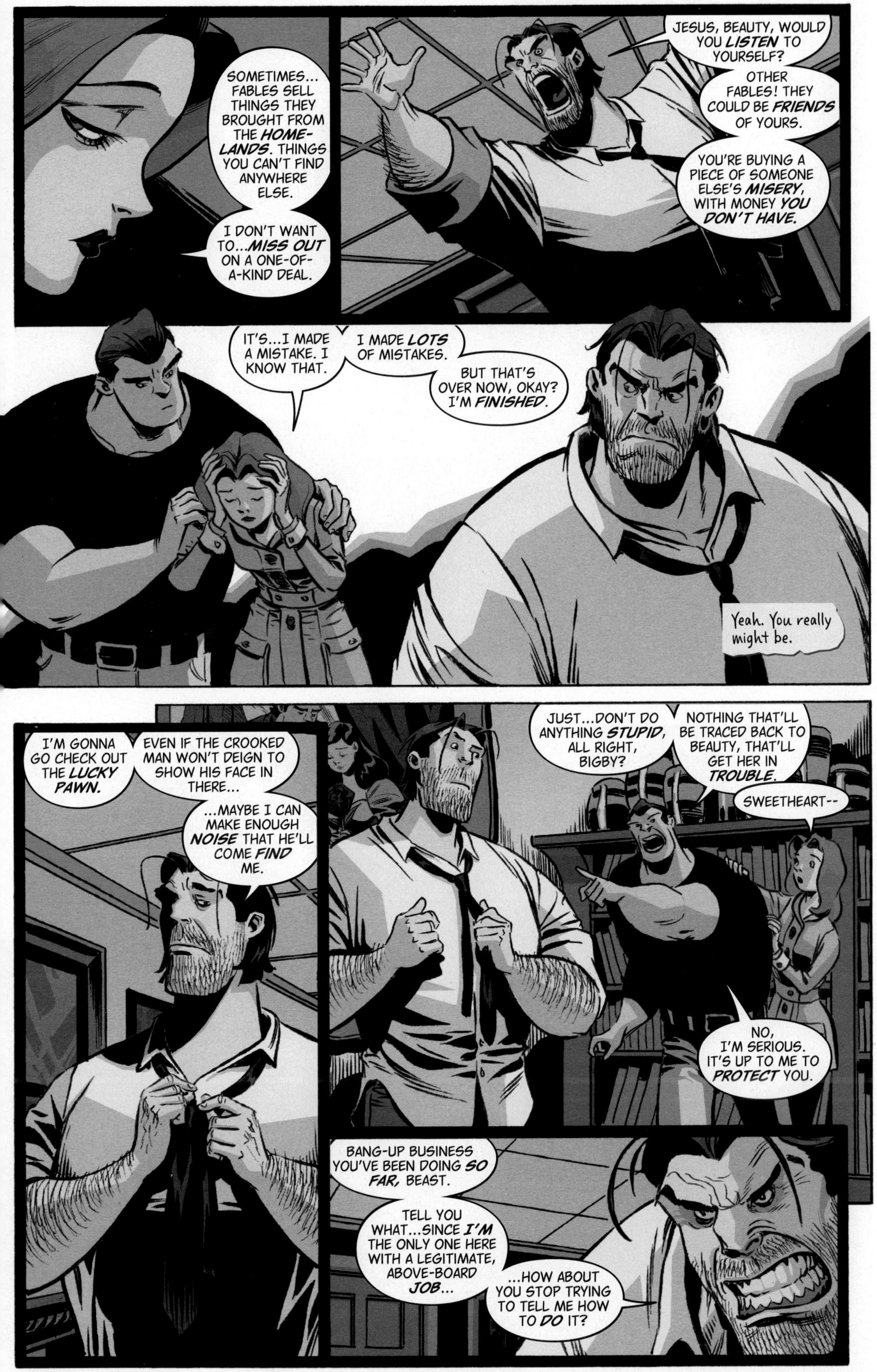
SOMETIMES... FABLES SELL THINGS THEY BROUGHT FROM THE HOME-LANDS. THINGS YOU CAN'T FIND ANYWHERE ELSE.
I DON'T WANT TO...MISS OUT ON A ONE-OF-A-KIND DEAL.
JESUS, BEAUTY, WOULD YOU LISTEN TO YOURSELF?
OTHER FABLES! THEY COULD BE FRIENDS OF YOURS.
YOU'RE BUYING A PIECE OF SOMEONE ELSE'S MISERY, WITH MONEY YOU DON'T HAVE.
IT'S...I MADE A MISTAKE. I KNOW THAT.
I MADE LOTS OF MISTAKES.
BUT THAT'S OVER NOW, OKAY? I'M FINISHED.
Yeah. You really might be.
I'M GONNA GO CHECK OUT THE LUCKY PAWN.
EVEN IF THE CROOKED MAN WON'T DEIGN TO SHOW HIS FACE IN THERE...
...MAYBE I CAN MAKE ENOUGH NOISE THAT HE'LL COME FIND ME.
JUST...DON'T DO ANYTHING STUPID, ALL RIGHT, BIGBY?
NOTHING THAT'LL BE TRACED BACK TO BEAUTY, THAT'LL GET HER IN TROUBLE.
SWEETHEART--
NO, I'M SERIOUS. IT'S UP TO ME TO PROTECT YOU.
BANG-UP BUSINESS YOU'VE BEEN DOING SO FAR, BEAST.
TELL YOU WHAT...SINCE I'M THE ONLY ONE HERE WITH A LEGITIMATE, ABOVE-BOARD JOB...
...HOW ABOUT YOU STOP TRYING TO TELL ME HOW TO DO IT?

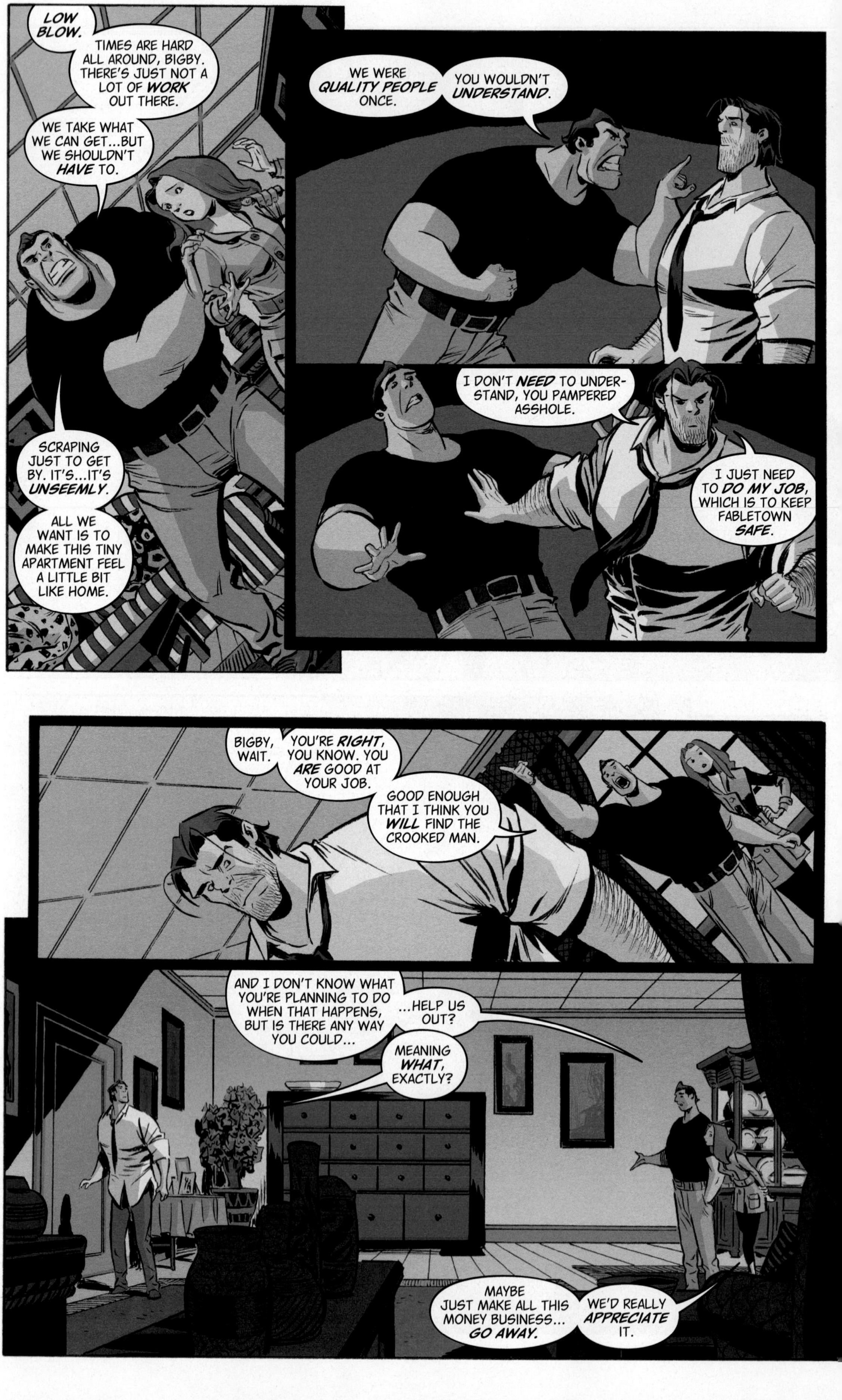
LOW BLOW.
TIMES ARE HARD ALL AROUND, BIGBY. THERE'S JUST NOT A LOT OF WORK OUT THERE.
WE TAKE WHAT WE CAN GET...BUT WE SHOULDN'T HAVE TO.
SCRAPING JUST TO GET BY. IT'S...IT'S UNSEEMLY.
ALL WE WANT IS TO MAKE THIS TINY APARTMENT FEEL A LITTLE BIT LIKE HOME.
WE WERE QUALITY PEOPLE ONCE.
YOU WOULDN'T UNDERSTAND.
I DON'T NEED TO UNDER-STAND, YOU PAMPERED ASSHOLE.
I JUST NEED TO DO MY JOB, WHICH IS TO KEEP FABLETOWN SAFE.
BIGBY, WAIT.
YOU'RE RIGHT, YOU KNOW. YOU ARE GOOD AT YOUR JOB.
GOOD ENOUGH THAT I THINK YOU WILL FIND THE CROOKED MAN.
AND I DON'T KNOW WHAT YOU'RE PLANNING TO DO WHEN THAT HAPPENS, BUT IS THERE ANY WAY YOU COULD...
...HELP US OUT?
MEANING WHAT, EXACTLY?
MAYBE JUST MAKE ALL THIS MONEY BUSINESS... GO AWAY.
WE'D REALLY APPRECIATE IT.

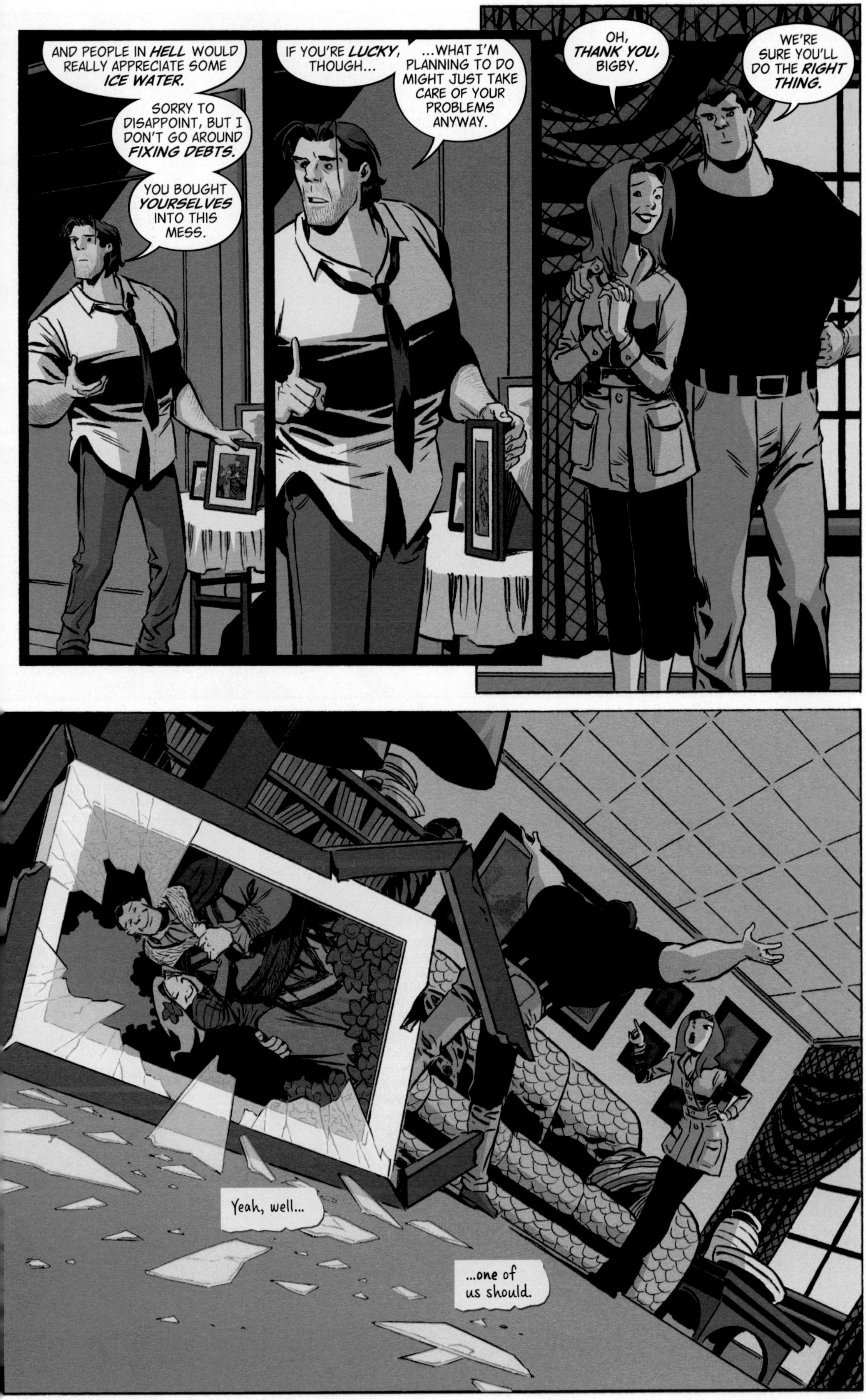
AND PEOPLE IN HELL WOULD REALLY APPRECIATE SOME ICE WATER.
SORRY TO DISAPPOINT, BUT I DON'T GO AROUND FIXING DEBTS.
YOU BOUGHT YOURSELVES INTO THIS MESS.
IF YOU'RE LUCKY, THOUGH...
...WHAT I'M PLANNING TO DO MIGHT JUST TAKE CARE OF YOUR PROBLEMS ANYWAY.
OH, THANK YOU, BIGBY.
WE'RE SURE YOU'LL DO THE RIGHT THING.
Yeah, well...
...one of us should.

THE SILVERING.

NOW, *MARY*, IT'S CLEAR FOR ANYONE TO SEE THAT YOU'VE BEEN THROUGH THE PROVERBIAL WRINGER.

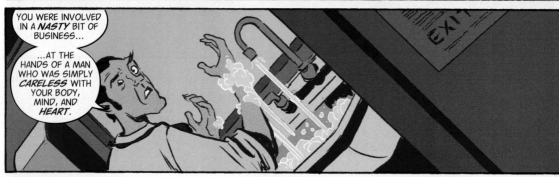

YOU WERE INVOLVED IN A *NASTY* BIT OF BUSINESS...

...AT THE HANDS OF A MAN WHO WAS SIMPLY *CARELESS* WITH YOUR BODY, MIND, AND *HEART*.

THERE ARE INJURIES IN OUR PASTS THAT WE CLING TO, THOUGH, WELL PAST THE POINT OF PRACTICALITY.

AND THOUGH WE CLAIM ALOUD THAT WE WISH TO BE *FREE* OF SUCH PAINS...

...WE WHISPER TO OURSELVES THAT PERHAPS WE ARE *UNREADY* TO SURRENDER THEM *ENTIRELY*.

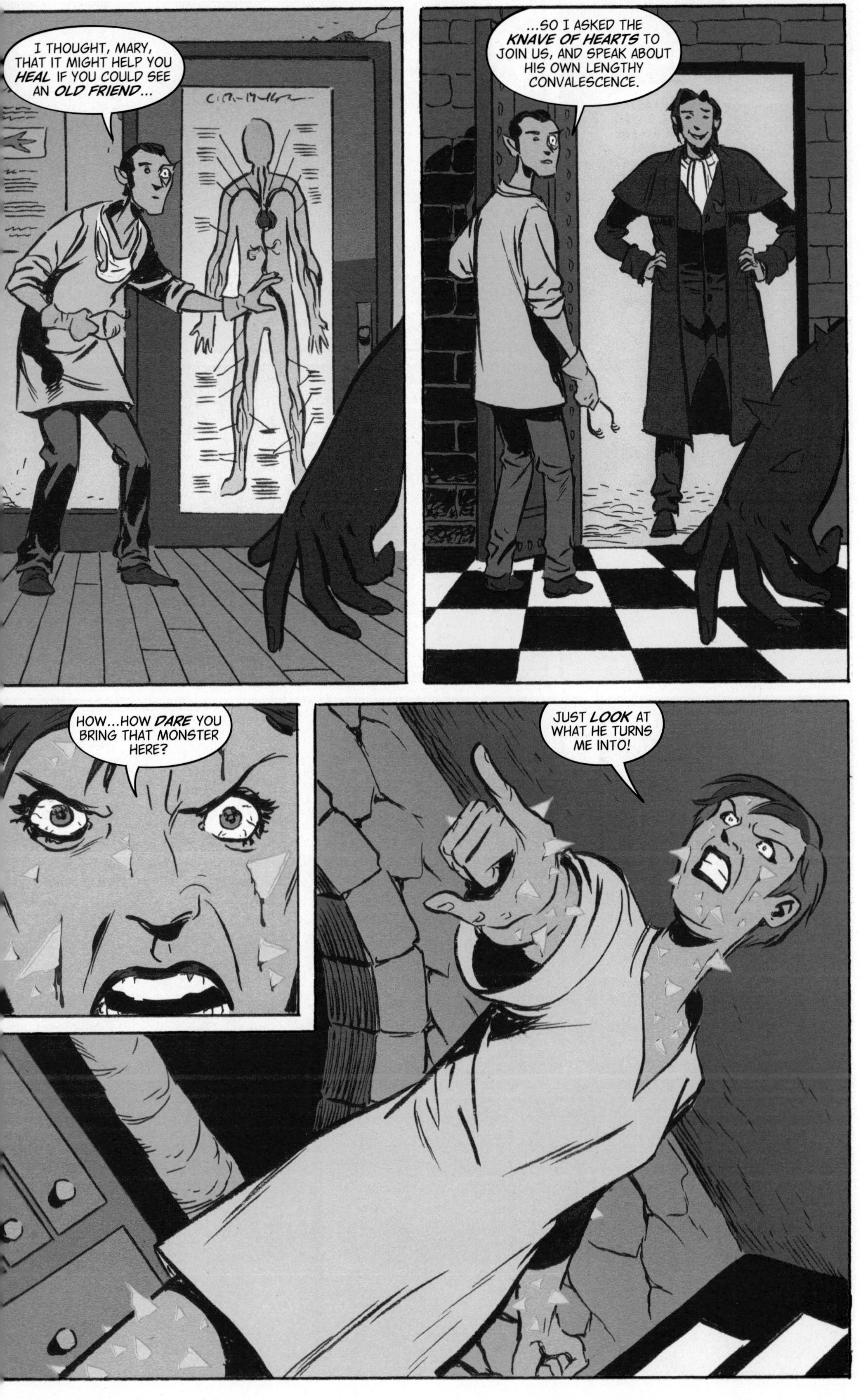
I THOUGHT, MARY, THAT IT MIGHT HELP YOU *HEAL* IF YOU COULD SEE AN *OLD FRIEND*...
...SO I ASKED THE *KNAVE OF HEARTS* TO JOIN US, AND SPEAK ABOUT HIS OWN LENGTHY CONVALESCENCE.
HOW...HOW *DARE* YOU BRING THAT MONSTER HERE?
JUST *LOOK* AT WHAT HE TURNS ME INTO!

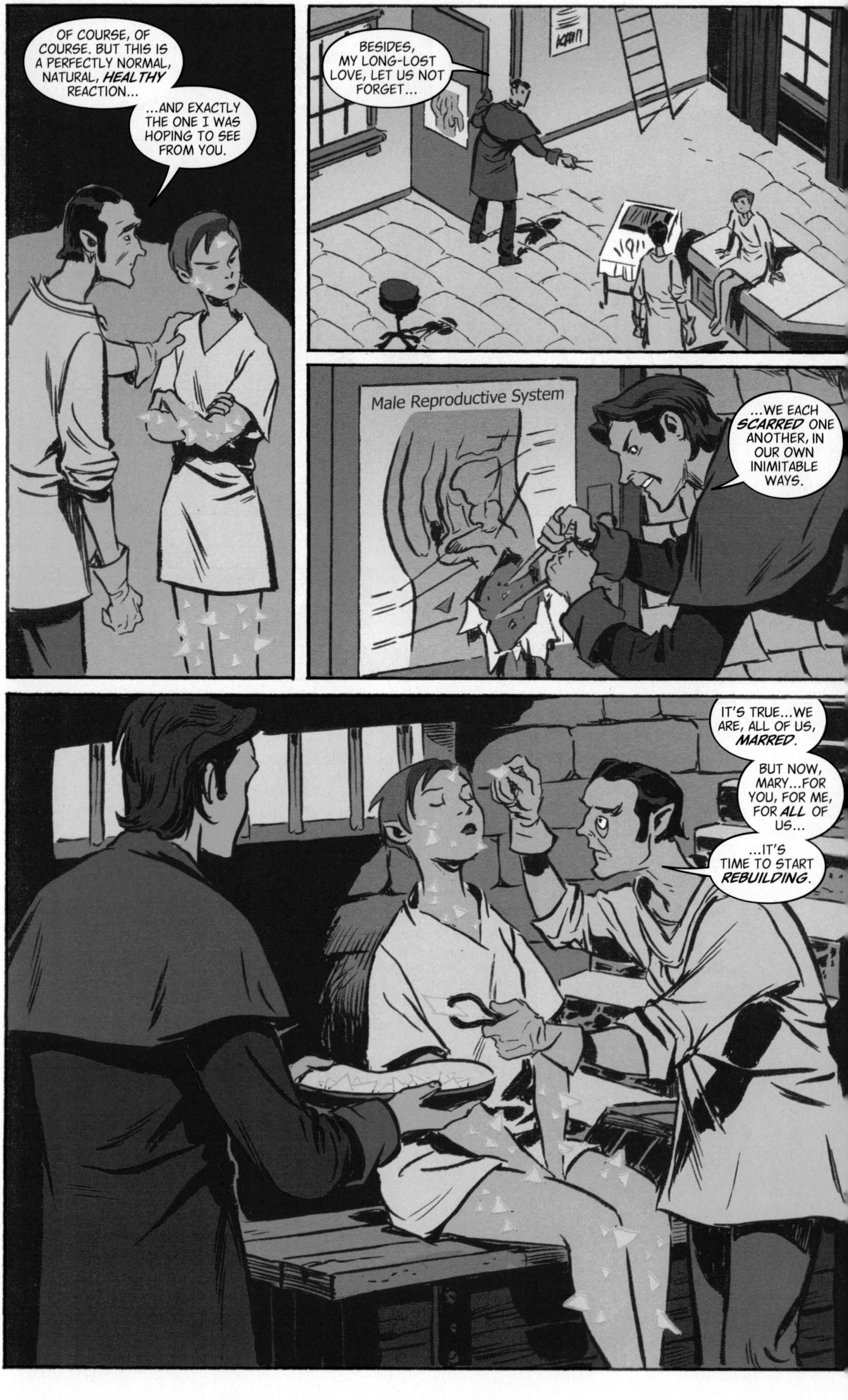

OF COURSE, OF COURSE. BUT THIS IS A PERFECTLY NORMAL, NATURAL, HEALTHY REACTION...
...AND EXACTLY THE ONE I WAS HOPING TO SEE FROM YOU.
BESIDES, MY LONG-LOST LOVE, LET US NOT FORGET...
Male Reproductive System
...WE EACH SCARRED ONE ANOTHER, IN OUR OWN INIMITABLE WAYS.
IT'S TRUE...WE ARE, ALL OF US, MARRED.
BUT NOW, MARY...FOR YOU, FOR ME, FOR ALL OF US...
...IT'S TIME TO START REBUILDING.

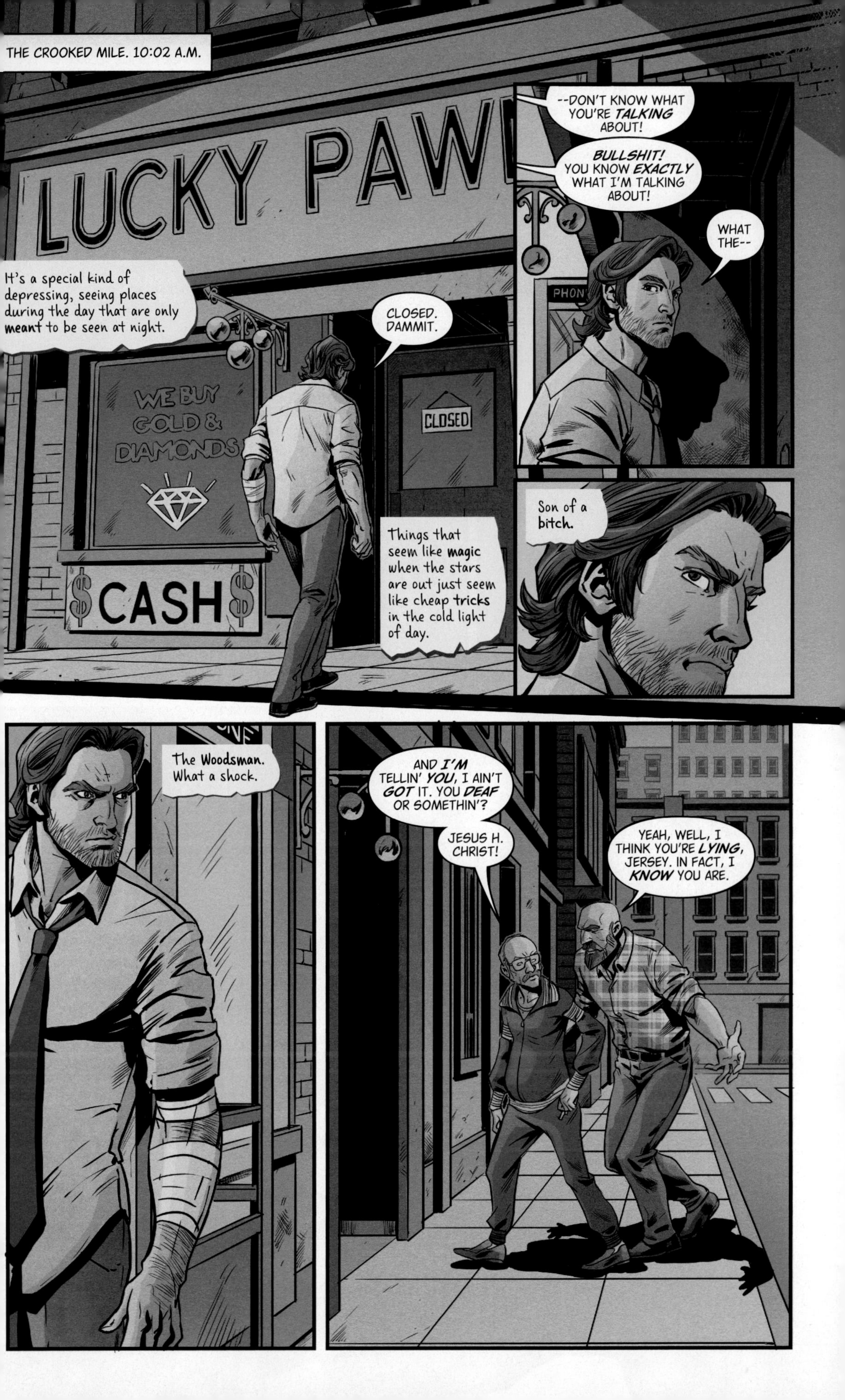

THE CROOKED MILE. 10:02 A.M.
LUCKY PAW
It's a special kind of depressing, seeing places during the day that are only meant to be seen at night.
WE BUY GOLD & DIAMONDS
$CASH$
CLOSED. DAMMIT.
CLOSED
Things that seem like magic when the stars are out just seem like cheap tricks in the cold light of day.
--DON'T KNOW WHAT YOU'RE TALKING ABOUT!
BULLSHIT! YOU KNOW EXACTLY WHAT I'M TALKING ABOUT!
WHAT THE--
PHON
Son of a bitch.
The Woodsman. What a shock.
AND I'M TELLIN' YOU, I AIN'T GOT IT. YOU DEAF OR SOMETHIN'?
JESUS H. CHRIST!
YEAH, WELL, I THINK YOU'RE LYING, JERSEY. IN FACT, I KNOW YOU ARE.

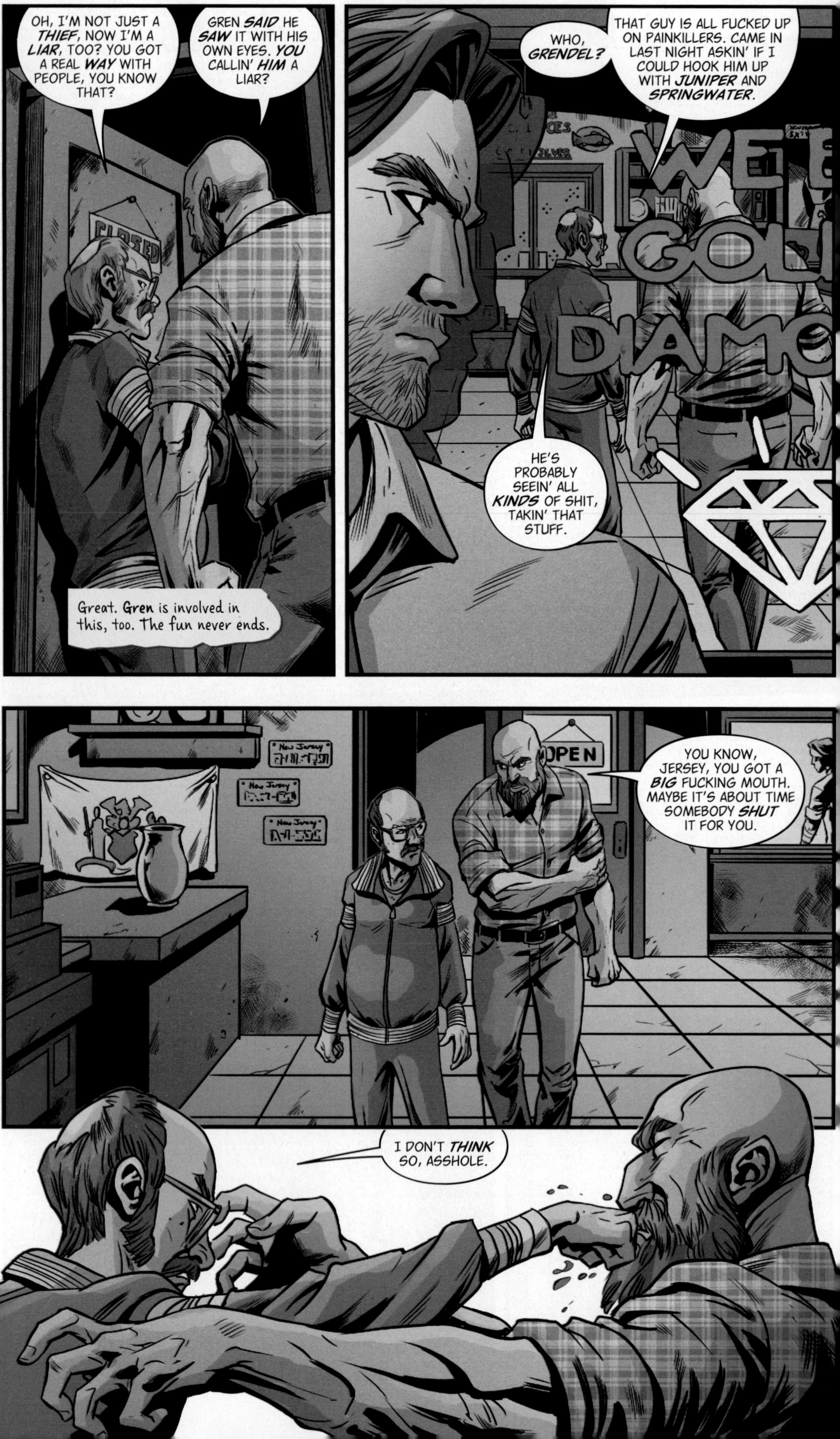
OH, I'M NOT JUST A THIEF, NOW I'M A LIAR, TOO? YOU GOT A REAL WAY WITH PEOPLE, YOU KNOW THAT?
GREN SAID HE SAW IT WITH HIS OWN EYES. YOU CALLIN' HIM A LIAR?
Great. Gren is involved in this, too. The fun never ends.
WHO, GRENDEL?
THAT GUY IS ALL FUCKED UP ON PAINKILLERS. CAME IN LAST NIGHT ASKIN' IF I COULD HOOK HIM UP WITH JUNIPER AND SPRINGWATER.
HE'S PROBABLY SEEIN' ALL KINDS OF SHIT, TAKIN' THAT STUFF.
OPEN
YOU KNOW, JERSEY, YOU GOT A BIG FUCKING MOUTH. MAYBE IT'S ABOUT TIME SOMEBODY SHUT IT FOR YOU.
I DON'T THINK SO, ASSHOLE.

THAT'S ENOUGH! WHAT THE *HELL* IS GOING ON HERE?

AW, *FUCK!* YOU CALL THE *COPS* ON ME, WOODY?

YEAH, *RIGHT.* LIKE CALLING *HIM* WOULD EVER DO *ME* ANY GOOD.

ALL RIGHT, FINE. YOU WANNA GET THE *FUZZ* INVOLVED?

I WANT TO FILE A *COMPLAINT* AGAINST THIS *ASSHOLE* FOR *HARASSMENT.* FOLLOWS ME ALL THE WAY FROM BATTERY PARK BADGERING ME ABOUT SOME *AXE* I AIN'T EVEN *GOT.*

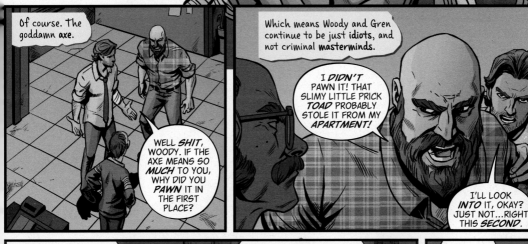

Of course. The goddamn axe.

Which means Woody and Gren continue to be just **idiots**, and not criminal **masterminds**.

WELL *SHIT,* WOODY. IF THE AXE MEANS SO *MUCH* TO YOU, WHY DID YOU *PAWN* IT IN THE FIRST PLACE?

I *DIDN'T* PAWN IT! THAT SLIMY LITTLE PRICK *TOAD* PROBABLY STOLE IT FROM MY *APARTMENT!*

I'LL LOOK *INTO* IT, OKAY? JUST NOT...RIGHT THIS *SECOND.*

LOOK AT YOU, WOODY. IT'S TEN IN THE MORNING AND YOU ALREADY SMELL LIKE A *BREWERY.*

WHY DON'T YOU GO *DRY OUT* SOMEPLACE, HUH? WE'LL FORGET THIS WHOLE THING HAPPENED.

I NEED TO TALK TO JERSEY *ALONE,* WOODY. CAN YOU JUST...ANOTHER *TIME,* MAYBE?

SCREW THE *BOTH* OF YOU.

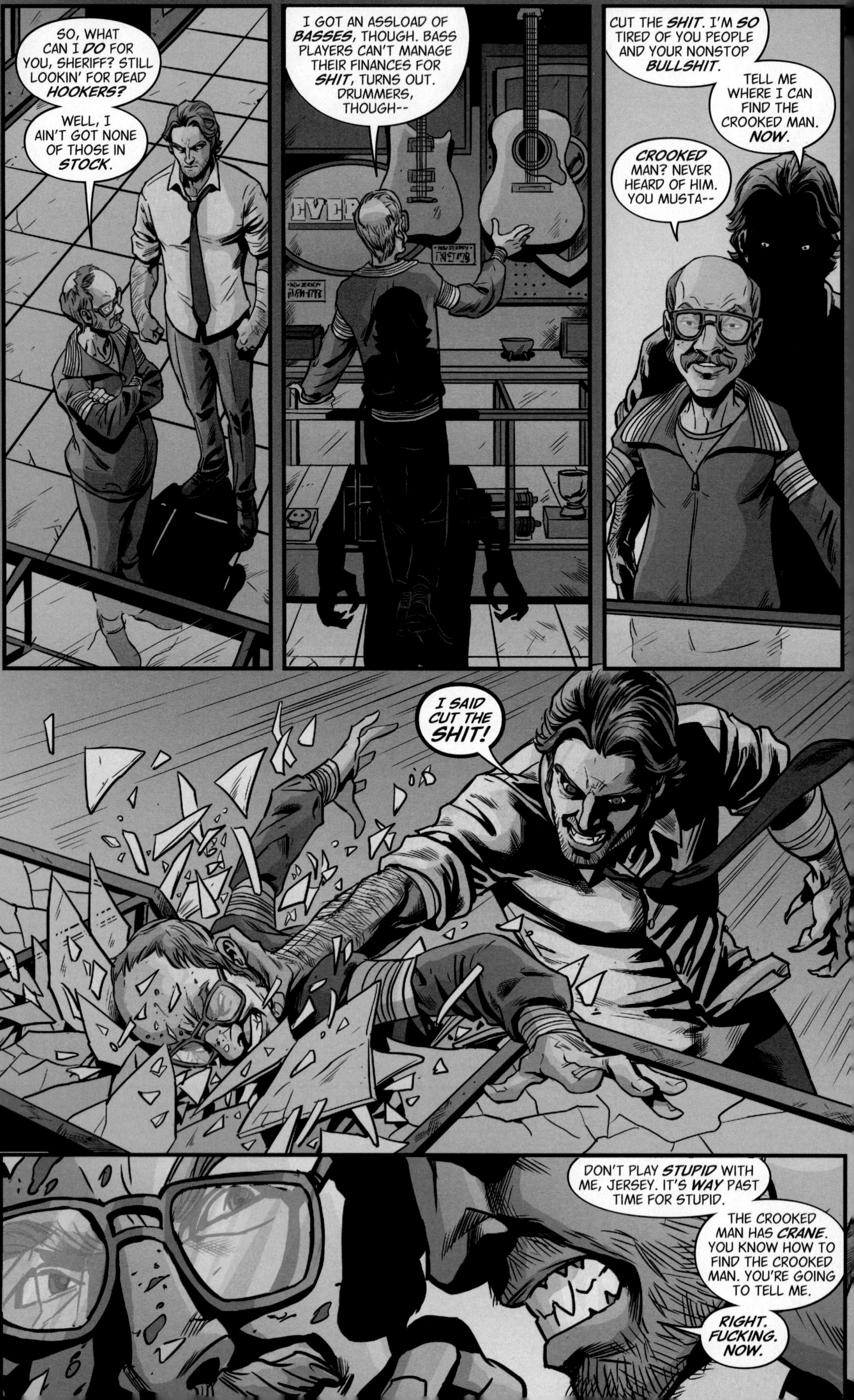
SO, WHAT CAN I DO FOR YOU, SHERIFF? STILL LOOKIN' FOR DEAD HOOKERS?
WELL, I AIN'T GOT NONE OF THOSE IN STOCK.
I GOT AN ASSLOAD OF BASSES, THOUGH. BASS PLAYERS CAN'T MANAGE THEIR FINANCES FOR SHIT, TURNS OUT. DRUMMERS, THOUGH--
CUT THE SHIT. I'M SO TIRED OF YOU PEOPLE AND YOUR NONSTOP BULLSHIT.
TELL ME WHERE I CAN FIND THE CROOKED MAN. NOW.
CROOKED MAN? NEVER HEARD OF HIM. YOU MUSTA--
I SAID CUT THE SHIT!
DON'T PLAY STUPID WITH ME, JERSEY. IT'S WAY PAST TIME FOR STUPID.
THE CROOKED MAN HAS CRANE. YOU KNOW HOW TO FIND THE CROOKED MAN. YOU'RE GOING TO TELL ME.
RIGHT. FUCKING. NOW.

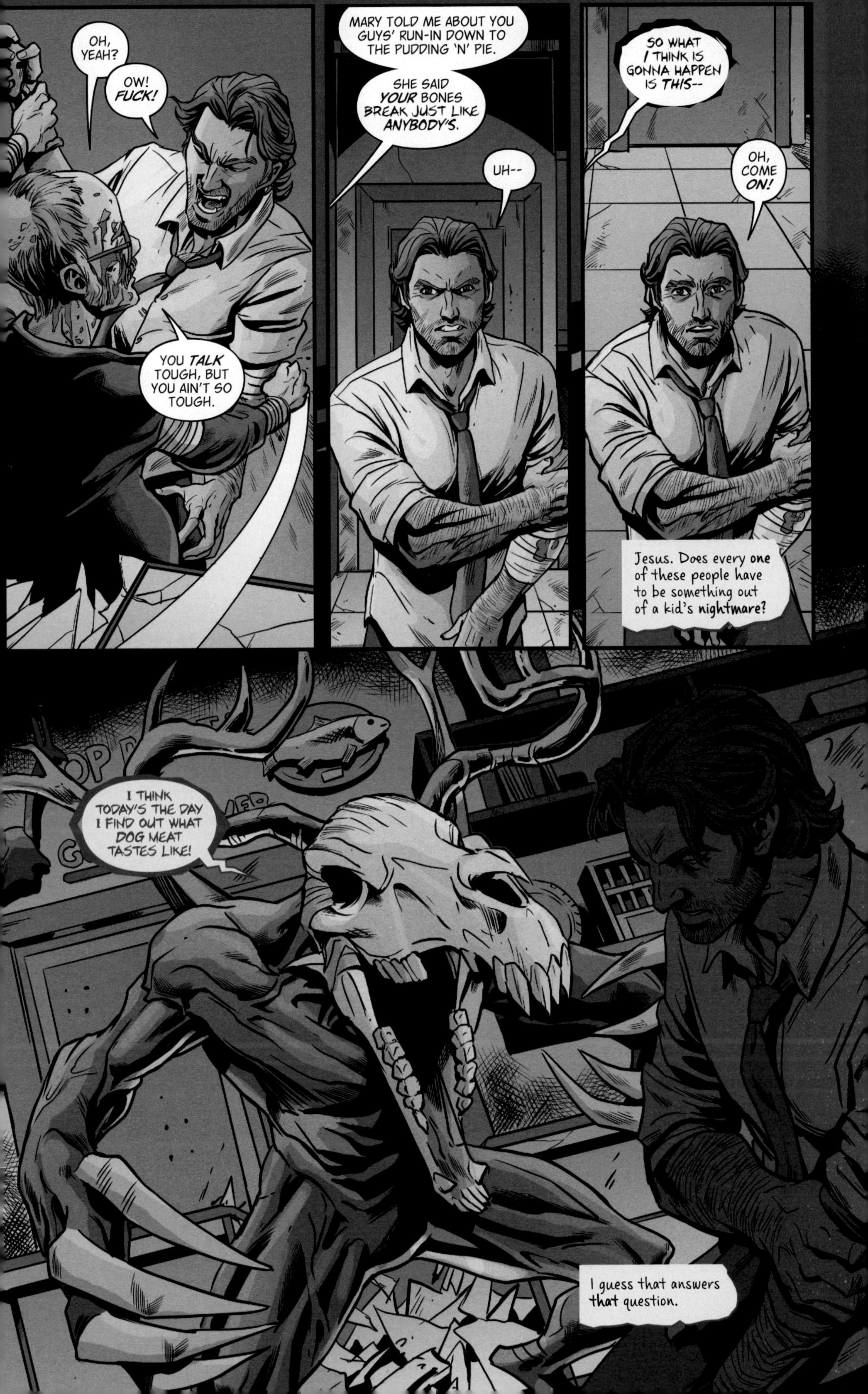
OH, YEAH?
OW! FUCK!
YOU TALK TOUGH, BUT YOU AIN'T SO TOUGH.
MARY TOLD ME ABOUT YOU GUYS' RUN-IN DOWN TO THE PUDDING 'N' PIE.
SHE SAID YOUR BONES BREAK JUST LIKE ANYBODY'S.
UH--
SO WHAT I THINK IS GONNA HAPPEN IS THIS--
OH, COME ON!
Jesus. Does every one of these people have to be something out of a kid's nightmare?
I THINK TODAY'S THE DAY I FIND OUT WHAT DOG MEAT TASTES LIKE!
I guess that answers that question.

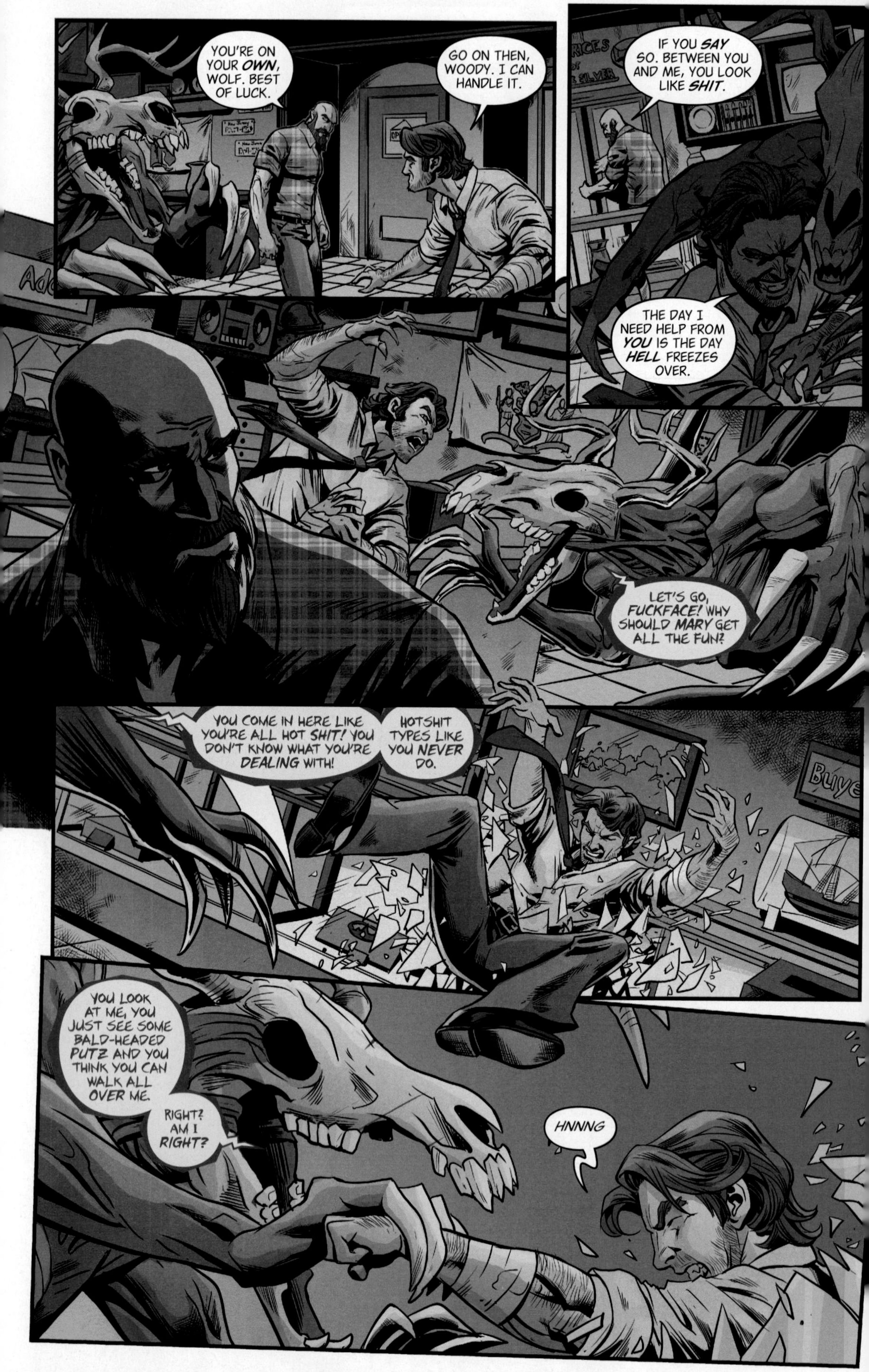
YOU'RE ON YOUR OWN, WOLF. BEST OF LUCK.
GO ON THEN, WOODY. I CAN HANDLE IT.
IF YOU SAY SO. BETWEEN YOU AND ME, YOU LOOK LIKE SHIT.
THE DAY I NEED HELP FROM YOU IS THE DAY HELL FREEZES OVER.
LET'S GO, FUCKFACE! WHY SHOULD MARY GET ALL THE FUN?
YOU COME IN HERE LIKE YOU'RE ALL HOT SHIT! YOU DON'T KNOW WHAT YOU'RE DEALING WITH!
HOTSHIT TYPES LIKE YOU NEVER DO.
YOU LOOK AT ME, YOU JUST SEE SOME BALD-HEADED PUTZ AND YOU THINK YOU CAN WALK ALL OVER ME.
RIGHT? AM I RIGHT?
HNNNG

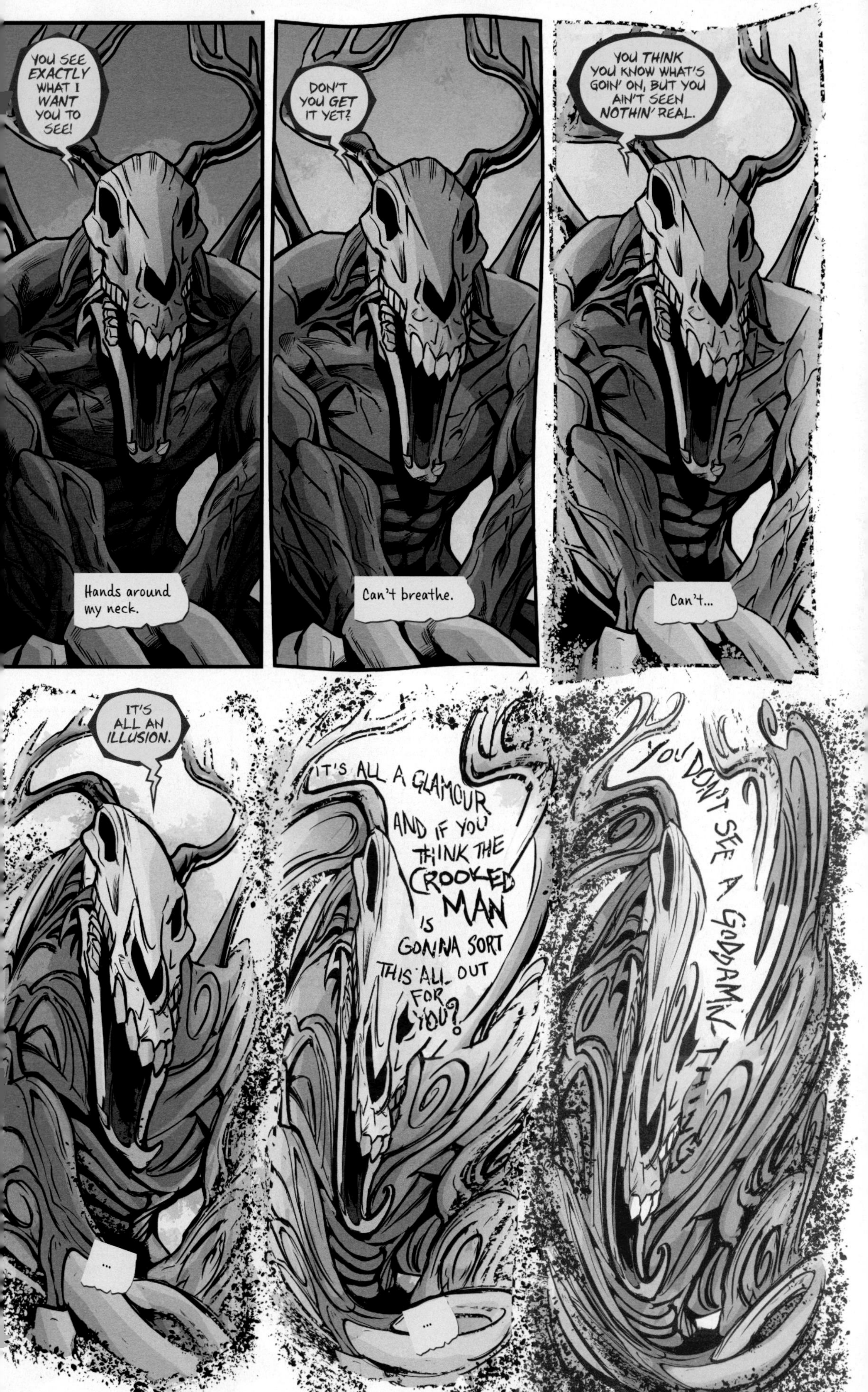
YOU SEE EXACTLY WHAT I WANT YOU TO SEE!
Hands around my neck.
DON'T YOU GET IT YET?
Can't breathe.
YOU THINK YOU KNOW WHAT'S GOIN' ON, BUT YOU AIN'T SEEN NOTHIN' REAL.
Can't...
IT'S ALL AN ILLUSION.
...
IT'S ALL A GLAMOUR AND IF YOU THINK THE CROOKED MAN IS GONNA SORT THIS ALL OUT FOR YOU?
...
YOU DON'T SEE A GODDAMN THING.

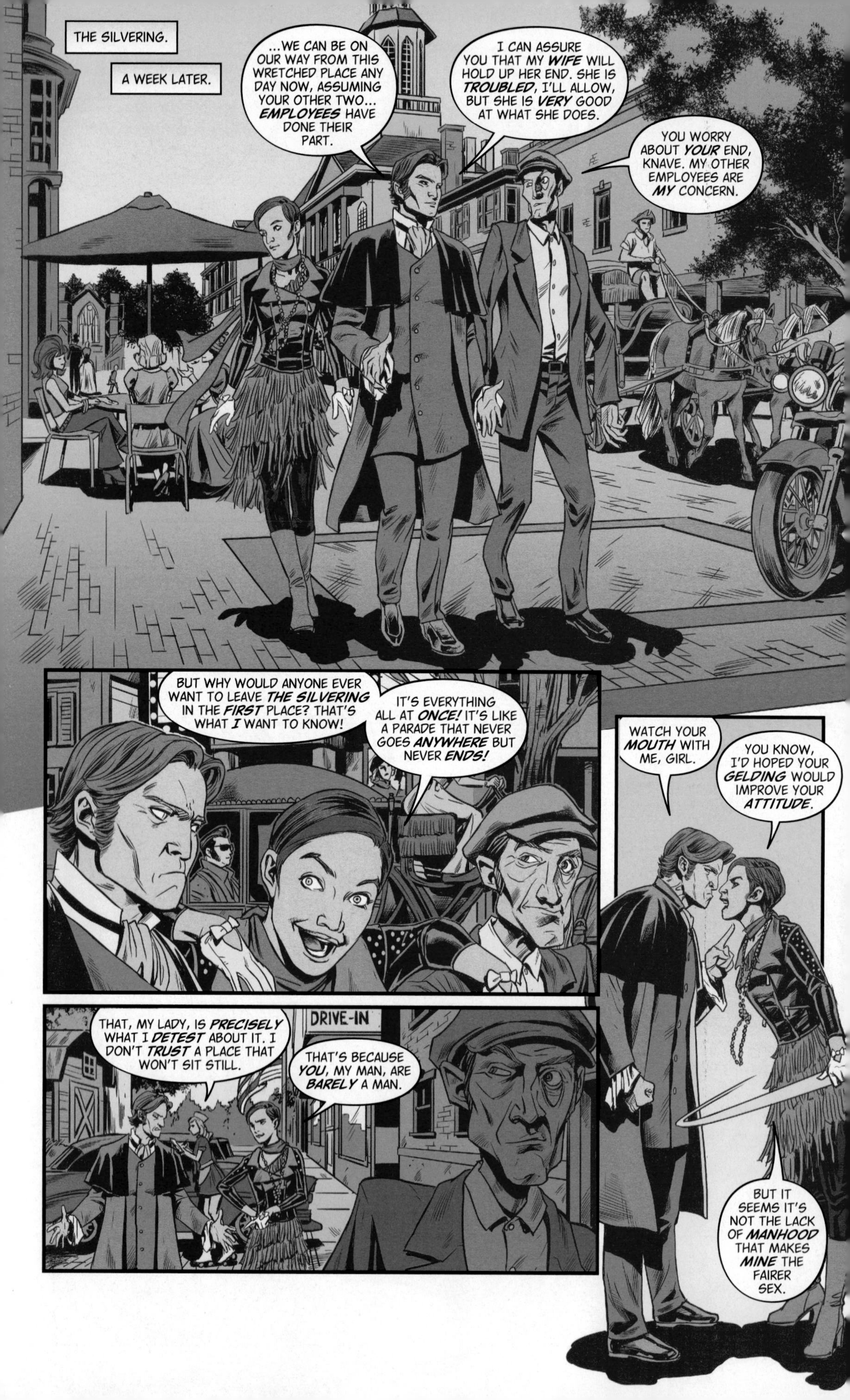
THE SILVERING.
A WEEK LATER.
...WE CAN BE ON OUR WAY FROM THIS WRETCHED PLACE ANY DAY NOW, ASSUMING YOUR OTHER TWO... EMPLOYEES HAVE DONE THEIR PART.
I CAN ASSURE YOU THAT MY WIFE WILL HOLD UP HER END. SHE IS TROUBLED, I'LL ALLOW, BUT SHE IS VERY GOOD AT WHAT SHE DOES.
YOU WORRY ABOUT YOUR END, KNAVE. MY OTHER EMPLOYEES ARE MY CONCERN.
BUT WHY WOULD ANYONE EVER WANT TO LEAVE THE SILVERING IN THE FIRST PLACE? THAT'S WHAT I WANT TO KNOW!
IT'S EVERYTHING ALL AT ONCE! IT'S LIKE A PARADE THAT NEVER GOES ANYWHERE BUT NEVER ENDS!
THAT, MY LADY, IS PRECISELY WHAT I DETEST ABOUT IT. I DON'T TRUST A PLACE THAT WON'T SIT STILL.
DRIVE-IN
THAT'S BECAUSE YOU, MY MAN, ARE BARELY A MAN.
WATCH YOUR MOUTH WITH ME, GIRL.
YOU KNOW, I'D HOPED YOUR GELDING WOULD IMPROVE YOUR ATTITUDE.
BUT IT SEEMS IT'S NOT THE LACK OF MANHOOD THAT MAKES MINE THE FAIRER SEX.

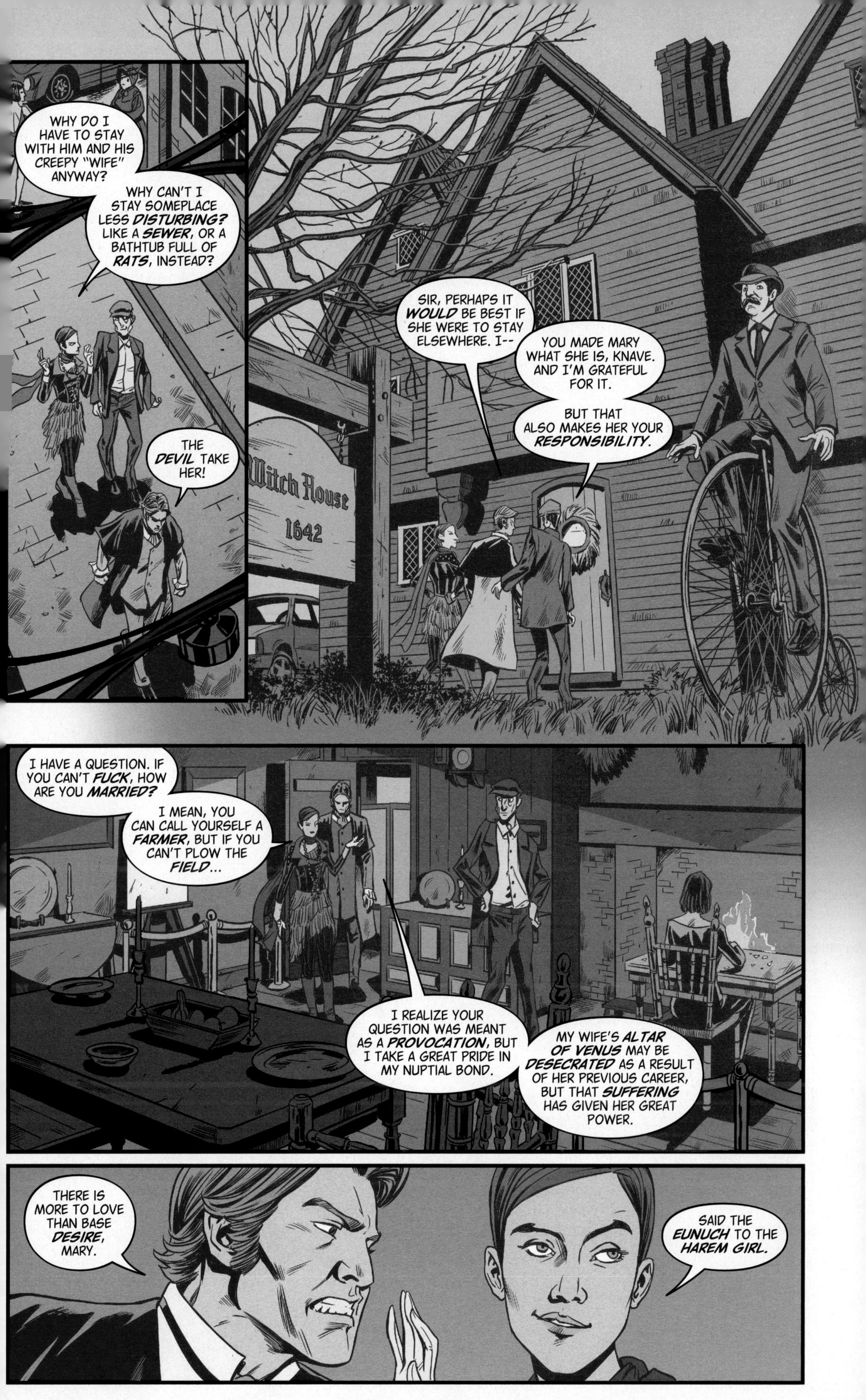
WHY DO I HAVE TO STAY WITH HIM AND HIS CREEPY "WIFE" ANYWAY?
WHY CAN'T I STAY SOMEPLACE LESS DISTURBING? LIKE A SEWER, OR A BATHTUB FULL OF RATS, INSTEAD?
THE DEVIL TAKE HER!
Witch House 1642
SIR, PERHAPS IT WOULD BE BEST IF SHE WERE TO STAY ELSEWHERE. I--
YOU MADE MARY WHAT SHE IS, KNAVE. AND I'M GRATEFUL FOR IT.
BUT THAT ALSO MAKES HER YOUR RESPONSIBILITY.
I HAVE A QUESTION. IF YOU CAN'T FUCK, HOW ARE YOU MARRIED?
I MEAN, YOU CAN CALL YOURSELF A FARMER, BUT IF YOU CAN'T PLOW THE FIELD...
I REALIZE YOUR QUESTION WAS MEANT AS A PROVOCATION, BUT I TAKE A GREAT PRIDE IN MY NUPTIAL BOND.
MY WIFE'S ALTAR OF VENUS MAY BE DESECRATED AS A RESULT OF HER PREVIOUS CAREER, BUT THAT SUFFERING HAS GIVEN HER GREAT POWER.
THERE IS MORE TO LOVE THAN BASE DESIRE, MARY.
SAID THE EUNUCH TO THE HAREM GIRL.

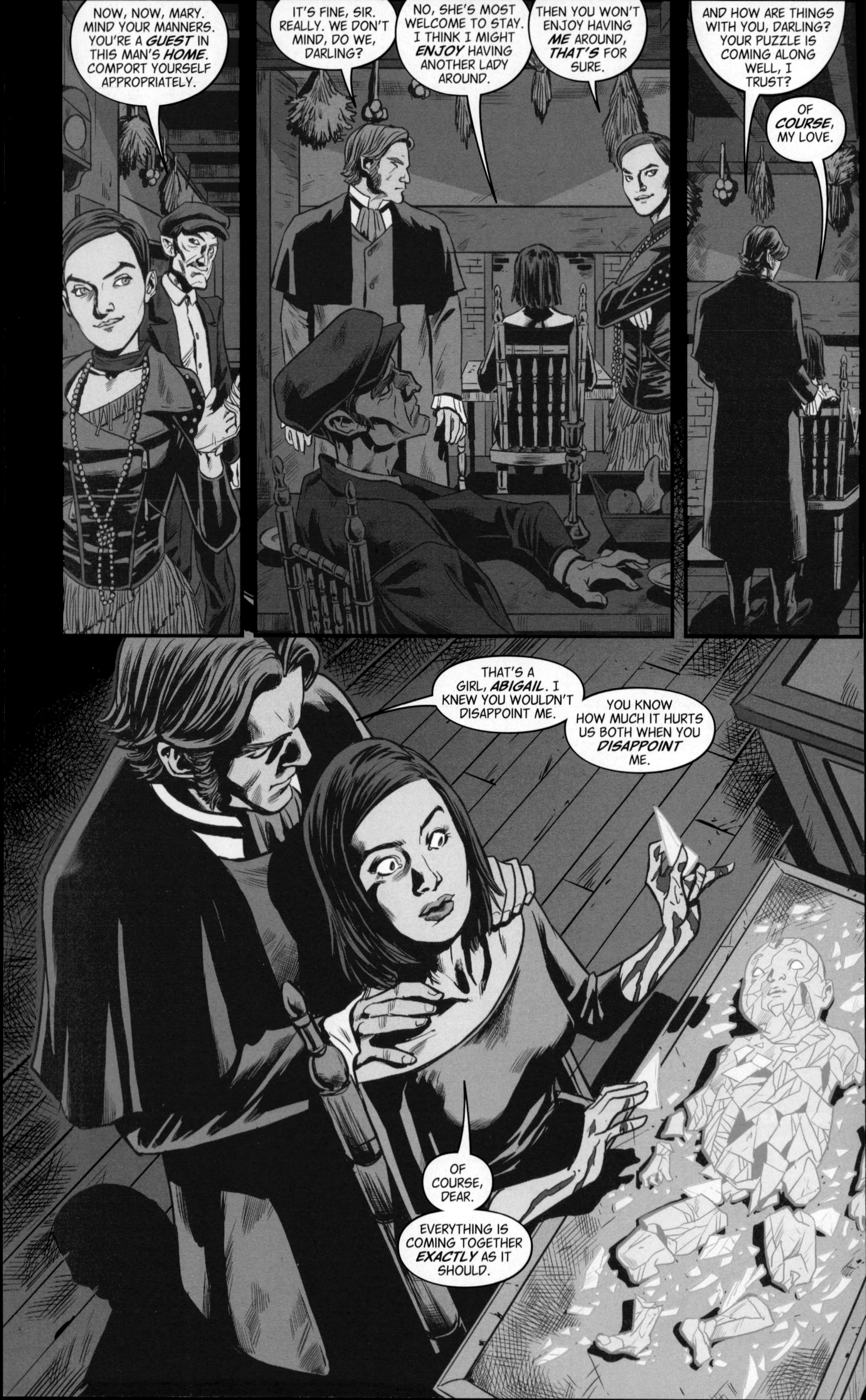
NOW, NOW, MARY. MIND YOUR MANNERS. YOU'RE A GUEST IN THIS MAN'S HOME. COMPORT YOURSELF APPROPRIATELY.
IT'S FINE, SIR. REALLY. WE DON'T MIND, DO WE, DARLING?
NO, SHE'S MOST WELCOME TO STAY. I THINK I MIGHT ENJOY HAVING ANOTHER LADY AROUND.
THEN YOU WON'T ENJOY HAVING ME AROUND, THAT'S FOR SURE.
AND HOW ARE THINGS WITH YOU, DARLING? YOUR PUZZLE IS COMING ALONG WELL, I TRUST?
OF COURSE, MY LOVE.
THAT'S A GIRL, ABIGAIL. I KNEW YOU WOULDN'T DISAPPOINT ME.
YOU KNOW HOW MUCH IT HURTS US BOTH WHEN YOU DISAPPOINT ME.
OF COURSE, DEAR.
EVERYTHING IS COMING TOGETHER EXACTLY AS IT SHOULD.

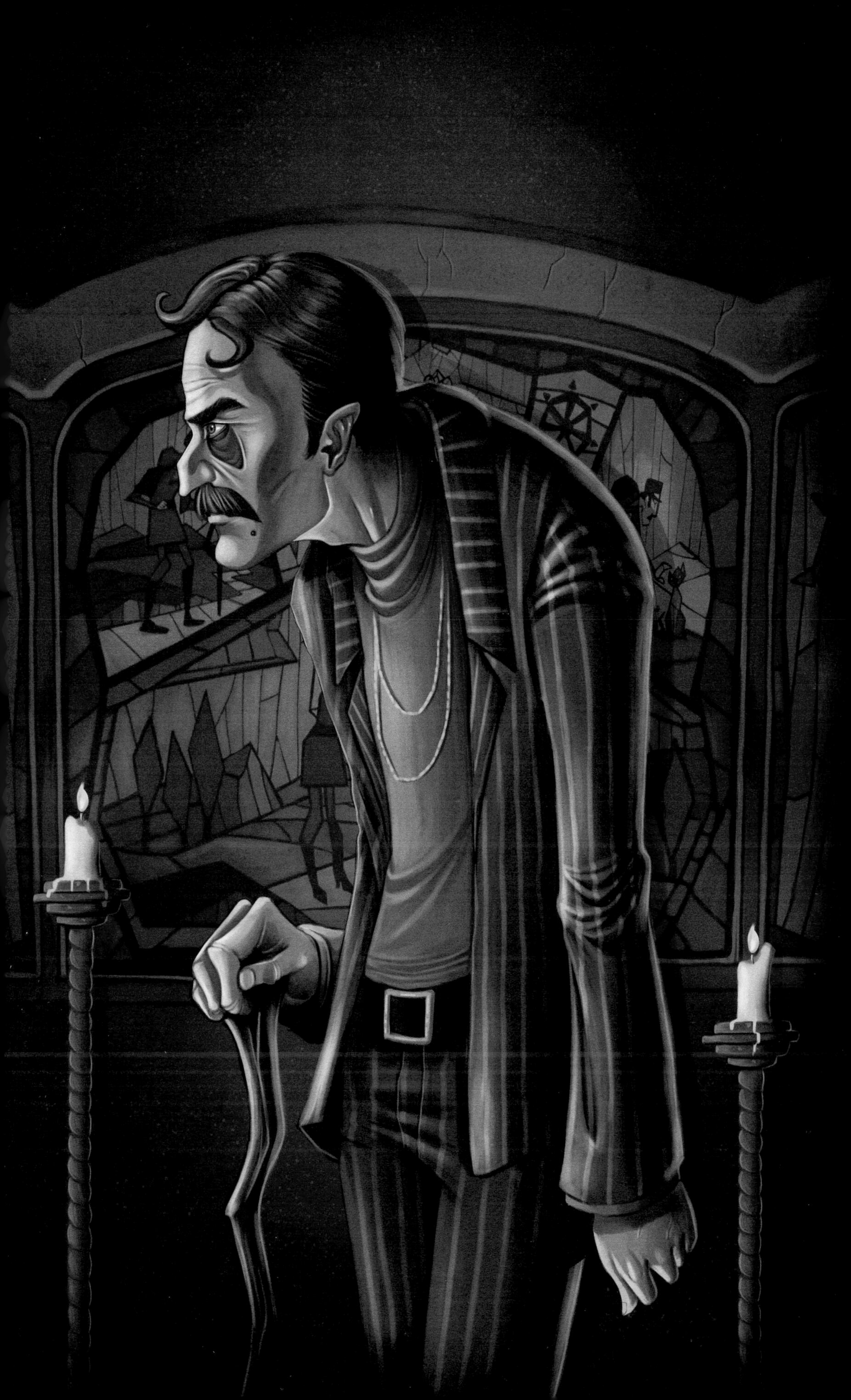

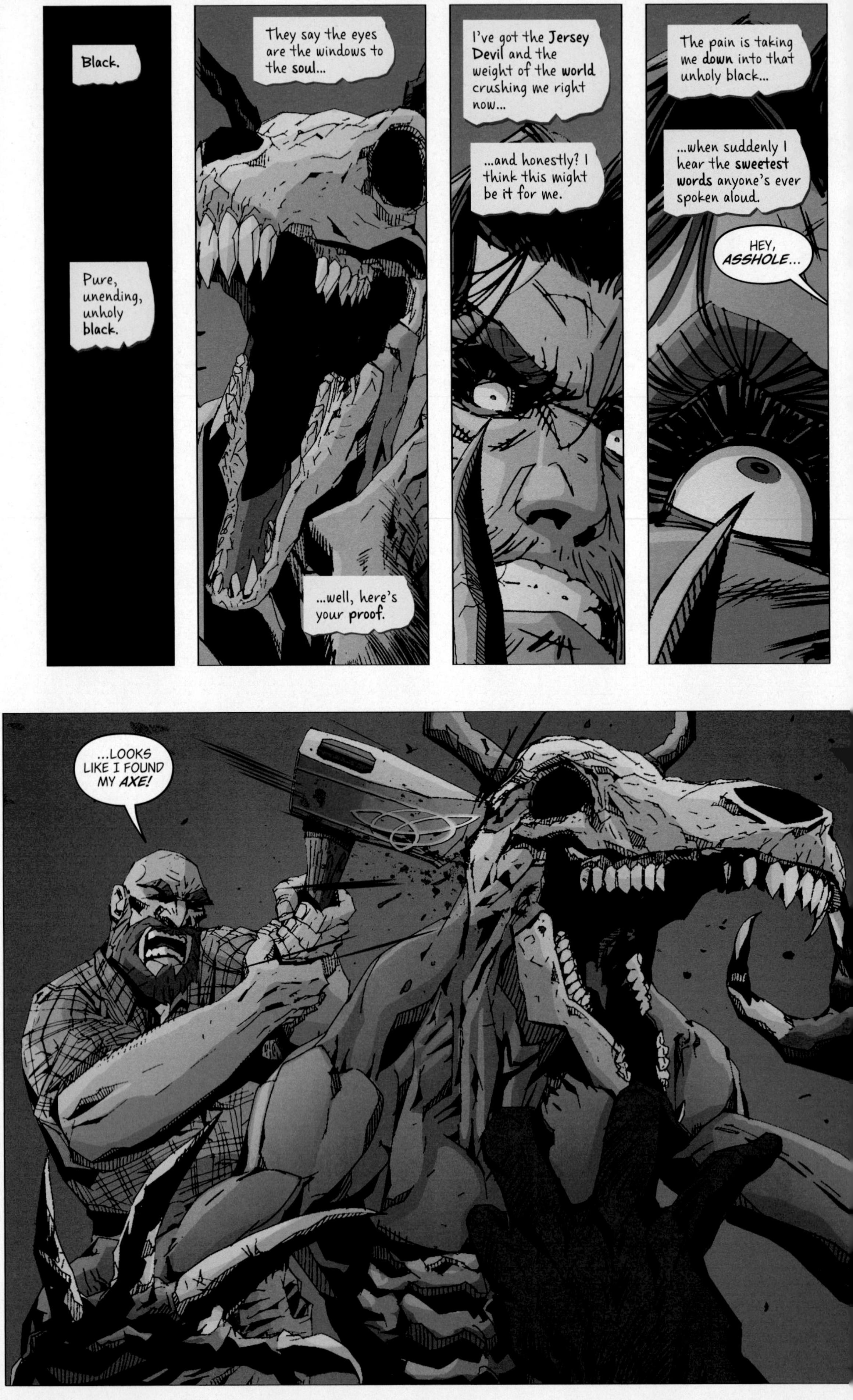
Black.
Pure, unending, unholy black.
They say the eyes are the windows to the soul...
...well, here's your proof.
I've got the Jersey Devil and the weight of the world crushing me right now...
...and honestly? I think this might be it for me.
The pain is taking me down into that unholy black...
...when suddenly I hear the sweetest words anyone's ever spoken aloud.
HEY, ASSHOLE...
...LOOKS LIKE I FOUND MY AXE!

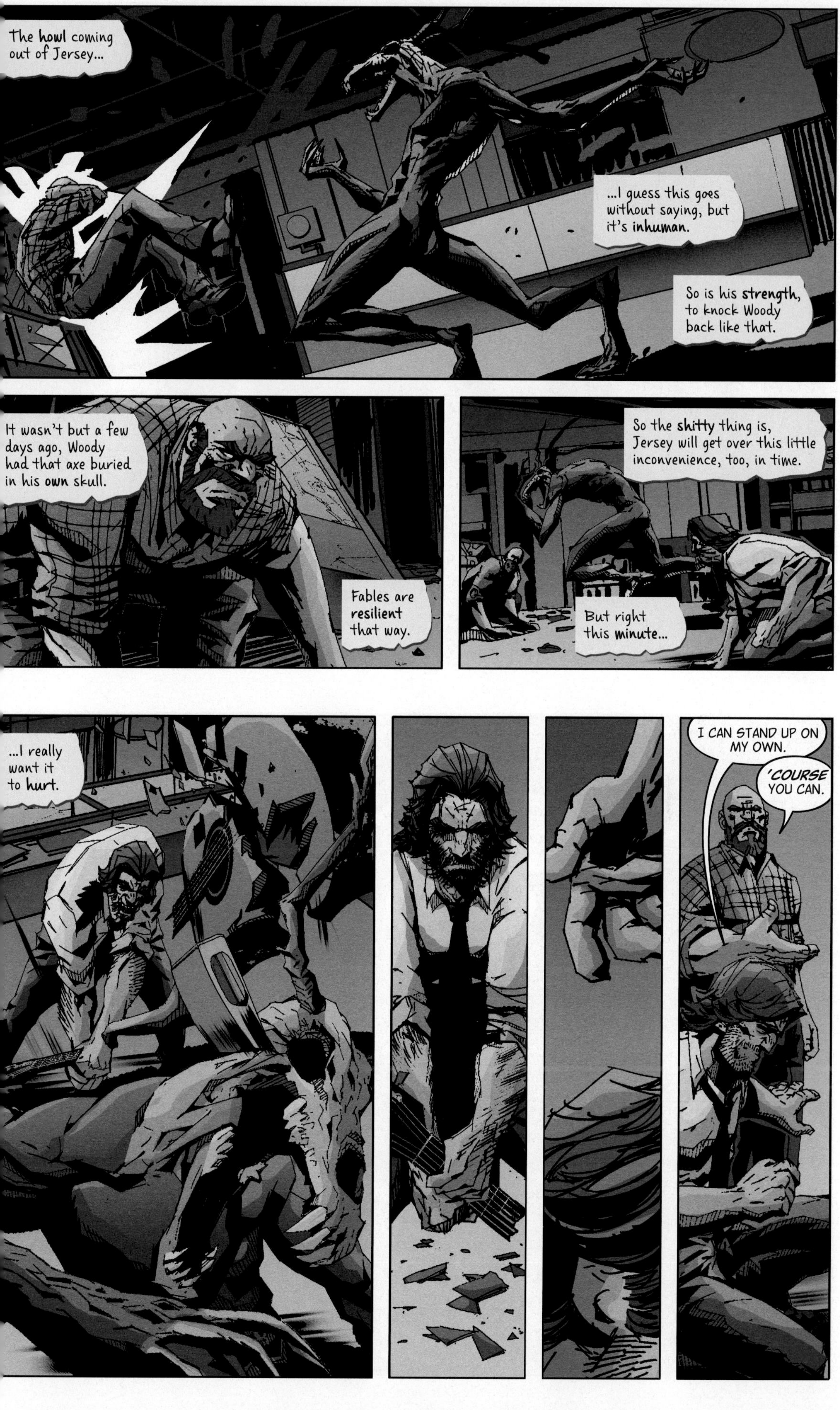
The howl coming out of Jersey...
...I guess this goes without saying, but it's inhuman.
So is his strength, to knock Woody back like that.
It wasn't but a few days ago, Woody had that axe buried in his own skull.
Fables are resilient that way.
So the shitty thing is, Jersey will get over this little inconvenience, too, in time.
But right this minute...
...I really want it to hurt.
I CAN STAND UP ON MY OWN.
'COURSE YOU CAN.

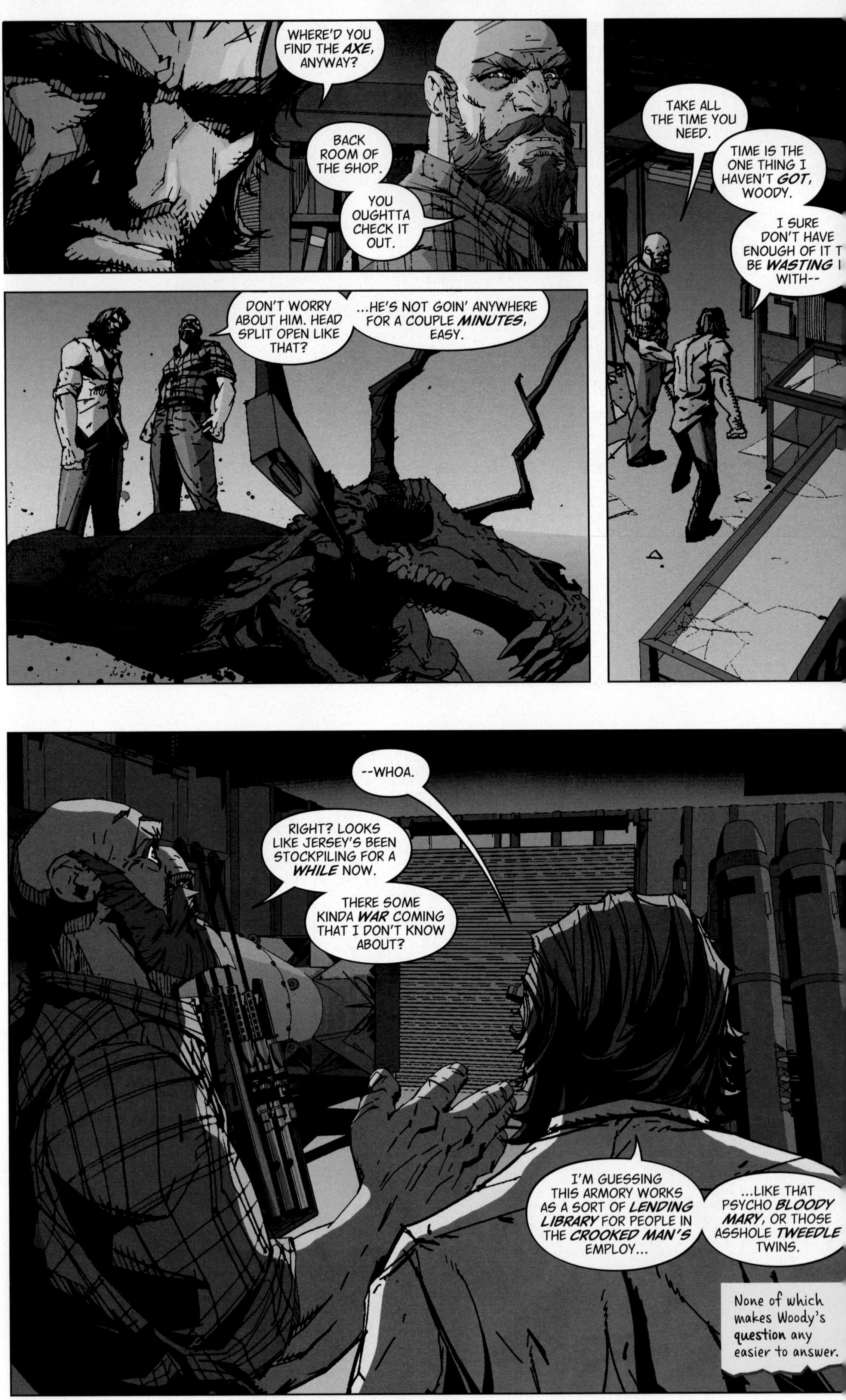

WHERE'D YOU FIND THE AXE, ANYWAY?
BACK ROOM OF THE SHOP.
YOU OUGHTTA CHECK IT OUT.
DON'T WORRY ABOUT HIM. HEAD SPLIT OPEN LIKE THAT?
...HE'S NOT GOIN' ANYWHERE FOR A COUPLE MINUTES, EASY.
TAKE ALL THE TIME YOU NEED.
TIME IS THE ONE THING I HAVEN'T GOT, WOODY.
I SURE DON'T HAVE ENOUGH OF IT T BE WASTING I WITH--
--WHOA.
RIGHT? LOOKS LIKE JERSEY'S BEEN STOCKPILING FOR A WHILE NOW.
THERE SOME KINDA WAR COMING THAT I DON'T KNOW ABOUT?
I'M GUESSING THIS ARMORY WORKS AS A SORT OF LENDING LIBRARY FOR PEOPLE IN THE CROOKED MAN'S EMPLOY...
...LIKE THAT PSYCHO BLOODY MARY, OR THOSE ASSHOLE TWEEDLE TWINS.
None of which makes Woody's question any easier to answer.

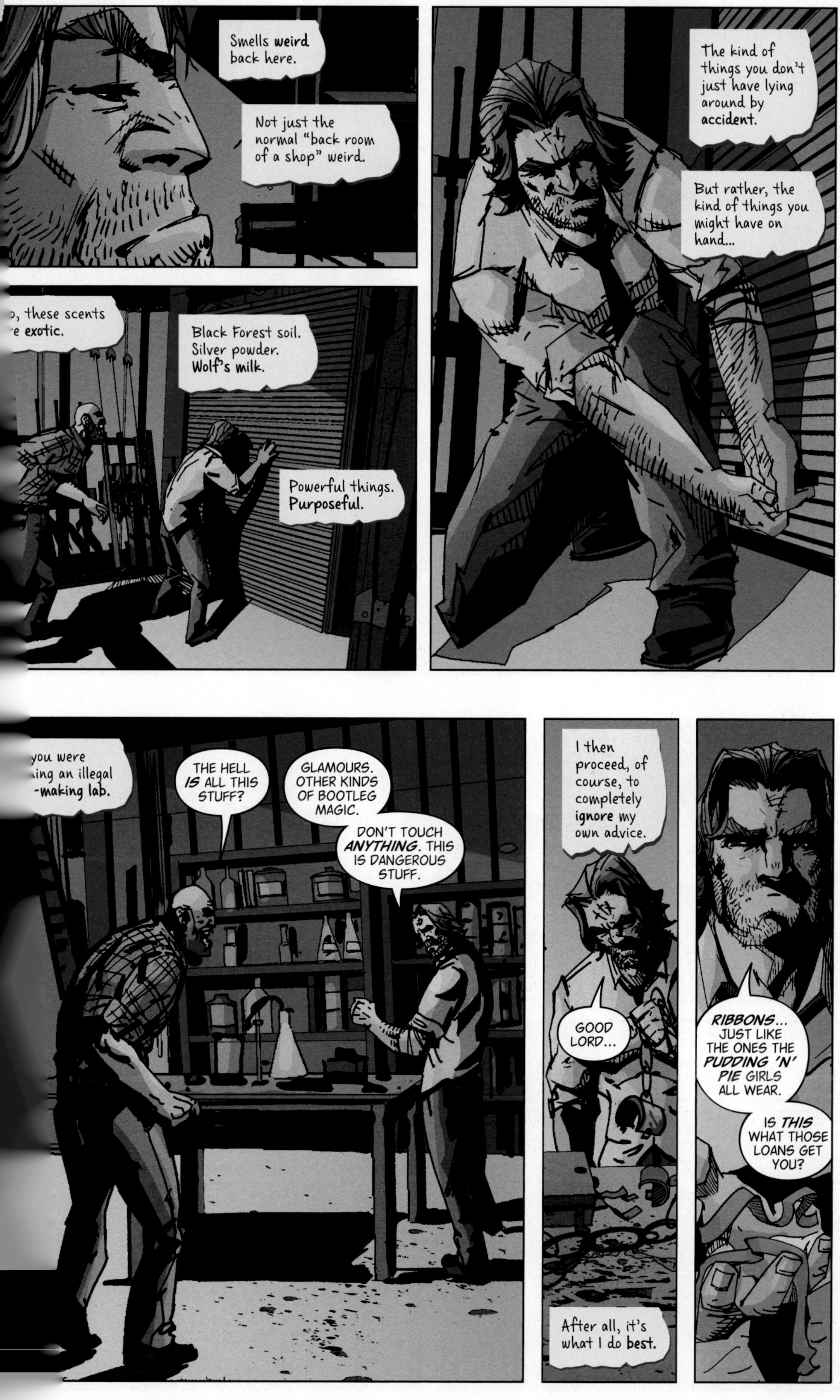
Smells weird back here.
Not just the normal "back room of a shop" weird.
The kind of things you don't just have lying around by accident.
But rather, the kind of things you might have on hand...
o, these scents e exotic.
Black Forest soil. Silver powder. Wolf's milk.
Powerful things. Purposeful.
you were ing an illegal -making lab.
THE HELL IS ALL THIS STUFF?
GLAMOURS. OTHER KINDS OF BOOTLEG MAGIC.
DON'T TOUCH ANYTHING. THIS IS DANGEROUS STUFF.
I then proceed, of course, to completely ignore my own advice.
GOOD LORD...
After all, it's what I do best.
RIBBONS... JUST LIKE THE ONES THE PUDDING 'N' PIE GIRLS ALL WEAR.
IS THIS WHAT THOSE LOANS GET YOU?

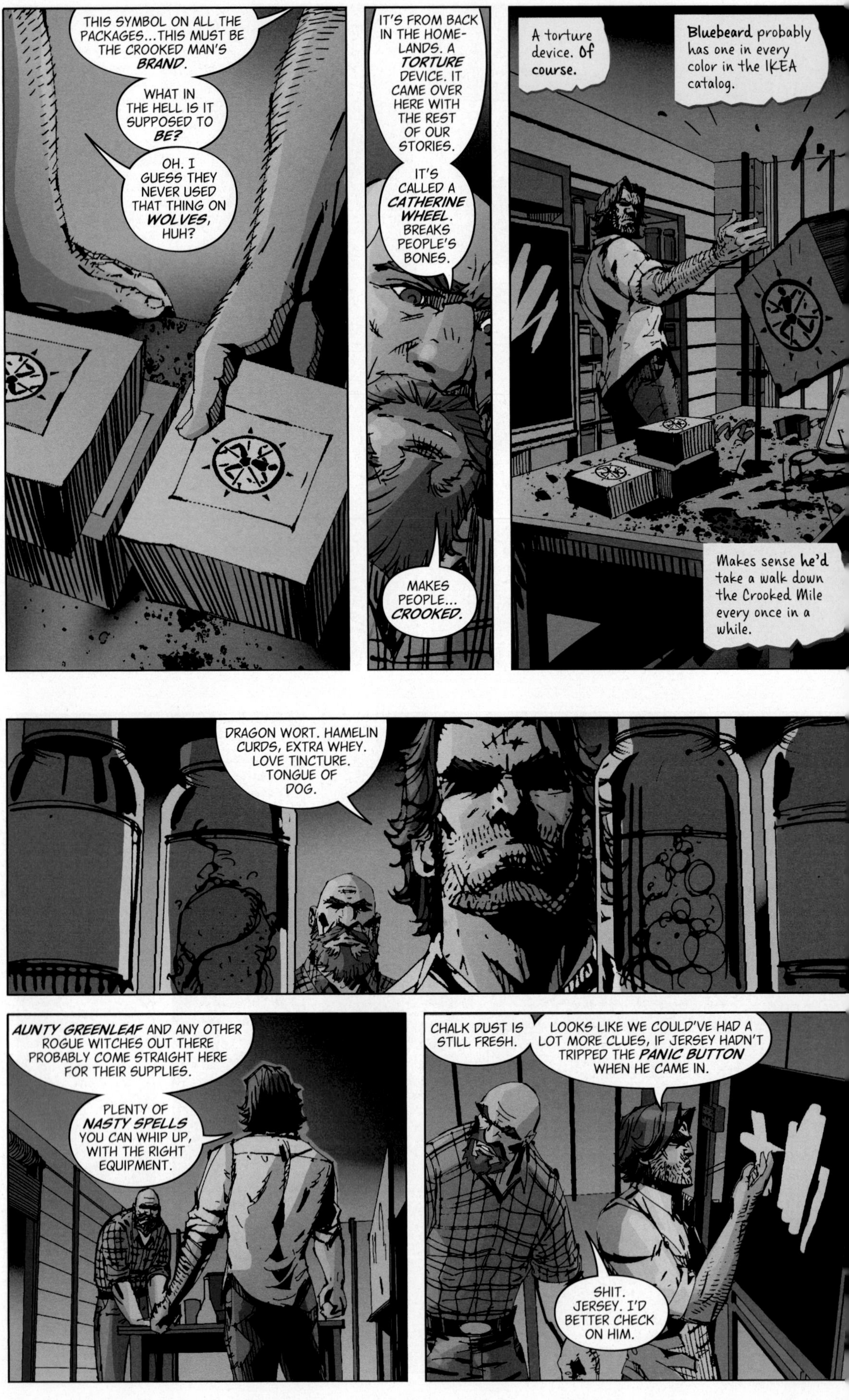

THIS SYMBOL ON ALL THE PACKAGES...THIS MUST BE THE CROOKED MAN'S BRAND.
WHAT IN THE HELL IS IT SUPPOSED TO BE?
OH. I GUESS THEY NEVER USED THAT THING ON WOLVES, HUH?
IT'S FROM BACK IN THE HOME-LANDS. A TORTURE DEVICE. IT CAME OVER HERE WITH THE REST OF OUR STORIES.
IT'S CALLED A CATHERINE WHEEL. BREAKS PEOPLE'S BONES.
MAKES PEOPLE... CROOKED.
A torture device. Of course.
Bluebeard probably has one in every color in the IKEA catalog.
Makes sense he'd take a walk down the Crooked Mile every once in a while.
DRAGON WORT. HAMELIN CURDS, EXTRA WHEY. LOVE TINCTURE. TONGUE OF DOG.
AUNTY GREENLEAF AND ANY OTHER ROGUE WITCHES OUT THERE PROBABLY COME STRAIGHT HERE FOR THEIR SUPPLIES.
PLENTY OF NASTY SPELLS YOU CAN WHIP UP, WITH THE RIGHT EQUIPMENT.
CHALK DUST IS STILL FRESH.
LOOKS LIKE WE COULD'VE HAD A LOT MORE CLUES, IF JERSEY HADN'T TRIPPED THE PANIC BUTTON WHEN HE CAME IN.
SHIT. JERSEY. I'D BETTER CHECK ON HIM.

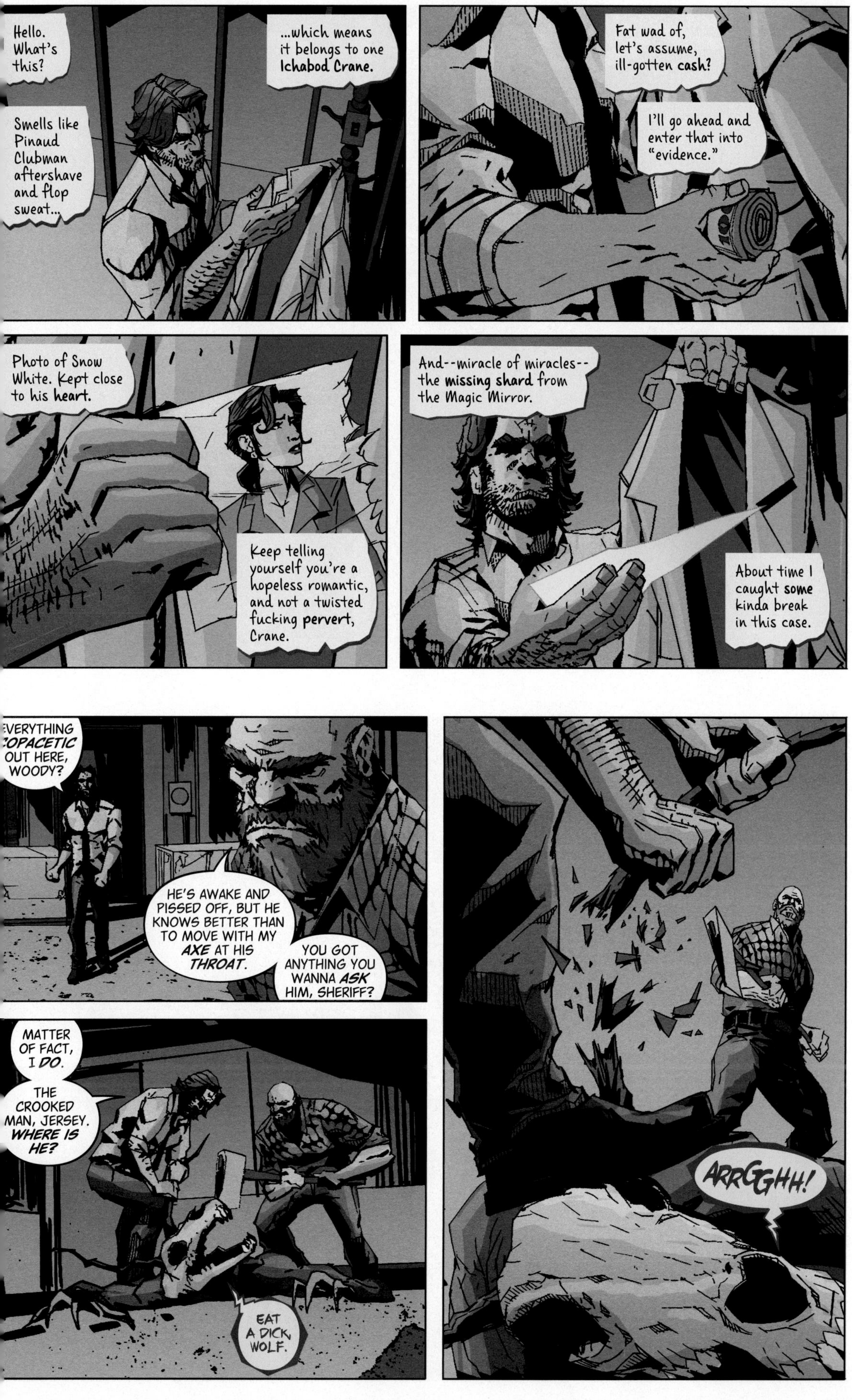

Hello. What's this?
...which means it belongs to one Ichabod Crane.
Smells like Pinaud Clubman aftershave and flop sweat...
Fat wad of, let's assume, ill-gotten cash?
I'll go ahead and enter that into "evidence."
Photo of Snow White. Kept close to his heart.
Keep telling yourself you're a hopeless romantic, and not a twisted fucking pervert, Crane.
And--miracle of miracles--the missing shard from the Magic Mirror.
About time I caught some kinda break in this case.
EVERYTHING COPACETIC OUT HERE, WOODY?
HE'S AWAKE AND PISSED OFF, BUT HE KNOWS BETTER THAN TO MOVE WITH MY AXE AT HIS THROAT.
YOU GOT ANYTHING YOU WANNA ASK HIM, SHERIFF?
MATTER OF FACT, I DO.
THE CROOKED MAN, JERSEY. WHERE IS HE?
EAT A DICK, WOLF.
ARRGGHH!

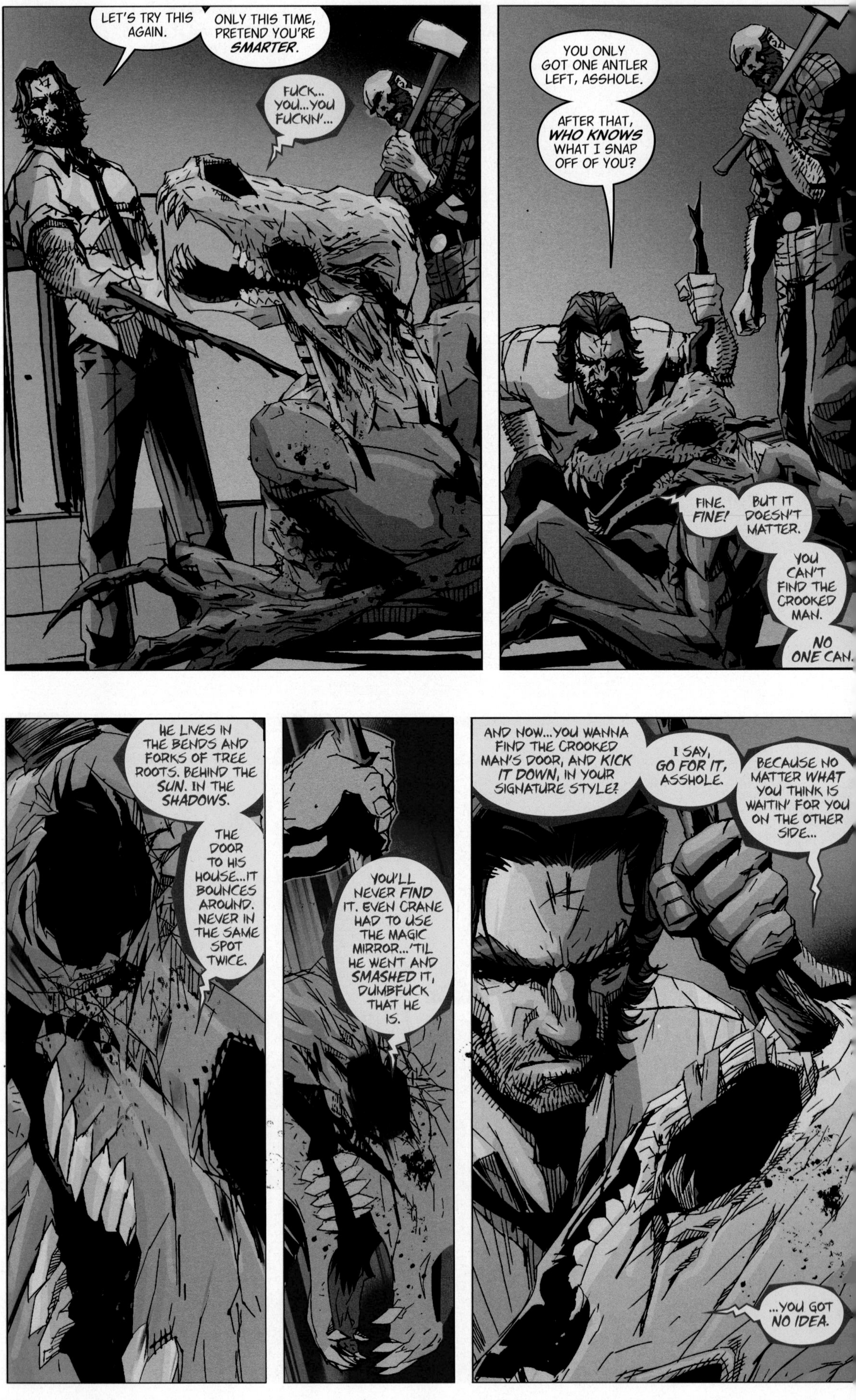
LET'S TRY THIS AGAIN.
ONLY THIS TIME, PRETEND YOU'RE SMARTER.
FUCK... YOU...YOU FUCKIN'...
YOU ONLY GOT ONE ANTLER LEFT, ASSHOLE.
AFTER THAT, WHO KNOWS WHAT I SNAP OFF OF YOU?
FINE. FINE!
BUT IT DOESN'T MATTER.
YOU CAN'T FIND THE CROOKED MAN.
NO ONE CAN.
HE LIVES IN THE BENDS AND FORKS OF TREE ROOTS. BEHIND THE SUN. IN THE SHADOWS.
THE DOOR TO HIS HOUSE...IT BOUNCES AROUND. NEVER IN THE SAME SPOT TWICE.
YOU'LL NEVER FIND IT. EVEN CRANE HAD TO USE THE MAGIC MIRROR...'TIL HE WENT AND SMASHED IT, DUMBFUCK THAT HE IS.
AND NOW...YOU WANNA FIND THE CROOKED MAN'S DOOR, AND KICK IT DOWN, IN YOUR SIGNATURE STYLE?
I SAY, GO FOR IT, ASSHOLE.
BECAUSE NO MATTER WHAT YOU THINK IS WAITIN' FOR YOU ON THE OTHER SIDE...
...YOU GOT NO IDEA.

SO THERE'S THE INFORMATION YOU WERE AFTER, FOR WHATEVER IT'S WORTH.

NOW HERE'S SOME OPINION TO GO ALONG WITH IT.

NOT INTERESTED.

TOO BAD. BECAUSE HEY, GUESS WHAT, SHERIFF?

THOSE GIRLS? THEY'RE STILL DEAD.

AND THERE AIN'T A GODDAMN THING YOU CAN DO TO BRING 'EM BACK.

AND I DON'T KNOW WHAT THEY DID, BUT I DO KNOW THIS...

...IF THEY'RE DEAD, IT'S BECAUSE THE CROOKED MAN WANTED 'EM DEAD.

THAT'S ALL IT TAKES.

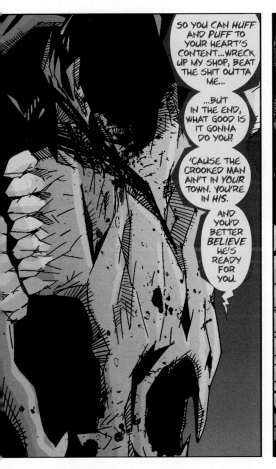

SO YOU CAN HUFF AND PUFF TO YOUR HEART'S CONTENT...WRECK UP MY SHOP, BEAT THE SHIT OUTTA ME...

...BUT IN THE END, WHAT GOOD IS IT GONNA DO YOU?

'CAUSE THE CROOKED MAN AIN'T IN YOUR TOWN. YOU'RE IN HIS.

AND YOU'D BETTER BELIEVE HE'S READY FOR YOU.

MAYBE IN FABLETOWN PROPER, YOU'RE USED TO BEING THE "GOOD GUY," THE WHITE KNIGHT, THE HERO WHO ALWAYS WINS.

BUT HERE ON THE CROOKED MILE, YOU'RE JUST A TINY SPECK OF WHITE...

...IN A WHOLE OCEAN OF BLACK.

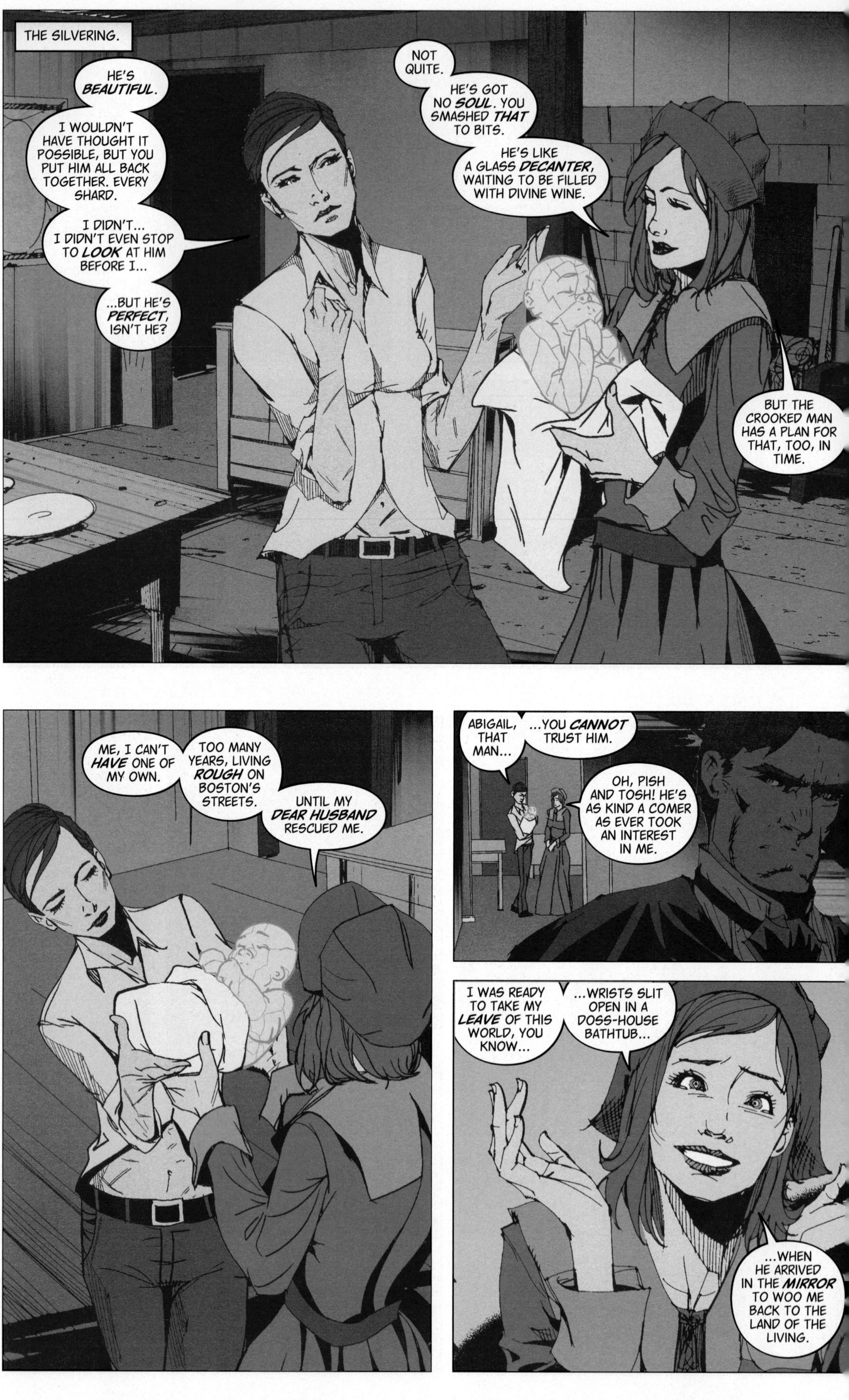
THE SILVERING.
HE'S BEAUTIFUL.
I WOULDN'T HAVE THOUGHT IT POSSIBLE, BUT YOU PUT HIM ALL BACK TOGETHER. EVERY SHARD.
I DIDN'T... I DIDN'T EVEN STOP TO LOOK AT HIM BEFORE I...
...BUT HE'S PERFECT, ISN'T HE?
NOT QUITE.
HE'S GOT NO SOUL. YOU SMASHED THAT TO BITS.
HE'S LIKE A GLASS DECANTER, WAITING TO BE FILLED WITH DIVINE WINE.
BUT THE CROOKED MAN HAS A PLAN FOR THAT, TOO, IN TIME.
ME, I CAN'T HAVE ONE OF MY OWN.
TOO MANY YEARS, LIVING ROUGH ON BOSTON'S STREETS.
UNTIL MY DEAR HUSBAND RESCUED ME.
ABIGAIL, THAT MAN...
...YOU CANNOT TRUST HIM.
OH, PISH AND TOSH! HE'S AS KIND A COMER AS EVER TOOK AN INTEREST IN ME.
I WAS READY TO TAKE MY LEAVE OF THIS WORLD, YOU KNOW...
...WRISTS SLIT OPEN IN A DOSS-HOUSE BATHTUB...
...WHEN HE ARRIVED IN THE MIRROR TO WOO ME BACK TO THE LAND OF THE LIVING.

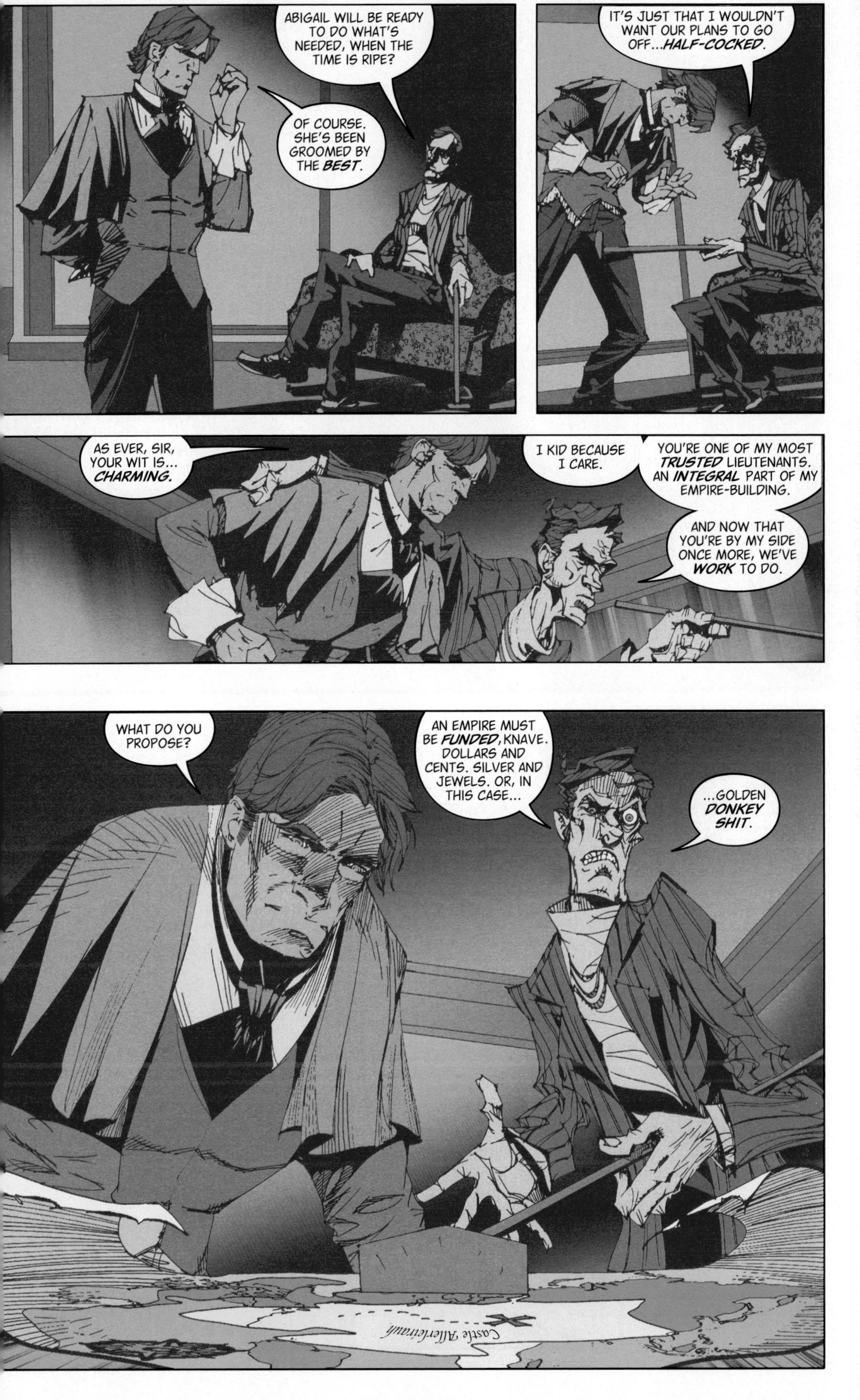

ABIGAIL WILL BE READY TO DO WHAT'S NEEDED, WHEN THE TIME IS RIPE?
OF COURSE. SHE'S BEEN GROOMED BY THE *BEST*.
IT'S JUST THAT I WOULDN'T WANT OUR PLANS TO GO OFF...*HALF-COCKED*.
AS EVER, SIR, YOUR WIT IS... *CHARMING*.
I KID BECAUSE I CARE.
YOU'RE ONE OF MY MOST *TRUSTED* LIEUTENANTS. AN *INTEGRAL* PART OF MY EMPIRE-BUILDING.
AND NOW THAT YOU'RE BY MY SIDE ONCE MORE, WE'VE *WORK* TO DO.
WHAT DO YOU PROPOSE?
AN EMPIRE MUST BE *FUNDED*, KNAVE. DOLLARS AND CENTS. SILVER AND JEWELS. OR, IN THIS CASE...
...GOLDEN *DONKEY SHIT*.

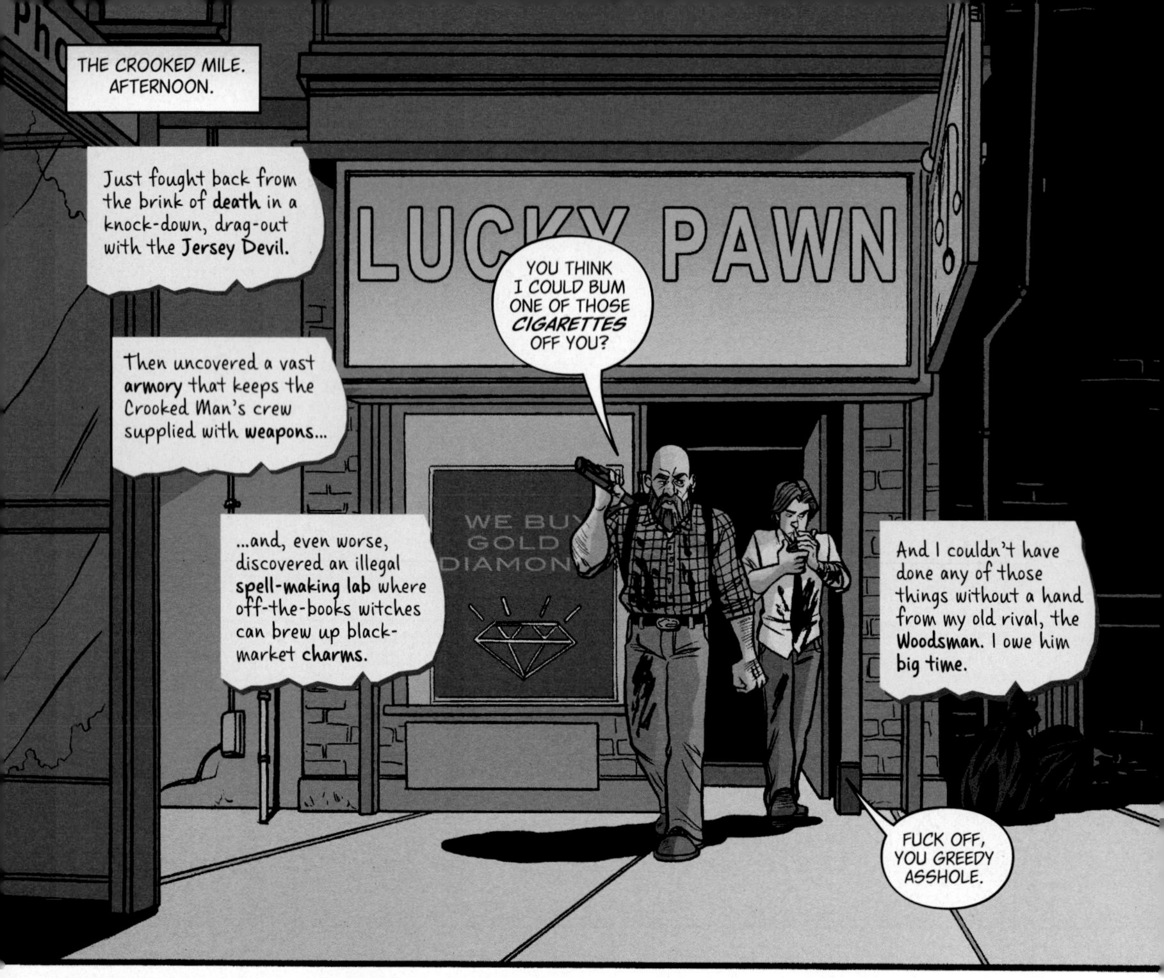

THE CROOKED MILE.
AFTERNOON.
Just fought back from the brink of death in a knock-down, drag-out with the Jersey Devil.
Then uncovered a vast armory that keeps the Crooked Man's crew supplied with weapons...
...and, even worse, discovered an illegal spell-making lab where off-the-books witches can brew up black-market charms.
LUCKY PAWN
YOU THINK I COULD BUM ONE OF THOSE CIGARETTES OFF YOU?
WE BUY GOLD DIAMON
And I couldn't have done any of those things without a hand from my old rival, the Woodsman. I owe him big time.
FUCK OFF, YOU GREEDY ASSHOLE.

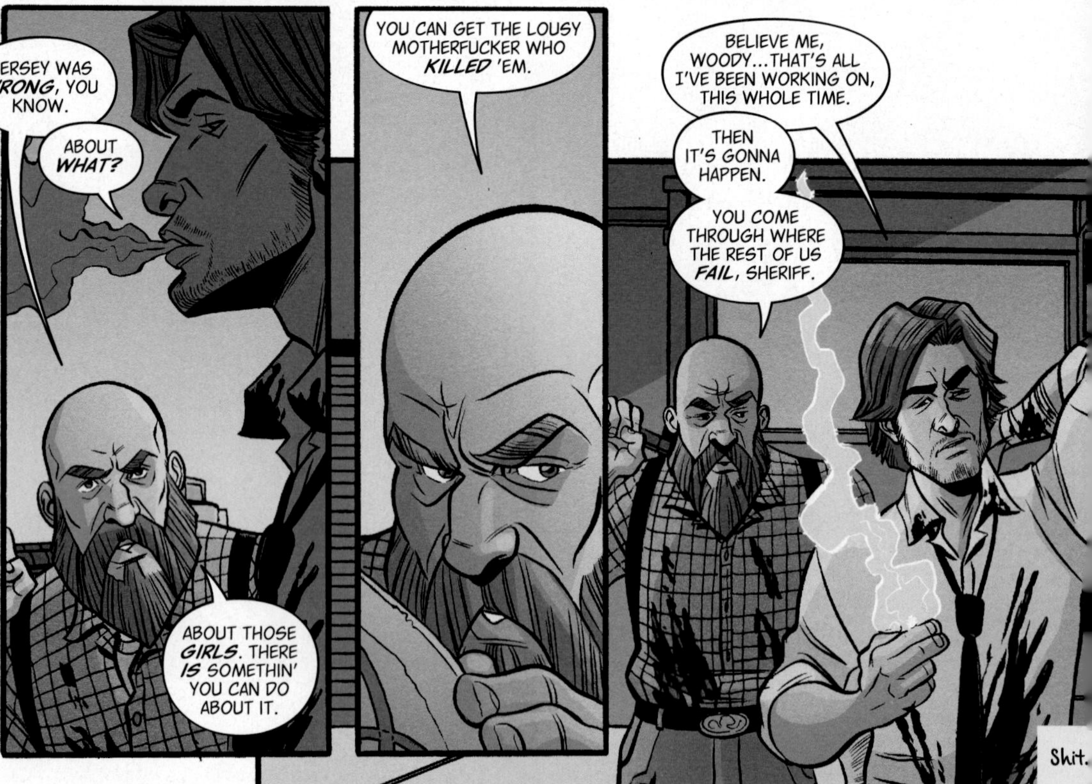

JERSEY WAS WRONG, YOU KNOW.
ABOUT WHAT?
ABOUT THOSE GIRLS. THERE IS SOMETHIN' YOU CAN DO ABOUT IT.
YOU CAN GET THE LOUSY MOTHERFUCKER WHO KILLED 'EM.
BELIEVE ME, WOODY...THAT'S ALL I'VE BEEN WORKING ON, THIS WHOLE TIME.
THEN IT'S GONNA HAPPEN.
YOU COME THROUGH WHERE THE REST OF US FAIL, SHERIFF.
Shit.

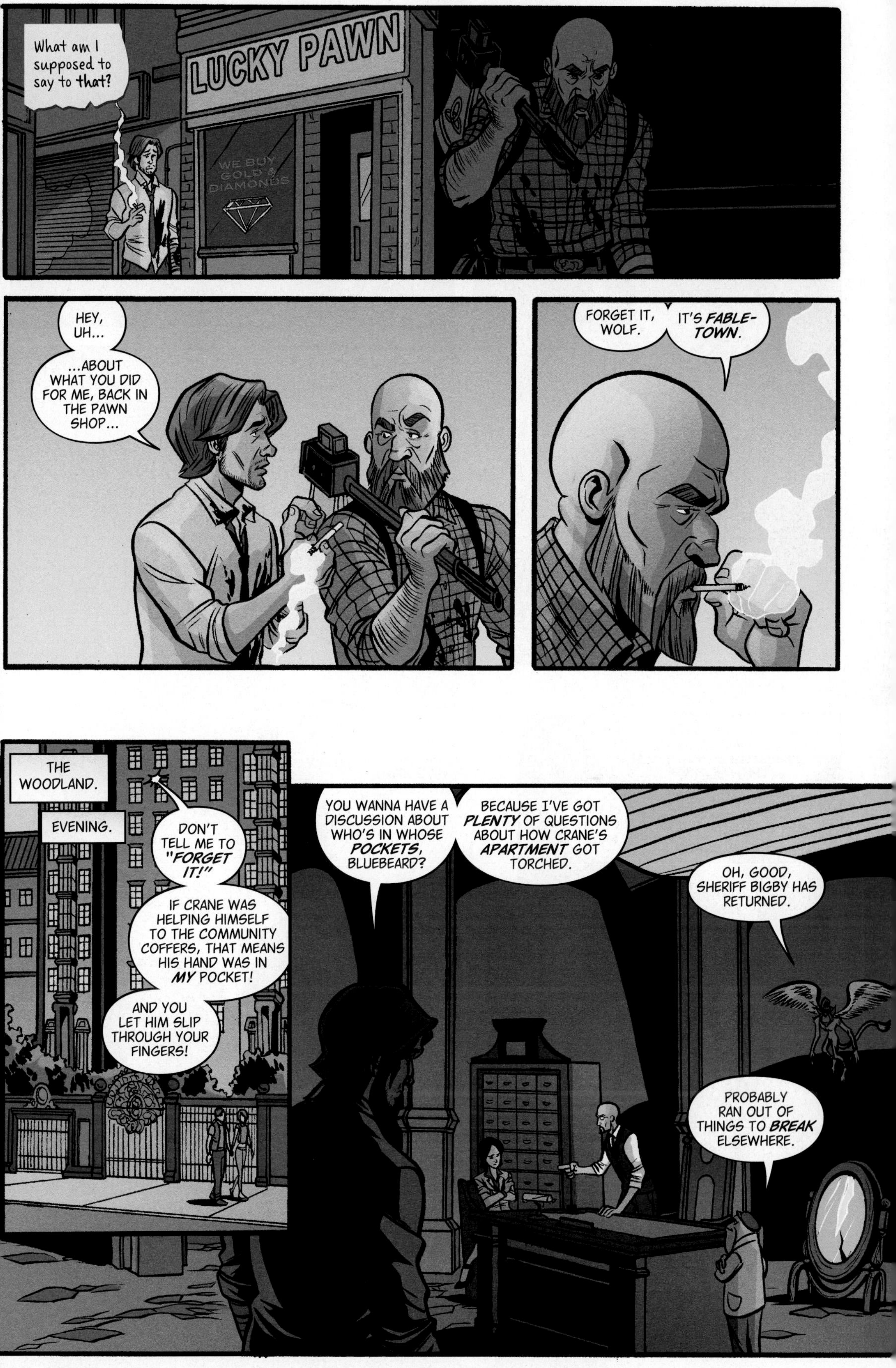
What am I supposed to say to that?
LUCKY PAWN
WE BUY GOLD & DIAMONDS
HEY, UH...
...ABOUT WHAT YOU DID FOR ME, BACK IN THE PAWN SHOP...
FORGET IT, WOLF.
IT'S FABLETOWN.
THE WOODLAND.
EVENING.
DON'T TELL ME TO "FORGET IT!"
IF CRANE WAS HELPING HIMSELF TO THE COMMUNITY COFFERS, THAT MEANS HIS HAND WAS IN MY POCKET!
AND YOU LET HIM SLIP THROUGH YOUR FINGERS!
YOU WANNA HAVE A DISCUSSION ABOUT WHO'S IN WHOSE POCKETS, BLUEBEARD?
BECAUSE I'VE GOT PLENTY OF QUESTIONS ABOUT HOW CRANE'S APARTMENT GOT TORCHED.
OH, GOOD, SHERIFF BIGBY HAS RETURNED.
PROBABLY RAN OUT OF THINGS TO BREAK ELSEWHERE.

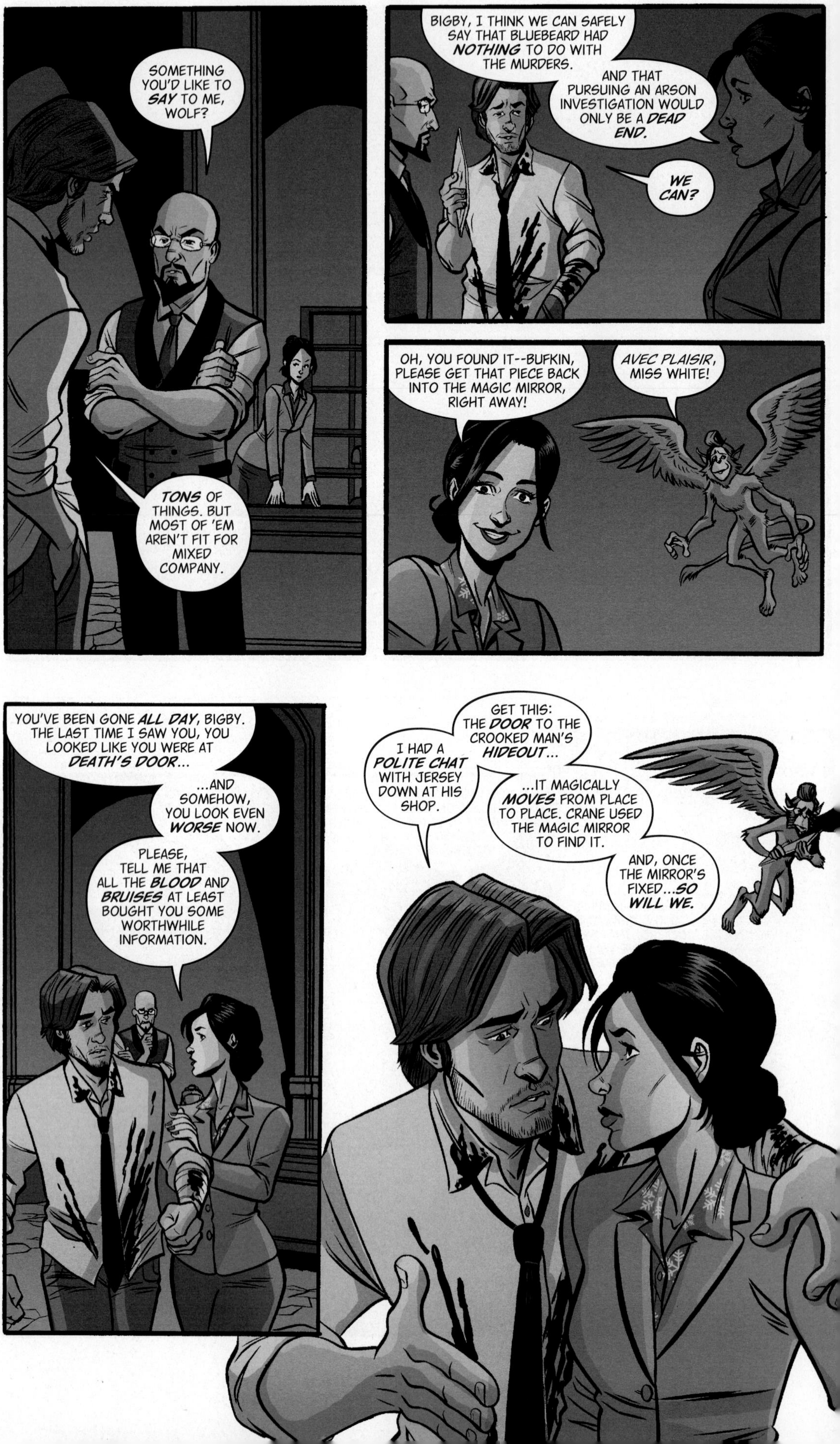
SOMETHING YOU'D LIKE TO SAY TO ME, WOLF?
TONS OF THINGS. BUT MOST OF 'EM AREN'T FIT FOR MIXED COMPANY.
BIGBY, I THINK WE CAN SAFELY SAY THAT BLUEBEARD HAD NOTHING TO DO WITH THE MURDERS.
AND THAT PURSUING AN ARSON INVESTIGATION WOULD ONLY BE A DEAD END.
WE CAN?
OH, YOU FOUND IT--BUFKIN, PLEASE GET THAT PIECE BACK INTO THE MAGIC MIRROR, RIGHT AWAY!
AVEC PLAISIR, MISS WHITE!
YOU'VE BEEN GONE ALL DAY, BIGBY. THE LAST TIME I SAW YOU, YOU LOOKED LIKE YOU WERE AT DEATH'S DOOR...
...AND SOMEHOW, YOU LOOK EVEN WORSE NOW.
PLEASE, TELL ME THAT ALL THE BLOOD AND BRUISES AT LEAST BOUGHT YOU SOME WORTHWHILE INFORMATION.
I HAD A POLITE CHAT WITH JERSEY DOWN AT HIS SHOP.
GET THIS: THE DOOR TO THE CROOKED MAN'S HIDEOUT...
...IT MAGICALLY MOVES FROM PLACE TO PLACE. CRANE USED THE MAGIC MIRROR TO FIND IT.
AND, ONCE THE MIRROR'S FIXED...SO WILL WE.

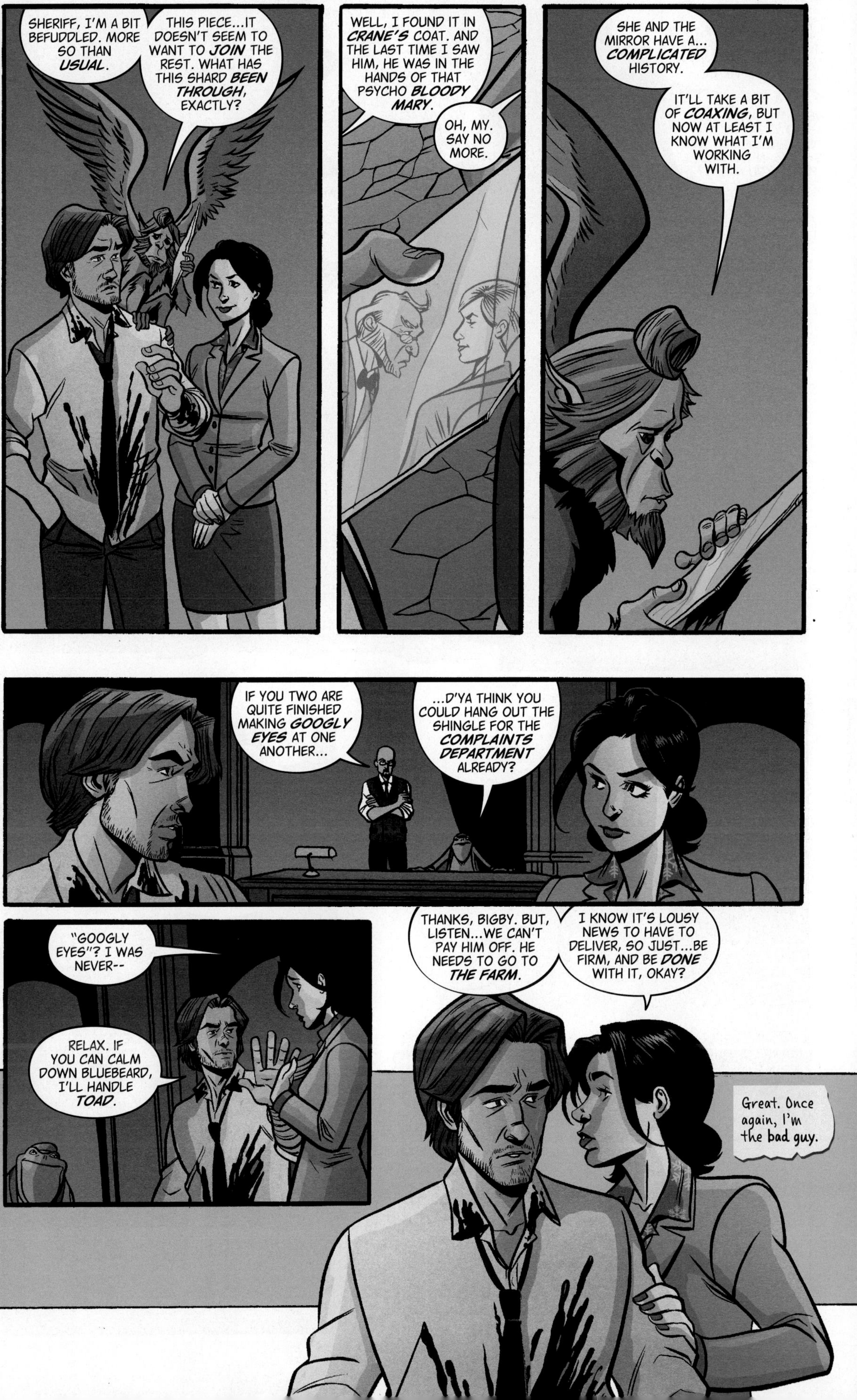
SHERIFF, I'M A BIT BEFUDDLED. MORE SO THAN USUAL.
THIS PIECE...IT DOESN'T SEEM TO WANT TO JOIN THE REST. WHAT HAS THIS SHARD BEEN THROUGH, EXACTLY?
WELL, I FOUND IT IN CRANE'S COAT. AND THE LAST TIME I SAW HIM, HE WAS IN THE HANDS OF THAT PSYCHO BLOODY MARY.
OH, MY. SAY NO MORE.
SHE AND THE MIRROR HAVE A... COMPLICATED HISTORY.
IT'LL TAKE A BIT OF COAXING, BUT NOW AT LEAST I KNOW WHAT I'M WORKING WITH.
IF YOU TWO ARE QUITE FINISHED MAKING GOOGLY EYES AT ONE ANOTHER...
...D'YA THINK YOU COULD HANG OUT THE SHINGLE FOR THE COMPLAINTS DEPARTMENT ALREADY?
"GOOGLY EYES"? I WAS NEVER--
RELAX. IF YOU CAN CALM DOWN BLUEBEARD, I'LL HANDLE TOAD.
THANKS, BIGBY. BUT, LISTEN...WE CAN'T PAY HIM OFF. HE NEEDS TO GO TO THE FARM.
I KNOW IT'S LOUSY NEWS TO HAVE TO DELIVER, SO JUST...BE FIRM, AND BE DONE WITH IT, OKAY?
Great. Once again, I'm the bad guy.

OH, I SEE. I GET PASSED OFF TO AN *UNDERLING*. TYPICAL BUREAUCRACY AT WORK.

IT'S JUST AS WELL, THOUGH, SEEIN' AS HOW *YOU'RE* THE ONE WHAT CAUSED THE DAMAGE IN THE FIRST PLACE, YOU MIGHTY LUMMOX.

LET'S TALK *REMUNERATION*.

OR, IF THAT'S TOO BIG A WORD FOR YOU, LET'S JUST TALK *CASH*.

TOAD, THIS IS THE BUSINESS OFFICE. NOT A BANK.

I'M NOT LOOKIN' FOR A *HANDOUT*, YOU NINNY. YOU SMASHED MY CAR TO FLINDERS. I JUST WANT YOU TO MAKE IT *RIGHT*.

LOOK...I'M NOT EVEN GONNA SPEND THE DOSH ON A *NEW RIDE*, YOU SAVVY?

YOU'RE ALWAYS ON ME ABOUT THE *GLAMOURS*, THE *GLAMOURS*. I JUST NEED THE RESOURCES TO AFFORD THOSE SPELLS, MATE.

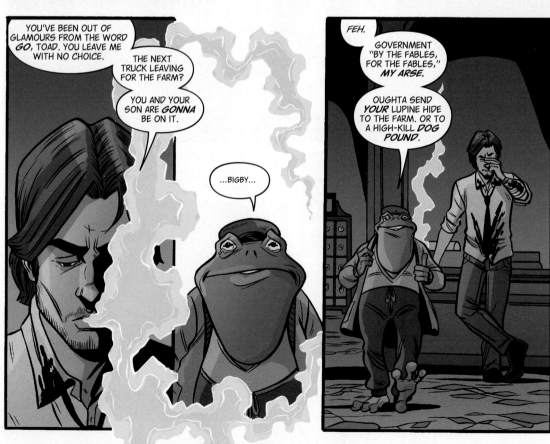

YOU'VE BEEN OUT OF GLAMOURS FROM THE WORD *GO*, TOAD. YOU LEAVE ME WITH NO CHOICE.

THE NEXT TRUCK LEAVING FOR THE FARM?

YOU AND YOUR SON ARE *GONNA* BE ON IT.

...BIGBY...

FEH.

GOVERNMENT "BY THE FABLES, FOR THE FABLES," *MY ARSE*.

OUGHTA SEND *YOUR* LUPINE HIDE TO THE FARM. OR TO A HIGH-KILL *DOG POUND*.

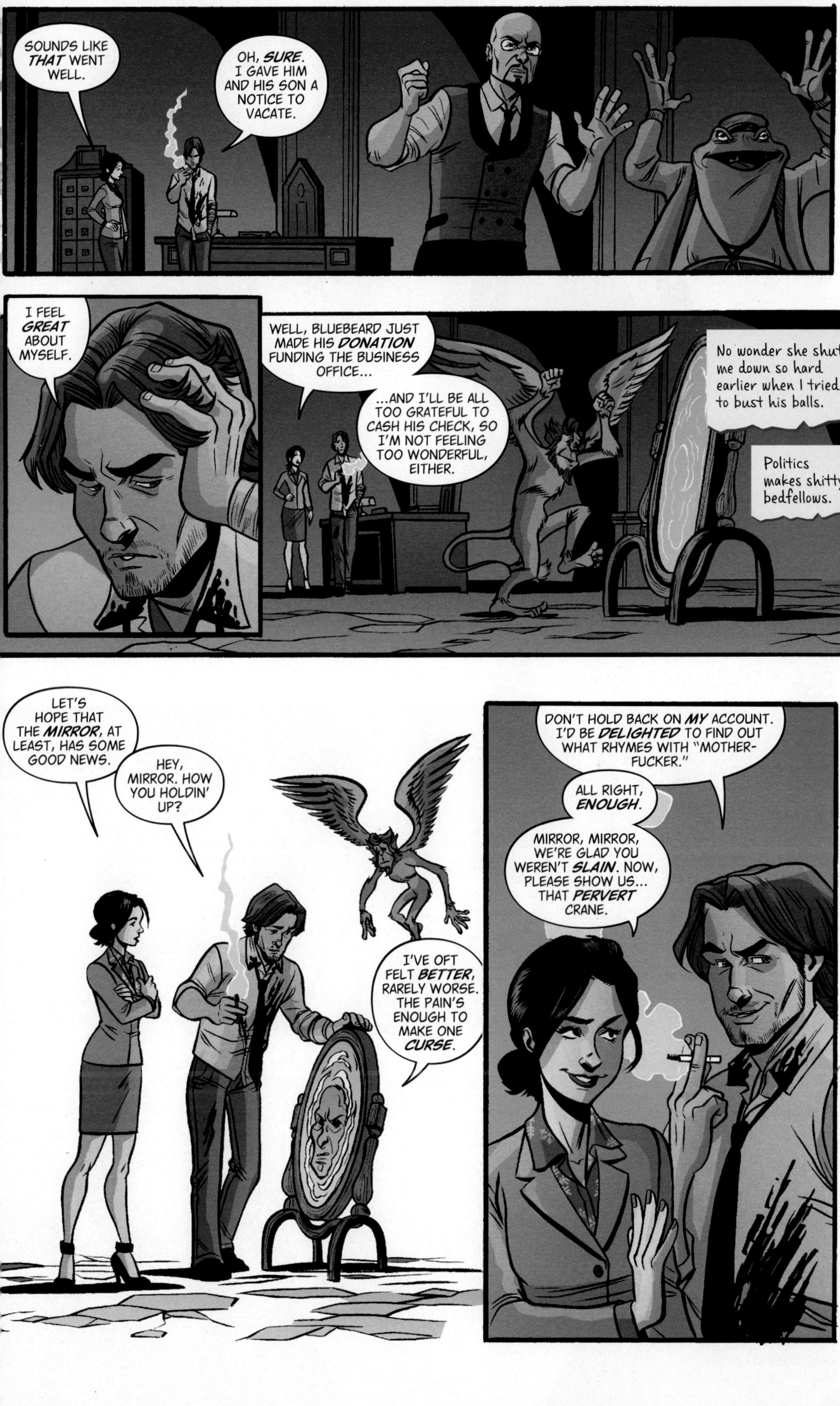
SOUNDS LIKE THAT WENT WELL.
OH, SURE. I GAVE HIM AND HIS SON A NOTICE TO VACATE.
I FEEL GREAT ABOUT MYSELF.
WELL, BLUEBEARD JUST MADE HIS DONATION FUNDING THE BUSINESS OFFICE...
...AND I'LL BE ALL TOO GRATEFUL TO CASH HIS CHECK, SO I'M NOT FEELING TOO WONDERFUL, EITHER.
No wonder she shut me down so hard earlier when I tried to bust his balls.
Politics makes shitty bedfellows.
LET'S HOPE THAT THE MIRROR, AT LEAST, HAS SOME GOOD NEWS.
HEY, MIRROR. HOW YOU HOLDIN' UP?
I'VE OFT FELT BETTER, RARELY WORSE. THE PAIN'S ENOUGH TO MAKE ONE CURSE.
DON'T HOLD BACK ON MY ACCOUNT. I'D BE DELIGHTED TO FIND OUT WHAT RHYMES WITH "MOTHER-FUCKER."
ALL RIGHT, ENOUGH.
MIRROR, MIRROR, WE'RE GLAD YOU WEREN'T SLAIN. NOW, PLEASE SHOW US... THAT PERVERT CRANE.

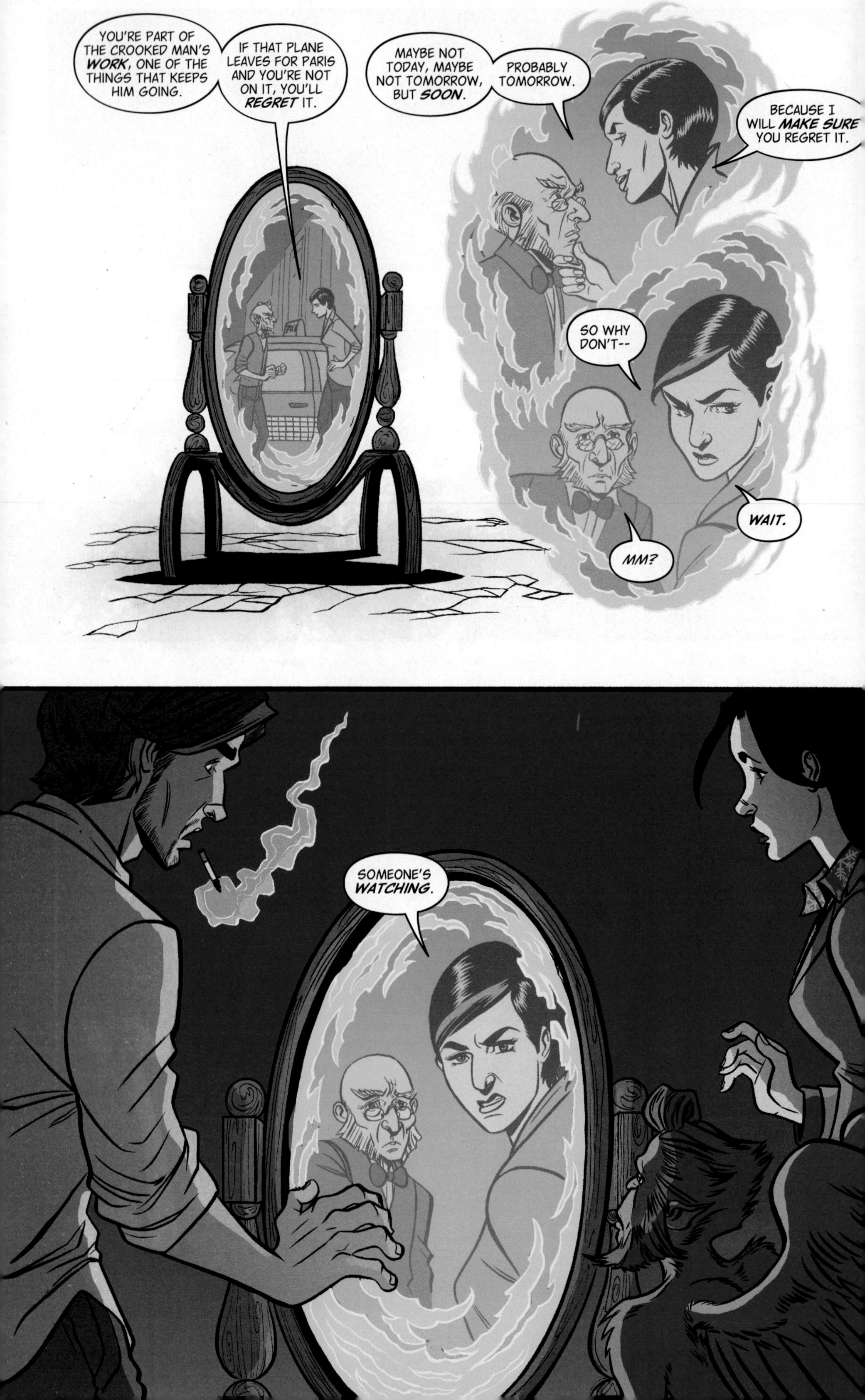
YOU'RE PART OF THE CROOKED MAN'S **WORK**, ONE OF THE THINGS THAT KEEPS HIM GOING.
IF THAT PLANE LEAVES FOR PARIS AND YOU'RE NOT ON IT, YOU'LL **REGRET** IT.
MAYBE NOT TODAY, MAYBE NOT TOMORROW, BUT **SOON**.
PROBABLY TOMORROW.
BECAUSE I WILL **MAKE SURE** YOU REGRET IT.
SO WHY DON'T--
WAIT.
MM?
SOMEONE'S **WATCHING**.

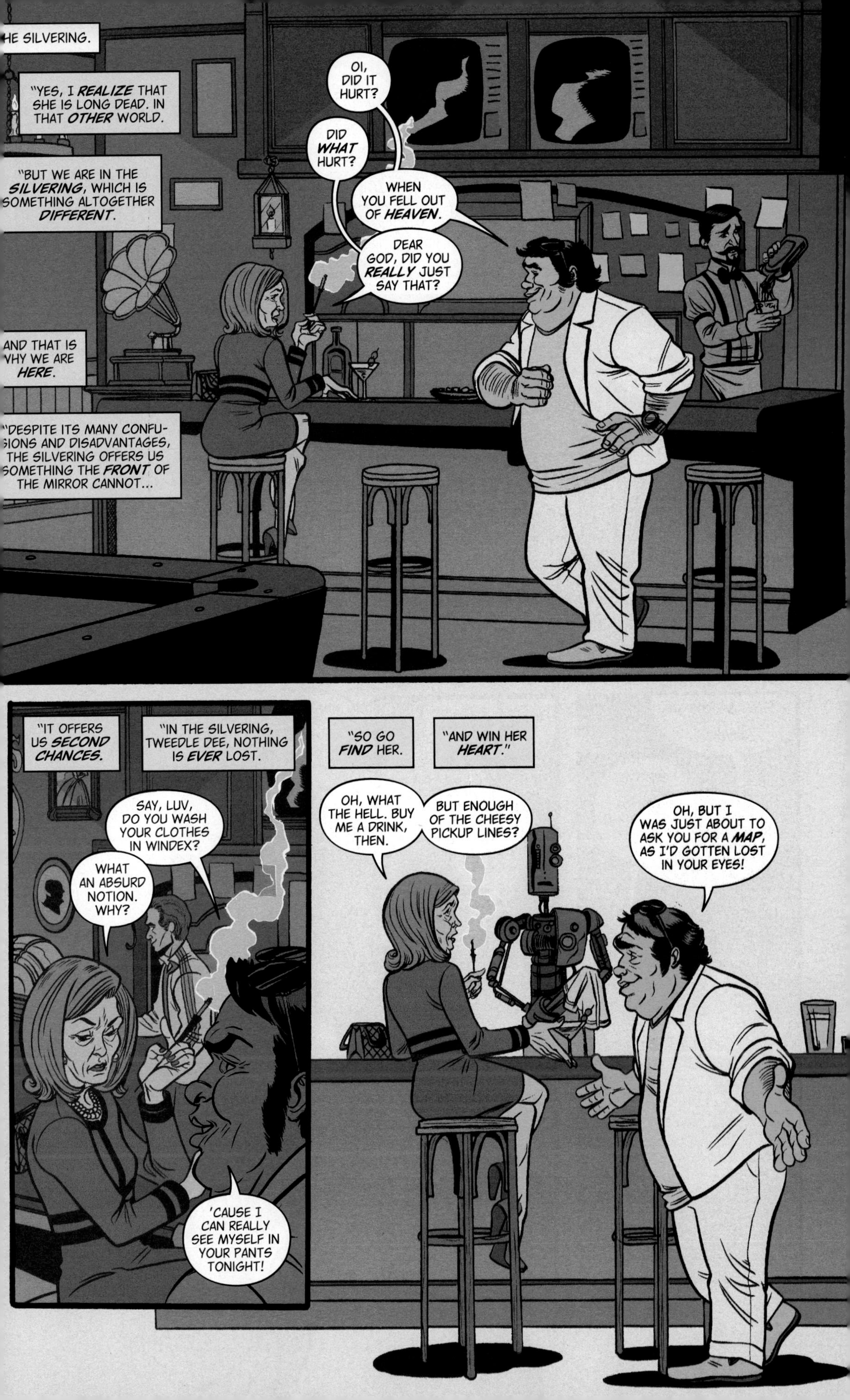
HE SILVERING.
"YES, I REALIZE THAT SHE IS LONG DEAD. IN THAT OTHER WORLD.
"BUT WE ARE IN THE SILVERING, WHICH IS SOMETHING ALTOGETHER DIFFERENT.
OI, DID IT HURT?
DID WHAT HURT?
WHEN YOU FELL OUT OF HEAVEN.
DEAR GOD, DID YOU REALLY JUST SAY THAT?
AND THAT IS VHY WE ARE HERE.
"DESPITE ITS MANY CONFUSIONS AND DISADVANTAGES, THE SILVERING OFFERS US SOMETHING THE FRONT OF THE MIRROR CANNOT...
"IT OFFERS US SECOND CHANCES.
"IN THE SILVERING, TWEEDLE DEE, NOTHING IS EVER LOST.
SAY, LUV, DO YOU WASH YOUR CLOTHES IN WINDEX?
WHAT AN ABSURD NOTION. WHY?
'CAUSE I CAN REALLY SEE MYSELF IN YOUR PANTS TONIGHT!
"SO GO FIND HER.
"AND WIN HER HEART."
OH, WHAT THE HELL. BUY ME A DRINK, THEN.
BUT ENOUGH OF THE CHEESY PICKUP LINES?
OH, BUT I WAS JUST ABOUT TO ASK YOU FOR A MAP, AS I'D GOTTEN LOST IN YOUR EYES!

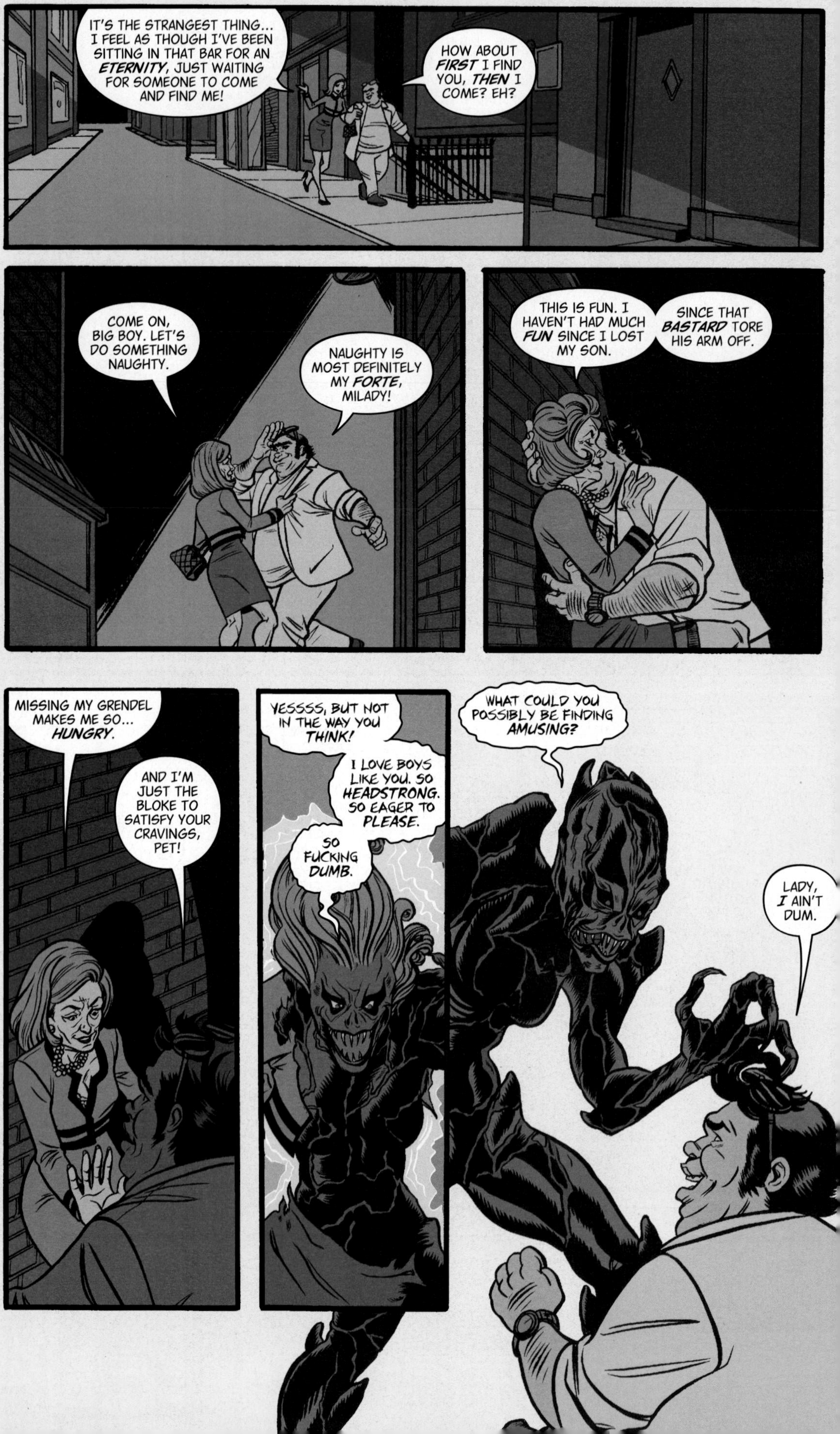
IT'S THE STRANGEST THING... I FEEL AS THOUGH I'VE BEEN SITTING IN THAT BAR FOR AN ETERNITY, JUST WAITING FOR SOMEONE TO COME AND FIND ME!
HOW ABOUT FIRST I FIND YOU, THEN I COME? EH?
COME ON, BIG BOY. LET'S DO SOMETHING NAUGHTY.
NAUGHTY IS MOST DEFINITELY MY FORTE, MILADY!
THIS IS FUN. I HAVEN'T HAD MUCH FUN SINCE I LOST MY SON.
SINCE THAT BASTARD TORE HIS ARM OFF.
MISSING MY GRENDEL MAKES ME SO... HUNGRY.
AND I'M JUST THE BLOKE TO SATISFY YOUR CRAVINGS, PET!
YESSSS, BUT NOT IN THE WAY YOU THINK!
I LOVE BOYS LIKE YOU. SO HEADSTRONG. SO EAGER TO PLEASE.
SO FUCKING DUMB.
WHAT COULD YOU POSSIBLY BE FINDING AMUSING?
LADY, I AIN'T DUM.

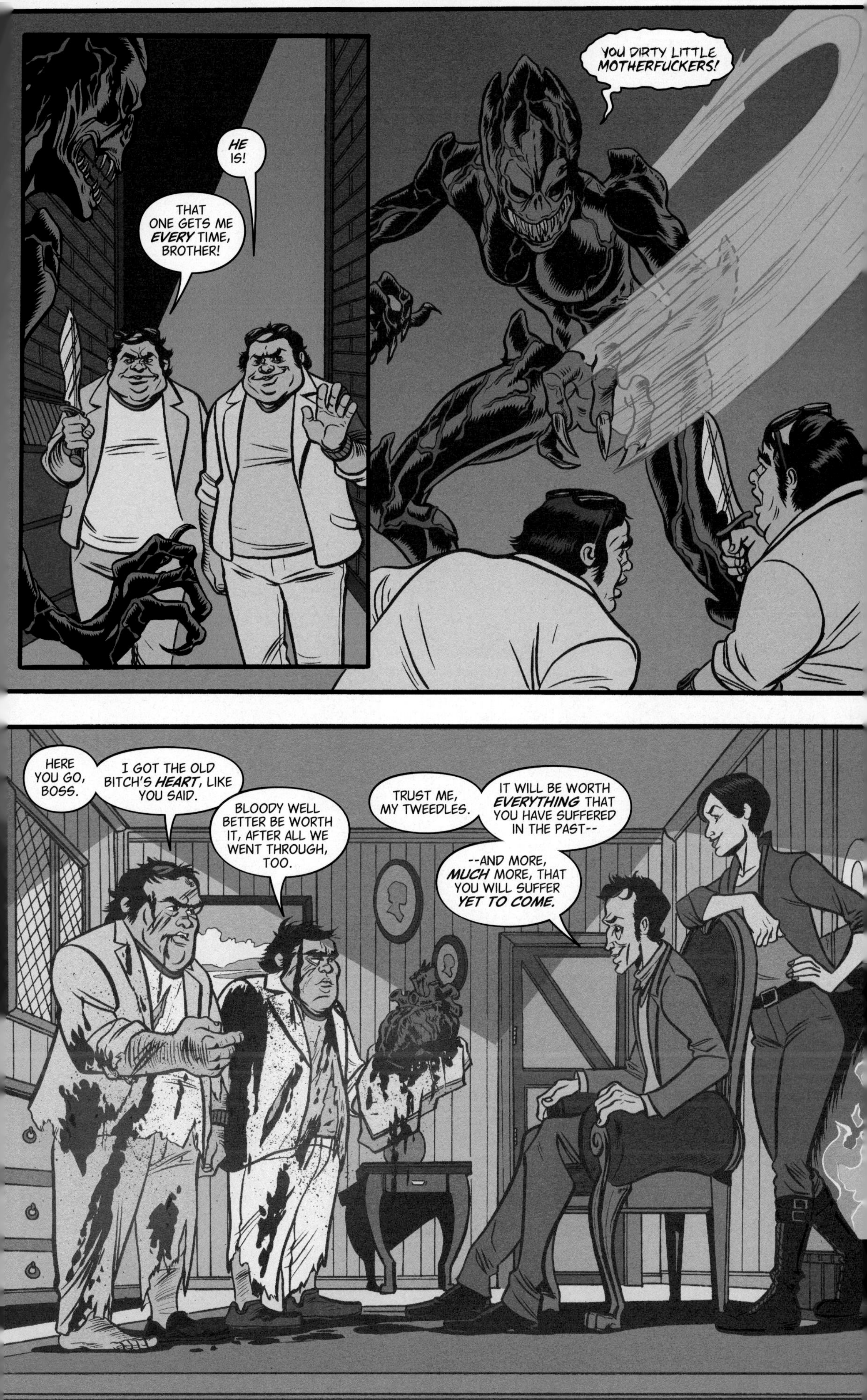
HE IS!
THAT ONE GETS ME EVERY TIME, BROTHER!
YOU DIRTY LITTLE MOTHERFUCKERS!
HERE YOU GO, BOSS.
I GOT THE OLD BITCH'S HEART, LIKE YOU SAID.
BLOODY WELL BETTER BE WORTH IT, AFTER ALL WE WENT THROUGH, TOO.
TRUST ME, MY TWEEDLES.
IT WILL BE WORTH EVERYTHING THAT YOU HAVE SUFFERED IN THE PAST--
--AND MORE, MUCH MORE, THAT YOU WILL SUFFER YET TO COME.

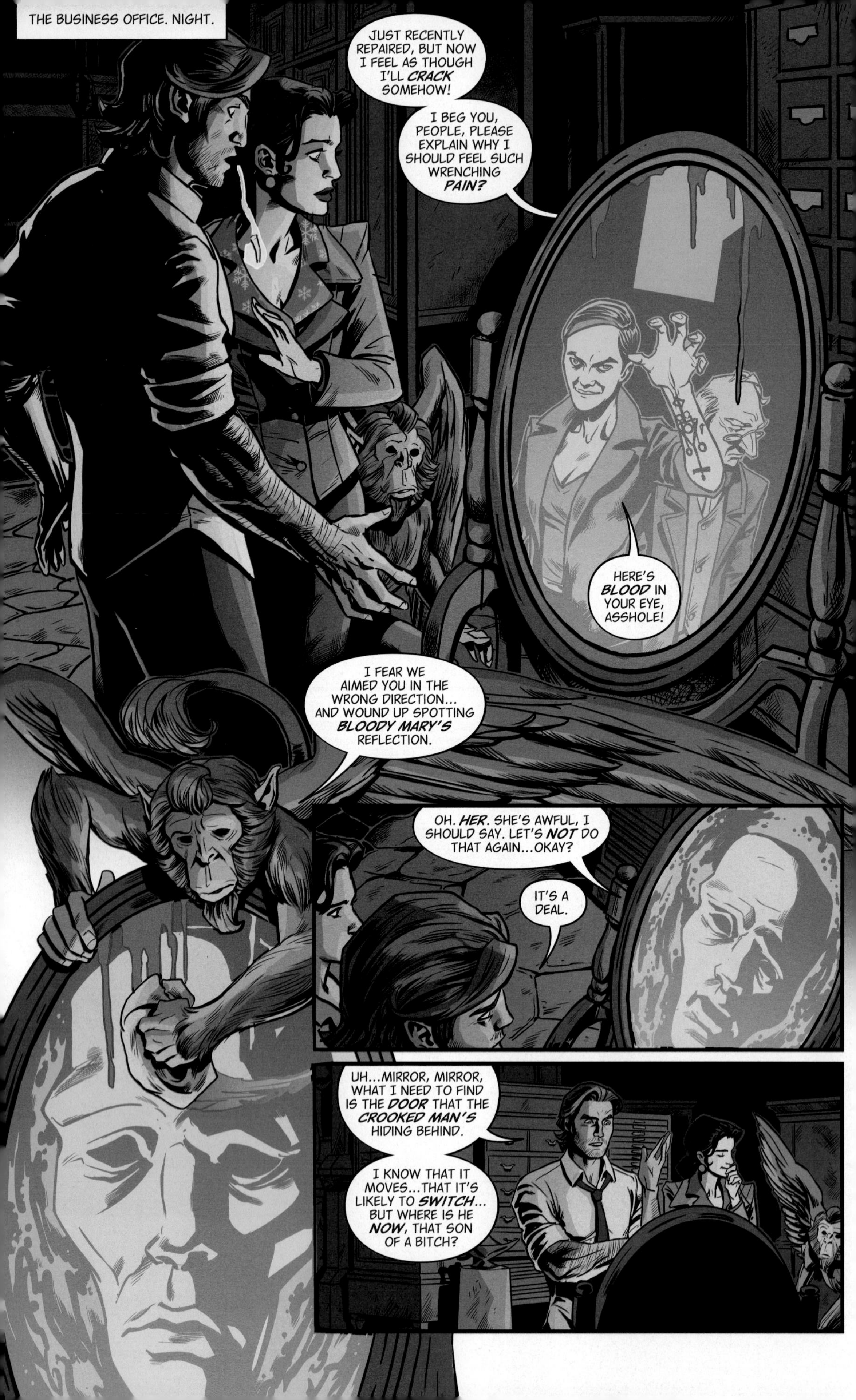
THE BUSINESS OFFICE. NIGHT.
JUST RECENTLY REPAIRED, BUT NOW I FEEL AS THOUGH I'LL CRACK SOMEHOW!
I BEG YOU, PEOPLE, PLEASE EXPLAIN WHY I SHOULD FEEL SUCH WRENCHING PAIN?
HERE'S BLOOD IN YOUR EYE, ASSHOLE!
I FEAR WE AIMED YOU IN THE WRONG DIRECTION... AND WOUND UP SPOTTING BLOODY MARY'S REFLECTION.
OH. HER. SHE'S AWFUL, I SHOULD SAY. LET'S NOT DO THAT AGAIN...OKAY?
IT'S A DEAL.
UH...MIRROR, MIRROR, WHAT I NEED TO FIND IS THE DOOR THAT THE CROOKED MAN'S HIDING BEHIND.
I KNOW THAT IT MOVES...THAT IT'S LIKELY TO SWITCH... BUT WHERE IS HE NOW, THAT SON OF A BITCH?

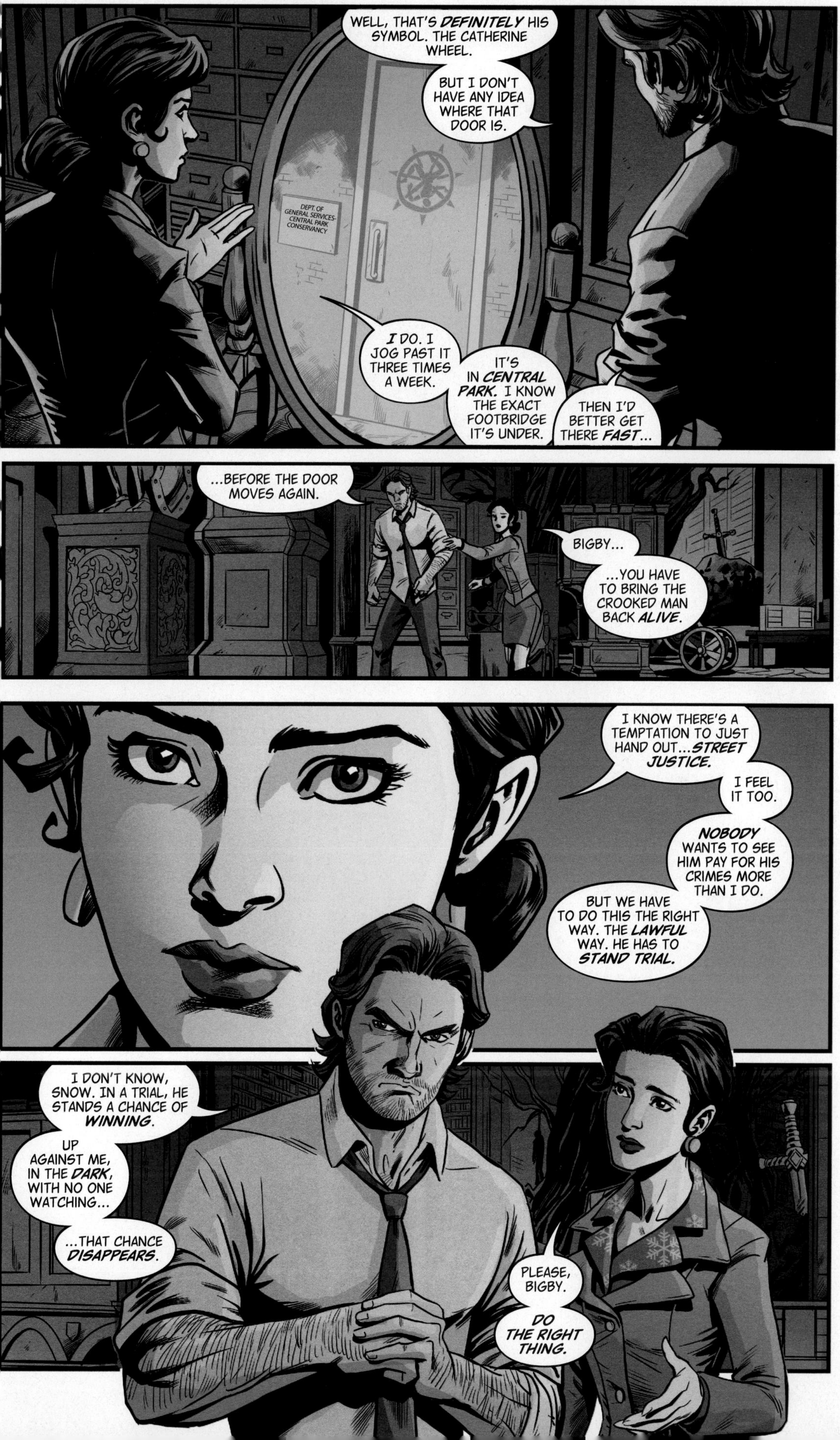
WELL, THAT'S DEFINITELY HIS SYMBOL. THE CATHERINE WHEEL.
BUT I DON'T HAVE ANY IDEA WHERE THAT DOOR IS.
DEPT. OF GENERAL SERVICES- CENTRAL PARK CONSERVANCY
I DO. I JOG PAST IT THREE TIMES A WEEK.
IT'S IN CENTRAL PARK. I KNOW THE EXACT FOOTBRIDGE IT'S UNDER.
THEN I'D BETTER GET THERE FAST...
...BEFORE THE DOOR MOVES AGAIN.
BIGBY...
...YOU HAVE TO BRING THE CROOKED MAN BACK ALIVE.
I KNOW THERE'S A TEMPTATION TO JUST HAND OUT...STREET JUSTICE.
I FEEL IT TOO.
NOBODY WANTS TO SEE HIM PAY FOR HIS CRIMES MORE THAN I DO.
BUT WE HAVE TO DO THIS THE RIGHT WAY. THE LAWFUL WAY. HE HAS TO STAND TRIAL.
I DON'T KNOW, SNOW. IN A TRIAL, HE STANDS A CHANCE OF WINNING.
UP AGAINST ME, IN THE DARK, WITH NO ONE WATCHING...
...THAT CHANCE DISAPPEARS.
PLEASE, BIGBY.
DO THE RIGHT THING.

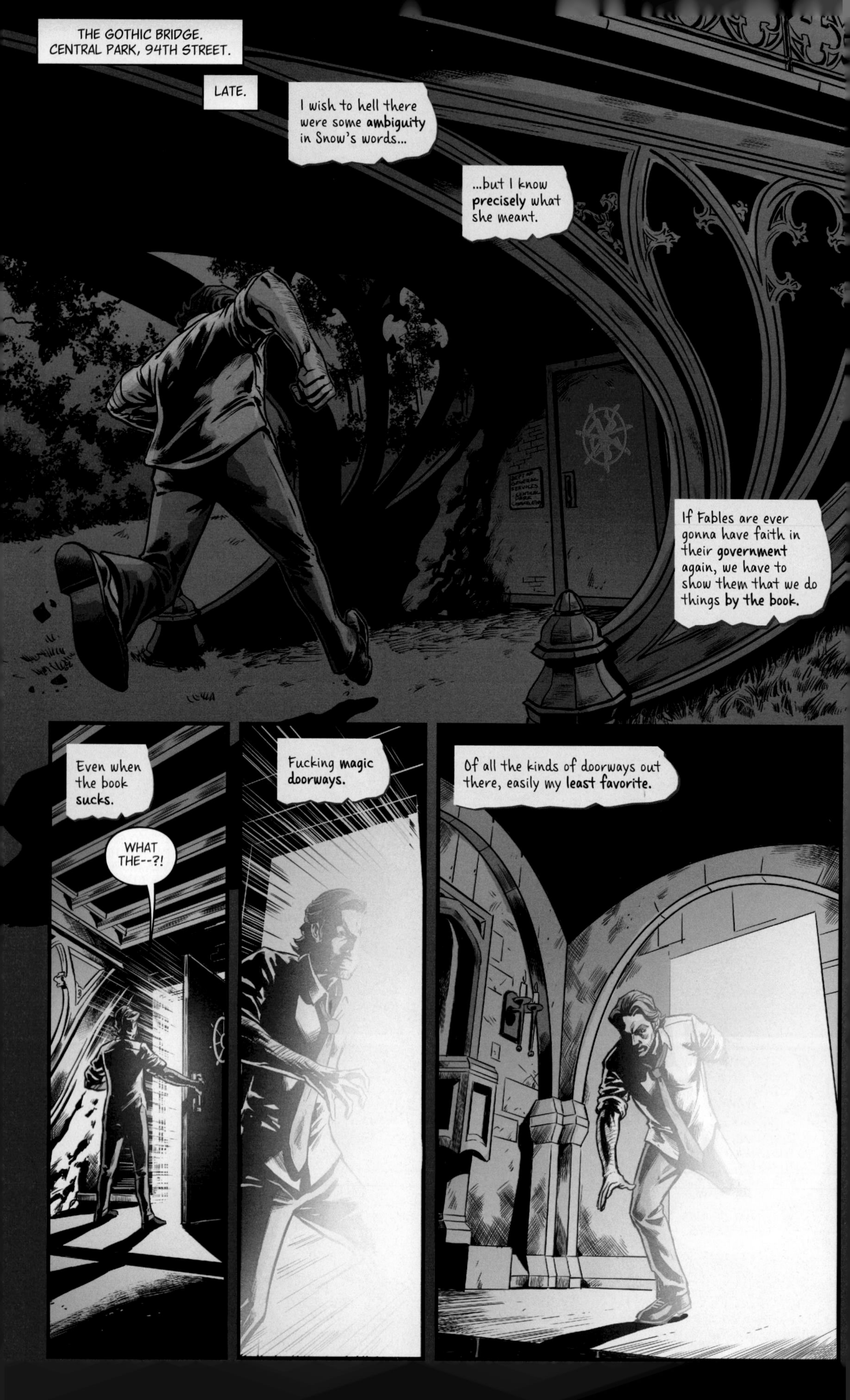
THE GOTHIC BRIDGE. CENTRAL PARK, 94TH STREET.
LATE.
I wish to hell there were some ambiguity in Snow's words...
...but I know precisely what she meant.
If Fables are ever gonna have faith in their government again, we have to show them that we do things by the book.
Even when the book sucks.
WHAT THE--?!
Fucking magic doorways.
Of all the kinds of doorways out there, easily my least favorite.

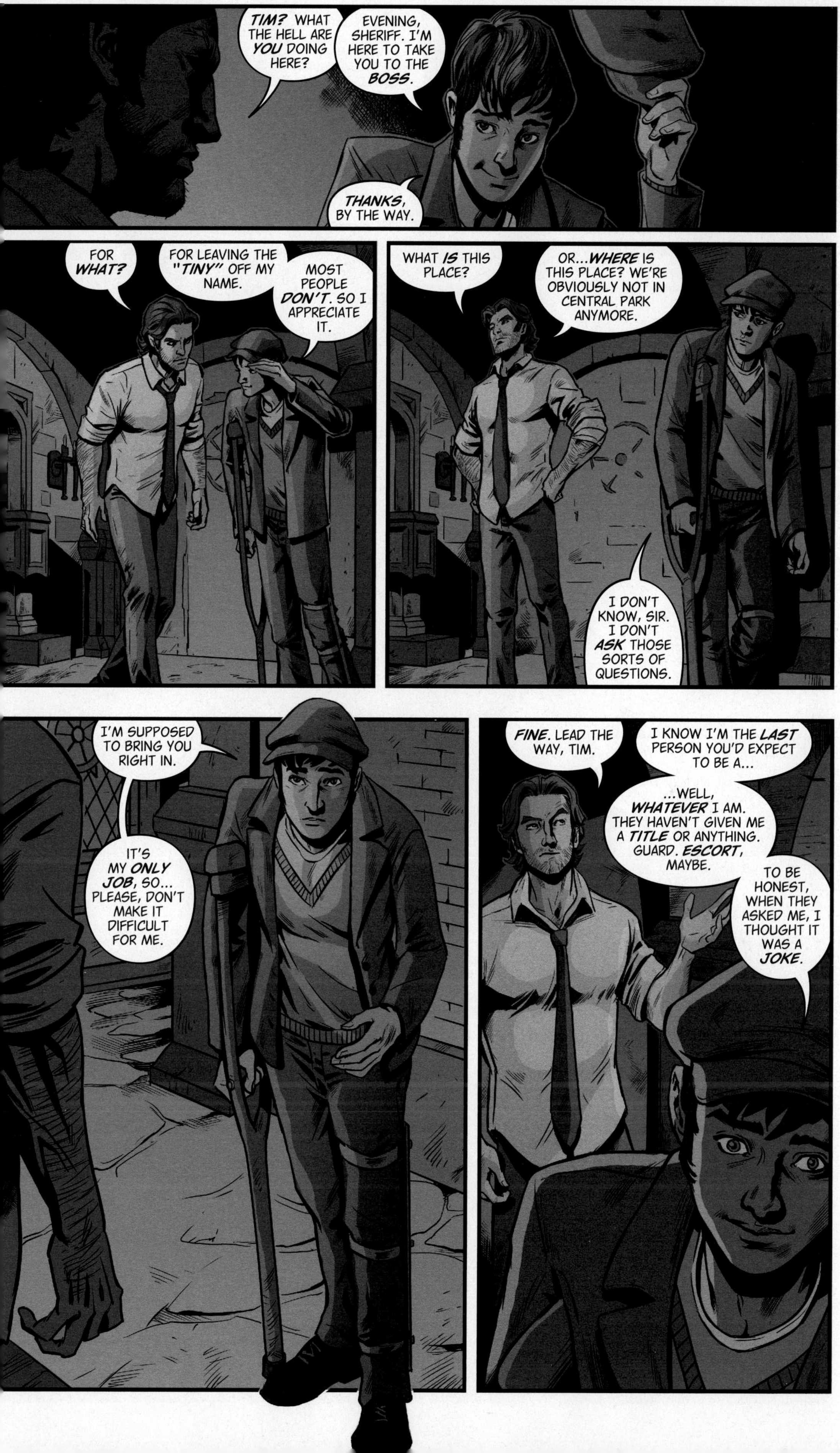
TIM? WHAT THE HELL ARE YOU DOING HERE?
EVENING, SHERIFF. I'M HERE TO TAKE YOU TO THE BOSS.
THANKS, BY THE WAY.
FOR WHAT?
FOR LEAVING THE "TINY" OFF MY NAME.
MOST PEOPLE DON'T. SO I APPRECIATE IT.
WHAT IS THIS PLACE?
OR...WHERE IS THIS PLACE? WE'RE OBVIOUSLY NOT IN CENTRAL PARK ANYMORE.
I DON'T KNOW, SIR. I DON'T ASK THOSE SORTS OF QUESTIONS.
I'M SUPPOSED TO BRING YOU RIGHT IN.
IT'S MY ONLY JOB, SO... PLEASE, DON'T MAKE IT DIFFICULT FOR ME.
FINE. LEAD THE WAY, TIM.
I KNOW I'M THE LAST PERSON YOU'D EXPECT TO BE A...
...WELL, WHATEVER I AM. THEY HAVEN'T GIVEN ME A TITLE OR ANYTHING. GUARD. ESCORT, MAYBE.
TO BE HONEST, WHEN THEY ASKED ME, I THOUGHT IT WAS A JOKE.

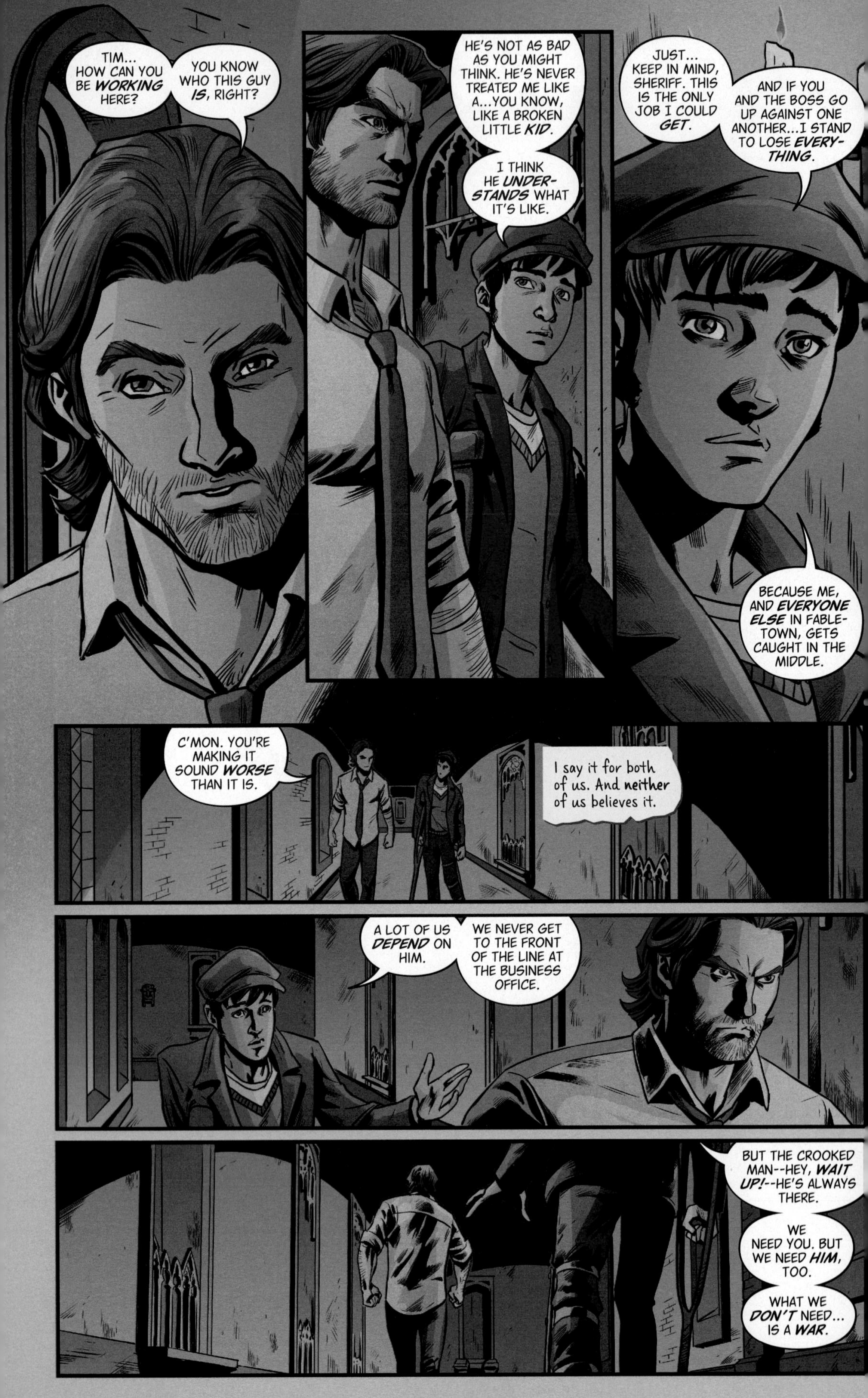

TIM... HOW CAN YOU BE *WORKING* HERE?
YOU KNOW WHO THIS GUY *IS*, RIGHT?
HE'S NOT AS BAD AS YOU MIGHT THINK. HE'S NEVER TREATED ME LIKE A...YOU KNOW, LIKE A BROKEN LITTLE *KID*.
I THINK HE *UNDERSTANDS* WHAT IT'S LIKE.
JUST... KEEP IN MIND, SHERIFF. THIS IS THE ONLY JOB I COULD *GET*.
AND IF YOU AND THE BOSS GO UP AGAINST ONE ANOTHER...I STAND TO LOSE *EVERYTHING*.
BECAUSE ME, AND *EVERYONE ELSE* IN FABLETOWN, GETS CAUGHT IN THE MIDDLE.
C'MON. YOU'RE MAKING IT SOUND *WORSE* THAN IT IS.
I say it for both of us. And **neither** of us believes it.
A LOT OF US *DEPEND* ON HIM.
WE NEVER GET TO THE FRONT OF THE LINE AT THE BUSINESS OFFICE.
BUT THE CROOKED MAN--HEY, *WAIT UP!*--HE'S ALWAYS THERE.
WE NEED YOU. BUT WE NEED *HIM*, TOO.
WHAT WE *DON'T* NEED... IS A *WAR*.

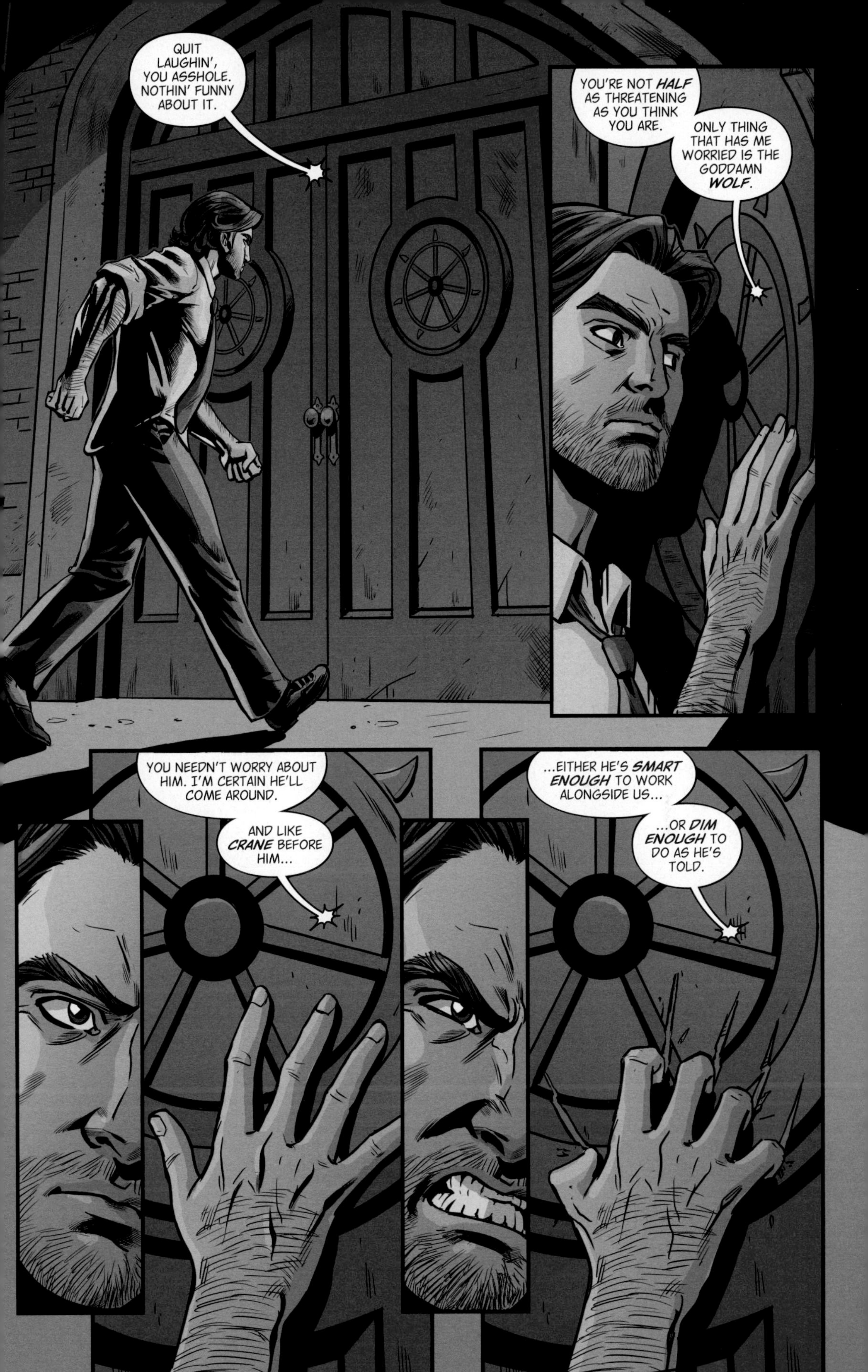
QUIT LAUGHIN', YOU ASSHOLE. NOTHIN' FUNNY ABOUT IT.
YOU'RE NOT HALF AS THREATENING AS YOU THINK YOU ARE.
ONLY THING THAT HAS ME WORRIED IS THE GODDAMN WOLF.
YOU NEEDN'T WORRY ABOUT HIM. I'M CERTAIN HE'LL COME AROUND.
AND LIKE CRANE BEFORE HIM...
...EITHER HE'S SMART ENOUGH TO WORK ALONGSIDE US...
...OR DIM ENOUGH TO DO AS HE'S TOLD.

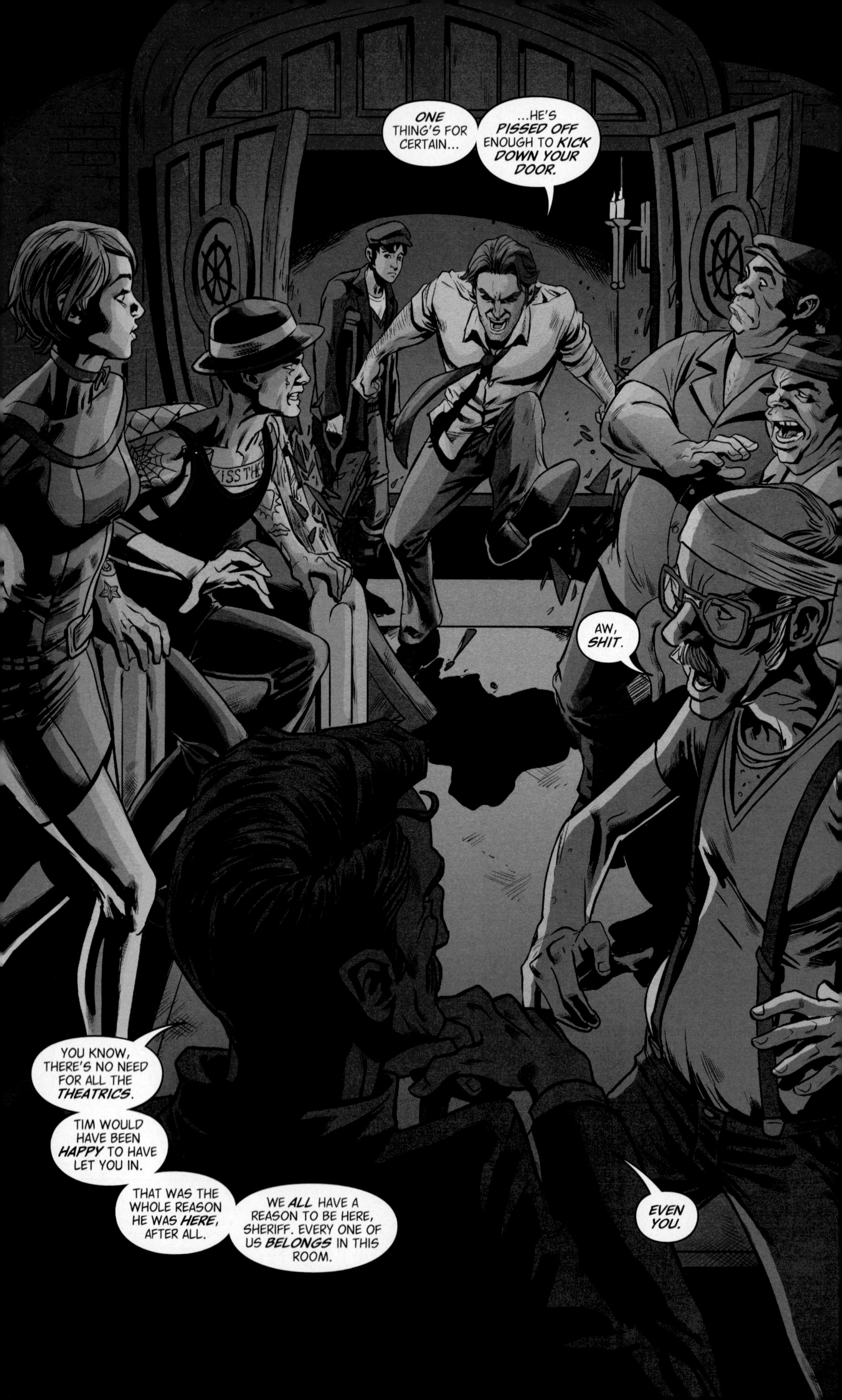
ONE THING'S FOR CERTAIN...
...HE'S PISSED OFF ENOUGH TO KICK DOWN YOUR DOOR.
AW, SHIT.
YOU KNOW, THERE'S NO NEED FOR ALL THE THEATRICS.
TIM WOULD HAVE BEEN HAPPY TO HAVE LET YOU IN.
THAT WAS THE WHOLE REASON HE WAS HERE, AFTER ALL.
WE ALL HAVE A REASON TO BE HERE, SHERIFF. EVERY ONE OF US BELONGS IN THIS ROOM.
EVEN YOU.

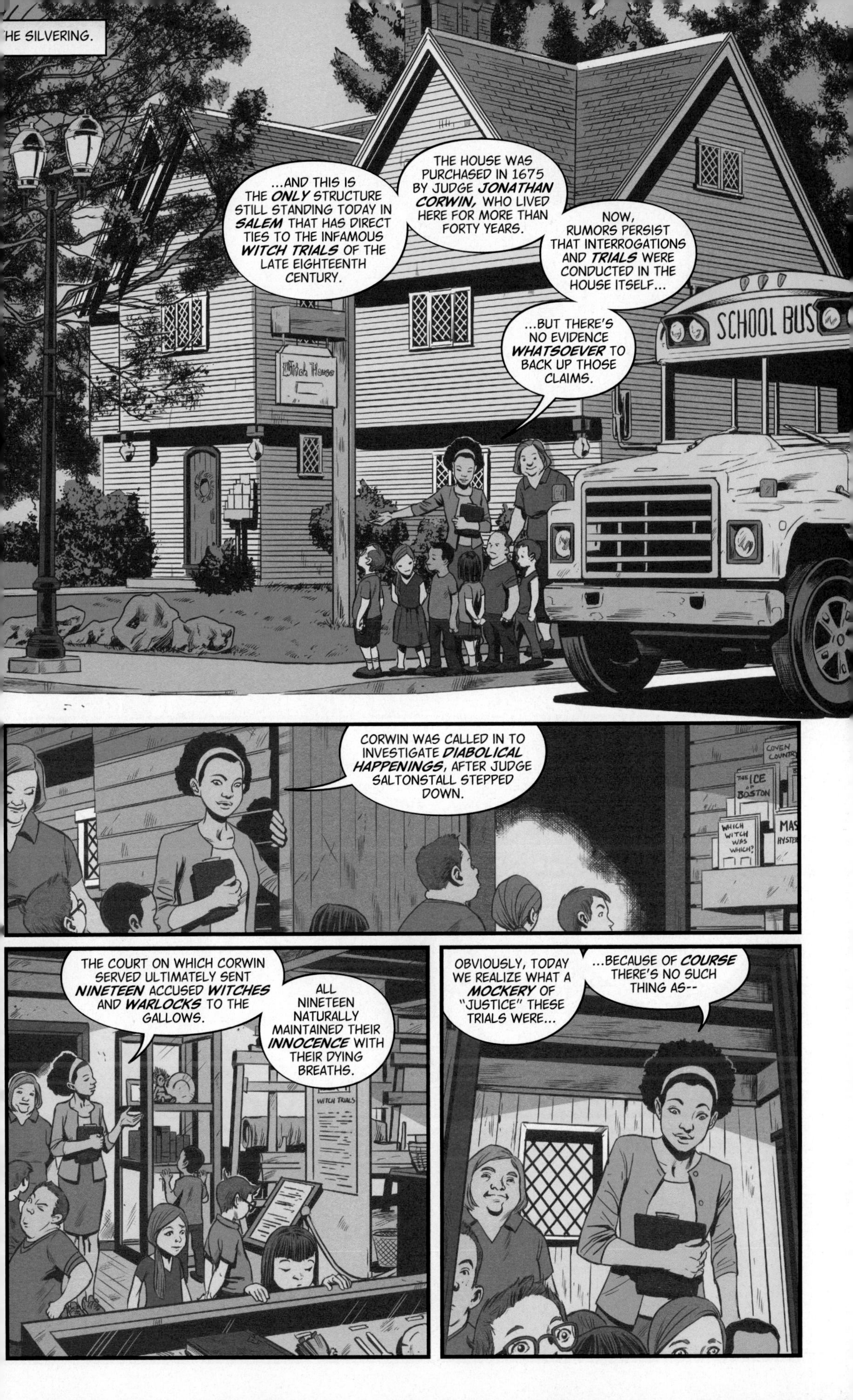
HE SILVERING.
...AND THIS IS THE ONLY STRUCTURE STILL STANDING TODAY IN SALEM THAT HAS DIRECT TIES TO THE INFAMOUS WITCH TRIALS OF THE LATE EIGHTEENTH CENTURY.
THE HOUSE WAS PURCHASED IN 1675 BY JUDGE JONATHAN CORWIN, WHO LIVED HERE FOR MORE THAN FORTY YEARS.
NOW, RUMORS PERSIST THAT INTERROGATIONS AND TRIALS WERE CONDUCTED IN THE HOUSE ITSELF...
...BUT THERE'S NO EVIDENCE WHATSOEVER TO BACK UP THOSE CLAIMS.
Witch House
SCHOOL BUS
CORWIN WAS CALLED IN TO INVESTIGATE DIABOLICAL HAPPENINGS, AFTER JUDGE SALTONSTALL STEPPED DOWN.
COVEN COUNTRY
THE ICE OF BOSTON
WHICH WITCH WAS WHICH?
MAS HYSTER
THE COURT ON WHICH CORWIN SERVED ULTIMATELY SENT NINETEEN ACCUSED WITCHES AND WARLOCKS TO THE GALLOWS.
ALL NINETEEN NATURALLY MAINTAINED THEIR INNOCENCE WITH THEIR DYING BREATHS.
WITCH TRIALS
OBVIOUSLY, TODAY WE REALIZE WHAT A MOCKERY OF "JUSTICE" THESE TRIALS WERE...
...BECAUSE OF COURSE THERE'S NO SUCH THING AS--

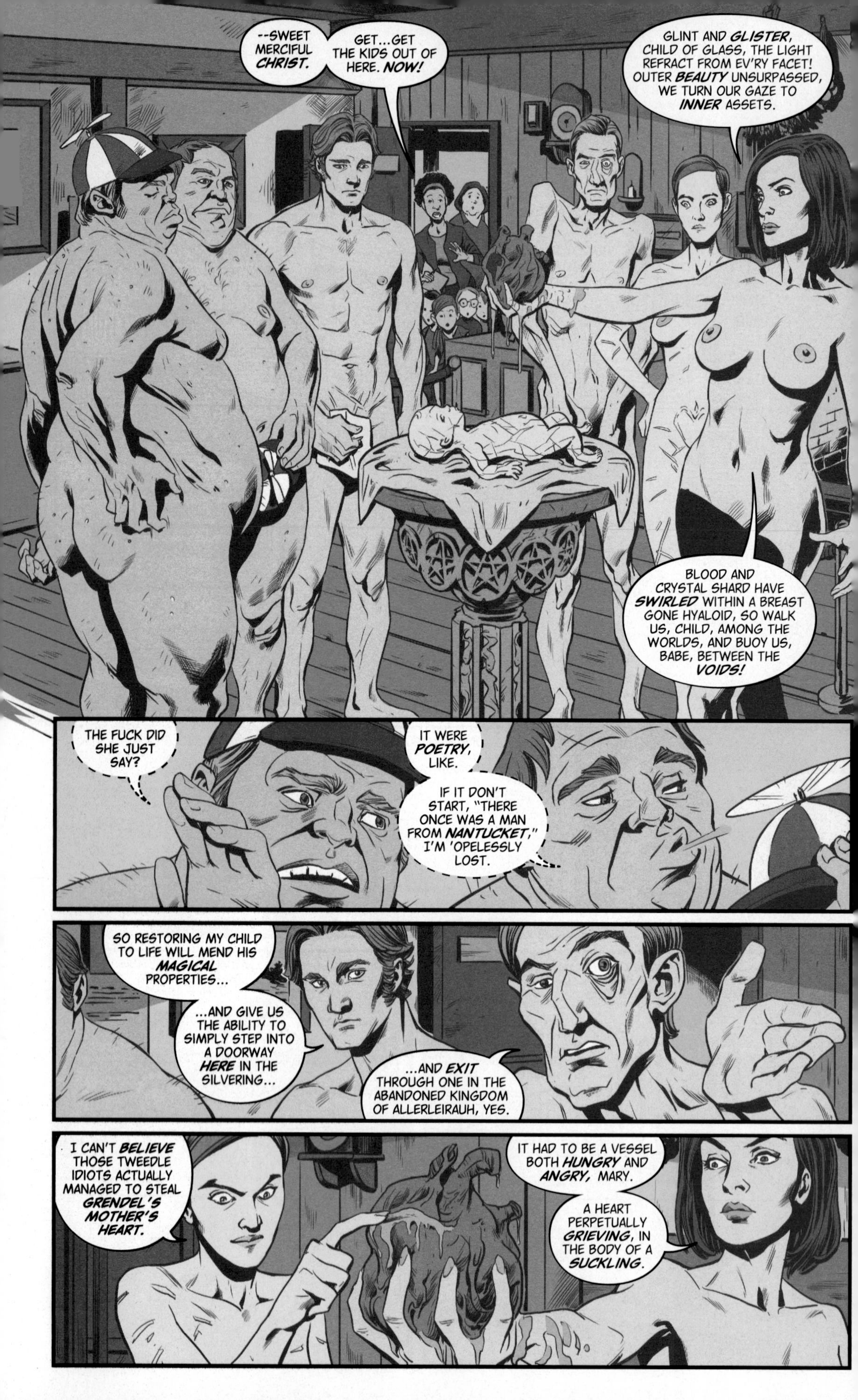
--SWEET MERCIFUL CHRIST.
GET...GET THE KIDS OUT OF HERE. NOW!
GLINT AND GLISTER, CHILD OF GLASS, THE LIGHT REFRACT FROM EV'RY FACET! OUTER BEAUTY UNSURPASSED, WE TURN OUR GAZE TO INNER ASSETS.
BLOOD AND CRYSTAL SHARD HAVE SWIRLED WITHIN A BREAST GONE HYALOID, SO WALK US, CHILD, AMONG THE WORLDS, AND BUOY US, BABE, BETWEEN THE VOIDS!
THE FUCK DID SHE JUST SAY?
IT WERE POETRY, LIKE.
IF IT DON'T START, "THERE ONCE WAS A MAN FROM NANTUCKET," I'M 'OPELESSLY LOST.
SO RESTORING MY CHILD TO LIFE WILL MEND HIS MAGICAL PROPERTIES...
...AND GIVE US THE ABILITY TO SIMPLY STEP INTO A DOORWAY HERE IN THE SILVERING...
...AND EXIT THROUGH ONE IN THE ABANDONED KINGDOM OF ALLERLEIRAUH, YES.
I CAN'T BELIEVE THOSE TWEEDLE IDIOTS ACTUALLY MANAGED TO STEAL GRENDEL'S MOTHER'S HEART.
IT HAD TO BE A VESSEL BOTH HUNGRY AND ANGRY, MARY.
A HEART PERPETUALLY GRIEVING, IN THE BODY OF A SUCKLING.

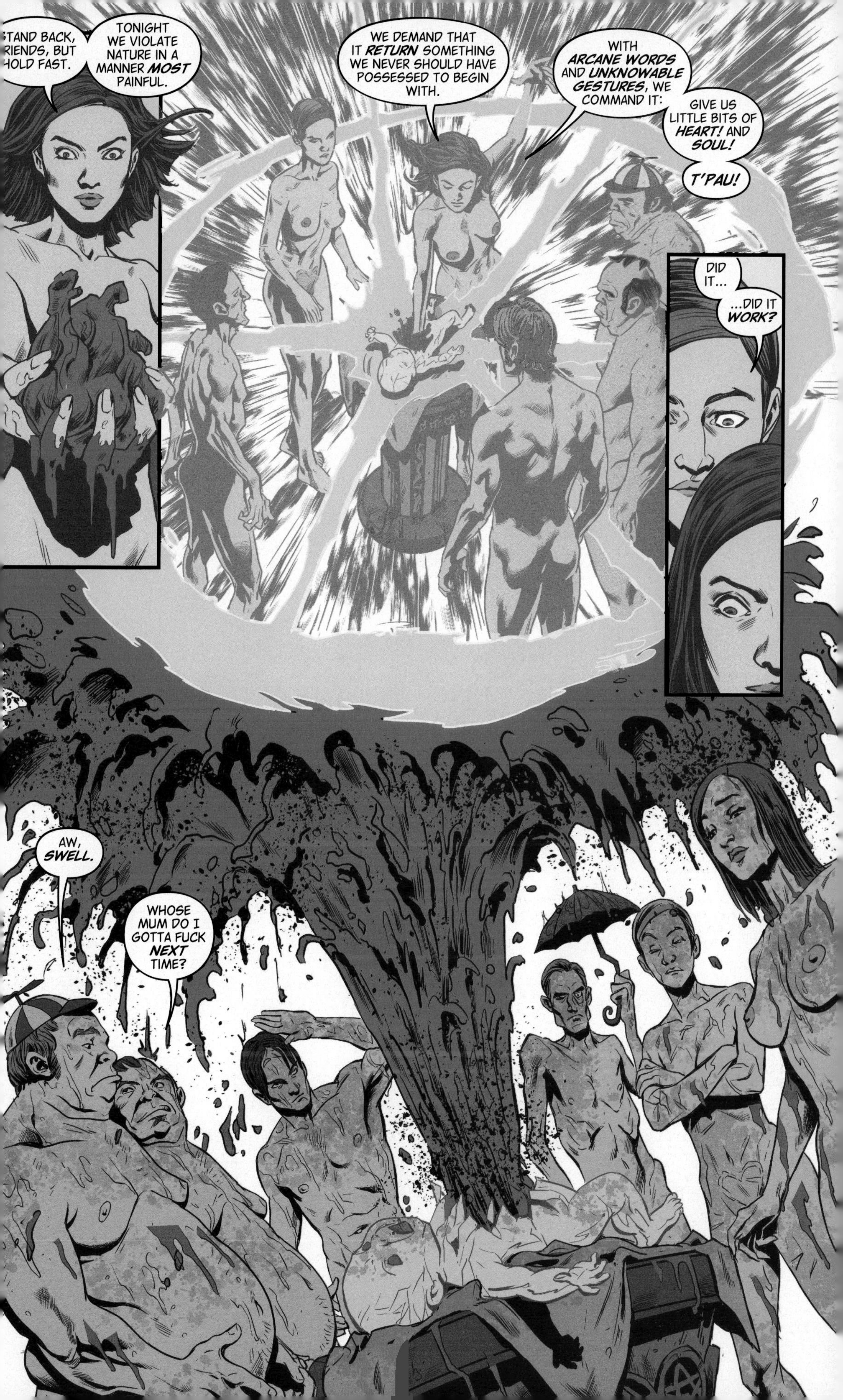
STAND BACK, FRIENDS, BUT HOLD FAST.
TONIGHT WE VIOLATE NATURE IN A MANNER MOST PAINFUL.
WE DEMAND THAT IT RETURN SOMETHING WE NEVER SHOULD HAVE POSSESSED TO BEGIN WITH.
WITH ARCANE WORDS AND UNKNOWABLE GESTURES, WE COMMAND IT:
GIVE US LITTLE BITS OF HEART! AND SOUL!
T'PAU!
DID IT...
...DID IT WORK?
AW, SWELL.
WHOSE MUM DO I GOTTA FUCK NEXT TIME?

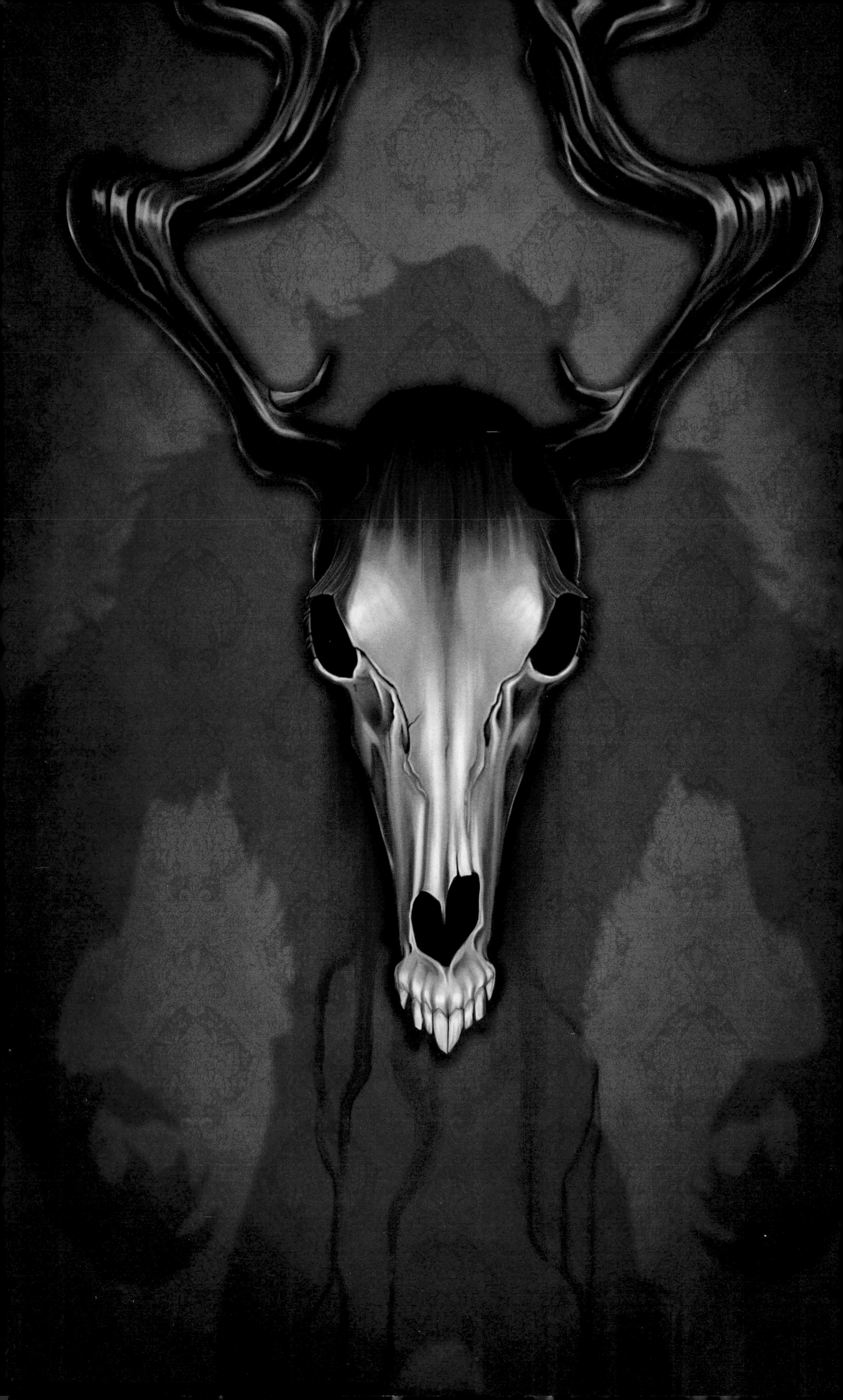

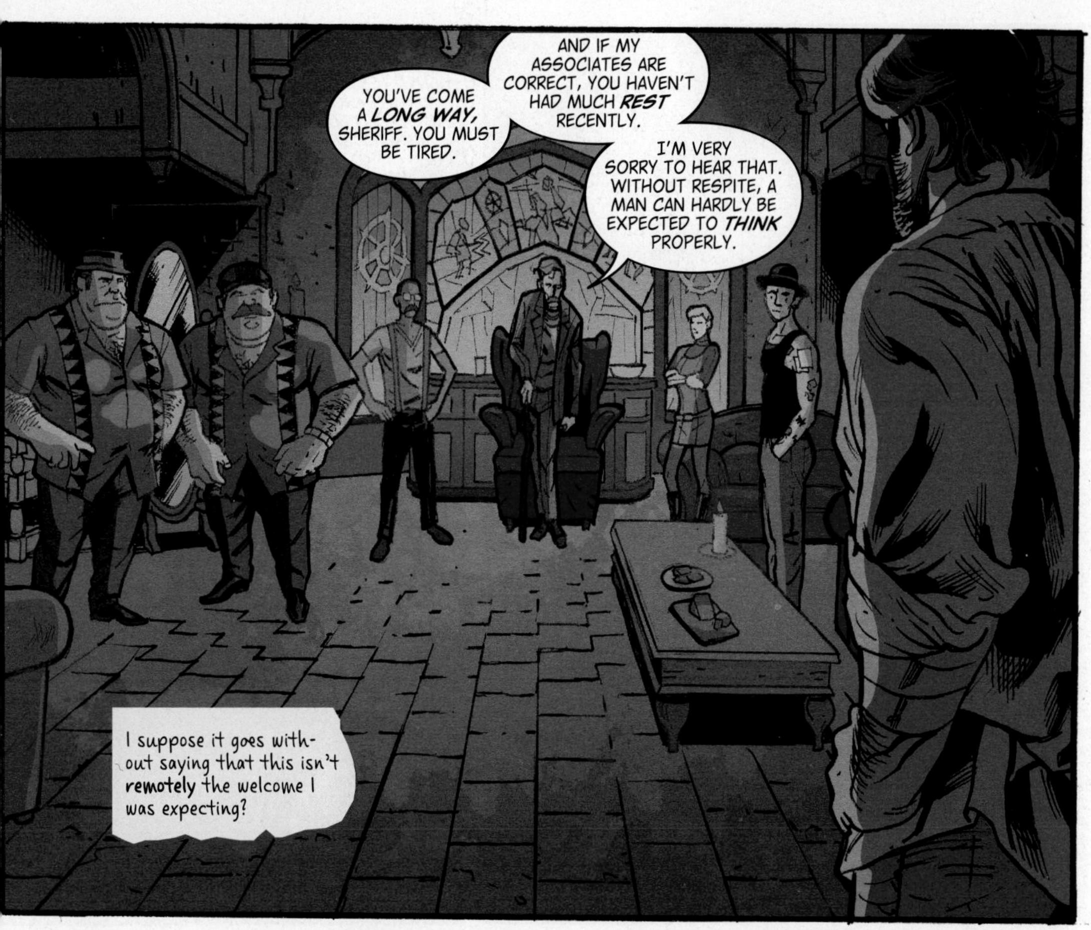
YOU'VE COME A **LONG WAY,** SHERIFF. YOU MUST BE TIRED.
AND IF MY ASSOCIATES ARE CORRECT, YOU HAVEN'T HAD MUCH **REST** RECENTLY.
I'M VERY SORRY TO HEAR THAT. WITHOUT RESPITE, A MAN CAN HARDLY BE EXPECTED TO **THINK** PROPERLY.
I suppose it goes without saying that this isn't **remotely** the welcome I was expecting?

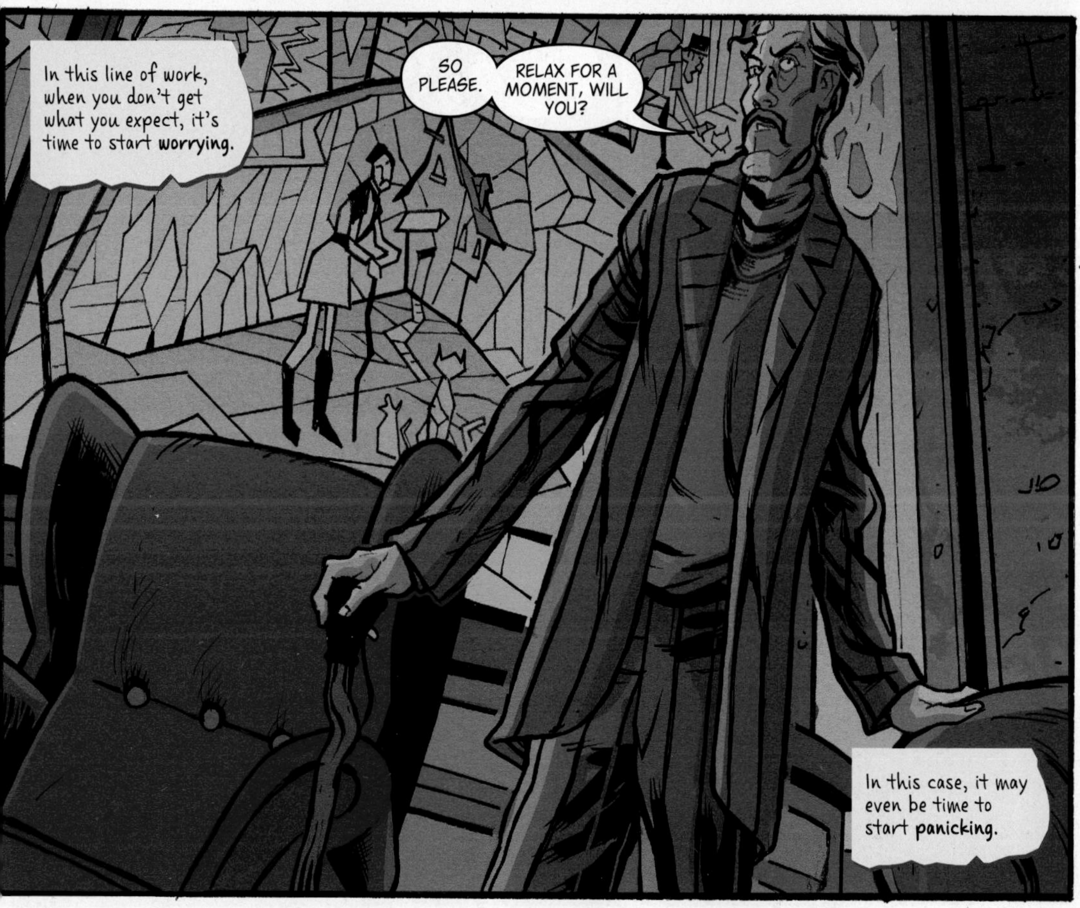
In this line of work, when you don't get what you expect, it's time to start **worrying**.
SO PLEASE.
RELAX FOR A MOMENT, WILL YOU?
In this case, it may even be time to start **panicking**.

I PREFER TO *STAND*, THANKS.

WOULD YOU CARE FOR A *DRINK?* SOMETHING TO *EAT?*

VIVIAN HERE MAKES AN EXCELLENT *CARPACCIO.*

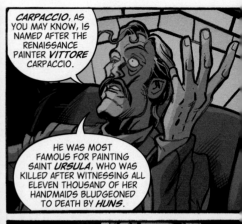

CARPACCIO, AS YOU MAY KNOW, IS NAMED AFTER THE RENAISSANCE PAINTER *VITTORE* CARPACCIO.

HE WAS MOST FAMOUS FOR PAINTING SAINT *URSULA*, WHO WAS KILLED AFTER WITNESSING ALL ELEVEN THOUSAND OF HER HANDMAIDS BLUDGEONED TO DEATH BY *HUNS.*

ANYWAY, CARPACCIO IS POUNDED *RAW MEAT*, IN CASE YOU WEREN'T AWARE.

I'M ONLY HERE FOR *ONE* THING, CROOKED MAN. AND IT'S NOT THE FUCKING *CRUDO.*

IS THAT *SO?*

THAT'S ENOUGH OF THIS--

JERSEY, PLEASE. THIS MAN IS OUR *GUEST.*

OF COURSE. SORRY, SIR.

FOR TRANSPARENCY'S SAKE, *DO* TELL US WHY YOU'RE HERE, SHERIFF. PERHAPS IT WILL PUT MY *COMPANIONS* AT EASE.

YOU *KNOW* WHY I'M HERE. THE TWO *DEAD* GIRLS. *FAITH* AND *LILY*. EVERYTHING IN THIS INVESTIGATION LEADS BACK TO YOU.

I SEE. HOW *DREADFUL*.

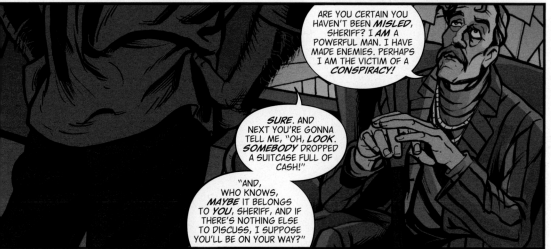

ARE YOU CERTAIN YOU HAVEN'T BEEN *MISLED*, SHERIFF? I *AM* A POWERFUL MAN. I HAVE MADE ENEMIES. PERHAPS I AM THE VICTIM OF A *CONSPIRACY*!

SURE. AND NEXT YOU'RE GONNA TELL ME, "OH, *LOOK*. *SOMEBODY* DROPPED A SUITCASE FULL OF CASH!"

"AND, WHO KNOWS, *MAYBE* IT BELONGS TO *YOU*, SHERIFF, AND IF THERE'S NOTHING ELSE TO DISCUSS, I SUPPOSE YOU'LL BE ON YOUR WAY?"

A CASH-LADEN SUITCASE! MY, WHAT AN *IMAGINATION* YOU HAVE!

I HAVE NO *NEED* FOR SUCH ANTICS, MISTER WOLF. AND IT'S CLEAR THAT YOU ARE NOT SO EASILY PUT OFF, REGARDLESS.

I *DO* APOLOGIZE FOR ALL THE *TROUBLE* YOU'VE GONE THROUGH. AND I INTEND TO MAKE IT *UP* TO YOU.

UH-HUH.

THE *CRIMES* OF WHICH YOU SPEAK...

...WERE *INDEED* PERPETRATED BY AN EMPLOYEE OF MINE.

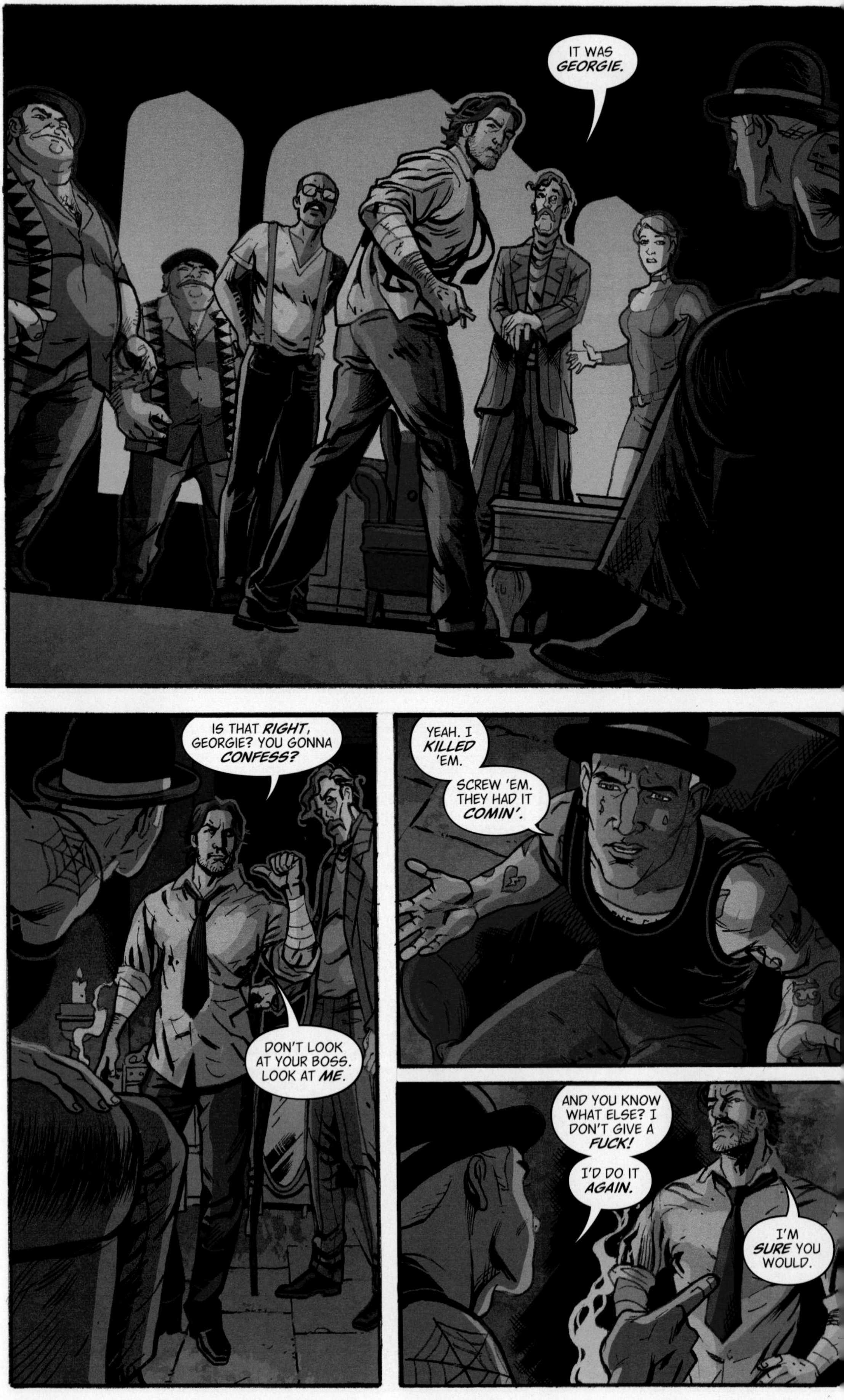
IT WAS GEORGIE.
IS THAT RIGHT, GEORGIE? YOU GONNA CONFESS?
DON'T LOOK AT YOUR BOSS. LOOK AT ME.
YEAH. I KILLED 'EM.
SCREW 'EM. THEY HAD IT COMIN'.
AND YOU KNOW WHAT ELSE? I DON'T GIVE A FUCK!
I'D DO IT AGAIN.
I'M SURE YOU WOULD.

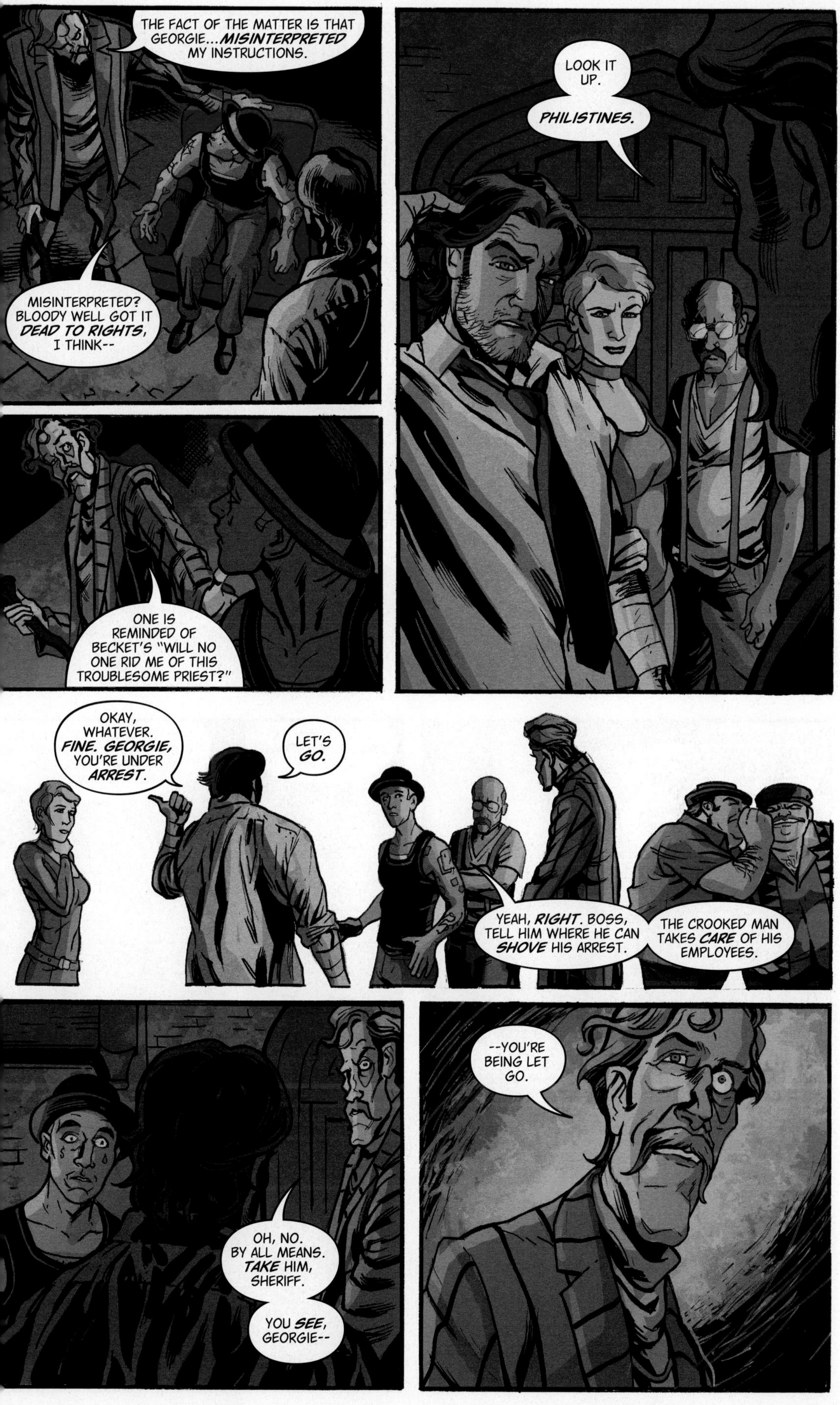
THE FACT OF THE MATTER IS THAT GEORGIE... MISINTERPRETED MY INSTRUCTIONS.
MISINTERPRETED? BLOODY WELL GOT IT DEAD TO RIGHTS, I THINK--
ONE IS REMINDED OF BECKET'S "WILL NO ONE RID ME OF THIS TROUBLESOME PRIEST?"
LOOK IT UP.
PHILISTINES.
OKAY, WHATEVER. FINE. GEORGIE, YOU'RE UNDER ARREST.
LET'S GO.
YEAH, RIGHT. BOSS, TELL HIM WHERE HE CAN SHOVE HIS ARREST.
THE CROOKED MAN TAKES CARE OF HIS EMPLOYEES.
OH, NO. BY ALL MEANS. TAKE HIM, SHERIFF.
YOU SEE, GEORGIE--
--YOU'RE BEING LET GO.

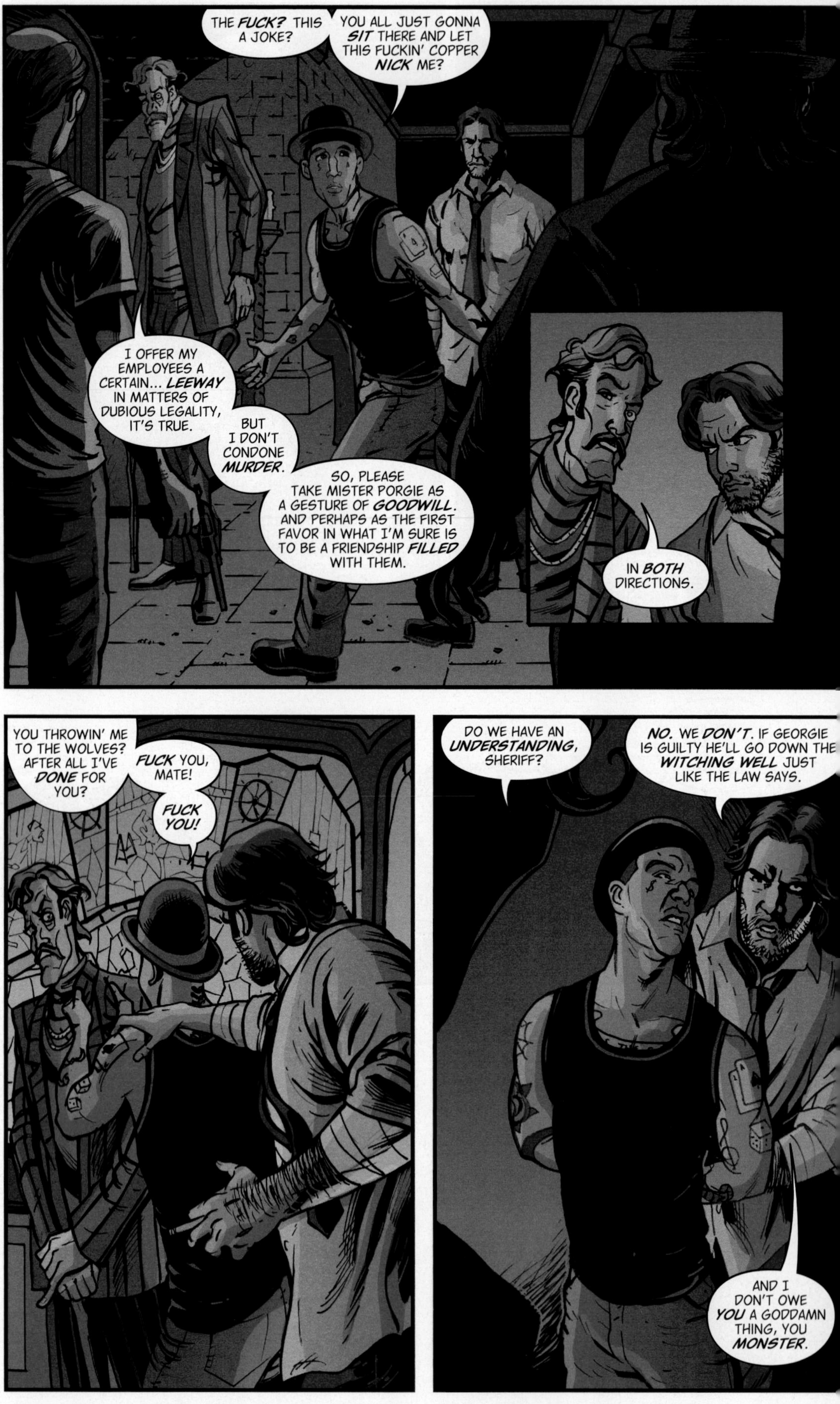
THE FUCK? THIS A JOKE?
YOU ALL JUST GONNA SIT THERE AND LET THIS FUCKIN' COPPER NICK ME?
I OFFER MY EMPLOYEES A CERTAIN... LEEWAY IN MATTERS OF DUBIOUS LEGALITY, IT'S TRUE.
BUT I DON'T CONDONE MURDER.
SO, PLEASE TAKE MISTER PORGIE AS A GESTURE OF GOODWILL. AND PERHAPS AS THE FIRST FAVOR IN WHAT I'M SURE IS TO BE A FRIENDSHIP FILLED WITH THEM.
IN BOTH DIRECTIONS.
YOU THROWIN' ME TO THE WOLVES? AFTER ALL I'VE DONE FOR YOU?
FUCK YOU, MATE!
FUCK YOU!
DO WE HAVE AN UNDERSTANDING, SHERIFF?
NO. WE DON'T. IF GEORGIE IS GUILTY HE'LL GO DOWN THE WITCHING WELL JUST LIKE THE LAW SAYS.
AND I DON'T OWE YOU A GODDAMN THING, YOU MONSTER.

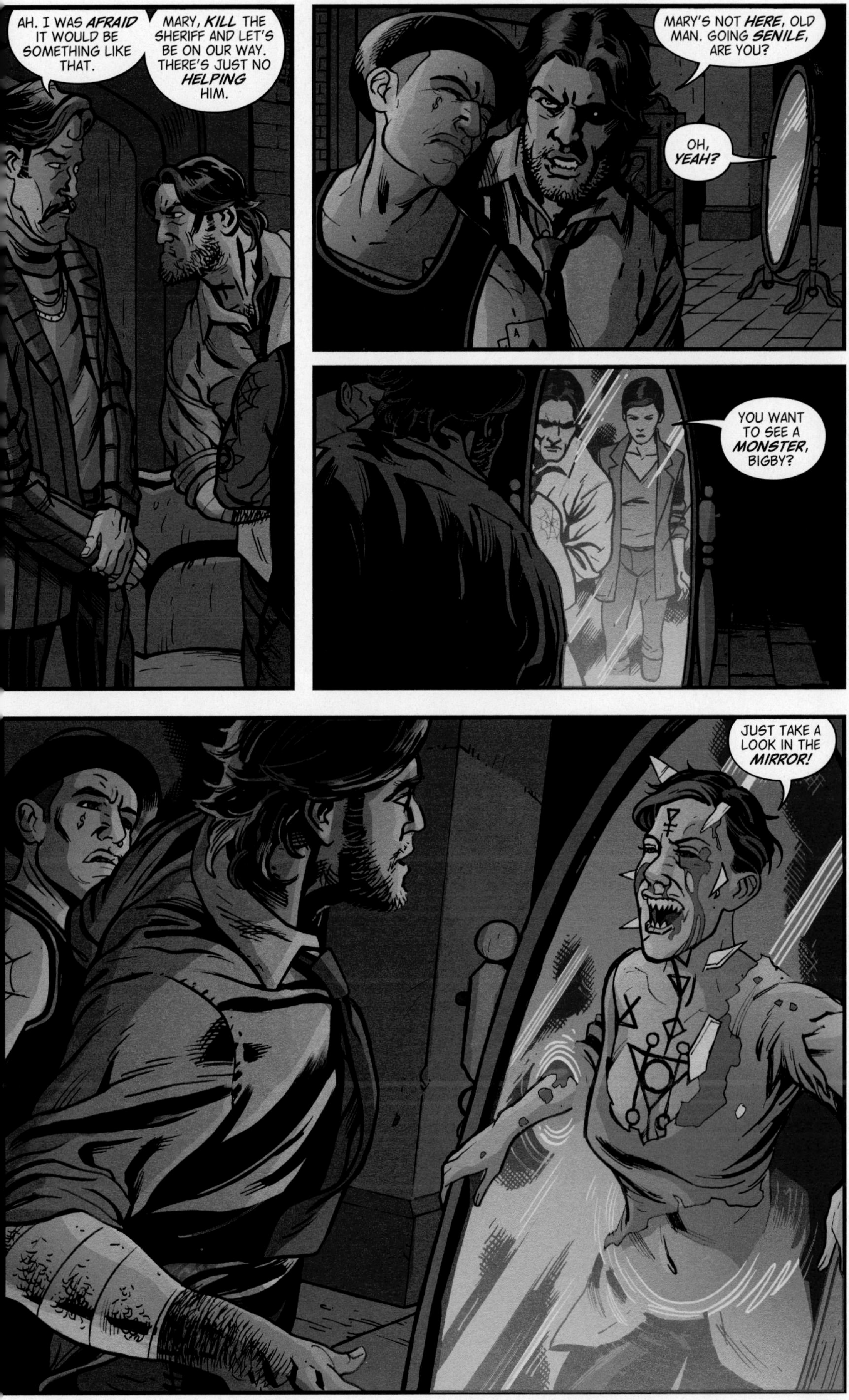
AH. I WAS AFRAID IT WOULD BE SOMETHING LIKE THAT.
MARY, KILL THE SHERIFF AND LET'S BE ON OUR WAY. THERE'S JUST NO HELPING HIM.
MARY'S NOT HERE, OLD MAN. GOING SENILE, ARE YOU?
OH, YEAH?
YOU WANT TO SEE A MONSTER, BIGBY?
JUST TAKE A LOOK IN THE MIRROR!

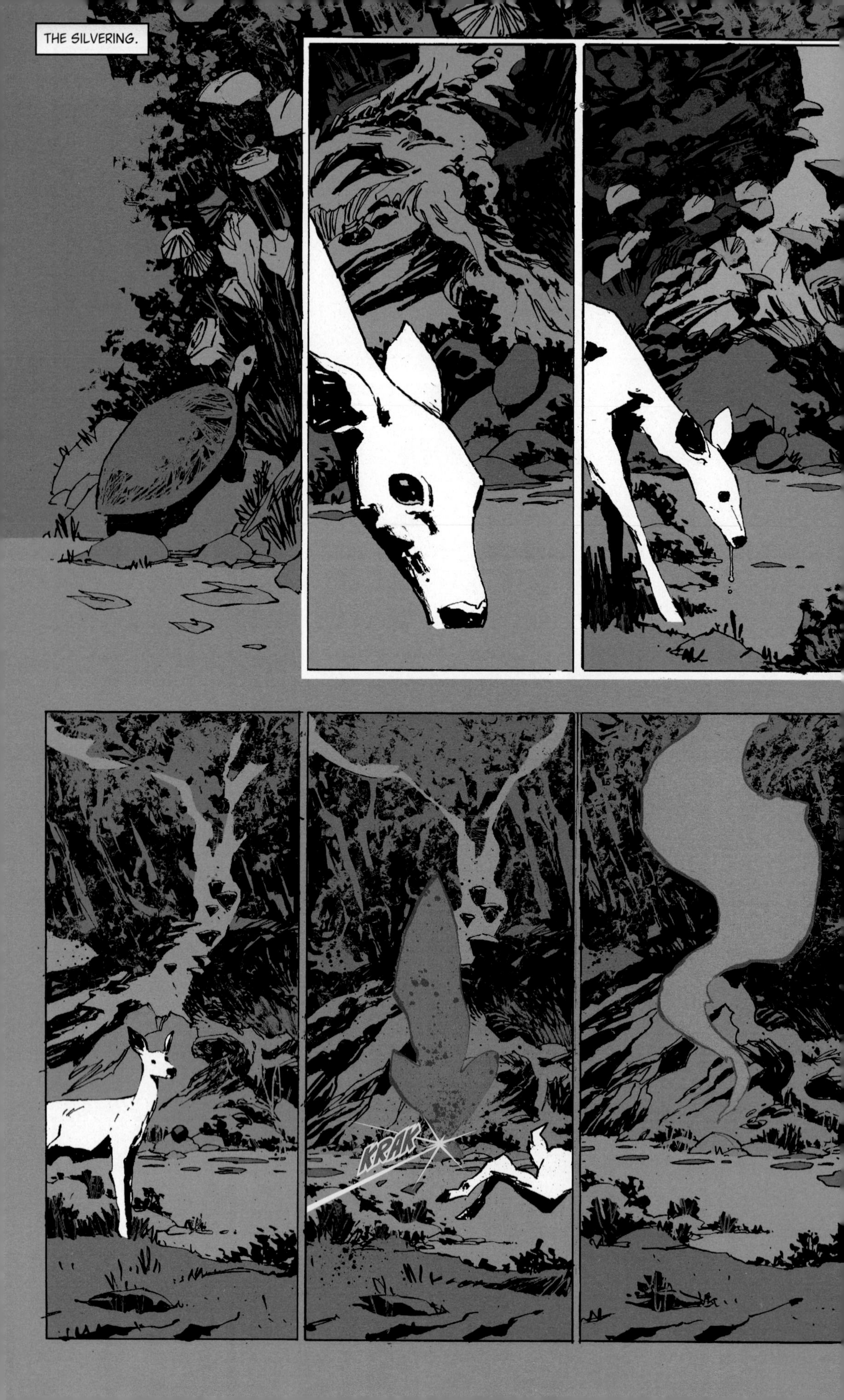
THE SILVERING.
K-RAK

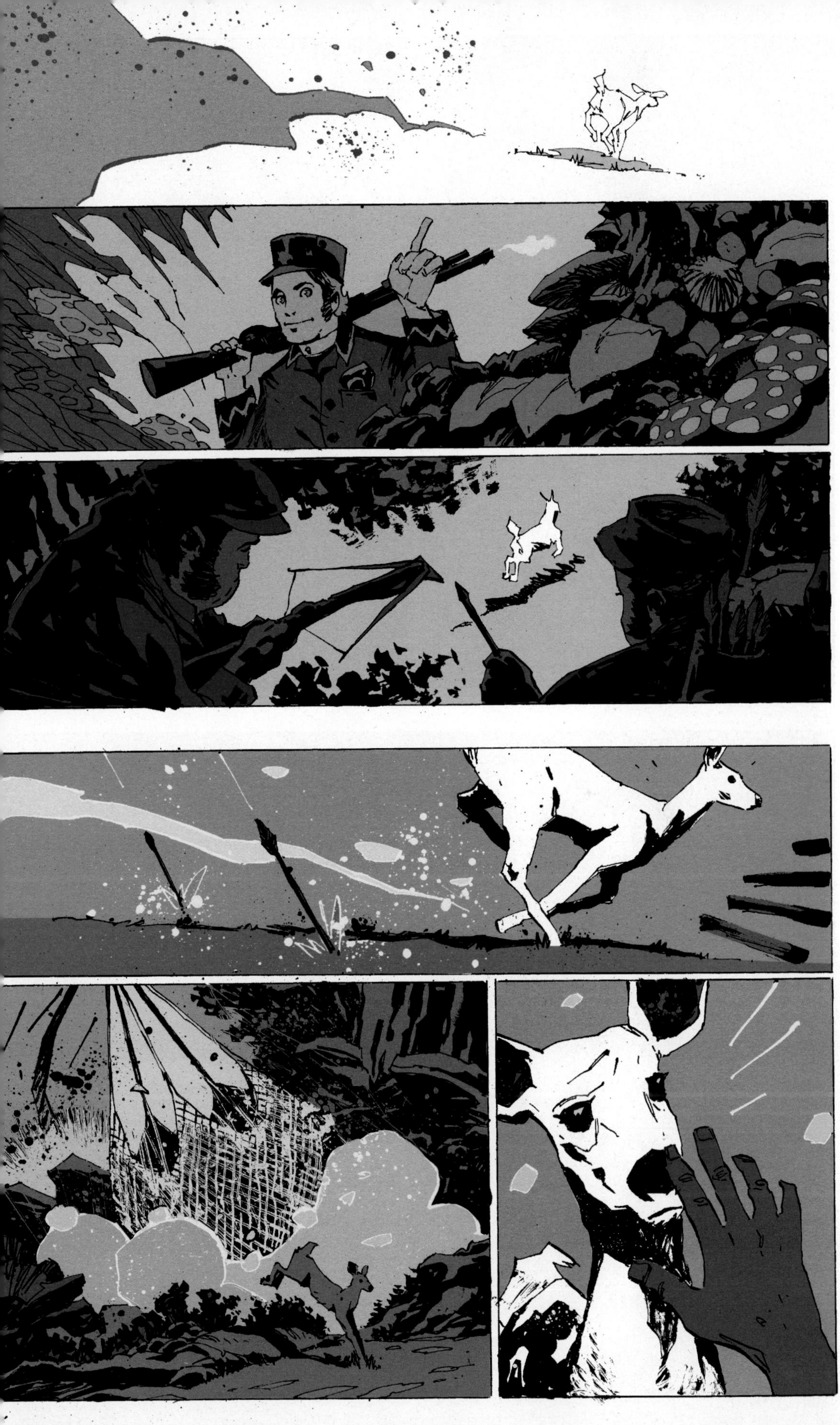

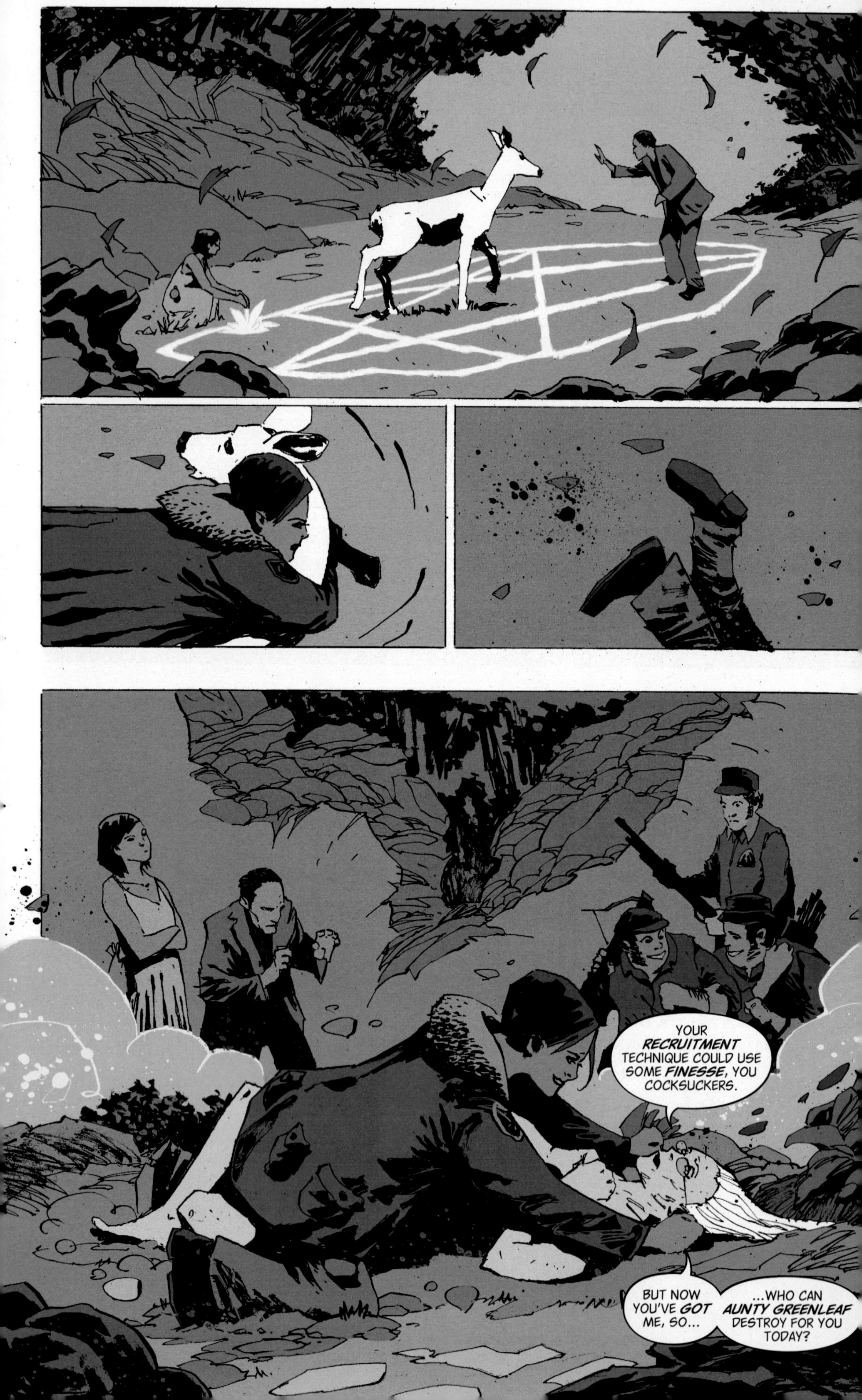
YOUR *RECRUITMENT* TECHNIQUE COULD USE SOME *FINESSE*, YOU COCKSUCKERS.
BUT NOW YOU'VE *GOT* ME, SO...
...WHO CAN *AUNTY GREENLEAF* DESTROY FOR YOU TODAY?

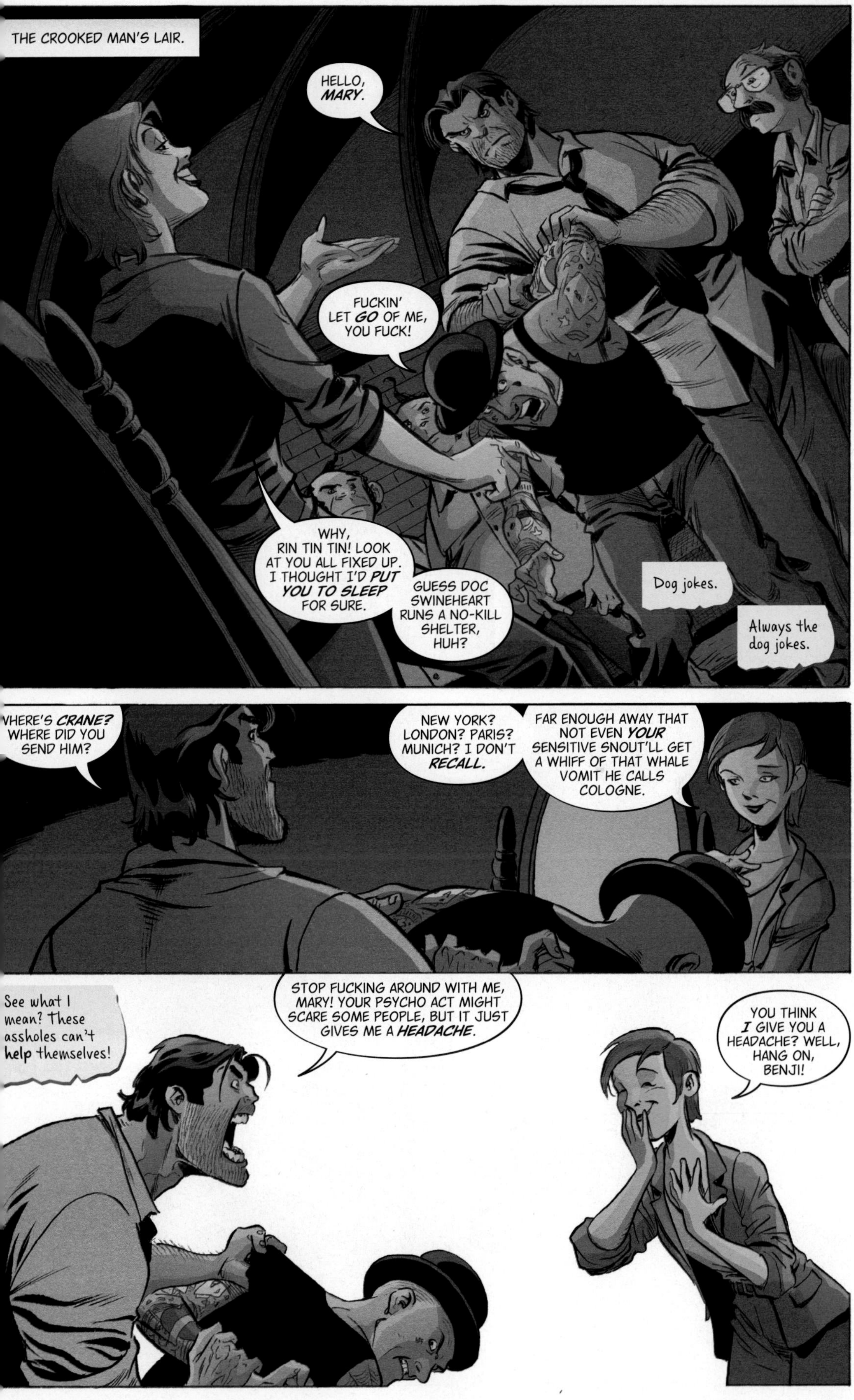
THE CROOKED MAN'S LAIR.
HELLO, MARY.
FUCKIN' LET GO OF ME, YOU FUCK!
WHY, RIN TIN TIN! LOOK AT YOU ALL FIXED UP. I THOUGHT I'D PUT YOU TO SLEEP FOR SURE.
GUESS DOC SWINEHEART RUNS A NO-KILL SHELTER, HUH?
Dog jokes.
Always the dog jokes.
WHERE'S CRANE? WHERE DID YOU SEND HIM?
NEW YORK? LONDON? PARIS? MUNICH? I DON'T RECALL.
FAR ENOUGH AWAY THAT NOT EVEN YOUR SENSITIVE SNOUT'LL GET A WHIFF OF THAT WHALE VOMIT HE CALLS COLOGNE.
See what I mean? These assholes can't help themselves!
STOP FUCKING AROUND WITH ME, MARY! YOUR PSYCHO ACT MIGHT SCARE SOME PEOPLE, BUT IT JUST GIVES ME A HEADACHE.
YOU THINK I GIVE YOU A HEADACHE? WELL, HANG ON, BENJI!

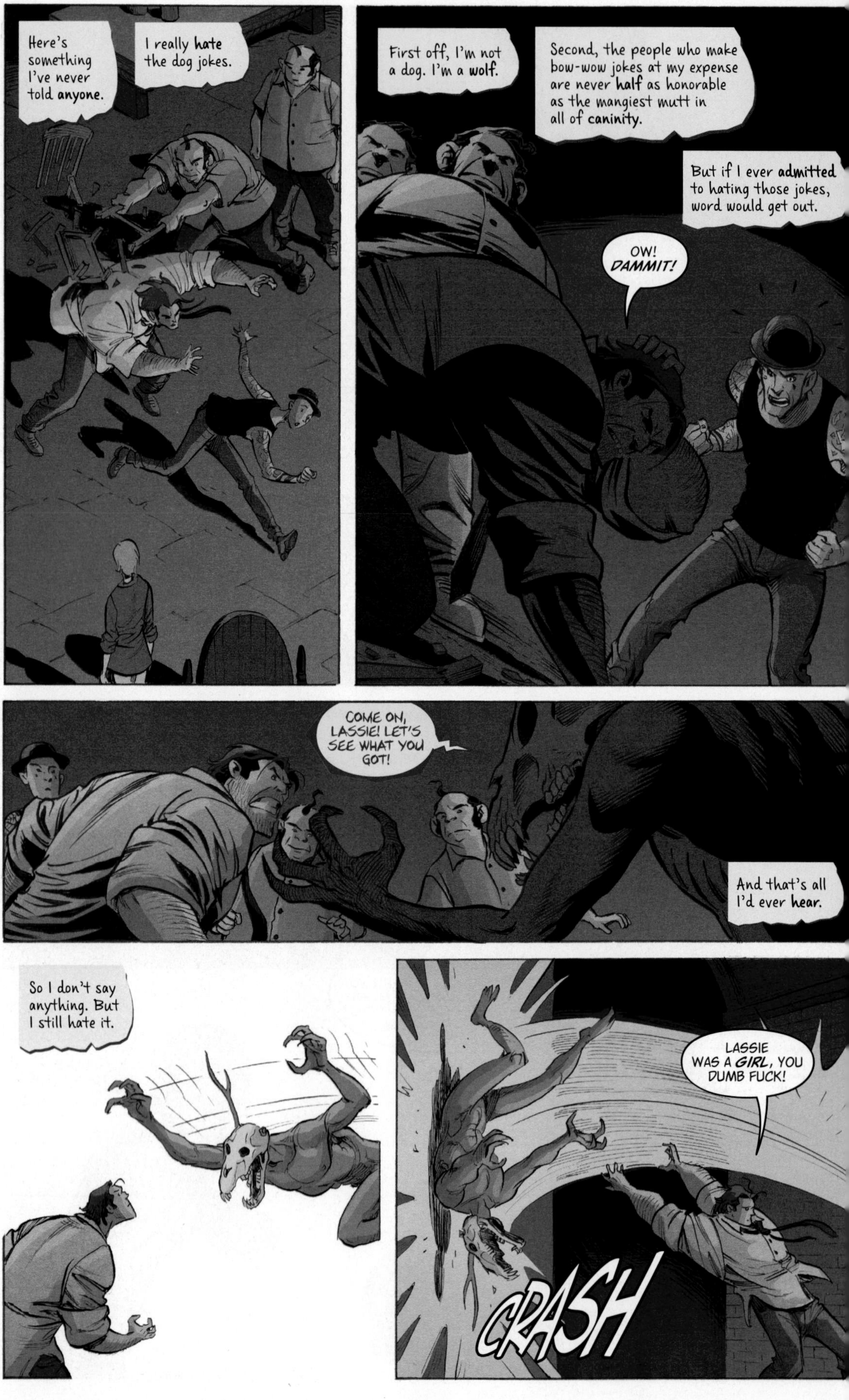
Here's something I've never told **anyone**.
I really **hate** the dog jokes.
First off, I'm not a dog. I'm a **wolf**.
Second, the people who make bow-wow jokes at my expense are never **half** as honorable as the mangiest mutt in all of **caninity**.
But if I ever **admitted** to hating those jokes, word would get out.
OW! *DAMMIT!*
COME ON, LASSIE! LET'S SEE WHAT YOU GOT!
And that's all I'd ever **hear**.
So I don't say anything. But I still hate it.
LASSIE WAS A *GIRL*, YOU DUMB FUCK!
CRASH

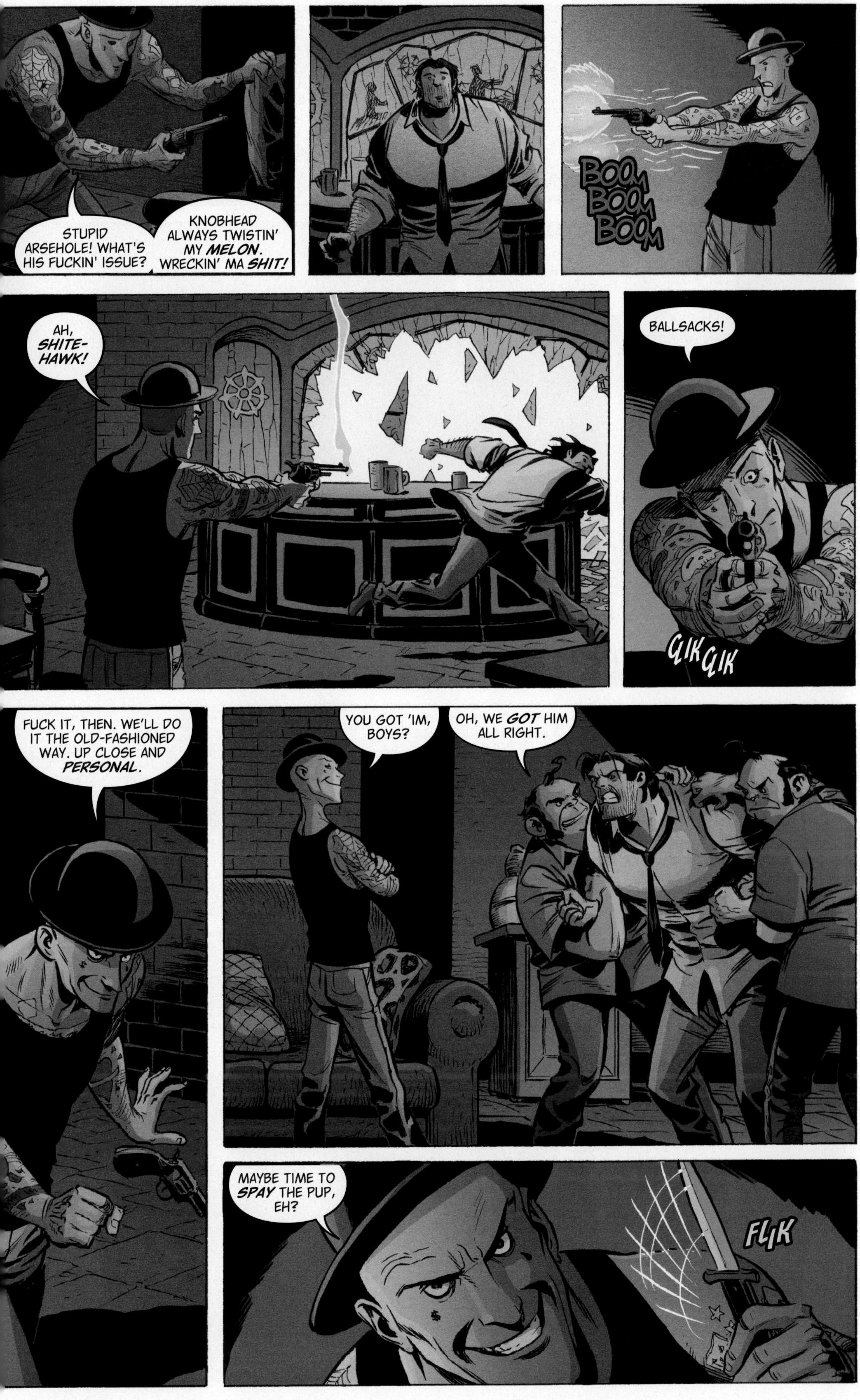
STUPID ARSEHOLE! WHAT'S HIS FUCKIN' ISSUE?
KNOBHEAD ALWAYS TWISTIN' MY MELON. WRECKIN' MA SHIT!
BOOM BOOM BOOM
AH, SHITE-HAWK!
BALLSACKS!
CLIK CLIK
FUCK IT, THEN. WE'LL DO IT THE OLD-FASHIONED WAY. UP CLOSE AND PERSONAL.
YOU GOT 'IM, BOYS?
OH, WE GOT HIM ALL RIGHT.
MAYBE TIME TO SPAY THE PUP, EH?
FLIK

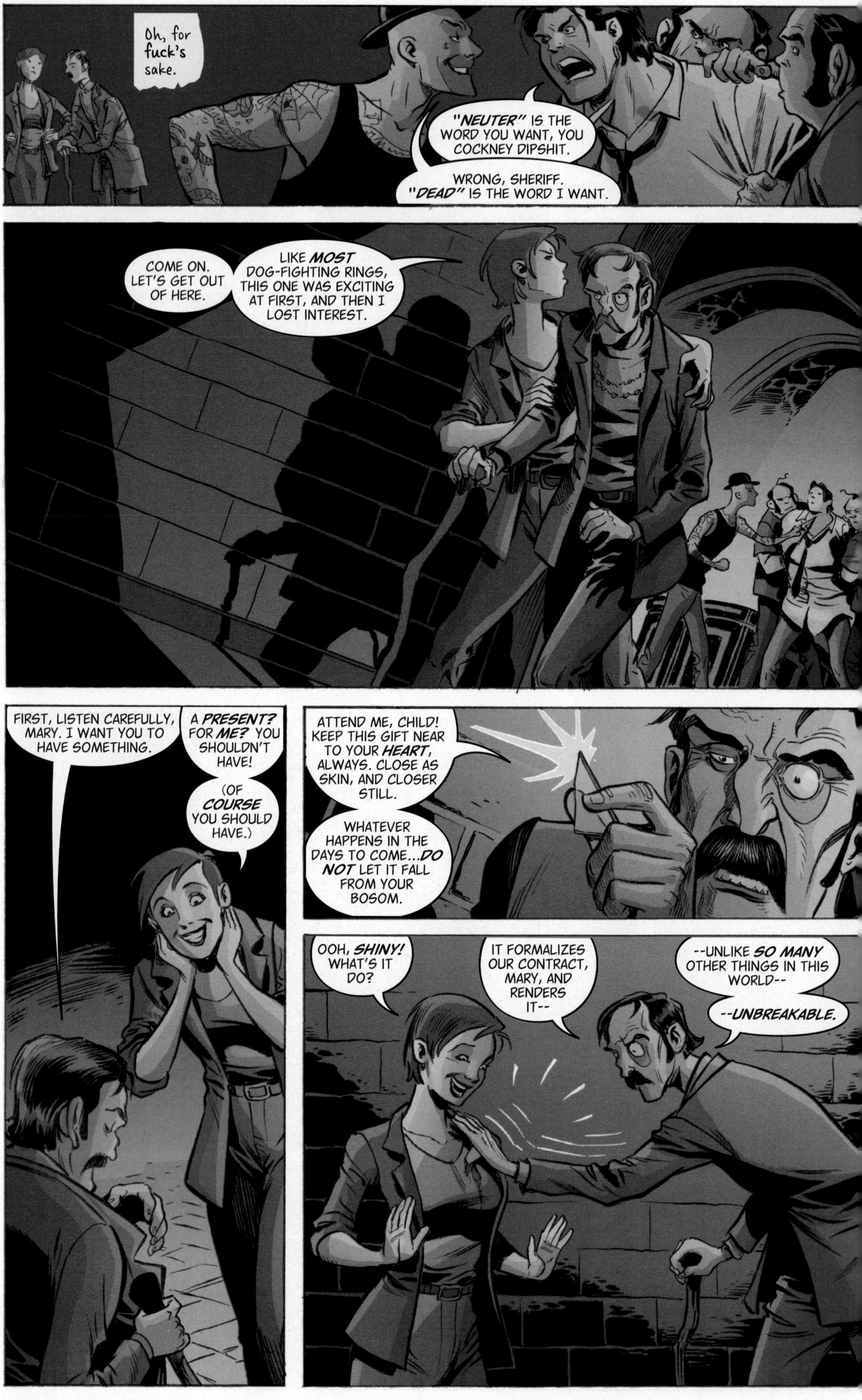
Oh, for fuck's sake.
"NEUTER" IS THE WORD YOU WANT, YOU COCKNEY DIPSHIT.
WRONG, SHERIFF. "DEAD" IS THE WORD I WANT.
COME ON. LET'S GET OUT OF HERE.
LIKE MOST DOG-FIGHTING RINGS, THIS ONE WAS EXCITING AT FIRST, AND THEN I LOST INTEREST.
FIRST, LISTEN CAREFULLY, MARY. I WANT YOU TO HAVE SOMETHING.
A PRESENT? FOR ME? YOU SHOULDN'T HAVE!
(OF COURSE YOU SHOULD HAVE.)
ATTEND ME, CHILD! KEEP THIS GIFT NEAR TO YOUR HEART, ALWAYS. CLOSE AS SKIN, AND CLOSER STILL.
WHATEVER HAPPENS IN THE DAYS TO COME...DO NOT LET IT FALL FROM YOUR BOSOM.
OOH, SHINY! WHAT'S IT DO?
IT FORMALIZES OUR CONTRACT, MARY, AND RENDERS IT--
--UNLIKE SO MANY OTHER THINGS IN THIS WORLD--
--UNBREAKABLE.

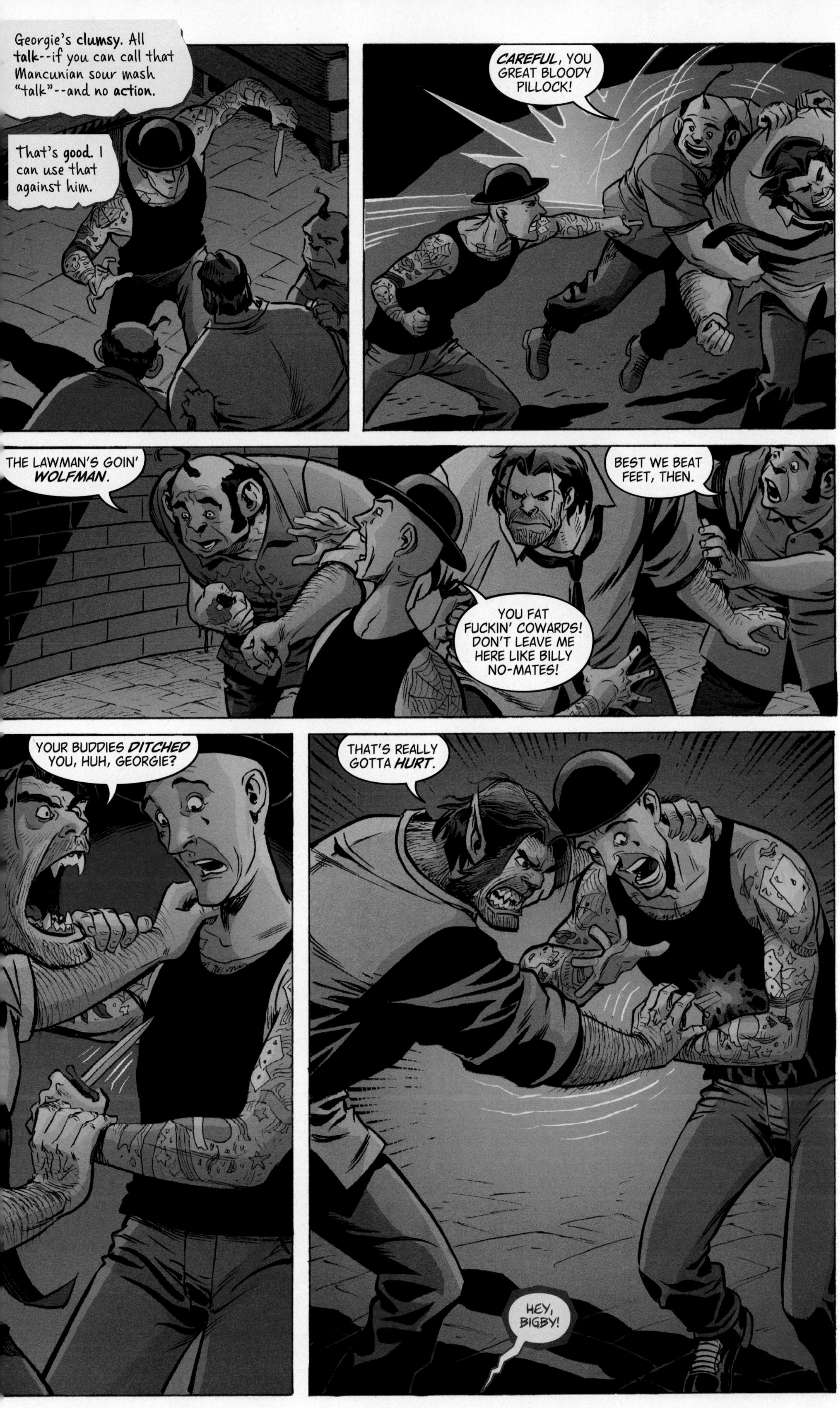

Georgie's **clumsy**. All **talk**--if you can call that Mancunian sour mash "talk"--and no **action**.
That's **good**. I can use that against him.
CAREFUL, YOU GREAT BLOODY PILLOCK!
THE LAWMAN'S GOIN' ***WOLFMAN***.
BEST WE BEAT FEET, THEN.
YOU FAT FUCKIN' COWARDS! DON'T LEAVE ME HERE LIKE BILLY NO-MATES!
YOUR BUDDIES ***DITCHED*** YOU, HUH, GEORGIE?
THAT'S REALLY GOTTA ***HURT***.
HEY, BIGBY!

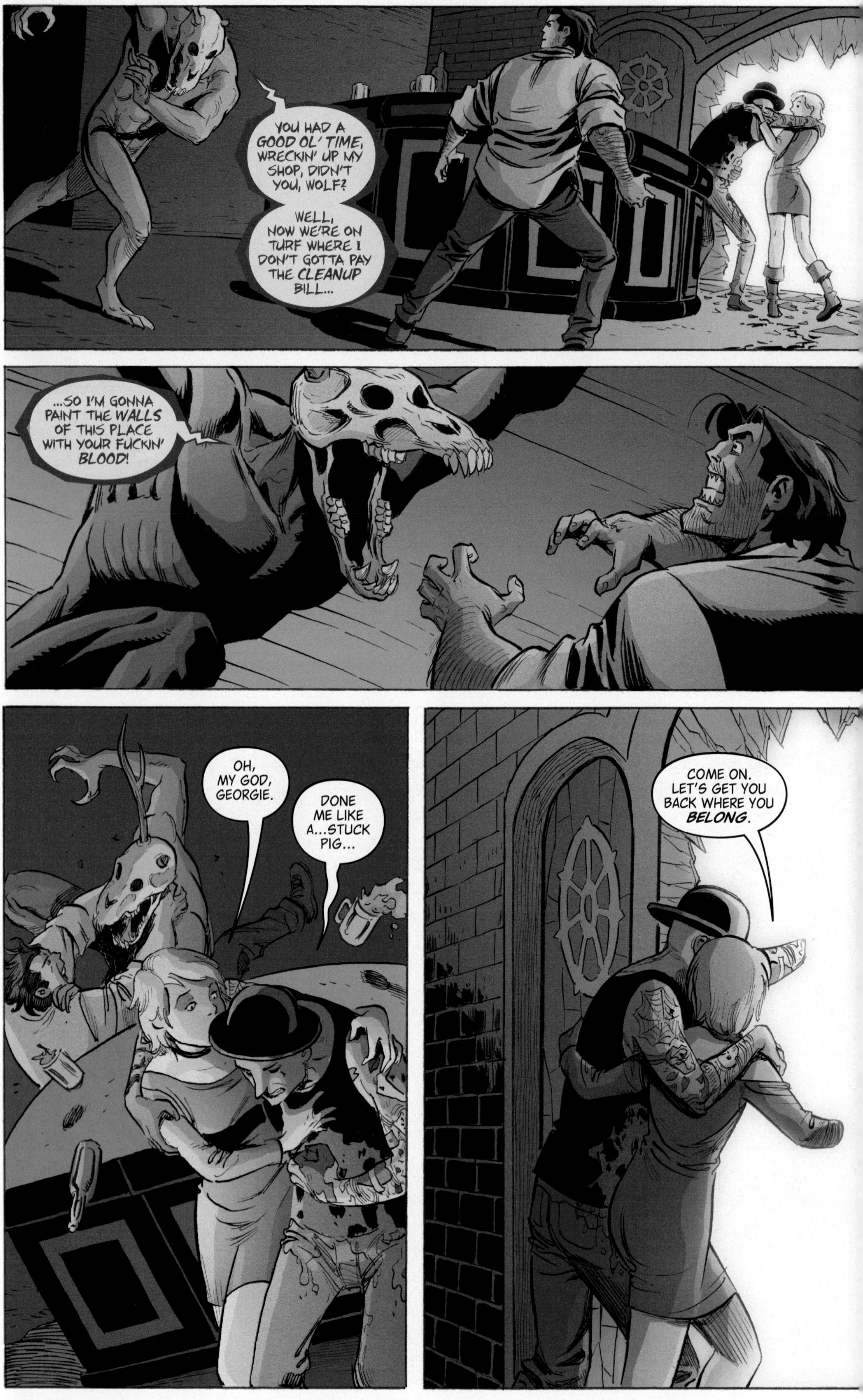
YOU HAD A GOOD OL' TIME, WRECKIN' UP MY SHOP, DIDN'T YOU, WOLF?
WELL, NOW WE'RE ON TURF WHERE I DON'T GOTTA PAY THE CLEANUP BILL...
...SO I'M GONNA PAINT THE WALLS OF THIS PLACE WITH YOUR FUCKIN' BLOOD!
OH, MY GOD, GEORGIE.
DONE ME LIKE A...STUCK PIG...
COME ON. LET'S GET YOU BACK WHERE YOU BELONG.

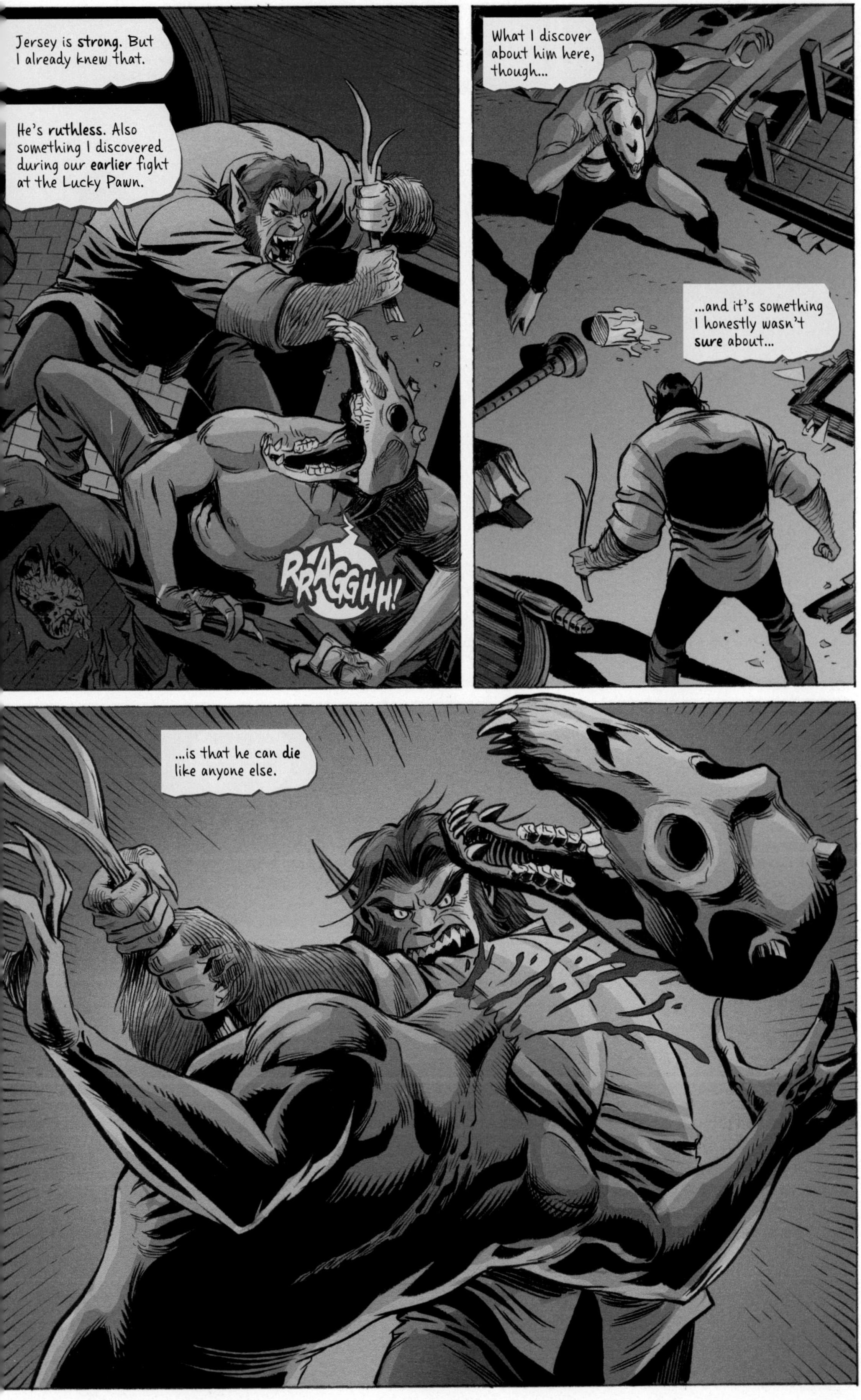
Jersey is strong. But I already knew that.
He's ruthless. Also something I discovered during our earlier fight at the Lucky Pawn.
RRRAGGHH!
What I discover about him here, though...
...and it's something I honestly wasn't sure about...
...is that he can die like anyone else.

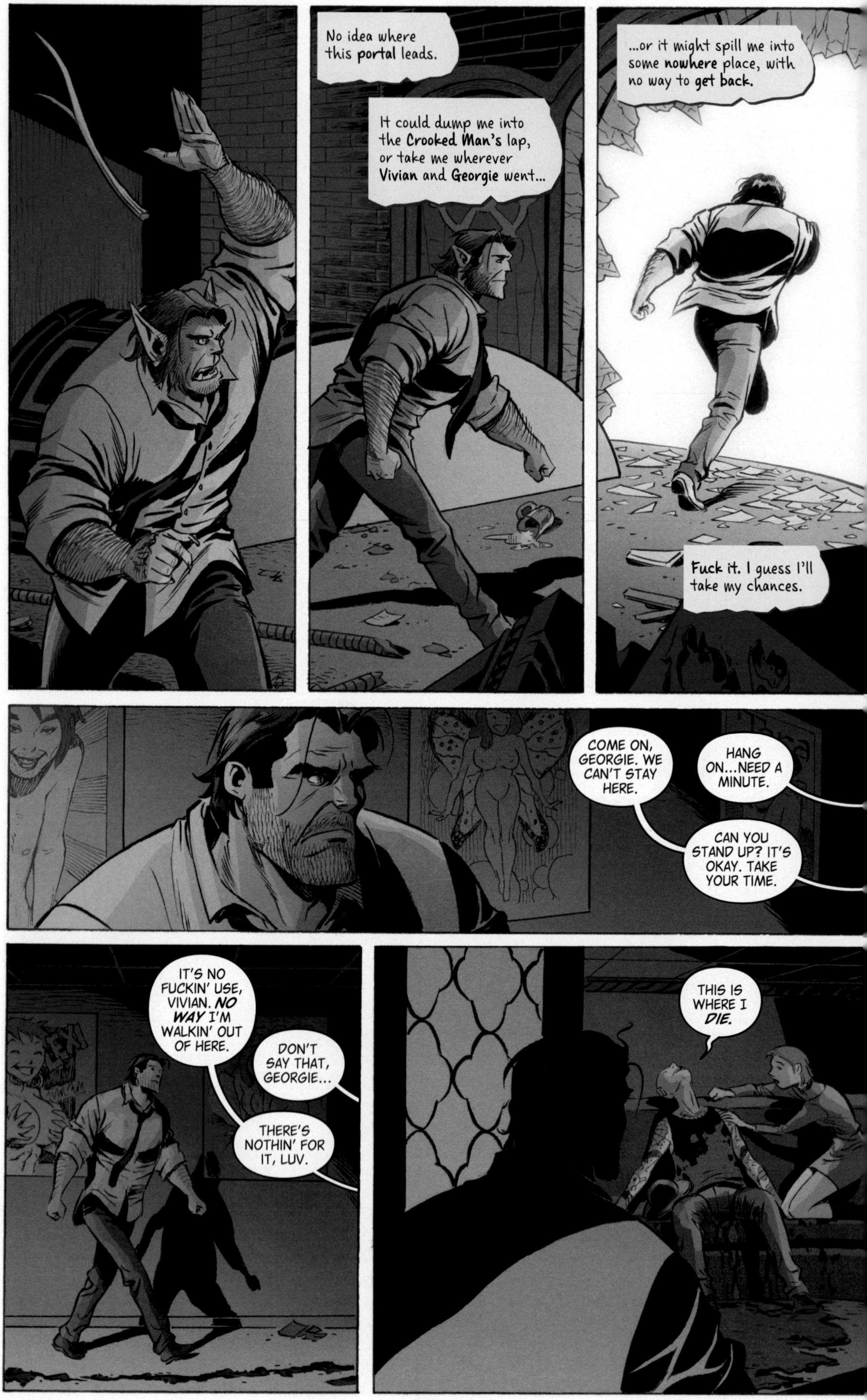
No idea where this portal leads.
It could dump me into the Crooked Man's lap, or take me wherever Vivian and Georgie went...
...or it might spill me into some nowhere place, with no way to get back.
Fuck it. I guess I'll take my chances.
COME ON, GEORGIE. WE CAN'T STAY HERE.
HANG ON...NEED A MINUTE.
CAN YOU STAND UP? IT'S OKAY. TAKE YOUR TIME.
IT'S NO FUCKIN' USE, VIVIAN. NO WAY I'M WALKIN' OUT OF HERE.
DON'T SAY THAT, GEORGIE...
THERE'S NOTHIN' FOR IT, LUV.
THIS IS WHERE I DIE.

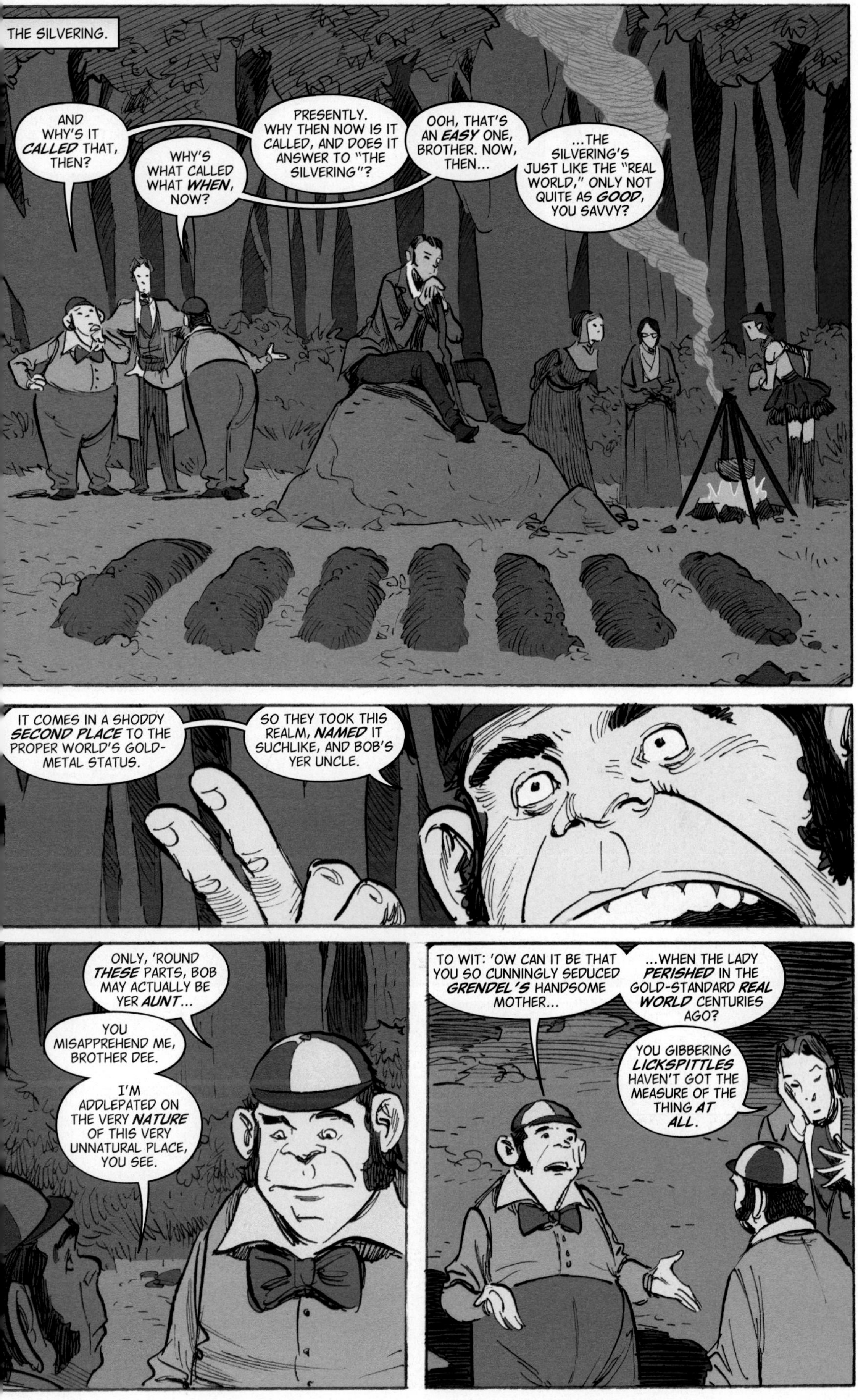
THE SILVERING.
AND WHY'S IT CALLED THAT, THEN?
WHY'S WHAT CALLED WHAT WHEN, NOW?
PRESENTLY. WHY THEN NOW IS IT CALLED, AND DOES IT ANSWER TO "THE SILVERING"?
OOH, THAT'S AN EASY ONE, BROTHER. NOW, THEN...
...THE SILVERING'S JUST LIKE THE "REAL WORLD," ONLY NOT QUITE AS GOOD, YOU SAVVY?
IT COMES IN A SHODDY SECOND PLACE TO THE PROPER WORLD'S GOLD-METAL STATUS.
SO THEY TOOK THIS REALM, NAMED IT SUCHLIKE, AND BOB'S YER UNCLE.
ONLY, 'ROUND THESE PARTS, BOB MAY ACTUALLY BE YER AUNT...
YOU MISAPPREHEND ME, BROTHER DEE.
I'M ADDLEPATED ON THE VERY NATURE OF THIS VERY UNNATURAL PLACE, YOU SEE.
TO WIT: 'OW CAN IT BE THAT YOU SO CUNNINGLY SEDUCED GRENDEL'S HANDSOME MOTHER...
...WHEN THE LADY PERISHED IN THE GOLD-STANDARD REAL WORLD CENTURIES AGO?
YOU GIBBERING LICKSPITTLES HAVEN'T GOT THE MEASURE OF THE THING AT ALL.

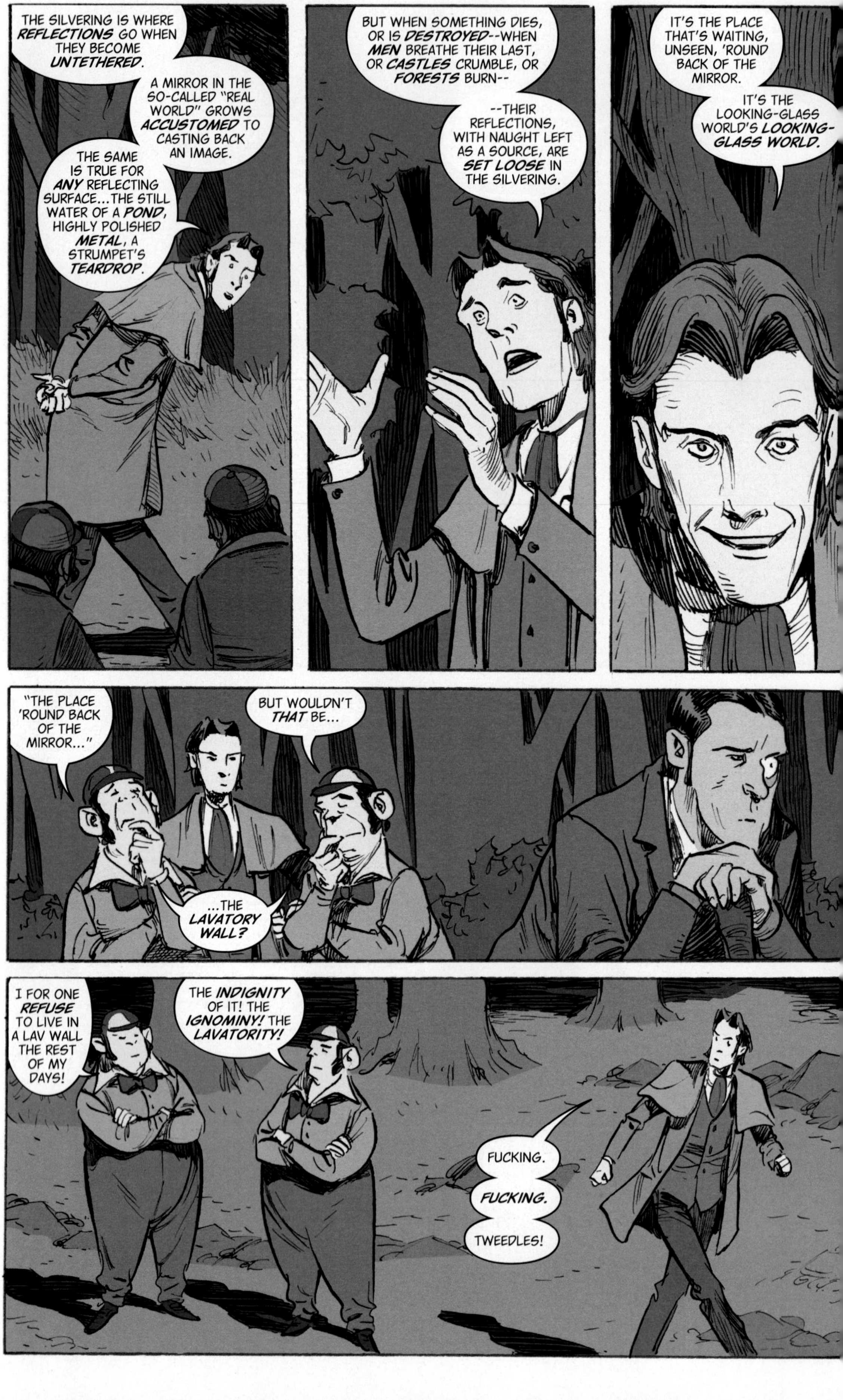

THE SILVERING IS WHERE *REFLECTIONS* GO WHEN THEY BECOME *UNTETHERED*.
A MIRROR IN THE SO-CALLED "REAL WORLD" GROWS *ACCUSTOMED* TO CASTING BACK AN IMAGE.
THE SAME IS TRUE FOR *ANY* REFLECTING SURFACE...THE STILL WATER OF A *POND*, HIGHLY POLISHED *METAL*, A STRUMPET'S *TEARDROP*.
BUT WHEN SOMETHING DIES, OR IS *DESTROYED*--WHEN *MEN* BREATHE THEIR LAST, OR *CASTLES* CRUMBLE, OR *FORESTS* BURN--
--THEIR REFLECTIONS, WITH NAUGHT LEFT AS A SOURCE, ARE *SET LOOSE* IN THE SILVERING.
IT'S THE PLACE THAT'S WAITING, UNSEEN, 'ROUND BACK OF THE MIRROR.
IT'S THE LOOKING-GLASS WORLD'S *LOOKING-GLASS WORLD.*
"THE PLACE 'ROUND BACK OF THE MIRROR..."
BUT WOULDN'T *THAT* BE...
...THE *LAVATORY WALL?*
I FOR ONE *REFUSE* TO LIVE IN A LAV WALL THE REST OF MY DAYS!
THE *INDIGNITY* OF IT! THE *IGNOMINY!* THE *LAVATORITY!*
FUCKING.
FUCKING.
TWEEDLES!

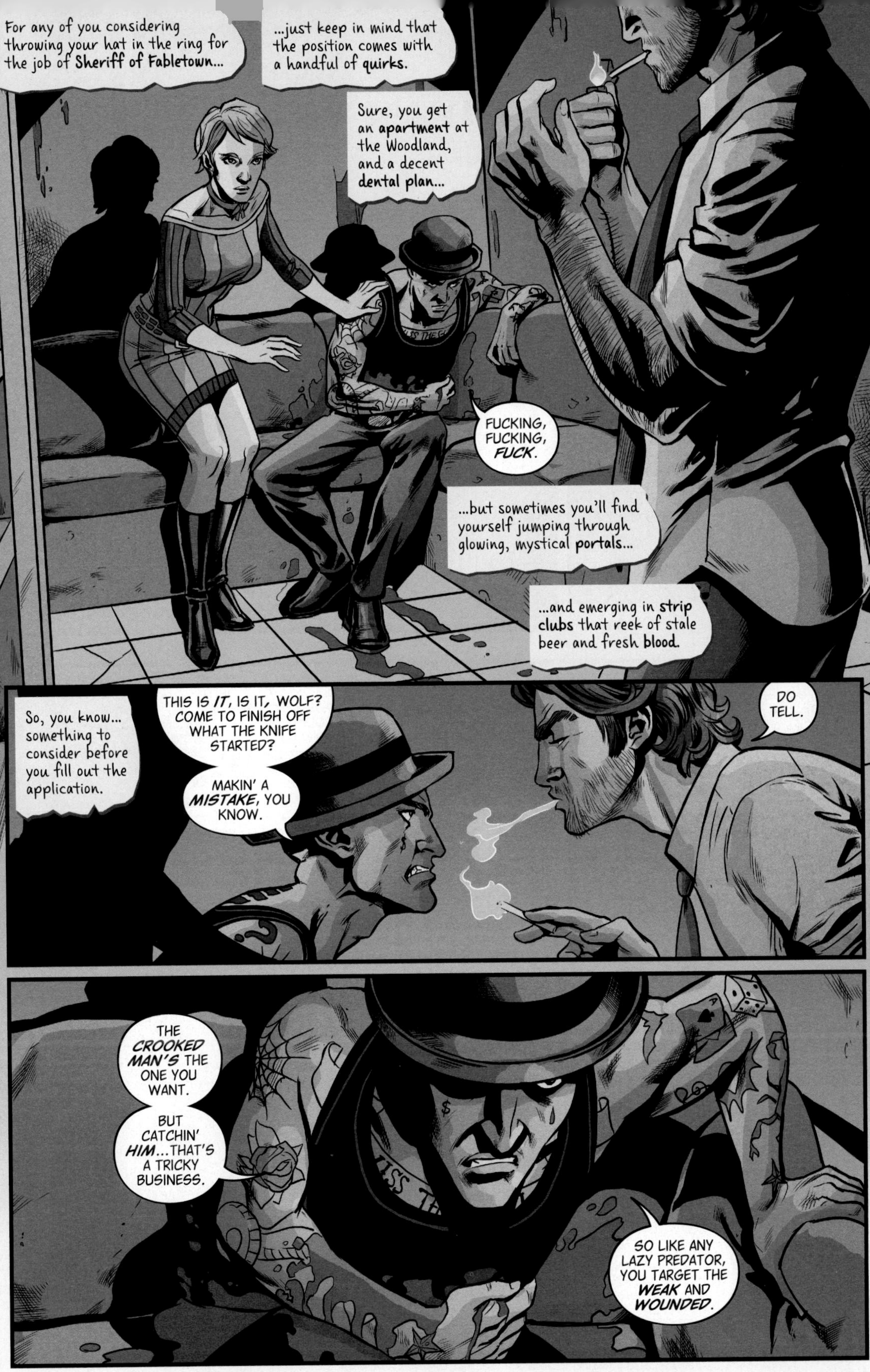
For any of you considering throwing your hat in the ring for the job of Sheriff of Fabletown...
...just keep in mind that the position comes with a handful of quirks.
Sure, you get an apartment at the Woodland, and a decent dental plan...
FUCKING, FUCKING, FUCK.
...but sometimes you'll find yourself jumping through glowing, mystical portals...
...and emerging in strip clubs that reek of stale beer and fresh blood.
So, you know... something to consider before you fill out the application.
THIS IS IT, IS IT, WOLF? COME TO FINISH OFF WHAT THE KNIFE STARTED?
MAKIN' A MISTAKE, YOU KNOW.
DO TELL.
THE CROOKED MAN'S THE ONE YOU WANT.
BUT CATCHIN' HIM...THAT'S A TRICKY BUSINESS.
SO LIKE ANY LAZY PREDATOR, YOU TARGET THE WEAK AND WOUNDED.

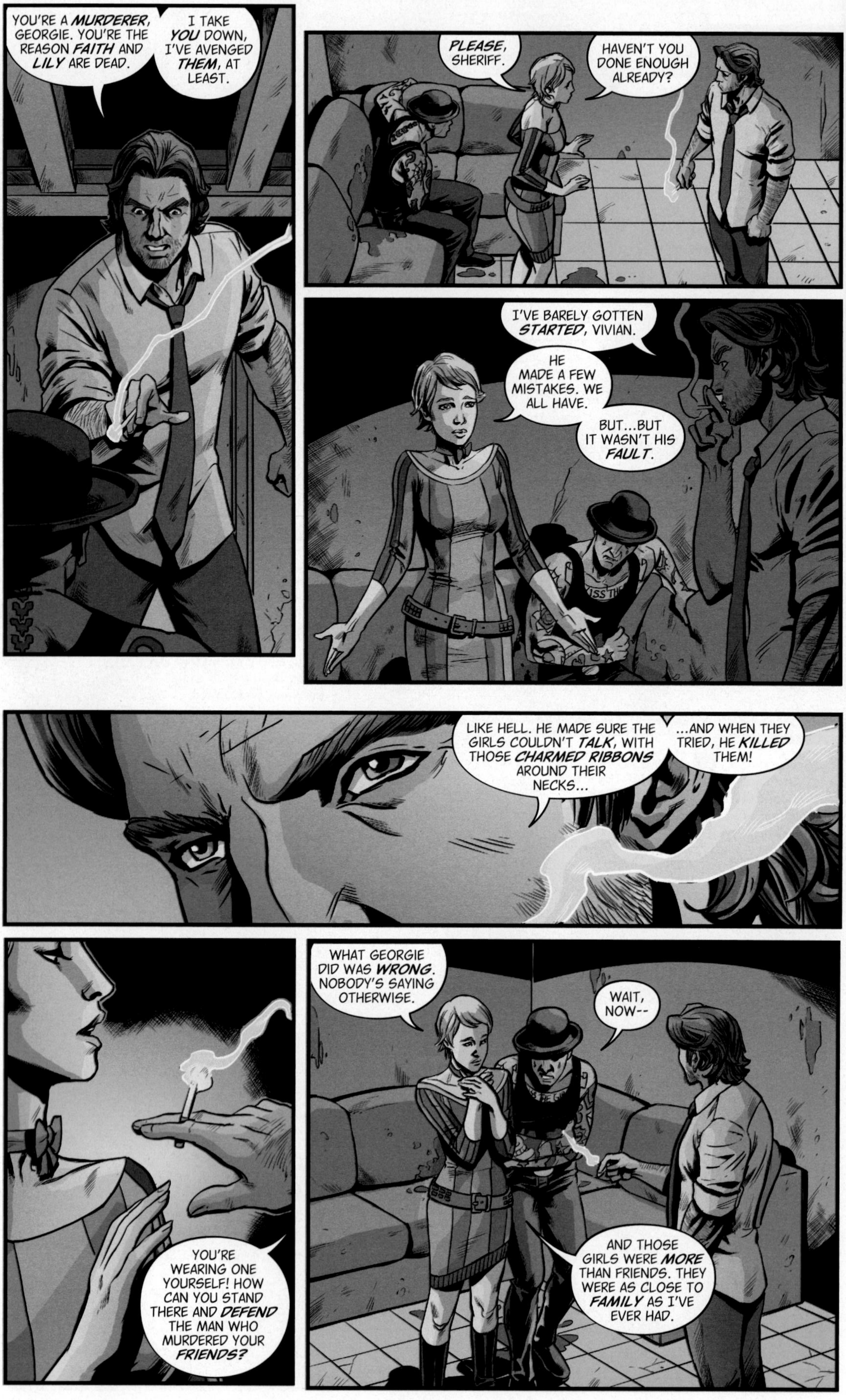

YOU'RE A MURDERER, GEORGIE. YOU'RE THE REASON FAITH AND LILY ARE DEAD.
I TAKE YOU DOWN, I'VE AVENGED THEM, AT LEAST.
PLEASE, SHERIFF.
HAVEN'T YOU DONE ENOUGH ALREADY?
I'VE BARELY GOTTEN STARTED, VIVIAN.
HE MADE A FEW MISTAKES. WE ALL HAVE.
BUT...BUT IT WASN'T HIS FAULT.
LIKE HELL. HE MADE SURE THE GIRLS COULDN'T TALK, WITH THOSE CHARMED RIBBONS AROUND THEIR NECKS...
...AND WHEN THEY TRIED, HE KILLED THEM!
YOU'RE WEARING ONE YOURSELF! HOW CAN YOU STAND THERE AND DEFEND THE MAN WHO MURDERED YOUR FRIENDS?
WHAT GEORGIE DID WAS WRONG. NOBODY'S SAYING OTHERWISE.
WAIT, NOW--
AND THOSE GIRLS WERE MORE THAN FRIENDS. THEY WERE AS CLOSE TO FAMILY AS I'VE EVER HAD.

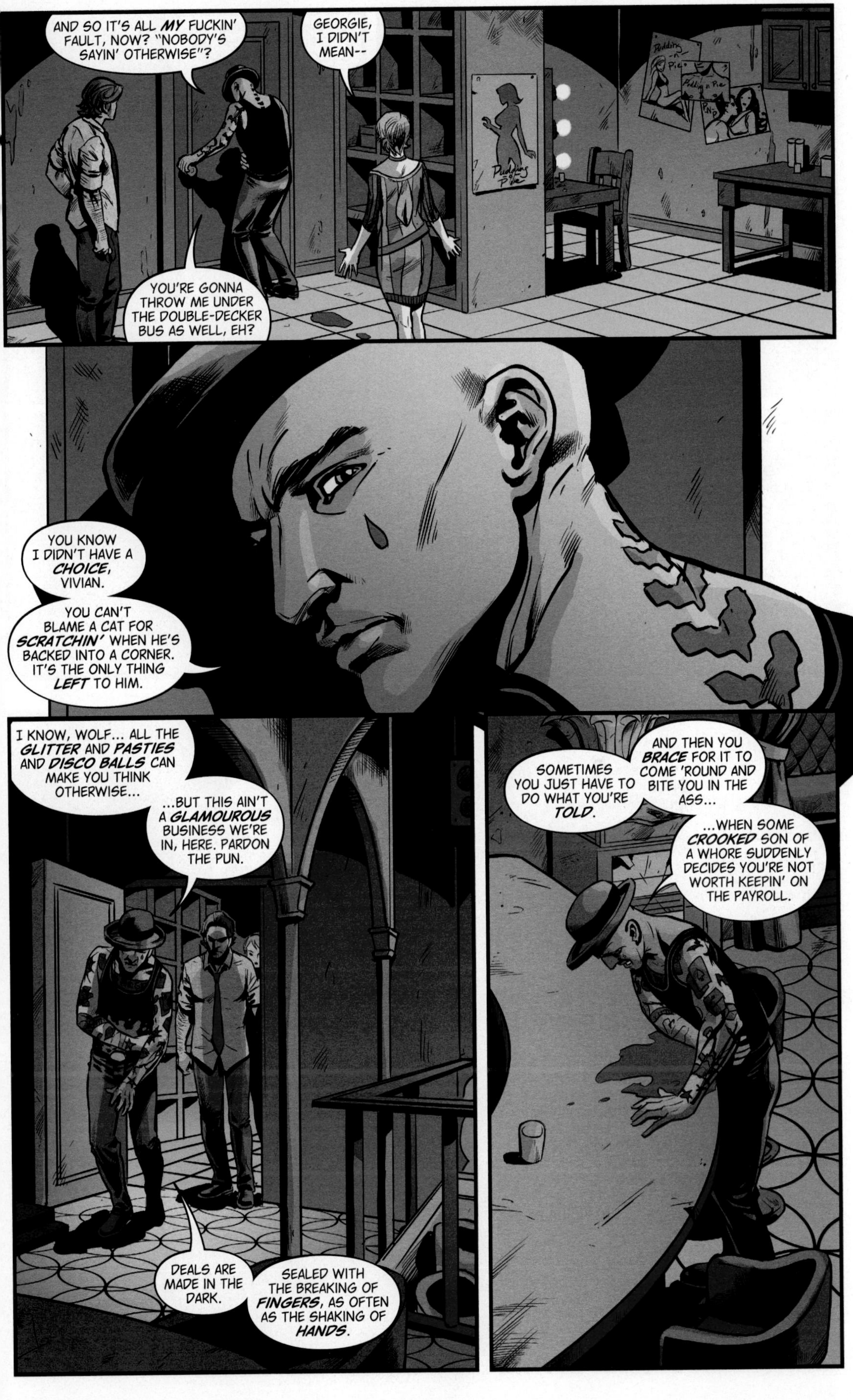
AND SO IT'S ALL MY FUCKIN' FAULT, NOW? "NOBODY'S SAYIN' OTHERWISE"?
GEORGIE, I DIDN'T MEAN--
YOU'RE GONNA THROW ME UNDER THE DOUBLE-DECKER BUS AS WELL, EH?
Pudding n Pie
YOU KNOW I DIDN'T HAVE A CHOICE, VIVIAN.
YOU CAN'T BLAME A CAT FOR SCRATCHIN' WHEN HE'S BACKED INTO A CORNER. IT'S THE ONLY THING LEFT TO HIM.
I KNOW, WOLF... ALL THE GLITTER AND PASTIES AND DISCO BALLS CAN MAKE YOU THINK OTHERWISE...
...BUT THIS AIN'T A GLAMOUROUS BUSINESS WE'RE IN, HERE. PARDON THE PUN.
DEALS ARE MADE IN THE DARK.
SEALED WITH THE BREAKING OF FINGERS, AS OFTEN AS THE SHAKING OF HANDS.
SOMETIMES YOU JUST HAVE TO DO WHAT YOU'RE TOLD.
AND THEN YOU BRACE FOR IT TO COME 'ROUND AND BITE YOU IN THE ASS...
...WHEN SOME CROOKED SON OF A WHORE SUDDENLY DECIDES YOU'RE NOT WORTH KEEPIN' ON THE PAYROLL.

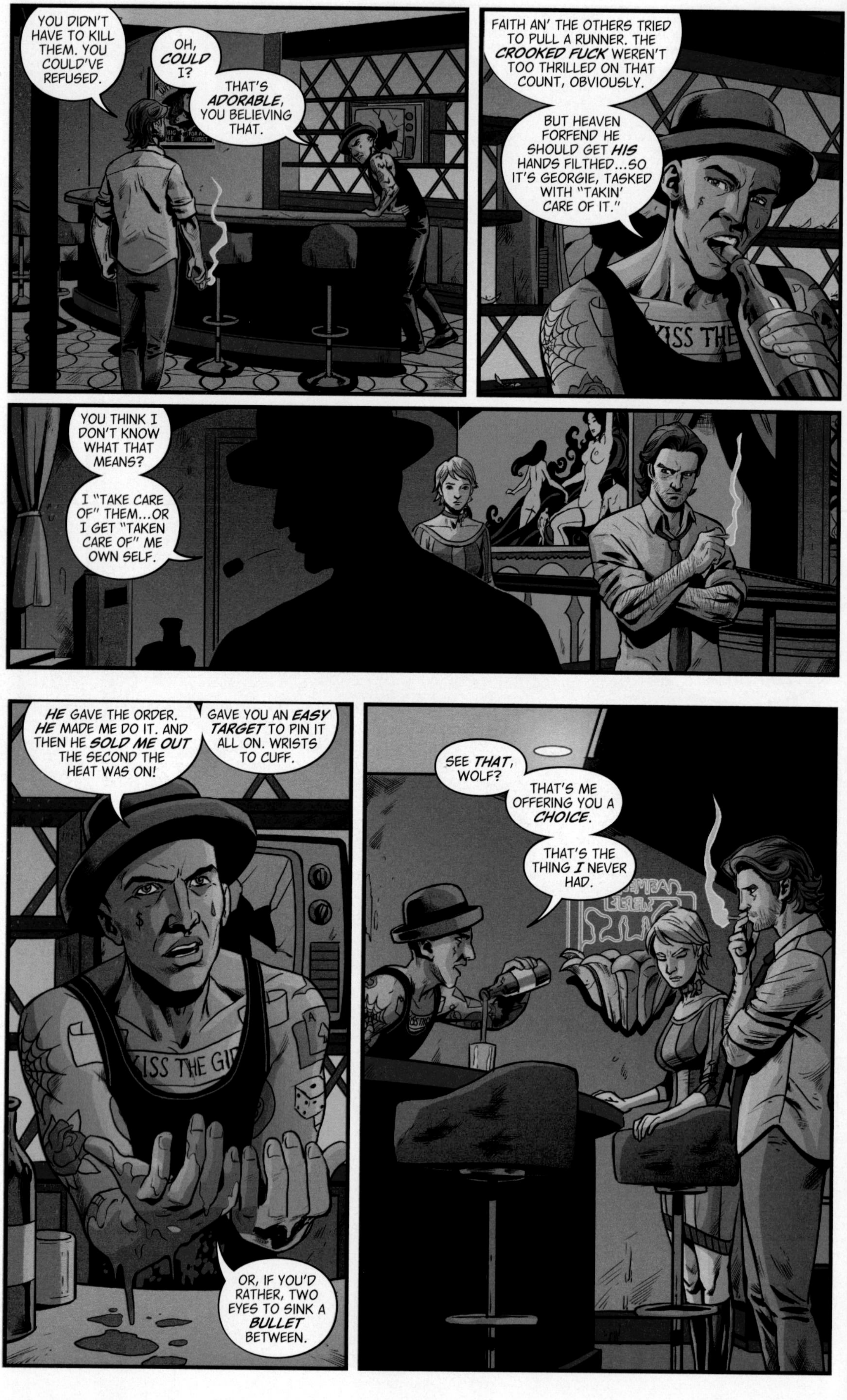
YOU DIDN'T HAVE TO KILL THEM. YOU COULD'VE REFUSED.
OH, *COULD* I?
THAT'S *ADORABLE*, YOU BELIEVING THAT.
FAITH AN' THE OTHERS TRIED TO PULL A RUNNER. THE *CROOKED FUCK* WEREN'T TOO THRILLED ON THAT COUNT, OBVIOUSLY.
BUT HEAVEN FORFEND HE SHOULD GET *HIS* HANDS FILTHED...SO IT'S GEORGIE, TASKED WITH "TAKIN' CARE OF IT."
YOU THINK I DON'T KNOW WHAT THAT MEANS?
I "TAKE CARE OF" THEM...OR I GET "TAKEN CARE OF" ME OWN SELF.
HE GAVE THE ORDER. *HE* MADE ME DO IT. AND THEN HE *SOLD ME OUT* THE SECOND THE HEAT WAS ON!
GAVE YOU AN *EASY TARGET* TO PIN IT ALL ON. WRISTS TO CUFF.
OR, IF YOU'D RATHER, TWO EYES TO SINK A *BULLET* BETWEEN.
SEE *THAT*, WOLF?
THAT'S ME OFFERING YOU A *CHOICE*.
THAT'S THE THING *I* NEVER HAD.

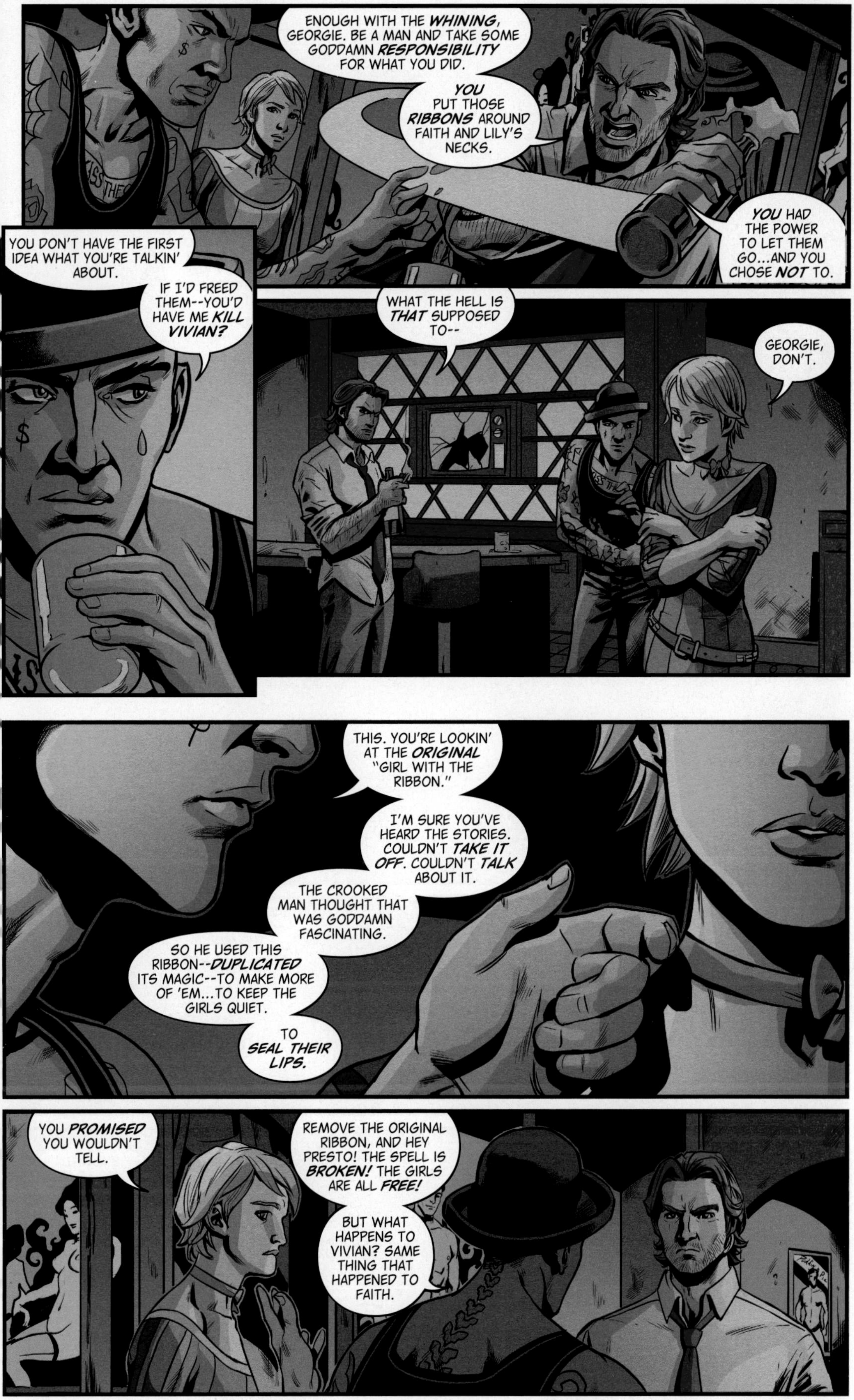

ENOUGH WITH THE WHINING, GEORGIE. BE A MAN AND TAKE SOME GODDAMN RESPONSIBILITY FOR WHAT YOU DID.
YOU PUT THOSE RIBBONS AROUND FAITH AND LILY'S NECKS.
YOU HAD THE POWER TO LET THEM GO...AND YOU CHOSE NOT TO.
YOU DON'T HAVE THE FIRST IDEA WHAT YOU'RE TALKIN' ABOUT.
IF I'D FREED THEM--YOU'D HAVE ME KILL VIVIAN?
WHAT THE HELL IS THAT SUPPOSED TO--
GEORGIE, DON'T.
THIS. YOU'RE LOOKIN' AT THE ORIGINAL "GIRL WITH THE RIBBON."
I'M SURE YOU'VE HEARD THE STORIES. COULDN'T TAKE IT OFF. COULDN'T TALK ABOUT IT.
THE CROOKED MAN THOUGHT THAT WAS GODDAMN FASCINATING.
SO HE USED THIS RIBBON--DUPLICATED ITS MAGIC--TO MAKE MORE OF 'EM...TO KEEP THE GIRLS QUIET.
TO SEAL THEIR LIPS.
YOU PROMISED YOU WOULDN'T TELL.
REMOVE THE ORIGINAL RIBBON, AND HEY PRESTO! THE SPELL IS BROKEN! THE GIRLS ARE ALL FREE!
BUT WHAT HAPPENS TO VIVIAN? SAME THING THAT HAPPENED TO FAITH.

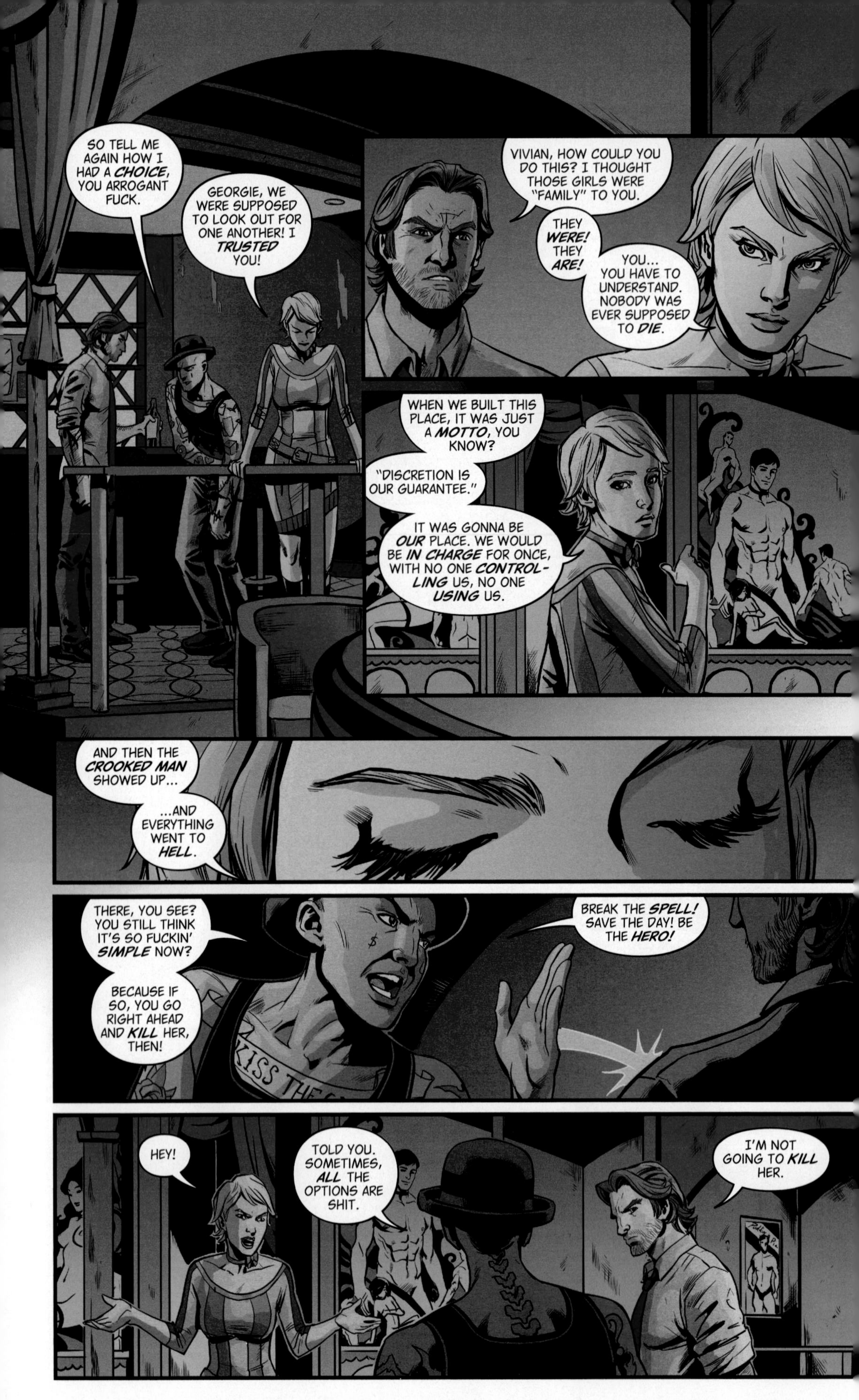
SO TELL ME AGAIN HOW I HAD A CHOICE, YOU ARROGANT FUCK.
GEORGIE, WE WERE SUPPOSED TO LOOK OUT FOR ONE ANOTHER! I TRUSTED YOU!
VIVIAN, HOW COULD YOU DO THIS? I THOUGHT THOSE GIRLS WERE "FAMILY" TO YOU.
THEY WERE! THEY ARE!
YOU... YOU HAVE TO UNDERSTAND. NOBODY WAS EVER SUPPOSED TO DIE.
WHEN WE BUILT THIS PLACE, IT WAS JUST A MOTTO, YOU KNOW?
"DISCRETION IS OUR GUARANTEE."
IT WAS GONNA BE OUR PLACE. WE WOULD BE IN CHARGE FOR ONCE, WITH NO ONE CONTROLLING US, NO ONE USING US.
AND THEN THE CROOKED MAN SHOWED UP...
...AND EVERYTHING WENT TO HELL.
THERE, YOU SEE? YOU STILL THINK IT'S SO FUCKIN' SIMPLE NOW?
BECAUSE IF SO, YOU GO RIGHT AHEAD AND KILL HER, THEN!
BREAK THE SPELL! SAVE THE DAY! BE THE HERO!
HEY!
TOLD YOU. SOMETIMES, ALL THE OPTIONS ARE SHIT.
I'M NOT GOING TO KILL HER.

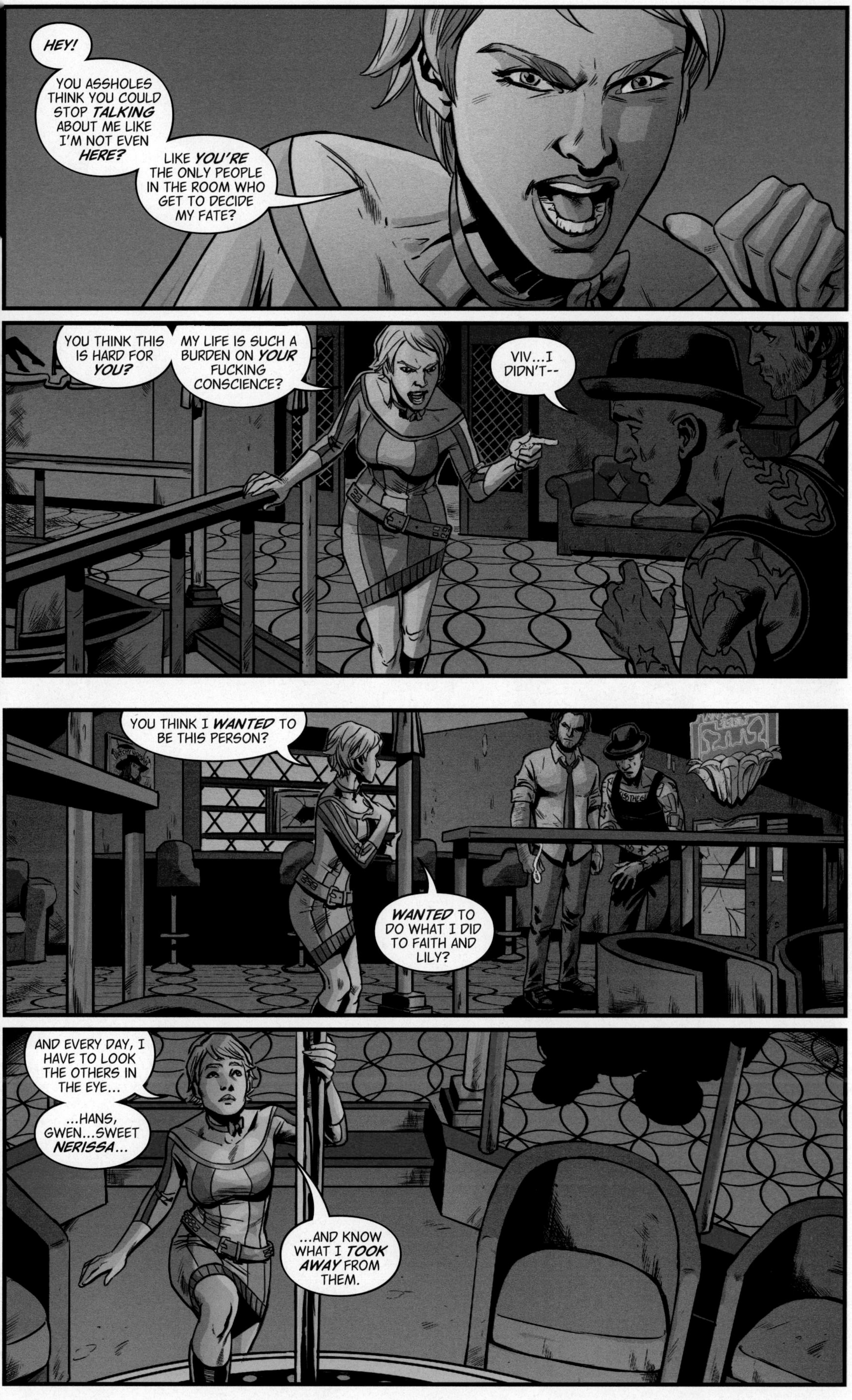
HEY!
YOU ASSHOLES THINK YOU COULD STOP TALKING ABOUT ME LIKE I'M NOT EVEN HERE?
LIKE YOU'RE THE ONLY PEOPLE IN THE ROOM WHO GET TO DECIDE MY FATE?
YOU THINK THIS IS HARD FOR YOU?
MY LIFE IS SUCH A BURDEN ON YOUR FUCKING CONSCIENCE?
VIV...I DIDN'T--
YOU THINK I WANTED TO BE THIS PERSON?
WANTED TO DO WHAT I DID TO FAITH AND LILY?
AND EVERY DAY, I HAVE TO LOOK THE OTHERS IN THE EYE...
...HANS, GWEN...SWEET NERISSA...
...AND KNOW WHAT I TOOK AWAY FROM THEM.

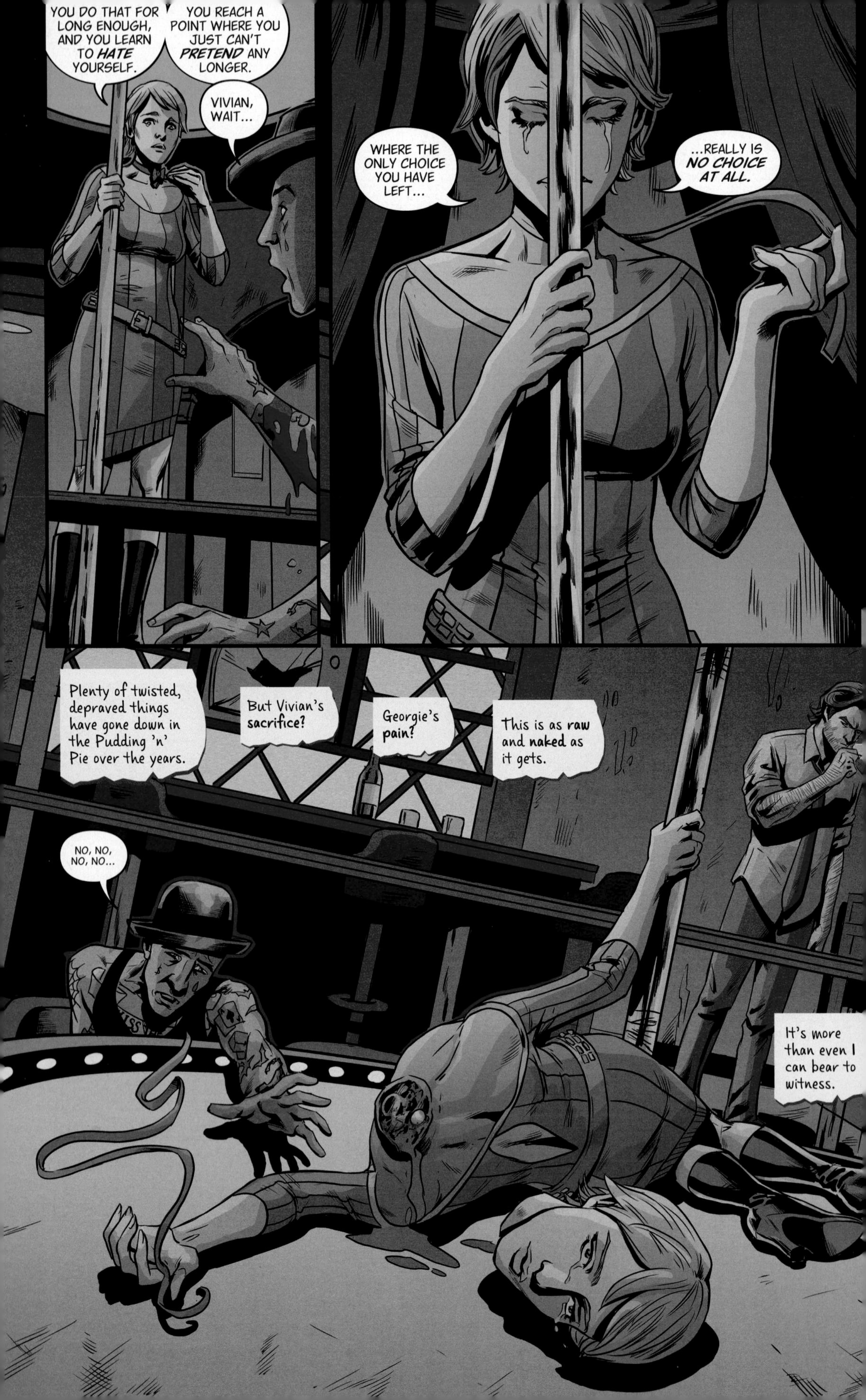
YOU DO THAT FOR LONG ENOUGH, AND YOU LEARN TO *HATE* YOURSELF.
YOU REACH A POINT WHERE YOU JUST CAN'T *PRETEND* ANY LONGER.
VIVIAN, WAIT...
WHERE THE ONLY CHOICE YOU HAVE LEFT...
...REALLY IS *NO CHOICE AT ALL.*
Plenty of twisted, depraved things have gone down in the Pudding 'n' Pie over the years.
But Vivian's **sacrifice?**
Georgie's **pain?**
This is as **raw** and **naked** as it gets.
NO, NO, NO, NO...
It's more than even I can bear to witness.

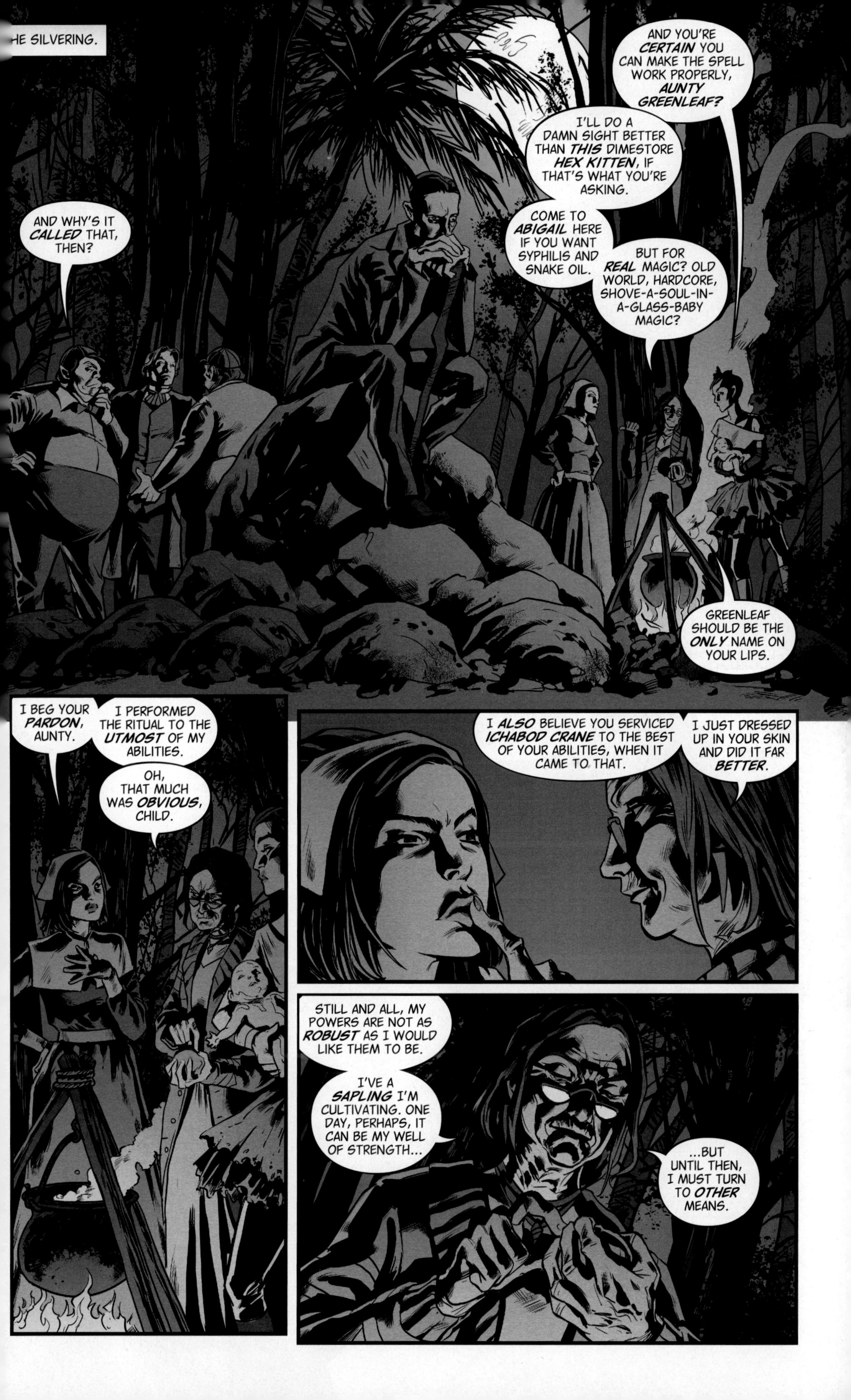
HE SILVERING.
AND YOU'RE CERTAIN YOU CAN MAKE THE SPELL WORK PROPERLY, AUNTY GREENLEAF?
I'LL DO A DAMN SIGHT BETTER THAN THIS DIMESTORE HEX KITTEN, IF THAT'S WHAT YOU'RE ASKING.
COME TO ABIGAIL HERE IF YOU WANT SYPHILIS AND SNAKE OIL.
BUT FOR REAL MAGIC? OLD WORLD, HARDCORE, SHOVE-A-SOUL-IN-A-GLASS-BABY MAGIC?
AND WHY'S IT CALLED THAT, THEN?
GREENLEAF SHOULD BE THE ONLY NAME ON YOUR LIPS.
I BEG YOUR PARDON, AUNTY.
I PERFORMED THE RITUAL TO THE UTMOST OF MY ABILITIES.
OH, THAT MUCH WAS OBVIOUS, CHILD.
I ALSO BELIEVE YOU SERVICED ICHABOD CRANE TO THE BEST OF YOUR ABILITIES, WHEN IT CAME TO THAT.
I JUST DRESSED UP IN YOUR SKIN AND DID IT FAR BETTER.
STILL AND ALL, MY POWERS ARE NOT AS ROBUST AS I WOULD LIKE THEM TO BE.
I'VE A SAPLING I'M CULTIVATING. ONE DAY, PERHAPS, IT CAN BE MY WELL OF STRENGTH...
...BUT UNTIL THEN, I MUST TURN TO OTHER MEANS.

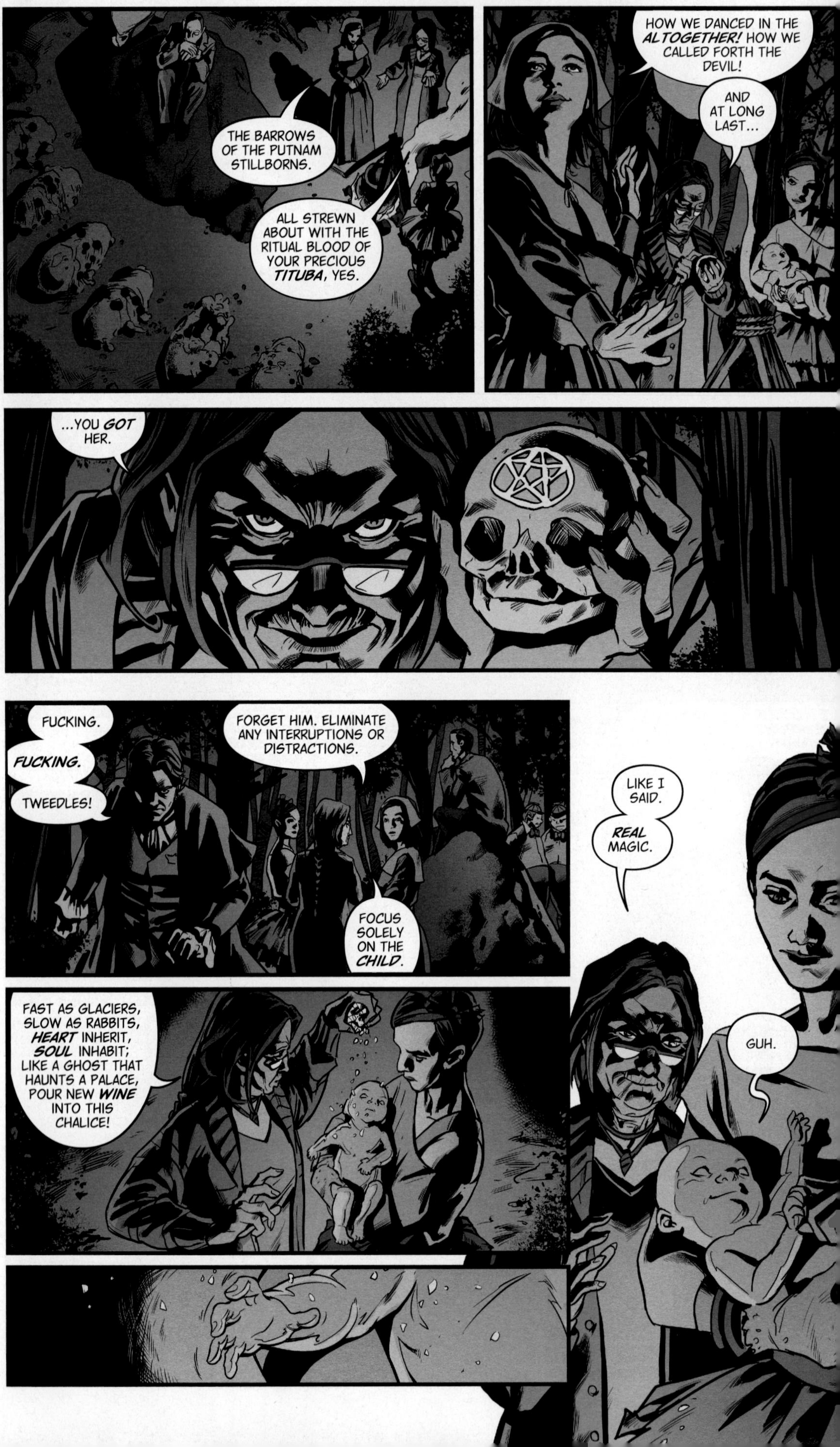

THE BARROWS OF THE PUTNAM STILLBORNS.
ALL STREWN ABOUT WITH THE RITUAL BLOOD OF YOUR PRECIOUS TITUBA, YES.
HOW WE DANCED IN THE ALTOGETHER! HOW WE CALLED FORTH THE DEVIL!
AND AT LONG LAST...
...YOU GOT HER.
FUCKING.
FUCKING.
TWEEDLES!
FORGET HIM. ELIMINATE ANY INTERRUPTIONS OR DISTRACTIONS.
FOCUS SOLELY ON THE CHILD.
LIKE I SAID.
REAL MAGIC.
FAST AS GLACIERS, SLOW AS RABBITS, HEART INHERIT, SOUL INHABIT; LIKE A GHOST THAT HAUNTS A PALACE, POUR NEW WINE INTO THIS CHALICE!
GUH.

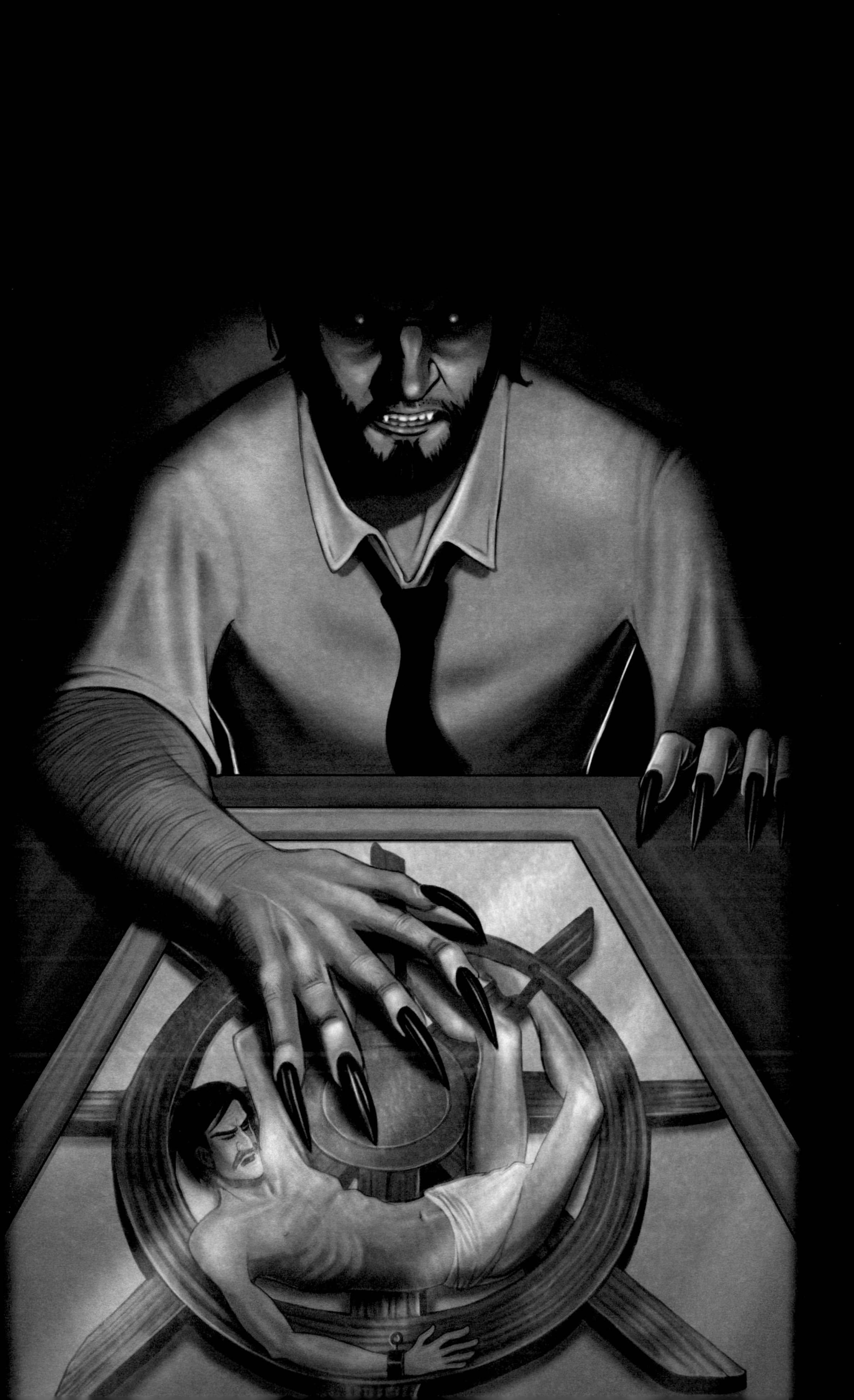

THE PUDDING & PIE.

LATER.

JESUS, *VIVIAN!* WHY'D YOU HAVE TO GO AN' DO THAT?

WHY'D YOU HAVE TO TAKE OFF THE BLOODY *RIBBON?*

HOW DID EVERYTHING GET SO *FUCKED?*

COME ON, GEORGIE. IT'S TIME TO GO.

I DON'T THINK SO, SHERIFF.

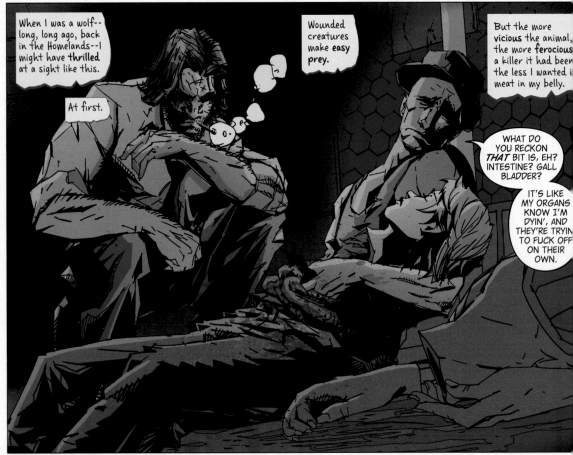

When I was a wolf--long, long ago, back in the Homelands--I might have **thrilled** at a sight like this.

At first.

Wounded creatures make **easy** prey.

But the more **vicious** the animal, the more **ferocious** a killer it had been the less I wanted i meat in my belly.

WHAT DO YOU RECKON *THAT* BIT IS, EH? INTESTINE? GALL BLADDER?

IT'S LIKE MY ORGANS KNOW I'M DYIN', AND THEY'RE TRYIN TO FUCK OFF ON THEIR OWN.

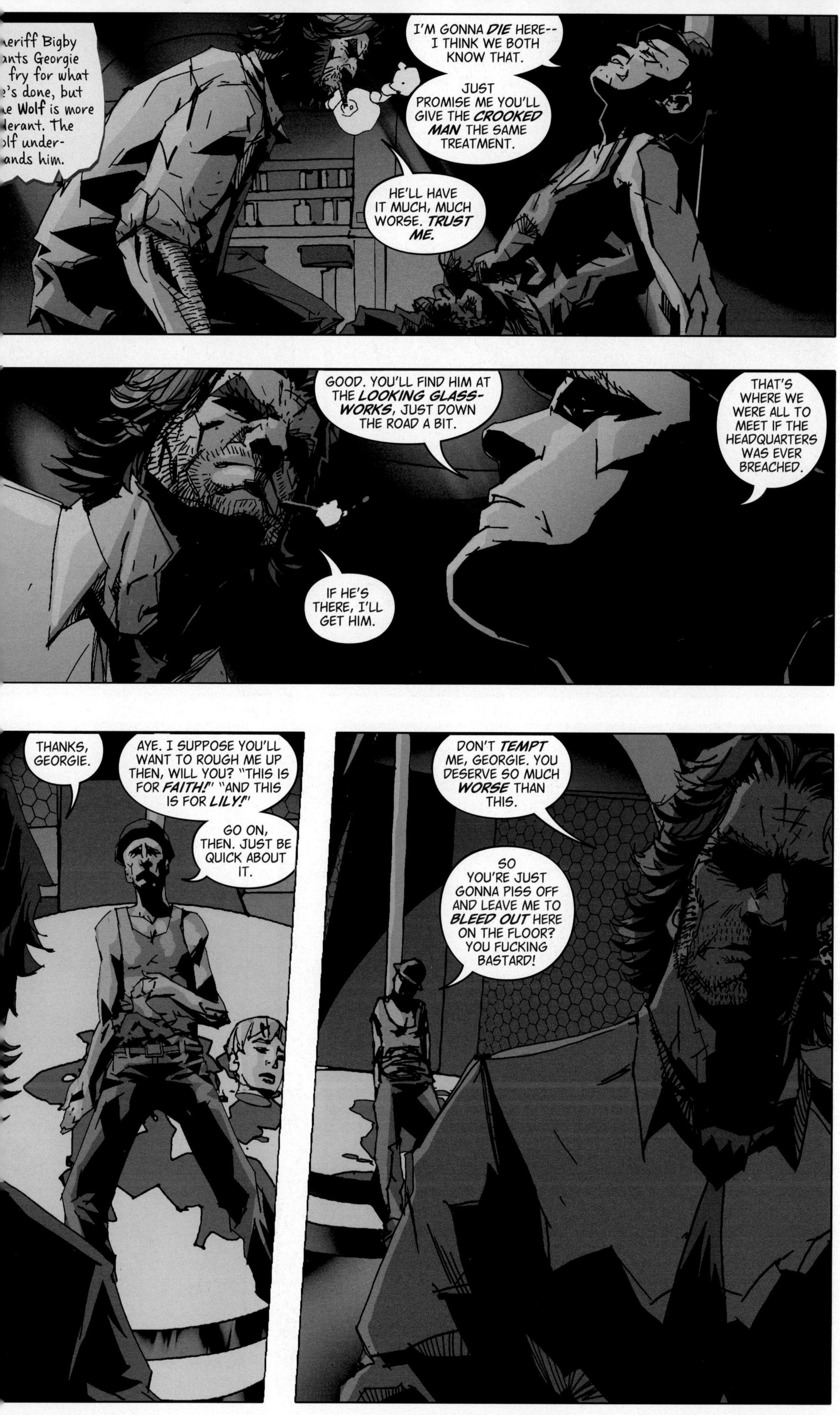

eriff Bigby ants Georgie fry for what e's done, but e Wolf is more lerant. The olf under- ands him.
I'M GONNA DIE HERE-- I THINK WE BOTH KNOW THAT.
JUST PROMISE ME YOU'LL GIVE THE CROOKED MAN THE SAME TREATMENT.
HE'LL HAVE IT MUCH, MUCH WORSE. TRUST ME.
GOOD. YOU'LL FIND HIM AT THE LOOKING GLASS-WORKS, JUST DOWN THE ROAD A BIT.
THAT'S WHERE WE WERE ALL TO MEET IF THE HEADQUARTERS WAS EVER BREACHED.
IF HE'S THERE, I'LL GET HIM.
THANKS, GEORGIE.
AYE. I SUPPOSE YOU'LL WANT TO ROUGH ME UP THEN, WILL YOU? "THIS IS FOR FAITH!" "AND THIS IS FOR LILY!"
GO ON, THEN. JUST BE QUICK ABOUT IT.
DON'T TEMPT ME, GEORGIE. YOU DESERVE SO MUCH WORSE THAN THIS.
SO YOU'RE JUST GONNA PISS OFF AND LEAVE ME TO BLEED OUT HERE ON THE FLOOR? YOU FUCKING BASTARD!

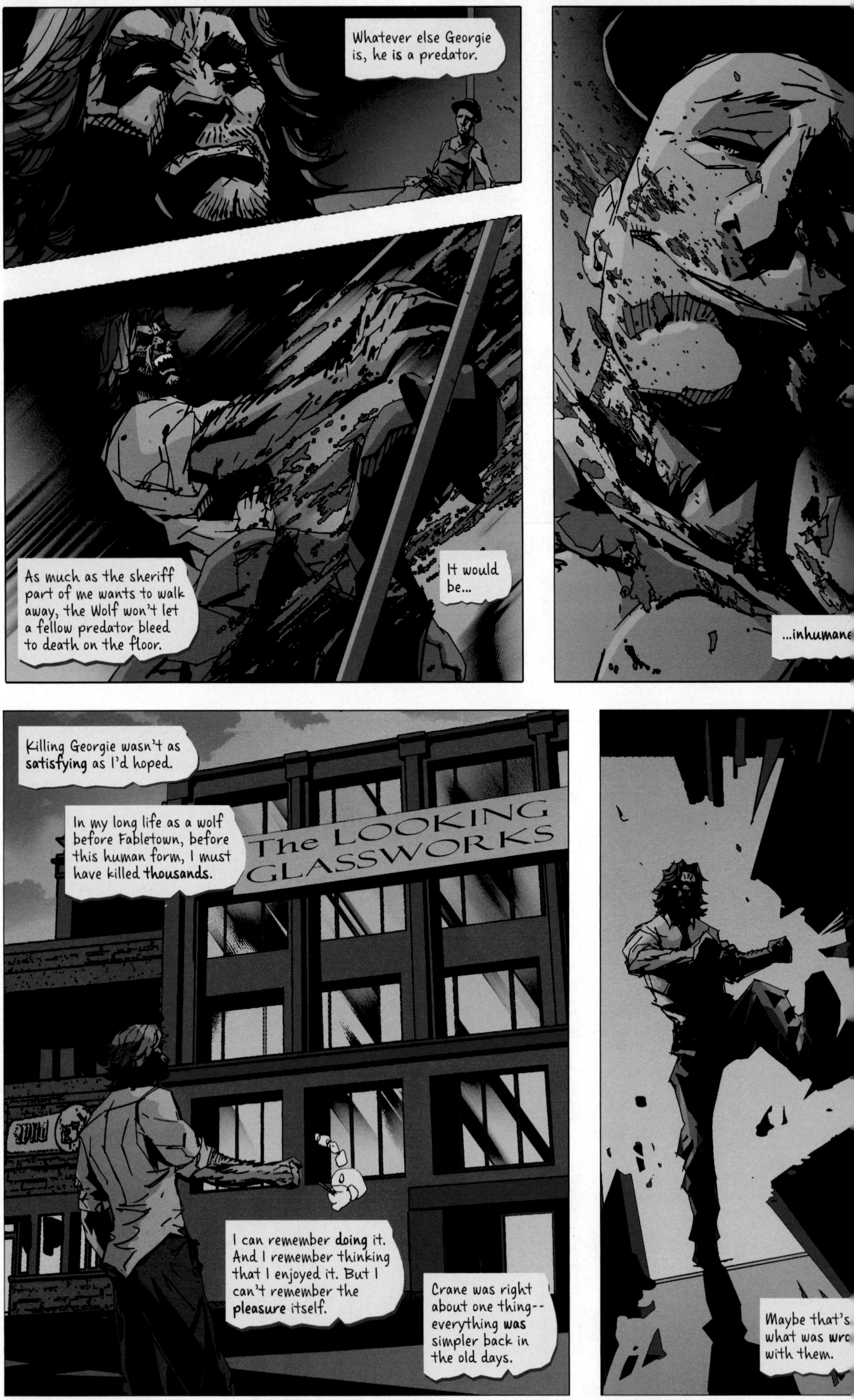

Whatever else Georgie is, he is a predator.
As much as the sheriff part of me wants to walk away, the Wolf won't let a fellow predator bleed to death on the floor.
It would be...
...inhumane
Killing Georgie wasn't as **satisfying** as I'd hoped.
In my long life as a wolf before Fabletown, before this human form, I must have killed **thousands**.
The LOOKING GLASSWORKS
I can remember **doing** it. And I remember thinking that I enjoyed it. But I can't remember the **pleasure** itself.
Crane was right about one thing-- everything **was** simpler back in the old days.
Maybe that's what was wro
with them.

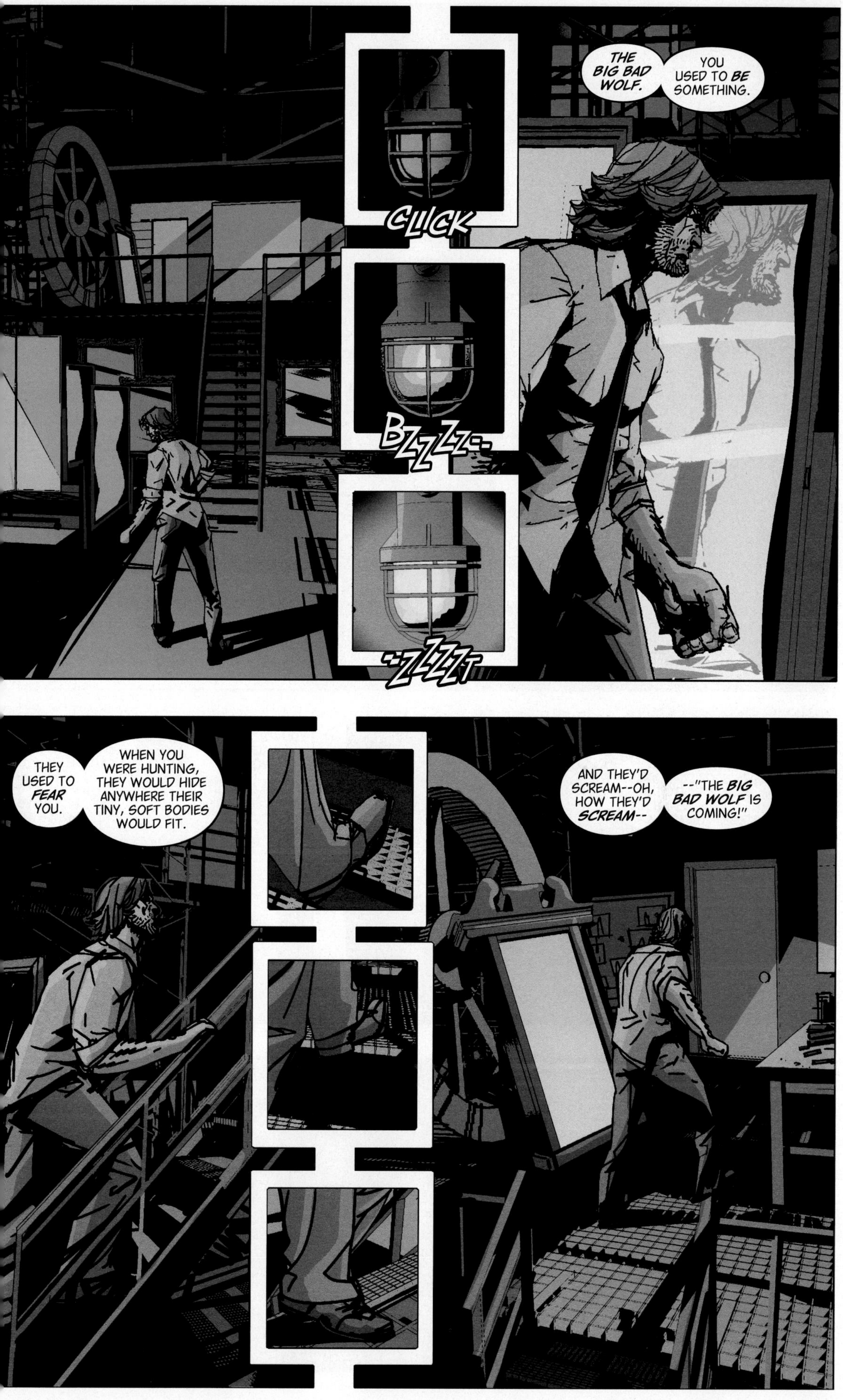
THE BIG BAD WOLF.
YOU USED TO BE SOMETHING.
CLICK
BZZZZ--
--ZZZZT
THEY USED TO FEAR YOU.
WHEN YOU WERE HUNTING, THEY WOULD HIDE ANYWHERE THEIR TINY, SOFT BODIES WOULD FIT.
AND THEY'D SCREAM--OH, HOW THEY'D SCREAM--
--"THE BIG BAD WOLF IS COMING!"

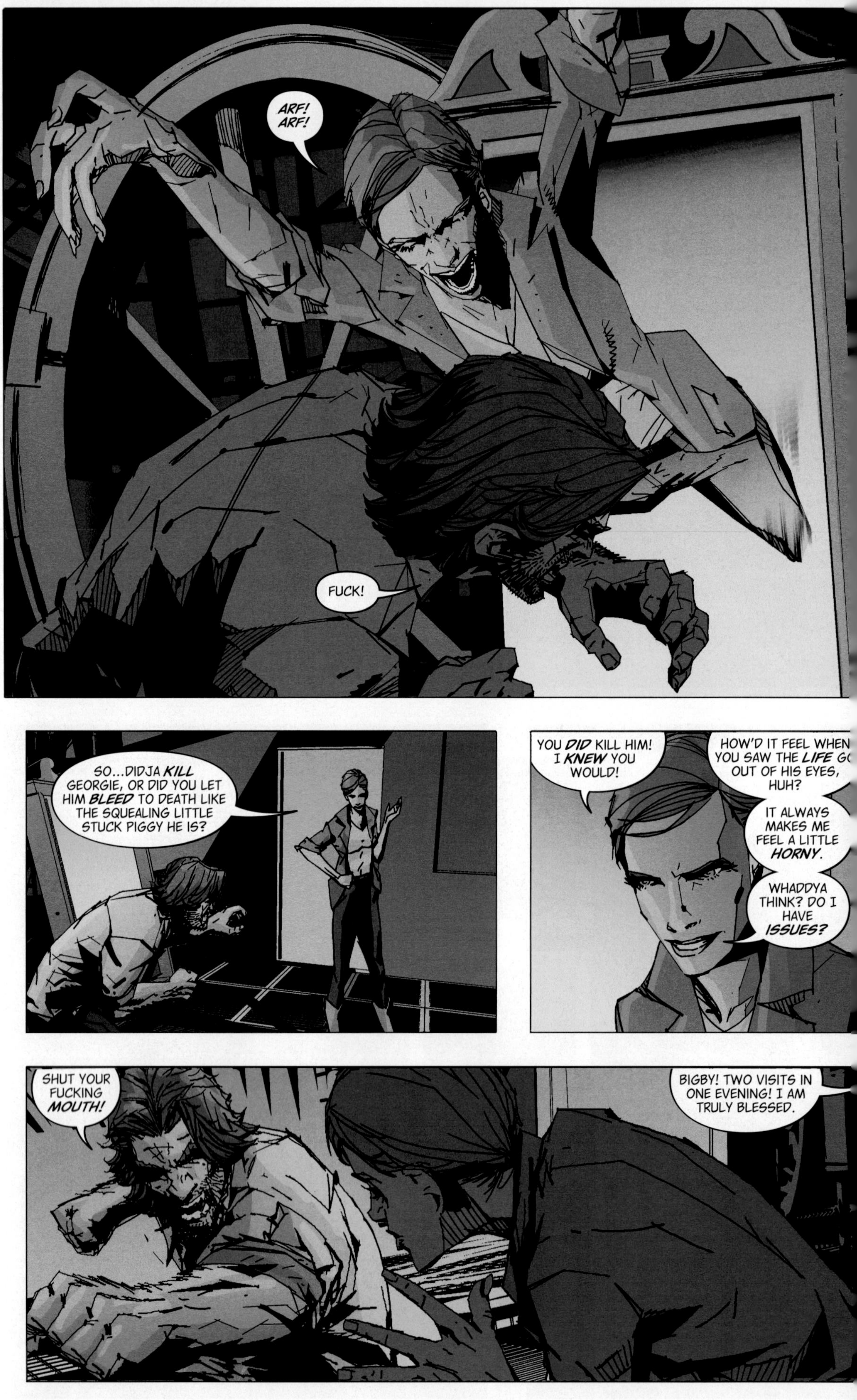
ARF! ARF!
FUCK!
SO...DIDJA KILL GEORGIE, OR DID YOU LET HIM BLEED TO DEATH LIKE THE SQUEALING LITTLE STUCK PIGGY HE IS?
YOU DID KILL HIM! I KNEW YOU WOULD!
HOW'D IT FEEL WHEN YOU SAW THE LIFE GO OUT OF HIS EYES, HUH?
IT ALWAYS MAKES ME FEEL A LITTLE HORNY.
WHADDYA THINK? DO I HAVE ISSUES?
SHUT YOUR FUCKING MOUTH!
BIGBY! TWO VISITS IN ONE EVENING! I AM TRULY BLESSED.

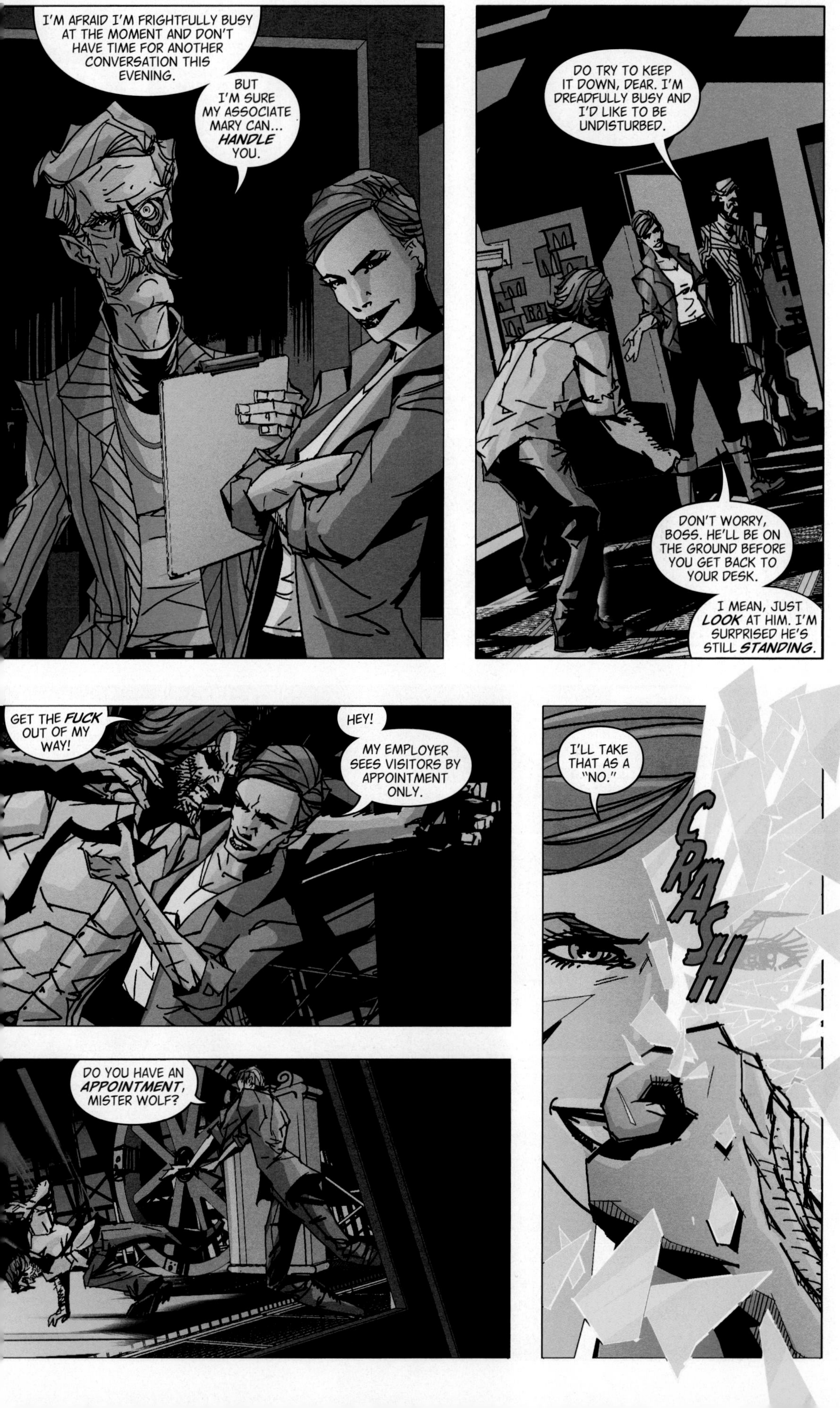
I'M AFRAID I'M FRIGHTFULLY BUSY AT THE MOMENT AND DON'T HAVE TIME FOR ANOTHER CONVERSATION THIS EVENING.
BUT I'M SURE MY ASSOCIATE MARY CAN... HANDLE YOU.
DO TRY TO KEEP IT DOWN, DEAR. I'M DREADFULLY BUSY AND I'D LIKE TO BE UNDISTURBED.
DON'T WORRY, BOSS. HE'LL BE ON THE GROUND BEFORE YOU GET BACK TO YOUR DESK.
I MEAN, JUST LOOK AT HIM. I'M SURPRISED HE'S STILL STANDING.
GET THE FUCK OUT OF MY WAY!
HEY!
MY EMPLOYER SEES VISITORS BY APPOINTMENT ONLY.
DO YOU HAVE AN APPOINTMENT, MISTER WOLF?
I'LL TAKE THAT AS A "NO."
CRASH

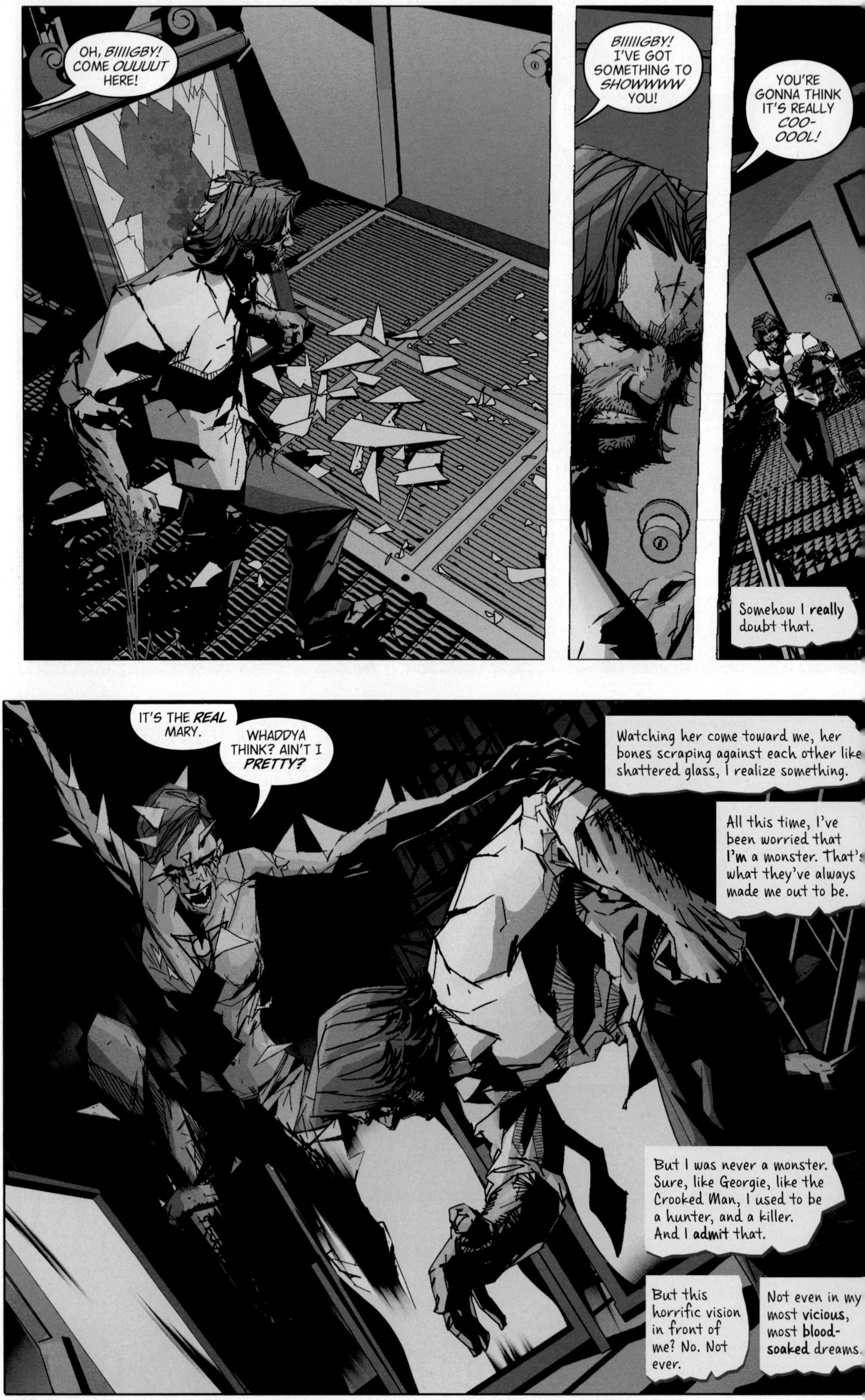
OH, BIIIIGBY! COME OUUUUT HERE!
BIIIIGBY! I'VE GOT SOMETHING TO SHOWWWW YOU!
YOU'RE GONNA THINK IT'S REALLY COO-OOOL!
Somehow I really doubt that.
IT'S THE REAL MARY.
WHADDYA THINK? AIN'T I PRETTY?
Watching her come toward me, her bones scraping against each other like shattered glass, I realize something.
All this time, I've been worried that I'm a monster. That's what they've always made me out to be.
But I was never a monster. Sure, like Georgie, like the Crooked Man, I used to be a hunter, and a killer. And I admit that.
But this horrific vision in front of me? No. Not ever.
Not even in my most vicious, most blood-soaked dreams.

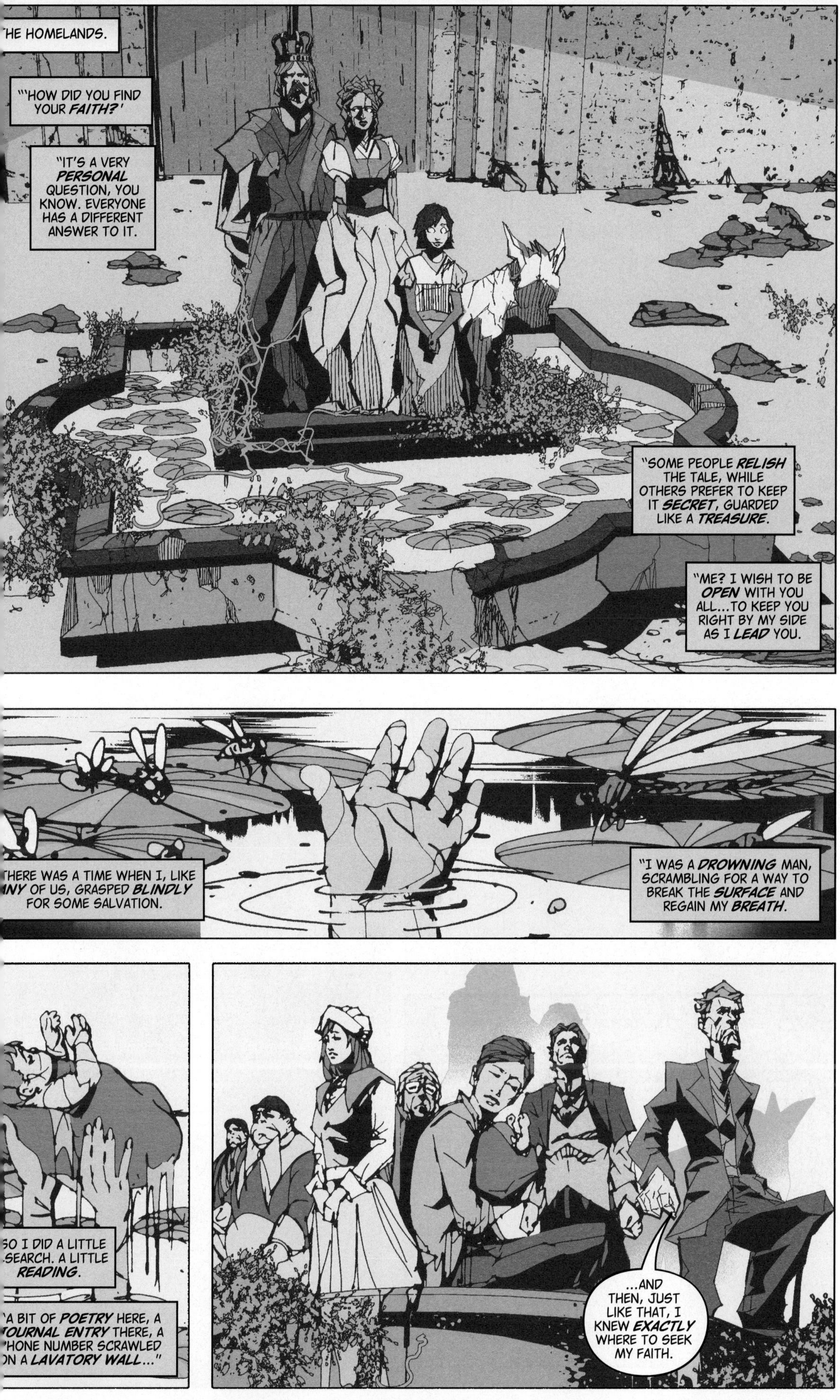
THE HOMELANDS.
"'HOW DID YOU FIND YOUR FAITH?'
"IT'S A VERY PERSONAL QUESTION, YOU KNOW. EVERYONE HAS A DIFFERENT ANSWER TO IT.
"SOME PEOPLE RELISH THE TALE, WHILE OTHERS PREFER TO KEEP IT SECRET, GUARDED LIKE A TREASURE.
"ME? I WISH TO BE OPEN WITH YOU ALL...TO KEEP YOU RIGHT BY MY SIDE AS I LEAD YOU.
THERE WAS A TIME WHEN I, LIKE NY OF US, GRASPED BLINDLY FOR SOME SALVATION.
"I WAS A DROWNING MAN, SCRAMBLING FOR A WAY TO BREAK THE SURFACE AND REGAIN MY BREATH.
SO I DID A LITTLE SEARCH. A LITTLE READING.
"A BIT OF POETRY HERE, A JOURNAL ENTRY THERE, A PHONE NUMBER SCRAWLED ON A LAVATORY WALL..."
...AND THEN, JUST LIKE THAT, I KNEW EXACTLY WHERE TO SEEK MY FAITH.

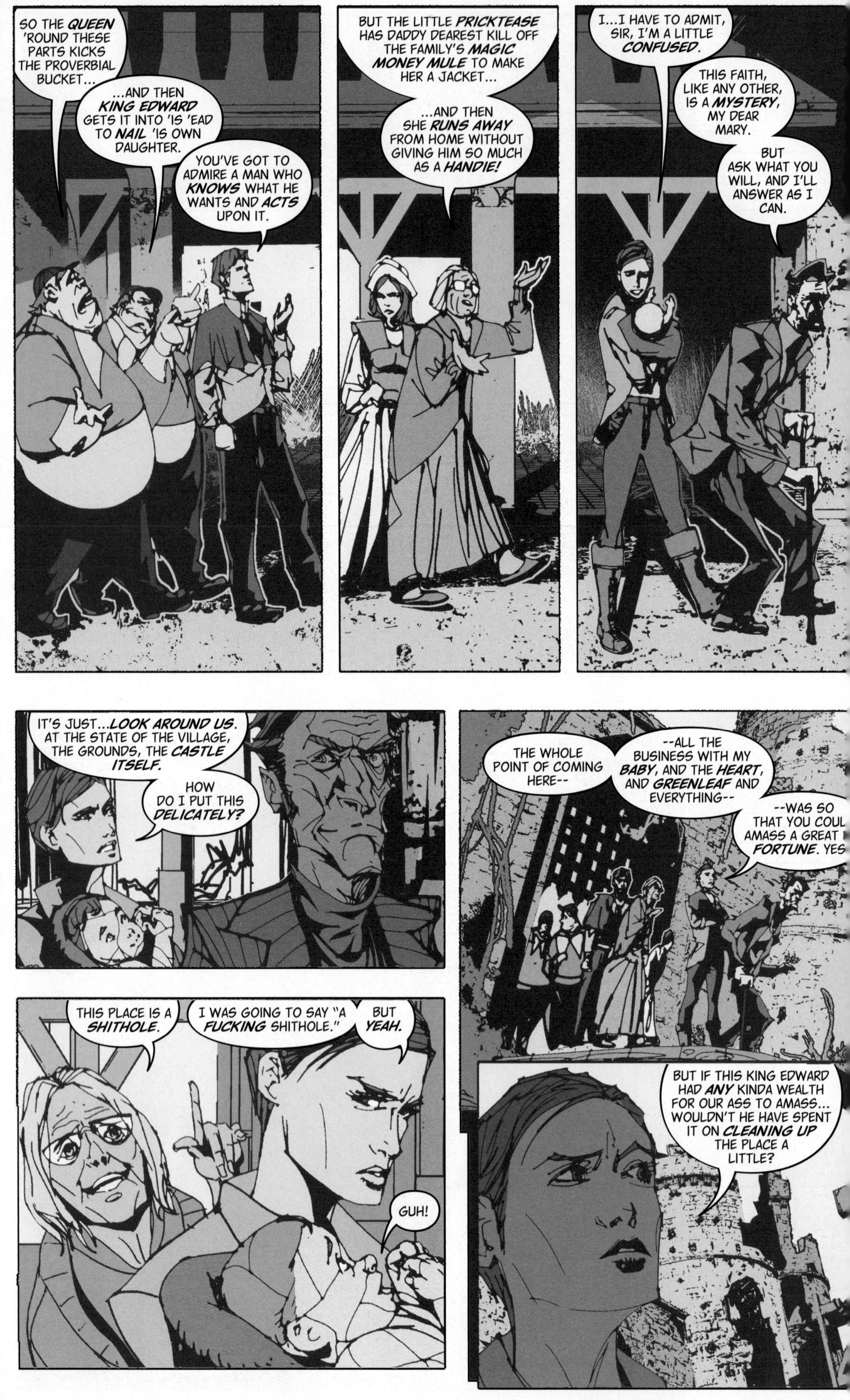

SO THE QUEEN 'ROUND THESE PARTS KICKS THE PROVERBIAL BUCKET...
...AND THEN KING EDWARD GETS IT INTO 'IS 'EAD TO NAIL 'IS OWN DAUGHTER.
YOU'VE GOT TO ADMIRE A MAN WHO KNOWS WHAT HE WANTS AND ACTS UPON IT.
BUT THE LITTLE PRICKTEASE HAS DADDY DEAREST KILL OFF THE FAMILY'S MAGIC MONEY MULE TO MAKE HER A JACKET...
...AND THEN SHE RUNS AWAY FROM HOME WITHOUT GIVING HIM SO MUCH AS A HANDIE!
I...I HAVE TO ADMIT, SIR, I'M A LITTLE CONFUSED.
THIS FAITH, LIKE ANY OTHER, IS A MYSTERY, MY DEAR MARY.
BUT ASK WHAT YOU WILL, AND I'LL ANSWER AS I CAN.
IT'S JUST...LOOK AROUND US. AT THE STATE OF THE VILLAGE, THE GROUNDS, THE CASTLE ITSELF.
HOW DO I PUT THIS DELICATELY?
THE WHOLE POINT OF COMING HERE--
--ALL THE BUSINESS WITH MY BABY, AND THE HEART, AND GREENLEAF AND EVERYTHING--
--WAS SO THAT YOU COUL AMASS A GREAT FORTUNE. YES
THIS PLACE IS A SHITHOLE.
I WAS GOING TO SAY "A FUCKING SHITHOLE."
BUT YEAH.
GUH!
BUT IF THIS KING EDWARD HAD ANY KINDA WEALTH FOR OUR ASS TO AMASS... WOULDN'T HE HAVE SPENT IT ON CLEANING UP THE PLACE A LITTLE?

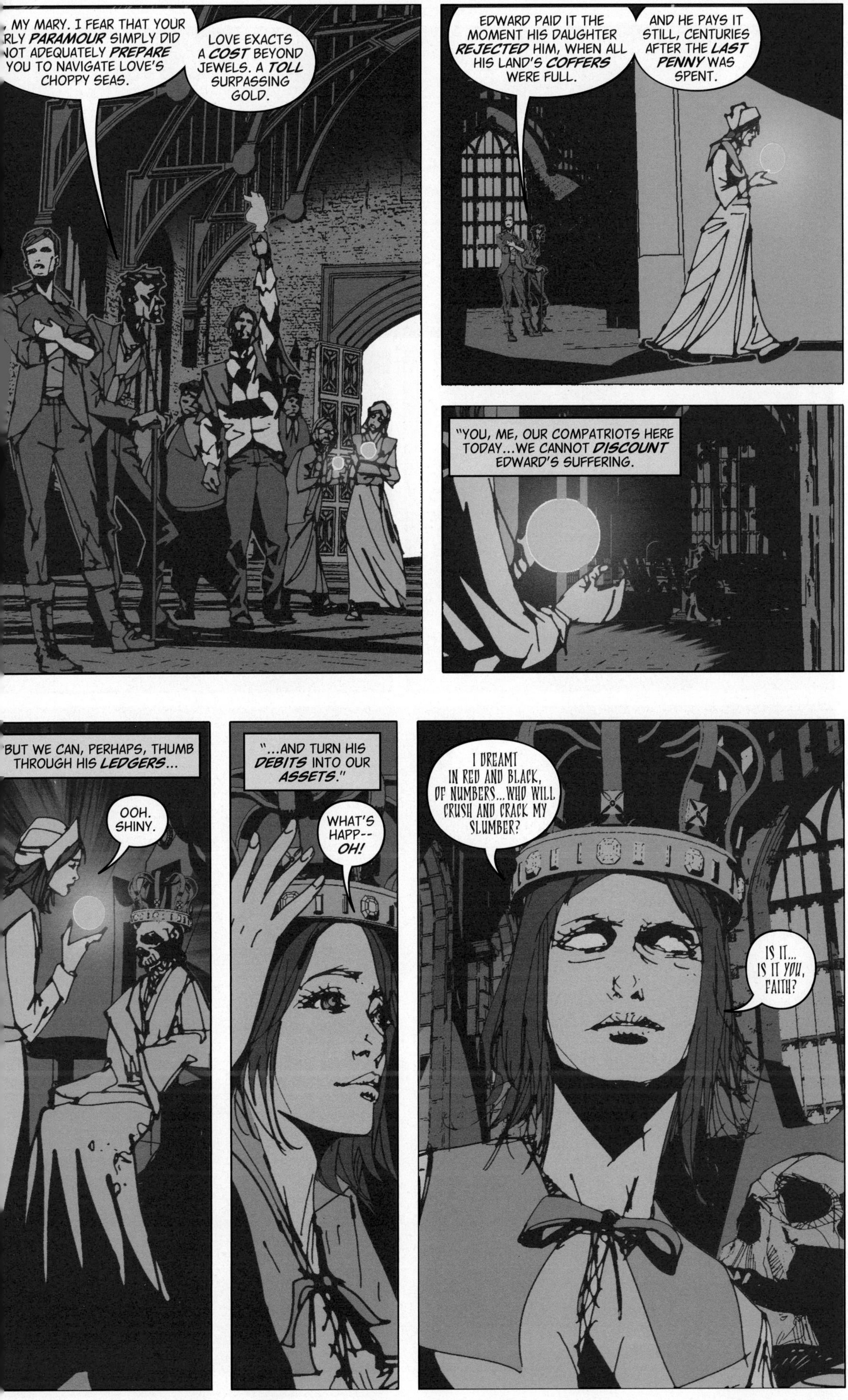

, MY MARY. I FEAR THAT YOUR RLY PARAMOUR SIMPLY DID NOT ADEQUATELY PREPARE YOU TO NAVIGATE LOVE'S CHOPPY SEAS.
LOVE EXACTS A COST BEYOND JEWELS. A TOLL SURPASSING GOLD.
EDWARD PAID IT THE MOMENT HIS DAUGHTER REJECTED HIM, WHEN ALL HIS LAND'S COFFERS WERE FULL.
AND HE PAYS IT STILL, CENTURIES AFTER THE LAST PENNY WAS SPENT.
"YOU, ME, OUR COMPATRIOTS HERE TODAY...WE CANNOT DISCOUNT EDWARD'S SUFFERING.
"BUT WE CAN, PERHAPS, THUMB THROUGH HIS LEDGERS...
OOH. SHINY.
"...AND TURN HIS DEBITS INTO OUR ASSETS."
WHAT'S HAPP-- OH!
I DREAMT IN RED AND BLACK, OF NUMBERS...WHO WILL CRUSH AND CRACK MY SLUMBER?
IS IT... IS IT YOU, FAITH?

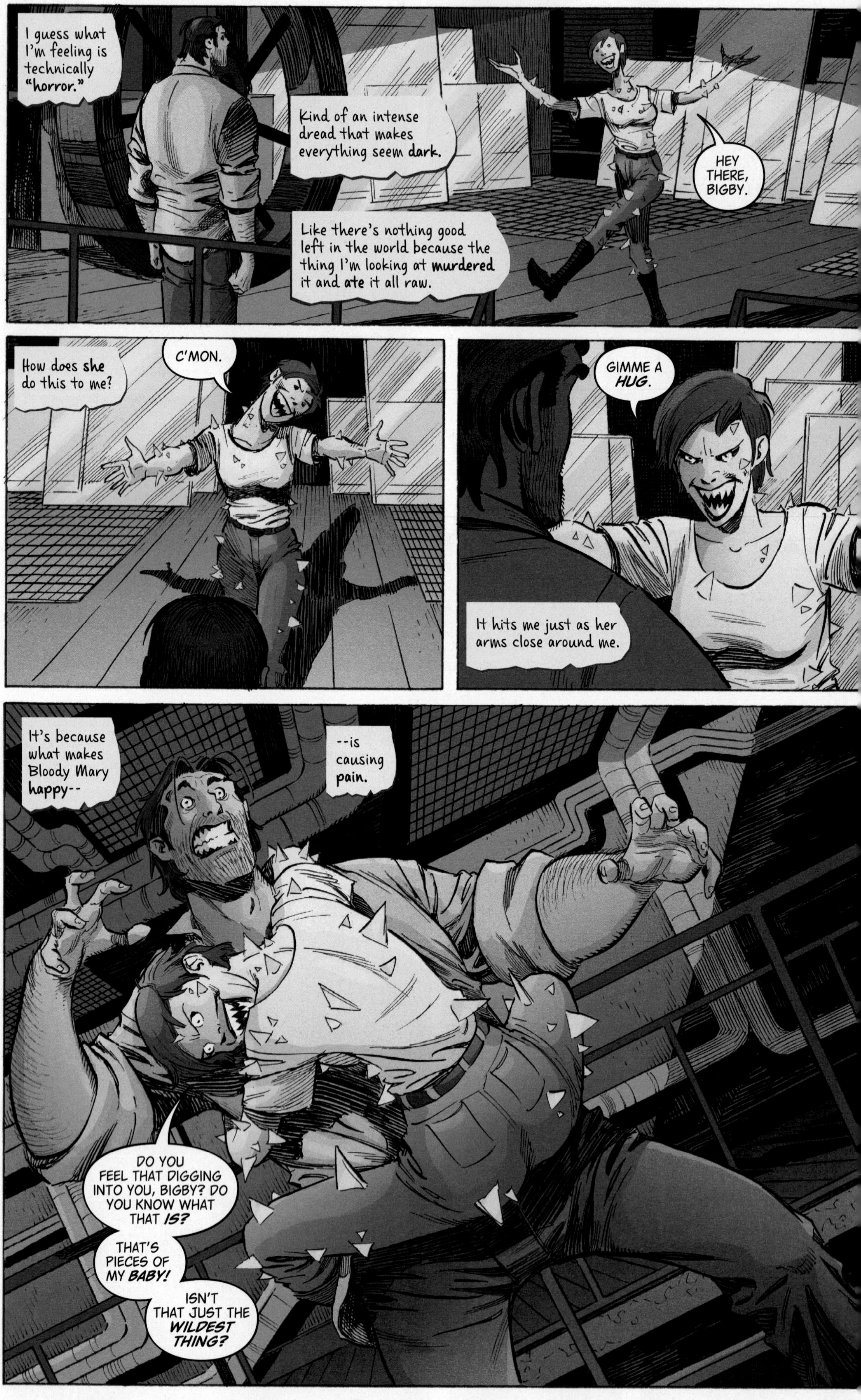
I guess what I'm feeling is technically "horror."
Kind of an intense dread that makes everything seem dark.
Like there's nothing good left in the world because the thing I'm looking at murdered it and ate it all raw.
HEY THERE, BIGBY.
How does she do this to me?
C'MON.
GIMME A HUG.
It hits me just as her arms close around me.
It's because what makes Bloody Mary happy--
--is causing pain.
DO YOU FEEL THAT DIGGING INTO YOU, BIGBY? DO YOU KNOW WHAT THAT IS?
THAT'S PIECES OF MY BABY!
ISN'T THAT JUST THE WILDEST THING?

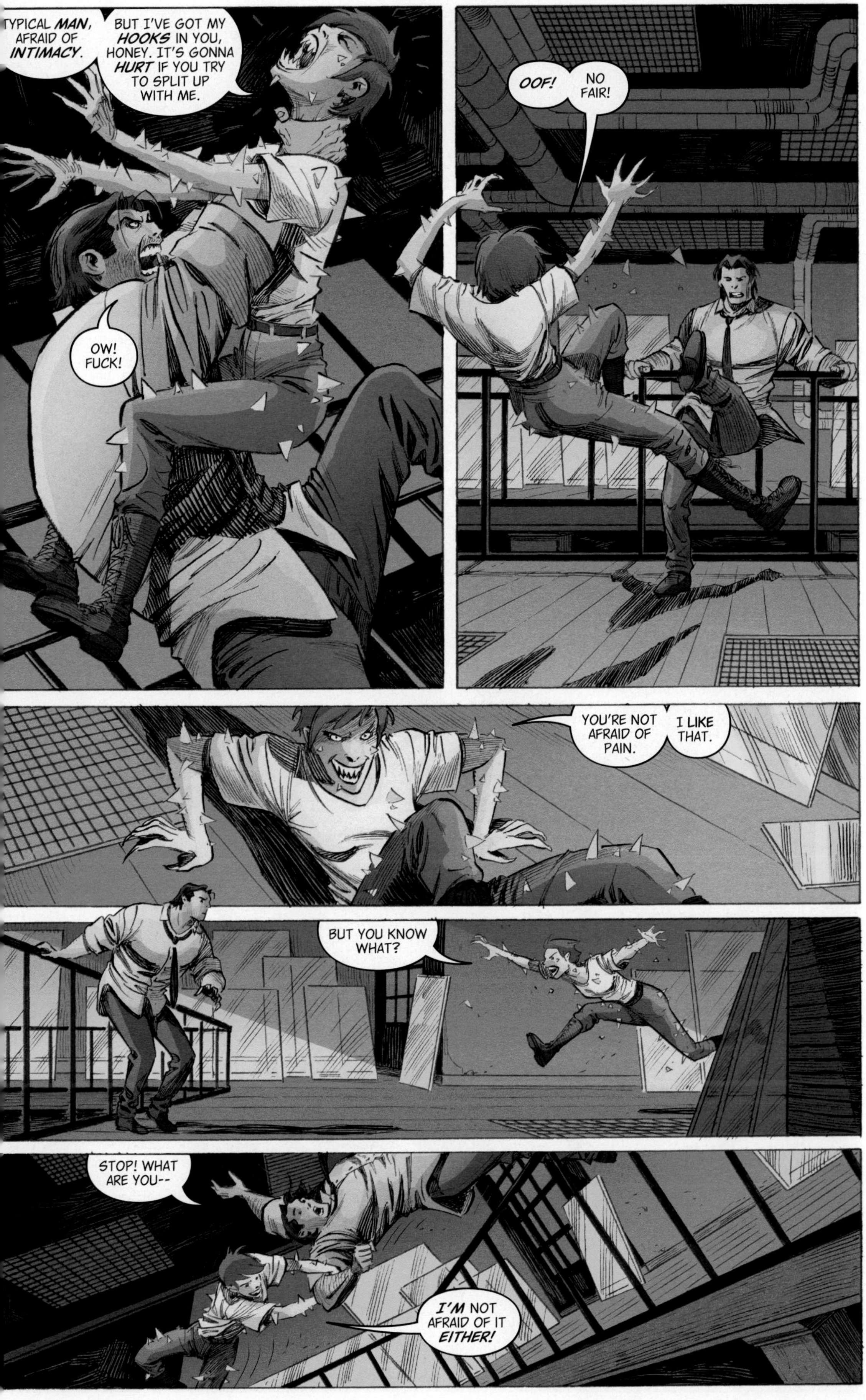
TYPICAL MAN, AFRAID OF INTIMACY.
BUT I'VE GOT MY HOOKS IN YOU, HONEY. IT'S GONNA HURT IF YOU TRY TO SPLIT UP WITH ME.
OW! FUCK!
OOF!
NO FAIR!
YOU'RE NOT AFRAID OF PAIN.
I LIKE THAT.
BUT YOU KNOW WHAT?
STOP! WHAT ARE YOU--
I'M NOT AFRAID OF IT EITHER!

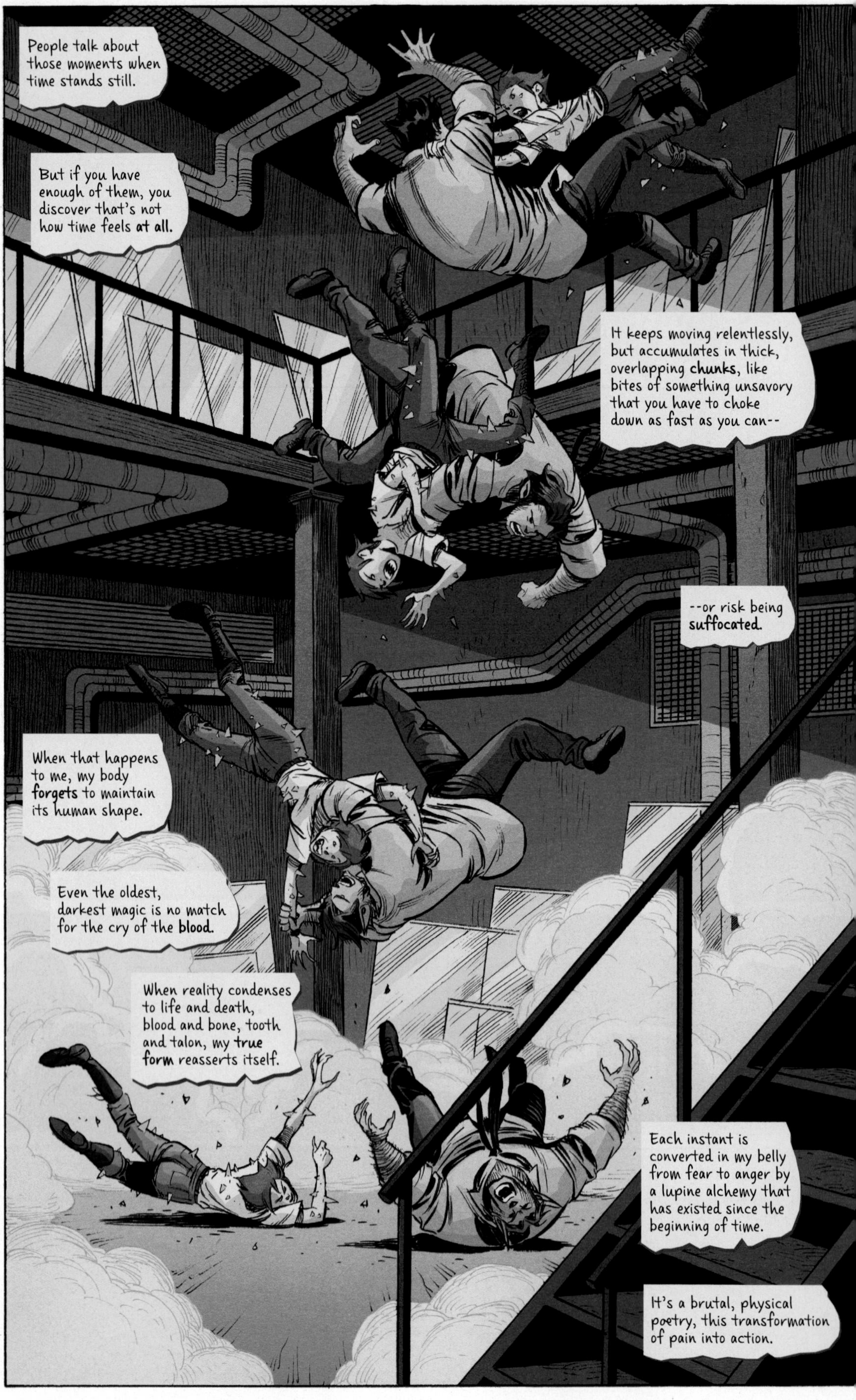
People talk about those moments when time stands still.
But if you have enough of them, you discover that's not how time feels **at all**.
It keeps moving relentlessly, but accumulates in thick, overlapping **chunks**, like bites of something unsavory that you have to choke down as fast as you can--
--or risk being **suffocated**.
When that happens to me, my body **forgets** to maintain its human shape.
Even the oldest, darkest magic is no match for the cry of the **blood**.
When reality condenses to life and death, blood and bone, tooth and talon, my **true form** reasserts itself.
Each instant is converted in my belly from fear to anger by a lupine alchemy that has existed since the beginning of time.
It's a brutal, physical poetry, this transformation of pain into action.

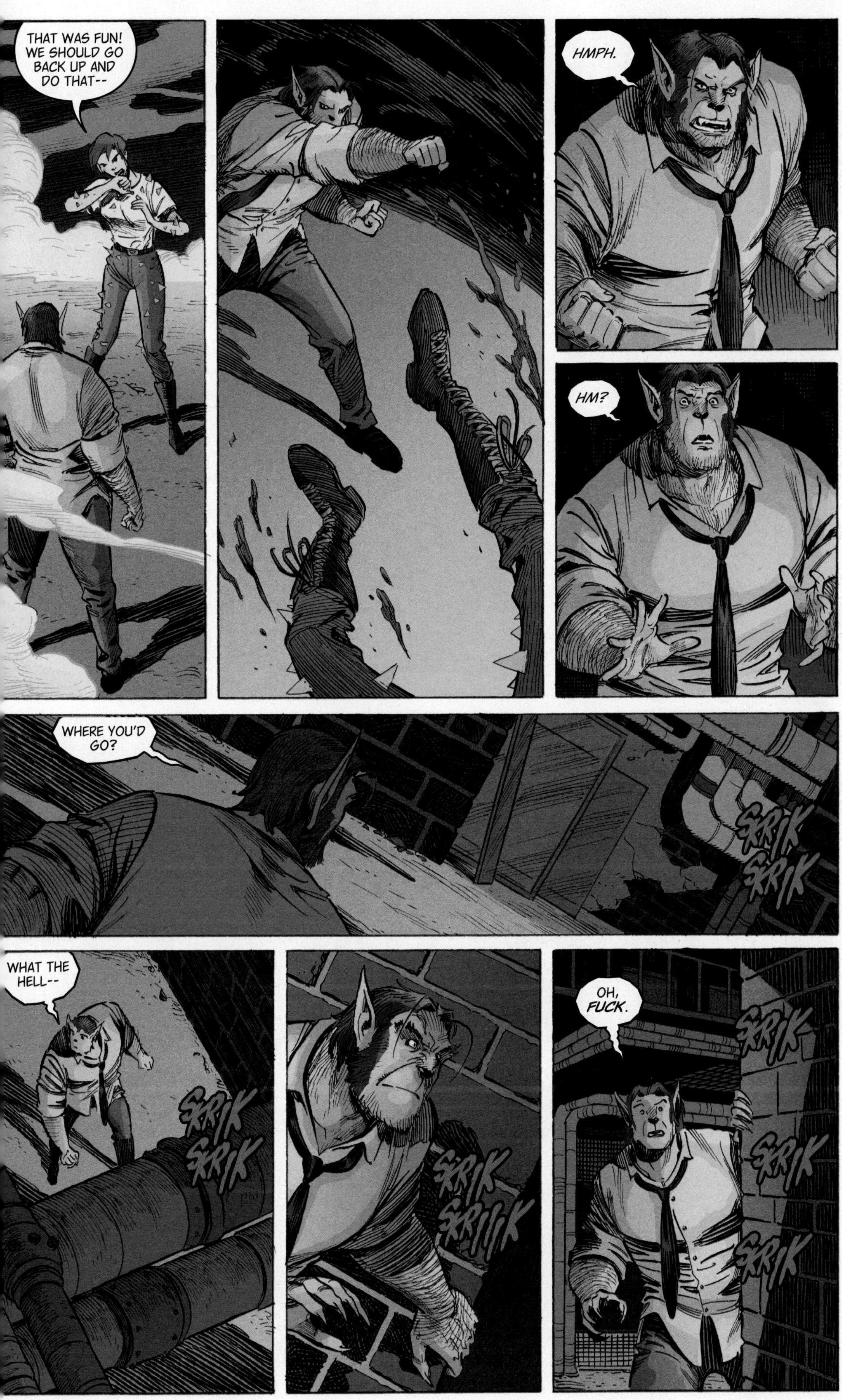
THAT WAS FUN! WE SHOULD GO BACK UP AND DO THAT--
HMPH.
HM?
WHERE YOU'D GO?
SKRIK SKRIK
WHAT THE HELL--
SKRIK SKRIK
SKRIK SKRIIIK
OH, FUCK.
SKRIK
SKRIK
SKRIK

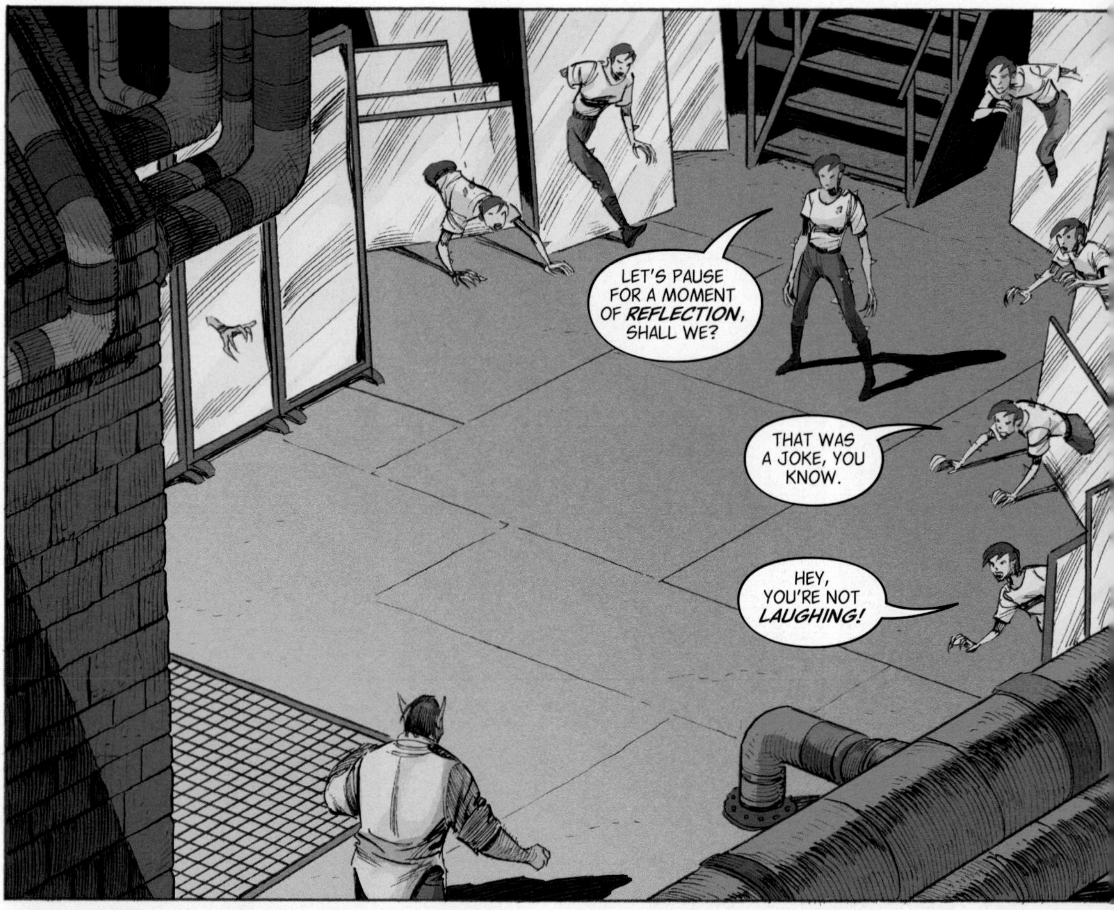
LET'S PAUSE FOR A MOMENT OF *REFLECTION*, SHALL WE?
THAT WAS A JOKE, YOU KNOW.
HEY, YOU'RE NOT *LAUGHING!*

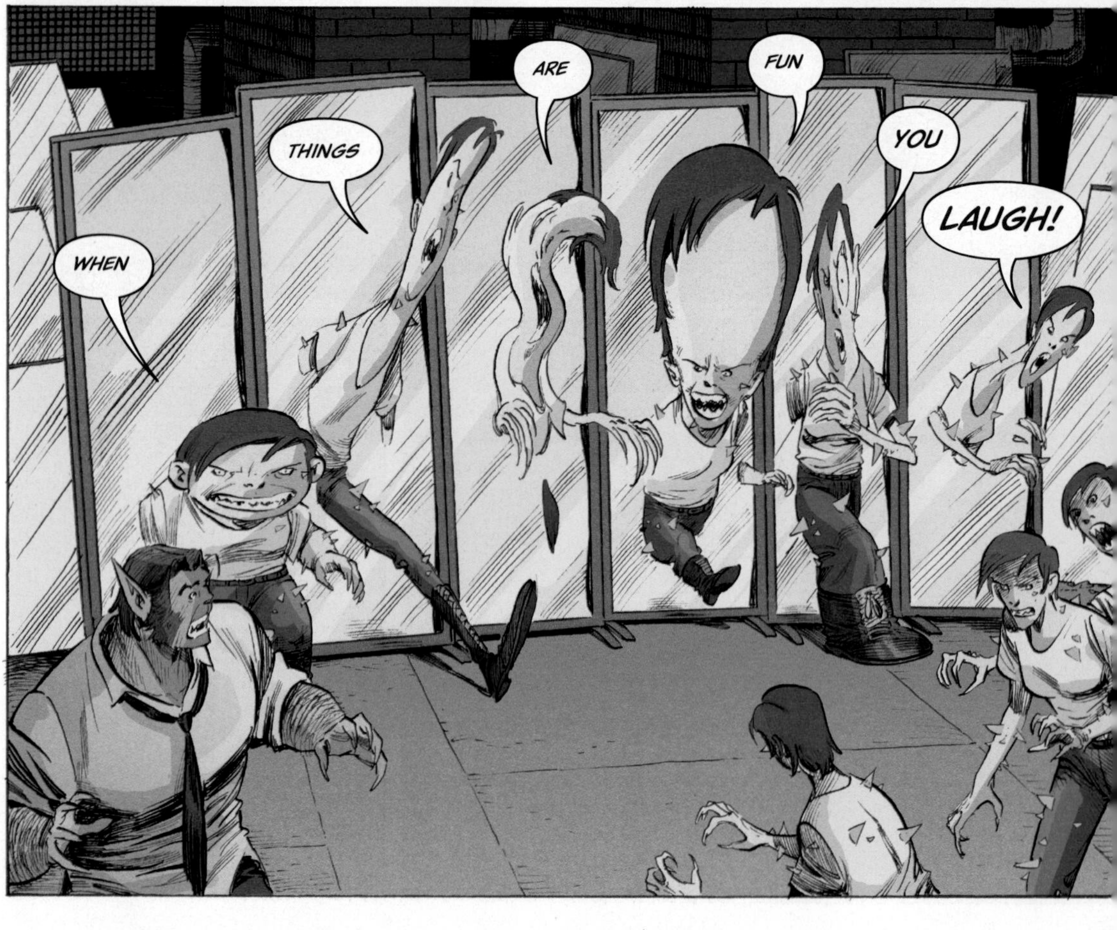
WHEN
THINGS
ARE
FUN
YOU
LAUGH!

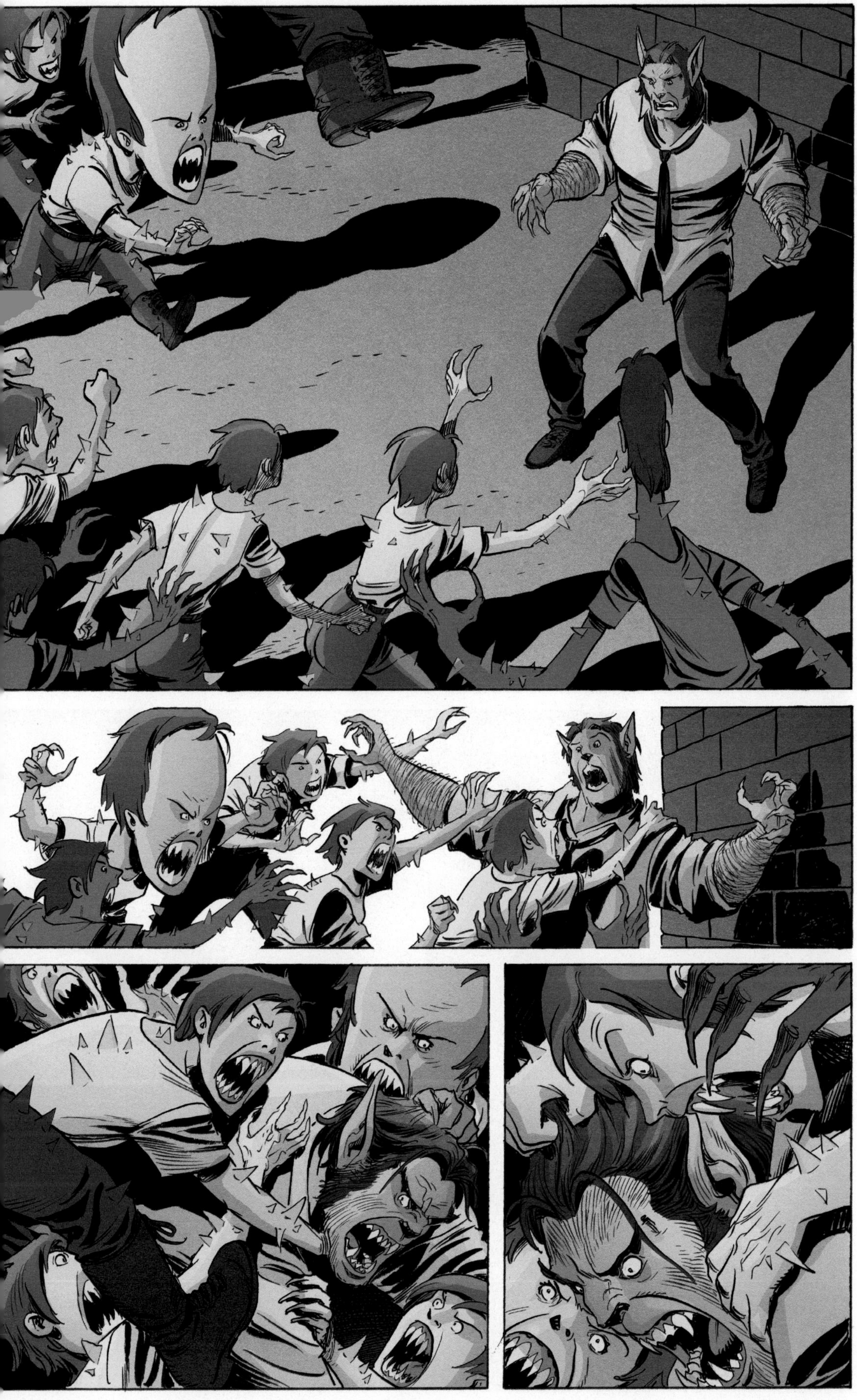

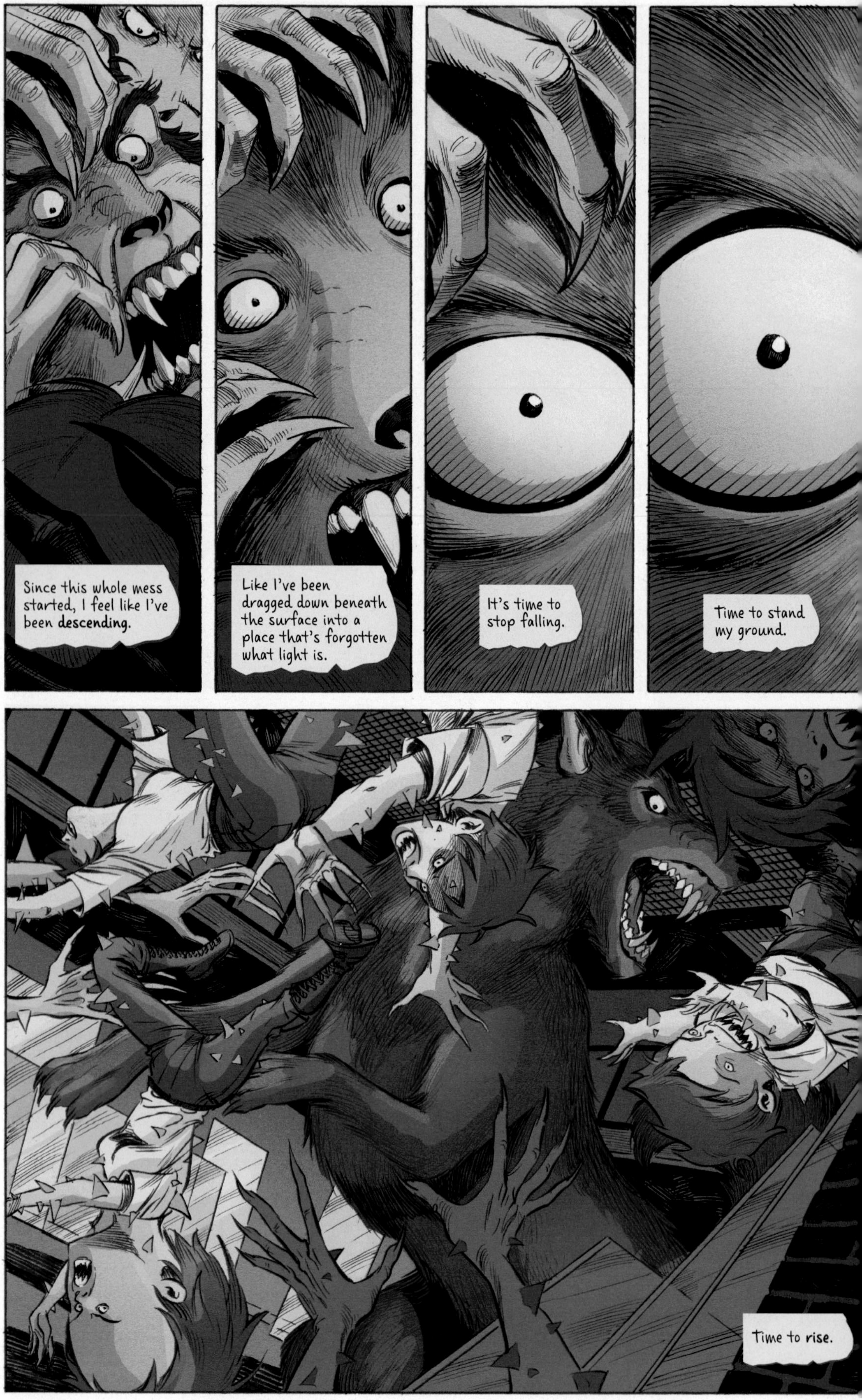
Since this whole mess started, I feel like I've been descending.
Like I've been dragged down beneath the surface into a place that's forgotten what light is.
It's time to stop falling.
Time to stand my ground.
Time to rise.

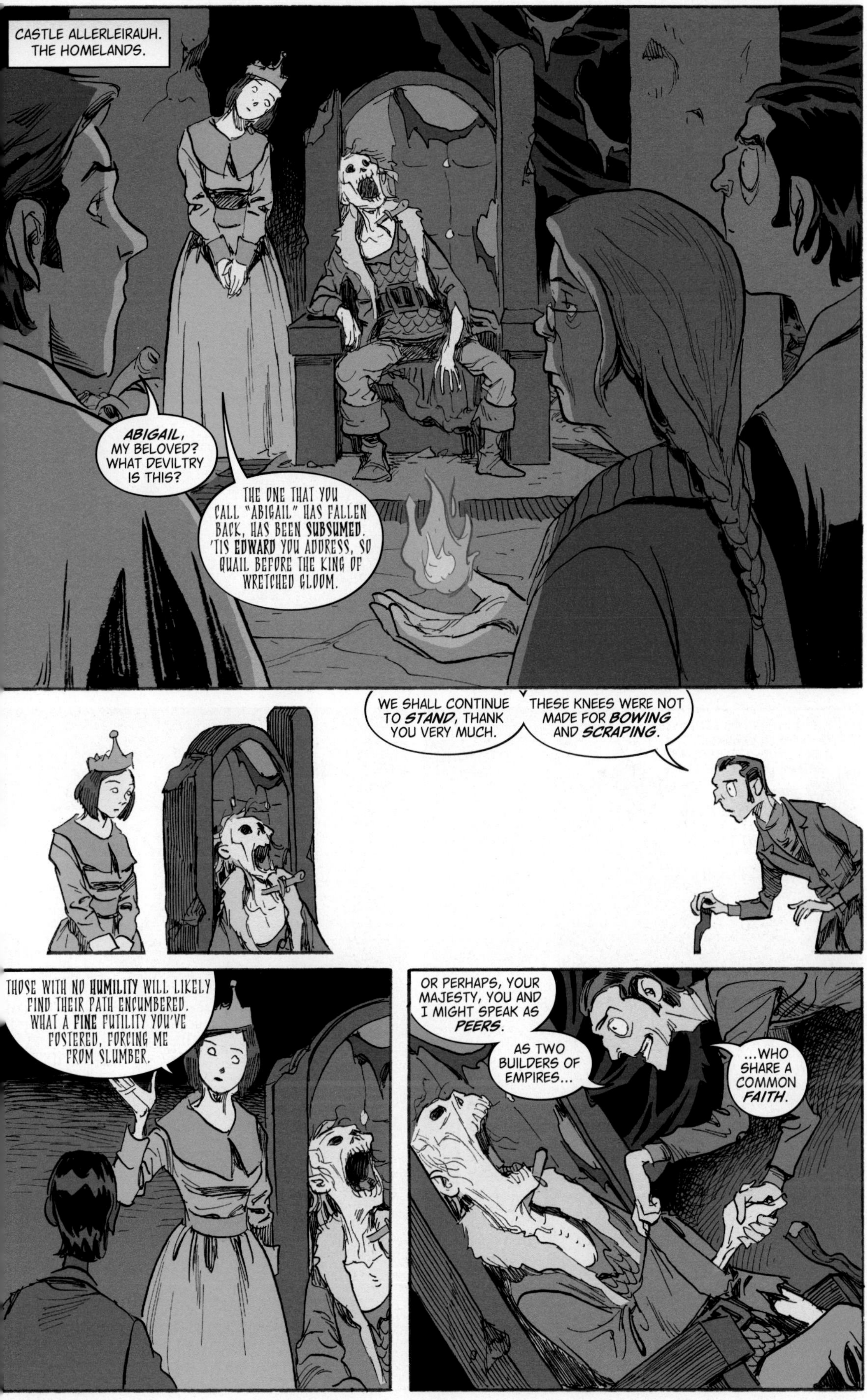

CASTLE ALLERLEIRAUH. THE HOMELANDS.
ABIGAIL, MY BELOVED? WHAT DEVILTRY IS THIS?
THE ONE THAT YOU CALL "ABIGAIL" HAS FALLEN BACK, HAS BEEN SUBSUMED. 'TIS EDWARD YOU ADDRESS, SO QUAIL BEFORE THE KING OF WRETCHED GLOOM.
WE SHALL CONTINUE TO STAND, THANK YOU VERY MUCH.
THESE KNEES WERE NOT MADE FOR BOWING AND SCRAPING.
THOSE WITH NO HUMILITY WILL LIKELY FIND THEIR PATH ENCUMBERED. WHAT A FINE FUTILITY YOU'VE FOSTERED, FORCING ME FROM SLUMBER.
OR PERHAPS, YOUR MAJESTY, YOU AND I MIGHT SPEAK AS PEERS.
AS TWO BUILDERS OF EMPIRES...
...WHO SHARE A COMMON FAITH.

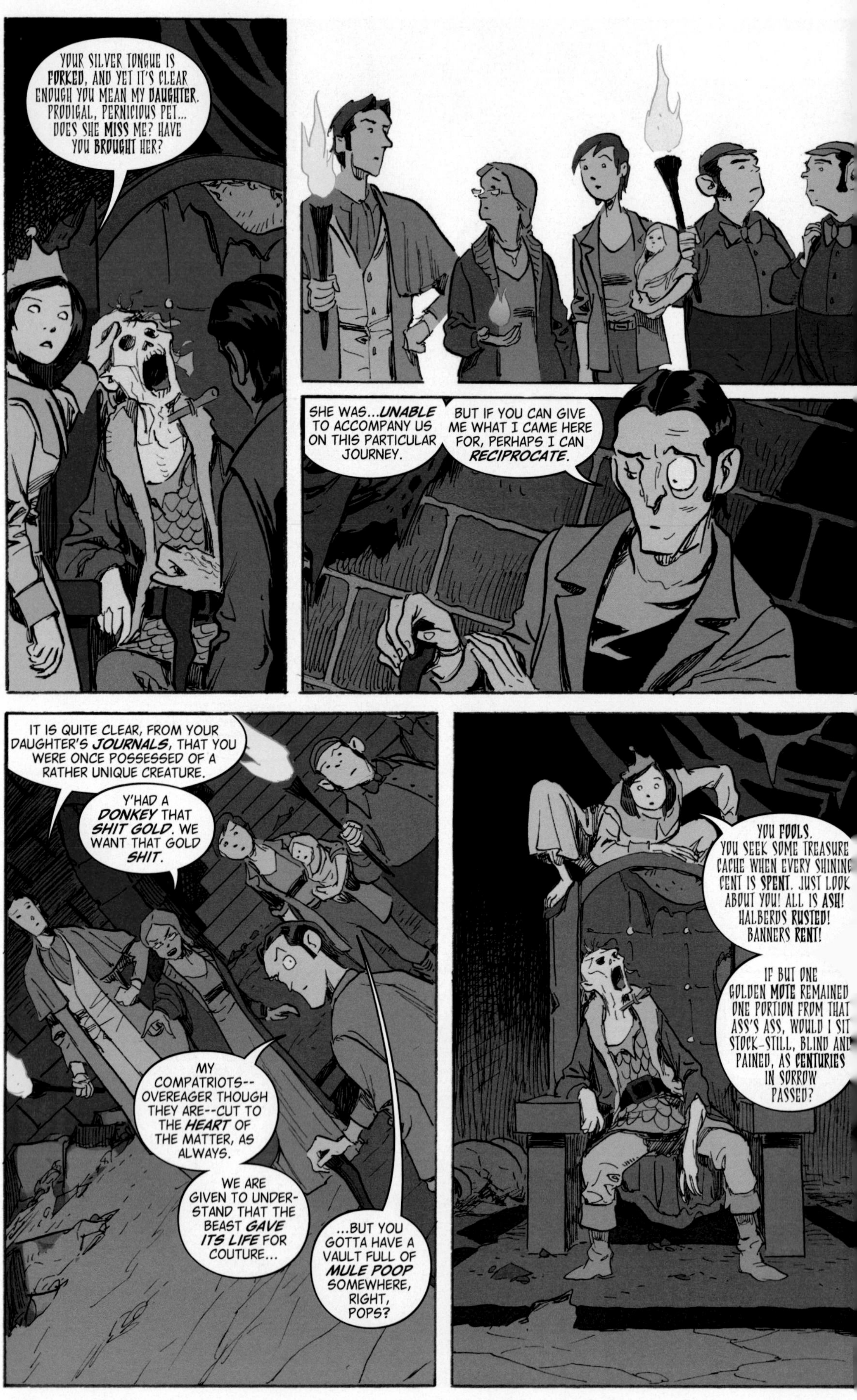
YOUR SILVER TONGUE IS FORKED, AND YET IT'S CLEAR ENOUGH YOU MEAN MY DAUGHTER. PRODIGAL, PERNICIOUS PET... DOES SHE MISS ME? HAVE YOU BROUGHT HER?
SHE WAS...UNABLE TO ACCOMPANY US ON THIS PARTICULAR JOURNEY.
BUT IF YOU CAN GIVE ME WHAT I CAME HERE FOR, PERHAPS I CAN RECIPROCATE.
IT IS QUITE CLEAR, FROM YOUR DAUGHTER'S JOURNALS, THAT YOU WERE ONCE POSSESSED OF A RATHER UNIQUE CREATURE.
Y'HAD A DONKEY THAT SHIT GOLD. WE WANT THAT GOLD SHIT.
MY COMPATRIOTS--OVEREAGER THOUGH THEY ARE--CUT TO THE HEART OF THE MATTER, AS ALWAYS.
WE ARE GIVEN TO UNDERSTAND THAT THE BEAST GAVE ITS LIFE FOR COUTURE...
...BUT YOU GOTTA HAVE A VAULT FULL OF MULE POOP SOMEWHERE, RIGHT, POPS?
YOU FOOLS. YOU SEEK SOME TREASURE CACHE WHEN EVERY SHINING CENT IS SPENT. JUST LOOK ABOUT YOU! ALL IS ASH! HALBERDS RUSTED! BANNERS RENT!
IF BUT ONE GOLDEN MOTE REMAINED ONE PORTION FROM THAT ASS'S ASS, WOULD I SIT STOCK-STILL, BLIND AND PAINED, AS CENTURIES IN SORROW PASSED?

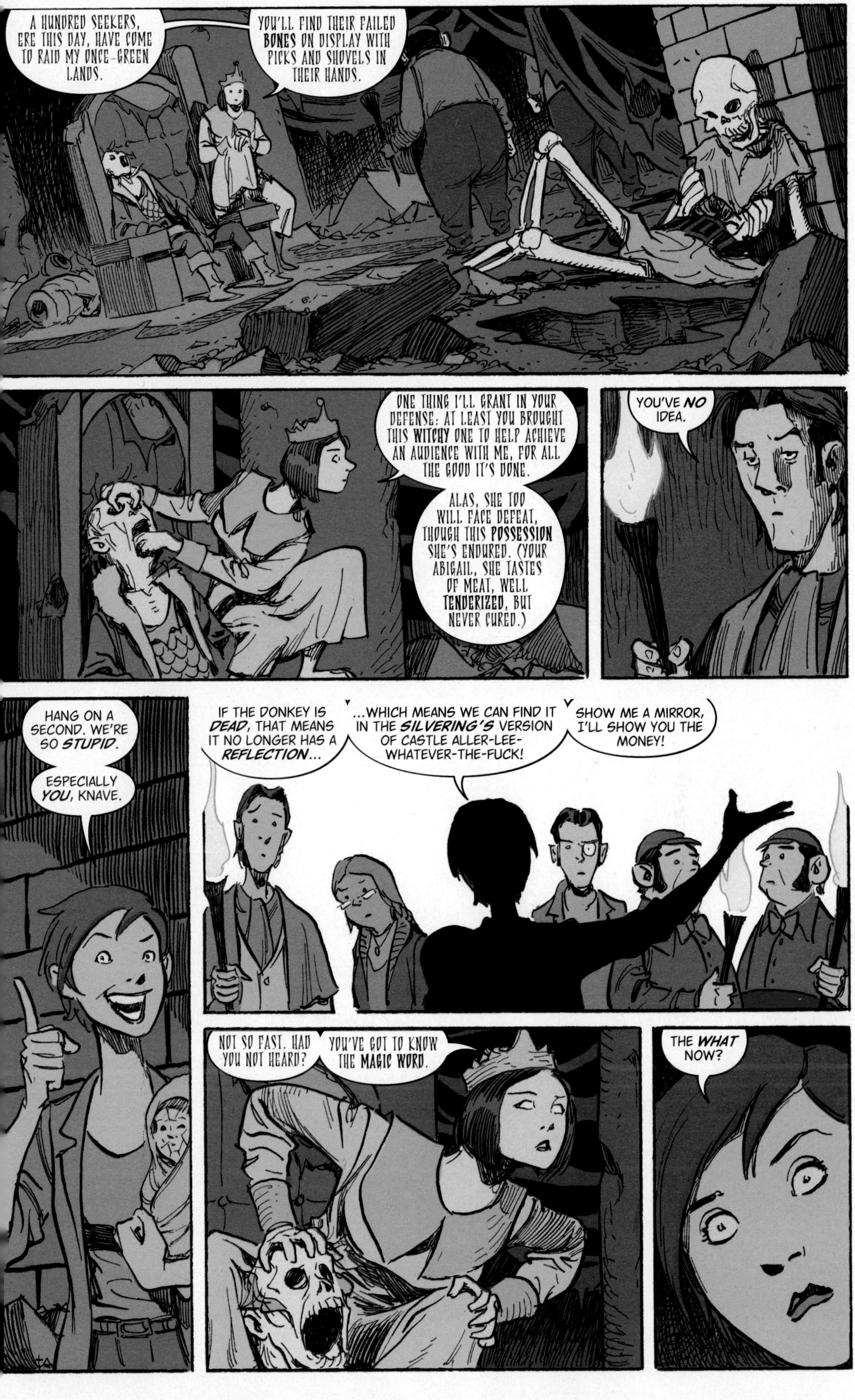
A HUNDRED SEEKERS, ERE THIS DAY, HAVE COME TO RAID MY ONCE-GREEN LANDS.
YOU'LL FIND THEIR FAILED BONES ON DISPLAY WITH PICKS AND SHOVELS IN THEIR HANDS.
ONE THING I'LL GRANT IN YOUR DEFENSE: AT LEAST YOU BROUGHT THIS WITCHY ONE TO HELP ACHIEVE AN AUDIENCE WITH ME, FOR ALL THE GOOD IT'S DONE.
ALAS, SHE TOO WILL FACE DEFEAT, THOUGH THIS POSSESSION SHE'S ENDURED. (YOUR ABIGAIL, SHE TASTES OF MEAT, WELL TENDERIZED, BUT NEVER CURED.)
YOU'VE NO IDEA.
HANG ON A SECOND. WE'RE SO STUPID.
ESPECIALLY YOU, KNAVE.
IF THE DONKEY IS DEAD, THAT MEANS IT NO LONGER HAS A REFLECTION...
...WHICH MEANS WE CAN FIND IT IN THE SILVERING'S VERSION OF CASTLE ALLER-LEE-WHATEVER-THE-FUCK!
SHOW ME A MIRROR, I'LL SHOW YOU THE MONEY!
NOT SO FAST. HAD YOU NOT HEARD?
YOU'VE GOT TO KNOW THE MAGIC WORD.
THE WHAT NOW?

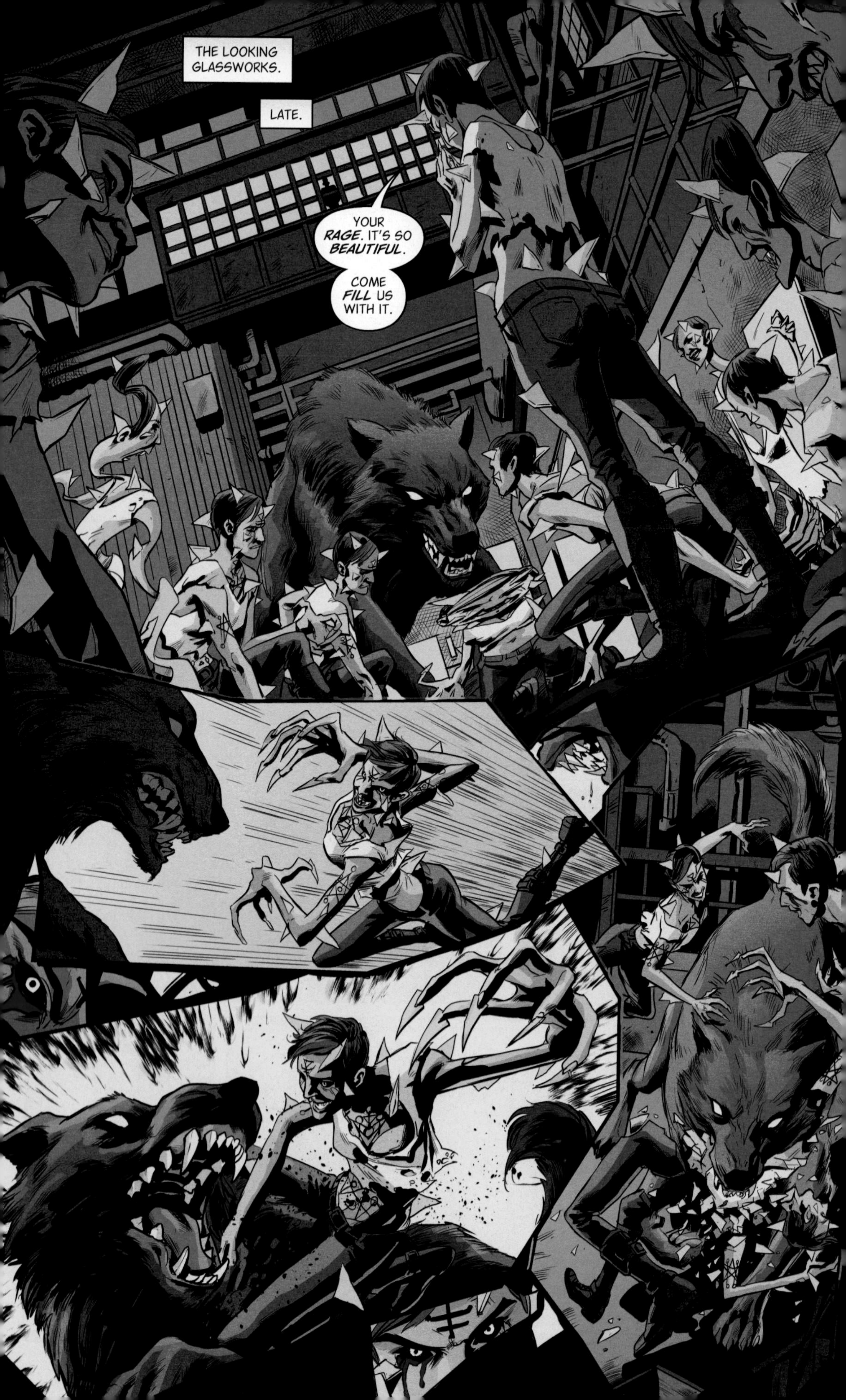
THE LOOKING GLASSWORKS.
LATE.
YOUR RAGE. IT'S SO BEAUTIFUL.
COME FILL US WITH IT.

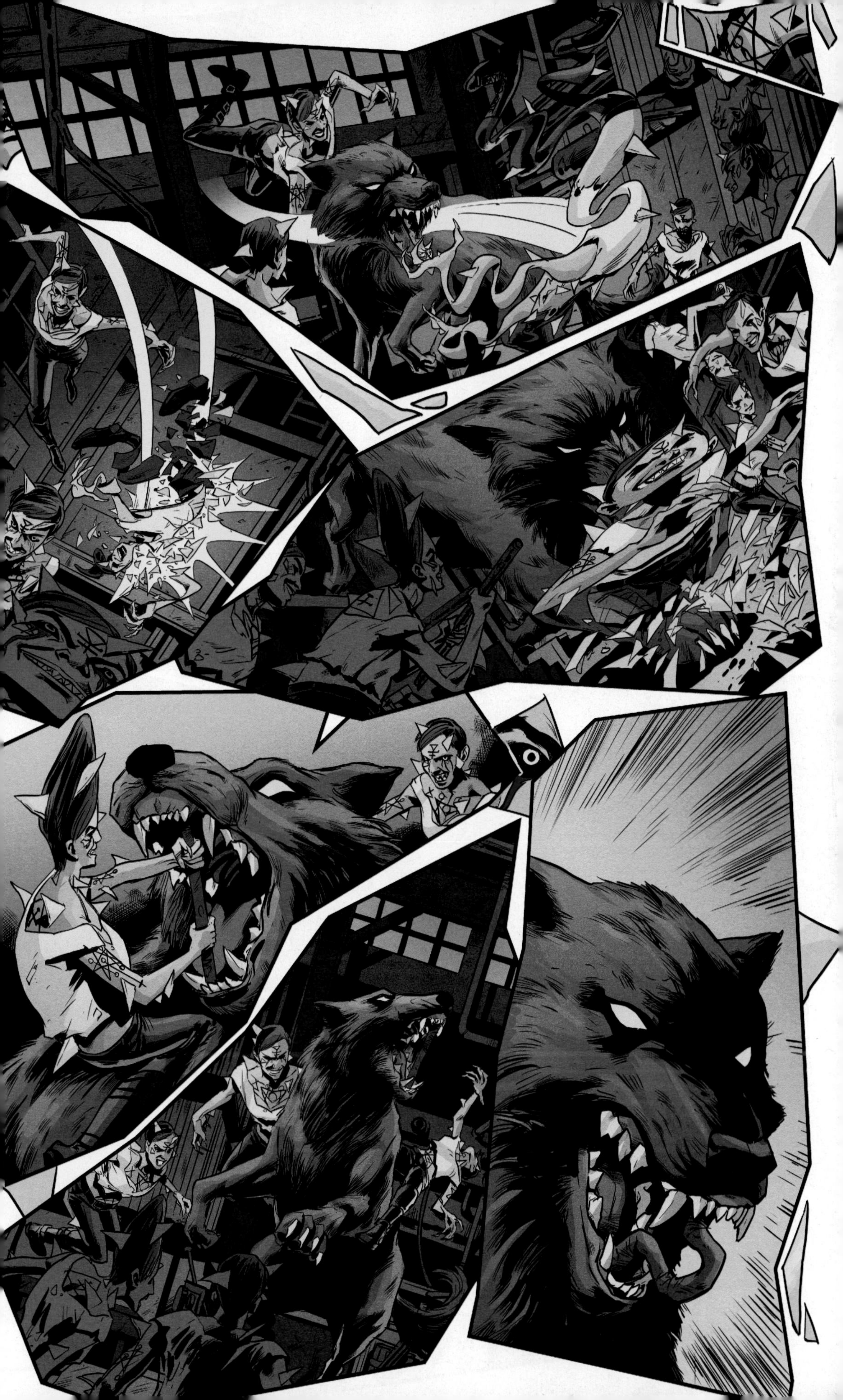

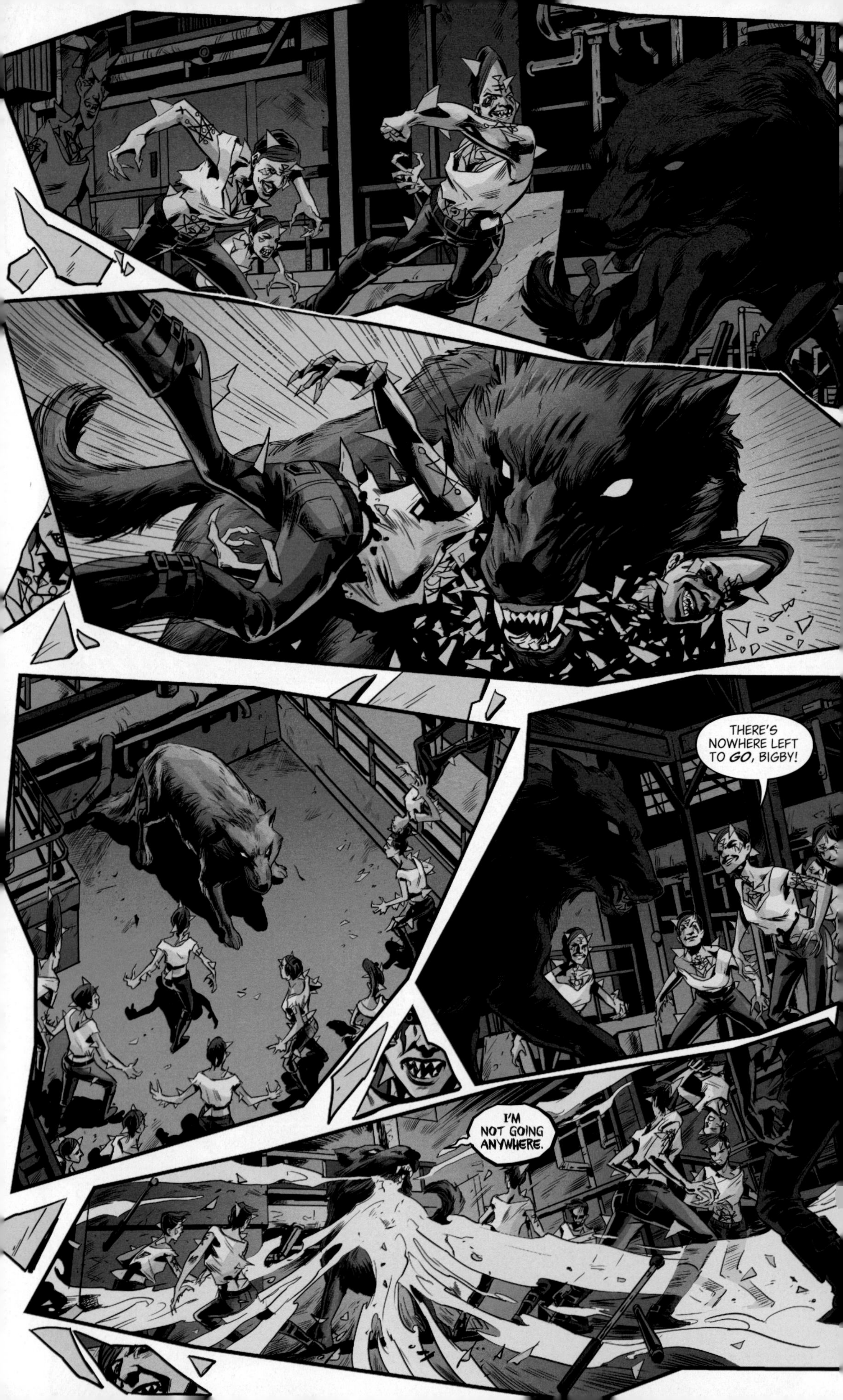
THERE'S NOWHERE LEFT TO GO, BIGBY!
I'M NOT GOING ANYWHERE.

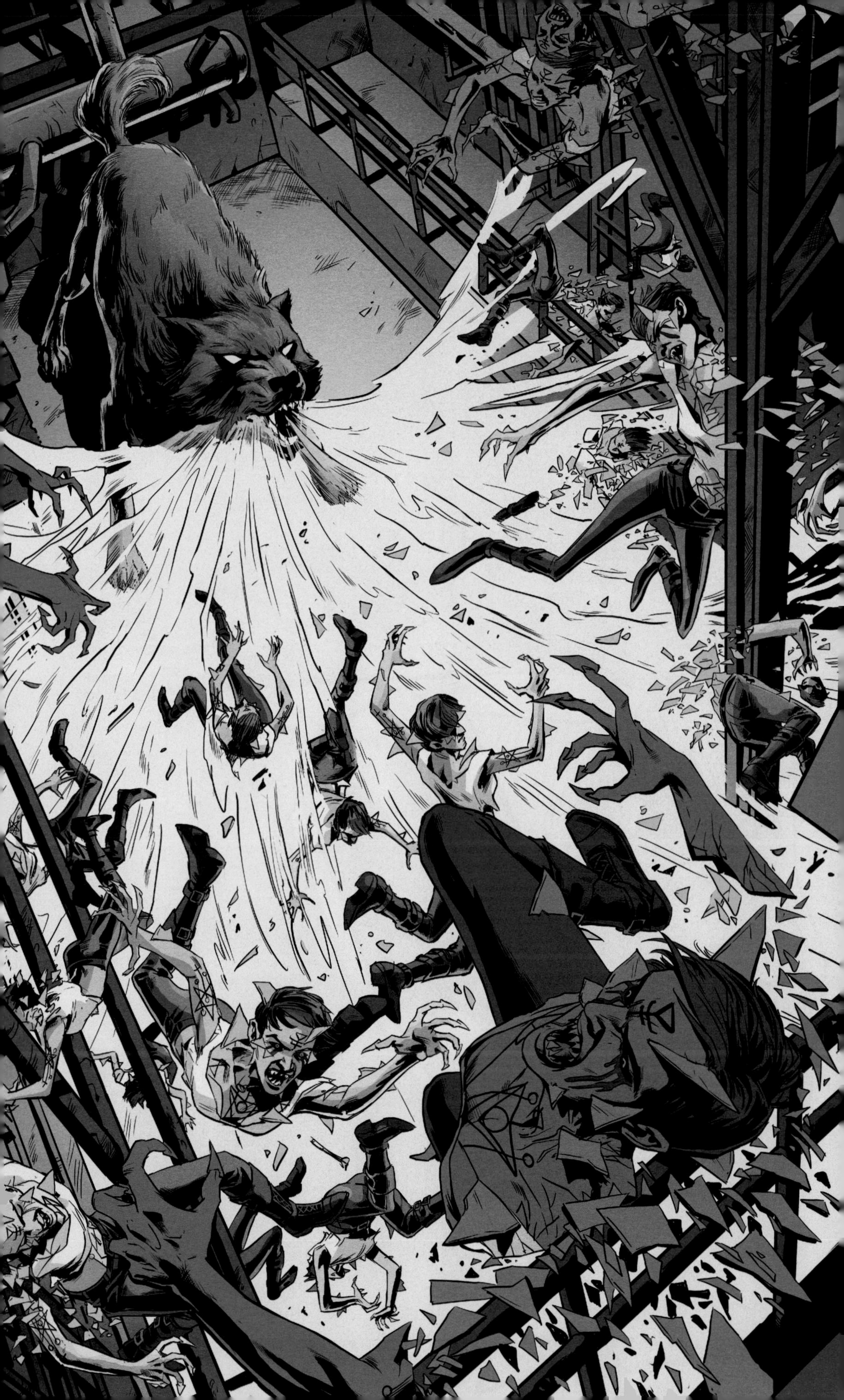

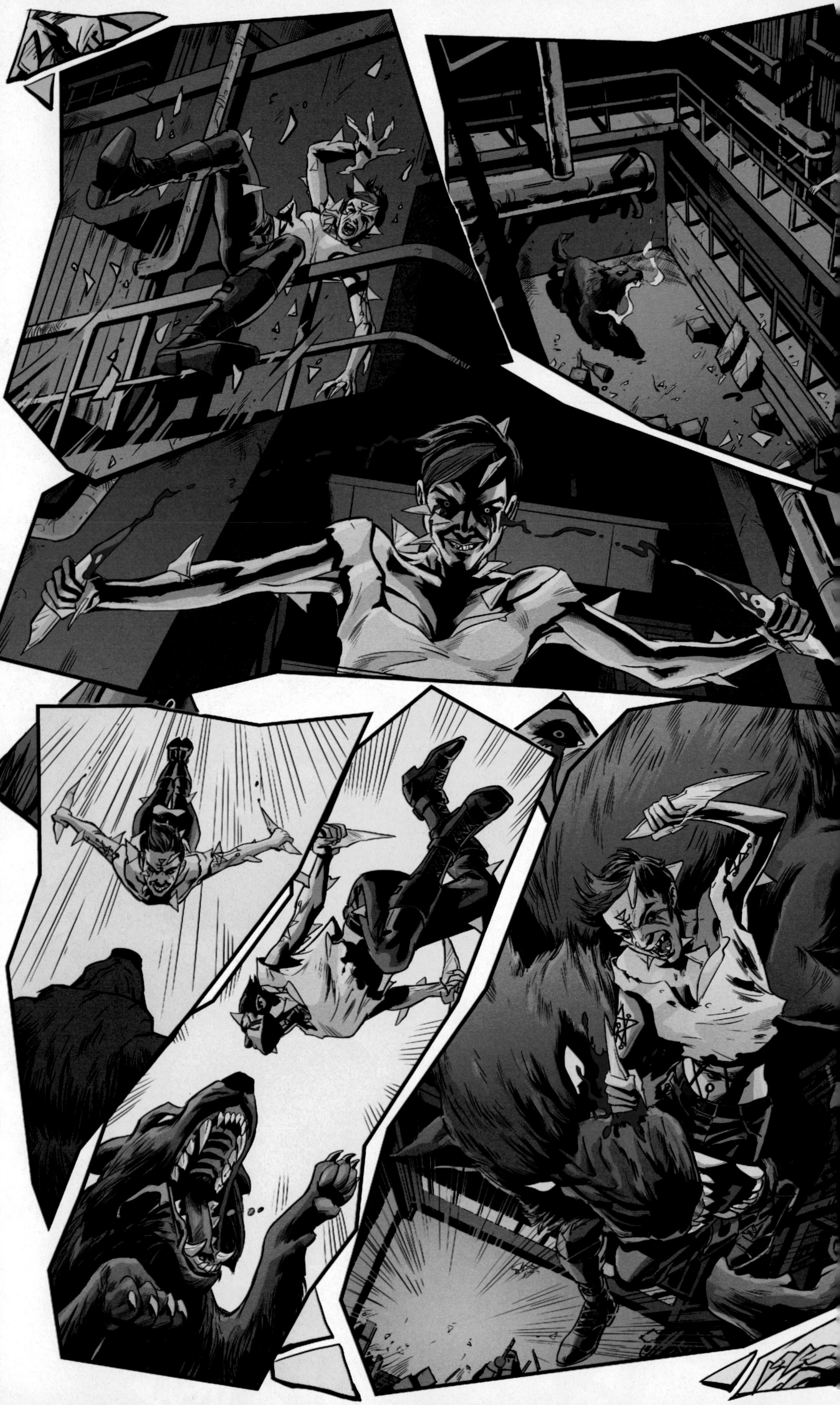

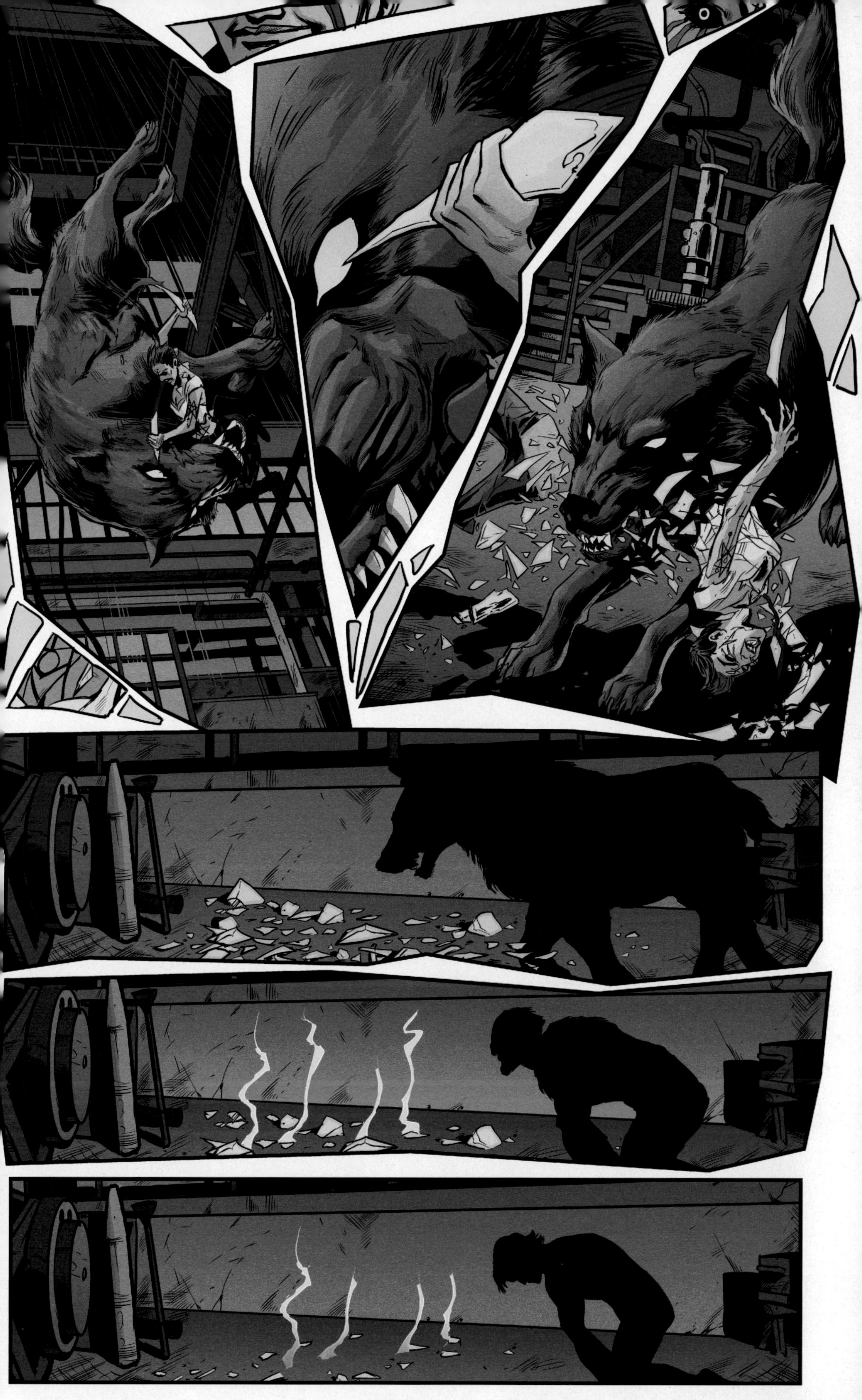

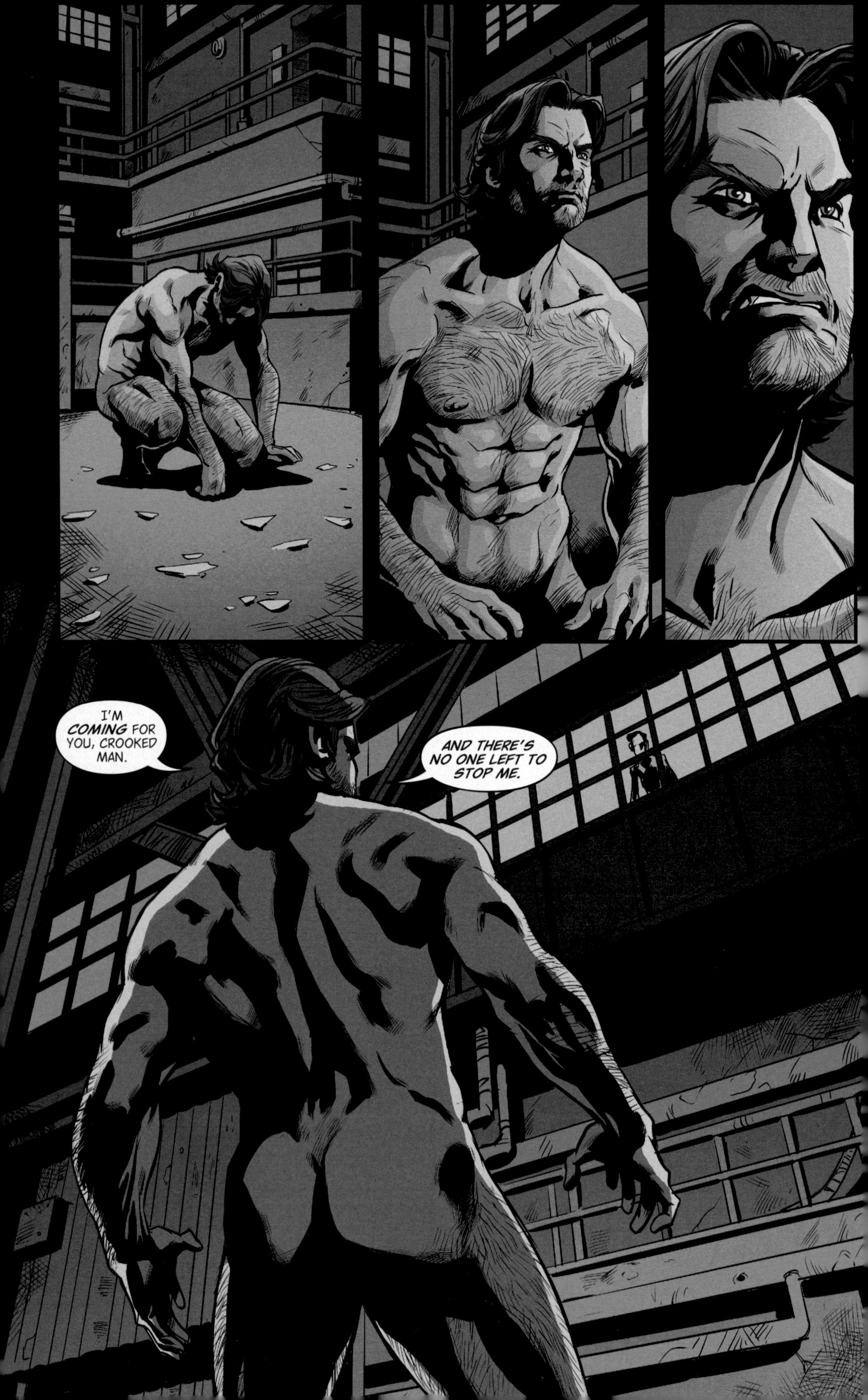
I'M COMING FOR YOU, CROOKED MAN.
AND THERE'S NO ONE LEFT TO STOP ME.

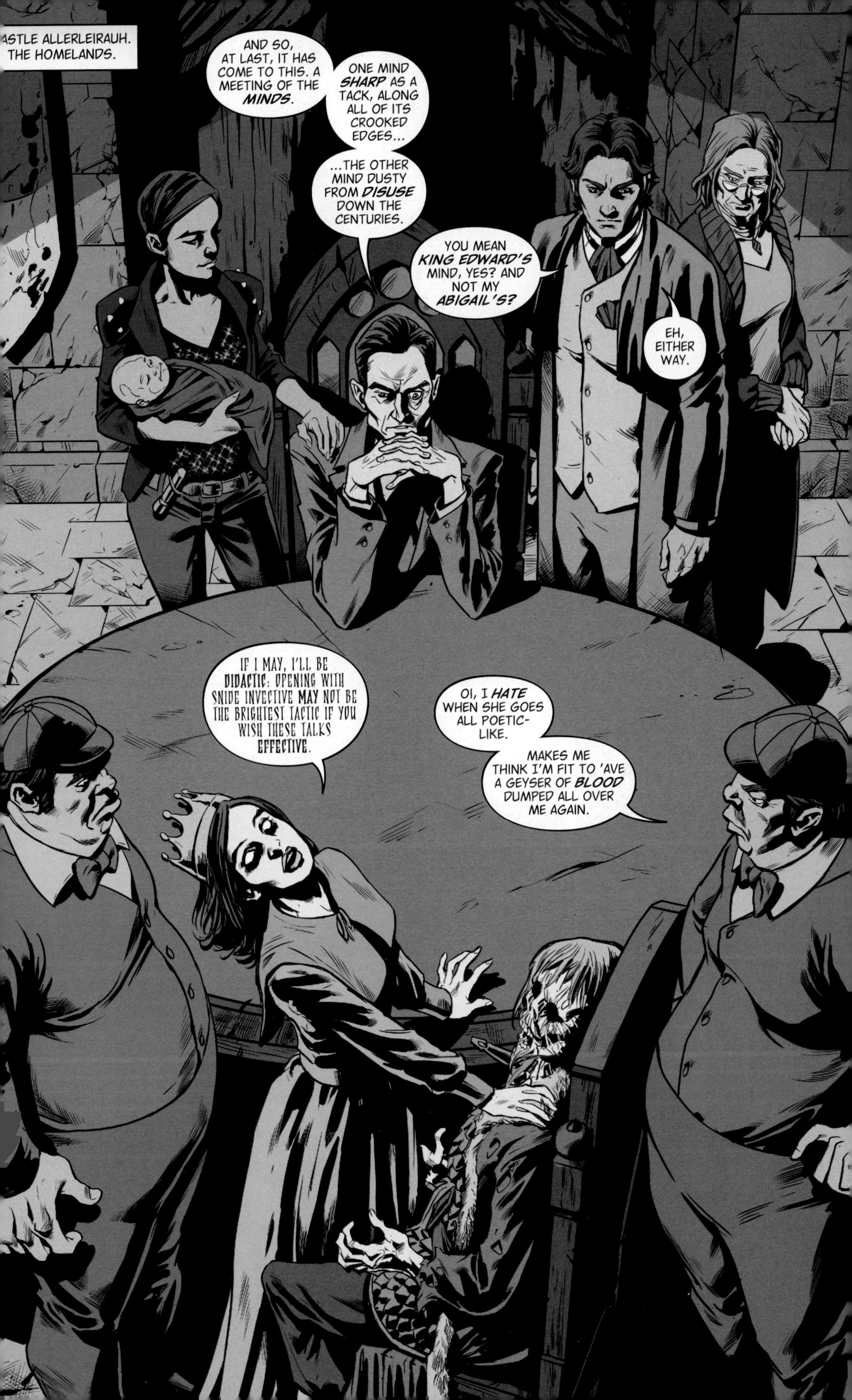

ASTLE ALLERLEIRAUH. THE HOMELANDS.
AND SO, AT LAST, IT HAS COME TO THIS. A MEETING OF THE MINDS.
ONE MIND SHARP AS A TACK, ALONG ALL OF ITS CROOKED EDGES...
...THE OTHER MIND DUSTY FROM DISUSE DOWN THE CENTURIES.
YOU MEAN KING EDWARD'S MIND, YES? AND NOT MY ABIGAIL'S?
EH, EITHER WAY.
IF I MAY, I'LL BE DIDACTIC: OPENING WITH SNIDE INVECTIVE MAY NOT BE THE BRIGHTEST TACTIC IF YOU WISH THESE TALKS EFFECTIVE.
OI, I HATE WHEN SHE GOES ALL POETIC-LIKE.
MAKES ME THINK I'M FIT TO 'AVE A GEYSER OF BLOOD DUMPED ALL OVER ME AGAIN.

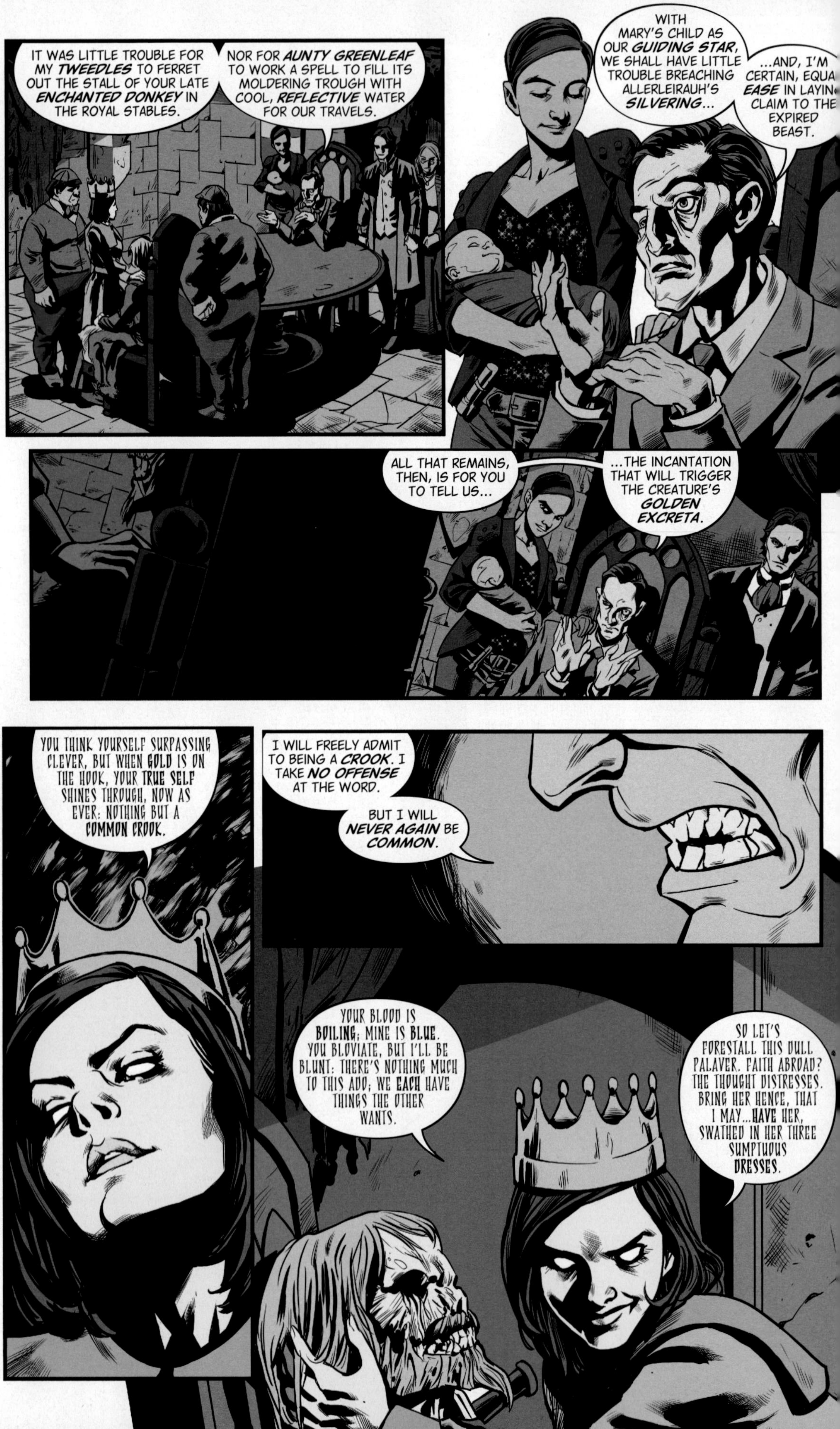
IT WAS LITTLE TROUBLE FOR MY TWEEDLES TO FERRET OUT THE STALL OF YOUR LATE ENCHANTED DONKEY IN THE ROYAL STABLES.
NOR FOR AUNTY GREENLEAF TO WORK A SPELL TO FILL ITS MOLDERING TROUGH WITH COOL, REFLECTIVE WATER FOR OUR TRAVELS.
WITH MARY'S CHILD AS OUR GUIDING STAR, WE SHALL HAVE LITTLE TROUBLE BREACHING ALLERLEIRAUH'S SILVERING...
...AND, I'M CERTAIN, EQUA EASE IN LAYIN CLAIM TO THE EXPIRED BEAST.
ALL THAT REMAINS, THEN, IS FOR YOU TO TELL US...
...THE INCANTATION THAT WILL TRIGGER THE CREATURE'S GOLDEN EXCRETA.
YOU THINK YOURSELF SURPASSING CLEVER, BUT WHEN GOLD IS ON THE HOOK, YOUR TRUE SELF SHINES THROUGH, NOW AS EVER: NOTHING BUT A COMMON CROOK.
I WILL FREELY ADMIT TO BEING A CROOK. I TAKE NO OFFENSE AT THE WORD.
BUT I WILL NEVER AGAIN BE COMMON.
YOUR BLOOD IS BOILING; MINE IS BLUE. YOU BLOVIATE, BUT I'LL BE BLUNT: THERE'S NOTHING MUCH TO THIS ADO; WE EACH HAVE THINGS THE OTHER WANTS.
SO LET'S FORESTALL THIS DULL PALAVER. FAITH ABROAD? THE THOUGHT DISTRESSES. BRING HER HENCE, THAT I MAY...HAVE HER, SWATHED IN HER THREE SUMPTUOUS DRESSES.

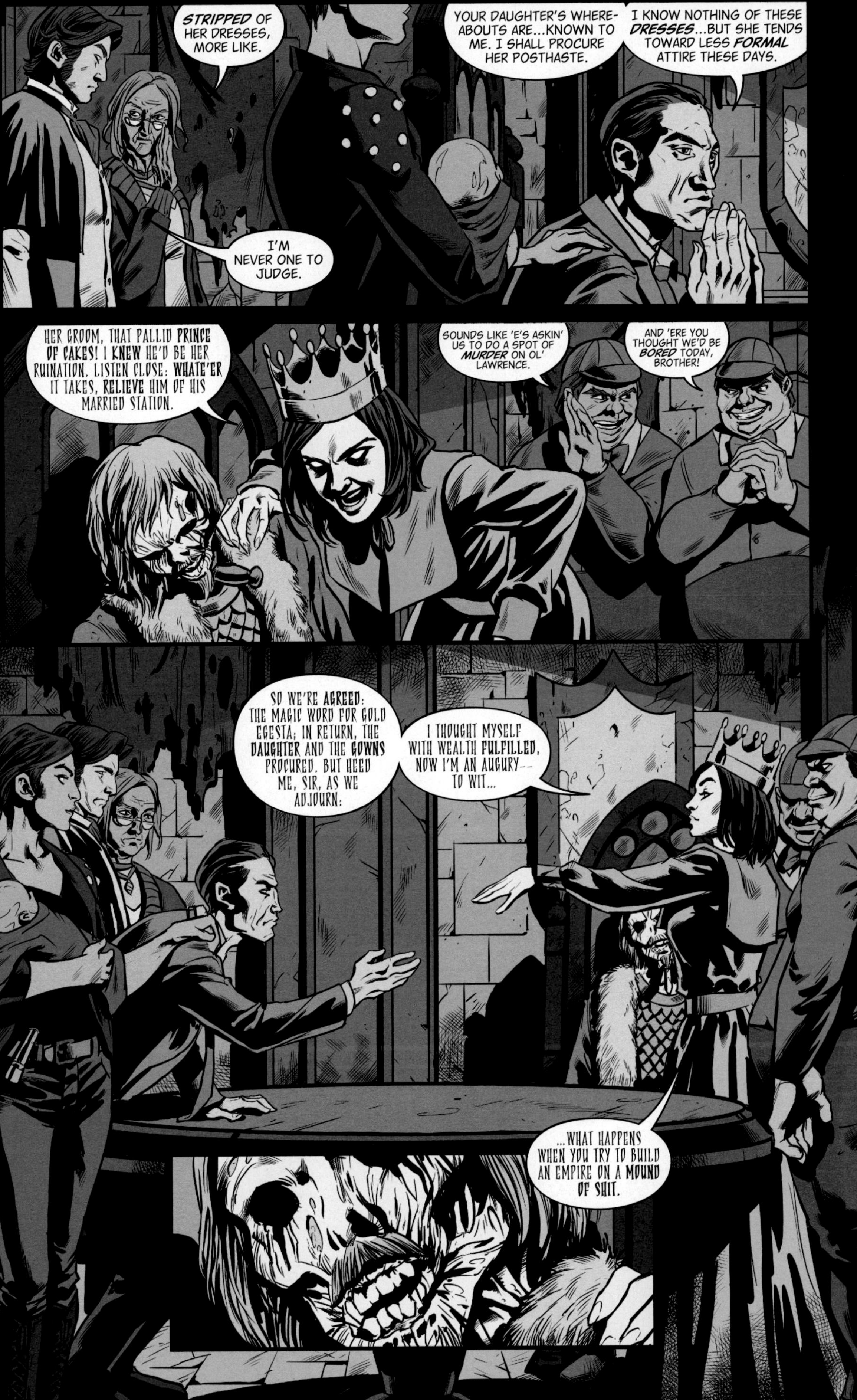
STRIPPED OF HER DRESSES, MORE LIKE.
I'M NEVER ONE TO JUDGE.
YOUR DAUGHTER'S WHERE-ABOUTS ARE...KNOWN TO ME. I SHALL PROCURE HER POSTHASTE.
I KNOW NOTHING OF THESE DRESSES...BUT SHE TENDS TOWARD LESS FORMAL ATTIRE THESE DAYS.
HER GROOM, THAT PALLID PRINCE OF CAKES! I KNEW HE'D BE HER RUINATION. LISTEN CLOSE: WHATE'ER IT TAKES, RELIEVE HIM OF HIS MARRIED STATION.
SOUNDS LIKE 'E'S ASKIN' US TO DO A SPOT OF MURDER ON OL' LAWRENCE.
AND 'ERE YOU THOUGHT WE'D BE BORED TODAY, BROTHER!
SO WE'RE AGREED: THE MAGIC WORD FOR GOLD EGESTA; IN RETURN, THE DAUGHTER AND THE GOWNS PROCURED. BUT HEED ME, SIR, AS WE ADJOURN:
I THOUGHT MYSELF WITH WEALTH FULFILLED, NOW I'M AN AUGURY-- TO WIT...
...WHAT HAPPENS WHEN YOU TRY TO BUILD AN EMPIRE ON A MOUND OF SHIT.

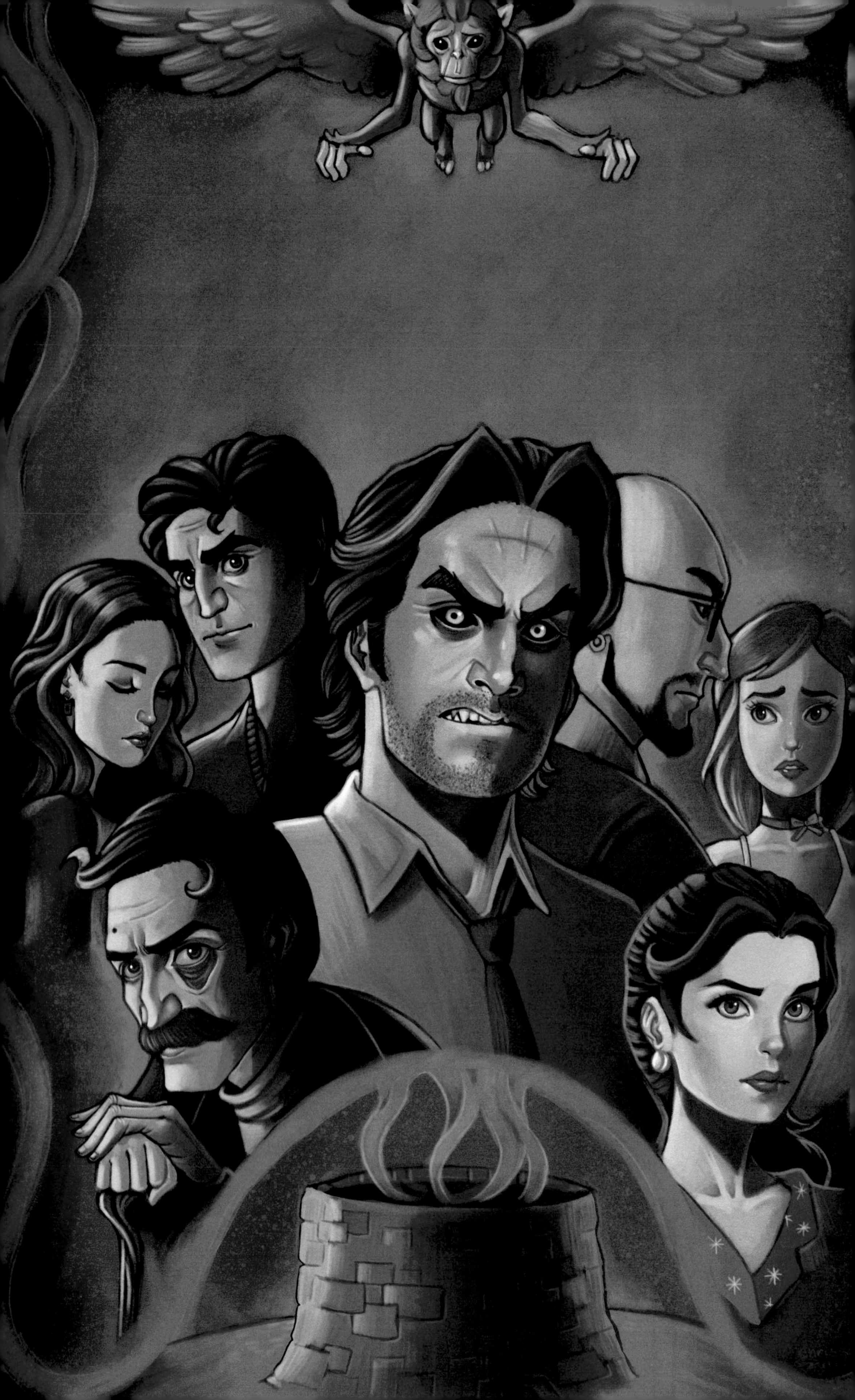

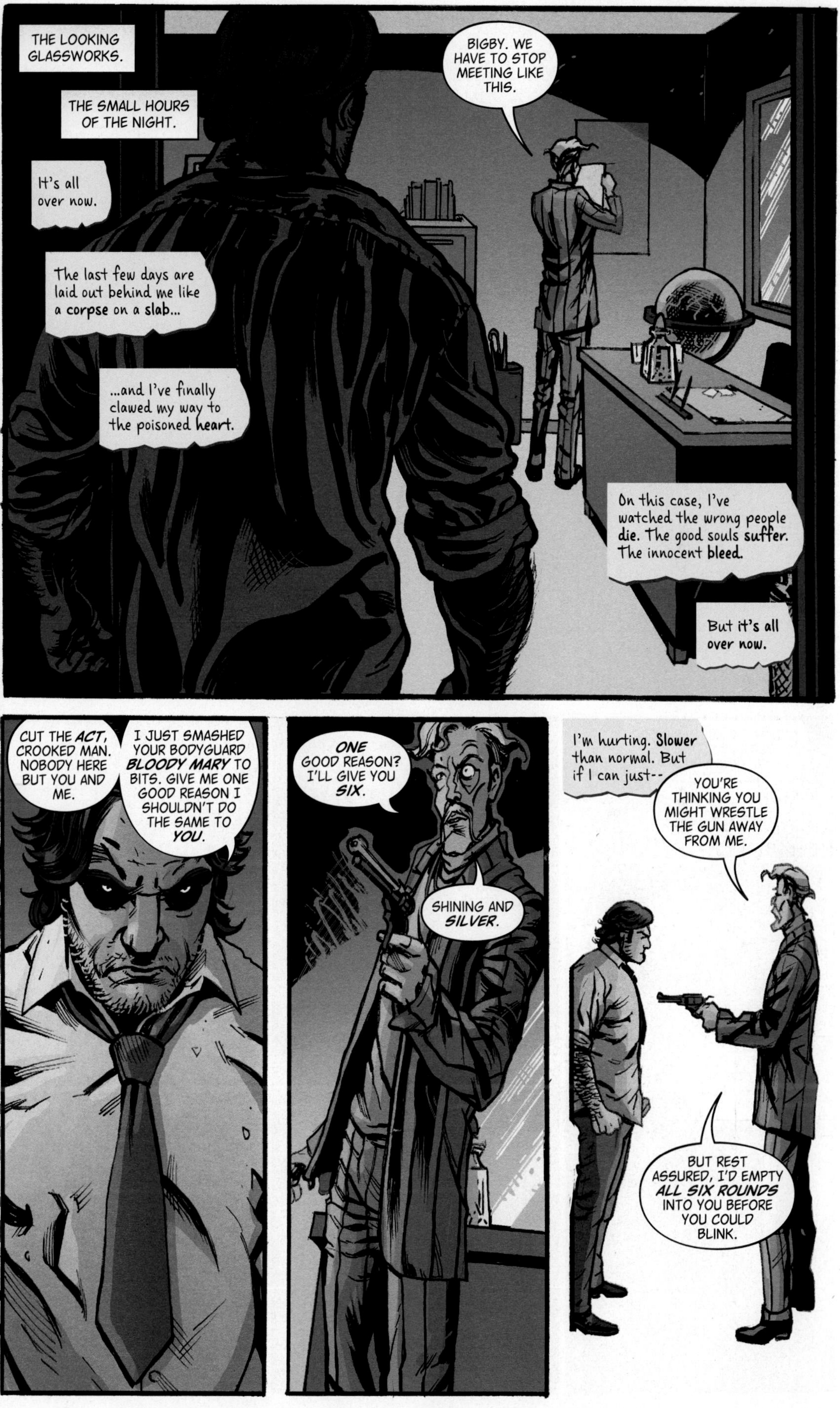
THE LOOKING GLASSWORKS.
THE SMALL HOURS OF THE NIGHT.
It's all over now.
The last few days are laid out behind me like a corpse on a slab...
...and I've finally clawed my way to the poisoned heart.
BIGBY. WE HAVE TO STOP MEETING LIKE THIS.
On this case, I've watched the wrong people die. The good souls suffer. The innocent bleed.
But it's all over now.
CUT THE ACT, CROOKED MAN. NOBODY HERE BUT YOU AND ME.
I JUST SMASHED YOUR BODYGUARD BLOODY MARY TO BITS. GIVE ME ONE GOOD REASON I SHOULDN'T DO THE SAME TO YOU.
ONE GOOD REASON? I'LL GIVE YOU SIX.
SHINING AND SILVER.
I'm hurting. Slower than normal. But if I can just--
YOU'RE THINKING YOU MIGHT WRESTLE THE GUN AWAY FROM ME.
BUT REST ASSURED, I'D EMPTY ALL SIX ROUNDS INTO YOU BEFORE YOU COULD BLINK.

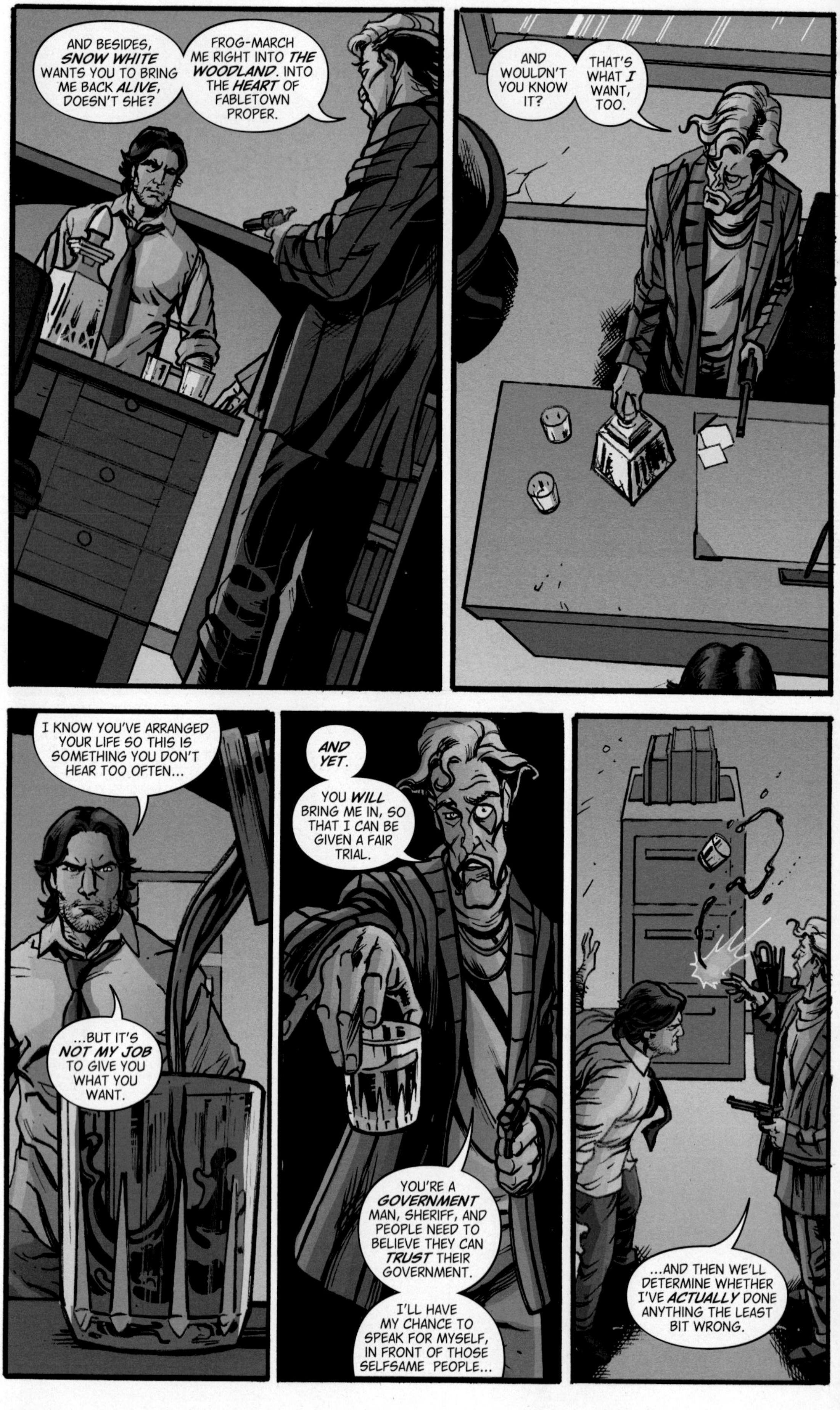
AND BESIDES, SNOW WHITE WANTS YOU TO BRING ME BACK ALIVE, DOESN'T SHE?
FROG-MARCH ME RIGHT INTO THE WOODLAND. INTO THE HEART OF FABLETOWN PROPER.
AND WOULDN'T YOU KNOW IT?
THAT'S WHAT I WANT, TOO.
I KNOW YOU'VE ARRANGED YOUR LIFE SO THIS IS SOMETHING YOU DON'T HEAR TOO OFTEN...
...BUT IT'S NOT MY JOB TO GIVE YOU WHAT YOU WANT.
AND YET.
YOU WILL BRING ME IN, SO THAT I CAN BE GIVEN A FAIR TRIAL.
YOU'RE A GOVERNMENT MAN, SHERIFF, AND PEOPLE NEED TO BELIEVE THEY CAN TRUST THEIR GOVERNMENT.
I'LL HAVE MY CHANCE TO SPEAK FOR MYSELF, IN FRONT OF THOSE SELFSAME PEOPLE...
...AND THEN WE'LL DETERMINE WHETHER I'VE ACTUALLY DONE ANYTHING THE LEAST BIT WRONG.

FUNNY THING...MOST FOLKS WITH A *CLEAN CONSCIENCE* DON'T GO POKING *LOADED GUNS* INTO PEOPLE'S CHESTS.

WHAT, *THIS* OLD THING? IT'S MERELY A *PRECAUTION.*

I'M NO *MURDERER.* I DIDN'T KILL THOSE WOMEN, OR ANYONE ELSE.

AND I THINK YOU *KNOW* THAT BY NOW.

I TALKED TO *GEORGIE.* I KNOW YOU GAVE THE ORDER.

THEY MIGHT NOT BE DEAD BY YOUR *HAND,* BUT THEY'RE DEAD ON YOUR *WORD.*

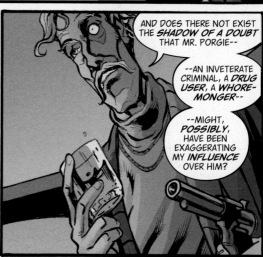

AND DOES THERE NOT EXIST THE *SHADOW OF A DOUBT* THAT MR. PORGIE--

--AN INVETERATE CRIMINAL, A *DRUG USER,* A *WHORE-MONGER*--

--MIGHT, *POSSIBLY,* HAVE BEEN EXAGGERATING MY *INFLUENCE* OVER HIM?

AS FOR *ME,* SHERIFF...I HAVE LITTLE ELSE TO SAY TO YOU HERE IN PRIVATE.

MY SIDE OF THE STORY DEMANDS AN *AUDIENCE.* I'LL TELL IT TO THE *COMMUNITY* AT MY TRIAL...

...WHERE I'M CONFIDENT THAT YOU WILL FIND YOURSELF *SWAYED* ALONG WITH THE REST OF THEM.

I'M PUTTING THE *GUN* AWAY NOW, AS A SHOW OF GOOD FAITH.

HEH. *"FAITH."*

BUT--AND I *DON'T* WISH TO BELABOR THIS POINT--

--YOU *CERTAINLY* SHOULDN'T TAKE THIS AS YOUR SIGNAL TO DO SOMETHING... *REGRETTABLE.*

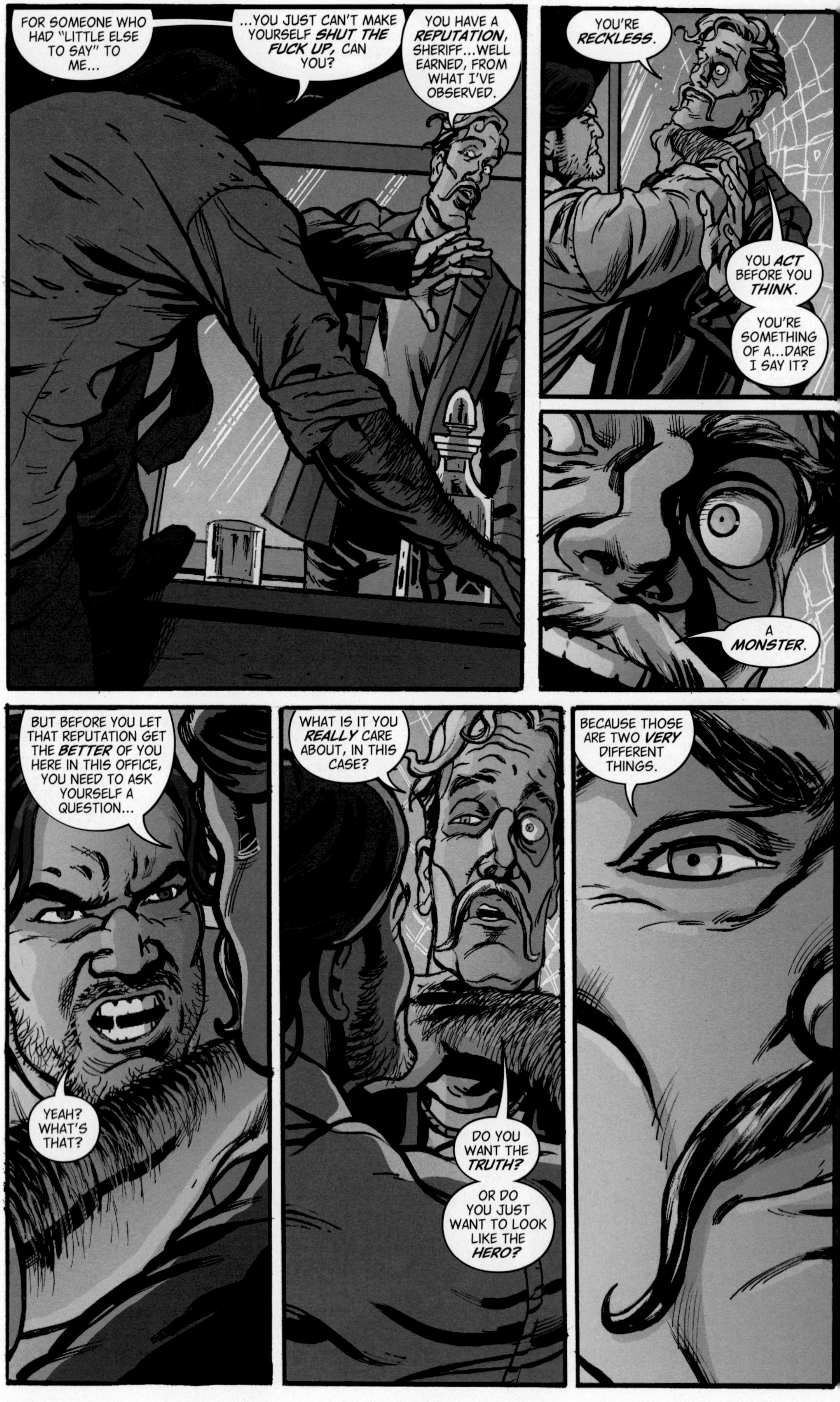
FOR SOMEONE WHO HAD "LITTLE ELSE TO SAY" TO ME...
...YOU JUST CAN'T MAKE YOURSELF SHUT THE FUCK UP, CAN YOU?
YOU HAVE A REPUTATION, SHERIFF...WELL EARNED, FROM WHAT I'VE OBSERVED.
YOU'RE RECKLESS.
YOU ACT BEFORE YOU THINK.
YOU'RE SOMETHING OF A...DARE I SAY IT?
A MONSTER.
BUT BEFORE YOU LET THAT REPUTATION GET THE BETTER OF YOU HERE IN THIS OFFICE, YOU NEED TO ASK YOURSELF A QUESTION...
YEAH? WHAT'S THAT?
WHAT IS IT YOU REALLY CARE ABOUT, IN THIS CASE?
DO YOU WANT THE TRUTH?
OR DO YOU JUST WANT TO LOOK LIKE THE HERO?
BECAUSE THOSE ARE TWO VERY DIFFERENT THINGS.

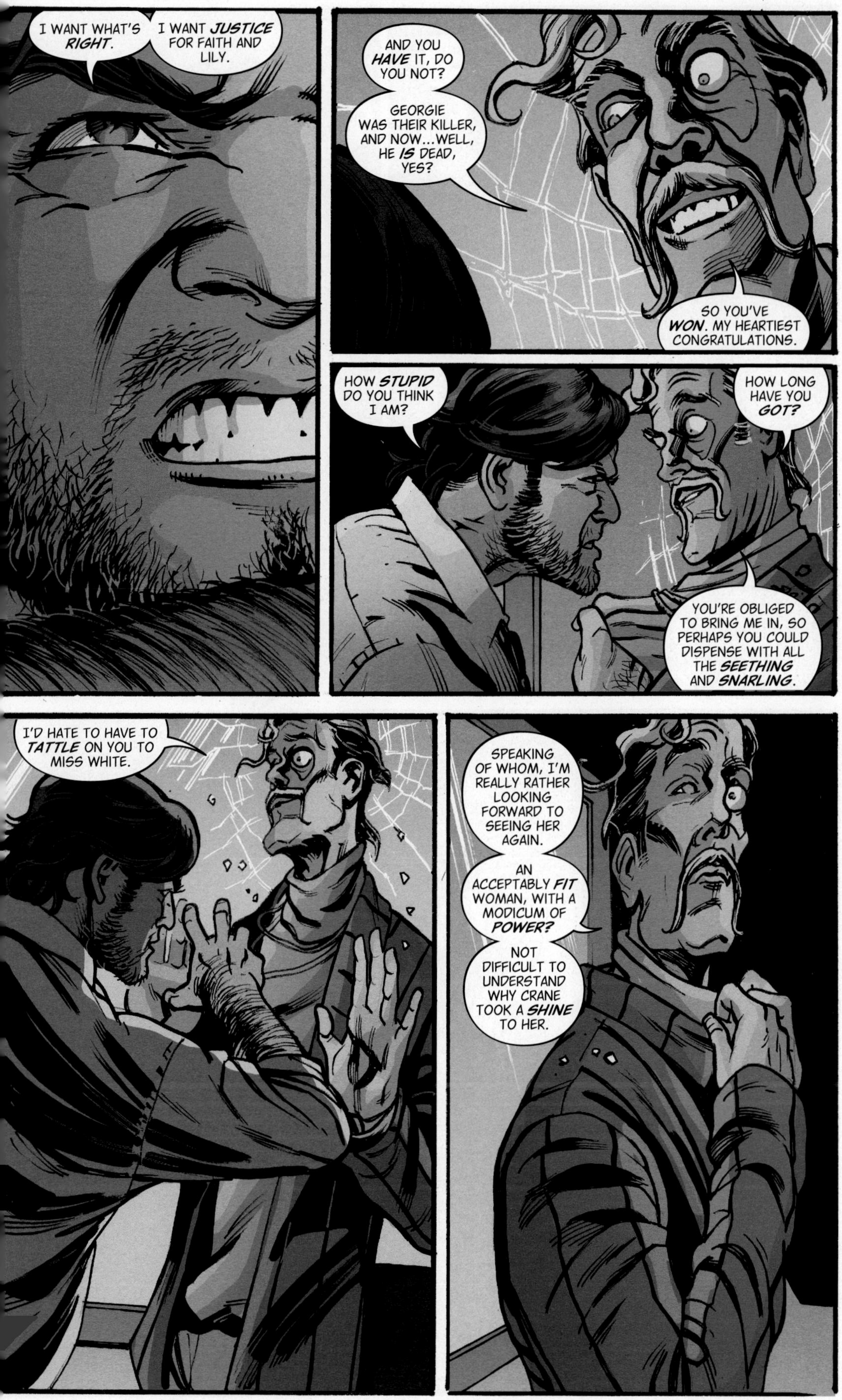
I WANT WHAT'S *RIGHT*.
I WANT *JUSTICE* FOR FAITH AND LILY.
AND YOU *HAVE* IT, DO YOU NOT?
GEORGIE WAS THEIR KILLER, AND NOW...WELL, HE *IS* DEAD, YES?
SO YOU'VE *WON*. MY HEARTIEST CONGRATULATIONS.
HOW *STUPID* DO YOU THINK I AM?
HOW LONG HAVE YOU *GOT?*
YOU'RE OBLIGED TO BRING ME IN, SO PERHAPS YOU COULD DISPENSE WITH ALL THE *SEETHING* AND *SNARLING*.
I'D HATE TO HAVE TO *TATTLE* ON YOU TO MISS WHITE.
SPEAKING OF WHOM, I'M REALLY RATHER LOOKING FORWARD TO SEEING HER AGAIN.
AN ACCEPTABLY *FIT* WOMAN, WITH A MODICUM OF *POWER?*
NOT DIFFICULT TO UNDERSTAND WHY CRANE TOOK A *SHINE* TO HER.

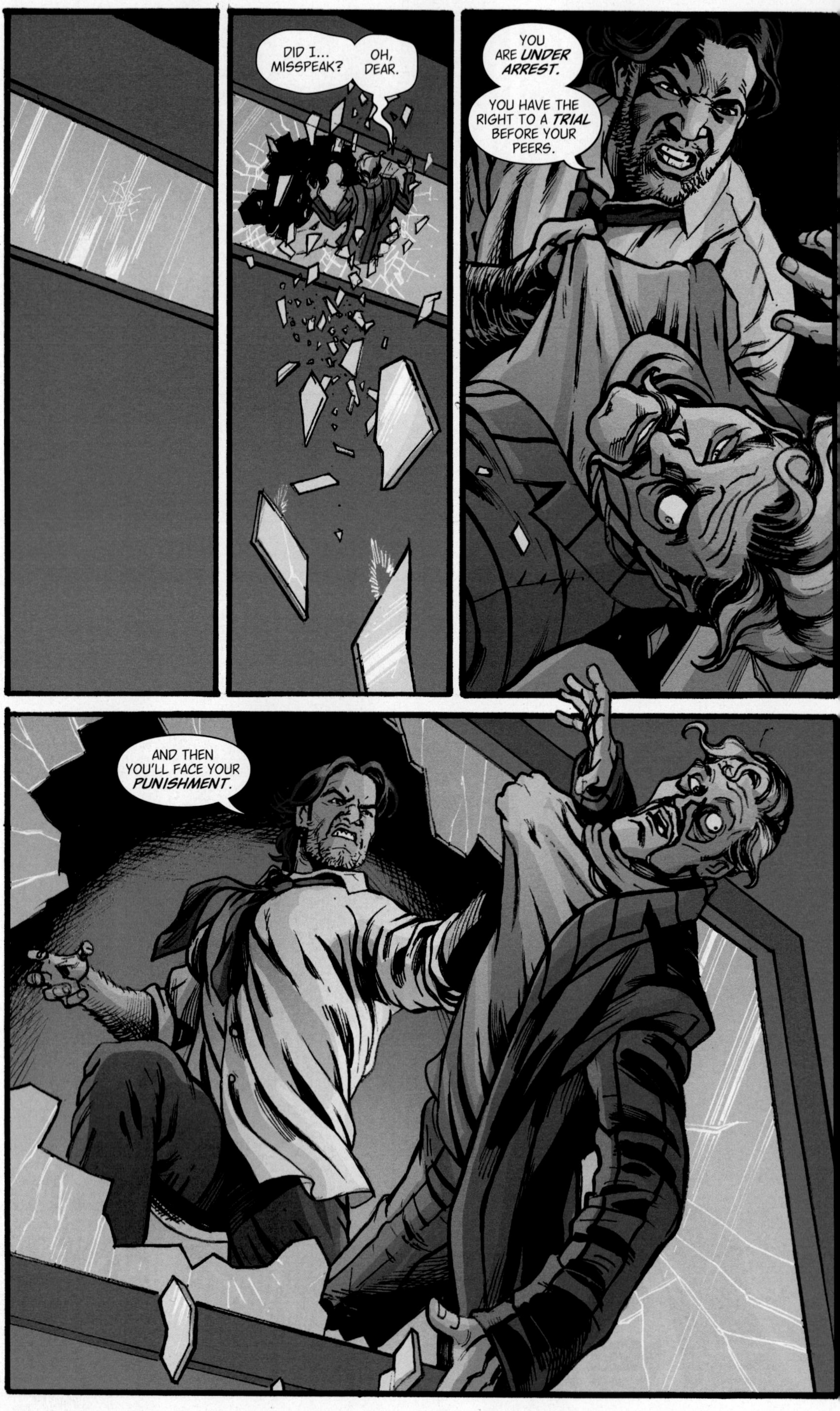
DID I... MISSPEAK?
OH, DEAR.
YOU ARE *UNDER ARREST.*
YOU HAVE THE RIGHT TO A *TRIAL* BEFORE YOUR PEERS.
AND THEN YOU'LL FACE YOUR *PUNISHMENT*.

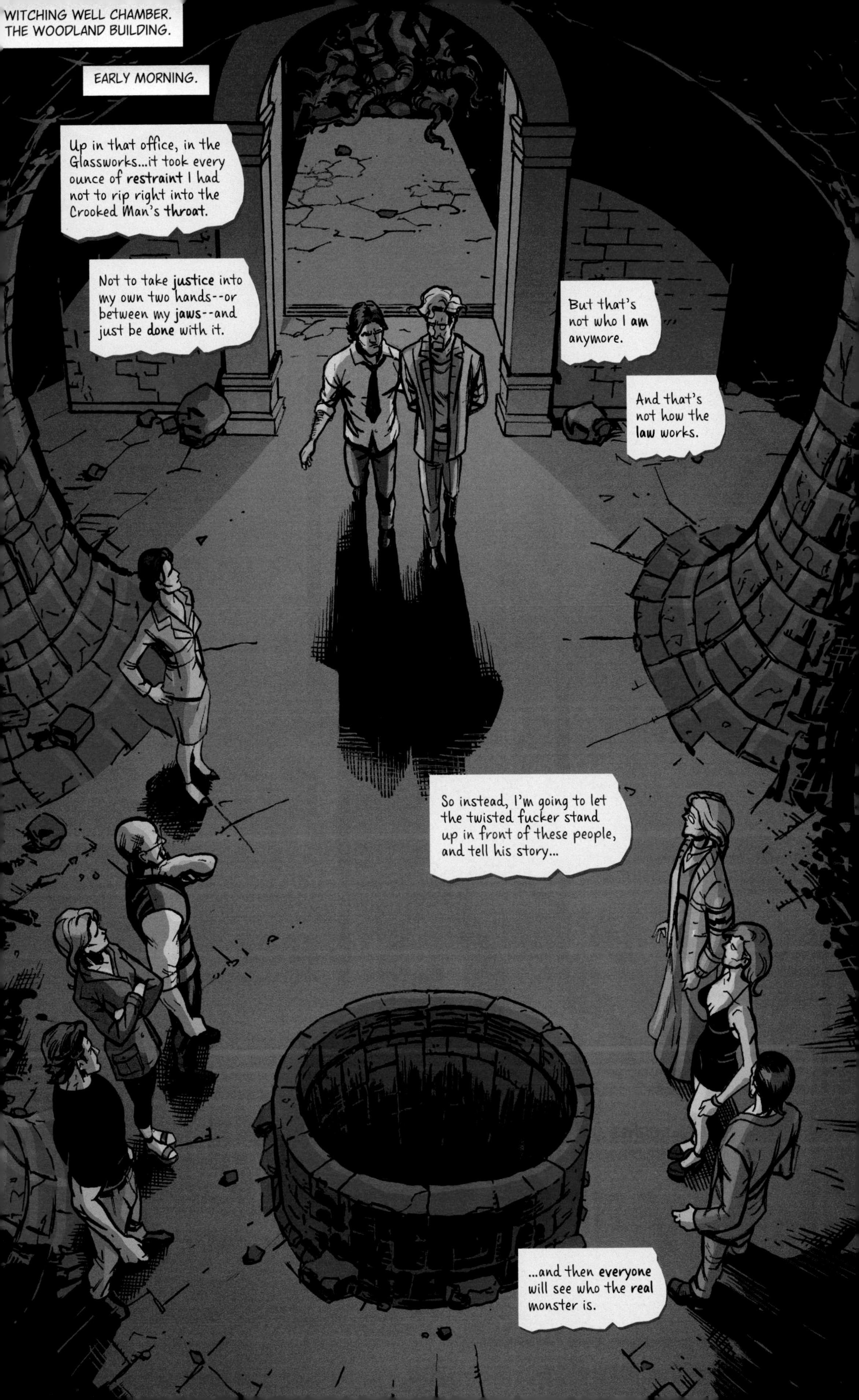
WITCHING WELL CHAMBER.
THE WOODLAND BUILDING.
EARLY MORNING.
Up in that office, in the Glassworks...it took every ounce of **restraint** I had not to rip right into the Crooked Man's **throat**.
Not to take **justice** into my own two hands--or between my **jaws**--and just be **done** with it.
But that's not who I **am** anymore.
And that's not how the **law** works.
So instead, I'm going to let the twisted fucker stand up in front of these people, and tell his story...
...and then **everyone** will see who the **real** monster is.

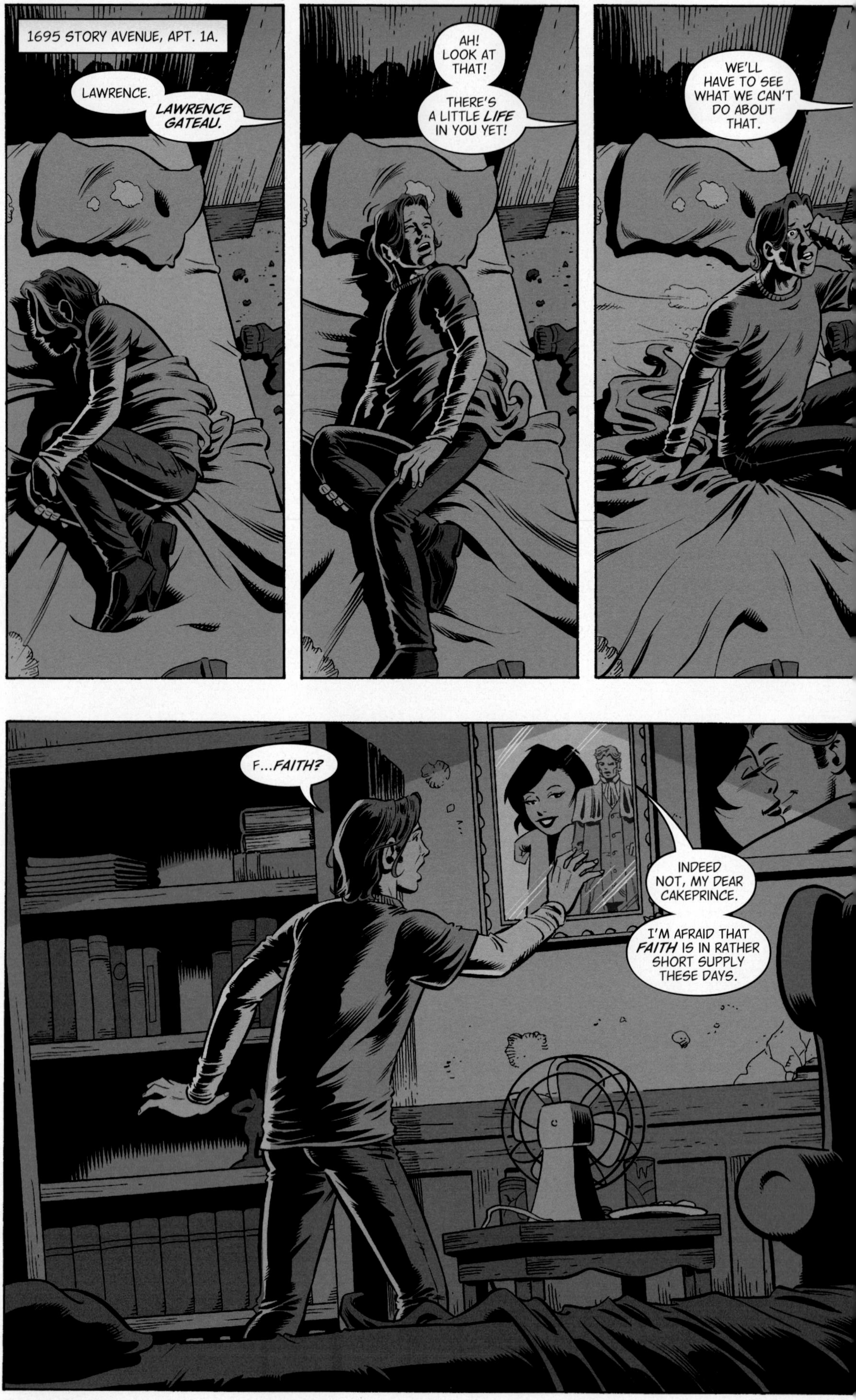
1695 STORY AVENUE, APT. 1A.
LAWRENCE.
LAWRENCE GATEAU.
AH! LOOK AT THAT!
THERE'S A LITTLE LIFE IN YOU YET!
WE'LL HAVE TO SEE WHAT WE CAN'T DO ABOUT THAT.
F...FAITH?
INDEED NOT, MY DEAR CAKEPRINCE.
I'M AFRAID THAT FAITH IS IN RATHER SHORT SUPPLY THESE DAYS.

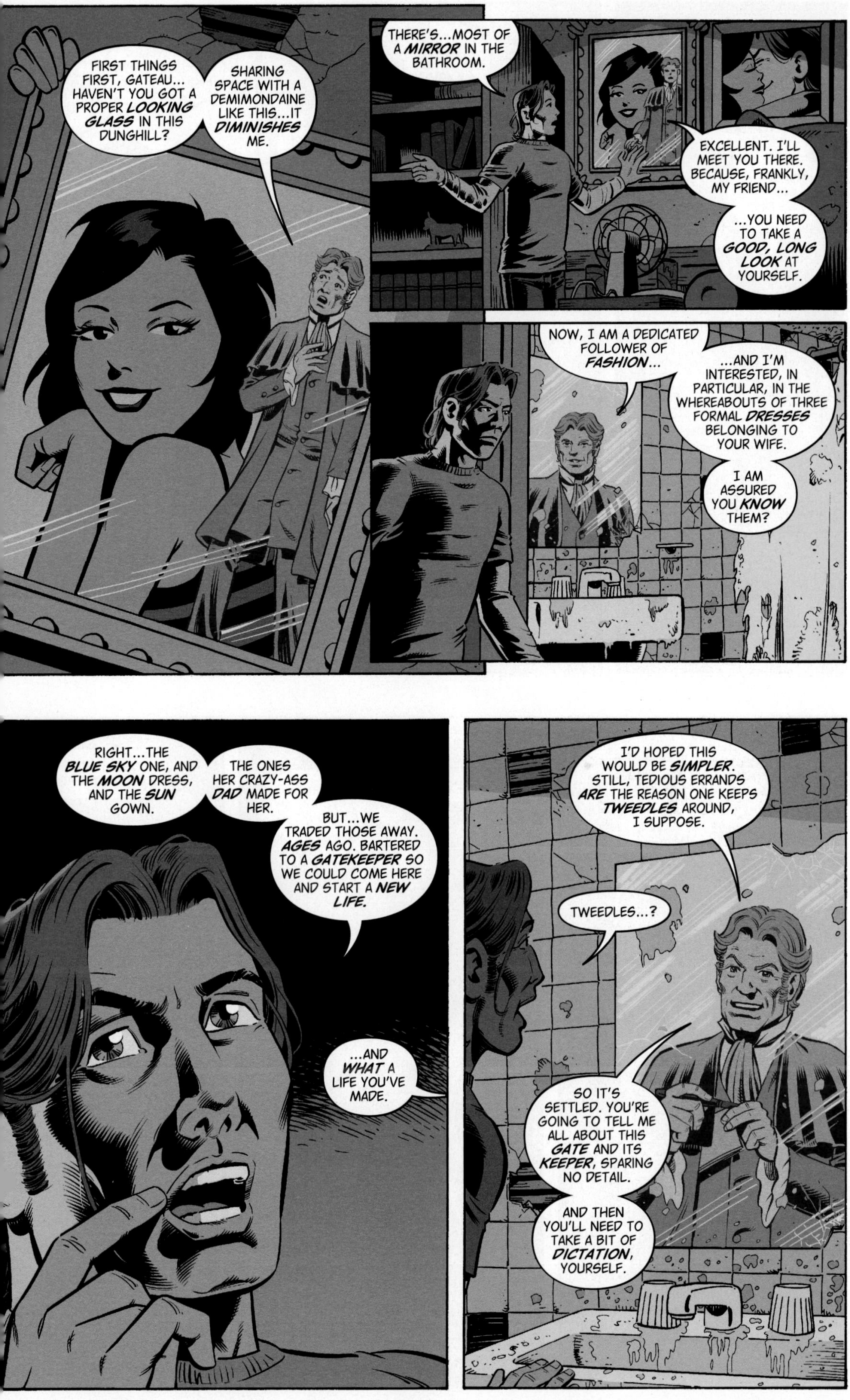
FIRST THINGS FIRST, GATEAU... HAVEN'T YOU GOT A PROPER LOOKING GLASS IN THIS DUNGHILL?
SHARING SPACE WITH A DEMIMONDAINE LIKE THIS...IT DIMINISHES ME.
THERE'S...MOST OF A MIRROR IN THE BATHROOM.
EXCELLENT. I'LL MEET YOU THERE. BECAUSE, FRANKLY, MY FRIEND...
...YOU NEED TO TAKE A GOOD, LONG LOOK AT YOURSELF.
NOW, I AM A DEDICATED FOLLOWER OF FASHION...
...AND I'M INTERESTED, IN PARTICULAR, IN THE WHEREABOUTS OF THREE FORMAL DRESSES BELONGING TO YOUR WIFE.
I AM ASSURED YOU KNOW THEM?
RIGHT...THE BLUE SKY ONE, AND THE MOON DRESS, AND THE SUN GOWN.
THE ONES HER CRAZY-ASS DAD MADE FOR HER.
BUT...WE TRADED THOSE AWAY. AGES AGO. BARTERED TO A GATEKEEPER SO WE COULD COME HERE AND START A NEW LIFE.
...AND WHAT A LIFE YOU'VE MADE.
I'D HOPED THIS WOULD BE SIMPLER. STILL, TEDIOUS ERRANDS ARE THE REASON ONE KEEPS TWEEDLES AROUND, I SUPPOSE.
TWEEDLES...?
SO IT'S SETTLED. YOU'RE GOING TO TELL ME ALL ABOUT THIS GATE AND ITS KEEPER, SPARING NO DETAIL.
AND THEN YOU'LL NEED TO TAKE A BIT OF DICTATION, YOURSELF.

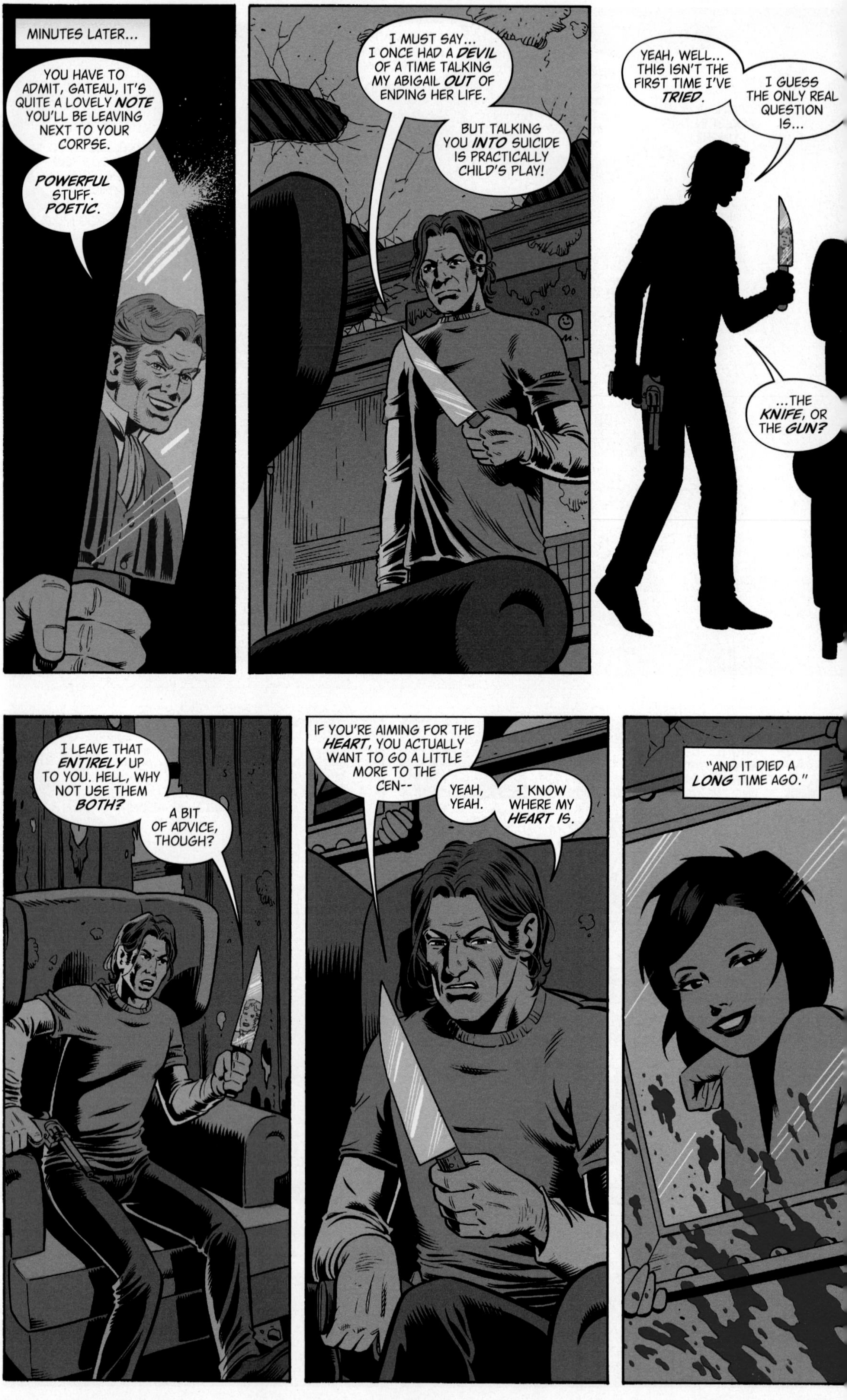
MINUTES LATER...
YOU HAVE TO ADMIT, GATEAU, IT'S QUITE A LOVELY NOTE YOU'LL BE LEAVING NEXT TO YOUR CORPSE.
POWERFUL STUFF. POETIC.
I MUST SAY... I ONCE HAD A DEVIL OF A TIME TALKING MY ABIGAIL OUT OF ENDING HER LIFE.
BUT TALKING YOU INTO SUICIDE IS PRACTICALLY CHILD'S PLAY!
YEAH, WELL... THIS ISN'T THE FIRST TIME I'VE TRIED.
I GUESS THE ONLY REAL QUESTION IS...
...THE KNIFE, OR THE GUN?
I LEAVE THAT ENTIRELY UP TO YOU. HELL, WHY NOT USE THEM BOTH?
A BIT OF ADVICE, THOUGH?
IF YOU'RE AIMING FOR THE HEART, YOU ACTUALLY WANT TO GO A LITTLE MORE TO THE CEN--
YEAH, YEAH.
I KNOW WHERE MY HEART IS.
"AND IT DIED A LONG TIME AGO."

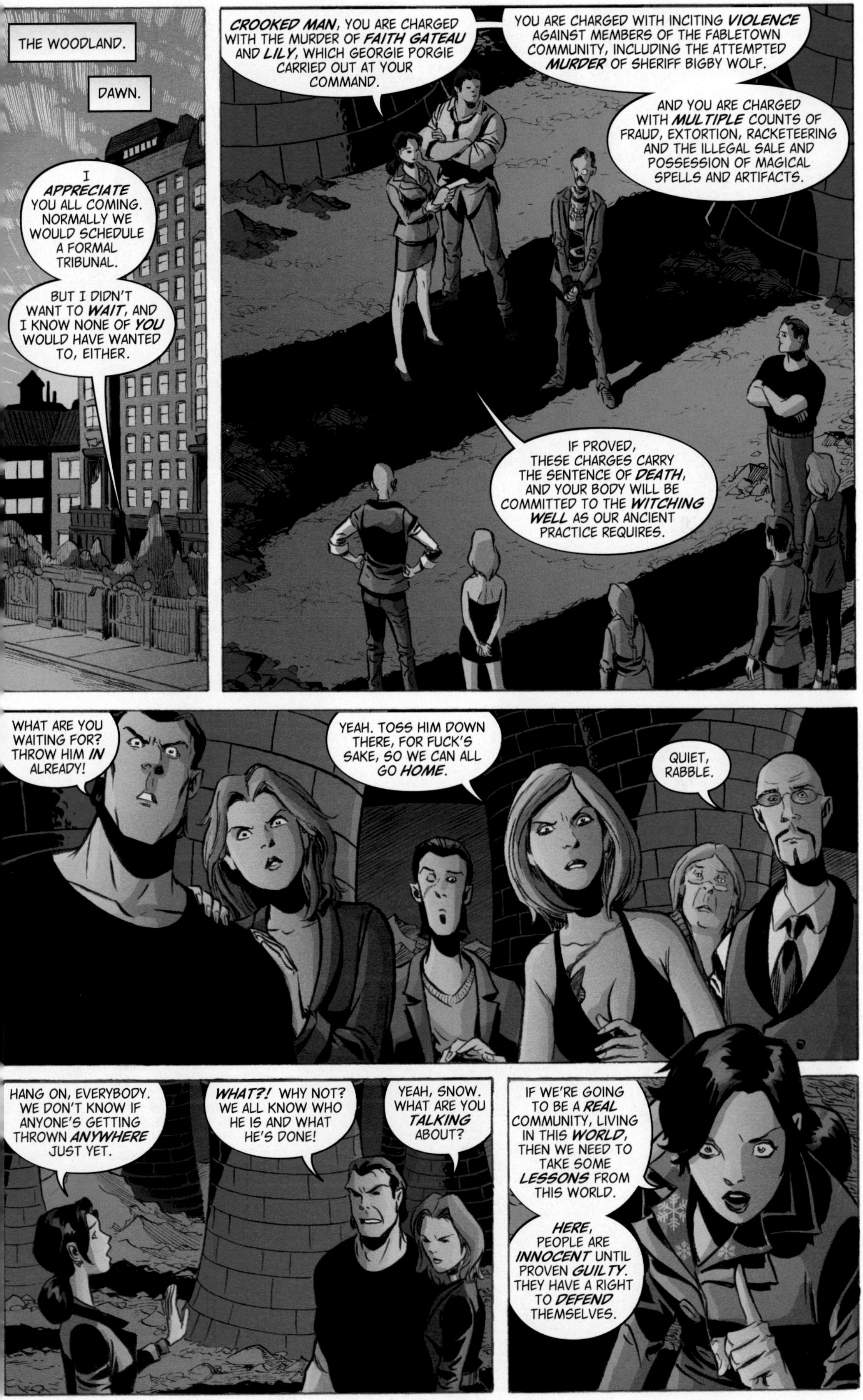
THE WOODLAND.
DAWN.
I APPRECIATE YOU ALL COMING. NORMALLY WE WOULD SCHEDULE A FORMAL TRIBUNAL.
BUT I DIDN'T WANT TO WAIT, AND I KNOW NONE OF YOU WOULD HAVE WANTED TO, EITHER.
CROOKED MAN, YOU ARE CHARGED WITH THE MURDER OF FAITH GATEAU AND LILY, WHICH GEORGIE PORGIE CARRIED OUT AT YOUR COMMAND.
YOU ARE CHARGED WITH INCITING VIOLENCE AGAINST MEMBERS OF THE FABLETOWN COMMUNITY, INCLUDING THE ATTEMPTED MURDER OF SHERIFF BIGBY WOLF.
AND YOU ARE CHARGED WITH MULTIPLE COUNTS OF FRAUD, EXTORTION, RACKETEERING AND THE ILLEGAL SALE AND POSSESSION OF MAGICAL SPELLS AND ARTIFACTS.
IF PROVED, THESE CHARGES CARRY THE SENTENCE OF DEATH, AND YOUR BODY WILL BE COMMITTED TO THE WITCHING WELL AS OUR ANCIENT PRACTICE REQUIRES.
WHAT ARE YOU WAITING FOR? THROW HIM IN ALREADY!
YEAH. TOSS HIM DOWN THERE, FOR FUCK'S SAKE, SO WE CAN ALL GO HOME.
QUIET, RABBLE.
HANG ON, EVERYBODY. WE DON'T KNOW IF ANYONE'S GETTING THROWN ANYWHERE JUST YET.
WHAT?! WHY NOT? WE ALL KNOW WHO HE IS AND WHAT HE'S DONE!
YEAH, SNOW. WHAT ARE YOU TALKING ABOUT?
IF WE'RE GOING TO BE A REAL COMMUNITY, LIVING IN THIS WORLD, THEN WE NEED TO TAKE SOME LESSONS FROM THIS WORLD.
HERE, PEOPLE ARE INNOCENT UNTIL PROVEN GUILTY. THEY HAVE A RIGHT TO DEFEND THEMSELVES.

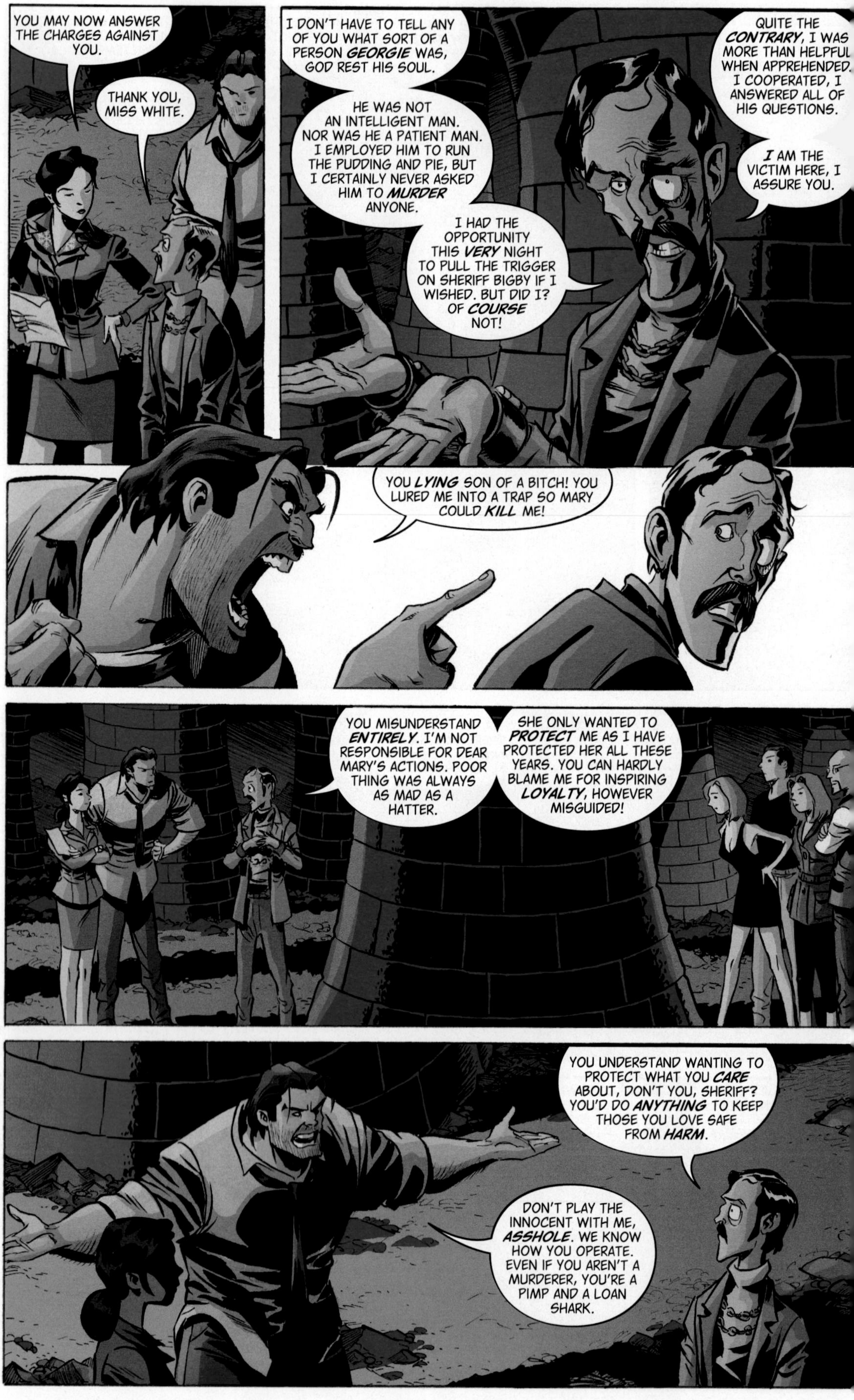
YOU MAY NOW ANSWER THE CHARGES AGAINST YOU.
THANK YOU, MISS WHITE.
I DON'T HAVE TO TELL ANY OF YOU WHAT SORT OF A PERSON GEORGIE WAS, GOD REST HIS SOUL.
HE WAS NOT AN INTELLIGENT MAN. NOR WAS HE A PATIENT MAN. I EMPLOYED HIM TO RUN THE PUDDING AND PIE, BUT I CERTAINLY NEVER ASKED HIM TO MURDER ANYONE.
I HAD THE OPPORTUNITY THIS VERY NIGHT TO PULL THE TRIGGER ON SHERIFF BIGBY IF I WISHED. BUT DID I? OF COURSE NOT!
QUITE THE CONTRARY, I WAS MORE THAN HELPFUL WHEN APPREHENDED. I COOPERATED, I ANSWERED ALL OF HIS QUESTIONS.
I AM THE VICTIM HERE, I ASSURE YOU.
YOU LYING SON OF A BITCH! YOU LURED ME INTO A TRAP SO MARY COULD KILL ME!
YOU MISUNDERSTAND ENTIRELY. I'M NOT RESPONSIBLE FOR DEAR MARY'S ACTIONS. POOR THING WAS ALWAYS AS MAD AS A HATTER.
SHE ONLY WANTED TO PROTECT ME AS I HAVE PROTECTED HER ALL THESE YEARS. YOU CAN HARDLY BLAME ME FOR INSPIRING LOYALTY, HOWEVER MISGUIDED!
YOU UNDERSTAND WANTING TO PROTECT WHAT YOU CARE ABOUT, DON'T YOU, SHERIFF? YOU'D DO ANYTHING TO KEEP THOSE YOU LOVE SAFE FROM HARM.
DON'T PLAY THE INNOCENT WITH ME, ASSHOLE. WE KNOW HOW YOU OPERATE. EVEN IF YOU AREN'T A MURDERER, YOU'RE A PIMP AND A LOAN SHARK.

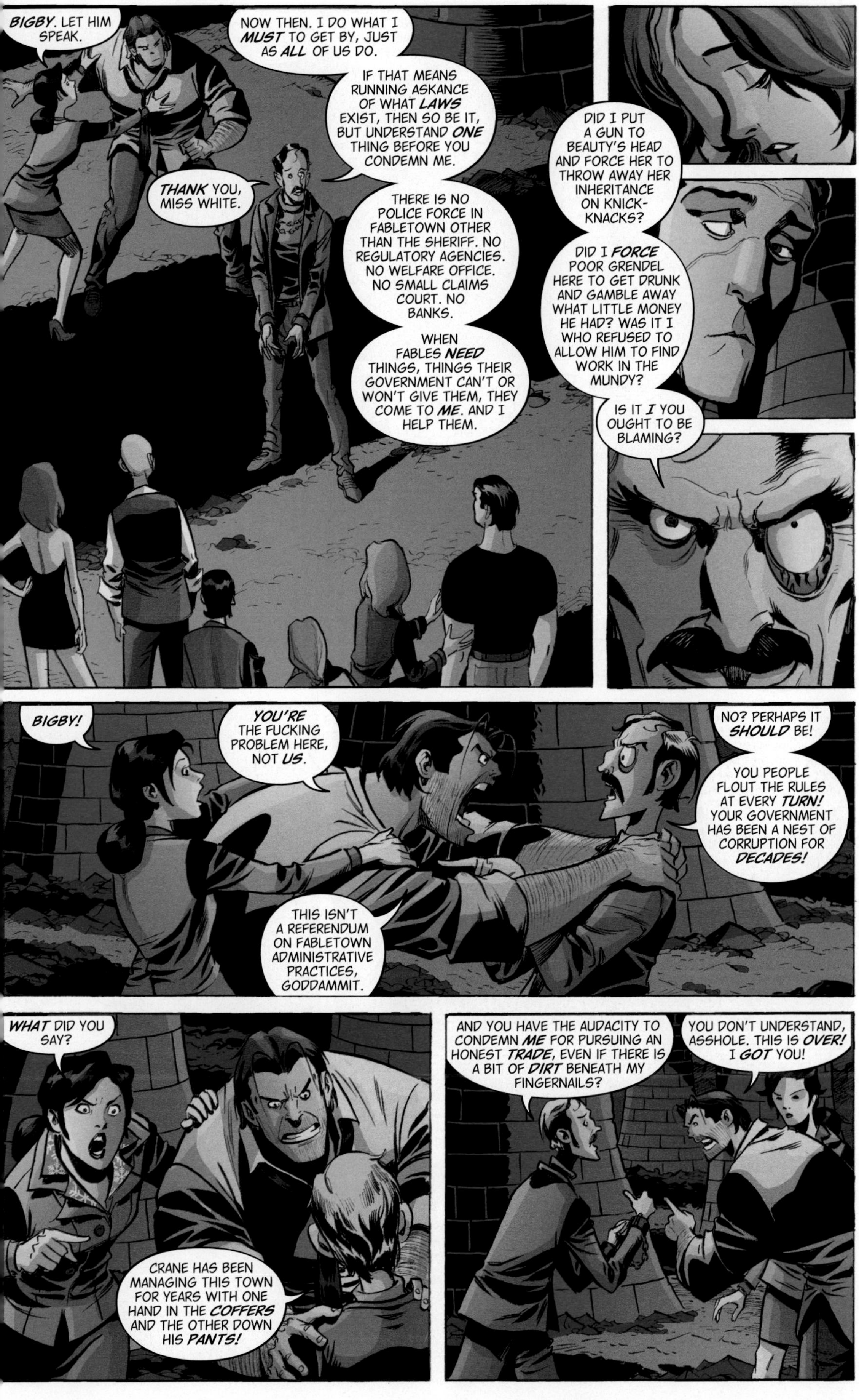
BIGBY. LET HIM SPEAK.
NOW THEN. I DO WHAT I MUST TO GET BY, JUST AS ALL OF US DO.
IF THAT MEANS RUNNING ASKANCE OF WHAT LAWS EXIST, THEN SO BE IT, BUT UNDERSTAND ONE THING BEFORE YOU CONDEMN ME.
THANK YOU, MISS WHITE.
THERE IS NO POLICE FORCE IN FABLETOWN OTHER THAN THE SHERIFF. NO REGULATORY AGENCIES. NO WELFARE OFFICE. NO SMALL CLAIMS COURT. NO BANKS.
WHEN FABLES NEED THINGS, THINGS THEIR GOVERNMENT CAN'T OR WON'T GIVE THEM, THEY COME TO ME. AND I HELP THEM.
DID I PUT A GUN TO BEAUTY'S HEAD AND FORCE HER TO THROW AWAY HER INHERITANCE ON KNICK-KNACKS?
DID I FORCE POOR GRENDEL HERE TO GET DRUNK AND GAMBLE AWAY WHAT LITTLE MONEY HE HAD? WAS IT I WHO REFUSED TO ALLOW HIM TO FIND WORK IN THE MUNDY?
IS IT I YOU OUGHT TO BE BLAMING?
BIGBY!
YOU'RE THE FUCKING PROBLEM HERE, NOT US.
NO? PERHAPS IT SHOULD BE!
YOU PEOPLE FLOUT THE RULES AT EVERY TURN! YOUR GOVERNMENT HAS BEEN A NEST OF CORRUPTION FOR DECADES!
THIS ISN'T A REFERENDUM ON FABLETOWN ADMINISTRATIVE PRACTICES, GODDAMMIT.
WHAT DID YOU SAY?
CRANE HAS BEEN MANAGING THIS TOWN FOR YEARS WITH ONE HAND IN THE COFFERS AND THE OTHER DOWN HIS PANTS!
AND YOU HAVE THE AUDACITY TO CONDEMN ME FOR PURSUING AN HONEST TRADE, EVEN IF THERE IS A BIT OF DIRT BENEATH MY FINGERNAILS?
YOU DON'T UNDERSTAND, ASSHOLE. THIS IS OVER! I GOT YOU!

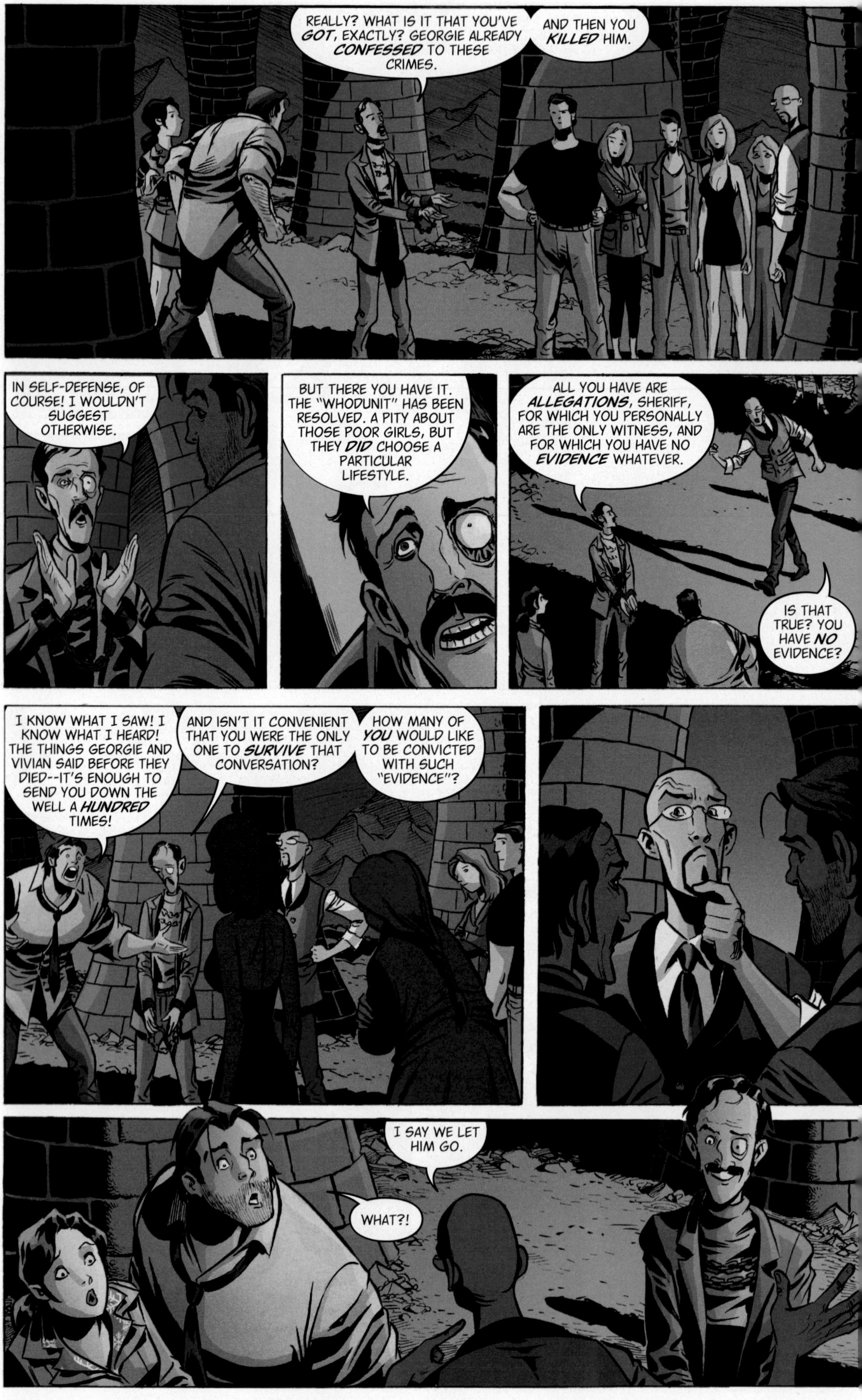
REALLY? WHAT IS IT THAT YOU'VE GOT, EXACTLY? GEORGIE ALREADY CONFESSED TO THESE CRIMES.
AND THEN YOU KILLED HIM.
IN SELF-DEFENSE, OF COURSE! I WOULDN'T SUGGEST OTHERWISE.
BUT THERE YOU HAVE IT. THE "WHODUNIT" HAS BEEN RESOLVED. A PITY ABOUT THOSE POOR GIRLS, BUT THEY DID CHOOSE A PARTICULAR LIFESTYLE.
ALL YOU HAVE ARE ALLEGATIONS, SHERIFF, FOR WHICH YOU PERSONALLY ARE THE ONLY WITNESS, AND FOR WHICH YOU HAVE NO EVIDENCE WHATEVER.
IS THAT TRUE? YOU HAVE NO EVIDENCE?
I KNOW WHAT I SAW! I KNOW WHAT I HEARD! THE THINGS GEORGIE AND VIVIAN SAID BEFORE THEY DIED--IT'S ENOUGH TO SEND YOU DOWN THE WELL A HUNDRED TIMES!
AND ISN'T IT CONVENIENT THAT YOU WERE THE ONLY ONE TO SURVIVE THAT CONVERSATION?
HOW MANY OF YOU WOULD LIKE TO BE CONVICTED WITH SUCH "EVIDENCE"?
I SAY WE LET HIM GO.
WHAT?!

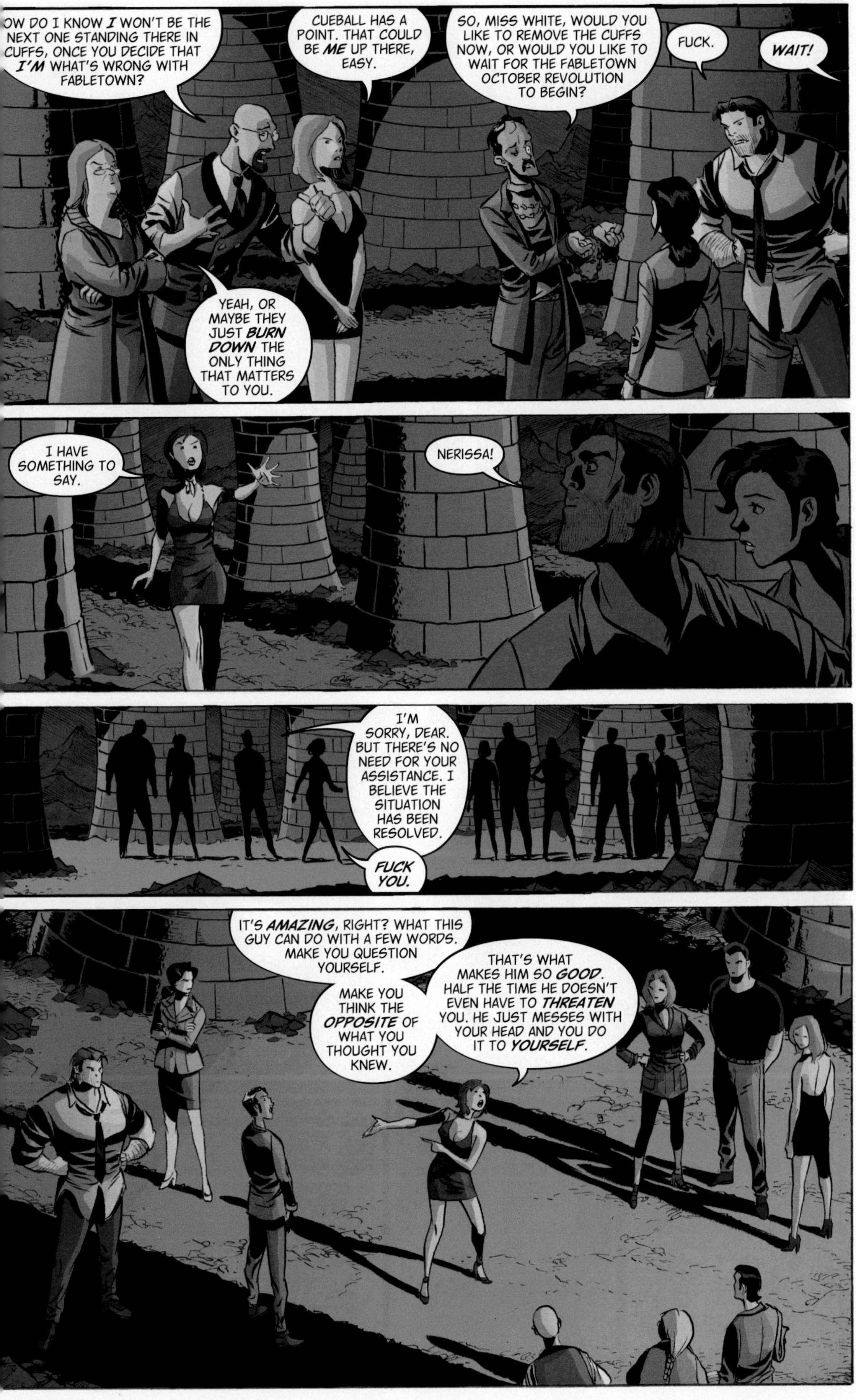
OW DO I KNOW I WON'T BE THE NEXT ONE STANDING THERE IN CUFFS, ONCE YOU DECIDE THAT I'M WHAT'S WRONG WITH FABLETOWN?
YEAH, OR MAYBE THEY JUST BURN DOWN THE ONLY THING THAT MATTERS TO YOU.
CUEBALL HAS A POINT. THAT COULD BE ME UP THERE, EASY.
SO, MISS WHITE, WOULD YOU LIKE TO REMOVE THE CUFFS NOW, OR WOULD YOU LIKE TO WAIT FOR THE FABLETOWN OCTOBER REVOLUTION TO BEGIN?
FUCK.
WAIT!
I HAVE SOMETHING TO SAY.
NERISSA!
I'M SORRY, DEAR. BUT THERE'S NO NEED FOR YOUR ASSISTANCE. I BELIEVE THE SITUATION HAS BEEN RESOLVED.
FUCK YOU.
IT'S AMAZING, RIGHT? WHAT THIS GUY CAN DO WITH A FEW WORDS. MAKE YOU QUESTION YOURSELF.
MAKE YOU THINK THE OPPOSITE OF WHAT YOU THOUGHT YOU KNEW.
THAT'S WHAT MAKES HIM SO GOOD. HALF THE TIME HE DOESN'T EVEN HAVE TO THREATEN YOU. HE JUST MESSES WITH YOUR HEAD AND YOU DO IT TO YOURSELF.

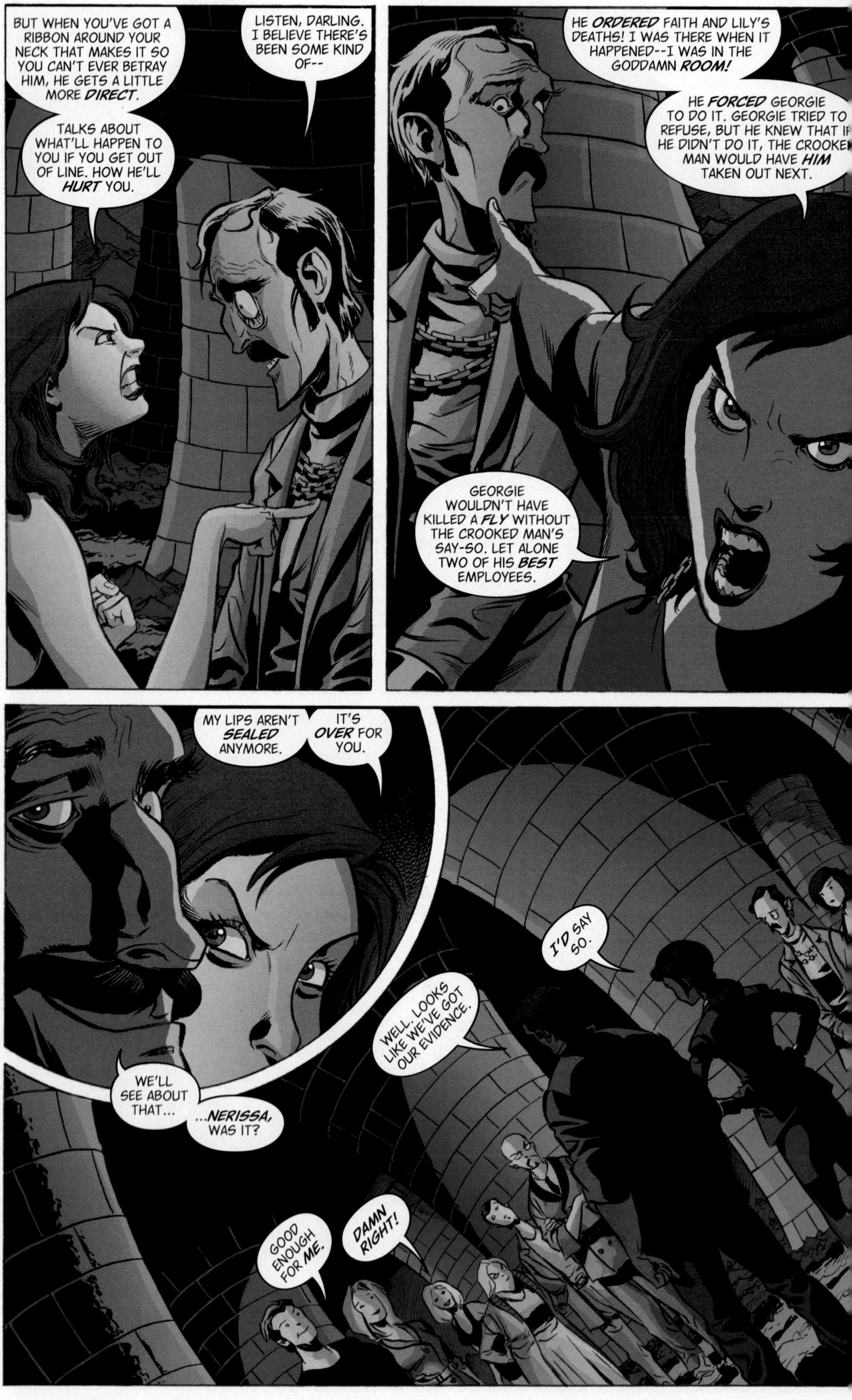

BUT WHEN YOU'VE GOT A RIBBON AROUND YOUR NECK THAT MAKES IT SO YOU CAN'T EVER BETRAY HIM, HE GETS A LITTLE MORE DIRECT.
TALKS ABOUT WHAT'LL HAPPEN TO YOU IF YOU GET OUT OF LINE. HOW HE'LL HURT YOU.
LISTEN, DARLING. I BELIEVE THERE'S BEEN SOME KIND OF--
HE ORDERED FAITH AND LILY'S DEATHS! I WAS THERE WHEN IT HAPPENED--I WAS IN THE GODDAMN ROOM!
HE FORCED GEORGIE TO DO IT. GEORGIE TRIED TO REFUSE, BUT HE KNEW THAT IF HE DIDN'T DO IT, THE CROOKED MAN WOULD HAVE HIM TAKEN OUT NEXT.
GEORGIE WOULDN'T HAVE KILLED A FLY WITHOUT THE CROOKED MAN'S SAY-SO. LET ALONE TWO OF HIS BEST EMPLOYEES.
MY LIPS AREN'T SEALED ANYMORE.
IT'S OVER FOR YOU.
WE'LL SEE ABOUT THAT...
...NERISSA, WAS IT?
I'D SAY SO.
WELL. LOOKS LIKE WE'VE GOT OUR EVIDENCE.
GOOD ENOUGH FOR ME.
DAMN RIGHT!

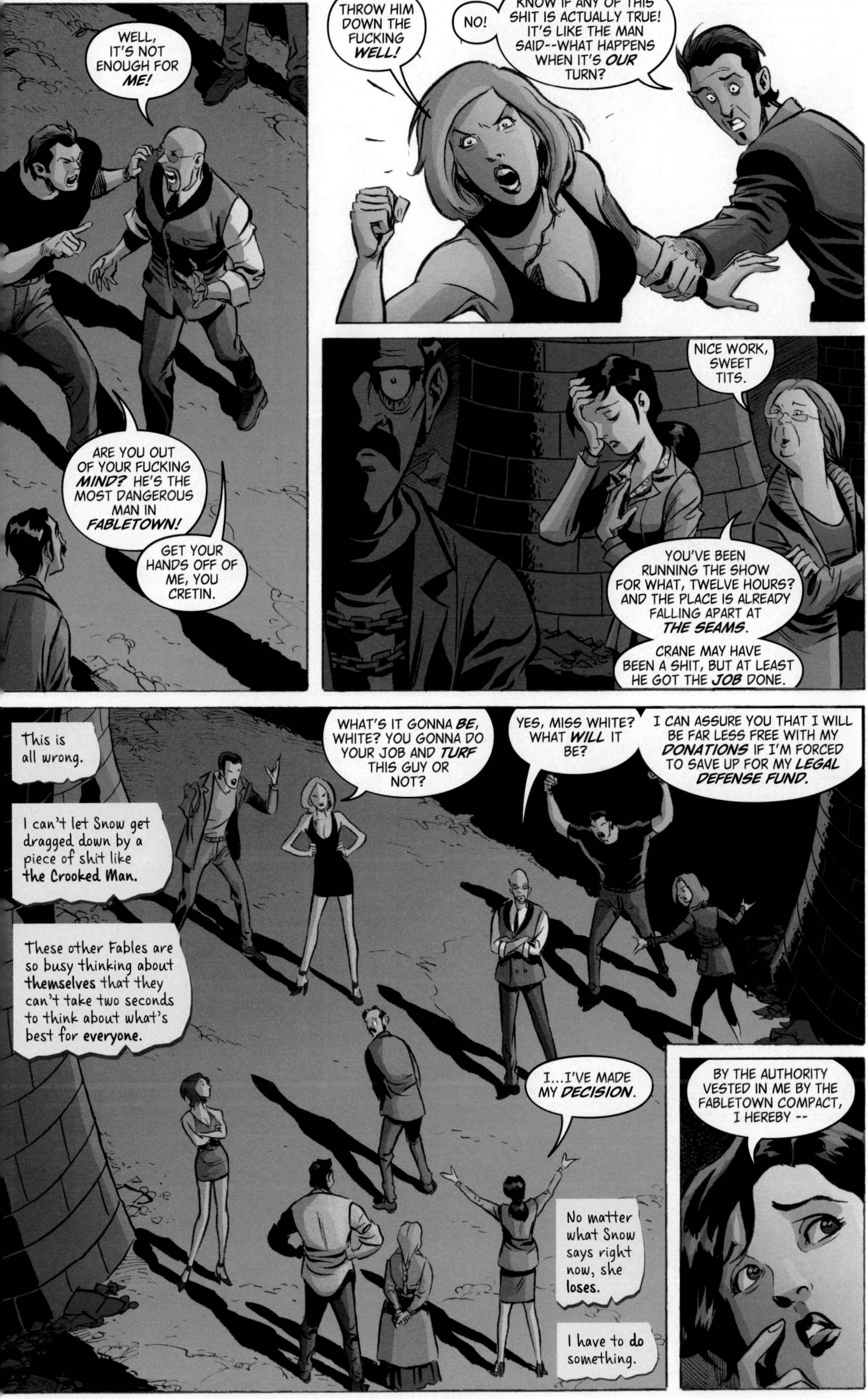

WELL, IT'S NOT ENOUGH FOR ME!
ARE YOU OUT OF YOUR FUCKING MIND? HE'S THE MOST DANGEROUS MAN IN FABLETOWN!
GET YOUR HANDS OFF OF ME, YOU CRETIN.
THROW HIM DOWN THE FUCKING WELL!
NO!
WE DON'T KNOW IF ANY OF THIS SHIT IS ACTUALLY TRUE! IT'S LIKE THE MAN SAID--WHAT HAPPENS WHEN IT'S OUR TURN?
NICE WORK, SWEET TITS.
YOU'VE BEEN RUNNING THE SHOW FOR WHAT, TWELVE HOURS? AND THE PLACE IS ALREADY FALLING APART AT THE SEAMS.
CRANE MAY HAVE BEEN A SHIT, BUT AT LEAST HE GOT THE JOB DONE.
This is all wrong.
I can't let Snow get dragged down by a piece of shit like the Crooked Man.
These other Fables are so busy thinking about themselves that they can't take two seconds to think about what's best for everyone.
WHAT'S IT GONNA BE, WHITE? YOU GONNA DO YOUR JOB AND TURF THIS GUY OR NOT?
YES, MISS WHITE? WHAT WILL IT BE?
I CAN ASSURE YOU THAT I WILL BE FAR LESS FREE WITH MY DONATIONS IF I'M FORCED TO SAVE UP FOR MY LEGAL DEFENSE FUND.
I...I'VE MADE MY DECISION.
No matter what Snow says right now, she loses.
I have to do something.
BY THE AUTHORITY VESTED IN ME BY THE FABLETOWN COMPACT, I HEREBY --

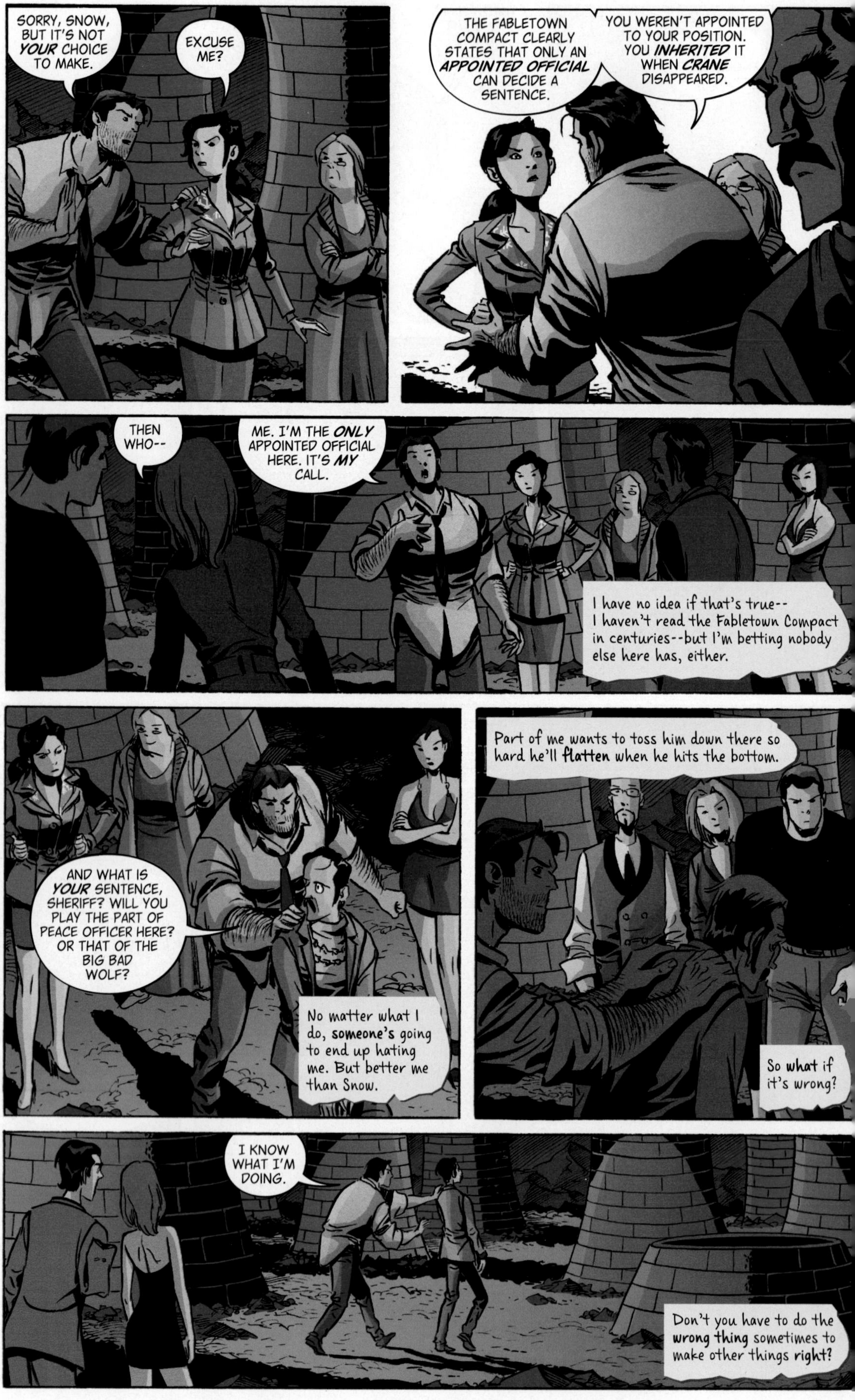
SORRY, SNOW, BUT IT'S NOT *YOUR* CHOICE TO MAKE.
EXCUSE ME?
THE FABLETOWN COMPACT CLEARLY STATES THAT ONLY AN *APPOINTED OFFICIAL* CAN DECIDE A SENTENCE.
YOU WEREN'T APPOINTED TO YOUR POSITION. YOU *INHERITED* IT WHEN *CRANE* DISAPPEARED.
THEN WHO--
ME. I'M THE *ONLY* APPOINTED OFFICIAL HERE. IT'S *MY* CALL.
I have no idea if that's true--I haven't read the Fabletown Compact in centuries--but I'm betting nobody else here has, either.
AND WHAT IS *YOUR* SENTENCE, SHERIFF? WILL YOU PLAY THE PART OF PEACE OFFICER HERE? OR THAT OF THE BIG BAD WOLF?
No matter what I do, **someone's** going to end up hating me. But better me than Snow.
Part of me wants to toss him down there so hard he'll **flatten** when he hits the bottom.
So **what** if it's wrong?
I KNOW WHAT I'M DOING.
Don't you have to do the **wrong thing** sometimes to make other things **right**?

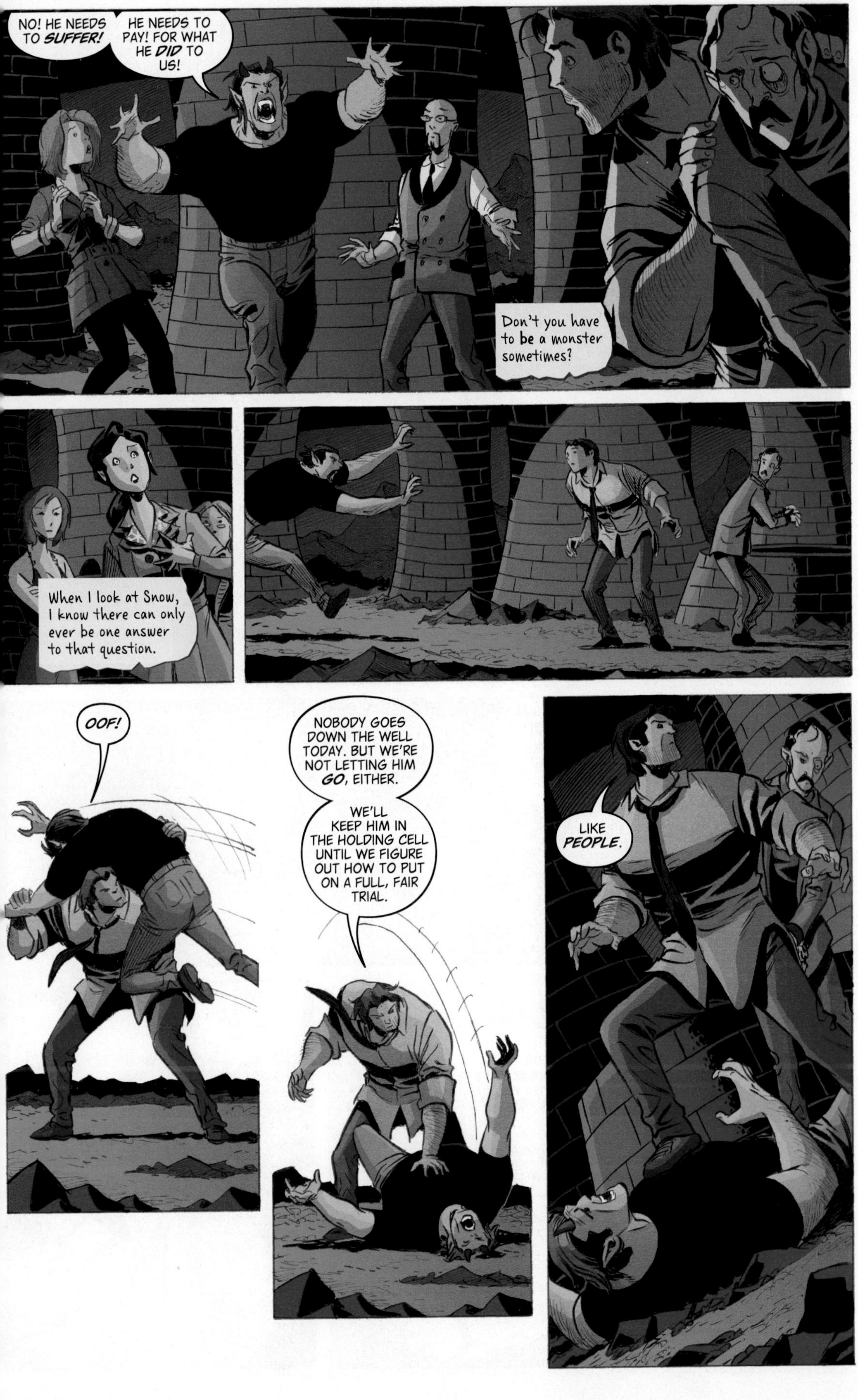
NO! HE NEEDS TO SUFFER!
HE NEEDS TO PAY! FOR WHAT HE DID TO US!
Don't you have to be a monster sometimes?
When I look at Snow, I know there can only ever be one answer to that question.
OOF!
NOBODY GOES DOWN THE WELL TODAY. BUT WE'RE NOT LETTING HIM GO, EITHER.
WE'LL KEEP HIM IN THE HOLDING CELL UNTIL WE FIGURE OUT HOW TO PUT ON A FULL, FAIR TRIAL.
LIKE PEOPLE.

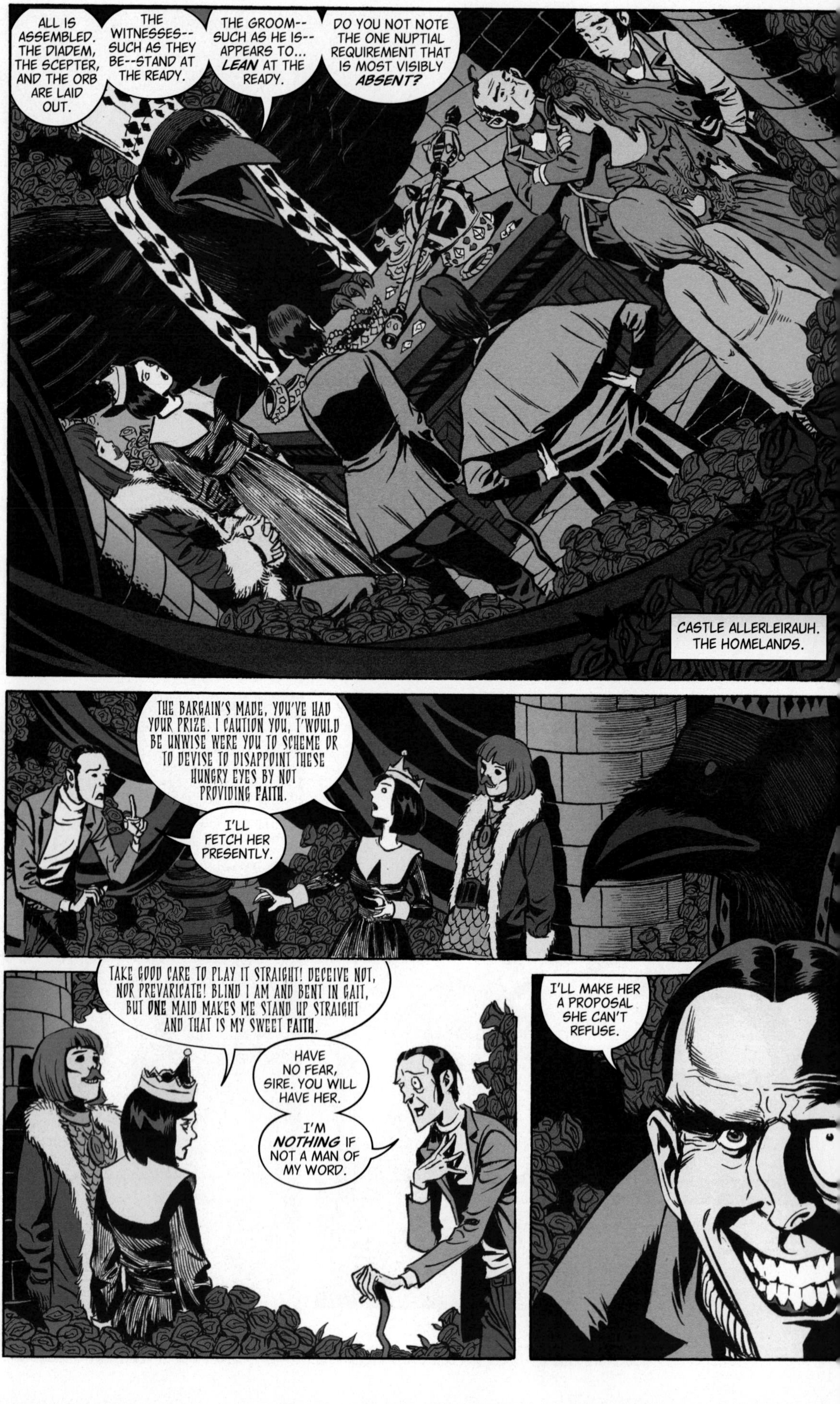
ALL IS ASSEMBLED. THE DIADEM, THE SCEPTER, AND THE ORB ARE LAID OUT.
THE WITNESSES-- SUCH AS THEY BE--STAND AT THE READY.
THE GROOM-- SUCH AS HE IS-- APPEARS TO... LEAN AT THE READY.
DO YOU NOT NOTE THE ONE NUPTIAL REQUIREMENT THAT IS MOST VISIBLY ABSENT?
CASTLE ALLERLEIRAUH. THE HOMELANDS.
THE BARGAIN'S MADE, YOU'VE HAD YOUR PRIZE. I CAUTION YOU, T'WOULD BE UNWISE WERE YOU TO SCHEME OR TO DEVISE TO DISAPPOINT THESE HUNGRY EYES BY NOT PROVIDING FAITH.
I'LL FETCH HER PRESENTLY.
TAKE GOOD CARE TO PLAY IT STRAIGHT! DECEIVE NOT, NOR PREVARICATE! BLIND I AM AND BENT IN GAIT, BUT ONE MAID MAKES ME STAND UP STRAIGHT AND THAT IS MY SWEET FAITH.
HAVE NO FEAR, SIRE. YOU WILL HAVE HER.
I'M NOTHING IF NOT A MAN OF MY WORD.
I'LL MAKE HER A PROPOSAL SHE CAN'T REFUSE.

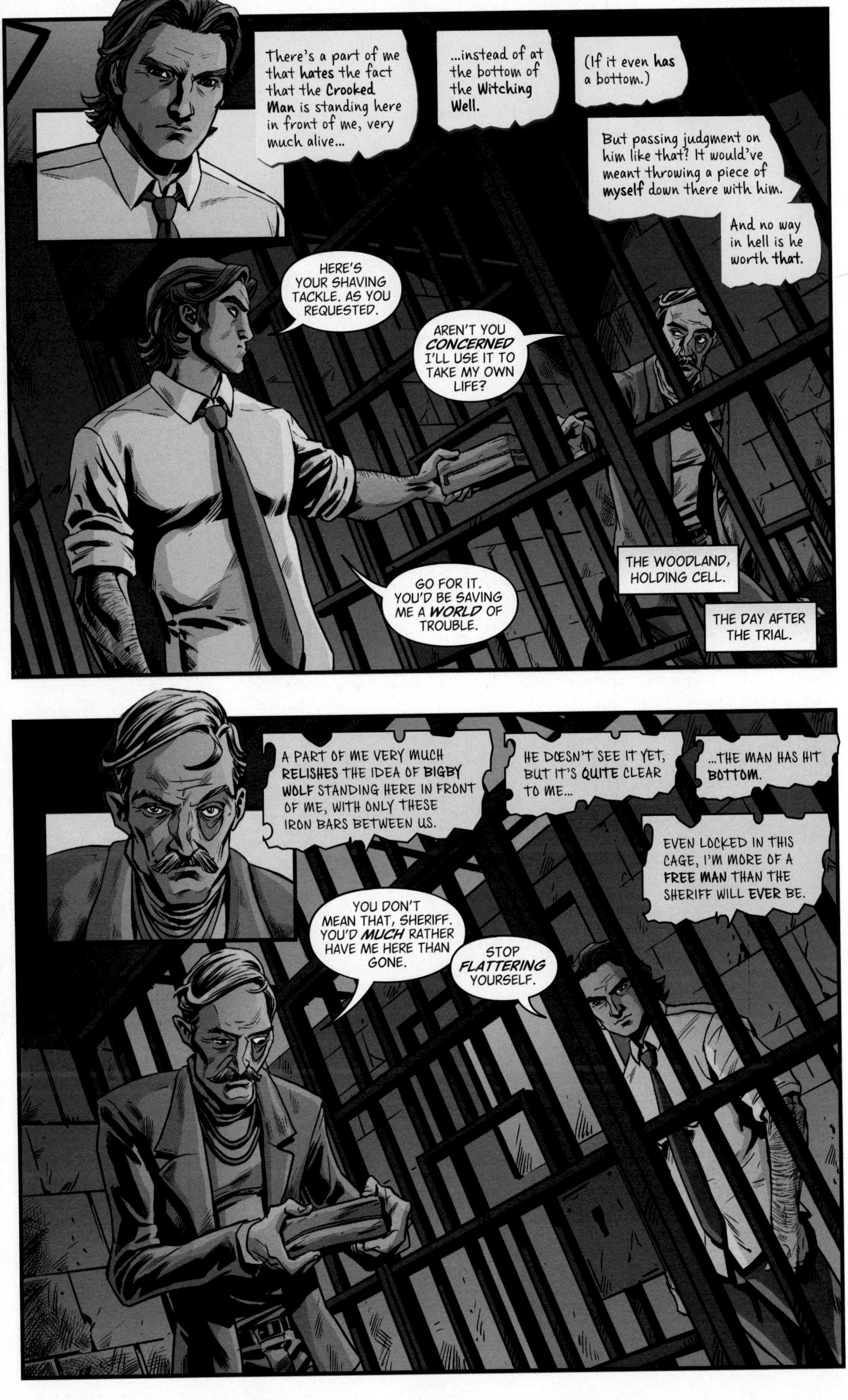
There's a part of me that hates the fact that the Crooked Man is standing here in front of me, very much alive...
...instead of at the bottom of the Witching Well.
(If it even has a bottom.)
But passing judgment on him like that? It would've meant throwing a piece of myself down there with him.
And no way in hell is he worth that.
HERE'S YOUR SHAVING TACKLE. AS YOU REQUESTED.
AREN'T YOU CONCERNED I'LL USE IT TO TAKE MY OWN LIFE?
GO FOR IT. YOU'D BE SAVING ME A WORLD OF TROUBLE.
THE WOODLAND, HOLDING CELL.
THE DAY AFTER THE TRIAL.
A PART OF ME VERY MUCH RELISHES THE IDEA OF BIGBY WOLF STANDING HERE IN FRONT OF ME, WITH ONLY THESE IRON BARS BETWEEN US.
HE DOESN'T SEE IT YET, BUT IT'S QUITE CLEAR TO ME...
...THE MAN HAS HIT BOTTOM.
EVEN LOCKED IN THIS CAGE, I'M MORE OF A FREE MAN THAN THE SHERIFF WILL EVER BE.
YOU DON'T MEAN THAT, SHERIFF. YOU'D MUCH RATHER HAVE ME HERE THAN GONE.
STOP FLATTERING YOURSELF.

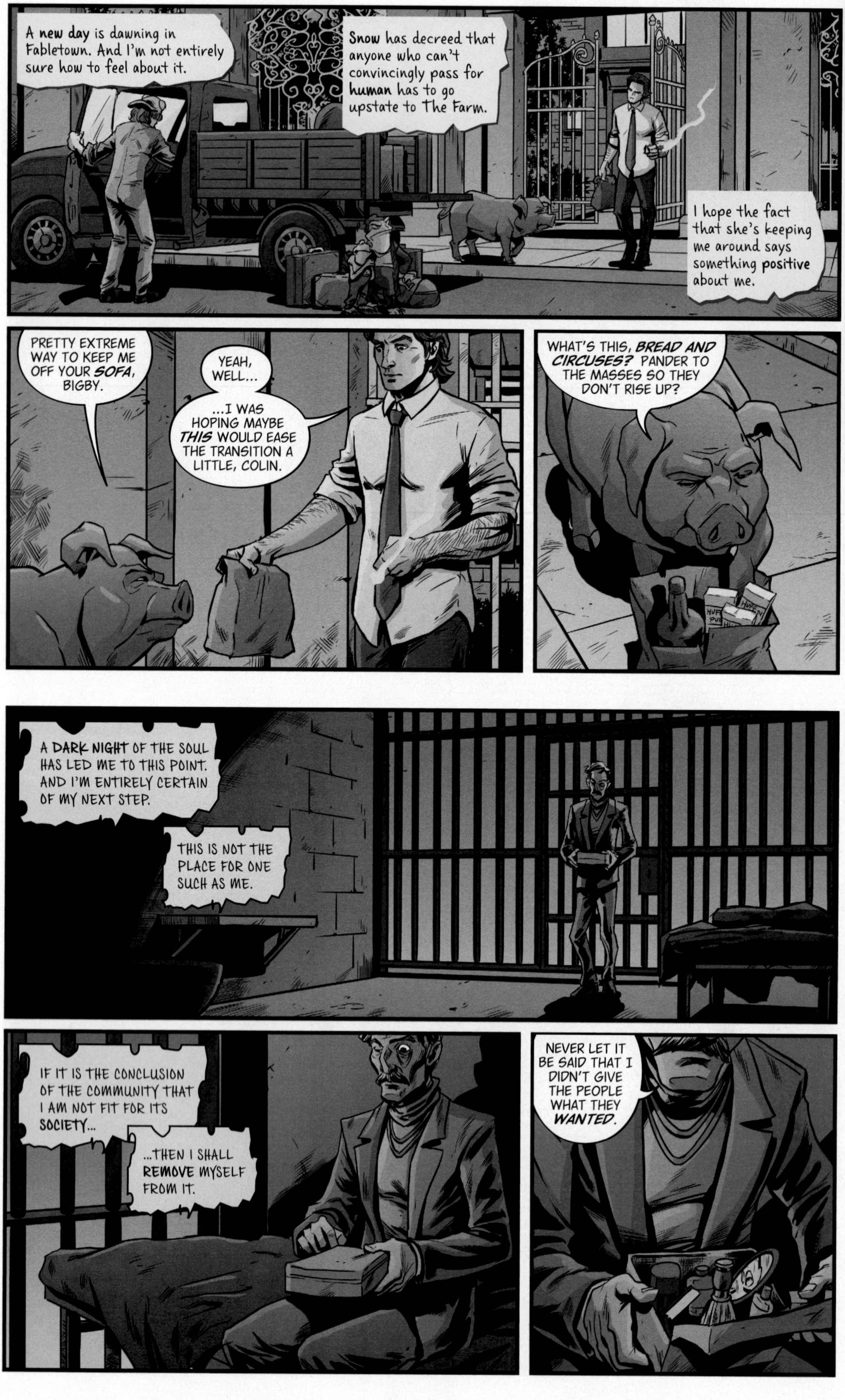

A new day is dawning in Fabletown. And I'm not entirely sure how to feel about it.
Snow has decreed that anyone who can't convincingly pass for human has to go upstate to The Farm.
I hope the fact that she's keeping me around says something positive about me.
PRETTY EXTREME WAY TO KEEP ME OFF YOUR SOFA, BIGBY.
YEAH, WELL...
...I WAS HOPING MAYBE THIS WOULD EASE THE TRANSITION A LITTLE, COLIN.
WHAT'S THIS, BREAD AND CIRCUSES? PANDER TO THE MASSES SO THEY DON'T RISE UP?
A DARK NIGHT OF THE SOUL HAS LED ME TO THIS POINT. AND I'M ENTIRELY CERTAIN OF MY NEXT STEP.
THIS IS NOT THE PLACE FOR ONE SUCH AS ME.
IF IT IS THE CONCLUSION OF THE COMMUNITY THAT I AM NOT FIT FOR ITS SOCIETY...
...THEN I SHALL REMOVE MYSELF FROM IT.
NEVER LET IT BE SAID THAT I DIDN'T GIVE THE PEOPLE WHAT THEY WANTED.

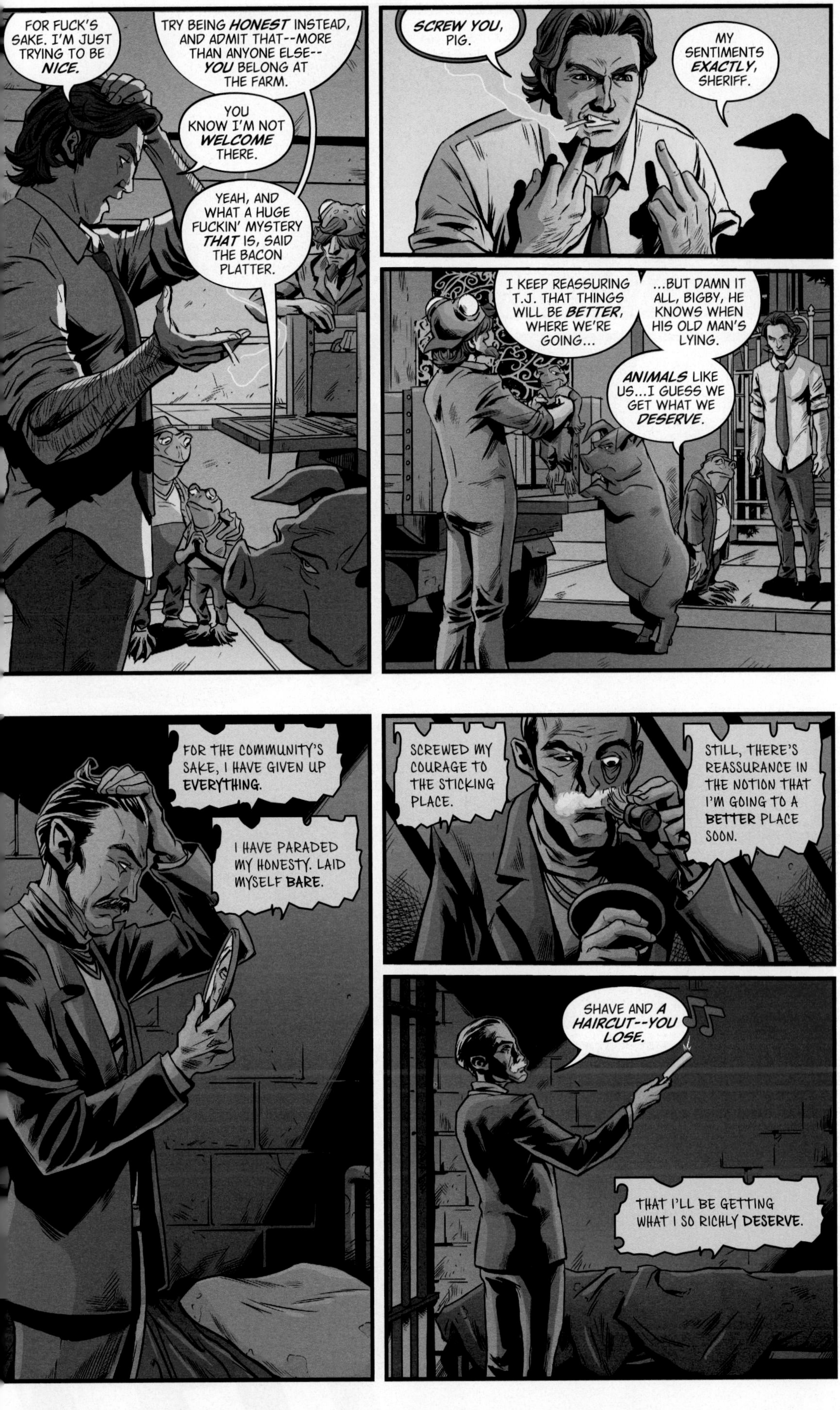
FOR FUCK'S SAKE. I'M JUST TRYING TO BE NICE.
TRY BEING HONEST INSTEAD, AND ADMIT THAT--MORE THAN ANYONE ELSE--YOU BELONG AT THE FARM.
YOU KNOW I'M NOT WELCOME THERE.
YEAH, AND WHAT A HUGE FUCKIN' MYSTERY THAT IS, SAID THE BACON PLATTER.
SCREW YOU, PIG.
MY SENTIMENTS EXACTLY, SHERIFF.
I KEEP REASSURING T.J. THAT THINGS WILL BE BETTER, WHERE WE'RE GOING...
...BUT DAMN IT ALL, BIGBY, HE KNOWS WHEN HIS OLD MAN'S LYING.
ANIMALS LIKE US...I GUESS WE GET WHAT WE DESERVE.
FOR THE COMMUNITY'S SAKE, I HAVE GIVEN UP EVERYTHING.
I HAVE PARADED MY HONESTY. LAID MYSELF BARE.
SCREWED MY COURAGE TO THE STICKING PLACE.
STILL, THERE'S REASSURANCE IN THE NOTION THAT I'M GOING TO A BETTER PLACE SOON.
SHAVE AND A HAIRCUT--YOU LOSE.
THAT I'LL BE GETTING WHAT I SO RICHLY DESERVE.

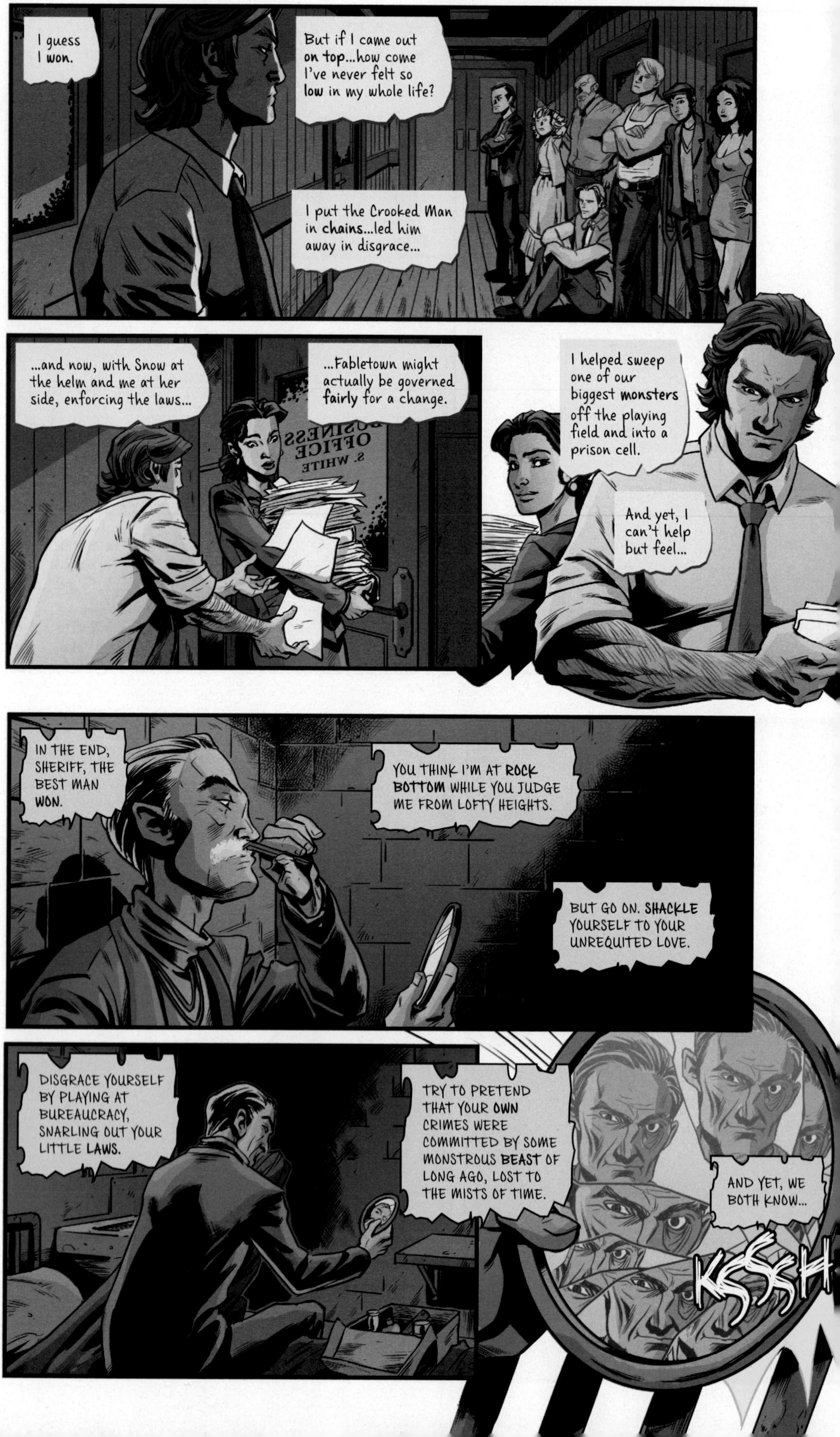

I guess I won.
But if I came out on top...how come I've never felt so low in my whole life?
I put the Crooked Man in chains...led him away in disgrace...
...and now, with Snow at the helm and me at her side, enforcing the laws...
...Fabletown might actually be governed fairly for a change.
BUSINESS OFFICE S. WHITE
I helped sweep one of our biggest monsters off the playing field and into a prison cell.
And yet, I can't help but feel...
IN THE END, SHERIFF, THE BEST MAN WON.
YOU THINK I'M AT ROCK BOTTOM WHILE YOU JUDGE ME FROM LOFTY HEIGHTS.
BUT GO ON. SHACKLE YOURSELF TO YOUR UNREQUITED LOVE.
DISGRACE YOURSELF BY PLAYING AT BUREAUCRACY, SNARLING OUT YOUR LITTLE LAWS.
TRY TO PRETEND THAT YOUR OWN CRIMES WERE COMMITTED BY SOME MONSTROUS BEAST OF LONG AGO, LOST TO THE MISTS OF TIME.
AND YET, WE BOTH KNOW...
KSSH

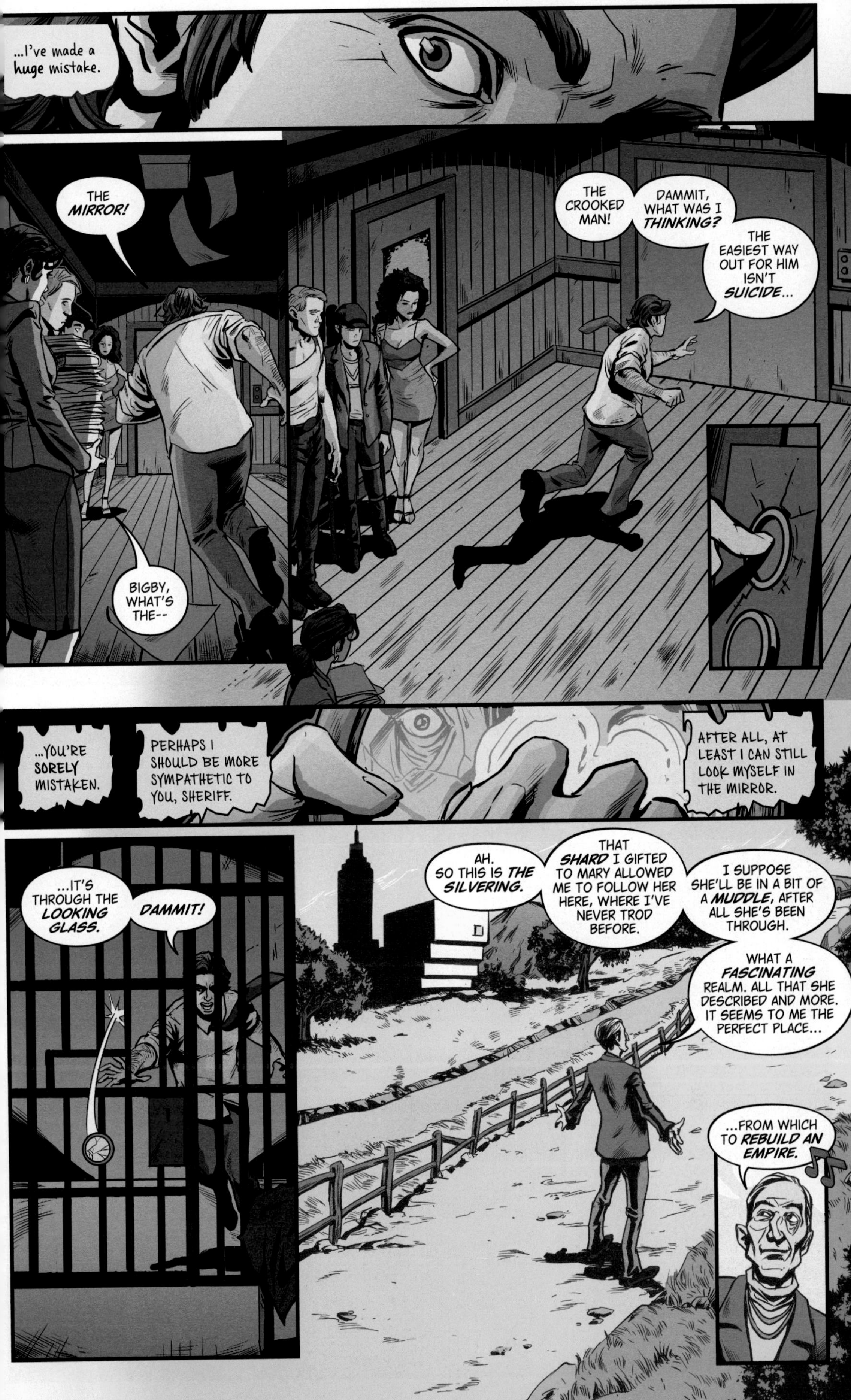
...I've made a huge mistake.
THE MIRROR!
BIGBY, WHAT'S THE--
THE CROOKED MAN!
DAMMIT, WHAT WAS I THINKING?
THE EASIEST WAY OUT FOR HIM ISN'T SUICIDE...
...YOU'RE SORELY MISTAKEN.
PERHAPS I SHOULD BE MORE SYMPATHETIC TO YOU, SHERIFF.
AFTER ALL, AT LEAST I CAN STILL LOOK MYSELF IN THE MIRROR.
...IT'S THROUGH THE LOOKING GLASS.
DAMMIT!
AH. SO THIS IS THE SILVERING.
THAT SHARD I GIFTED TO MARY ALLOWED ME TO FOLLOW HER HERE, WHERE I'VE NEVER TROD BEFORE.
I SUPPOSE SHE'LL BE IN A BIT OF A MUDDLE, AFTER ALL SHE'S BEEN THROUGH.
WHAT A FASCINATING REALM. ALL THAT SHE DESCRIBED AND MORE. IT SEEMS TO ME THE PERFECT PLACE...
...FROM WHICH TO REBUILD AN EMPIRE.

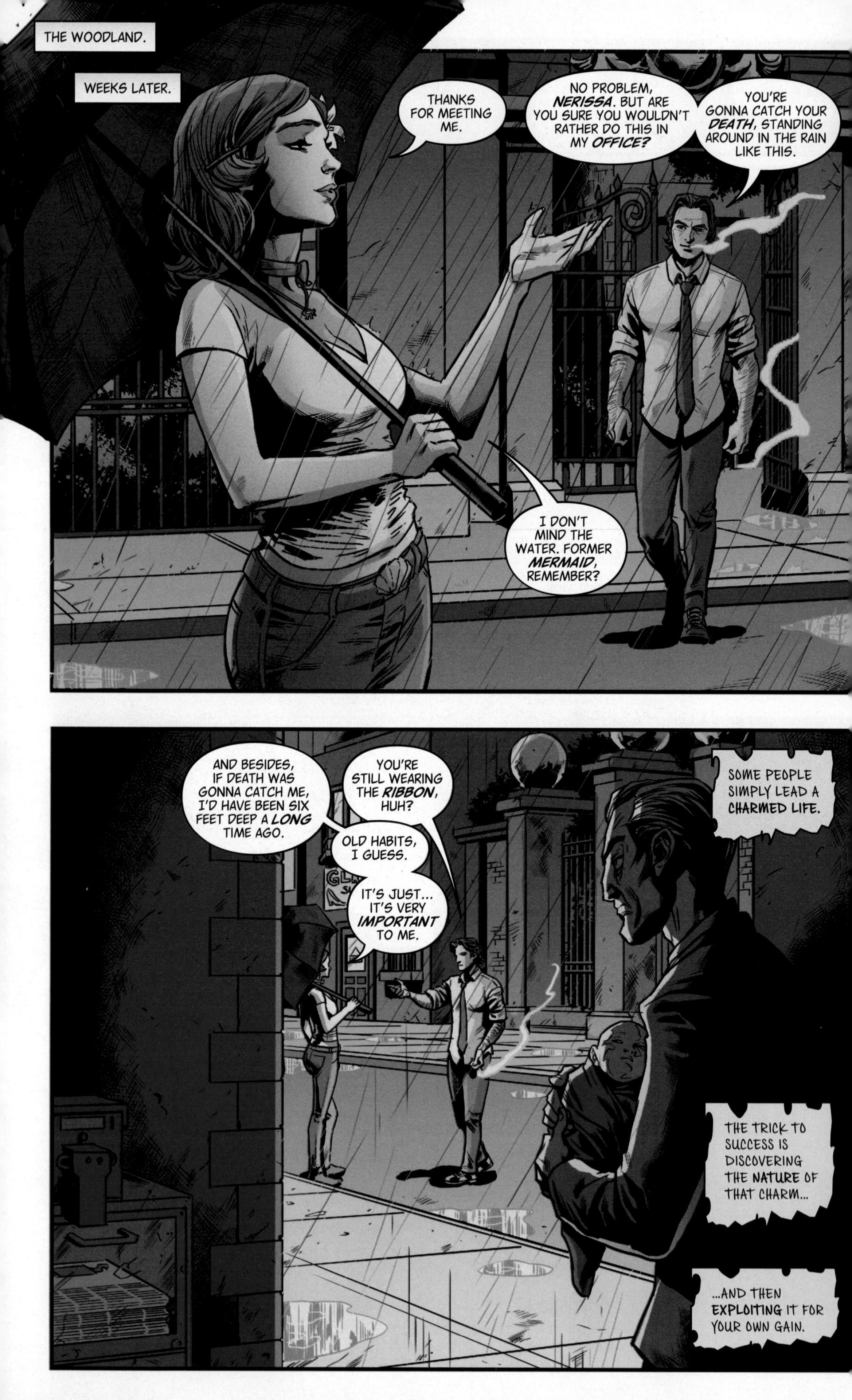
THE WOODLAND.
WEEKS LATER.
THANKS FOR MEETING ME.
NO PROBLEM, NERISSA. BUT ARE YOU SURE YOU WOULDN'T RATHER DO THIS IN MY OFFICE?
YOU'RE GONNA CATCH YOUR DEATH, STANDING AROUND IN THE RAIN LIKE THIS.
I DON'T MIND THE WATER. FORMER MERMAID, REMEMBER?
AND BESIDES, IF DEATH WAS GONNA CATCH ME, I'D HAVE BEEN SIX FEET DEEP A LONG TIME AGO.
YOU'RE STILL WEARING THE RIBBON, HUH?
OLD HABITS, I GUESS.
IT'S JUST... IT'S VERY IMPORTANT TO ME.
SOME PEOPLE SIMPLY LEAD A CHARMED LIFE.
THE TRICK TO SUCCESS IS DISCOVERING THE NATURE OF THAT CHARM...
...AND THEN EXPLOITING IT FOR YOUR OWN GAIN.

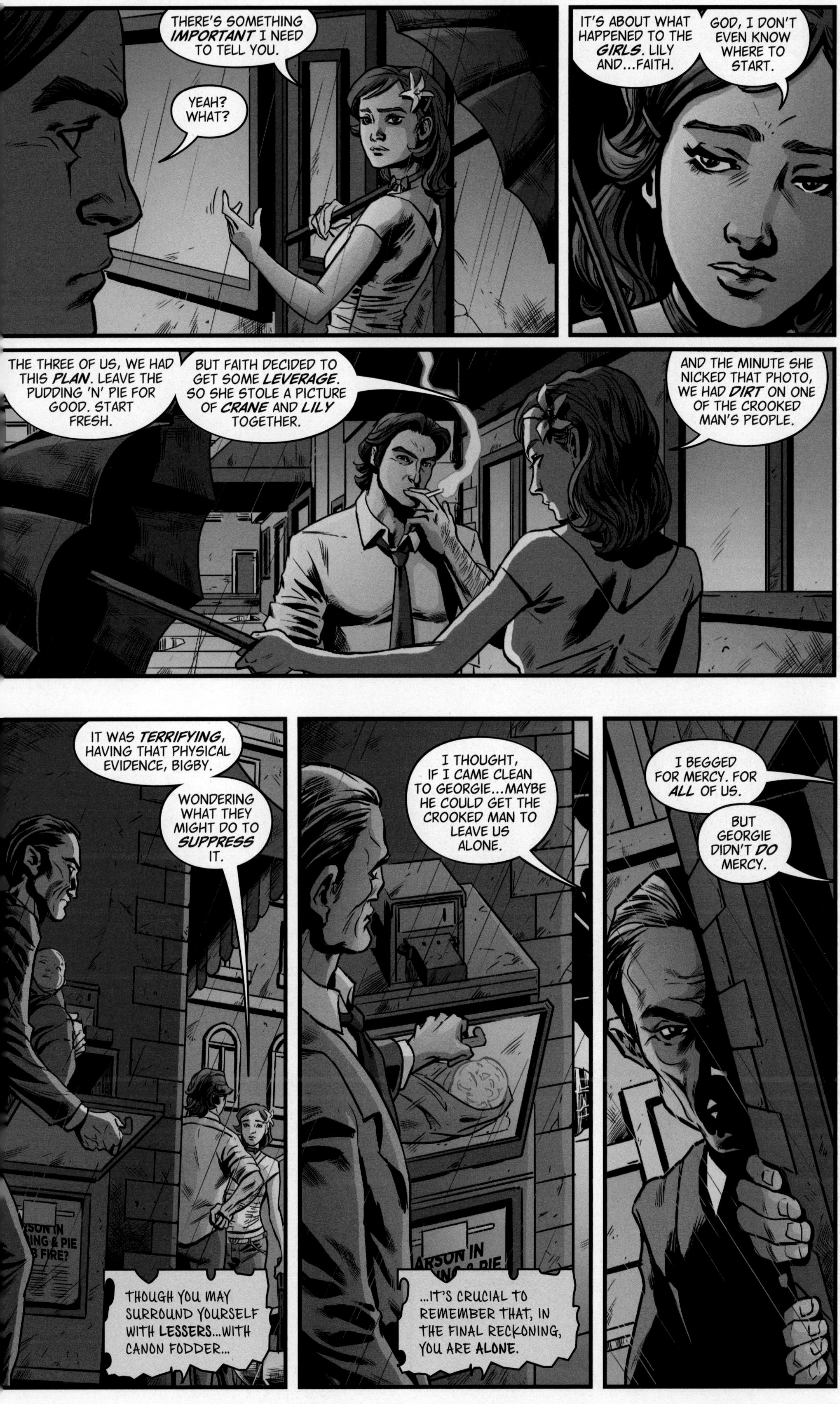
THERE'S SOMETHING IMPORTANT I NEED TO TELL YOU.
YEAH? WHAT?
IT'S ABOUT WHAT HAPPENED TO THE GIRLS. LILY AND...FAITH.
GOD, I DON'T EVEN KNOW WHERE TO START.
THE THREE OF US, WE HAD THIS PLAN. LEAVE THE PUDDING 'N' PIE FOR GOOD. START FRESH.
BUT FAITH DECIDED TO GET SOME LEVERAGE. SO SHE STOLE A PICTURE OF CRANE AND LILY TOGETHER.
AND THE MINUTE SHE NICKED THAT PHOTO, WE HAD DIRT ON ONE OF THE CROOKED MAN'S PEOPLE.
IT WAS TERRIFYING, HAVING THAT PHYSICAL EVIDENCE, BIGBY.
WONDERING WHAT THEY MIGHT DO TO SUPPRESS IT.
THOUGH YOU MAY SURROUND YOURSELF WITH LESSERS...WITH CANON FODDER...
I THOUGHT, IF I CAME CLEAN TO GEORGIE...MAYBE HE COULD GET THE CROOKED MAN TO LEAVE US ALONE.
...IT'S CRUCIAL TO REMEMBER THAT, IN THE FINAL RECKONING, YOU ARE ALONE.
I BEGGED FOR MERCY. FOR ALL OF US.
BUT GEORGIE DIDN'T DO MERCY.

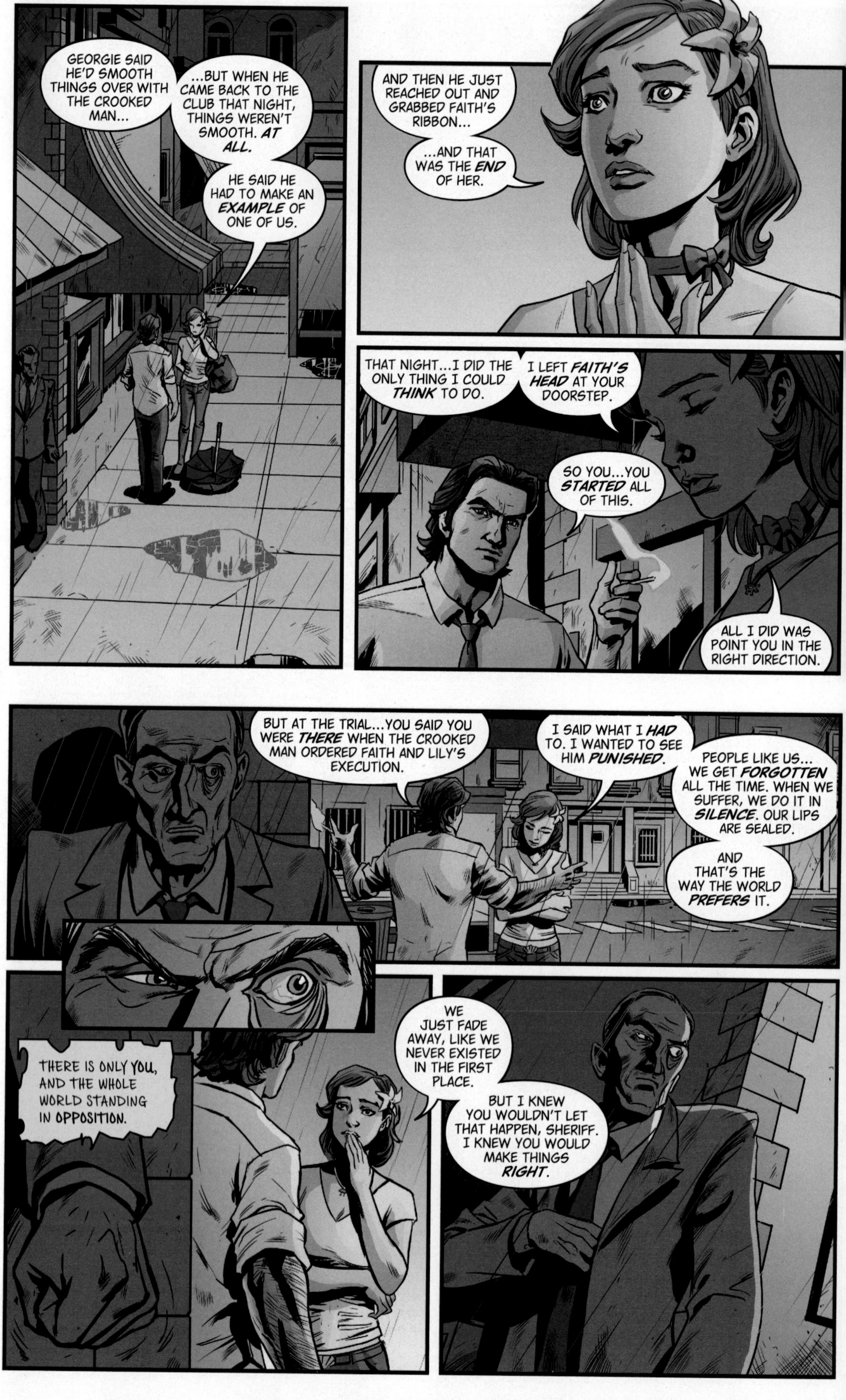
GEORGIE SAID HE'D SMOOTH THINGS OVER WITH THE CROOKED MAN...
...BUT WHEN HE CAME BACK TO THE CLUB THAT NIGHT, THINGS WEREN'T SMOOTH. AT ALL.
HE SAID HE HAD TO MAKE AN EXAMPLE OF ONE OF US.
AND THEN HE JUST REACHED OUT AND GRABBED FAITH'S RIBBON...
...AND THAT WAS THE END OF HER.
THAT NIGHT...I DID THE ONLY THING I COULD THINK TO DO.
I LEFT FAITH'S HEAD AT YOUR DOORSTEP.
SO YOU...YOU STARTED ALL OF THIS.
ALL I DID WAS POINT YOU IN THE RIGHT DIRECTION.
BUT AT THE TRIAL...YOU SAID YOU WERE THERE WHEN THE CROOKED MAN ORDERED FAITH AND LILY'S EXECUTION.
I SAID WHAT I HAD TO. I WANTED TO SEE HIM PUNISHED.
PEOPLE LIKE US... WE GET FORGOTTEN ALL THE TIME. WHEN WE SUFFER, WE DO IT IN SILENCE. OUR LIPS ARE SEALED.
AND THAT'S THE WAY THE WORLD PREFERS IT.
THERE IS ONLY YOU, AND THE WHOLE WORLD STANDING IN OPPOSITION.
WE JUST FADE AWAY, LIKE WE NEVER EXISTED IN THE FIRST PLACE.
BUT I KNEW YOU WOULDN'T LET THAT HAPPEN, SHERIFF. I KNEW YOU WOULD MAKE THINGS RIGHT.

FABLETOWN **NEEDS** YOU, BIGBY. YOU AND SNOW, BOTH.

YOU LOOK OUT FOR EACH OTHER...AND YOU LOOK OUT FOR THE **REST** OF US, TOO.

...YOU'RE NOT AS **BAD** AS EVERYONE SAYS YOU ARE.

YOU **LISTENED**, WHEN NO ONE ELSE WOULD. YOU PROTECTED THOSE WHO COULDN'T PROTECT THEMSELVES.

AND YOU BROUGHT A LITTLE **LAW** AND **ORDER** TO THIS FUCKED-UP TOWN.

AND THAT'S WHY I LEFT FAITH ON YOUR DOORSTEP. BECAUSE I KNEW, DEEP DOWN...

THE SECRET LIES IN KNOWING THAT YOU ARE **STRONGER** THAN THAT OPPOSITION.

MORE CUNNING. MORE RESOURCEFUL.

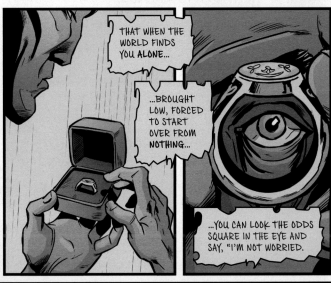

THAT WHEN THE WORLD FINDS YOU ALONE...

...BROUGHT LOW, FORCED TO START OVER FROM NOTHING...

...YOU CAN LOOK THE ODDS SQUARE IN THE EYE AND SAY, "I'M NOT WORRIED."

SEE YOU AROUND, **WOLF**.

"I KNOW I'LL WIN, IN THE END. AFTER ALL..."

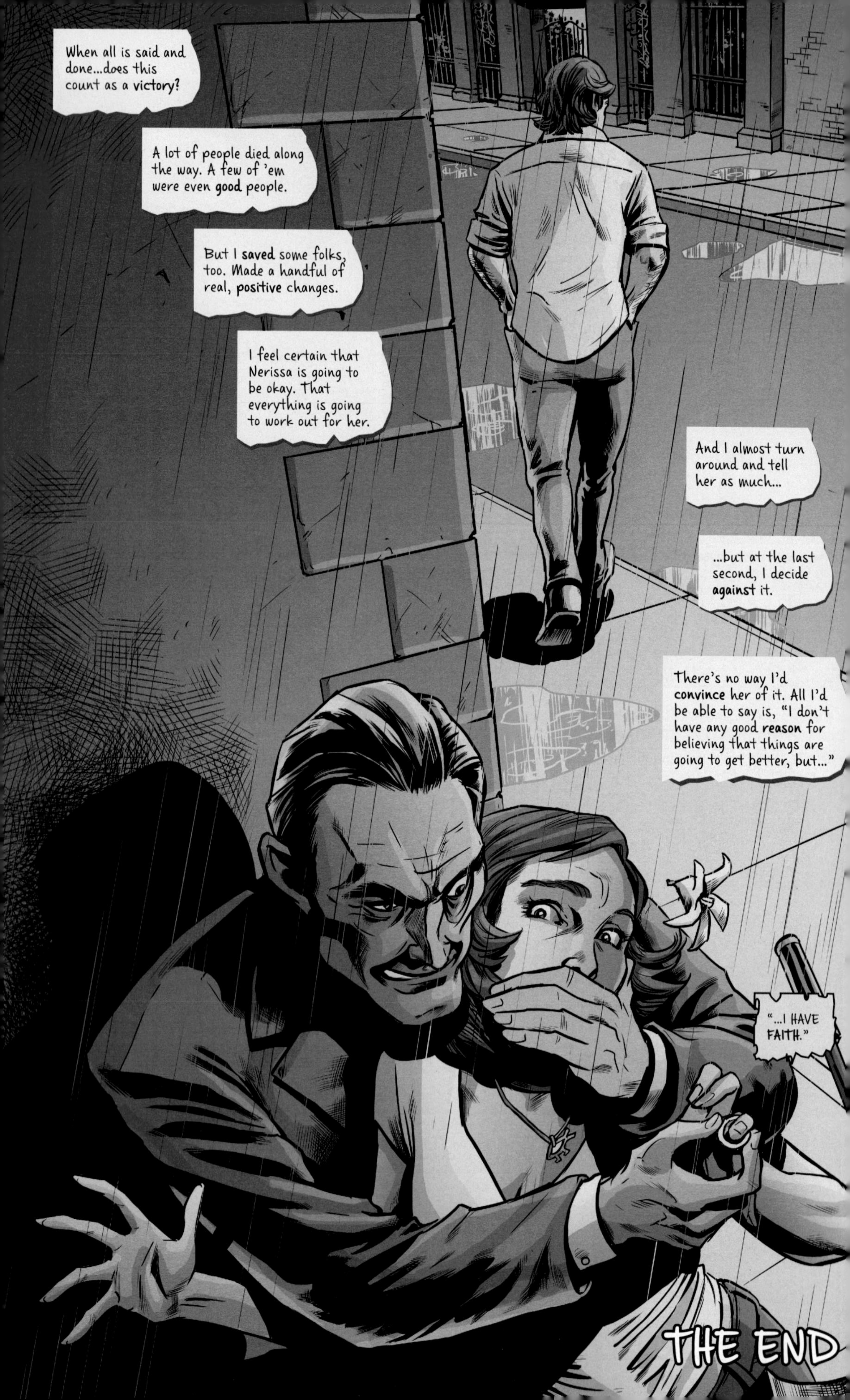
When all is said and done...does this count as a victory?
A lot of people died along the way. A few of 'em were even good people.
But I saved some folks, too. Made a handful of real, positive changes.
I feel certain that Nerissa is going to be okay. That everything is going to work out for her.
And I almost turn around and tell her as much...
...but at the last second, I decide against it.
There's no way I'd convince her of it. All I'd be able to say is, "I don't have any good reason for believing that things are going to get better, but..."
"...I HAVE FAITH."
THE END

VERTIGO

"FABLES is an excellent series in the tradition of SANDMAN, one that rewards careful attention and loyalty."
—PUBLISHERS WEEKLY

"[A] wonderfully twisted concept...features fairy tale characters banished to the noirish world of present-day New York."
—WASHINGTON POST

"Great fun." —BOOKLIST

READ THE ENTIRE SERIES!

FABLES VOL. 2: ANIMAL FARM

FABLES VOL. 3: STORYBOOK LOVE

FABLES VOL. 4: MARCH OF THE WOODEN SOLDIERS

FABLES VOL. 5: THE MEAN SEASONS

FABLES VOL. 6: HOMELANDS

FABLES VOL. 7: ARABIAN NIGHTS (AND DAYS)

FABLES VOL. 8: WOLVES

FABLES VOL. 9: SONS OF EMPIRE

FABLES VOL. 10: THE GOOD PRINCE

FABLES VOL. 11: WAR AND PIECES

FABLES VOL. 12: THE DARK AGES

FABLES VOL. 13: THE GREAT FABLES CROSS-OVER

FABLES VOL. 14: WITCHES

FABLES VOL. 15: ROSE RED

FABLES VOL. 16: SUPER TEAM

FABLES VOL. 17: INHERIT THE WIND

FABLES VOL. 18: CUBS IN TOYLAND

FABLES VOL. 19: SNOW WHITE

FABLES: 1001 NIGHTS OF SNOWFALL

FABLES: WEREWOLVES OF THE HEARTLAND

PETER & MAX: A FABLES NOVEL

THE FABLES ENCYCLOPEDIA

BILL WILLINGHAM

FABLES VOL. 1: LEGENDS IN EXILE

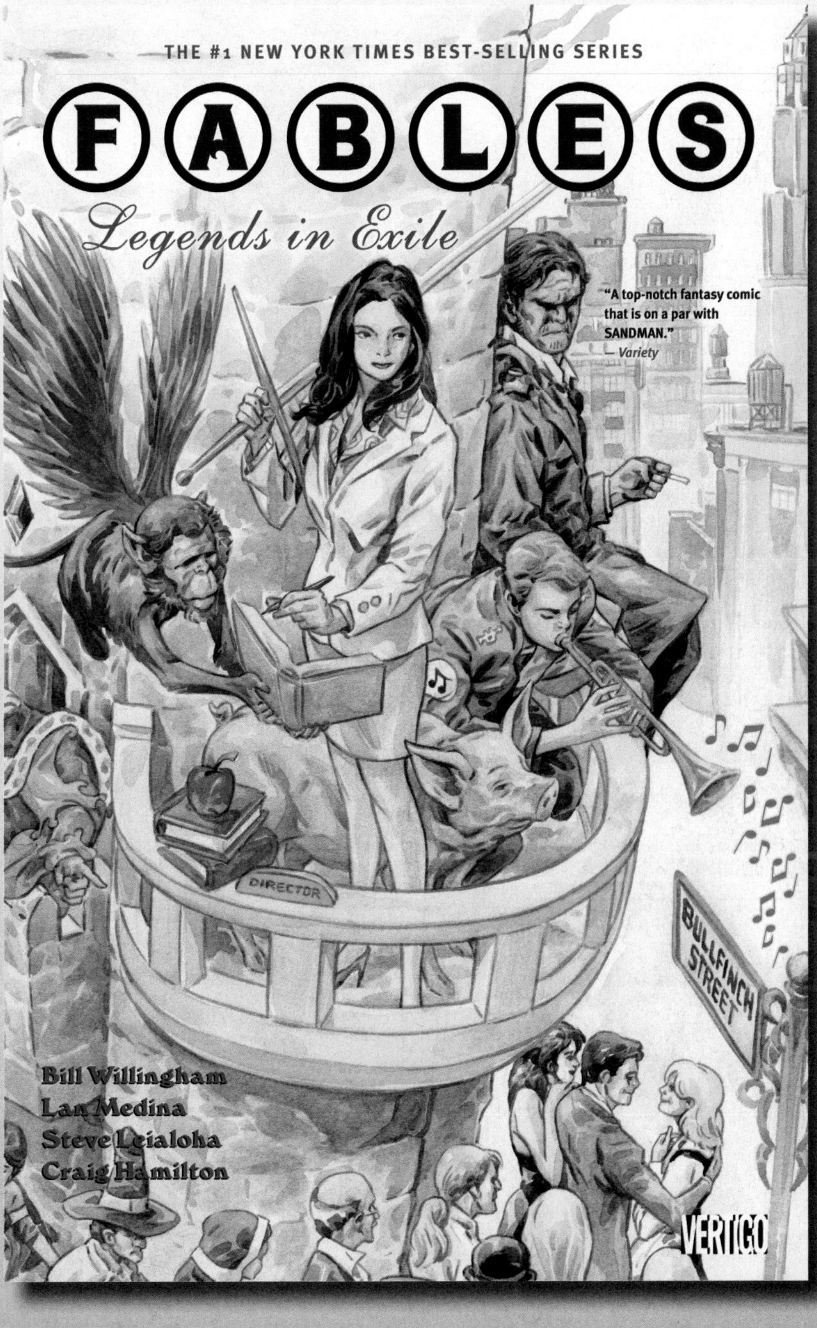

THE #1 NEW YORK TIMES BEST-SELLING SERIES
FABLES
Legends in Exile
"A top-notch fantasy comic that is on a par with SANDMAN." — Variety
DIRECTOR
BULLFINCH STREET
Bill Willingham
Lan Medina
Steve Leialoha
Craig Hamilton
VERTIGO

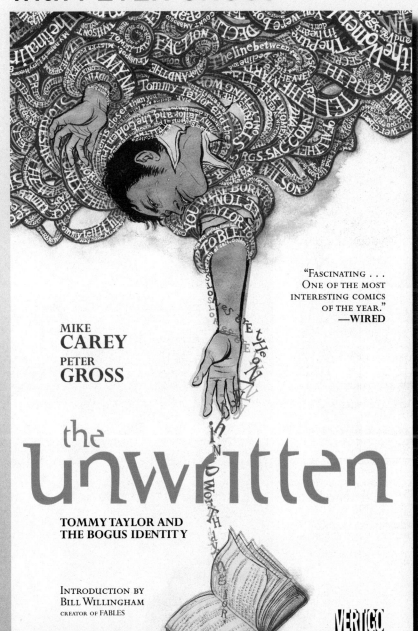